Principles of Equity and Trusts

Principles of Equity and Trusts is a concise new textbook from Alastair Hudson – the author of the definitive classic, *Equity and Trusts*. Through clear and careful analysis, the author explains what the law is, its foundational principles, and its social and economic effect. By beginning with the core principles on which this field is based, even the most complex academic debates concerning express, resulting and constructive trusts, the family home, charities law and other equitable doctrines become comprehensible and interesting. This book offers a fresh, lively and often humorous account of Equity and Trusts.

Through easy-to-follow worked examples and analysis of the case law, Alastair helps you to answer problem questions and to prepare coursework. The author shows how the law affects real people in real situations. Each chapter begins with a clear and concise introduction to the core principles. It contains numbered headings for ease of navigation and advice on studying this subject. Students also have access to Professor Hudson's ever-popular supporting website www.alastairhudson.com which has had hundreds of thousands of hits over the years. It has over 50 brief podcasts on key issues which have been specially re-recorded to coincide with the publication of this book. That website also contains detailed lectures, a variety of videos explaining the law and guidance on tackling assessments.

Characterised by the passion and enthusiasm for his subject matter that make Alastair Hudson's classic textbook so popular, *Principles of Equity and Trusts* is sure to be a winner with both academics and students alike.

Alastair Hudson is Professor of Equity & Finance Law at the University of Exeter. He is a National Teaching Fellow, a Fellow of the Higher Education Academy, a Fellow of the Royal Society of Arts, and has been voted UK Law Teacher of the Year. He has been Professor of Equity & Law at Queen Mary University of London and Professor of Equity & Finance Law at the University of Southampton.

Principles of Equity and Trusts

Alastair Hudson

LLB LLM PhD FHEA FRSA

Professor of Equity & Finance Law
University of Exeter
National Teaching Fellow

 Routledge
Taylor & Francis Group

LONDON AND NEW YORK

First edition published 2016
by Routledge
2 Park Square, Milton Park, Abingdon, Oxon, OX14 4RN

and by Routledge
711 Third Avenue, New York, NY 10017

Routledge is an imprint of the Taylor & Francis Group, an informa business

© 2016 Alastair Hudson

British Library Cataloguing in Publication Data
A catalogue record for this book is available from the British Library

Library of Congress Cataloging-in-Publication Data
Names: Hudson, Alastair, author.
Title: Principles of equity and trusts / Alastair Hudson.
Description: New York, NY : Routledge, 2016.
Identifiers: LCCN 2016001821 | ISBN 9781138122628 (hbk) |
    ISBN 9781138122635 (pbk)
Subjects: LCSH: Equity – England. | Trusts and trustees – England.
Classification: LCC KD674 .H835 2016 | DDC 346.42/004 – dc23
LC record available at http://lccn.loc.gov/2016001821

ISBN: 978-1-138-12262-8 (hbk)
ISBN: 978-1-138-12263-5 (pbk)
ISBN: 978-1-315-65040-1 (ebk)

Typeset in Times New Roman
by Apex CoVantage, LLC

MIX
Paper from
responsible sources
FSC® C013604

Printed and bound by CPI Group (UK) Ltd, Croydon, CR0 4YY

Outline contents

Detailed Contents

4 The beneficiary principle

Preface

This book is a clear, lively account of equity and the law of trusts. It sets out all of the key principles, explains all of the key cases, and analyses all of the key issues which they raise. The rules are brought to life by clear examples. The practical application of those rules and the reasoning behind the principles is laid bare. The fascinating stories behind the cases fuel the text. I love this area of law and have made it my mission to make you love it too.

Equity and trusts is one of the most interesting and rewarding subjects on the law school syllabus. Its reputation for being difficult and complex is unfair. Equity is based on a number of straightforward principles which are illustrated by the cases. By starting with the principles and working through the cases which illustrate them, it is possible to bring the subject to life and to connect it with real life. That is what this book does.

This book is connected to a large number of new podcasts and lectures which are available free through my website (www.alastairhudson.com) and on the publisher's companion website for this book. I also have a blog and other social media feeds which you can access through my website. I have tried to approach this subject from as many different ways as possible so that you can find the approach which suits you. I have peppered this book with a number of essays to consider the effect of the law on women; its connection with international terrorism; and to think about some of the deeper issues such as what a conscience really is, how it shapes equity, and why it is a necessary part of becoming a real girl or boy.

From Routledge Law, I would like to thank Fiona Briden for her support, her professionalism and especially for the sunflowers. I would not like to thank the driver of the refrigerated truck who drove up behind me, while I was walking along the pavement thinking about Ch 19 of this book, with his rear doors swinging open so that the left-hand door hit me – wham! – on the back of the head and knocked me flying across the pavement. Work on this book (and its companion books) halted for nearly five months so that I could recover. I would like to thank Fiona and Emily Wells for the way in which they helped me to reorganise the writing and delivery of the five books I was contracted to write for Routledge at the time.

Alastair Hudson
Professor of Equity & Finance Law
University of Exeter
New Year's Eve 2015

Introduction: Learning equity and trusts

Why you will enjoy studying equity and trusts, and reading this book

Why equity and trusts is enjoyable

You are probably studying equity and trusts because it is a compulsory 'module' on your undergraduate law degree. You may well have heard about its fearsome reputation for being difficult, obscure and even boring. None of these things is true. The pleasant surprise that awaits you is that equity is a fascinating field of English law which will enable you to learn an enormous amount about yourself as a lawyer and about very practical legal skills which will be useful when advising clients. It is a very practical subject. The cases discussed in Chapters 3 through 5 of this book are very good examples of the sort of things that most civil lawyers do in practice: drafting documents to achieve their clients' goals, balancing different analyses to achieve the right outcome, and identifying weaknesses in other people's arguments. This subject also opens up interesting jurisprudential debates about 'fairness versus predictability' in our legal system and 'morality versus positivism'. You will learn a lot about your own attitude to law from those debates.

Equity and trusts is predominantly a case law subject. You will be asked to analyse different wording in documents to see whether or not it complies with the rules, or to re-word documents and show that you understand how different structures can lead to different outcomes. That is a very creative process. Equity is also a subject which is built on moral principles, some of which have hardened into formal rules, so that you can switch between different ways of thinking. You will come to identify different approaches – whether literalist readings or flexible, purposive readings – with different judges. You will analyse how property passes on death, how property can be shielded from taxation, how disputes about ownership of the home are resolved, and so forth. You will analyse cases involving the largest investment banks in the middle of the largest financial crisis we have ever known, and you will analyse cases involving ordinary human beings in the smallest homes we have ever known arguing about their money, their possessions and their livelihoods. You can only be inspired by all of this.

How studying equity and trusts through this book can be central to developing your mind

A university law degree is about giving you an education. That education is about much more than just the grades you receive at the end of your three years. A law degree helps you to develop your mind and to follow whichever direction you want to follow in life. You are doing this at a time when, as the neuroscientists like Professor Sarah-Jayne Blakemore now confirm, your brain is reorganising itself radically between the ages of 18 and 22. The reason why university is such an important time in any person's life is because you and your brain are learning about yourself all over again. The most exciting aspect of that process is that you are able to become the person you want to be. Your brain will retain this 'plasticity' through-out the rest of your life. I was very aware of all of this while writing this book and therefore this is a book which will help you during that process.

Beneath the surface, a good law degree challenges you with problems from the outside world, it enables you to develop the skills you need to form your own mind, and it helps you to follow your own pathway. This book is designed to help you to do exactly that. On the surface, a law degree will fill your head with knowledge about a lot of rules and principles too. This book will certainly help you to do that. Unlike most textbooks, however, it is also written to talk directly to your experience and to your needs as a law student.

How this book was written

This book is intended to be a clear, lively account of equity and the law of trusts. I have had three rules in writing it.

First, be clear. I have attempted (in what can be a complicated and subtle area of law) to write in direct, Anglo-Saxon sentences so as to make the principles clear. However, nothing will beat reading the case law for yourself (perhaps simply by reading the extracts in my *Text, Cases and Materials on Equity & Trusts* or listening to the *Talking Cases* podcasts on my website where I discuss individual cases).

Second, make a clear distinction between what the law *is* and what the law *ought to be*. Like the famous equity judge Sir Robert Megarry, I shall focus primarily on the principles which the judges have actually held, even if they are contentious. Where there are competing authorities or competing approaches to the same question (which frequently happens) then I will state the competing points of view clearly, and illustrate why those differences matter. You should not fret when the judges are in disagreement with one another because that always provides you with a great opportunity to get good marks by showing that you understand what those differ-ences are and how they can lead to different outcomes on the same sets of facts.

This would be a very tedious book if it ignored all of the fascinating arguments which sur-round the law. However, before getting caught up in those subtle arguments this book will state the principles of equity and trusts law clearly and directly. This area of law is bedevilled by debates among people who are often more concerned to state what they think the law *ought to be* before actually acknowledging what the law *is*. We shall not make that mistake. By beginning with the core principles, everything becomes much more straightforward.

Third, be fun. I find this area of the law fascinating. The cases are thought-provoking, moving and sometimes very funny. The central concepts of equity (for example, in relation to the conscience and Aristotle's ethical idea of manoeuvring around unjust laws) are juris-prudentially and philosophically fascinating. So, this book will let you wallow in the joy that can be had from studying equity – but only after explaining the law clearly.

How this book is structured

Human beings learn by repetition. Studies of the brains of concert violinists and elite sportspeople show that their brains have particularly strong bonds between synapses which connect regularly when playing the violin or taking a free-kick. A substance called myelin wraps round and round those connections between brain cells the more that they are used. The same is true of lawyers: the more you use particular parts of your brain, the more you will develop your brain to be good at the things you want it to do. (I discuss all this on my website.)

Consequently, this textbook follows patterns in each chapter so that you can become used to a way of working and train your brain to be better at it. Each time you start a new topic in this course, you will follow your preferred pattern for doing your work and you will become better at it.

Each chapter starts with a 'Capsule Summary' which summarises the key legal principles in that chapter. You should have a basic idea of the principles before you start to read the full text because it makes the text and the case law easier to understand. Then the chapter gives you a clear example of how that area of law works and it introduces some of the key issues which will arise. Then the text goes through the principles in detail, providing you with suggested structures for answering exam problems or writing essays towards the end.

The best way to work at university is to work steadily through the year, and not simply to cram before you have a coursework deadline or in that panicky period before exams. All law degree courses are intended to develop skills as well as knowledge. Both skills and knowledge will be developed throughout the course like a bricklayer builds a wall: each new topic will build on earlier topics like bricks are laid on top of bricks. So, you will benefit from working consciously to a rhythm throughout the course by laying knowledge on top of knowledge and skills on top of skills steadily. Your legal skills and your knowledge will be better if you work steadily as opposed to working in short bursts because you cannot really develop your mind in short, panicky bursts.

Some advice on how to work using this book

Read, don't write at the start

My principal advice in using this book is simple. Just read the book first. Many students read a textbook line by line and make notes on it simultaneously line by line. This is a really inefficient way of working. You should read the assigned section of the textbook first. Turn off all distractions and just focus on the text. This book has been written so that it can be read easily like an ordinary book. Only after you have read everything should you start making notes.

Students often assume that each individual sentence is supposed to make an independent point which should be noted separately, rather than understanding that the writer intended each paragraph or section to be read as a whole. So, just read the appropriate section in this book before starting to make your notes.

If you cannot stop yourself making notes, or if you panic that you will forget a great idea when you eventually sit down at your desk, then use the 'voice recorder' function on your phone to make quick, verbal notes as you go along. Just sit down and read in the first place. In a busy world, you need to identify a place where you can be genuinely quiet and work effectively: a favourite chair, a favourite place, or a favourite seat on the train with your headphones on. When you find that place, you will understand a lot about yourself. This is a new you that is developing at university.

There is nothing much to be gained by spending eight hours typing a copy of your textbook into your notes if that information is not going into your brain. The key test for you should be: when I sit in seminars, did I know the answers or did I have to keep looking them up in my notes? If you had to keep looking them up then your work method is not helping you to know enough. Think of it this way. If you want to answer a problem question, then you must know the law so that you can identify the issues that arise in the problem question. Any information which is in your notes but not in your brain is simply *passive knowledge*. It is not helping you to learn or to become more skilful or to identify issues in problems. More to the point, this expensive university education should be about developing your knowledge and your skills as a legal thinker; not simply amassing notes which you do not really know.

My top tip

My top tip for success is that you should read ahead before your lectures. If you read the appropriate section which will be covered in lectures in a textbook then two things will happen. First, your notes will be much better because you will recognise the case names and concepts when your lecturer mentions them, and therefore you will be able to organise your notes much better. Second, you will be able to identify the aspects which are the particular focus of your course. You will be able to spot the areas which your lecturer prioritises. This will make it much easier for you to identify the topics which are likely to form the focus of your examinations. A third effect will be a massive increase in your confidence because you will feel that you understand the course as it is going along.

Use my podcasts

If you are unsure what you are supposed to be taking from the reading, then listen to my introductory podcast on the particular topic before you start your reading. (You will find them on my website.) That podcast will be approximately 15 minutes long. Or, if it helps, listen to my longer podcasts or lectures on that topic before you start your reading; or listen to them afterwards (on the way to class perhaps) to confirm your knowledge.

If you want explanation in another format, I have recorded a series of 'pathway podcasts' (which discuss the key academic issues in this area) and my *Talking Cases* podcasts (which analyse individual cases in detail). I also have a blog which discusses new developments in the law and other interesting issues. There are also several videos available through my website presenting short documentaries on various aspects of trusts law and explaining specific areas of law (using Smurfs on occasion, using Harry Potter on others) based on my belief that if I make the law seem fun then that will make it easier to understand. Different people learn in different ways: therefore, I have tried to connect with you in as many different ways as possible.

Tens of thousands of students have listened to my podcasts over the last ten years, and tens of thousands of students have watched my videos online. (Some practitioners use them for continuing education or as refreshers.) I know those students have found them useful because hundreds of them have been kind enough to email me to tell me so. Some people listen to my podcasts on their journey into college, or when tidying their room at weekends, or when jogging, or in the gym, or even in the bath. I know that because people have told me all of this too. (Even the bath thing.)

The important thing is that you are an individual. If you can get the point simply by reading the textbook and attending to lectures, then that is wonderful. I hope this textbook is the textbook which connects with you. However, if you are one of the many people who need something more than a textbook, then try my online materials. I have written long books and short books, and blogs and essays (free online), books for practitioners and books for students. Across all of these books and all of the online resources I hope that I can connect with you somehow.

The point is this: if you are struggling to understand your studies, then you need to approach them (and your tutors) in a different way. Let me help you to do that.

Glossary

Equity and trusts law is a language. Therefore, it is important for you to understand its vocabulary. This is a glossary of some of the main terms which arise in the early days of an equity and trusts course, especially in the older cases, together with appropriate cross-references to the text that follows where particularly important terms are considered in some detail.

Absolute title   ownership of all of the property rights, legal and equitable, in property.

Administrator   the person who administers the estate of someone who died without making a will.

Beneficiary   as discussed in section 2.3.4, the person (or people) for whose benefit property is held on trust, such that they have the equitable interest in that property. The nature of the rights of beneficiaries is discussed in Chapter 4 in detail.

Beneficial interest   a synonym for 'equitable interest'.

Bequest   a gift made under a will.

Certainty of intention   the requirement, considered in Chapter 3, that the settlor intended to create a trust, as opposed to something else. The court may infer the existence of an express trust from the circumstances: there is not obligation for the settlor to use any specific form of words nor to use writing to create a trust in all circumstances.

Certainty of objects   the requirement, considered in Chapter 3, that the beneficiaries of a trust or power must be sufficiently certain.

Certainty of subject matter   the requirement, considered in Chapter 3, that the property comprising the trust fund is sufficiently certain, i.e. that it must be separately identifiable from other property.

Cestui que trust   a Latin synonym for 'beneficiary'.

Chose in action   a form of intangible property, such as a debt, which constitutes an item of property in itself formed of the rights and obligations created between two (or more) parties.

Constructive trust   a trust created by operation of law (rather than by the conscious intention of the parties) when a person has knowledge of some factor affecting their conscience in relation to property, considered in Chapter 12.

Declaration of trust   the action performed by a settlor in creating a trust. In relation to some kinds of property, there are formalities for a proper declaration of trust, see Chapter 5. In relation to most property the settlor needs only to manifest an intention to create a trust.

Deed   a formal document signed and delivered as a deed (s 1 of the Law of Property (Miscellaneous Provisions) Act 1989) required, for example, to create a valid will (s 9 of the

Wills Act 1837) and to effect a valid conveyance of land (s 53 of the Law of Property Act 1925).

Equity   as discussed in section 1.1 and thereafter, a system of rules developed to counterbalance the rigours of statute and common law by the Courts of Chancery so as to allow for fairness in individual cases. It is a legal technique based on ensuring the good conscience of the individual defendant.

Equitable interest   a right in property classically recognised by the courts of equity. Beneficiaries under trusts have equitable interests in the trust property in ordinary circumstances.

Executor   a fiduciary under a will trust. (The feminine form is 'executrix'.)

Express trust   a trust created voluntarily by a settlor such that a trustee holds property on trust for a beneficiary or beneficiaries.

Injunction   an equitable remedy either requiring or precluding some action, considered in Chapter 24.

Intellectual property   copyright, patent and trademarks, being forms of chose in action constituting intangible property.

Inter vivos   some relation, such as a trust, taking effect while the settlor is alive. Literally, it is Latin for 'between living people'.

Legal title   the property rights acquired by a trustee which enables that trustee to manage and administer the trust fund for the benefit of the beneficiaries.

Legatee   a beneficiary under a will.

Next of kin   a person specified under the intestacy rules as being a deceased's nearest relative for the purposes of distributing the estate of a person who has died intestate.

Personal property   property other than land and intellectual property, such as chattels. Sometimes referred to as 'personalty'.

Personal representative   one who is appointed to administer a deceased's estate.

Real property   land; referred to as 'real property' because historically to acquire rights in land one had to bring a 'real action'; technically 'real property' does not include leases.

Restitution   either the common law process of restoring specific property to its original owner; or more generally the contested principle of effecting restitution of unjust enrichment by way, *inter alia*, of subtracting that enrichment from the defendant, discussed in Chapter 25.

Resulting trust   a trust arising to return an equitable interest in property automatically to its original owner where no trust has been created, or a trust arising in favour of a person who has contributed to the purchase price of property, as considered in Chapter 11.

Settlement   a synonym for trust in most circumstances, with a technical meaning in relation to the law of taxation and under the now-repealed Settled Land Act 1925. Family settlements were the way in which wealthy families organised the ownership and use of property down the generations, they were often created on the marriage of family members.

Settlor   one who creates an express trust.

Specific performance   an equitable remedy enforcing the intention of the parties to a contract.

Subrogation   an equitable remedy permitting a person to sue on obligations originally owed to another person where the court considers it just to do so, considered in Chapter 20.

Testamentary   taking effect after death; such as a trust, for example, coming into effect by means of a will after a person's death.

Testator   one who creates a will, a settlor of will trusts. (The feminine form is 'testratrix'.)

Tracing   the process of identifying and recovering either specific or substitute property transferred in breach of trust, prior to the imposition of an equitable remedy to recover that property or its substitute, considered in Chapter 20.

Trust   defined in full in section 2.2.1, an equitable institution arising so as to require a trustee to hold property for the benefit of a beneficiary, or beneficiaries, arising either expressly at the instigation of a settlor or being implied by a court as a resulting trust or as a constructive trust.

Trustee   a fiduciary who holds property on trust for the benefit of a beneficiary or beneficiaries.

Unjust enrichment   an alternative explanation of some equitable claims and remedies; a doctrine which achieves restitution by means of the subtraction of an unjust enrichment which the defendant has acquired at the claimant's expense, discussed in Chapter 25.

Vesting property   transferring property rights to a person.

Volunteer   one who receives property or a benefit without giving consideration for it.

Will   an attested document which provides for the manner in which the testator's property is to be divided on death, created in accordance with statute.

Table of cases

Table of statutes

Part 1

Fundamentals

Chapter 1

The nature of equity

CAPSULE SUMMARY

The English legal system distinguishes between common law and equity. The role of equity since the time of the ancient Greek philosopher Aristotle has been to ensure that strict legal rules are not applied in a way that causes injustice. Equity can be understood today as having three roles. First, to prevent strict legal rules being applied unjustly; second, as creating substantive rules itself, especially in the law of trusts; and, third, as creating procedural rules and remedies.

The general principle which English equity uses in this context is to 'correct' the defendant's conscience: that means, the court measures the defendant's behaviour against the standards which the law requires. This root principle informs the way in which more detailed rules are developed and interpreted. The historical root of this word 'conscience' can be identified in 16th century English history, but it remains important today in the ways that the courts have developed it in decided cases.

1.1 THE FOUNDATIONS OF EQUITY

1.1.1 The nature of equity

Equity is the means by which a system of law balances out the need for certainty in rule-making with the need to achieve fair results in individual circumstances. A society needs clear rules but it also needs to be just. In his *Ethics*, the ancient Greek philosopher Aristotle identified 'equity' as being 'superior' to formal legal rules precisely because equity enables a court to reach a fair result in individual circumstances in which that formal rule would otherwise have led to unfairness. This idea was central to the earliest forms of equity in English law.[1] An expression which has been commonly used to describe the way in which English equity functions is that it 'mitigates the rigour of the common law' so that the letter of the law is not applied in so strict a way that it may cause injustice in individual cases.[2] Equity does this by asking what the conscience of the individual defendant should have told them to do, with the result that a strict legal rule may not be applied if its application would be unconscionable.

There are three different ways of understanding equity's role as part of the English legal system. First, equity can be understood as the means by which English law ensures that the strict application of a common law or a statutory rule does not result in any unfairness when applied to a specific case. To this extent equity has been described as being a form of natural justice[3] and as operating on a moral basis.[4] Second, equity can be considered, in its formal sense, as constituting the collection of *substantive* principles and rules developed over the centuries by the courts of equity, principally the Court of Chancery, to measure people's actions against the standards that society expects of them.[5] This principle has given rise the law of trusts, the law on confidences, the law on injunctions and so forth, all of which are

---

1 Browne, 1933.

2 See, for example, *Earl of Oxford's Case* (1615) 1 Ch Rep 1, *per* Lord Ellesmere LC: 'to soften and mollify the extremity of the law', considered below.

3 *Lord Dudley v Lady Dudley* (1705) Prec Ch 241, 244, *per* Lord Cowper. See, in similar vein, Story, 1839, 1.

4 See, for example, Spry, 2001, 1, who advances the proposition that 'equitable principles have above all a distinctive ethical quality, reflecting as they do the prevention of unconscionable conduct'.

5 *Earl of Oxford's Case* (1615) 1 Ch Rep 1.

discussed in this book. In this sense, equity should be understood as being a code of techni-cal, substantive rules and not simply as a pool of general, moral principles.[6] Third, equity can be understood as comprising the *procedural* rules and forms of action developed by the Courts of Chancery over the centuries under the authority of the Lord Chancellor (such as the law on injunctions).

Equity's particular moral purpose was described by Lord Ellesmere in the *Earl of Oxford's Case*[7] in 1615 as being to 'correct men's consciences for frauds, breach of trusts, wrongs and oppressions' as well as to 'soften and mollify the extremity of the law'. This is a moral objective in that it both prevents a defendant from taking unconscionable advantage of a situ-ation and also in that it prevents the law inadvertently permitting an unconscionable result by sticking with the application of a rigid rule which had not anticipated the needs of a particular case. As we shall see, this idea of 'conscience' stands behind all of the more detailed rules of equity and trusts law. We shall understand what that word means by examining the ways in which it has been used in the case law. Importantly, however, we can identify that this conscience is an objective statement of the views which the law considers that an individual should have had and not the subjective opinions of any individual defendant (as is discussed in section 1.1.4 below).

The underlying argument of this book is that we should embrace the elegant simplicity of equity because the legal system is being asked to consider very difficult questions arising in an ever more complex world. Those questions (all of which arise in the cases discussed in this book) range from international investment banks seeking to recover money through to disputes about ownership of the family home; from questions about the proper management of pension funds right through to provision of care for the elderly. The only way to cope with constant social change and that breadth of issues is to use 'high-level principles' to guide the courts, as well as a doctrine of precedent to develop predictable rules in appropriate contexts. A 'high-level principle' is a general principle which guides the nature and application of more detailed rules: for example, the high-level principle that no person shall be allowed to take unconscionable advantage of another person leads to the detailed rule that no-one can be allowed to take a profit from receiving a bribe. This is how equity uses the idea of con-science: it stands as the central moral principle which underpins all of the detailed case law principles and rules. That central moral principle – of good conscience – creates the flexibil-ity in this area; whereas the doctrine of precedent creates the stability and the predictability that runs through each of its specific doctrines by defining what those central principles mean in practice. Equity has been operating this methodology for centuries in a remarkably diverse range of fields, from the operation of pensions and investment trusts, through to ownership of the home, and into detailed remedies such as injunctions, specific performance, the recovery of property and so forth with great success.

Equity's flexibility is important in ensuring that the legal system retains sufficient supple-ness to cope with the social developments over which the court is asked to sit in judgment. It is often a different way of 'doing law' from the common law model of strict tests and hard-and-fast rules (although equity does develop hard-and-fast rules in appropriate contexts as we shall see) but it is none the worse for that. The English legal system has always main-tained a distinction between common law (including contract law and tort law) and equity.

---

6   The tendency to think of equity simply in terms of general principles as opposed to technical devices and strict case law rules was criticised by Megarry VC in *Re Montagu's Settlement* [1987] Ch 264.

7   (1615) 1 Ch Rep 1.

Historically, as we shall see below, there were entirely different courts which administered each of these traditions: the courts of common law (such as the Courts of King's Bench) and the courts of equity (principally the Courts of Chancery). While this formal distinction between the courts was removed by the Judicature Act in 1873, the intellectual distinction between common law and equity remains very important in practice today.

Another important argument which underpins this book is that our legal system is at its most effective when it synthesises strict rule-making with the ability to produce just outcomes in individual cases. That is, our legal system is at its most effective when it can synthesise the common law with equity. That is exactly what Aristotle had in mind originally as we shall see in section 1.1.3 below.

1.1.2 The scope of this book: Equity and trusts

This book considers both the general doctrines and remedies which form part of equity, and more particularly the law of trusts. To acquire a 'qualifying law degree' for professional purposes in England and Wales you are currently required to have studied trusts law. It is impossible to understand trusts law properly unless you understand the equitable soil in which it is grown. This book covers the entirety of any 'equity and trusts', 'trusts law', or 'equity and trusts law' course or module. We begin with an analysis of the core principles of equity (and the equitable maxims which are considered in section 1.4 of this chapter). The bulk of the book is then devoted to trusts law and the equitable principles which are significant in the principles of trusts law.

1.1.3 Concepts of equity in ancient Greek philosophy

It is commonly said that there is something uniquely English about this area of law. For example, Professor Maitland, in lectures delivered at the turn of the 20th century, wanted us to believe that equity is founded on 'ancient English elements' and rejected the idea that equity was taken from Roman law.[8] In truth, the provenance of the English courts of equity is a mixture of ecclesiastical law and a body of law which, as Maitland suggested, developed in terms of a line of precedent from 1557 onwards.[9] So, there were ancient English elements in the creation of the jurisprudence which we shall consider in this book (if by 'ancient' we mean the period leading up to mid-16th century). However, the idea of 'equity' can be found in the work of Aristotle nearly 3,000 years ago. Many early English texts on equity, such as Ashburner's *Equity*, identify Aristotle's model of equity as being the root of the English idea. The concept is simple: even in a formal system of justice (such as the common law or statute) there will arise some circumstances which the creator of those rules of justice could not have anticipated. Equity operates so as to correct those formal rules for the circumstances of that particular case. Aristotle's *Ethics* described equity in the following terms:

> For equity, though superior to justice, is still just . . . justice and equity coincide, and although both are good, equity is superior. What causes the difficulty is the fact that equity is just, but not what is legally just: it is a rectification of legal justice.[10]

8   Maitland, 1936, 6.
9   *Ibid*, 8.
10 Aristotle, 1955, 198.

In this way, Aristotle considered that equity provides a better form of justice because it provides for a more specific judgment as to right and wrong in individual cases which rectifies any errors or similar unfairness which the common law or statute would otherwise have produced. The superiority of equity, on Aristotle's account, emerges in the following passage which continues on from the last quoted passage:

> The explanation of this is that all law is universal, and there are some things about which it is not possible to pronounce rightly in general terms; therefore in cases where it is necessary to make a general pronouncement, but impossible to do so rightly, the law takes account of the majority of cases, though not unaware that in this way errors are made . . . So when the law states a general rule, and a case arises under this that is exceptional, then it is right, where the legislator owing to the generality of his language has erred in not covering that case, to correct the omission by a ruling such as the legislator himself would have given if he had been present there, and as he would have enacted if he had been aware of the circumstances.[11]

So, the people who create rules do so only for the general case (i.e. their rules are universal in that sense) although that will result in an 'error' in some cases because the outcome they produce will be unjust. A good example of this can be derived from the case of *Rochefoucauld v Boustead*[12] where there was a formal rule that rights in land would only be protected if they were properly registered. The claimant failed to register their right in property having paid for it when buying it from the defendant. The defendant realised there had been no registration and therefore purported to sell the same land again to a third party. The formal rule did not prevent that sale because there had been no registration of the claimant's rights. It was held, on the equitable principle that 'statute may not be used as an engine of fraud', that the defendant was about to commit a fraud against the claimant by purporting to sell the land to someone else and therefore that good conscience required that the claimant's rights should bind the defendant. This general principle of equity (about statute not being used as an engine of fraud) was applied to a specific case so as to produce a just outcome which the statute would otherwise have prevented.

It is worth noting that Aristotle refers only to the role of a legislator here, and not to judge-made law in a common law system like that in England and Wales. However, the core point transfers perfectly well: if the common law or a statute has failed to anticipate a particular situation, or if it would produce unfairness or allow unconscionability to persist without a remedy, then equity will intervene to correct that universal rule. Aristotle refers to these as 'errors' in the law, which shows us that he lived in a different time when there was neither the volume of law nor the breadth of legal rights among all citizens which we see today.

It is worth noticing that English judges do not quote Aristotle as an authority. Nevertheless, Aristotle's model of equity was significant in the formation of the English model. Lord Chancellor Ellesmere held the following in the *Earl of Oxford's Case* in 1615: 'men's actions are so diverse and infinite that it is impossible to make a general law which may aptly meet with every particular and not fail in some circumstances'.[13] This model of equity, which was the root of the reported English case law, clearly used Aristotle's ideas and language.

---

11 *Ibid.*
12 [1897] 1 Ch 196.
13 (1615) 1 Ch Rep 1, at 6.

Therefore, Aristotle was important as an inspiration for English equity. Indeed, for educated people in the 17th century, knowledge of Aristotle's thought would have been a keystone of their education and therefore it is no surprise that Aristotle's ideas would have been influential on them. (The Aristotelian model of equity is considered in greater detail in Chapter 26.)

1.1.4 Equity and trusts are based on conscience

The principal difference between English equity and the model of equity which Aristotle presented is that English equity is organised around a central principle of 'conscience'. The idea of 'conscience' remains central to all of the law which we shall consider in this book to this day. So, it is important that we consider the emergence of this idea in the early case law if we are to understand the modern principles.

The reason for the importance of conscience is twofold. First, any group of moral principles requires a central concept to bind them together. For example, in financial regulation that word is 'integrity', whereas in much of the common law it is 'reasonableness'. In equity, the key concept is 'conscience'. Second, when equity was beginning to formalise itself in the 17th century (in reaction to criticism from some common law judges) the word 'conscience' was particularly important because it was central to the debates about whether England and Wales should be a Protestant or a Catholic country. Many people were executed for their religious beliefs and the succession of monarchs (including Lady Jane Grey who was executed after having been Queen of England for only nine days in 1553) saw the official religion bounce between the Catholic and the Protestant traditions. This created questions of conscience for everyone in England about whether they should agree to change religion when the monarch changed, or whether they should risk death by sticking to their beliefs. Reading historical accounts of the period, the word 'conscience' rings like a bell in letters written by family members, speeches given in Parliament and so forth. So, it is no surprise that this concept of 'conscience' was important when equity was being formalised in the 16th and 17th centuries.

The Lord Chancellors who presided over the courts of equity were mostly clergymen during this period and therefore the language of 'conscience' came naturally to them, as part of these theological discussions, when they were reaching for a central concept for equity. The courts of equity – deploying this idea of conscience – saw the defendant's conscience as being something which was overseen directly by God, such that the defendant needed to convinced to confess their misdeeds so as to the cleanse their conscience before God. Therefore, when the early courts of equity were assessing 'conscience' they were doing so as ecclesiastics sitting as judges who were also considering what God would require a defendant to do in response to the demands of conscience. As we shall see, our idea of conscience is different today.

This idea of a conscience is not just moral window-dressing. The leading case on the nature of trusts (which form the principal focus of this book) is the decision of the House of Lords in 1996 in *Westdeutsche Landesbank v Islington LBC*[14] in which Lord Browne-Wilkinson reminded us that trusts arise when the person who is recognised by the law as being the owner of property has their conscience affected in some way: either by knowledge that they are holding that property on trust for other people's benefit, or because they have

---

14   [1996] AC 669.

acquired that property by unconscionable means (such as stealing it). This idea of the trust is discussed in detail in the next chapter. What is important is that it is 'conscience' which is the trigger for the creation of these obligations in relation to property. As we shall see, this idea of conscience may also trigger the imposition of an injunction, the removal of property rights, and so forth. So precise is this idea of conscience in some contexts that the very point in time at which a person's conscience is affected may be important. In the *Westdeutsche* case itself the defendant local authority had not known that it and the claimant bank had made a mistake about the validity of their contract when the defendant had spent all of the money it had acquired under that contract. Lord Browne-Wilkinson held that the defendant's conscience had not been affected before it spent the money because it had not known that the contract was void, and therefore it was not subject to any equitable obligations to the claimant. We shall explore this idea of conscience in detail (and summarise what we have learned in Chapter 26). All that is important to note at this stage is that the idea of 'conscience' is central to the operation of the legal principles in this area.

1.1.5 The many senses of conscience

Conscience and 'unconscionability' in equity

Given that the whole of English equity is based on the idea of 'conscience' it would be worthwhile to set out a working understanding of what that word means from the outset. The task of establishing a meaning for the term 'conscience' will be, as we shall see throughout the course of this book, an interesting one. It will be important to notice the judges' frequent reference to 'conscience' and to the technical concept of 'unconscionability' (which is used in many different contexts in cases such as *Jennings v Rice*[15] in relation to estoppel and *BBCI v Akindele*[16] in relation to liability for breach of trust). Judges like Megarry VC in *Re Montagu*,[17] Lord Browne-Wilkinson in *Westdeutsche Landesbank v Islington*,[18] and the root judgment of Lord Ellesmere in the *Earl of Oxford's Case*[19] talk more generally of 'conscience'. Judges like Lord Denning in the 20th century were more comfortable with general talk of morality than many other judges. Reaching judgment on the basis of broadly-based moral principles is a very different way of 'doing law' than applying hard-and-fast rules or strict tests. Even within equity, as we shall see, there are situations in which hard-and-fast rules are applied (for example, *Certainties* discussed in Chapter 3) and other situations in which general principles are applied (for example, *Constructive Trusts* discussed in Chapter 12).

It is a matter of general preference, and you personally should develop your own opinion (after a study of the law), as to whether you prefer a 'positivist' approach based on technical concepts applied strictly to individual cases or a 'natural justice' approach based on moral concepts applied flexibly in individual cases. This is one of the (often unspoken) ways in which the study of equity and trusts contributes to your legal education and to your

---

15 [2002] EWCA Civ 159.
16 [2001] Ch 437.
17 [1987] Ch 264.
18 [1996] AC 669.
19 (1615) 1 Ch Rep 1; (1615) 21 ER 485.

understanding of your own attitudes as a future legal practitioner because you will come to realise whether you are more comfortable with general principles of the sort used in equity, international treaties or family law, or the detail which is pursued (for example) by commercial lawyers and tax lawyers.

The roots of the conscience in English history

We outlined the use of the word 'conscience' above in relation to religious conflicts in English society in the 16th and 17th centuries. It would be useful to expand a little on that history so that we can understand how equity developed into its modern form. From its earliest days in the English legal system, equity was administered by the Lord Chancellor as its principal judge through the Court of Chancery. The genesis of the term 'conscience' is in the early statements of English jurists that the courts of equity were 'courts of conscience' and, more significantly, that the Lord Chancellor was also the keeper of the monarch's conscience as well as being a judge. This is important. The role of Lord Chancellor used to be very significant in England and Wales. The Lord Chancellor was usually a bishop but he also acted as the monarch's prime minister. As prime minister, the Lord Chancellor used to oversee the Chancery, which was a department of state which issued writs and carried out a large amount of administration using the Great Seal of England as its authority. This was particularly significant when the monarch was out of the country, as monarchs before the 16th century tended to be. Over time, the Chancery began to function as a court as well as a bureaucratic department. Therefore, the Lord Chancellor had a role as a politician and bureaucrat overseeing the activities of the Chancery, as well as being a judge overseeing the Court of Chancery, and as well as ministering to the monarch's personal conscience as a spiritual advisor. The most famous holders of this post served during the reign of Henry VIII and were particularly important in negotiating his many marriages and divorces.

The post of Lord Chancellor was frequently referred to as the position of 'Lord Keeper'.[20] Sir Christopher Hatton was known during his time as Lord Chancellor during a part of the reign of Elizabeth I as being 'the Keeper of the Queen's Conscience'. Therefore, the work of the Court of Chancery was concerned with the monarch's personal conscience as exercised through the law. This meant that the Queen's conscience was something which could exist outside her mind and which could be administered by her officials. This is an interesting idea which we shall consider next.

The meaning of the word 'conscience'

The English word 'conscience' is an amalgam of 'con' and 'science': literally, 'knowledge with'. Its meaning is drawn from the ancient Greek word 'suneidenai' which itself carried a meaning of 'knowledge with' which meant more precisely 'knowledge of oneself *with oneself*'. That means there are two voices inside each mind: the conscious mind and the conscience. Those two different voices talk to one another. More particularly, the conscience is

---

20   Thomas, 1976, 506.

part of the mind but it comes unbidden to you when it wants to nag at you about something that you have done or not done. So, the meaning of the word 'conscience' necessarily incorporates the idea that the conscience is outside the conscious mind even though we all experience the naggings of our own consciences inside our heads. Therefore, it is commonly supposed by legal scholars that the conscience is something entirely subjective. However, the philosophical literature, the psychological literature, the theological literature, and even mainstream pop culture (like Walt Disney's *Pinocchio*) understand the conscience as being something that is *outside* the conscious mind. For example, the famous psychoanalyst Sigmund Freud explained the conscience as being part of the 'super-ego' which held the 'ego' in check: that is, the conscience controlled the behaviour of the conscious mind by nagging at it. Moreover, the conscience is understood as being formulated by absorbing objective messages about right and wrong from the world around us, which are then synthesised into the psychological phenomenon of our own conscience which nags us when it thinks that we have done something wrong. So, very importantly for us, the conscience is an objectively-formed phenomenon which nevertheless lodges inside our individual minds. This objective constitution of the conscience (even though we experience it subjectively inside our own heads) is why it is possible to think of Queen Elizabeth I's conscience as being something which can be detached from the Queen and administered by her Lord Chancellor on her behalf. For Sir Christopher Hatton to administer the Queen's conscience meant that the Queen's conscience was understood as being something detachable from her own brain because it expressed her interaction with her god, her role as monarch, and also her existence as a human being. This duality matches the modern psychological understanding of a conscience. This conception of the conscience is discussed in greater detail in Chapter 26, although a summary of the ideas is given in the next section.

The psychological idea of a conscience in popular culture and in equity

Among the legal commentators in the 21st century, there is some concern about whether or not the idea of conscience is too uncertain to act as the base for equity. Much of the confusion about the idea of conscience among these modern commentators is based on two things. First, those commentators tend to prefer a form of law which is rigid and laid out in a clear framework, whereas equity operates by reference to a high-level principle of 'conscience' which informs the various principles within equity. Their caricature of equity as something which is entirely discretionary and arbitrary is simply that: a caricature.

Second, those commentators fail to understand what a conscience is. Their assumption is that a conscience is an entirely random and entirely subjective phenomenon. That is not what a conscience is. The leading psycho-analysts Freud[21] and Jung[22] both conceived of the conscience as something which sits *outside* the conscious mind and calls the conscious mind to account. Freud described the conscience as being like a garrison left by an invading army inside a captured town because the contents of that conscience are mainly placed there by our parents, our education and society around us, but the contents of that conscience nevertheless hold us to account inside our own brains. The conscience may only be small within the

---

21 Freud, 1923 and 1930.
22 Jung, 1927.

mind but it is powerful and can hold the entirety of the conscious mind to account. Similarly, the philosopher Immanuel Kant considered the conscience to be a sort of guard that holds the conscious mind prisoner. The point is that while the conscience may be experienced as a subjective phenomenon inside our minds, it is nevertheless constituted by a range of ideas that come from outside it. The influential Catholic priest Cardinal Newman understood this when he described the conscience as being 'the aboriginal vicar of Christ'. What he meant was that Roman Catholics have such a complete education in their moral responsibilities from their church that those teachings are hardwired into their brains; and therefore wherever they may wander, those attitudes go with them and hold them accountable to the teachings they have had throughout their lives. This Christian understanding of the conscience was important in the 17th century case law which laid the foundations for the modern idea of equity being based on conscience.

This idea of the conscience as being distinct from the conscious mind is also a staple of our popular culture. Walt Disney's *Pinocchio* is perhaps the best example. Pinocchio was a wooden boy made by the craftsman Gepetto who was brought to life by the Blue Fairy at the start of the film. The one thing that stopped Pinocchio from becoming 'a real boy' was his lack of a conscience. So, the Fairy appointed Jiminy Cricket, a small cricket who happened to be in the corner of the room at the time, to act as Pinocchio's conscience. And that is what Jiminy Cricket does throughout the film: he nags at Pinocchio when he misbehaves. When Pinocchio falls in with some bad boys, it is Jiminy Cricket who rescues him just in time by telling him to stop being a jackass (as the other boys are transformed literally into jackasses). Jiminy Cricket is a literal conscience within that story. He stands outside Pinocchio's conscious mind, warning him about the outcome of his behaviour; and he even receives a badge at the end of the film which reads 'Official Conscience'. If you were to watch this film now (you may not have seen it since you were young) then you will realise that it is 'conscience, conscience, conscience' throughout. The Italian novel on which that film is based was cautionary tale for young boys without any heart-warming songs or amusing cartoon cats. (The cat is probably the best thing in the Disney film.) There are many other examples of a conscience of this sort in our culture (as discussed in Chapter 26) ranging from high-cultural examples such as the character of the Fool in Shakespeare's *King Lear*, who holds Lear's actions to account through a series of sarcastic riddles and songs, right the way through to comic book characters like Marvel's anti-hero Deadpool, who has more than one voice in his head questioning his behaviour as he kills people for money.

Given that the conscience is accepted by psychologists, philosophers, theologians and even Walt Disney as being something that is separate from our conscious minds, and which is filled with societal attitudes and mores, then it is possible to think in legal terms that the conscience is something which *ought to* contain certain ideas and attitudes. And if the conscience ought to contain certain attitudes (do not kill, do not steal, and so forth) then it is appropriate for the law to have a system of principles – embodied in part by equity in England and Wales – which measure whether or not an individual defendant has behaved in a way that is suitable according to those objective standards of conscience. The argument which sustains this book is that the idea of conscience is not a subjective one which differs from person to person, but rather that it is naturally an objective measurement of whether or not a person has acted properly in a given set of circumstances. These ideas are amplified in Chapter 26 by reference to the cases which we will have analysed in this book in the meantime.

1.1.6 Equity as a moral virtue

Equity was understood from its earliest incarnations as being concerned with the imposition of moral principles. The following description of equity was provided by Lord Chancellor Cowper in *Dudley v Dudley* in 1705:[23]

> Now equity is no part of the [common] law, but a moral virtue, which qualifies, moderates, and reforms the rigour, hardness, and edge of the law, and is an universal truth; it does also assist the law where it is defective and weak in the constitution (which is the life of the law) and defends the law from crafty evasions, delusions, and new subtleties, invested and contrived to evade and delude the common law, whereby such as have undoubted right are made remediless: and this is the office of equity, to support and protect the common law from shifts and crafty contrivances against the justice of the law. Equity therefore does not destroy the law, nor create it, but assist it.

What is significant about this description of equity is that it considers equity itself to be a moral virtue. Equity is presented here as a means of making the common law stronger by supplying it with moral principles and with weapons against the 'craft contrivances' which lawyers may bring to it. This is similar in tone to Aristotle's approach to equity as a means of preventing any unfairness which might otherwise result from the rigid application of formal legal rules. It should not be forgotten that for many equity jurists, the assertion that its principles constitute a 'universal truth' is a very significant part of the legal concept of equity.[24]

1.2 THE BIRTH OF EQUITY

1.2.1 The development of two systems: Common law and equity

Professor Story, in his 19th century American history of equity, described the court of equity as being 'an original and fundamental court, as ancient as the kingdom itself'.[25] This gives the subject an appealingly *Game of Thrones* feeling. This section sets out a short, potted history of the development of equity (which is important on some equity and trusts law courses). (A longer treatment is set out in Ch 1 of Alastair Hudson, *Equity & Trusts*.)

Henry II created the courts of King's Bench to hear matters otherwise brought before the Crown. From these early, medieval courts the principles of the common law began. There remained, however, a right to petition the King directly if it was thought that the decision of the common law court was unfair or unjust. During the medieval period the position of Lord Chancellor was created, among other things, to hear those petitions which would otherwise have been taken directly to the monarch. The medieval Lord Chancellor was empowered to issue royal writs on behalf of the Crown through the use of the Great Seal, but gradually acquired power to hear petitions directly during the 13th and 14th centuries. Over time, the bureaucratic department which the Lord Chancellor headed – known as the Chancery – became a court, known as the Court of Chancery. It was this court which was primarily responsible for developing the principles of equity.

---

23 *Lord Dudley v Lady Dudley* (1705) Prec Ch 241, 244, *per* Lord Cowper LC.
24 E.g. Kames, *Principles of Equity*, 1778, 41.
25 Story, *Equity Jurisprudence*, 1st edn, 1835; 13th edn, 1886.

As a result the Lord Chancellor's discretion broadened, until some lawyers began to comment that it had begun to place too much power in the hands of one person. It is also interesting to note that the early courts of equity did not necessarily concern themselves with a doctrine of precedent or strict rules at all, but rather concerned themselves with inquiring specifically into the defendant's conscience. For example, Chief Justice Fortescue declared in 1452 that:

> We are to argue conscience here, not the law.[26]

By contrast, equity had many critics among the common lawyers who disliked its tendency to use discretion to reach judgments. Selden is reputed to have said:

> Equity is a roguish thing. For [common] law we have a measure . . . equity is according to the conscience of him that is Chancellor, and as that is longer or narrower, so is equity. 'Tis all one as if they should make the standard for the measure a Chancellor's foot.[27]

This statement implied that Lords Chancellor were thought to ignore precedent and to decide what judgments to make entirely in accordance with their own whims. There were furious arguments between the judges of the common law, especially Lord Coke at the turn of the 17th century, and this Court of Chancery. The *Earl of Oxford's Case* was very important in deciding in 1615, with the agreement of King James I, that the courts of equity had the power to set aside judgments of the common law courts where appropriate – just as Aristotle had had in mind.

It was Lord Chancellor Nottingham who first undertook the work, in cases like *Cook v Fountain* in 1676,[28] of regularising the principles of equity and in particular the principles of trusts law. Previously, those judgments had been very poorly reported and many judges tended to treat their principles very loosely. There was even a debate about whether or not courts of equity should be obliged to follow precedent at all. When he became Lord Chancellor, Lord Nottingham was important in following precedent and regularising equity more than had been the case previously, although he too tended to construe the existence of trusts on moral grounds on occasion. Lord Chancellors like Lord Hardwicke and Lord Eldon in the 19th century continued this work of battening down many of the general principles of equity into hard-and-fast rules, particularly in relation to the creation of trusts. Chapters 3 through 5 of this book bear the stamp of Lord Eldon's strict judgments during the 19th century. Since that time the rules of equity, and in particular the rules relating to the law of trusts, have become far more rigidified[29] – a tendency which will be considered in detail in this book.[30] The Court of Chancery had only comprised the Lord Chancellor and his assistant, the Master of the Rolls, until 1813 when the first Vice-Chancellor was appointed.[31] Consequently, even after that time, until the creation of the Chancery Division

---

26   Mitch 31 Hen VI, Fitz Abr, *Subpena*, pl 23, cited by Baker, 2002, 108.
27   *Table Talk of John Selden*, 1927.
28   (1676) 3 Swan 585.
29   Croft, 1989, 29.
30   See Chapter 7.
31   There were no official, methodical law reports of Chancery cases before 1557: Maitland, 1936, 8.

of the High Court in 1873, the direction of equity was very much under the control of one or two judges.

As mentioned above, the early Lord Chancellors were all clerics.[32] Latterly, the Lords Chancellor were secular appointments, some of whom were attracted to the post by the profits which were available to the less scrupulous holders of the post. Indeed the Georgian Lords Chancellor used to charge for the award of the position of Master in the Courts of Chancery. This was clearly corrupt. No modern judge or government minister could take bribes to make someone a judge in this brazen way. Nevertheless, the Earl of Macclesfield, when Lord Chancellor, was convicted by the House of Lords of embezzling court funds in the early 18th century.[33] Lord Bacon was also found to have accepted 'presents' (which today we would consider to be bribes) when he was Lord Chancellor so that he would grant posts to his donors. We should not allow the irony of a person who sat as the sole judge in the court of conscience accepting 'presents'[34] to escape us. By today's standards the courts in this period were very corrupt.

1.2.2 The effect of the Judicature Act 1873

The Judicature Act 1873 was very important (and it still features in some university equity courses). It is worth observing that before 1813 there was only one full judge for chancery matters: that was the Lord Chancellor. Consequently, it could take an enormously long time for a case to be heard before that one judge. As mentioned above, the Lord Chancellor was assisted by the Master of the Rolls, who in time acquired judicial status. It was only in 1813 that the weight of cases waiting to be heard by these two people led to the appointment of a Vice-Chancellor for the first time, and later to the appointment of two Vice-Chancellors.

Through this passage of time, however, the popular conception of equity – and one which accords with the reality – was that the chancery courts were expensive and caused extraordinary delays. By 1873 pressure had built to change the court structure. The sorts of delays and other nonsense which occurred were portrayed brilliantly by Charles Dickens in *Bleak House*. The opening pages of that novel describe the Court of Chancery as being hidden in a fog and mired in confusion and delay. The upshot was genuine hardship for litigants who might be forced to live in poverty while the court took its time (often several years) to reach judgment. A great campaign developed to challenge this awful delay and confusion. This led to the enactment of the Judicature Act 1873. There were two particular objectives behind that Act: one to fuse the administration of equity and common law, and the second to reorganise the courts. The fusion of common law and equity took the shape of permitting any court to award common law remedies or equitable remedies without the need to petition one particular court or another.[35] Instead proceedings were simply begun in the High Court, which was divided into the divisions we recognise today. Lord Watson explained that the purpose of the Judicature Act was 'to enable the parties to a suit to obtain in that suit and without the necessity of resorting to another court, all remedies to which they are entitled in respect of any legal or equitable claim or defence properly advanced by them, so as to avoid a multiplicity of legal proceedings.'[36]

---

32 Thomas, 1976.
33 Hibbert, 1957, 126.
34 Baker, 2002.
35 Judicature Act 1873, s 24.
36 *Ind, Coope & Co v Emmerson* (1887) 12 App Cas 300, 308.

Significantly section 25 of the Supreme Court of Judicature Act 1873 provided:

> Generally, in all matters not hereinbefore particularly mentioned in which there is any conflict or variance between the rules of equity and the rules of common law with reference to the same matter, the rules of equity shall prevail.

Thus the principles of equity prevail over the principles of common law. The decision in the *Earl of Oxford's Case* thus received a statutory form.

Historically, the position of Lord Chancellor encompassed the constitutionally confusing roles of House of Lords judge, politically-appointed Cabinet minister and speaker of the House of Lords. It is worth noting that this position has changed with the creation of the Supreme Court by means of the Constitutional Reform Act 2005. These constitutional changes have had no effect on the substance of equity, however.

1.2.3 The continuing distinction between equity and common law

The distinction between equity and the common law was both practically and intellectually significant before the Judicature Act 1873. Before that Act came into full effect in 1875 it was necessary for a litigant to decide whether her claim related to common law or to equity. To select the wrong jurisdiction would mean that the claim would be thrown out and sent to the other court. So, if a claim for an equitable remedy were brought before a common law court, that common law court would dismiss the claim and the claimant would be required to go to the Court of Equity instead. The result of the Judicature Act 1873 was that the *practical* distinction between common law and equity disappeared. However, it is vitally important to understand that the *intellectual* distinction remains. As considered below, there remains a division between certain claims and remedies which are available only at common law, and other claims and remedies available only in equity.

1.2.4 The impact of the distinction between common law and equity

The main result of the distinction between common law and equity is that each has distinct claims and distinct remedies. Common law is the system which is able to award cash damages for loss. This is the pre-eminent common law remedy, for example in cases concerning breach of contract or the tort of negligence. On the other hand, a claimant seeking, for example, an injunction, or specific performance, or a trust must rely on equity because those are equitable remedies awarded at the court's discretion.

Therefore, it is necessary to make a distinction between common law and equity. The division might be rendered diagrammatically as shown in the table below. The detail of the available remedies is considered below and variously through this book. What is apparent from this list is that it is only in equity that it is possible to receive tailor-made awards of the various types of remedy on that very long list.

Common law	Equity
Examples of claims:	
Breach of contract	Breach of trust
Negligence	Tracing property
Fraud	Claiming property on insolvency

Examples of remedies and responses available:

Damages
Common law tracing
Money had and received

Compensation
Equitable tracing
Specific performance
Injunction
Rescission
Rectification
Imposition of constructive trust
Imposition of resulting trust
Subrogation
Account
Lien
Charge (fixed and floating)
Specific restitution

The impression we might take from this list is that equity is much more creative than the common law.

1.3 UNDERSTANDING EQUITY

1.3.1 Equity: An ethical construct

At its root, equity is concerned to prevent a defendant from acting unconscionably (literally, contrary to conscience) in circumstances in which the common law would otherwise allow the defendant to do so. To put that point another way, the courts will intervene to stop a fraudster, shyster or wrongdoer from taking advantage of the rights of another person.

Equity is therefore interfering to protect some underlying right of the victim either because of a contract with the shyster, or because the shyster has control over some property which rightfully belongs to the victim, or because we can assume that the actions of the shyster will affect the victim in the future in some way. In any of these cases, equity will attempt to intervene to stop the shyster from acting unconscionably. It will then impose a remedy which both prevents the shyster's wrongdoing and compensates the victim for any consequential loss.

1.3.2 Equity acts *in personam*

The core of the equitable jurisdiction is the principle that it acts *in personam*. That means that a Court of Equity is concerned to prevent any given individual from acting unconscionably. The Court of Equity is therefore making an order, based on the facts of an individual case, to prevent that particular defendant from continuing to act unconscionably. If that person does not refrain from acting in that way then he or she will be in contempt of court. The order, though, is addressed to that person in respect of the particular issue complained of. It is best thought of as a form of judicial control of that particular person's conscience. The study of equity is concerned with the isolation of the principles upon which judges in particular cases seek to implement this idea of conscience or other rules. It is always important to *read* the leading cases and the anomalous cases in the law reports to understand *the reasons why* judges have reached particular conclusions.

1.3.3 The nature of equity: A running river

It is sometimes said, in criticism of this moral equity, that it is arbitrary because too much discretion is given to the judges. This is to misunderstand equity. Equity is like a river. It rises from a series of small springs in ancient precedents and has flowed through hundreds of cases over the centuries. Rivers flow. Their waters flow incessantly. If you stand in the middle of a river with the water up to your chin, then it looks even more powerful and indifferent to you than it looked from the bank. Yet, rivers do not run freely wherever they choose. Instead they are controlled by their banks. In the same way, the principles of equity occasionally develop in a new way. In the same way, rivers are contained, just as equity is contained by the doctrine of precedent and the principles which govern its doctrines. The judges in courts of equity do not have unfettered discretion. Instead, the principles of equity are controlled by those precedents just as the course of a river is controlled by its banks. As we shall see throughout this book, the courts observe precedent and tend to limit their own discretions rather than allowing them to run free.

While equity is contained by precedent, every once in a while equity will create a new doctrine or strike out in a new direction when societal pressures require it. This potential for creativity is a part of equity's strength within the legal system. Intermittently, social changes demand change from equity. By way of example, in the 1970s there was a need for a new doctrine which would allocate rights in the family home before divorce law was created in its modern form. Consequently, the decision of the House of Lords in *Gissing v Gissing*[37] provided that response, as is discussed in Chapter 15, by providing that ownership of the home should be governed by the 'common intention' of the parties. As we shall see, one of the weaknesses of this creative system can be that judges in subsequent cases took that concept of 'common intention' in so many different directions that it became difficult to know what it meant. Another example of societal pressure arose in the 1990s in relation to domestic mortgages. There were too many mortgagees seeking repossession of properties against women who had been the subject of undue influence and duress and so the House of Lords in *Barclays Bank v O'Brien*[38] provided a response by clarifying the situations in which the claimant could have a mortgage contract set aside. The development of freezing injunctions, search orders, common intention constructive trusts, equitable tracing, floating charges, *Quistclose* trusts and other doctrines have come to the aid of people seeking answers to familial problems and commercial problems. Equity has reacted creatively to all of these social pressures. Significantly, those judges did not create these new doctrines on a whim. Rather, their development was planned to meet important social needs.

This is like a river in flood. When sufficient pressure for change builds up, then the river bursts its banks or it erodes the river banks and cuts a new course for itself. Or, preferably, a new course is cut for that river by humans so that it does not cause harm to the surrounding land. Similarly, equity cuts a new path when there is a need for it. Its capacity for change is important. There is nothing arbitrary in this continuous pulse of equitable principle: its sources are well known and it is bound by predictable precedents which act like a river's banks.

37 [1971] AC 886.
38 [1994] 1 AC 180.

1.4 THE CORE EQUITABLE PRINCIPLES

Thinking of equity as being based on its ancient[39] maxims has been a feature of some of the oldest books in the field. Snell's *Equity* published since 1868 still begins with a survey of the equitable maxims in its recent editions; Francis in his *Maxims of Equity* published in 1739 organised the entirety of his discussion of the case law in equity around 14 maxims. Not all of Francis' 14 maxims are still in existence today, although most of them are. My favourite of the disappeared maxims from 1739 is that 'equity prevents mischief'. It sounds like a rule to deal with naughty schoolboys but in fact it tended to refer to cases where one person would intrude on another person's commercial rights, such as publishing law textbooks in contravention of the exclusive right of the stationers' guild to do so.[40] There is something gloriously equitable in the idea that a court would seek to 'prevent mischief' generally. However, it is a sign of the changing nature of equity in the modern era that its principles are generally more clearly described than that. This section considers the most significant maxims which are still important today. They illustrate the way in which equity operates on the basis of 'high-level', broadly-stated principles which are applied flexibly on a case-by-case basis. By reading the cases which have used these maxims, we can assemble an understanding of what those maxims and those principles mean, and how they will be used in future cases.

The sub-headings for the subsections to follow state those ancient principles and then the text explains their meaning and relevance. These principles will occur and reoccur at various stages throughout this book.

1.4.1 Equity will not suffer a wrong to be without a remedy

This principle is at the very heart of equity: where the common law or statute do not provide for the remedying of a wrong, it is equity which intercedes to ensure that a fair result is reached.[41] In that sense, equity will not allow a wrong to be committed without there being some sort of remedy to address it. Hence, the scope for the courts to apply flexible doctrines like injunctions in any circumstance in which it is necessary to do justice between the parties.[42] The authorities demonstrate that equity will intervene in circumstances in which there is no apparent remedy but where the court is of the view that justice demands that there must be some remedy made available to the complainant.[43]

1.4.2 Equity follows the law – but not slavishly or always

This principle means simply that equity will ordinarily come to the same answer as the common law (e.g. concerning the ownership of land) unless there is a compelling reason not to do so. Nevertheless, the fact that equity will not follow the common law answer if there is a compelling reason not to do so is a demonstration that it is not always slavish.[44] Let us take an example of the leading case from Chapter 15, *Trusts of Homes*. When deciding who owns

---

39   If Maitland can use the word 'ancient' to describe equity, then so can I.
40   Francis, 1739, 30.
41   E.g., *Sanders v Sanders* (1881) 19 Ch D 373, 381.
42   *Mercedes Benz AG v Leiduck* [1996] AC 284, at 308, *per* Lord Nicholls.
43   *Seddon v Commercial Salt Co Ltd* [1925] Ch 187.
44   *Graf v Hope Building Corp* 254 NY 1, 9 (1930), *per* Cardozo CJ.

the home, the approach taken in *Jones v Kernott*[45] was that the true ownership of the home should be presumed to be the same as the entry on the Land Register. In that sense, equity is following the law because it is statute which provides for the Land Register to record the proprietor of land. However, Lady Hale and Lord Walker held in *Jones v Kernott* that equity would not follow the law (i.e. it would not presume the person entered as the proprietor was the beneficial owner of the home in equity) if there was some evidence that the parties had a different common intention as to the ownership of the property, or if there were some other demands of fairness which required the court to find otherwise. This is an example of equity – in the guise of the true, beneficial ownership of the home – following the law, but it could not be said to be following the law slavishly because evidence of a common intention or the demands of fairness empower the court to come to another conclusion.

1.4.3 Where there is equal equity, the law shall prevail

In a situation in which there is no clear distinction to be drawn between parties as to which of them has the better claim in equity, the common law principle which best fits the case is applied. In that sense, where the equitable doctrines produce an equal result, then the common law prevails.

1.4.4 Where the equities are equal, the first in time shall prevail

Where two claimants have equally strong cases, equity will favour the person who acquired their rights first. In that sense, the first in time prevails. Thus, if two equitable mortgagees each seek to enforce their security rights under the mortgage ahead of the other mortgagee, the court will give priority to the person who had created their mortgage first.

1.4.5 Delay defeats equities

An example of the importance of time in equity is the principle relating to delay. It is said that 'delay defeats equity' in the sense that too much delay will prevent access to an equitable remedy. The underpinning of the principle is that if a claimant allows too much time to elapse between the facts giving rise to her claim and the service of proceedings to protect that claim, then the court will not protect her rights.[46]

1.4.6 He who seeks equity must do equity

Another theme in the general principles of equity is that a claimant will not receive the court's support unless she has acted entirely fairly herself. Therefore, in relation to injunctions, for example, the court will award an injunction to an applicant during litigation only where that would be fair to the respondent and where the applicant herself undertakes to carry out her own obligations under any court judgment. A court of equity will not act in favour of someone who has, for example, committed an illegal act.[47]

---

45 [2011] UKSC 53.
46 *Smith v Clay* (1767) 3 Bro CC 639.
47 *Nessom v Clarkson* (1845) 4 Hare 97.

1.4.7 He who comes to equity must come with clean hands

Equity requires that a claimant comes to equity 'with clean hands' in the sense that that person must not have acted improperly or unconscionably if she is seeking an equitable remedy. As a development of the preceding principle of fairness, an applicant for an equitable remedy will not receive that remedy where she has not acted equitably herself.[48] So, for example, an applicant will not be entitled to an order for specific performance of a lease if that applicant is already in breach of a material term of that lease.[49] The principle means that you cannot act hypocritically by asking for equitable relief when you are not acting equitably yourself.

1.4.8 Equality is equity

Typically, in relation to claims to specific property, where two people have equal claims to that property, equity will order an equal division of title in that property between the claimants in furtherance of an ancient principle that 'equity did delight in equality'.[50] In that sense, the touchstone of equity is equality between the parties. Vaisey J considered the doctrine of 'equality is equity' in the following way: 'I think that the principle which applies here is Plato's definition of equality as a "sort of justice": if you cannot find any other, equality is the proper basis.'[51]

1.4.9 Equity looks to the intent rather than to the form

It is a common principle of English law that the courts will seek to look through any artifice and give effect to the substance of any transaction rather than merely to its surface appearance.[52] In this sense, equity will consider the parties' intentions and not simply the form which any documents may have taken. Equity will not ignore formalities altogether – for example, in relation to the law of express trusts, equity is particularly astute to observe formalities[53] – but it will not observe unnecessary formalities.[54]

1.4.10 Equity looks on as done that which ought to have been done

One of the key techniques deployed by the courts in recent years has been the principle that equity will consider that something has been done if the court believes that it ought to have been done.[55] So, if (as in *Walsh v Lonsdale*[56]) a landlord had contractually undertaken to grant a lease then equity would recognise the existence of a lease on the basis that the landlord was bound by specific performance of that contract to grant a lease.[57]

---

48 *Jones v Lenthal* (1669) 1 Ch Cas 154, authority for the proposition that equitable remedies may be denied to those who have acted inequitably and which has become accepted authority for the 'clean hands' doctrine in this context.
49 *Coatsworth v Johnson* (1886) 54 LT 520.
50 *Petit v Smith* (1695) 1 P Wms 7, 9, *per* Lord Somers LC.
51 *Jones v Maynard* [1951] Ch 572, 575.
52 *Midland Bank v Wyatt* [1995] 1 FLR 697.
53 *Milroy v Lord* (1862) 4 De GF & J 264.
54 *Sprange v Lee* [1908] 1 Ch 424.
55 See *Banks v Sutton* (1732) 2 P Wms 700, 715.
56 (1882) 21 Ch D 9.
57 *Re Antis* (1886) 31 Ch D 596.

1.4.11 Equity imputes an intention to fulfil an obligation

This doctrine assumes an intention in a person bound by an obligation to carry out that obligation, such that acts not strictly required by the obligation may be deemed to be in performance of the obligation.[58]

1.4.12 Equity acts *in personam*

As was considered above, it is a key feature of equity that it acts *in personam*.[59] As Lord Selbourne held:

> The courts of Equity in England are, and always have been, courts of conscience, operating *in personam* and not *in rem*; and in the exercise of this personal jurisdiction they have always been accustomed to compel the performance of contracts and trusts . . . [60]

The focus of a court of equity in making a judgment is to act on the conscience of the particular defendant involved in the particular case before it. Therefore, equity is acting against that particular person and not seeking, in theory, to set down general rules as to the manner in which the law should deal with similar cases in the future. Of course, over the centuries, the courts have come to adopt specific practices and rules of precedent as to the manner in which equitable principles will be imposed. Consequently, many aspects of equity are now bound by precedent. This topic will, in effect, occupy us for much of the remainder of this book.

1.4.13 Equity will not permit statute or common law to be used as an engine of fraud

Equity will not allow a defendant to use a statutory principle so as to effect a fraud in relation to someone else. Slightly more lyrically, equity will not permit statute to be used as an engine of fraud. The best example is probably the secret trust, considered in Chapter 6 below. Secret trusts arise in situations in which a person making a will has sought to create a trust while concealing their real purpose – historically, this tended to be a trust created by a man with a mistress and an illegitimate child by her who wanted to leave property to his best friend so that the friend would actually pay that money to his mistress for the child's maintenance. In those cases, the friend would often try to keep the money for themselves. Equity would intervene to require the friend to hold that property on trust for the mistress for the benefit of the child.[61] The best friend would otherwise seek to rely on the statutory principle that only the will could dictate who was to be the owner of the property; but that statutory provision would facilitate that man's fraud unless equity intervened.

---

58 *Sowden v Sowden* (1785) 1 Bro CC 582.
59 See section 1.3.3 above.
60 *Ewing v Orr Ewing (No 1)* (1883) 9 App Cas 34, 40.
61 *Blackwell v Blackwell* [1929] AC 318.

1.4.14 Equity will not permit a person who is trustee of property to take benefit from that property as though a beneficiary

As considered in detail in Chapter 2, a trust is created by transferring the common law title in property to a trustee to hold that property on trust for identified beneficiaries.[62]

1.4.15 Equity will not assist a volunteer

The principle that equity will not assist a volunteer occurs frequently in this book. In line with the commercial roots of many of these doctrines, equity will not assist a person who has given no consideration for the benefits which she is claiming. Therefore, someone who is the intended recipient of a gift, for example, will not have a failed gift completed by equity interpreting the incomplete gift to be a trust or some other equitable structure.[63]

1.4.16 Equity abhors a vacuum

In considering rights to property, equity will not allow there to be some property rights which are not owned by some identifiable person.[64] Thus, a trustee must hold property on trust for identifiable beneficiaries, or else there is no valid trust. Similarly, it is generally considered at English law that no person can simply abandon their rights in property – rather, that person retains those proprietary rights until they are transferred to another person. To do otherwise would be to create a vacuum in the ownership of property. The doctrine of resulting trusts operates so as to carry property rights back to the person who was their last owner.[65]

1.4.17 A trust operates on the conscience of the legal owner of property

The most significant of the equitable doctrines is the trust, under which a beneficiary is able to assert equitable rights to particular property and thus control the way in which the common law owner of that property is entitled to deal with it. The trust is considered in the next chapter. As will emerge, the key tenets of the trust are that the legal owner of property will be obliged to hold it on trust for any persons beneficially entitled to it where good conscience so requires: this can be due to an express declaration of trust, or to the imposition of a trust implied by law by the courts.[66]

---

62 *Fletcher v Fletcher* (1844) 4 Hare 67.
63 *Milroy v Lord* (1862) 4 De GF & J 264.
64 *Vandervell v IRC* [1967] 2 AC 291, HL.
65 *Ibid.*
66 *Westdeutsche Landesbank Girozentrale v Islington LBC* [1996] AC 669.

The nature of trusts

2.1 THE BIRTH OF THE TRUST

2.1.1 The medieval roots of the trust

The easiest way of understanding the nature of the trust is to understand some of the legends about the way in which the trust came to exist in English law. The story was told to me in the following way, and I understood what was going on immediately. So, excuse me if I tell the story to you in the same way. In the 12th century, English and other European noblemen ('the knights') travelled to the Middle East to fight wars which are still known somewhat distastefully among historians as 'the crusades'. Typically, they spent many years in the Middle East and learned many things. It is from the Middle East that we in the West acquired our concepts of arithmetic and civilised ideas like hospitals. Many of these knights were some of the most significant landowners in England at the time. While they were to be absent from the country for several years, the knights had to transfer the common law ownership rights associated with their land to someone else (their '*trustee*') to look after the property for them, to raise rents, and so forth. When the knight eventually returned from the Middle East it seems that many of these trustees argued that the land belonged to them at common law and they were not going to transfer the property back to the returning knight. The common law courts could do nothing to help the knight.

It was the courts of equity which identified the unconscionability in this situation: the trustee was never intended to be the real owner of the land, just to administer it while the knight was abroad. The trustee knew that he was only intended to look after the property temporarily and was never intended to become its outright owner permanently. So, the courts of equity recognised, to use modern language, that the trustee was really holding an equitable interest (that is, a right recognised by the courts of equity) in that land *on trust* for the knight. That meant that while the trustee did have a form of ownership which was recognised by the common law, equity recognised that the knight had the true ownership of the property. The trustee was only the owner at common law, whereas the real beneficial ownership took effect in equity. As a result we have one person, the trustee, who has rights recognised by the common law holding property on trust for the benefit of someone else (whom we shall call the 'beneficiary') so that the beneficiary has rights in that property which are recognised by equity.

Therefore, trusts were created to prevent unconscionability. Thomas Lewin, in the first edition of his important work *A Practical Treatise on the Law of Trusts and Trustees*, published in 1837, identified the birth of the trust as being based on the determination of the Court of Chancery to prevent fraud and consequently that 'the parents of the trust were Fraud and Fear, and a court of conscience was the Nurse'.[1] What Lewin meant was that the law of trusts developed in the courts of equity to prevent people committing fraud. In his lectures delivered in Cambridge at the turn of the 20th century, Professor Maitland considered that the trust was English law's greatest gift to jurisprudence and also that it was comprised of these sorts of ancient English elements.

However, there is reason to suppose that the idea which underpins the trust was in fact in existence in other countries before the English developed it into the form which caused Professor Maitland such excitement. It is possible that the knights, when they were in the Middle East, encountered the idea of the Islamic 'waqf'. This institution was a form of charitable institution within a family which permitted property to be held to one side for the benefit of impoverished members of that family. It was this basic structure which is used in the English concept of the trust. (In its earliest form, the trust was known as a 'use' in England.) So, when the knight returned from the Middle East and sought to recover his land, it was found by the courts of equity that the trustee was treated as holding the land for the benefit of the knight. It is possible that the inspiration for this idea came from the waqf. Similarly, when people wanted to give money or other property to the Franciscan order of monks, they encountered the problem that Franciscan monks had taken a vow of poverty and therefore could not become the owners of any property. Therefore, it was common for the abbot (who was in charge of a monastery) to hold that property as trustee for the benefit of the monastic community's members. In all of these examples, property is held by one person as a form of steward for the benefit of someone else. That is the core idea behind the trust.

---

1 Lewin, 1837, 2.

What is important is that the trustee is able to control, maintain and use the property, while the beneficiary has the ultimate entitlement to it. Consequently, the trustee has 'the legal title' to the property that is held on trust so that they can, for example, decide which crops are grown on the knight's land, grant tenancies over the land to individual farmers, and collect rents from those farmers. Without rights recognised by common law, the trustee would not be able to manage the property that is held on trust in this way. However, the beneficiary simultaneously must also have those property rights which are recognised by equity to take the ultimate benefit from the trust property. Therefore, the trustee is empowered to raise income from the trust property (and to do a thousand other things besides as we shall see), while that income is paid ultimately to the beneficiary. The simple trick which the English trust performs is recognising that two people can have proprietary rights in the same item of property at the same time so that one person is responsible for the maintenance of that property, while the other person takes the ultimate benefit from it. That simple idea is the basis for pension funds (where trustees invest the trust fund so as to generate incomes for the beneficiaries), investment funds, the ownership of co-owned homes, and so on.

This basic concept is endlessly flexible and the law of trusts has been almost endlessly creative. The key pieces of jargon which we have identified so far are as follows. The people who hold the common law rights in the property are known as '*trustees*' and it is they who act as stewards of the property; while the people who are ultimately intended to take a benefit from the arrangement are known as '*beneficiaries*'. Equity protects the interests of the beneficiaries. We shall encounter these ideas again and again throughout this book.

2.1.2 The development of the family settlement

If we fast-forward to the 18th century, then we encounter the world of English novelist Jane Austen. Two of her finest novels – *Sense and Sensibility* and *Pride and Prejudice* – are based on the problems caused by two trusts. It was usual in this period for the landed classes (that is, the aristocracy and the wealthy upper-middle classes) to have all of their property (their homes, their chattels and their investments) organised on the basis of complex trusts which controlled the rights of each family member to access and use that property. These trusts were also called '*settlements*'.

The person who creates a trust is known as the '*settlor*'. At the time of creating the trust (or, settlement) the settlor must be the absolute owner of all of the property that is intended to be held on the terms of that trust.

In the world of Jane Austen, it would usually be a family patriarch who was the owner of the family property (possibly under a family settlement which required amendment or which was about to expire during his lifetime) and it was therefore his responsibility to draft a settlement (usually with advice from his solicitors who would do the actual drafting) which would make plain how the family house, any other houses or cottages on their land, their silverware, their crockery, their heirlooms and their other property and investments, should be held for other family members down the generations until the settlement reached the time at which it was legally required to expire. Therefore, that family patriarch would be the settlor of this family settlement. Family settlements were created to organise the use and ownership of family property down the generations. (These settlements were only used by the wealthy because the poor had no property to settle on trust and could not afford the necessary legal advice in any event.)

It was common for these settlements to identify that, after the death of the settlor, the eldest son of the settlor would be the person who would become the beneficial owner (and therefore the occupant) of the main house during his lifetime. He would be known as the '*life tenant*' as a result. Other members of the family would be identified as taking rights in that same property after the death of the life tenant: they were known as '*remainder*' beneficiaries because their interest was in the property which remained after the death of the life tenant. Provision would be made for the rights of other family members (that son's sisters and brothers, his mother, their maiden aunts, their cousins, and so forth) to receive incomes from the trust or to occupy other property held on the terms of the settlement. If you were to picture the television programme *Downton Abbey* then that might give you an idea of the sorts of enormous houses and the range of adult children and elderly aunts who might require housing in small houses on the edge of the grounds or in the main house, and the vast amount of expensive heirlooms that were owned by these families and the number of servants that they appeared to require. None of these people would have jobs in the conventional sense. Instead, their livelihoods were dependent on these family settlements.

The settlor and his solicitors would have to anticipate all of the problems which might beset the family in future generations, ranging from their rights to income, the risk of people dying unexpectedly early, the risk of unfortunate marriages being contracted, and the risk of other family members falling on hard times. Given the danger of unexpected changes in the family's fortunes (such as premature death, the failure of the trust's investments or changes in the law), then the settlement would need to have flexibility built into its terms and there might be occasions when the settlement would need to be amended with the leave of the courts. (Those mechanisms for change are discussed in Chapter 10.) Even in the modern age, very well-known settlements held by wealthy families (in this book we shall consider the Nestle and the Vestey family settlements, for example) require regular updating to account for changes in tax law and so forth.

The drama in Jane Austen's novels *Sense and Sensibility* and *Pride and Prejudice* is grounded in the fact that these sort of family settlements meant that well-to-do young women would be forced to leave their houses when their fathers (the life tenants under those settlements) died because the family settlement would specify that another *male* relative was entitled to vacant possession of the house as soon as the life tenant died. The risk of their father dying and leaving them without a penny (because all of his money was tied up in the family settlement anyway) hung over their young lives like a shadow. The young women would therefore be required to find wealthy husbands in good time, or to rely on the charity of other family members after their father died, or to live in genteel poverty for the rest of their days. Everything turned on the opinions and the words used by that patriarch, the settlor, in the family settlement. Even young male relatives whose incomes were dominated by the wealth held in the family settlement might find themselves penniless if the trust's investments failed or if the trustees exercised a power in the trust document in favour of another relative whom they considered to be more deserving or needy. These sorts of trusts governed the lives of upper echelons of British society as a result. This sort of issue illustrates the sort of sociological and political problems which seethed beneath the placid surface of trusts law.

2.1.3 Modern trusts

The family settlements dominated the lives and the fortunes of the wealthy in England and Wales. Through the Victorian period, the wealthy continued to have their property held on trust. For example, Charles Dickens's novel *Bleak House* focused on a lengthy dispute about a family settlement which was so complex that no two lawyers could agree on any of the issues which it raised. Eventually the litigation took so long and was so complex that the entire fortune that had been settled on trust was exhausted in paying lawyers' fees. Dickens based that element of the story on a real case. There have been several others like it since.

Over time, the law of trusts has also become the field of law which dominates situations as disparate as pensions and unit trusts, taking security over property in commercial transactions, and ownership of the family home. It is no longer limited to the settlements in wealthy families. When a pension is created, there are trustees who hold the pension fund on trust for the pensioners as beneficiaries; when a mutual investment fund is created, there are trustees appointed who invest the investors' money on their behalf and then hold those moneys and the profits on trust for the investors as the beneficiaries. Ownership of co-owned homes is decided by reference to trusts law principles, so that anyone identified as a 'proprietor' on the legal title over the land (i.e. the Land Register) holds that property on trust for anyone who is recognised by trusts law as having rights in that home. Pension fund and mutual investment funds (in the form of unit trusts) are some of the most significant participants in the stock market; seeking protection against the insolvency of counterparties in commercial transactions is central to commercial activity; wills and trusts dominate the way in which property is left after death within families; and ownership of privately-owned homes now dominates the UK economy and covers a large part of the population. All of these situations are governed by trusts law. Trusts have always been significant in England and Wales, and they continue to be so.

2.2 THE DEFINITION OF A TRUST

2.2.1 The definition of a trust

The following definition of a trust is given in Thomas and Hudson's *The Law of Trusts*:[2]

> The essence of a trust is the imposition of an equitable obligation on a person who is the legal owner of property (a trustee) which requires that person to act in good conscience when dealing with that property in favour of any person (the beneficiary) who has a beneficial interest recognised by equity in the property. The trustee is said to 'hold the property on trust' for the beneficiary. There are four significant elements to the trust: that it is equitable, that it provides the beneficiary with rights in property, that it also imposes obligations on the trustee, and that those obligations are fiduciary in nature.

Trusts are enforced by equity and therefore the beneficiary is said to have an 'equitable interest' in the trust property (sometimes this right in a beneficiary is referred to as a 'beneficial interest'), whereas the trustee will be treated by the common law as holding the 'legal title' in the trust property, thus enabling the trustee to deal with the trust property so as to achieve the objectives of the trust.[3] In general terms we can observe that a trustee is the officer under a trust who is obliged to carry out the terms of the trust and who owes strict fiduciary duties of the utmost good faith to the beneficiaries.

---

2 Thomas and Hudson, 2010, para 1.01.
3 See section 1.2 on the distinction between equity and common law.

2.2.2 The different types of trust

There are three principal types of trust: express trusts, resulting trusts, and constructive trusts. (There was a category of 'implied trusts' but they are rarely discussed today.) The most significant distinction between these types of trust is that express trusts can be created deliberately by a settlor (as considered in Part 2 *Express Trusts* of this book), whereas resulting and constructive trusts are implied by a court in appropriate circumstances (as considered in Part 4 *Trusts Implied by Law* of this book).

Express trusts

In general terms, express trusts are trusts which are declared intentionally by the settlor. Typically, the settlor will intend to settle specific property on trust for clearly identifiable beneficiaries, to be held by appointed trustees according to terms set out by the settlor.[4] A well-organised express trust will be drafted with legal advice and will be contained in a written 'trust instrument'. That trust instrument will contain all of the duties of the trustees, the rights of the beneficiaries and any other provisions expressed in full legal language. The advantage of writing all of these provisions down is that all of the parties involved then know the detail of their rights and obligations. However, it is not necessary that an express trust is contained in writing for it to come validly into existence (except for a few circumstances discussed in Chapter 5). There are situations (discussed in section 3.3) in which the settlor might not even realise that their actions would be analysed by a lawyer as creating a trust but which the courts will interpret as creating an express trust nevertheless.[5] It is necessary that the trust property is sufficiently identifiable[6] and that there is no uncertainty as to the identity of the beneficiaries (as discussed in detail in Chapter 3).[7] Similarly, legal title in the trust property must be transferred to the trustees before the trust can be effective.[8]

Resulting trusts

Resulting trusts arise 'by operation of law' – which means that they are not created intentionally by the settlor but rather their existence is inferred from the circumstances by the courts. The House of Lords in *Westdeutsche Landesbank Girozentrale v Islington LBC* held that resulting trusts arise in two situations.[9] First, where the settlor fails to create a valid transfer of property then the unallocated property will bounce back to the settlor on resulting trust.[10] Second, where two or more people contribute to the purchase price of property, such that those people acquire equitable interests in the property in proportion to the size of their contributions to the purchase price.[11] Resulting trusts are considered in detail in Chapter 11.

---

4 *Milroy v Lord* (1862) 4 De GF & J 264.
5 *Paul v Constance* [1977] 1 WLR 527.
6 *Re Goldcorp Exchange Ltd* [1995] 1 AC 74; *Westdeutsche Landesbank Girozentrale v Islington LBC* [1996] AC 669.
7 *Morice v Bishop of Durham* (1805) 10 Ves 522; *McPhail v Doulton* [1970] 2 WLR 1110.
8 *Milroy v Lord* (1862) 4 De GF&J 264.
9 [1996] AC 669.
10 *Vandervell v IRC* [1967] 2 AC 291, HL.
11 *Dyer v Dyer* (1788) 2 Cox Eq Cas 92.

Constructive trusts

Constructive trusts also arise by operation of law. They are imposed by the courts in situations in which a person acts unconscionably in relation to property. The constructive trust comes into existence when the defendant has knowledge that some unconscionable act has taken place in relation to an item of property.[12] So, by way of example, if a person steals property then that property will be deemed by the court to be held on constructive trust for its original owner because the theft was an unconscionable act.[13] Constructive trusts arise in many situations, including the following: where property is bought with a bribe; where money is paid mistakenly to the recipient and the recipient realises the mistake; where property is acquired by killing its owner; where property is acquired by stealing it; where the co-owners of a home form a common intention as to the way in which they want to own that property; where commercial people agree to develop property together; where payment for a house has been made but the sale not completed; where trust money has been paid into a mixed account; and personal liabilities to account as constructive trustee will arise where the defendant has dishonestly assisted a breach of trust or has received property unconscionably with knowledge of a breach of trust. This doctrine is very broad and its various sub-categories are considered in Chapters 12, 15, 19 and 20. It is also open-ended so that new categories of constructive trust can be created from time to time.

Proprietary estoppel

Where a representation has been made to a person about an item of property on which they rely to their detriment, then that person will be entitled to rely on proprietary estoppel. The court may then fashion any remedy it pleases either to give effect to the promise made in the representation, or to compensate the claimant for their detriment, or to prevent unconscionable advantage being taken of the claimant. This may result in an award of the freehold in the property at issue, or a mere award of financial compensation, or some combination of the two. That award will only take effect from the date of the court order prospectively. Proprietary estoppel is clearly a very open-textured doctrine. It is discussed in Chapter 13.

2.2.3 The mechanism by which an express trust comes into existence

We shall focus on express trusts for the time being. An express trust comes into existence by means of the settlor, a person who was the absolute owner of property before the creation of the trust, showing an intention to create a trust. Alternatively, an express trust may be created by virtue of some action of the settlor which the court interprets to have been sufficient to create a trust but which the settlor himself did not know was a trust.[14] There is no magic formula for the creation of a trust. The court must simply be convinced that the settlor had the appropriate intention to create a trust, as is discussed in section 3.3. The legal title in the trust property is passed to the trustee (or trustees). The trustees are responsible for holding that property on trust for the beneficiary (or beneficiaries). The beneficiaries acquire an equitable interest in the trust property.

---

12 *Ibid.*
13 *Westdeutsche Landesbank Girozentrale v Islington LBC* [1996] AC 669.
14 *Paul v Constance* [1977] 1 WLR 527.

Consequently, the trustees are the owners of the legal title in the trust property and simultaneously the beneficiaries are the owners of the equitable proprietary interest in the trust property.

2.3 EXPRESS TRUSTS – THE MAGIC TRIANGLE

2.3.1 How the express trust is structured

We shall consider the creation of express trusts in a little more detail in this section. Chapters 3 through 10 of this book consider express trusts in more detail yet. A description of the creation of an express trust runs as follows: a trust is created when the absolute owner of property (the settlor) passes the legal title in that property to a person (the trustee) to hold that property on trust for the benefit of another person (the beneficiary) in accordance with terms set out by the settlor. There are consequently three legal capacities to bear in mind in the creation of a trust: that of the settlor, the trustee, and the beneficiary. These three capacities form the 'magic triangle'. The 'magic triangle' looks like this:

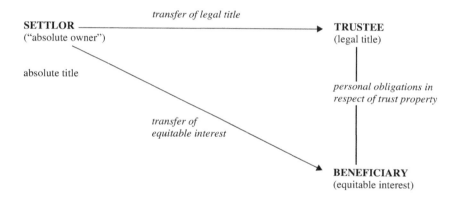

The following sections summarise some of the key requirements for the creation of an express trust, and the roles of the settlor, trustee and beneficiary. Each of these principles is discussed in detail later in the book. For the moment, we are only trying to create some familiarity with the basic concepts. Let us begin with the settlor and the creation of an express trust.

2.3.2 The settlor

Before the creation of an express trust, the settlor holds absolute title in the property which is to be settled on trust. There is no magic formula for the creation of a trust, in the sense that there is no specific formality which must be performed for all trusts to be valid. Instead, the settlor must demonstrate certainty that their intention is to create a trust (not something else), certainty as to the property which is to be held on trust, and certainty as to the identity of the intended beneficiaries (all of which are considered in Chapter 3). There must be a beneficiary or beneficiaries for a trust to be valid (as discussed in Chapter 4 this requirement is known as 'the beneficiary principle'). There are formalities for the valid declaration of trust only in relation to specific properties like land and shares (as discussed in Chapter 5). Aside from those specific formalities in relation to those types of property, trusts can be created either orally or in writing. However, as mentioned above, a well-organised trust will have a 'trust instrument' in which the terms of the trust are recorded in writing because that makes it clear what the trustees' powers and duties are, and what the beneficiaries' rights are. An oral trust will not usually specify what those rights are meant to be in that sort of detail and what the settlor said may be difficult to prove later as a purely practical matter.

A trust must be properly constituted by transferring the legal title in the trust property to the trustees: for example, in relation to a trust over money held in a bank account it is necessary that the name on the account and the signatories on that account must be the trustees; and in relation to land the trustees must be registered on the Land Register, as considered in Chapter 5. Thus all of the rights necessary to deal with the property must be 'vested' in the trustees. The beneficiary acquires the equitable interest in the trust fund at the same time.

Once a trust has been validly declared and constituted, the settlor ceases to have any active role in the trust in their capacity as settlor.[15] A little like a shipbuilder setting a new ship out to sea for the first time, once a settlor has created a trust and transferred the legal title in the trust property to the trustees then the trust has a life of its own over which the settlor, in their capacity as settlor, has no control.

There is one point which often puzzles students who have studied some property law and so it may be useful to dispose of it now. Does property have an equitable interest in it all of the time, even without a trust being declared over it? The answer is 'no'. There is no equitable interest in property until a trust (or some other equitable doctrine) is declared over it. We do not think of all property as having legal title and an equitable interest latent within it like an egg has albumen and yolk always existing within it. Instead, the legal title and the equitable interest are created at the moment when the trust is created by the settlor. So, when I buy a pair of shoes in a shop, I become the 'absolute owner' of those shoes: that is, I own all of the property rights in those shoes without needing to distinguish between legal and equitable rights. There is no question of the shoes having legal title and an equitable interest latent within them. I am simply the owner of the absolute interest in those shoes. I own all of the property rights in them outright. If I were, for some reason, to decide to settle those shoes on trust then there would be a trust created over those shoes for the first time and at that moment the person I nominate to be trustee would acquire the legal title in them and the beneficiary would acquire the equitable interest in those shoes.

2.3.3 The trustee

On creation of a trust, the legal title in the trust property must be vested in the trustee and the property rights making up the trust fund must be held by the trustee on trust for the beneficiaries. Any litigation involving the trust and third persons is conducted by the trustee as legal titleholder in the trust property. Therefore, in the remainder of this book we shall refer to the trustee as the 'legal owner' of property. This is a technical use of the term 'legal owner' which means that the trustee is vested with all of the common law or any statutory rights (that is, the 'legal title') in the property. It is not being used in opposition to the colloquial use of the word 'illegal'.

---

15 *Paul v Paul* (1882) 20 Ch D 742.

The most important feature of the trust is that the trustee is not entitled to assert personal, beneficial ownership in the trust property. Rather, it is the beneficiary who has all of the beneficial interest in property, as considered immediately below. Therefore, suppose that Susan dies leaving a will which appoints Tabitha to hold a house on trust as trustee for Susan's children with a power to sell it. Tabitha will be the person whose name appears on the legal title to the property at the Land Registry because the trustee takes the legal title in the trust property. However, Tabitha would not be entitled to sell the property and keep the money for herself beneficially because Tabitha is intended only to be trustee of the property in this example. Rather than keep that money for herself, Tabitha would be required to hold the sale proceeds on trust for the beneficiaries. The beneficiaries own the equitable interest in the trust property. In that sense, it is not Tabitha's property. She is merely trustee of it.

Two important points arise. First, a practical point. It will always be important to consider the precise terms of the trust (when there is a trust instrument). As will become apparent throughout this book, the courts will tend to look very closely at the precise written terms of a trust or at any evidence of the verbal expression of the settlor's intentions in an oral trust.[16] Second, the trustee is required to hold the original trust property, or any substitute property, on trust for the beneficiaries. So, if £10,000 was held on trust and if that money was used to buy shares, then the shares would be held on trust in place of the money. Therefore, a trust does not simply attach to one specific item of property and to that property only. Rather, the trust attaches to bundles of property rights which may be transferred from one piece of property to another.

The precise obligations on the trustee are therefore to be found in the trust instrument, if there is one. If there is no trust instrument, or if the trust instrument does not anticipate every issue, then there are more general obligations imposed on the trustee by the general law of trusts. These issues are considered in more detail in this book in Part 3 *Administration of Trusts* (in Chapters 8 through 10). Among the issues to be considered are the amount of information which trustees are required to give to beneficiaries, the manner in which the trust fund should be invested, the appointment and retirement of trustees, whether the terms of the trust can be varied to deal with unexpected events, and the termination of the trust. There are case law and some statutory principles dealing with these sorts of practical issues. As may have become apparent by now, much will depend upon the nature and terms of the trust. However, the most important types of express trusts are considered next.

Bare trust

The simplest form of trust is a 'bare trust'. A bare trust arises where the trustees hold property on trust for a single, absolutely entitled beneficiary. That beneficiary therefore owns the entire equitable interest in the trust fund. That means that the trustee has no discretion nor any obligation other than the stewardship of the trust property on behalf of that beneficiary. The beneficiary will hold 100% of the possible equitable interest in that property. The trustee in such a situation is generally referred to as being a 'nominee'; that is, one who holds property in the name of another.[17] As we shall see, it is common for there to be several beneficiaries with different rights under trusts which are not bare trusts, and consequently those types of trusts are usually more complex.

16 *Fuller v Evans* [2000] 1 All ER 636.
17 See section 3.5.6 below.

Fixed trust

The term 'fixed trust' refers to the situation in which the trustees hold property on trust for a certain, defined list of beneficiaries. The rights of the beneficiaries are fixed and the trustees consequently have no discretion as to those rights. An example of a definition of such a class of beneficiaries would be: 'on trust for my two children Anna and Bertha equally'. The 'fixed' nature of the trust refers then to the fixed list of people who can benefit from the trust. That Anna and Bertha share the equitable interest 'equally' means that the trustee has no discretion as to the rights which attach to each person. The role of trustee is comparatively straightforward in this situation because the trustee is required simply to perform the terms of the trust slavishly.[18] The trustee has no meaningful discretion in the operation of such a trust, in contrast to the trusts and powers considered next.

Discretionary trust and mere power of appointment

The settlor may want to give the trustees the flexibility to cope with unexpected future events by giving them some discretion. So, a 'discretionary trust' gives some discretion to the trustee as to the manner in which property is to be distributed and/or the people to whom that property is to be distributed. Suppose a situation in which a settlor has three adult children and wishes to require that the trustees use as much of a fund of money as they may think appropriate to help whichever one of the children earns the least money in any given calendar year. The trustee has discretion to distribute the amount of money necessary to make good that person's lack of funds. The role of trustee is therefore more complicated than in a fixed trust because the trustee is required to exercise some discretion.[19] Suppose the settlor set aside a fund of money 'such that my trustee *shall* pay £5,000 per year out of that fund to whichever of my children has the greatest need of it'. In such a situation, the trustee is compelled to make the payment because of the inclusion of the word 'shall', but she has discretion as to which child will receive it by assessing their level of need.

Alternatively, a settlor may decide that a trustee is to have a 'power of appointment' between a number of potential beneficiaries so that the trustees are only required to make a payment out of a trust fund if they consider it to be appropriate. That means that the trustee is empowered to decide which people from among an identified class of beneficiaries are entitled to take absolute title in any property which is appointed to them by the trustees. Suppose then that the settlor sets aside a fund 'to be held on trust by Trustee with a power such that Trustee *may* appoint the sum of £10,000 to whichever of the Exeter City FC first team has performed most consistently throughout the current season'. The trustee therefore has discretion to choose which of the identified class is to receive absolute title in that £10,000 per season, but unlike a discretionary trust power, the power of appointment does not require that any payment be made unless the trustee considers it to be necessary: because the trustee has a *power* to appoint that money, she will not be obliged to do so if she considers it inappropriate.[20] As discussed in Chapter 3 there are important differences between trusts and mere powers. By giving a trustee this sort of power to act, it is possible to build some flexibility into the trust and to allow the trustees to cope with unexpected future problems.

18   See section 3.5.5 below.
19   See section 3.5.4 below.
20   *Breadner v Granville-Grossman* [2000] 4 All ER 705.

Accumulation and maintenance trust

An accumulation and maintenance trust is one which seeks to earn income for beneficiaries which can be held back and applied when those beneficiaries need it. A settlor may seek to create an endowment trust from which, for example, the future needs and living expenses of the settlor's children are to be provided. Consequently, the principal responsibility of the trustee is to invest the trust property and then to apply it according to the needs identified in the terms of the trust. The beneficiaries have rights against the trustees to have the trust performed in accordance with the terms of the trust and to have property advanced for their benefit at the time identified in the trust (subject to any discretion vested in the trustees).

The nature of fiduciary duties

The office of trustee is a form of what English lawyers term a 'fiduciary'. There are four well-established examples of fiduciaries: a trustee in relation to their beneficiaries; a company director in relation to a company; an agent in relation to their principal; and a business partner in relation to other partners. One commonly used definition of a fiduciary office was given by Millett LJ:[21]

> A fiduciary is someone who has undertaken to act for or on behalf of another in a particular matter in circumstances which give rise to a relationship of trust and confidence. The distinguishing obligation of a fiduciary is the obligation of loyalty. The principal is entitled to the single-minded loyalty of his fiduciary. The core liability has several facets. A fiduciary must act in good faith; he must not make a profit out of his trust; he must not place himself in a position where his duty and his interest may conflict; he may not act for his own benefit or the benefit of a third person without the informed consent of his principal. This is not intended to be an exhaustive list, but it is sufficient to indicate the nature of fiduciary obligations. They are the defining characteristics of the fiduciary.

Therefore, we know that the obligations of acting in a fiduciary capacity arise in circumstances in which one person has undertaken to act loyally in the affairs of another. The clearest example of a fiduciary is a trustee who is obliged to obey the terms of the trust and who also owes duties not to take any unauthorised profit from her office of trustee, not to permit any conflict of interest between her own affairs and those of the trust, to act with impartiality among all of the beneficiaries to a trust, and so forth. These obligations are discussed in detail in Chapter 8.

Broadly then, a fiduciary is someone who owes legal duties of loyalty and utmost good faith in relation to another person. Yet, whether a fiduciary obligation exists in any specific set of circumstances is not always an easy question to answer. It is easy in relation to an express trust. In relation to a trustee carrying on trust business, once that trust is properly constituted, there will necessarily be a fiduciary relationship between trustee and beneficiary. However, the courts will impose fiduciary duties in many other contexts when it is considered to be appropriate (as considered in Chapter 12). The effect of there being a fiduciary relationship will be that the fiduciary will owe the beneficiary a range of obligations of good

21 *Bristol & West Building Society v Mothew* [1998] Ch 1 at 18, *per* Millett LJ.

faith and potential obligations to make good any loss suffered by the beneficiary.[22] It is an onerous role. In other contexts it is less easy to know how far any fiduciary obligations will extend.

2.3.4 The beneficiary

The rights of the beneficiary will depend on the specific terms of the trust. It is a pre-requisite of the creation of a valid trust that there be some person for whose benefit the court can decree performance of the trust (as discussed in Chapter 4).[23] Furthermore, the beneficiary has proprietary rights in the trust property.[24] Thus, the beneficiary's equitable interest is a right in property. If any loss is suffered by the trust as a result of some breach of trust, then the beneficiary also has a right against the trustee personally to compensate the beneficiary's loss.[25] This right to equitable compensation operates over and above the beneficiary's proprietary rights.[26] The beneficiary's proprietary rights also permit her to trace after her property and to assert rights over any property by which the original trust property has been substituted wrongfully[27] and against any people who participated in the breach of trust despite not being trustees.[28]

The rights of a beneficiary will depend upon the terms of their own particular trust and upon the type of trust which has been created. Thus, beneficiaries under a discretionary trust do not have vested rights to any particular property until the trustees decide to grant some property to them, whereas the sole beneficiary under a bare trust owns all of the equitable proprietary rights in the property held on trust. Therefore, the most important distinction is between 'vested' rights and rights which remain contingent on some eventuality provided for under the terms of the trust. The different types of trusts and powers of this sort are discussed in detail in section 3.3. The nature of the rights of beneficiaries is analysed in detail in section 4.1. As will be clear by this stage, everything will depend upon the precise terms of any trust instrument or the wishes expressed by the settlor in relation to a verbal trust.

2.3.5 Distinguishing between 'people' and 'legal capacities'

If you are going to become a lawyer then it will be important for you not to be concerned about seeing people as individuals.[29] Instead, you should see people (whether individuals or companies) in terms of the legal capacities in which they are acting. Let us take an example. Suppose that Brenda wants to create a trust over her home so that she will be the life tenant who is entitled to occupy that home during her lifetime but so that it will be held on trust in remainder for her adult daughters after her death. Brenda would be the settlor. However, Brenda might decide that she wants to be one of two trustees so that she can control how the property is managed (instead of trusting everything to third parties).

---

22   *Target Holdings v Redferns* [1996] 1 AC 421.
23   *Bowman v Secular Society Ltd* [1917] AC 406, 441, *per* Lord Parker.
24   *Saunders v Vautier* (1841) 4 Beav 115.
25   *Target Holdings v Redferns* [1996] 1 AC 421.
26   *Ibid.*
27   *Re Diplock's Estate* [1948] Ch 465.
28   *Royal Brunei Airlines v Tan* [1995] 2 AC 378.
29   I am joking, but only partly.

To ensure the legal niceties are obeyed, Brenda might pay her solicitor to act as the other trustee. So, Brenda can be both settlor and a trustee. Brenda would then identify herself as the life tenant and therefore would be one of the beneficiaries, with her daughters Petula and Petunia as the remainder beneficiaries. In this situation, Brenda is the settlor, one of the trustees, and also one of the beneficiaries. Trusts law prevents people like Brenda from benefiting themselves as beneficiaries to the detriment of other people when they are making decisions as trustees. Brenda may be one human being but she occupies three different legal capacities here: she is settlor, trustee and beneficiary. Therefore, she must separate off these different capacities in her mind. Whenever she makes a decision as trustee, she must be able to justify it and show that it is not to the detriment of the other beneficiaries. She must act without bias and impartially in the interests of all of the beneficiaries. The law of trusts will treat Brenda as being three different people whenever she acts in relation to the trust as a result. This is why, as a lawyer, you must not become distracted by people: instead, you must consider the capacities in which they are acting from time-to-time, and the rights and obligations which stick to them depending on the capacity in which they are acting.

2.4 FUNDAMENTALS OF THE LAW OF TRUSTS

2.4.1 The core principles of the trust

This section considers some of the central statements of the principles at the heart of trusts law. The most important judicial statement of the core principles of trusts law in recent times was made by Lord Browne-Wilkinson in *Westdeutsche Landesbank Girozentrale v Islington LBC*,[30] when his lordship sought to set out the framework upon which the trust operates:

The Relevant Principles of Trust Law:

(i)   Equity operates on the conscience of the owner of the legal interest. In the case of a trust, the conscience of the legal owner requires him to carry out the purposes for which the property was vested in him (express or implied trust) or which the law imposes on him by reason of his unconscionable conduct (constructive trust).

(ii)   Since the equitable jurisdiction to enforce trusts depends upon the conscience of the holder of the legal interest being affected, he cannot be a trustee of the property if and so long as he is ignorant of the facts alleged to affect his conscience . . .

(iii) In order to establish a trust there must be identifiable trust property . . .

(iv)   Once a trust is established, as from the date of its establishment the beneficiary has, in equity, a proprietary interest in the trust property, which proprietary interest will be enforceable in equity against any subsequent holder of the property (whether the original property or substituted property into which it can be traced) other than a purchaser for value of the legal interest without notice.

Four things emerge from these *dicta* and are considered in turn in the following paragraphs.

---

30 [1996] 2 All ER 961, 988.

2.4.2 The trust imposes equitable obligations on the conscience of the trustee

First, the source of the trustees' obligations are found in equity requiring that they act in good conscience whether as a result of a settlor having created an express trust, thus obliging the trustee to obey the terms of the trust in good conscience, or else a court having considered it appropriate to impose a trust in circumstances in which the trustee would otherwise have been permitted to act unconscionably. As has already been said in Chapter 1, equity acts *in personam* and thus operates on the conscience of the defendant.[31] The explanation of the trust as an equitable institution is that the trustee receives property in circumstances in which it would be against conscience for her to refuse to be bound by the terms of that trust. The trust can take one of two forms:

(a) It might be an express trust under which a settlor has consciously and deliberately created a trust. In such circumstances, equity would not permit a trustee to seek to act in contravention of the terms of such a trust or to act more generally in bad conscience.
(b) Alternatively, the trust might be one imposed by the courts, instead of by a settlor, because it is considered that it would be unconscionable to allow a person who has acquired common law rights in property to continue to control that property without some judicial action being taken against her. Thus, Lord Browne-Wilkinson refers to these constructive trusts as being imposed on a person 'by reason of his unconscionable conduct'. Such a person has the role of 'trusteeship' imposed on her by the court, thus creating the obligations of trustee and beneficiary between that person and others.

What can also be observed about trusts, however, is that the importance which they have acquired over the centuries has caused the courts to develop a number of strict principles surrounding the manner in which they are created and operated, as is considered in detail in Parts B and C of this book. This tendency towards increased rigidity of principle – which will become apparent when we consider the requirements of certainty in Chapter 3 and of formalities in Chapter 5 – might suggest a movement away from a general notion of an equitable, moral conscience as underpinning the trust. In truth the idea of conscience still governs the obligations of trustees even though it may appear to have been submerged at times behind the requirements of certainty and formality. This development emerges more clearly in the next paragraph.

2.4.3 Trusts create proprietary rights for the beneficiary and personal rights against the trustees

A trust must take effect over property in favour of a beneficiary

The trust is built on a combination of property law rules and personal obligations. First let us consider the proprietary aspects of the trust. As Lord Browne-Wilkinson held in *Westdeutsche Landesbank v Islington LBC*: 'in order to establish a trust there must be identifiable trust property'.[32] Thus, if a settlor purported to create a trust without having any rights in the trust property at the time of purporting to create that trust, then there would not be

---

31   *The Earl of Oxford's Case* (1615) 1 Ch Rep 1.
32   See section 2.4.1 above.

a valid trust created.[33] Once a trust is created, the trustee is required to hold the identified trust property on trust for the identified beneficiaries.[34] Secondly, however, the manner in which the trustee is required to behave in relation to the beneficiaries in the exercise of her fiduciary duties is a matter concerning a system of personal, equitable obligations as well as proprietary obligations. The obligations are equitable in that it is equity which recognises the rights of the beneficiaries. These obligations will stem from the proprietary rights of the beneficiaries in the trust property but go further than simply imposing proprietary obligations on the trustees. The trustees also owe personal obligations to the beneficiaries to account to the beneficiaries for the value of the trust property if the trustees commit some breach of trust.[35] This has the effect that the trustees are personally liable to pay into the trust fund an amount equal to any loss suffered by the trust, as considered in Chapter 18.[36] The distinction between personal and proprietary obligations is considered in greater detail next.

The division between property rights and personal obligations

The beneficiary under a trust will have rights in property (or, 'proprietary rights' or 'rights *in rem*') provided that she is validly a beneficiary with some rights vested in her at the material time. In English law, if the defendant owes only a personal obligation to the claimant (or, a 'right *in personam*') then the defendant will be liable either to pay damages at common law (in the form of a breach of contract or a tort) or to pay some equitable compensation in equity to the claimant (for example in relation to a breach of trust) in the event that that obligation is breached.[37]

The trust, whether express or implied, will grant proprietary rights to the beneficiary. Significantly, rights in property entitle the beneficial owner to title to the property regardless of the value of that property. Therefore, it is also preferable to retain title in property which is likely to increase in value instead of relying on common law damages or some other personal claim. Conversely, if the property is likely to decrease in value, then it would be preferable to recover monetary compensation equal to the beneficiaries' loss measured at a level before the property decreases in value. Rights to compensation for a breach of trust by the trustees are discussed in Chapter 18.

2.5 THE BENEFITS AND USES OF TRUSTS

2.5.1 Family uses of trusts

As was explained in section 2.1, the early history of trusts law concerned the creation of family settlements to pass property down the generations. Chesterman and Moffat described the trust as being a gift over the plane of time. What they meant was that a settlor is effectively making a gift to the members of their family so that the trustees administer the trust for the full period of time which trusts law permits that trust to last (which is currently 125 years under

---

33 *Re Brooks' Settlement Trusts* [1939] 1 Ch 993.
34 *Milroy v Lord* (1862) 4 De GF & J 264.
35 *Clough v Bond* (1838) 3 My & Cr 490.
36 *Target Holdings v Redferns* [1996] 1 AC 421.
37 *Ibid.*

the Perpetuities and Accumulations Act 2009). The family settlements which we discussed above are designed to control the ownership and use of property down the generations. Significantly, will trusts have also been used for centuries to pass property on death. The will appoints 'executors' who act as trustees over any property which is left on the terms of this 'testamentary trust' (i.e. a trust created by a will). The settlor (or, 'testator' in relation to will trusts) identifies the terms on which that property is held for the identified beneficiaries who receive bequests under that will. It is more common for well-advised, wealthy individuals to organise the passage of their property by means of '*inter vivos*' trusts (i.e. trusts created during their lifetime) because such trusts used to be more tax efficient than wills in many circumstances.

2.5.2 Commercial uses of trusts, insolvency

Trusts can conduct businesses (and, before the creation of the modern company in 1897, they were the principal form of business enterprise in tandem with the partnership). The principal commercial use of the trust today is something different. The principal commercial use of the trust today is taking security against the failure of commercial counterparties (i.e. the other party to a contract). If a commercial person is concerned about the solvency of their counterparty, then having property held on trust for them by that counterparty will mean that the trust will survive the insolvency and so the trust property will still be held protected.

A good illustration of trusts being used to take security is the case of *Re Kayford*,[38] discussed in section 3.2. In that case, a mail order company sold goods to the public through a catalogue. It received payments from customers through the post before sending out their goods. As a result, there was a period of time when the company held customers' money before the customer received their goods. The company's accountants and their managers became concerned that the company was on the brink of insolvency. Therefore, the accountants suggested that the customer moneys should be held in a separate bank account and not mixed in the company's general bank accounts until the customers had received their goods. Eventually the company did go into insolvency. It was held that the customers' money held in the separate bank account should be treated as having been held on trust by the company for those customers. The fate of the company's ordinary trade creditors was that they were 'unsecured creditors', which meant that they had no specific property which they could take from the company to discharge the debts that were owed to them. Unsecured creditors have to wait in the hope that there will be some money left to discharge their debts when the insolvency is wound up. Usually, unsecured creditors receive a few pennies for every pound that they are owed in an insolvency. Very importantly, however, beneficiaries under a trust still have that identified property held on trust for them by the insolvent person because the law of trusts holds trust property sacrosanct and protected from the claims of the unsecured creditors. Therefore, the customers whose money was held on trust were shielded against losing their money in the insolvency. A trust grants protection against another person's insolvency.

Trusts can be used by commercial people as part of their contracts from the beginning of their dealing so as to protect themselves. Let us take an example. Suppose that Peter is starting a new online business which needs a large amount of computer equipment each month as new staff are taken on. He meets Meg, who is starting up in business supplying the computer equipment which Peter needs. Meg's prices are very good but she is new to the business. Neither Peter nor Meg trust one another completely. Both of their businesses are new and both of them could easily go into insolvency in a weak economy. They agree that Peter will buy £10,000 of computer equipment from Meg each month for one year. However, Meg does not want to make delivery until Peter makes payment, and Peter does not want to make payment until he has received and tested the equipment. They are advised that they could solve their problems by creating a new trust bank account so that Peter can pay the money into that account until the equipment is delivered and tested. The trust money is held by the bank as trustee. (The bank will charge them for this service.) Peter pays the £10,000 into the trust account on terms that the money is held on trust for Peter until the computer equipment is delivered to him. Once the computer equipment has been received and tested, then that £10,000 is held on trust for Meg. In that way, Peter is protected against the risk of Meg going into insolvency, or simply failing to make delivery, because the trust will continue in existence even if Meg is bankrupt. Therefore, Peter could simply recover the money in the trust account if no delivery is made. Similarly, Meg is protected against Peter's failure to make payment to Meg because Peter is required to deposit the £10,000 into the trust account before Meg has to make delivery of the computer components to him. If Peter went into insolvency then Meg is entitled to any money held on trust for her in the account once she has made delivery. If Peter were to fail to deposit the £10,000 in the trust account then Meg would be absolved from the need to make any deliveries.

The trust is a very flexible way of permitting the parties to take security against the risk of the other party's failure to perform their contractual obligations. The beneficiary has an equitable proprietary interest in the trust property even if the trustee or their counterparty goes into insolvency. The trustee is obliged by their fiduciary duties to act in the best interests of the beneficiaries regardless of their own concerns. Over the centuries, the trust device has been honed into an incredibly useful tool for commercial situations as well as family situations.

Part 2

The creation of express trusts

Chapter 3

The three certainties

CAPSULE SUMMARY

There are three certainties required for the creation of a valid express trust. The settlor must demonstrate the following: (a) a clear intention to create a trust as opposed to creating something else ('certainty of intention'); (b) the trust property must be sufficiently segregated from other property so that the trust fund is certain ('certainty of subject matter'); (c) and the people who are to benefit from the trust must also be identified with sufficient certainty ('certainty of objects'). Without those three certainties being satisfied, any purported trust will be void. These certainties are required so that the courts can oversee the behaviour of the trustees: to be able to do that, it must be certain that a trust was intended, that the property is clearly identifiable, and that the identities of the intended beneficiaries are clear.

(a) *Certainty of intention.* The settlor must have had an intention to create a trust as opposed to something else. There is no requirement to use a specific form of words when creating a trust over property other than land. The court will be prepared to infer an intention to create a trust from the circumstances.

(b) *Certainty of subject matter.* The trust fund must be separately identifiable from other property. A purported trust in which the trust property is mixed with other property, so that it is impossible to identify precisely which property is to be held on trust, will be invalid. Exceptionally, it may be that where the property is intangible property made up of identical units (such as ordinary shares of the same class), it may not be necessary to segregate that trust property from other property. Similarly, a recent decision of the Supreme Court relating to the insolvency of an investment bank (Lehman Brothers) held that a huge mixed fund may be considered to be held on the terms of a single trust, with all of the bank's relevant customers as its beneficiaries, for the purposes of specific financial regulations (as opposed to there needing to be a separate trust for each customer). Consequently, the collapse of Lehman Brothers (which triggered the global financial crash of 2008) has put this area of law at the centre of the most significant corporate insolvency in history.

(c) *Certainty of objects.* To identify the beneficiaries, it is first necessary to identify the nature of the trust or power which is being exercised. (The various categories are discussed in the text.) In relation to fiduciary mere powers and in relation to discretionary trusts, it is required that it is possible to say of any person claiming to be a beneficiary that that person is or is not a member of the class of beneficiaries. Some exceptional cases have taken the view that the trust may be valid where it is possible to say that a substantial number of people do or do not fall within the class of beneficiaries. In relation to a fixed trust, it is necessary to be able to draw up a complete list of all the beneficiaries. Personal powers, on the authorities, will not be void for lack of certainty of objects. The case law has dealt with a variety of words and expressions which commonly cause uncertainty, as considered below.

3.1 INTRODUCTION

3.1.1 The need for certainty as trusts grew in importance

The subject of certainties (which we consider in this chapter) demonstrates that the law of trusts is built on a bedrock of clear rules. As with any case law system, however, the real world generates factual situations which challenge those rules. Consequently, this chapter lays out the rules in the leading cases governing the requirements of certainty in the creation of express private trusts, and then it considers other cases which have adapted, distinguished, modified or challenged those rules to fit their circumstances. In every topic in this Part 2 of this book we shall no sooner see a rule set out in a leading case to cover a particular issue before we shall see other cases test the limits of that rule. In that sense, this area of law is just like any other. In essence the key question is always whether the trust at issue will be valid or void depending on the certainty about its terms.

Trusts grew in importance across the centuries as they were used increasingly in the form of family settlements and will trusts, as was discussed in the previous chapter. That discussion also considered how the trust is now widely used in commercial situations as well as familial circumstances. The trust really is one of the fundamental techniques of English law: it allows property to cascade down the generations within families, it protects commercial parties against one another's insolvencies, and everything in between. Many of the newer cases considered in this chapter arise from banking transactions and the financial crisis of 2008 in particular. Significantly, the same trusts law principles apply in these different contexts.

In recognition of their social importance, the courts developed rules which required that three basic elements of express trusts needed to be sufficiently certain before those trusts would be valid. Consequently, there are three certainties required for the creation of a valid express trust.[1] The settlor must demonstrate a clear intention to create a trust as opposed to creating something else;[2] the trust property must be sufficiently segregated from other property so that the trust fund is certain;[3] and the people who are to benefit from the trust must also be identified with sufficient certainty.[4] These forms of certainty are, respectively: certainty of intention, certainty of subject matter and certainty of objects. These are 'the three certainties'. Without those three certainties being satisfied, the trust will be void.

3.1.2 The relationship of settlor, trustee and beneficiary

When an express trust is created then there are the three different capacities under that trust: settlor, trustee and beneficiary. These fundamentals of these capacities were considered in detail in Chapter 2. The central question considered in this chapter is the certainty that is necessary before an express trust will be said to exist. When considering express trusts – that is, situations in which the settlor *intends* to create a trust – we should recognise that there will be cases in which the court may analyse the actions of the settlor as demonstrating an intention to create an express trust even though the settlor might not have realised that that was what she was doing.[5] Thus, when we talk about express trusts, we are concerned with any situation in which the settlor performs actions which the courts consider demonstrates an intention to create a trust.

3.2 THE THREE CERTAINTIES

English law has a great affection for certainty: judges are concerned that the law promotes certainty in contracts, trusts and other dealings between persons. In terms of the trust specifically, the judges' concern is that the settlor makes her intention sufficiently certain so that the court

---

1 *Morice v Bishop of Durham* (1805) 10 Ves 522, at 539, *per* Lord Eldon.
2 *Knight v Knight* (1840) 3 Beav 148; *Knight v Boughton* (1840) 11 Cl & Fin 513.
3 *Re London Wine Co (Shippers) Ltd* [1986] PCC 121.
4 *IRC v Broadway Cottages Trust* [1955] 2 WLR 552; *Re Gulbenkian* [1968] Ch 126; *McPhail v Doulton* [1970] 2 WLR 1110.
5 *Paul v Constance* [1977] 1 WLR 527 – as considered in section 3.3.

will be able to direct the trustees how to act if there are problems with the administration of the trust. For the court to be able to make such directions, it is essential that it be certain:

(a) that the settlor intended to create a trust ('certainty of intention');
(b) which property is to comprise the trust fund ('certainty of subject matter'); and
(c) who the beneficiaries are ('certainty of objects').[6]

Each of these forms of certainty are considered in turn in the following sections.

3.3 CERTAINTY OF INTENTION

3.3.1 What form of intention?

Conscious creation of a trust

It is important that the settlor intends to create a trust as opposed to doing something else, such as making a gift or a contract.[7] The simplest manifestation of that intention would be for the settlor to take advice from a solicitor and sign a formal declaration of trust in the form of a deed.[8] Such a written manifestation of a trust is referred to as a 'trust instrument'. As is considered in Chapter 5, the creation of a written instrument is not a legal requirement in most situations;[9] however, the use of a well-drafted trust instrument does make it easier to prove that there is a trust.[10] In such a situation, if the settlor consciously intended to create a trust, then there is no difficulty in establishing that there was sufficient certainty of intention.[11] A verbal expression of an intention to create a trust will be sufficient for most forms of property except land.[12] The more difficult situations arise when a settlor unknowingly behaves in a way which might have created a trust, or where the settlor leaves her intention ambiguous in the terms of a will or other document. It is in those situations that the question of whether or not there was sufficient certainty of intention will be significant. Interestingly, there are many decided cases involving commercial parties with expensive legal advisors in which the intention to create a trust was not made clear because those advisors behaved incompetently.

Express trusts based on the inference of an intention to create a trust by the court

One of the best-known examples of a case involving certainty of intention is the decision of that excellent Chancery judge Megarry J in *Re Kayford*.[13] In that case, a mail order company used to receive money from customers buying items from their catalogues before those items were

---

6 *Knight v Knight* (1840) 3 Beav 148, *per* Lord Langdale.
7 *Milroy v Lord* (1862) 4 De GF & J 264.
8 Sometimes matters will be simple. The Australian High Court held in *Byrnes and another v Kendle* [2011] HCA 26, 14 ITELR 299 that the use of the term 'trust' should be interpreted quite simply as creating a trust.
9 There are, however, statutory exceptions which do require signed writing to create a trust, as discussed in Chapter 5, such as trusts of land: Law of Property 1925, s 53(1)(b).
10 See section 5.1 below.
11 E.g. *Slamon v Planchon* [2004] 4 All ER 407; [2004] EWCA Civ 799.
12 *Moore v Williamson* [2011] EWHC 672 (Ch).
13 [1975] 1 WLR 279.

sent out to the customers. The customers therefore bore the risk that they had paid their money but that they might not receive the items for which they had paid. The mail order company realised that it was in danger of going into insolvency and therefore segregated all of its customer prepayments into a separate bank account. Money was moved out of that bank account after the item had been sent to the customer. Eventually the company did go into insolvency.

Megarry J considered that the question for him to answer was 'whether the money in the bank account . . . is held on trust for those who paid it, or whether it forms part of the general assets of the company'. Put more briefly, the question was whether the money was held on trust for the customers or was owned absolutely by the company. If the money was owned absolutely by the insolvent company then it would be distributed among the company's many creditors. Alternatively, if the money was held on trust for the customers then the trust would protect the customer's equitable interests under the trust against the insolvency. The question for the purposes of certainty of intention was whether the decision to place the customers' prepayments into that separate bank account demonstrated an intention to create an express trust, even though no document to that effect had been created nor had any of the parties made a conscious, verbal declaration of trust. Nevertheless, Megarry J held that the parties' intention was to declare a trust over the money held in the separate bank account even though the parties did not explicitly declare a trust. His lordship analysed the circumstances and held that they disclosed something which a lawyer would consider to be an intention to create a trust.

Therefore, we can see that even in commercial circumstances where the parties have professional advice, the court will analyse the parties' behaviour and decide whether or not there is an intention which a court would characterise as creating a trust. The question is: what are these circumstances which the courts interpret as constituting a declaration of trust? I would suggest that it is the act of segregating property with an intention that that is being done for the benefit of a third party. So, when the company put the prepayments into a separate bank account while being concerned that their impending insolvency would lead to those customers losing that money, then that would suggest that money was being segregated for the benefit of those customers. As Megarry J put it, the customer 'may create a trust by using appropriate words when he sends the money . . . or the company may do it by taking suitable steps on or before receiving the money [such as paying the money into a separate account for the benefit of the customers]. If either is done, the obligations in respect of the money are transformed' into a trust.

Lord Millett summarised the principle relating to the identification of certainty of intention in the House of Lords in *Twinsectra Ltd v Yardley*:[14]

> A settlor must, of course, possess the necessary intention to create a trust, but his subjective intentions are irrelevant. If he enters into *arrangements* which have the effect of creating a trust, it is not necessary that he should appreciate that they do so; it is sufficient that he intends to enter into them.

Consequently, the court will infer the existence of a trust if the circumstances are the sort of circumstances or 'arrangements' which the court would interpret as constituting a trust.

14 [2002] 2 AC 164 at [71].

Such trusts will be express trusts, even if the parties did not know that that was what they were creating.

Another good example of the circumstances in which the courts will infer an intention to create an express trust is the non-commercial case of *Paul v Constance*.[15] Mr Dennis Constance left his wife (Brenda) to live with Mrs Doreen Paul. Dennis received a court award of £950 for an injury suffered at work, subsequent to which Dennis and Doreen decided to set up a joint bank account. When they visited the bank they were advised that the account should be set up in Dennis's name alone because the couple were not married. Therefore, Dennis was the common law owner of the account. The £950 lump sum was paid into the account and formed the bulk of the money held in it. The couple also added joint bingo winnings to the account and used some of the money to pay for a joint holiday. Importantly, evidence was also adduced at trial that Dennis had said to Doreen 'this money is as much yours as mine'.

In time, Dennis died. His wife, Brenda, sought to claim that the bank account belonged entirely to her deceased husband and that it therefore passed to her as his widow under the statutory Intestacy Rules. Doreen argued to the contrary that the money was held on trust by Dennis, as legal owner of the bank account, for both Dennis and Doreen as beneficiaries. Therefore, Doreen argued, the bank account should pass to her as sole surviving beneficiary. The litigation was therefore a staple of soap operas: the spurned wife was fighting with her dead husband's mistress over his money.

The Court of Appeal held that Dennis had declared a trust over the money in the bank account. Their rationale was that the words 'the money is as much yours as mine' manifested sufficient intention that Dennis would hold the property on trust for both himself and Doreen. Furthermore, that the couple had treated the money in the account as joint money was taken to be evidence of the intention to create a trust. As Scarman LJ held, the words Dennis did use, that the money was as much hers as his, 'convey clearly a present declaration that the existing fund was as much the plaintiff's as his own'. His lordship also observed that Dennis was a man of 'unsophisticated character' who did not know he was creating a trust. This was a part of the court interpreting the parties' intention as being the creation of an express trust even though they would not have known that that was what they were doing.

Let us take another example to illustrate the same point. As a law student you may well have worked in a restaurant. If so, you may well have participated in a 'tronc' system whereby (depending on the nature of the particular system operated in your restaurant) tips received from customers would have been collected by a nominated person and then distributed between all waiting staff and possibly kitchen staff too. The upmarket London nightspot Annabel's (as we learn from *Annabel's (Berkley Square) Ltd v Revenue and Customs Commissioners*[16]) operated a tronc system under which all cash tips left for waiting staff by customers were taken by a 'troncmaster'. The troncmaster was a senior member of the staff but they were not acting on behalf of their employer. Instead, in their role as troncmaster, they held all of those cash tips before distributing them among the waiting staff periodically in accordance with the terms of their tronc. An issue arose as to the nature of the troncmaster's duties when holding those cash tips before they were distributed. It was held that while the

---

15   [1977] 1 WLR 527.
16   [2009] EWCA Civ 361, [2009] 4 All ER 55.

troncmaster held those cash tips they were holding them on trust for the other waiting staff. In essence, the troncmaster had legal title over those cash sums but they were held ultimately for the benefit of other staff, and therefore it was found that they were held on trust. Again, the key feature of the finding of a trust was that property was being held by the troncmaster with the intention that it was being so held ultimately for the benefit of other people. It would not be possible, on this analysis, for the restaurant owners to claim title to the tronc and to use the contents of the tronc to pay a part of the wages of the waiting staff – a practice which is used by many disreputable restaurants in the UK to meet their obligations under the minimum wage legislation.

Failed gifts are not express trusts

Imagine you were expecting to receive a gift from someone. Imagine that you had been encouraged to believe that some delicious item of property was soon to be passed to you wrapped in exquisite, gossamer-thin paper. Imagine that you believed this object would change your life. And then imagine that the gift was never made. The injustice of it! The object resided in the other person's possession but they decided not to make a present of it to you. Being a passionate, vivacious human being you could be forgiven for claiming, in the heat of your distress, that this object should be treated as being held on trust for you. Perhaps you would argue through your tears that it would be unconscionable to deny this property to you after all that you had been led to believe. Unfortunately, the law of trusts does not agree with you. The law of trusts will not permit a failed gift to be re-characterised as an express trust. Rather, the transferor must have intended to declare a trust over the property for it to be held on trust for you. Otherwise, all that happened was a failure to make a gift.

In practice, everything will turn on the judge's assessment of the evidence and their observation of the witnesses in the witness box. In consequence, at the distance of many years from the facts of many of these cases it may be difficult to distinguish between one case and another. So, in *Jones v Lock*,[17] a father returned home from a business trip to Birmingham only to walk into an argument with his wife because he had not brought back a present for his infant son. In what appears to have been a fit of pique, he went upstairs, wrote a cheque out for a large sum of money in favour of himself as payee, came back downstairs, shouted 'Look you here, I give this to the baby', and thrust the cheque into the baby's crib. Under banking law this could not have been a gift of the amount of money stipulated on the cheque because the cheque was made out in favour of the father. Instead, the mother argued that the father had intended to create a trust over the money in favour of the infant child. Lord Cranworth held that there was no intention to create a trust here. Clearly, this was just another act in that most ancient and tedious form of theatre: the unhappy marriage. At best it was an intention to create a gift which was not completed. It was certainly not an intention to create a trust because the father did not intend to hold the benefit of the cheque for his infant child.

As Lord Jessel MR held in *Richards v Delbridge*,[18] the court will not uphold a failed gift by treating it as being a declaration of trust instead. In that case, a businessman decided to transfer his business outright to a member of his family and sought to demonstrate this

---

17 (1865) 1 Ch App 25.
18 (1874) LR 18 Eq 11.

intention by an endorsement on the lease over the business premises. The gift was never completed. The claimant argued that the business should be treated as having been held on trust for him. The court held that the failed gift would not be effected by means of inferring an intention to create a trust because a gift was what had been intended throughout. It has also been held that the use of the word 'trust' in an instrument will not necessarily mean that a court will deem that to be a trust;[19] although that will be a likely inference, particularly if one person is holding property for the benefit of another.

Commercial situations disclosing an intention to create a trust

As the leading case of *Re Kayford* shows, it is not uncommon for well-advised commercial parties to fail to specify that they intend to create trust rights over property used in their businesses. In cases of insolvency this can be particularly important because commercial people may well take security against their counterparties' insolvency by means of having property held on trust; or if they failed to have property held on trust, then they may want to argue that the existence of a trust should be inferred by the court.

The shattering financial crisis of 2008 generated two particularly significant cases in the area of certainty of intention. In *Brazzill v Willoughby*[20] Smith J considered the failure of the financial institution Kaupthing Singer Friedlander ('KSF'). KSF had been taken over by the Icelandic bank Kaupthing which collapsed during the financial crisis. There was concern, as a result, that KSF would go into insolvency itself. KSF was regulated by the Financial Services Authority ('FSA') in the UK. The FSA issued a 'supervisory order' under the Banking (Special Provisions) Act 2008[21] which required KSF to set up an account with the Bank of England into which it would pay amounts to match any deposits made with it by its customers. The purpose of this scheme was to ensure that there was money set aside to repay client deposits in case KSF did fail. Clause 2 of the supervisory order used the term 'trust' to describe this arrangement and the parties themselves also used the expression 'trust' to describe this arrangement. Unfortunately the order did not make it clear which deposits nor which customers were covered by this scheme and which were not. Subsequently, KSF did go into insolvency. The question arose whether or not there was a trust in existence over the money held in that account with the Bank of England. Smith J held, following *Re Kayford*, that putting those sums into that account constituted a voluntary intention to create a trust on the part of KSF, even though it was made in accordance with the FSA's supervisory order.

In *Mills v Sportsdirect.com Retail Ltd*[22] a second case arose in relation to KSF. KSF went into insolvency at precisely 14.21 hours on 8 October 2008. A question arose as to whether KSF held shares on trust for the claimant company before the time at which it went into insolvency. The claimant had entered into a 'repo' transaction with KSF whereby shares were deposited with KSF and cash paid to the claimant, before the shares were to have been returned to the claimant and an amount of cash repaid by the claimant. (In essence, a repo is a way of acquiring a short-term loan in exchange for lodging financial instruments like shares or bonds.) On these facts, because the claimant had been concerned about KSF's solvency during the financial crisis, the parties' representatives had agreed that the claimant would transfer the shares outright to KSF, but that KSF would pass legal title in those shares

---

19 *Tito v Waddell (No 2)* [1977] 1 Ch 106, 211, *per* Megarry VC.
20 [2009] EWHC 1633 (Ch), [2010] 1 BCLC 673.
21 On which see Alastair Hudson, *The Law of Finance*, Sweet & Maxwell, 2009, 29–41.
22 [2010] EWHC 1072 (Ch), [2010] 2 BCLC 143.

to a nominee, Sinjul Nominees Ltd, which would then hold the shares. While the parties' representatives negotiated the deal, they said that the shares would be transferred into '[the claimant] SD's box' within the holdings held by Sinjul so that those shares would be 'ringfenced' and so that 'you [the claimant] would own those shares outright'.[23] It was also made plain between the parties that the purpose of this arrangement was 'to keep the shares out of the hands of KSF's creditors'.[24] The term 'trust' was not used by the parties nor their advisors. Nevertheless, Lewison J held that these circumstances demonstrated an intention to create a trust over the shares in favour of the claimant. Sinjul was found to have acted as trustee and the references to the shares being 'ringfenced' and put 'in a box' were found to demonstrate an intention to hold them on trust. His lordship followed *Re Kayford* in reaching this decision.

The case of *Don King Productions Inc v Warren*[25] was another commercial case in which the parties' advisors failed to specify the existence of a trust. Here two famous boxing promoters entered into an agreement to promote a boxer in Europe. The two men formed a partnership agreement whereby they, and the companies which they controlled, agreed to exploit existing promotion agreements for their mutual advantage. The partnership agreement was very unclear as to the nature of the rights which the parties acquired. Simply put, each party was required to hold the benefit of any existing or future management promotion agreements for the benefit of the partnership. However, some of these promotion agreements were stated to be non-transferable. It was argued that a non-transferable contract of this sort could not be property of the sort which could be held on trust because, it was said, the ability to be transferred is key to being an item of property. Lightman J held that the best interpretation of the partnership agreement was that the intentions of the parties had been to hold the benefit derived from any such non-transferable contracts on trust for the partnership and not the contracts themselves. Thus, even though the contracts themselves were expressed to have been incapable of transfer (and so prima facie to have been incapable of forming the subject matter of a trust), it was held that any benefit received from them could be the subject matter of a trust and that this partnership arrangement evinced sufficient intention to create a trust. Lightman J made repeated reference to how poorly drafted the parties' agreements had been and how their frequent redrafting of their contracts had not made the position any clearer. This decision was affirmed in the Court of Appeal.[26]

By way of balance, we should acknowledge the unsatisfactory decision of the High Court just before Christmas 2006 on ostensibly similar facts to *Re Kayford* in *Re Farepak Food and Gifts Ltd.*[27] This case was very newsworthy and was decided very quickly. In short, Farepak operated a Christmas club which went into insolvency thus denying its members the goods to which they were contractually entitled at Christmas time. In essence, the members paid into the club throughout the year and then were entitled to order goods (food, presents and so forth) from the club in time for Christmas. Therefore, the members had made prepayments throughout the year and the management of Farepak had organised for those prepayments to be transferred into a separate bank account. Management did this in large part because they had become aware that the business was in danger of insolvency. Nevertheless, in a judgment which did not mention *Kayford* at all, Mann J held that there should *not* be a trust

---

23   [2010] EWHC 1072 (Ch), [2010] 2 BCLC 143, para [59].
24   [2010] EWHC 1072 (Ch), [2010] 2 BCLC 143, para [63].
25   [1998] 2 All ER 608.
26   [2000] Ch 291, CA.
27   [2006] EWHC 3272 (Ch), [2007] 2 BCLC 1.

found because the finding of a trust would disadvantage Farepak's other creditors by ring-fencing that segregated trust money for the sole benefit of the club's members who had made prepayments.

On the authority of *Re Kayford* (the facts of which were almost identical) an express trust should clearly have been found in *Farepak*. Instead, the case seems to have been argued by the barristers on the erroneous basis of *Quistclose* trusts (discussed in Chapter 22 – a type of trust imposed over loan moneys if the borrower goes into insolvency) and therefore one must feel sorry for Mann J who did not have the case argued properly in front of him. The case was argued in front of Mann J on Friday 15 December and he had to reach judgment by Monday 18 December in the eye of a tabloid news storm. So close to Christmas Day, the newspapers were in a state of high anticipation to see whether the High Court would order a merry Christmas for all of the club's members or whether Mann J would play Scrooge and deny everyone so much as a humbug.[28] He did the latter, even though the case law would have permitted him to play the role of Santa Claus. Much could have been learned by counsel consulting the opening chapters of any trusts law textbook. This is a lesson for us all: we must know our law and not rely on being able to search the internet for answers. If we do not know the law then we do not even know the terms for which we should search on the internet. Simply entering 'Ctrl+F' is rarely the answer; whereas knowing your stuff always is.

3.3.2 Precatory words: Moral obligations or trusts?

In many cases it may be difficult to know whether the settlor intended to create a trust or to make a gift of property, or something else entirely. If the settlor has instructed solicitors and had a trust instrument drafted, then the situation may be clear; although, as we noted earlier, the involvement of professional advisors does not always make things clear. In many older cases there were problems of so-called precatory words in documents: that is, a provision (usually in a will in those cases) which left it unclear whether the settlor had intended a family member who received property from them to hold that property on trust for the benefit of other family members or whether that family member was merely intended to be under some moral obligation which was not legally binding to use the property for the benefit of other people. For example, when a husband left property to his wife in his will it might be unclear whether she was intended to be trustee of that property for the family generally or whether he merely wanted to express a wish that would not be legally binding that she would look after the family.

In *Re Adams and Kensington Vestry*,[29] George Smith left property to his wife by means of a will which included a provision that he left the property to her 'in full confidence that she would do what was right' by his children. The question was whether these words created a trust over the property, or whether it expressed a non-binding wish that the wife[30]

---

28 Scrooge was the miserly character in Charles Dickens's wonderful novella *A Christmas Carol* who would have no truck with Christmas. In the story he says 'Humbug!' to anyone who wishes him a merry Christmas, suggesting that the Christmas holiday is just bunkum. A humbug is also a sort of mint sweet popular in my extended family at Christmas time. Many of the jokes in this book are, it is true, included primarily for my own amusement.

29 (1884) 27 Ch D 394.

30 I want to apologise for referring to Mrs Smith as 'the wife' but that is how she is referred to in the judgment and it is not clear what her name was.

would take an outright gift of this property and use it to look after the children. If a gift had been intended then the wife would become the absolute owner of the property and could do whatever she wanted with it in legal terms. If a trust had been created then the wife would hold the property on trust for the children and would not have been able to do whatever she liked with it because the terms of the trust would bind her. Cotton LJ took the view that George Smith intended to pass his role as head of the family to his wife and that she would therefore have the power to decide how she would look after their children in the future. Consequently, Cotton LJ considered that George Smith had intended to make an outright gift of his property to his wife together with a mere hope that she would benefit their children. His lordship considered, having listened to all the evidence, that George Smith had trusted his wife to care for the children appropriately and therefore that there was no need to have imposed a trust over her. The children had argued this provision should have created a trust but the Court of Appeal did not consider that to have been their father's intention and, what is more, they did not like the tendency in earlier cases to find trusts too easily. So, the court interpreted this provision to have created only a non-legal, moral obligation for the wife to use the money in a way which would benefit the children.

To illustrate a different approach we should consider the appeal in *Comiskey v Bowring-Hanbury*[31] where the testator, the Right Honourable RW Hanbury MP, left property by will to his wife, Ellen. The will was ambiguously worded. One provision suggested that the property was being left to Ellen 'absolutely' while another provision suggested that the property would pass in some way to the testator's nieces after Ellen's death. If the property was left to Ellen absolutely then that would mean she was receiving a gift (i.e. a transfer of absolute ownership of that property); whereas if the property had to be left to her husband's nieces then that would suggest that she was merely holding the property on trust. The question arose whether Ellen would be able to treat this property as being entirely hers such that she could pass it by will to people other than her former husband's nieces. Not unreasonably Ellen was seeking a declaration from the court as to the nature of her rights in this property. In essence, Ellen and the seven nieces fought this matter through the courts. The majority of the House of Lords held that RW Hanbury's will had created a trust. The Lord Chancellor, the Earl of Halsbury, was clear that he considered a natural reading of the will to require that the entirety of the property was intended to be passed ultimately to the nieces after Ellen had had the enjoyment of it during her lifetime.

As we consider these cases it is worth observing that the only principle which runs through them is that the trial judges in each case have formed their own opinion as to the best interpretation of the terms of the will from listening to the evidence, from watching the witnesses tell their stories in the witness box, and from making a judgment as to the best interpretation of the facts. There appears to be only a sliver of difference between these two cases in the abstract. There was a clear sense in the majority judgments in *Comiskey* that Ellen could not be relied upon to provide for her nieces and therefore that Hanbury must have intended to create a trust so that the property would definitely pass to his nieces after Ellen's death. That was the majority's interpretation of the circumstances. By contrast, the court in *Adams* considered that the testator's intention had been something different because the mother could be relied upon to provide for the children. Put simply, the court considered that it was reasonable to assume that a mother could be relied upon to care for her children so that an

---

31 [1905] AC 84.

outright gift of property could be made to her; whereas an aunt could not be trusted to show the same care for her relatives by marriage with the result that the court should interpret the testator as having imposed a trust over her so as to control her future behaviour.

As Lindley LJ held in *Re Hamilton*,[32] the approach taken by the court ought to be to 'take the will you have to construe and see what it means, and if you come to the conclusion that no trust was intended you say so'. Therefore, the courts are required to exercise judgment over what the best interpretation of the will must be. Another good example of this issue is the decision of the Court of Appeal in *Lambe v Eames*.[33] This case demonstrates that the court will form an interpretation of what the testator must have intended by considering all of the surrounding circumstances. A shopkeeper John Lambe had left all of his property by will to his wife 'to be at her disposal in any way she may think best, for the benefit of herself and her family'. The Court of Appeal held that the testator, John Lambe, should be taken to have intended to make a gift of the property to his wife and not to have imposed a trust on her. After considering all of the evidence, James LJ was very clear that John Lambe's intention here had been to make his wife the 'head of the family' by making an outright gift of all of his property to her so that she could deal with the property as she thought fit in the interests of the whole family. Consequently, the best interpretation was held not to be a trust.

3.3.3 Intention to create a trust, not something else

Charges and trusts

A charge is an equitable device which imposes rights over property to secure payment of money. If the money is not paid then the secured party may apply to the court for permission to seize the property and sell it. It is different from a trust in that beneficiaries under a trust acquire proprietary rights in the trust property which do not require a court order to be exercised, and trusts provide all of the rights considered in the remainder of this book which impose duties on the trustees. In *Clough Mill v Martin*[34] the claimant supplied a clothes manufacturer with fabric. That fabric was used to make clothes. Consequently, the fabric ceased to exist as separate property and was instead combined with the clothes. The supplier was concerned about the manufacturer's solvency while it was waiting to be paid for its supplies. Therefore, the parties agreed that the claimant would be granted rights of a given value over all of the stock of clothes held by the manufacturer. Importantly, the manufacturer could continue to sell clothes from its stock. When the manufacturer went into insolvency the claimant argued that it had a trust over the stock of clothes. Goff LJ held that there was no trust intended here because the rights did not take effect over any specific property such that that property could be considered to be owned in equity by the claimant. Instead, the parties should be taken to have intended to creating a floating charge: that is, a right to secure payment of money owed to the claimant for supplying fabric which floats over whatever property is held in the stockroom from time to time.

---

32 [1895] 2 Ch 370.
33 (1871) LR 6 Ch 597.
34 [1984] 3 All ER 982.

Trust used as a sham device will not be a valid trust

Equity looks to the substance of an arrangement, not to the form. So, when a person purports to create a trust but is really carrying on some alternative purpose using the trust as a sham for that purpose, then the court will not find a valid trust. For example, in *Midland Bank v Wyatt*[35] Mr Wyatt sought to protect himself against his textiles business failing by settling his share in the family home on trust for the benefit of his wife and his daughter. In time Mr Wyatt's business went into insolvency owing money to the claimant bank. Mr Wyatt sought to rely on the purported declaration of trust. However, it transpired that neither his wife nor his daughter had been told of the existence of the trust. Indeed, when the Wyatts had divorced the existence of this supposed trust had not been mentioned between them. Consequently, the court held that the trust had been a sham which had been created solely to put property beyond the reach of Mr Wyatt's creditors in the event of his insolvency. As a result, his share in the home was not protected against his insolvency (by being held on trust for his former wife and daughters) but rather was deemed to be owned by him still and therefore could be claimed by his creditors.

Diplock LJ held in *Snook v London and West Riding Investments Ltd* that a sham has the following meaning:[36] 'it means acts done or documents executed by the parties to the "sham" which are intended by them to give to third parties or to the court the appearance of creating between the parties legal rights and obligations different from the actual legal rights and obligations (if any) which the parties intended to create'. Furthermore, 'all the parties thereto must have a common intention that the acts or documents are not to create the legal rights or obligations which they give the appearance of creating'. Therefore, a sham is an arrangement which seeks to create the impression that the state of affairs something other than it actually is.[37] Shams are often used in insolvency situations[38] or in an attempt to avoid tax: in both cases the parties seek to conceal the true ownership of property.

3.4 CERTAINTY OF SUBJECT MATTER

3.4.1 Introduction

For a trust to be valid there must be sufficient 'certainty of subject matter'. That is ordinarily taken to mean that the property which is intended to constitute the trust fund must be segregated from all other property so that its identity is sufficiently certain. If the trust fund is not sufficiently segregated, with the result that there is no certainty of subject matter, then the trust will fail.[39] That is the traditional approach. As will emerge from the discussion to follow there are some cases which have found trusts in circumstances in which there was no segregation of the trust property from other property.

Much will depend on the nature of the property in question. If a trust is to be declared over my house *The Gables*, The Street, Wiverton, Devon then there is unlikely to be any confusion

---

35 [1995] 1 FLR 697.

36 *Snook v London and West Riding Investments Ltd* [1967] 2 QB 786, 802.

37 *Stokes v Mardner* [2011] EWHC 1179 (QB); *Soutzos v Asombang* [2010] EWHC 842 (Ch), [2010] BPIR 960, Newey J.

38 *Re Reynolds* [2007] NZCA 122, 10 ITELR 1064, New Zealand Court of Appeal.

39 *Re London Wine Co (Shippers) Ltd* [1986] PCC 121; *Re Goldcorp* [1995] 1 AC 74.

over the property which is intended to be held on trust (assuming I have the address correct and that I am indeed the lawful owner of that property). However, if a trust is to be declared over money held in a bank account then that is intangible property which is less easy to identify. If the trust is clear as to the identity of the bank account then matters will be simple, provided that the trust money is not mixed with any other money in that bank account. If the trust is intended to take effect over £1,000 which I paid into that account on Monday morning then matters will be complicated if there was already £500 in that account. The mainstream principle (as we shall see) is that there would not be a valid trust over the £1,000 because that money was not clearly identifiable within the £1,500 held in that account. The point to take at the outset is simply this: if the property which is to be held on trust is not separately identifiable from all other property (for example, if it is mixed with other property) then there cannot be a valid trust because there will be uncertainty of subject matter.

The simplest illustration of this principle is *Re London Wine Co.*[40] In that case, creditors of an insolvent wine merchant's business sought to establish trusts over bottles of wine held in the merchant's cellars. The wine merchant had contracted to sell wine to these customers and then to hold the wine in its cellar. The wine merchant went into insolvency. At that time the customers – who had now become creditors in the insolvency – realised that the wine merchant had not made clear which wine bottles were to be held for which customer, and that there was insufficient wine left to meet all their claims. Nevertheless, the creditors claimed that the terms of their contracts provided that they were supposed to have their bottles acquired for them and held in the cellars. Consequently, they argued that those contractual provisions meant that there should be a trust in their favours. The problem here was certainty of subject matter. Oliver J held that the creditors would only be entitled to assert proprietary claims as beneficiaries under a trust if they could demonstrate that particular, identifiable bottles of wine had been segregated for the purpose of their trust. If they could demonstrate such a segregation then those identifiable bottles of wine would be held on trust for them. By contrast, if no wine had been segregated for them then there would not be a trust in their favour over any bottles of wine held in the cellar. On these facts there had been no such segregation and therefore there was no trust. As Oliver J put it:

> to create a trust it must be possible to ascertain with certainty not only what the interest of the beneficiary is to be but to what property it is to attach.

The principle is clear: if the property which is to be held on trust is not separately identifiable from all other property then there is no trust. It did not matter in this case that one bottle of a particular kind of wine was effectively inter-changeable with any other bottle of the same type of wine. Just because you had ordered seven bottles of the Chateau Megarry 1948 would not mean that you could take any seven bottles of that type of wine if the cellar contained 40 bottles of Chateau Megarry 1948 all jumbled together on one shelf. To establish a trust over seven bottles of that wine then the claimant's seven bottles would have to be segregated from the other 33 bottles in the cellar for this purpose and ideally labelled as such. The question came down to a question of fact: had segregation of bottles of wine actually taken place so that a trust could be found to exist? On these facts no such segregation had taken place.

40 *Ibid.*

Re London Wine drew on a line of old cases.[41] In *Palmer v Simmonds*[42] a testatrix left 'the bulk' of her estate on a purported trust. It was held that the subject matter of this trust was too uncertain because of the vagueness of the expression 'the bulk'. Similarly, in *Sprange v Barnard*[43] it was held that there would not be a valid trust on terms that the testatrix's partner would receive 'the remaining part of what is left, that he does not want for his own wants and use' because that provision was too uncertain as to which property was intended to be held on trust for her partner.

3.4.2 The application of the orthodox approach

The *London Wine* case was followed in an appeal to the Privy Council in *Re Goldcorp*.[44] That case concerned a gold bullion exchange which went into insolvency. The Goldcorp exchange was well-known in New Zealand and had advertised itself aggressively to ordinary people by encouraging them to become investors in the commodities markets. The exchange acted for clients in acquiring gold and precious metals (known as 'bullion') for them. It also offered a further service in which it stored the customers' bullion once it had received an order from a customer. The exchange's standard-form customer contracts required the exchange to buy and hold all of the bullion specified in their clients' orders physically in its vaults. However, in breach of contract, the exchange slipped into the practice of only taking physical delivery of as much bullion as it usually needed to satisfy customers' day-to-day needs. Its business began to collapse and it had far too little bullion in its vaults to meet its customers' orders. It therefore broke its contracts by failing to buy in all of the bullion in its clients' orders. Consequently, when the exchange went into insolvency, it did not hold enough bullion to satisfy its clients' orders, even though it had taken their money for claiming to have done so.

The claimants were customers who wanted to demonstrate that bullion was held on trust for them on the terms of their contracts with the exchange. In consequence, they sought to avoid the exchange's insolvency by having themselves accepted as being secured creditors under a trust. These customers fell into three classes. The first class of claimants were fortunate that the exchange had actually held their bullion separately for them in its vaults. Consequently, this first class of customers were found to have proprietary rights in those specifically identifiable holdings of bullion. Segregation in this instance meant that there could be a valid trust.

The second class of customers did not, as a matter of fact, have their bullion segregated from the bulk of bullion held by the exchange. The general bulk of bullion held by the exchange was insufficient to satisfy these customers' claims. This second class of customers was unable to identify any particular stock of bullion in the vaults and show that it was held on trust for them. The only thing that was available to all of them as a group was a disappointingly small pile of bullion left in the middle of the floor. Instead, all they could show was a contractual entitlement to an amount of bullion bearing a specific monetary value but which was otherwise unidentifiable. They could not identify any property as being held separately for them. Therefore, this category of claimants did not satisfy the requirement

---

41 *Harland v Trigg* (1782) 1 Bro CC 142; *Choitheram International SA v Pagarani* [2001] 1 WLR 1.
42 (1854) 2 Drew 221.
43 (1789) 2 Bro CC 585.
44 [1995] 1 AC 74; *Associated Alloys Pty v CAN* (2000) 71 Aus LR 568.

of certainty of subject matter and therefore acquired no rights under a trust. Their counsel raised two further lines of argument, both of which failed. First, they argued that the customers' contracts entitled them to rights under the doctrine of specific performance against the exchange requiring them to acquire and segregate bullion to their account. So, it was argued that these customers ought to have received equitable rights in the bullion on the basis that 'equity looks upon as done that which ought to have been done'.[45] However, Lord Mustill held that the property was nevertheless unidentifiable, and therefore there could be no equitable proprietary rights because there was no identifiable property to which they could have attached. Second, counsel argued that there should have been proprietary estoppel rights on the basis that the exchange had represented to their clients that they would hold bullion for them, in reliance on which their clients had paid money. Lord Mustill refused to apply proprietary estoppel on the basis that there was no specific, segregated property over which those equitable proprietary rights could bite in any event, as before.

The third category of claimant was an individual, Mr Liggett. His plight highlights the rigidity of the traditional approach to this rule. Liggett had placed an order to buy gold coins in a Canadian denomination – a rare form of coin of which the exchange would not usually carry a large stock. Liggett's order was therefore an unusually large one. Moreover, it was agreed that the exchange would keep the coins in its vault on safe deposit. (Oh, if only Mr Liggett had decided to take them home with him! They would have been safer in a tin box in his kitchen cupboard.) There were, therefore, a handful of coins which the exchange ordinarily held which were mixed in together with the large order of coins acquired for Mr Liggett. Even though this large number of gold coins of this type must have comprised the coins that were bought specifically for Liggett, nevertheless Lord Mustill held that Liggett acquired no property rights over those coins because he could not identify precisely which coins were intended for him (so that they could be held on trust) and which coins belonged to the exchange.

We can divine that this rule revolves around the property itself *having actually* been segregated for the purpose of subjecting it to the trust arrangement, and does not revolve around it being logistically *possible* to identify the property. Suppose I contract to buy 1,000 coins from an exchange which ordinarily holds 52 such coins: there would therefore be 1,052 of these coins in the exchange's vaults. If my 1,000 coins are mixed with the 52 coins, then there will not be sufficient certainty of subject matter for me to have an equitable interest under a trust in those coins even though there is only such a large number of coins because of my unusually large order. My 1,000 coins would need to be physically separated from the exchange's 52 coins for me to have such an equitable interest under a trust in the 1,000 coins. We might feel sorry for Liggett but we should observe from his example how strict this principle of certainty of subject matter is intended to be in its traditional form.

3.4.3 An exception for fungible or for intangible property?

The problem with fungible and intangible property

The traditional approach to certainty of subject matter – considered in the previous section – operates well in relation to chattels like bottles of wine or bars of gold. That sort of property is tangible and predictable. It is easy to count and to locate. The earliest property law rules in

---

45   *Walsh v Lonsdale* (1882) 21 Ch D 9.

human civilisations are thought to have related to land (rules like 'stay out of my cave' and 'don't play on there, it's the burial ground') and then to have related to livestock (rules like 'you can't take that cow because it belongs to me' and 'thou shalt not covet thy neighbour's ox'). It is no coincidence that word 'chattel' has the same root as the word 'cattle', and that the word 'pecuniary' comes from the Greek word 'pecus' meaning 'cow', given the importance of livestock in early human societies. However, intangible property like money in an electronic bank account is more difficult to locate and identify because its only presence is as a record in a computer's memory. Similarly, fungible property like sugar or grain in a bowl or water in a pipe is difficult to segregate out into units. It is only if an amount of sugar or grain which is to be held on trust is emptied into a separate container where it is not mixed with any other property that there is sufficient segregation for certainty of subject matter on the traditional approach in *Re Goldcorp*. Similarly, 'money' in an electronic bank account is only a record of a debt owed by the bank to its customer and therefore it is only if that 'money' is recorded in a separate bank account without any other money being credited to that account that there can be a trust over it. These intangible and fungible forms of property have tended to present greater problems for certainty of subject matter in recent years.

The traditional rule in this context

The traditional rule was applied by the Court of Appeal in *MacJordan v Brookmount*.[46] In that case there was a complex construction contract, to simplify matters down to the essentials, under which payments which were to be made periodically to all of the sub-contractors who were responsible for different parts of the building work. The payments which were to be made to all of the sub-contractors were paid into a single bank account before they were distributed to the relevant subcontractors. The lead company went into insolvency before all of the outstanding payments had been made to the subcontractors. The claimant was a sub-contractor who wanted to be paid for their work. Consequently, the claimant sought to argue that there should be a trust over the money which was to have been paid to them. The claimant could demonstrate that the money which was to be used to pay them was held in that particular bank account. Unfortunately, the money that was to be paid to the claimant was mixed with the money that was to be paid to other people. Therefore, it was held that the claimant could not identify the money which was to be paid to it distinct from all of the other money in the bank account, and therefore its purported trust could not take effect due to uncertainty of subject matter. This was a straightforward application of the traditional principle to a case of intangible property (i.e. the money held in the bank account).

An alternative approach in Hunter v Moss

The decision of the Court of Appeal in *Hunter v Moss*[47] took a different approach from *Re Goldcorp* and the traditional approach cases. In that case, the claimant was employed by the defendant via his company. His contract of employment provided that a part of his payment for his work would include 50 shares in the company. Those 50 shares were to be taken from

46 [1992] BCLC 350.
47 [1994] 1 WLR 452.

the defendant's own holding of 950 shares in the company. The claimant and the defendant fell out and the claimant's employment was terminated, but the claimant was never given his shares. Therefore, the claimant sued the defendant for delivery of the shares. The argument was presented on the basis that the defendant must have held 50 shares on trust for the claimant out of his 950 shares. The defendant counter-argued that, because no 50 shares had ever been segregated out of the holding of 950 shares, then there could not be a trust over any 50 shares because there was no certainty of subject matter. Nevertheless, Dillon LJ held that there was a valid trust.

Dillon LJ suggested that the certainty of subject matter rule was not a strict rule which applied in *all* circumstances. For example, his lordship argued that in cases of a will the executors do not know which property was owned by the deceased for the purposes of the will until they start to administer the will, and yet no-one argues that wills fail to take effect on that basis. Consequently, his lordship claimed to have identified an exception to the rule requiring certainty of subject matter and therefore felt entitled to make another exception in relation to intangible, fungible property like shares. However, it should be noted that this argument relies on a sleight of hand. The executors *do* know as a question of law which property is held by the deceased: that is, all of the property which the deceased owned at the time of their death. The executors may not know as a question of fact precisely which property was owned by the deceased, but that does not make it uncertain as a matter of law.

Moreover, Dillon LJ sought to distinguish earlier cases like *Re London Wine* on the basis that they related to the 'appropriation of chattels' whereas, his lordship said, *Hunter v Moss* related to a 'declaration of trust'. This argument was also entirely spurious. The issue in *London Wine* had also been whether or not there was a valid trust over property (albeit chattels as opposed to shares). In consequence, although Dillon LJ himself had been careful not to say this explicitly, Neuberger J in the later case of *Re Harvard Securities*[48] was reluctantly forced to acknowledge that *Hunter v Moss* appeared to have created a test which established a different rule for intangible, fungible property from tangible property. It is difficult to see why a trust over shares should be different from a trust over a lorry-load of ball-bearings where each of the ball-bearings is functionally identical and of the same value. Why should the tangibility or the fungibility of the property necessarily make the difference? It would seem more appropriate to draw a distinction between cases where all the parties are solvent and there is enough property in existence to meet their claims (as in *Hunter v Moss*) and cases in which the parties are insolvent and there is insufficient property in existence to meet the parties' claims (as in *London Wine*, *Goldcorp* and *Mac-Jordan v Brookmount*).

Nevertheless, Dillon LJ appears to have arrived at the fairest conclusion (and this is equity after all). The defendant was simply attempting to renege on his contractual obligation to transfer 50 shares to the claimant once their relationship had broken down. Consequently, Dillon LJ bent over backwards (metaphorically speaking) to ensure that a trust was found so that the claimant would receive the shares to which he was otherwise entitled. Refusing to transfer those shares was equivalent to denying the claimant a part of his salary.

48 [1997] 2 BCLC 369.

The newer approach in White v Shortall

A better approach was taken in *White v Shortall*[49] by the New South Wales Supreme Court when it was presented with a similar problem to that in *Hunter v Moss*. Whereas the Court of Appeal in *Hunter v Moss* tried to draw poor distinctions with earlier cases and to avoid saying that fungible property had a different test from other types of property, in *White v Shortall* the court simply took a different approach to the facts. Suppose the following attempt to create a trust, by way of introduction: '£1,000 is to be held on trust separately for my adult children Aaron and Sharon'. One approach to that provision would be to say that the settlor's intention was to create two separate trusts – one for Aaron and a different one for Sharon – with the requirement that for certainty of subject matter purposes that the amount of money to be held on each trust must be put into a separate bank account. Failure to do so would render that trust void for uncertainty of subject matter. The alternative analysis would be to find that there is to be a single trust and that the entire fund of money is to be deemed to be held on equal shares for Aaron and Sharon as the two beneficiaries of that single trust.

In *White v Shortall* they did something very similar to this second analysis. In that case, the parties entered into a contract whereby the defendant was to declare a trust over a total holding of 1,500,000 shares so that the claimant would acquire an equitable interest in 222,000 of those shares. No transfer nor segregation of shares took place. Nevertheless, the claimant sought to enforce the trust. The defendant argued that, like *Hunter v Moss*, a distinct trust could take effect over just the 222,000 shares. Ordinarily, without segregation, that trust would be void. The claimant argued that, following *Hunter v Moss*, there did not need to be segregation of shares for there to be a valid trust over those shares. The court upheld the validity of the trust but explicitly disavowed the rationale in *Hunter v Moss*. Instead, looking closely at the facts, the court interpreted the parties' intention to be the creation of a single trust which took effect over the entire holding of 1,500,000 shares such that the trustees had a power to elect which 222,000 shares out of that entire shareholding were to be treated as being held for the claimant. This analysis dealt with the problem of certainty of subject matter because the trust took effect over the identified fund of 1,500,000 shares with no need to segregate out 222,000 shares. This analysis became very important when the UK Supreme Court considered certainty of subject matter in relation to the insolvency of US investment bank Lehman Brothers, as is discussed in section 3.4.5 below.

3.4.4 The nature of property: Trusts over non-transferable assets

It is a difficult question to know what will constitute 'property' capable of being held on trust in some circumstances. It is often said that the key defining feature of property is that it can be transferred to another person. Nevertheless, that is no longer English law. It has been held that even the benefit of non-transferable contracts can be property which can be the subject matter of a trust. In *Vandepitte v Preferred Accident Insurance Corporation of New York*[50] the Privy Council accepted that the benefit of a motor insurance contract could be transferred to another person even though the terms of the contract limited its rights to the

49 [2006] NSWSC 1379.
50 [1933] AC 70, PC.

original insured party. The principle was accepted that the benefit of a contract may itself be property even if the contract cannot be transferred. Similarly, in *Barbados Trust Co v Bank of Zambia*,[51] where a financial instrument provided that assets could only be transferred to specified types of entity, it was nevertheless held possible for the benefits to be derived from that instrument to be held on trust for another type of entity altogether.[52] Several cases have made the same point. In *Don King v Warren*, as considered above in section 3.3, it was held that cash flows which were expected to be earned from non-transferable boxing promotion contracts could form the subject matter of a trust. In *Swift v Dairywise*[53] milk quotas (which were non-transferable entitlements to sell milk) were held to give rise to benefits which themselves would constitute property. Finally, in *Re Celtic Extraction*[54] the benefits which derived from non-transferable government licences to do works and dispose of waste were held to constitute property.

3.4.5 Certainty of subject matter, insolvency and the law of finance

Introduction: From certainty to crisis

The financial crisis of 2007–09 led to the insolvency of several financial institutions and a seismic shock to the global economy from which it is still struggling to emerge.[55] The principal event was the insolvency of the huge US investment bank Lehman Brothers on 15 September 2008 which transformed a panic among bankers into a global economic catastrophe. When financial institutions go into insolvency there are huge amounts of money involved and large numbers of customers seeking to recover their money or other property. Evidently, those customers (who may range from other banks to private individuals) will seek to prove that property was held on trust for them so that they can take that property in the insolvency proceedings. Otherwise, insolvency creditors usually only receive a couple of pennies for every pound they are owed. Investment banks are complex – they may have thousands of subsidiary companies operating many hundreds of thousands of accounts for potentially millions of customers. Therefore, the practicalities of establishing which property might be held on trust for which customer are very difficult indeed.

Cases following the traditional approach

For the law on certainty of subject matter, this presents a challenge. As we shall see, in some cases the courts are concerned to reach the most convenient outcome so that the liquidators of the bank (who are the officials operating the insolvency process) can achieve an orderly distribution of the banks' remaining assets. In other cases, the judges have felt themselves bound by traditional trusts law principles (as exemplified in *Re Goldcorp* and *MacJordan v Brookmount*) to the effect that a valid trust may only be found if property has

---

51 *Barbados Trust Co Ltd v Bank of Zambia* [2006] EWHC 222 (Comm); [2006] 1 Lloyd's Rep 723, para [58].
52 See also *Law Debenture Trust Corporation v Elektrim Finance NV* [2006] EWHC 1305 (Ch).
53 [2000] 1 All ER 320.
54 [1999] 4 All ER 684.
55 See Alastair Hudson, *The Law of Finance*, Sweet & Maxwell, 2013, Chapter 45.

been clearly segregated for that purpose. If that money is still mixed with other property then no trust will be found. This was the approach taken in *Re Global Trader Europe Ltd (in liquidation)*[56] by Park J where Global Trader held money for the benefit of its many different customers. Under the financial regulations at the time – the Client Asset Sourcebook ('CASS') – Global Trader was supposed to hold customers' money on trust for each customer. In practice it happened that some of those moneys were held in segregated accounts and other moneys were not. It was a question of fact from client to client as to whether or not any given client's assets had actually been paid into a segregated account or were held in a general, mixed account. Global Trader was acting (as were most financial institutions at this time) in breach of its regulatory and contractual obligations in this regard. Park J held, in line with *Re Goldcorp*, that there could not be a trust for an individual customer over any money held in a mixed account. If the money had been segregated into a distinct account then a trust would be found.

Therefore, this judgment applied the traditional principle. Following *Re Global Trader*, Briggs J considered the poorly drafted regulations in Part 7 of the FSA rulebook CASS ('CASS 7') in *Re Lehman Bros International (Europe) (No 2)*.[57] These regulations (which became the feature of all the subsequent litigation in this area) required that client assets were held on trust. The terms of this regulatory trust were not clear, although the word 'trust' was used expressly. (Confusingly, the CASS regulations also permitted banks to hold client assets for a period in a single, mixed account, without making clear how that inter-acted with the obligation to hold client assets on trust. This ambiguity in the drafting occupies most of the judgments.) Lehman Brothers' failure to segregate client money was described as being 'spectacular' and 'staggering' in different courts. When Lehman Brothers went into insolvency, the question arose, *inter alia*, as to whether or not a valid trust had been imposed over the moneys held in this general account in favour of clients. Briggs J held that unless and until money was segregated there could not be a trust over it in favour of any given client. If money was actually held in a segregated account for a given client then there could be a valid trust over that segregated money in favour of that client.

The Lehman Brothers litigation was appealed to the Court of Appeal in relation to different, but related, legal questions concerning certainty of subject matter, the interpretation of the CASS regulations and insolvency law.[58] Eventually the question of certainty of subject matter came on before the Supreme Court in a case which may be interpreted in the future either as effecting seismic change in this area of law or as relating narrowly to the CASS regulations.

The decision of the Supreme Court in Lehman Brothers International (Europe) v CRC

The decision of the Supreme Court in *Lehman Brothers International (Europe) v CRC*[59] saw a difference of opinion between the majority that was led by Lord Dyson and who sought to generate a pragmatic solution to assist the orderly dismantling of the insolvent Lehman

---

56 [2009] EWHC 602 (Ch), [2009] 2 BCLC 18.
57 See the various judgments of Briggs J in this complex litigation at [2009] EWHC 3228 (Ch), [2010] EWHC 47 (Ch), [2010] 2 BCLC 301, and the supplemental judgment at [2010] EWHC 47 (Ch).
58 [2010] EWCA Civ 917 and [2011] EWCA Civ 1544.
59 [2012] UKSC 6, [2012] Bus LR 667.

Brothers, and the minority led by Lord Walker who sought to persist with the traditional principles of trusts law in this area requiring segregation of property. The facts were the same as those considered by Briggs J immediately above.

Lord Dyson approached this case strictly on the basis of the interpretation of the 'statutory trust' in the CASS regulations. The CASS regulations were interpreted by reference to the EU directive which had given birth to them: that is, the Markets in Financial Instruments Directive ('MiFID').[60] MiFID provided that the purpose of the CASS regulations was to provide protection for investors and therefore Lord Dyson held that a benign interpretation of the regulations should be taken which benefited investors. Therefore, his lordship sought to adopt an interpretation which offered the largest amount of protection to the largest possible number of clients of the bank.[61] In essence, Lord Dyson held that the CASS regulations should be interpreted as creating one vast trust over all of the client assets held by the bank, with each customer taking a proportionate share of the total equitable interest. This was different to the approach taken by Park J and Briggs J which had assumed that there was intended to be one trust for each individual customer and that therefore there needed to be segregation of assets for each individual customer.

The minority, in the form of Lord Walker (a specialist in trusts law) and Lord Hope, proceeded on the basis that the statutory trust which was required by CASS was 'erected on the foundation of the general law of trusts'.[62] Lord Walker doubted the efficacy of the large 'single trust' approach which had been taken in the Court of Appeal and which was taken by the majority of the Supreme Court.[63] Reading between the lines, it seemed to him to be a means of finding a trust where otherwise none existed. The minority did not agree that the CASS regulations permitted or required the creation of one colossal trust for all of the customers at once. Lord Walker was convinced of the dangers to trusts law, and to the orderly administration of insolvencies, if this 'single trust' approach was maintained in place of the rigour of requiring that trusts must be predicated on a clear segregation of the trust property. Lord Walker held that 'a trust without segregation is a very precarious form of protection', which was taken to be a reason for rejecting the possibility of such a trust. The minority argued that it was only by clinging to the traditional trusts law principle expressed in *Goldcorp* (that there could only be a trust in favour of a customer who could show that property had actually been segregated for her individual benefit) that it would be possible to know precisely which assets were held for those customers.

There is no perfect answer to this question: either the traditional logic of trusts law is protected, or all customers are treated equally badly. The fault, of course, lies with Lehman Brothers (and other banks like them) which broke their regulatory obligations with breathtaking arrogance. Lehman Brothers itself was correctly criticised by judges at all levels for its 'shocking underperformance' and its regulatory non-compliance 'on a truly spectacular scale'. That none of these issues have yet led to criminal prosecutions is an affront to our jurisprudence and to the rule of law itself.

---

60 *Ibid*, per Lord Clarke, at para [110].
61 *Ibid*, per Lord Dyson, at para [148]: 'If there are two possible interpretations of CASS 7, it seems to me to be axiomatic that the interpretation which more closely meets the purpose of the Directives should be adopted.' Similar sentiments are expressed at para [159] in his lordship's conclusions on this point.
62 [2012] UKSC 6, [2012] Bus LR 667, *per* Lord Walker, at para [84].
63 *Ibid, per* Lord Walker, at para [82].

3.5 CERTAINTY OF OBJECTS

3.5.1 Introduction

The question at issue

The rules on 'certainty of objects' relate to the requirement that the beneficiaries (or, 'objects' as they are often called in the cases in this context) must be sufficiently identifiable for the courts to be able to judge the appropriateness of the behaviour of the trustees in their management of the trust. In this section we will divide between the various forms of 'trusts' and mere 'powers', and then we will identify the tests for certainty of objects which applies to each of them. If the objects of a trust or power are insufficiently certain then that trust or power will be ineffective and therefore any purported trust will be void.

The suggested structure for addressing problem questions in this area

This subject is best approached in the following way. First, identify the nature of the trust or power at issue. We shall consider each of the categories in turn in the discussion to follow. The choice is broadly between fixed trusts, discretionary trusts, fiduciary mere powers (including powers of appointment) and purely personal powers. Second, apply the test for certainty of beneficiaries appropriate to that type of power or trust which is set out in the leading case (or cases). In some circumstances that test may appear to be overly strict and consequently it may appear to produce an unfair result. Third, consider alternative cases in the lower courts which have presented a different approach to that same issue (sometimes purporting to apply the principle from the leading case or sometimes applying a different test) after you have considered the effect of the principle set out in the leading case. These alternative approaches may offer a means of avoiding the unfairness in applying the leading case. Fourth, after analysing all of the above, consider one of the means of resolving the uncertainty which have been presented in the case law. If you use this structure when addressing problem questions then that should guide you through your analysis.

The distinction between trusts and powers

There is a distinction to be made between 'trusts' and 'powers'.[64] Trusts impose obligations on a trustee which the trustee is required to perform in obedience to the terms of that trust. The trustee owes fiduciary obligations to the beneficiary further to the trust.[65] Furthermore, under a trust the beneficiary acquires proprietary rights in the trust property (as is discussed in Chapter 4).[66] Trusts may be 'fixed trusts' in the sense that the trustees are given no discretion as to the acts which they are required to take; or trusts may be 'discretionary trusts' in that the trustees are given a discretion as to the manner in which they exercise the act.

By contrast, a power is not a trust. A power creates no proprietary rights for its objects. Powers are often referred to as 'mere powers' in the cases because they create no trust. A power is a legal ability to perform an act. There are two forms of power, for our purposes.

---

64   The most authoritative discussion of these principles is to be found in Thomas, 2012, paras 2.61–2.75.
65   *Westdeutsche Landesbank v Islington LBC* [1996] AC 669.
66   *Saunders v Vautier* (1841) 4 Beav 115.

The first form is a 'fiduciary power' which (because of the way it is worded) gives the power-holder an ability to perform an act – for example, to pay money to one of an identified class of people – and which requires the power-holder to act in a fiduciary capacity. The second type of power is a power which is given to a person *not* in a fiduciary capacity. This non-fiduciary power is described as being a 'personal power' to reflect the fact that the power-holder is act-ing in a purely personal capacity. The distinction between taking a power as a fiduciary and not taking it as a fiduciary is that a fiduciary is required to act in the utmost good faith and is prevented from acting capriciously or irrationally, whereas the holder of a non-fiduciary power is not bound in that way.[67]

The most useful authority in this area is the judgment of Megarry VC in *Re Hay's ST*.[68] His lordship presents a very clear discussion of the various forms of power in this area and gives clear indications of the applicable standards of certainty. A discussion of these various powers and trusts follows in the next sections.

The skills associated with studying certainty of objects

The topic of 'certainty of objects' is a particular favourite at exam time on most trusts law courses. This is because it requires you to exhibit a set of skills which are very important in all areas of legal practice but which are not necessarily the focus of many areas of your law degree. Those skills focus on the precise use of language and its legal effects. You must explore the meaning and impact of words with the attention to detail of a jeweller fixing a diamond into a ring or a computer engineer designing a microchip. This topic requires you to examine a specific form of words and to analyse the various possible constructions of those words in the light of the various case law analyses in this area. First you will need to analyse which category of power or trust is being used, then a leading case will set out the test for certainty of objects in that context, and then there will be other cases which take different approaches for different reasons. The skill is to identify, apply and manipulate the appropri-ate legal principles in the light of the specific wording and circumstances.

When I am working with my students I always stress that they have the ability to re-draft the words which have been placed before them: that is because I am asking my students to recognise the problematic parts of the wording, and to 'structure' different means of vali-dating that trust, while recognising the different effects which those changes will have on the parties in the real world. This is a very important part of the work which lawyers do in practice. In this sense, the verb 'to structure' means to use different legal models to achieve specific outcomes. In all areas of law, using different wording can lead to completely dif-ferent outcomes for clients. Consequently, trusts law practitioners are required to achieve their clients' goals (where possible) by manipulating their knowledge of the legal concepts to avoid 'heffalump traps'[69] (i.e. formulations which will lead to their purported trust being found to be invalid) and yet to achieve important outcomes in the real world.

---

67 *Re Hay's ST* [1981] 3 All ER 786.
68 [1981] 3 All ER 786.
69 The reference to 'heffalump traps' is used by Lord Hoffmann and others in different areas of law. It comes from AA Milne's *Winnie the Pooh* stories where Piglet and Pooh Bear set a clever trap to catch an elephant (or, 'hef-falump') but nevertheless fail to catch a heffalump. Lawyers use the term to refer to pitfalls in the law whereby a purported trust, for example, might be found to be void because of a rule of which the lawyer was ignorant.

The skills which you should be able to exhibit in using this material are the following: identify the different analyses of the appropriate tests set out in the leading cases and in other cases in the lower courts; demonstrate that you can apply those different analyses to factual situations; and demonstrate that you understand the different outcomes which may flow from applying those different analyses to the same set of facts.

The example on which this section is based

Certainty of objects is a very practical topic. We shall be considering words which a settlor intends to use and the outcomes which she hoped to achieve. We shall be doing that on the basis that it is still possible for us to adjust that wording so as to achieve the outcome which we want, instead of assuming that we are simply judging whether a trust is valid or void without needing to do anything more. The most interesting types of legal practice involve manipulating legal concepts so as to structure the most desirable outcome. As mentioned above, we shall be dividing our discussion in this section between the different types of trust and power which have been recognised in the cases.

So, let us suppose that Tanya is hoping to declare a trust for the benefit of members of her family. This is her situation:

> The Pratchett family live in a large town in Devon. Historically, they have always worked on farms although Tanya, the matriarch of this family, has aspirations for her family to establish themselves as comfortable professionals. She qualified as an accountant when she was in her 40s (after the last of her children had left home) and has worked for the last 30 years as a successful bookkeeper for local farms.
>
> Tanya is a widow in her 60s. She is well-known in the town, serving as a parish councillor and teaching a yoga class part-time in the community centre. She has two adult daughters who are in their late thirties. Those daughters (Emily and Sue) presented her with a grandson each when they were 20 years old. Each of those grandchildren is now in their mid-teens and is therefore thinking about going to university. Emily had been married to a soldier who was killed on active service. This traumatised their son, Edward, when he was younger. Sue brought up her son, Simon, as a single parent after his father had refused to pay maintenance before moving to South America. Tanya hopes that both of her grandsons will go to university and establish themselves in safe careers.
>
> Tanya also has two sons who are unmarried, who are in their late 30s, and who work as farm labourers. After many years working 'on the festival circuit' as roadies for bands and 'flipping burgers' during the summer months, they have come back home to Devon for a quieter life. Tanya has had a romantic relationship with Joe, whom she also employs to work in her garden once a week during the summer, for the last four years. Joe is in his late 20s.
>
> Tanya is not rich but she has managed to save a large amount of money because she inherited the house in which she lives. She has been advised that it would be tax efficient to establish a trust for each of these people during her lifetime.[70] She has appointed

---

70 At the time of writing, however, there have been changes made to the inheritance tax legislation which means that *inter vivos* trusts of this sort are less attractive for tax purposes than once they were.

her solicitor, Wendy, to act as trustee. It was suggested to Tanya that she could have appointed herself as one of the trustees so as to ensure that the property was used as she wished. However, she said that she preferred 'to leave all that complicated stuff' to Wendy. More to the point, Tanya has a dream that she might spend a few years travelling with Joe and therefore wants to leave Wendy in charge of the trust fund while she is overseas. So, Tanya has prepared a 'letter of wishes' to guide Wendy as to the exercise of her powers: that is, a document which is not a part of the trust but which explained her concerns about her sons' drug use, her grandsons' emotional difficulties, and her daughters' difficulties in finding work.

We shall consider the provisions which Tanya has drafted for this trust as we examine the detail of the law. In essence, this is problem-based learning in that we shall learn how the law operates in reaction to this hypothetical problem.

It is important to decide on the facts of any case into which category the settlor's directions fall. In determining which type of power is created, there is no simpler method than reading the provisions of the trust closely to analyse the settlor's intention. It is possible for a settlor to create a trust and to give different people different types of power over the trust fund. That is particularly important when different objects of the trust might be in different circumstances. The discussion which follows will divide between the four main forms of trust by analysing Tanya's trust provision. Imagine that Wendy has asked us for our technical advice on the trusts law aspects of what Tanya is proposing to write. Therefore, we will have the opportunity to amend these provisions as we go. So, suppose the following provisions were included in a trust instrument. Each of the four provisions illustrates a different category of trust or power, as is explained in the sections to follow.

> I, Tanya Pratchett of Little Nestling, Slugwash Lane, Nestleton, Devon, do settle four separate amounts of £25,000 each to be held by Wendy Denton, Solicitor of The Street, Nestleton, Devon (hereafter 'The Trustee') on trust as follows:
>
> Amount 1: so that The Trustee shall hold the £25,000 equally for my grandsons now that they have enrolled for full-time university degree courses.
>
> Amount 2: so that The Trustee may distribute all or part or none of the £25,000 to either of my daughters who shall find themselves in financial difficulties.
>
> Amount 3: so that The Trustee shall divide the £25,000 between any of my sons who become unemployed and who become deserving of help in the opinion of The Trustee.
>
> Amount 4: so that Xena, as an old family friend, shall be entirely free in a personal capacity to pay as much of the £25,000 as he sees fit to any of my relatives whom he deems worthy of it.
>
> Any amount held in remainder shall be held on trust for my lover.

Each provision is analysed in turn in the discussion to follow as an example of the four main types of powers and trusts. We shall take them in this order because that reflects the chronological order in which the leading cases were decided. That will make it easier to understand the issues which arose in those cases.

3.5.2 Fixed trusts

The nature of fixed trusts

A fixed trust is a trust which gives the trustees no discretion as to how they perform their duties. Typically a fixed trust is a trust which requires that the property be held for a fixed number of identified beneficiaries.[71] An example would be: '£25,000 to be held upon trust for my children in equal shares.' This is a fixed trust because the property is to be held 'in equal shares' for this class of people such that it is necessary to know how many of them there are and who they are before the trust can be administered. It is only possible to divide property equally if you know the number of people between whom that property is to be divided. Therefore, in this example, the number of people in the class is fixed. In such a situation, it is necessary for the trustees to be able to produce a complete list of all the potential beneficiaries for there to be sufficient certainty as to the beneficiaries.[72] So, let us consider, in the example relating to Tanya which was given at the start of this section:

> *Amount 1: so that The Trustee shall hold the £25,000 equally for my grandsons now that they have enrolled for full-time university degree courses.*

The trustees are required to distribute the property equally and therefore they have no discretion about the amount of property to be held for each beneficiary: rather, the trustees are obliged to act in the limited manner so described. In such situations the trustee has only an obligation to act in the manner identified in the trust instrument but no discretion of any sort. Consequently, this is a fixed trust. The beneficiaries have proprietary rights in the equitable interest of the trust fund in accordance with the terms of the trust instrument.

The test for certainty of objects in relation to fixed trusts

In relation to establishing the certainty of objects under a fixed trust, it is necessary for the trustees to be able to compile a complete list of the beneficiaries. This rule was confirmed by the Court of Appeal in *IRC v Broadway Cottages*,[73] and by *dicta* of Lord Upjohn and the House of Lords in *Re Gulbenkian*.[74] That means that the trustee must be able to name each possible beneficiary or to identify all of the members of the appropriate class. If there are any objects about whom the trustee could not be certain, or if the trustee is not able to compile such a complete list, then the trust will be void for uncertainty. If the identity of the membership of the class cannot be known until an identified time in the future at which the trust is to be performed, then that will be permitted provided that it will be possible to compile a complete list of the members of that class at that time.[75]

---

71 See Thomas, 2012, para 3–03 *et seq*.
72 *IRC v Broadway Cottages* [1955] Ch 20.
73 [1955] Ch 20, 29, *per* Jenkins LJ; and also required at first instance by Wynn-Parry J at [1954] 1 All ER 878, 881.
74 [1970] AC 508, at 524.
75 *Swain v Law Society* [1981] 3 All ER 797, 822, *per* Fox LJ.

3.5.3 Fiduciary mere powers: The power of appointment

The nature of fiduciary mere powers

Let us begin by defining a mere power and by distinguishing it from a trust. A 'mere power' is not a fully-fledged trust obligation. Rather, it gives the holder of the power the *ability* to exercise that power but without them having any obligation to do so. An example of a fiduciary mere power would be expressed by the words 'the trustee *may* advance £1,000 to Xena' whereby the power-holder is empowered to pay that money but is not obliged to do anything as a result of the word 'may'; whereas an example of a trust obligation would be 'the trustee *shall* pay £1,000 to Xena annually' whereby there is compulsion to act. In the former case, the power-holder is able to pay £1,000 but is under no compulsion to do so, and therefore has a mere power; whereas the second example compels the trustee to pay £1,000 to Xena and therefore the trustee bears a trust obligation.

Significantly, a fiduciary exercising a mere power is bound by fiduciary law. Consequently, the fiduciary power-holder must be able to justify their actions and decisions, and (as was outlined in Chapter 2) they may not take an unauthorised benefit for themselves and so forth. A further feature of being a fiduciary is that the power-holder may not act purely capriciously in relation to that power. Rather, the trustee is under an obligation to exercise that power reasonably and to be able to justify its exercise. As Megarry VC put it in *Re Hay's ST*:[76]

> A mere power is very different [from an ordinary trust obligation]. Normally the trustee is not bound to exercise it, and the court will not compel him to do so. That, however, does not mean that he can simply fold his hands and ignore it, for normally he must from time to time consider whether or not to exercise the power, and the court may direct him to do this.

It remains open to the power-holder to decide whether or not to exercise the power. In the second part of the example given above in relation to Tanya, the trustee is permitted to exercise a power of appointment over a fund of £25,000:

> *Amount 2: so that The Trustee may distribute all or part or none of the £25,000 to either of my daughters who shall find themselves in financial difficulties.*

There is a permission, evidenced by the word 'may', for the power-holder to pay nothing at all or a maximum of £25,000 to any one of a class of beneficiaries as the power-holder decides. Therefore, this is a mere power in which the power-holder is required to act as a fiduciary because their power comes to them as part of a trust. The problem which causes uncertainty here (as we shall discuss below) is what is meant by the concept 'financial difficulties' in this context. Therefore, we shall have to identify the appropriate test for certainty in relation to a fiduciary power (in the next paragraph) and apply it to the term 'who shall find themselves in financial difficulties' to see whether or not that will be sufficiently certain.

---

76 [1981] 3 All ER 786, 791.

The test for certainty of objects in relation to fiduciary mere powers

The leading case dealing with fiduciary mere powers is the decision of the House of Lords in *Re Gulbenkian*.[77] This case established a test which we shall refer to as the 'is or is not' test, which means that the trustees must be able to decide whether any hypothetical beneficiary is or is not within the class of objects.

The case of *Re Gulbenkian* itself was concerned with the estate of Mr Gulbenkian, who had created a will to provide bequests for 'any person and his remoter issue . . . and any person . . . in whose house or apartment or in whose company or under whose care or control or by or with whom [my son Nubar] may from time to time be employed or residing'. The question arose whether or not this expression was too uncertain because it did not define the class of objects of the trust sufficiently clearly. On the facts of this case it was held that this slightly odd provision was sufficiently certain. Lord Upjohn rejected a test previously propounded by the Court of Appeal in *Re Allen*[78] and in the Court of Appeal in *Re Gulbenkian* in which Lord Denning had held that a power could be valid even if only one person could be demonstrated to have satisfied the test.[79] Instead, Lord Upjohn approved a test outlined in *Re Gestetner*[80] to the effect that it must be possible to know whether 'any given postulant is or is not' within the class of beneficiaries. As Lord Reid described the test, with typical neatness:

> If the classes of beneficiaries are not defined with sufficient particularity to enable the court to determine whether a particular person is or is not, on the facts at a particular time, within one of the classes of beneficiaries, then the power must be bad for uncertainty.

So, if there is even one person in relation to whom the trustees cannot decide whether or not she falls within the class of objects, then the trust is invalid. To find that a fiduciary mere power is valid, you must be able to tell whether any given individual 'is' or alternatively 'is not' within the class of objects.[81] It is not required that everyone falls inside the class, merely that it is certain whether anyone would fall inside or would fall outside the class. A power which provided that 'only people over six feet in height shall be within the class' would be certain even though lots of people would not be sufficiently tall to fall within the class. Indeed, it is the clarity that people not over six feet tall would fall outside the class which makes the class itself sufficiently certain. It is only if a class is vaguely defined that there will be invalidity: for example, a power to benefit 'nice people' would fail because it would not be possible to know what the concept 'nice' means and therefore it could not be possible to know whether some people fell inside or outside the class. As Lord Upjohn put it: 'the trustees, or the court, must be able to say with certainty who is within and who is without the power'.[82] Thus the purpose of the rule is to ensure that the court can judge the behaviour of the fiduciary power-holder by knowing with certainty who the objects of that power were intended to be.

This 'is or is not' test is quite a strict one – even though it is slightly more relaxed than the old 'complete list' test, which we considered above in relation to fixed trusts. The reason

---

77 [1968] Ch 126.
78 In the Court of Appeal [1968] Ch 126, 134E.
79 *Ibid*, 133.
80 [1953] 2 WLR 1033.
81 *Re Gulbenkian* [1968] Ch 785, 787, *per* Lord Reid.
82 *Ibid* at 794, *per* Lord Upjohn.

for this relaxation in the test for fiduciary mere powers in *Re Gulbenkian*[83] was that in relation to mere powers the trustee is not compelled to make a payment under the trust. Consequently, it was considered inconsistent to require the trustee to draw up a fixed list of the potential beneficiaries in whose favour the discretion could be exercised when the trustee was not necessarily even required to perform her power.

Alternative approaches to certainty of objects in relation to fiduciary mere powers

In this section we consider a different approach in the High Court in *Re Barlow* to the approach that was taken in *Re Gulbenkian*.[84] The principal difficulty with the *Gulbenkian* test is that perfectly serviceable powers and trusts may be invalidated because of a minor defect in their drafting. Many trial judges will be tempted to give effect to the trust if they possibly can. A good example of this tendency is the judgment of Browne-Wilkinson J in *Re Barlow*. In that case, a testatrix had provided a power in her will for any of her 'family or friends' to purchase paintings at a specially low price. Under a strict application of the *Gulbenkian* test this power would have failed for uncertainty on the basis that the term 'friends' is too conceptually uncertain. (Lord Upjohn had even mentioned in *Re Gulbenkian* that the word 'friends' was a clear example of a word that would be void; but, oddly, the point was not taken in *Re Barlow*.) Nevertheless, Browne-Wilkinson J held that the bequest was valid, on three bases.

First, and most importantly, the bequest was construed by Browne-Wilkinson J as disclosing an intention to make a series of identical, individual *gifts* to anyone who could prove that they personally fell within the core of the beneficial class intended by the testatrix. Therefore, the bequest was found to constitute a series of gifts and not a power nor a trust at all. Because the transfer was a gift then the law on gift would apply to it, as opposed to the law on trusts and powers. Certainty of objects is only an issue in the law on trusts and powers. Cunningly, in this way, his lordship avoided the need to follow the 'is or is not' test. So, the first method for avoiding formalities required for the creation of a trust is to structure the disposition as something other than a trust.

Second, Browne-Wilkinson J was also persuaded *on the facts of that case specifically* that the proposed distribution of property which the trustees were seeking the court's permission to make was a reasonable one which would satisfy the testator's intention. The trustees had, in effect, drawn up a list of people who would be allowed to buy paintings and the court considered that that scheme was acceptable. His lordship considered that in relation to Ms Barlow specifically it was possible to ascertain whom she meant by her friends, even if it might not have been clear in relation to many other people. So, we can see here that the practice of trusts law may involve deciding on the best outcome in the case even if the abstract legal question may involve different considerations.

Third, his lordship found that term 'friends' could be rendered conceptually certain as is considered below in section 3.5.7. It should be noted that while Browne-Wilkinson J was able to validate the trust in his case, that does not mean that he was able to ignore the test in *Re Gulbenkian* – nor should you in writing problem answers.

---

83   [1968] Ch 126.
84   [1979] 1 WLR 278.

3.5.4 Discretionary trust

The obligatory nature of a discretionary trust

The discretionary trust *requires* that the trustees exercise their discretion and carry out their power, rather than being a fiduciary mere power which enables the power-holder to act but does not oblige them to do so. In the following example, the terms of the trust provide that the trustee 'shall' exercise the discretion, thus making its exercise by the trustee compulsory:

> *Amount 3: so that The Trustee shall divide the £25,000 between any of my sons who become unemployed and who become deserving of help in the opinion of The Trustee.*

In this example, T is subject to a trust because the wording provides that 'the Trustee shall divide the £25,000': the word 'shall' indicates compulsion and thereby a trust rather than a mere power. It is clear from the phrase that ends 'in the opinion of The Trustee' that the trustee is intended to have discretion as to whether or not (or to whom) this money is to be distributed. Consequently this is a discretionary trust because the wording grants the trustee that discretion.

The leading case in relation to certainty of objects under a discretionary trust power

The leading case regarding the test for certainty in relation to discretionary trusts is the decision of the House of Lords in *McPhail v Doulton*.[85] Their Lordships adopted the *Re Gulbenkian*[86] test (that is, the 'is or is not' test) for discretionary trusts. The tests for mere powers and discretionary trusts are therefore brought into line. Therefore, for this purpose, the need to divide strictly between the two has waned slightly. (Nevertheless, in answering problem questions it is still necessary that you show the analytical skills necessary to identify the precise category into which your problem question falls.)

The facts in *McPhail v Doulton*[87] were that payments were to be made in favour of 'employees, ex-officers or ex-employees of the Company or any relatives or dependants of any such persons'. The question of uncertainty surrounded the expression 'relatives and dependants'. The issue arose as to the nature of the power and, importantly, as to the appropriate test to decide the question of certainty of objects. Previously, it has always been the case that trusts had a stricter test than mere powers. The majority of the House of Lords in *McPhail v Doulton* adopted the 'is or is not' test set out in *Re Gulbenkian* in relation to discretionary trusts. Therefore, in considering the certainty of beneficiaries under a discretionary trust, it must be possible for the trustees to say of any postulant whether that person is or is not within the class of beneficiaries. Consequently, if it is impossible to tell whether or not one individual falls within the class or not, that trust power fails. On the facts of the case, the House of Lords decided that the term 'relative' could be rendered certain if it were interpreted to mean 'descendants of a common ancestor'. There were two dissenting judgments in the House of Lords which shall be considered below.

---

85   [1970] 2 WLR 1110.
86   [1968] Ch 126.
87   [1970] 2 WLR 1110.

The leading judgment was delivered by Lord Wilberforce. As his lordship held:

> the trust is valid if it can be said with certainty that any given individual is or is not a member of the class.

His lordship considered that there was no justification for having a completely different test for fiduciary mere powers and discretionary trusts when the two categories were so close to one another in practice. The previous approach (in *IRC v Broadway Cottages*) had required that the trustees be able to compile a complete list of the beneficiaries of a discretionary trust. The rationale behind that old rule was that the trustees could only be acting properly if they knew all of the people who could possibly take a benefit from the trust. However, Lord Wilberforce was more concerned to permit a relaxation of the rule so that more discretionary trusts would avoid being declared invalid due to some defect in the settlor's drafting. Moreover, Lord Wilberforce adopted the idea expressed by Harman J in *Re Gestetner* to the effect that the trustees should not need to 'survey the world from China to Peru' trying to come up with examples of people who might render the trust invalid. Rather, if the trust satisfied the 'is or is not' test then that would be sufficient.

The alternative approaches in Re Baden (No 2)

Despite this slight relaxation of the law in *McPhail v Doulton* from the strictness of the old 'complete list test', there continued to be situations in which there might be a single postulant who could not be categorised as being or not being within the class of beneficiaries such that that would invalidate the trust. There had been earlier decisions in other courts (such as *Re Allen*) in which judges like Birkett LJ (and Lord Denning in the Court of Appeal in *Re Gulbenkian*) had sought to broaden the appropriate test far beyond what *McPhail* would achieve. Consequently, there remained some debate among the judges as to the preferable test. When the facts of *McPhail v Doulton* returned to the courts on the slightly different question of what was meant by the term 'relatives', the Court of Appeal sought to mitigate the effect of the *McPhail* decision even further in *Re Baden (No 2)*.[88] On the facts it was held that the word 'relative' could be explained as referring to 'descendants of a common ancestor' and therefore rendered conceptually certain. However, the interest of that appeal rests in the different approaches which their lordships took to the law. They took three different approaches to it. This was remarkable given that the House of Lords had just given judgment in relation to those very same facts as to the meaning of the law. All three judges in the Court of Appeal gave separate judgments in which they each attempted to paint a gloss on the decision in *McPhail* which would validate the trust before them.

Sachs LJ took an imaginative approach to the law which appeared to follow the 'is or is not' test on its face but which placed the burden on the postulants of proving whether they fell within the class as opposed to leaving it to the trustees to prove that the trust was valid. In essence, Sachs LJ was saying that if a postulant could not prove that they fell within the class then the trustees should be entitled to assume that they did not fall within it. Consequently, a trust was more likely to be proved to be valid. In his lordship's words:

88 [1973] Ch 9.

Once the class of persons to be benefited is conceptually certain it then becomes a question of fact to be determined on evidence whether any postulant has on inquiry been proved to be within it; if he is not so proved, then he is not in it . . . [89]

Hence the doctrine of precedent appears to have been observed even though the effect of the test has been altered markedly. In short, the onus was placed on the claimants to prove themselves to be a 'relative' within the terms of the trust. If they could not, they were deemed not to be a relative. In this way, the literal meaning of the 'is or is not' test is preserved. Therefore, the test remains intact but many more trusts are likely to be validated because of the reversal of the onus of proof. Importantly, as Sachs LJ made plain in his judgment, this does not mean that every trust will be validated because there will still be trust provisions which are so vague that it will be impossible to know what the concept embodied in the provisions was intended to mean.

The judgment of Megaw LJ in *Re Baden (No 2)* returned to the logic of the decision in *Re Allen*[90] in seeking to validate those trusts in which there are a substantial number of postulants about whom one can be certain. The approach taken by Lord Denning in the Court of Appeal in *Re Gulbenkian* (which was overruled by the House of Lords) had been to accept any trust as being valid if only one person could be shown to satisfy the wording used to define the class. Megaw LJ held that the trust would be held to be valid despite some potential uncertainties as to a number of postulants, provided that there was a distinct core number of beneficiaries who could be said to satisfy the terms of the power: that is, the trust would be valid provided that there were a substantial number of postulants about whom one could be certain. The trust power would not be held to be void on the basis that there is a small number of postulants about whom the trustees are uncertain. The principal concern with the 'is or is not' test was the requirement that the trustees would be required, on a literal application of that test, to prove that someone 'is not' within the class of objects rather than focusing instead on the existence of an appreciable number of people who satisfy the class of objects.[91]

Stamp LJ held that the definition of 'relatives' should be restricted to 'statutory next of kin' rather than 'descendants of a common ancestor' because the latter was too broad. This approach concentrates specifically on the facts – although it doubts the approach to the term 'relatives' which was followed in the House of Lords.

(It should not be forgotten that the approach set out in *Re Barlow*[92] above – that is, identifying in the settlor an intention to make a gift rather than a trust – could also be deployed in relation to discretionary trusts. Equally, there is no reason in principle why the arguments in *Re Baden (No 2)* could not be applied to fiduciary mere powers.)

The rights of beneficiaries under discretionary trusts

The nature of the rights of the object of a discretionary trust is considered in section 4.1.2.

89 *Ibid*, 19.
90 [1953] Ch 810.
91 [1973] Ch 9, 22.
92 *Re Barlow* [1979] 1 WLR 278.

3.5.5 Personal powers

The non-fiduciary nature of a personal power

A personal power is a power that is not a fiduciary power. The power-holder acts in a purely personal capacity. A personal power can be identified by its wording which will indicate that it is not intended to make its holder act in a fiduciary capacity.[93] An example of a personal power would be as follows, quoting from the example given above:

> *Amount 4: so that Xena, as an old family friend, shall be entirely free in a personal capacity to pay as much of the £25,000 as he sees fit to any of my relatives whom she deems worthy of it.*

This is a personal power because the wording 'entirely free in a personal capacity' indicates that Xena is not intended to hold her power in a fiduciary capacity. She is free to act as she wishes within the terms of the power given to her (i.e. she cannot spend more than £25,000) and significantly she can act in her personal capacity.[94]

   In *Re Hay's ST*[95] Megarry VC held that the holder of a personal power cannot have it invalidated on the specific ground of uncertainty of objects. His lordship held that 'it is plain that if a power of appointment is given to a person who is not in a fiduciary position, there is nothing in the width of the power which invalidates it *per se*'. This means that a personal power will not be void for uncertainty no matter how vague its terms may be. This point is echoed in *Re Wright*[96] where it was held that the holder of the power 'is entitled to prefer one object to another from any motive he pleases, and however capriciously he exercises the power the Court will uphold it'. The rationale is that it is open to a holder of a personal power to exercise that power in any way that they see fit because they are not acting as a fiduciary. The power-holder is prevented from acting beyond the scope of their power, however. So, in the example quoted above, Xena may not purport to spend £26,000 because her power only enables her to spend £25,000. To act beyond the scope of her power is known as committing a 'fraud on the power' and that would be something which the court would intervene to prevent.[97] There is no limit, in the case law, based on uncertainty of objects in relation to personal powers.

3.5.6 Bare trusts

A bare trust is a trust where property is held for one beneficiary by the trustees. (This is sometimes referred to as a 'nominee trust'.) Clearly, the trustee must be able to identify the person who is intended to be that sole beneficiary or else the trust will be void for uncertainty of objects. Therefore, the remainder provision in the example given at the beginning of this section is a clear example of a bare trust 'the remainder shall be held on trust for my lover'.

---

93 *Re Hay's ST* [1981] 3 All ER 786.
94 *Ibid.*
95 *Ibid.*
96 [1920] 1 Ch 108, 118.
97 *Re Somes* [1896] 1 Ch 250, 255.

Any amount held in remainder shall be held on trust for my lover

The 'lover' is the sole beneficial owner of the property held in remainder. The question of uncertainty here is clearly identifying who Tanya means by 'my lover'. In the example given above, it is clear that she means Joe. In the real world she would be well-advised to make that explicit. If her affair was kept secret then it might not be obvious whom she intended to benefit. If she was that sort of Devon resident who often refers to acquaintances as 'my lover' in the local vernacular (just as people from the North-East of my grandmother's generation would refer to perfect strangers as 'pet') then this might cause even greater confusion.

3.5.7 Understanding the different approaches on the cases

At some point you will have studied the doctrine of precedent and you will have learned that English judges are supposed to follow the earlier judgments of higher courts or courts on their same level, unless there is something about their circumstances which permit them to distinguish their facts from those of earlier authorities. Nevertheless, you will have noticed throughout your studies in all courses (not just equity and trusts) that judges often try to elude earlier precedents or even defy earlier judgments (occasionally) if they consider it necessary to do justice on the facts in front of them. *Baden (No 2)* is just such a case. Sachs LJ was clearly upset (as he explained at the outset of his judgment) by the length of time it had taken for this case to make its way around the courts – 12 years in total – while the beneficiaries were still waiting for their money. This prompted him to take an imaginative approach to the law. No judge would bother to do that unless they considered it to be necessary to achieve justice on the facts in front of them.

  This area of law might seem very technical to you and it might be surprising to learn that different people (judges, legal practitioners, academics) have long-held views about what the law ought to be, and that they will argue passionately about them. Nevertheless, this is true. For example, in *Baden (No 2)*, Megaw LJ clearly preferred the more liberal test suggested by Lord Denning in earlier cases to the 'is or is not' test. He was prepared to defy the House of Lords by maintaining a version of that liberal approach in his judgment even though it appears to break with the doctrine of precedent. No judge would do that lightly. His lordship clearly had an opinion about the better direction for trusts law in the future. By reading the cases carefully, we can see that different judges simply have different opinions. The study of trusts law is about identifying and considering these different arguments. The pragmatism of Browne-Wilkinson J in *Re Barlow* is another approach to dealing with questions of this sort.

  Another passionate debate lurks just below the surface in *McPhail v Doulton*. There were two dissenting judgments by Lord Hodson and Lord Guest. Those two judges had been in the House of Lords in *Re Gulbenkian* when they agreed with Lord Upjohn, and Hodson LJ had been in the Court of Appeal in *IRC v Broadway Cottages* when the complete list test was accepted for fixed trusts. Importantly, Lord Hodson makes it plain in *McPhail v Doulton* that he did not agree with Lord Wilberforce's reading of what Lord Upjohn had intended to hold in *Re Gulbenkian*. Lord Hodson argues that Lord Upjohn did not intend to apply the 'is or is not' test to discretionary trusts and that therefore he must dissent. Nevertheless, because the majority of the House of Lords agree that that is the interpretation which they will place on Lord Upjohn's judgment then that is now the law. It is interesting, though, that Lords Hodson and Guest expressed the view that trusts should be treated differently from powers, and that in consequence there should be a stricter test for trusts than for powers because a trust places a greater burden on a trustee than a power places on a power-holder. Again, these two judges were presenting heart-felt opinions on this technical area of law. Equally, Lord Wilberforce wanted to make it easier for judges to validate discretionary trusts than the old complete list test would allow.

If you read the dissenting judgment of Lord Hodson then you will find a completely different approach to certainty of objects than is presented by Lord Wilberforce. When writing about English law, dissenting judgments always offer the law student a fertile source of opinion and argument which can be used in essays or to flavour your problem answers. An entirely different approach to this area of law was set out by Lord Denning in the Court of Appeal in *Re Gulbenkian*. In that case, Lord Denning held that it should be sufficient to validate a trust or power if any person can be shown to fall within the ambit of the class. In *Re Tuck's ST*, discussed below, Lord Denning advised us to 'cut out all the cackle' in this area of law (by which he meant we should move beyond the technicalities and confusions in the old judgments, and simply validate serviceable trusts and powers). That is a very different approach to Lord Hodson. Lord Hodson was concerned that, *inter alia*, it would be very difficult to hold trustees to account for breach of trust if we could not know what the precise ambit of their duties was intended to be. Lord Denning might have held lots of trusts and powers to be valid, but his approach would not have helped the trustees to know which people could take a benefit from them if the documents were poorly drafted. Lord Denning might have cut out the cackle, but only Lord Hodson would have prevented the confusion that would have come afterwards.

3.5.8 The problem with your so-called 'friends'

This section takes an example of a particular term which has caused problems in the case law: that is, the term 'friends'. This provides us with an example of how different courts will take different views to the certainty or uncertainty associated with the same word. In *Re Gulbenkian* Lord Upjohn simply accepted, without discussion, that the word 'friends' was an axiomatic example of something that would be uncertain. In *Brown v Gould*,[98] a trust in favour of 'old friends' was found to have been invalid by Megarry J. It was held that if the court cannot determine who an 'old friend' is, then the trustees will not be able to do so.[99]

Nevertheless, there are cases which have held the term 'friend' to be valid when used in the drafting of trusts or powers. In *Re Barlow*[100] Browne-Wilkinson J held that the term 'friends' might be sufficiently certain in relation to testamentary bequests which entitled 'friends' to buy paintings from the trustees. While Browne-Wilkinson J found that the term 'friend' in general terms would be uncertain, his lordship was nevertheless prepared to find in reliance on the test in *Re Allen*[101] that on the particular facts before him there were sufficient people who clearly would fall within the class of 'friends' in relation to that particular testator for the term to be validated. Browne-Wilkinson J held that the term 'friend' could be rendered certain if it was taken to mean people who had a long relationship with

98 [1972] Ch 53.
99 See also *Re Coates* [1955] Ch 495.
100 [1979] 1 WLR 278.
101 [1953] Ch 810.

the settlor, and whose relationship with the settlor was not built on business but rather on social contact. A lengthier definition of 'friend' was provided by Plowman J in *Re Gibbard* in a judgment which also upheld its certainty.[102] His lordship held that X would be a friend of the testator if 'the testator had been at prep school[103] with X and had gone on from prep school to public school with X, and then to university with X; each had become god-father to one of the other's children, perhaps lived in the same neighbourhood, perhaps belonged to the same club, perhaps played golf together, perhaps dined in each other's houses and had been doing that for fifty years'. That would be an example of a friend but is it a definition of what a friend must be in all circumstances? What if they had only met at university? What if they played squash but not golf? What if they had only dined in each other's houses for 30 years not 50?

The problem with the term 'friend' for the purposes of certainty of objects is that it is difficult to define what it will mean in all circumstances. So, Browne-Wilkinson J and Plowman J ultimately came to decide that they could define it on the facts of the cases before them specifically. However, that does not make clear distinctions between 'friend' and 'acquaintance', for example. Does a Facebook 'friend' constitute the same quality of friend as Plowman J had intended? Or does the idea of friend depend entirely on the circumstances? Take the example of Sheldon Cooper, the somewhat 'odd' character in the TV programme *The Big Bang Theory*. He maintains a list of all of his friends ranked in order of preference. For most people, it might be difficult to know who their friends are, even if many people would be able to distinguish between their closest friends and more distant acquaintances on social media. For many people there would be a mezzanine category of work colleagues, acquaintances at university, next-door neighbour and so forth about whom it would be difficult to say whether they were 'friends' or not. If Sheldon Cooper were to make a will identifying his 'friends' as the intended beneficiaries then for that particularly 'odd' person it would be possible to know whom he meant by his 'friends' because he has a clear list of them, even if it might not be possible in relation to you or I.

Recently, I made contact with an old friend from bar school. Immediately we lapsed into old jokes and nicknames, and then we were slightly surprised to realise that we had not spoken for 12 years. I would still consider him to be a friend even though we had not talked for several years. Would he count as a 'friend' for the purposes of certainty of objects? He is certainly a different category of friend from someone I see socially every week for dinner. It is exactly this sort of uncertainty which means that judges like Lord Upjohn and Megarry VC considered that word to be uncertain in the abstract; and yet other judges like Browne-Wilkinson J and Plowman J were prepared to find the concept workable on the particular facts in front of them. It is possible to find an authority which holds 'yes' or 'no' for most of these sorts of words if you search hard enough. The skill which you must develop, however, is the ability to establish why one judge decided as they did on the facts in front of them and then to apply that thinking to the facts in front of you. That is true of legal practice as well as the seminar and exam room.

---

102 [1966] 1 All ER 273, 279; [1967] 1 WLR 42, 48.

103 This is a reference to 'preparatory schools' which are private schools attended by some children before the age of 14 usually with the intention that those children will progress to English public schools thereafter.

3.5.9   Resolving the uncertainty: Use of an expert or trustee discretion

Means of seeking to resolve uncertainty used in trust instruments

This section considers different ways (over and above the cases considered so far) in which judges have resolved uncertainty on the facts in front of them and in which practitioners have sought to elude the rules on uncertainty when drafting trusts.

Lord Denning presented an elegant way of resolving uncertainty in cases in which it would be possible for an expert to rule on the meaning of a concept used to define a beneficial class. In *Re Tuck's Settlement Trusts*[104] Lord Denning held that a trust, which provided that money was left on trust for the benefit of such of the testator's issue who married into 'the Jewish faith', would be valid because it would be possible to ask the Chief Rabbi to rule as a question of Jewish law whether or not any given person would be considered to be a member of the Jewish faith. Because membership of that faith is a matter of Jewish law then it is possible to rule definitively on the question whether someone is or is not a member of that faith. By contrast, it would not be possible to appoint an expert to rule on a concept such as whether or not a postulant was sufficiently 'nice' to qualify as part of a class of 'nice people' because the term 'nice' is too vague to be capable of definition by an expert.

There are two devices which have been commonly used by practitioners to avoid the concept of uncertainty. First, to give the trustees a power to decide who will or will not fall within the class in the event of any alleged uncertainty. The problem with this device is that the courts will generally rule that if the court cannot decide what a concept means then it will be impossible to know whether or not the trustees have acted properly in the exercise of their power, as was held in *Re Coxen*.[105] Jenkins J held in *Re Coxen* that a concept was not made certain by leaving it to the trustees to decide who constituted, in that case, 'an old friend'. In *Re Wright's WT*,[106] a transfer of property had been made to trustees to help institutions which the trustees considered had assisted the testator during his lifetime. It was held that this bequest was uncertain as to its objects for the same reason.

The second is to provide that the trustees have a discretion to appoint property to anyone in the world, in the hope that the class will be logically certain (it simply means any person in the world) even if it will also be very broad. By way of example, in *Re Manisty's Settlement*[107] it was provided that the trustees could advance property to anyone in the world except some of the testator's identified relatives. Under tax law at the time it was important to make it clear that those relatives would not take an interest under the settlement. Templeman J held that there was no issue of uncertainty here precisely because it could be said with certainty which relatives were excluded and that they were the only people who were excluded from the ambit of the class of objects.[108] Similarly in *Re Hay's ST*[109] Megarry VC was asked to consider a power which could be exercised in favour of anyone 'except the settlor'. His lordship held that if the power was administratively workable, and provided that the trustees considered the exercise of their power appropriately, then such a power need not automatically be void.

---

104 [1978] 2 WLR 411.
105 [1948] Ch 747.
106 (1857) 3 K & J 419.
107 [1974] Ch 17.
108 Cf. *Mettoy Pension Trustees Ltd v Evans* [1990] 1 WLR 1587, 1617; [1991] 2 All ER 513, 549 *per* Warner J.
109 [1982] 1 WLR 202.

This approach may be logical but it creates other problems. So, in *Blausten v IRC*[110] taking the opposite approach, it was held that such a power would be void for uncertainty because it was simply too wide for the court to be able to know with any certainty whether or not the trustees had exercised their power properly. As Buckley LJ put it, the class of objects was 'so wide that it really did not amount to a class in any true sense at all'.[111] If the central principle here is to ensure that the court can exercise its inherent power to administer a trust and to assess the behaviour of the trustees,[112] then it cannot be possible to know whether or not a fiduciary has exercised a power properly if the power is expressed in overly broad terms.

3.5.10 The various forms of uncertainty

There are four different types of uncertainty which can be identified in the case law, as Emery described them in an article:[113] conceptual uncertainty; evidential uncertainty; 'ascertainability'; and 'administrative workability'. Emery's point is that differing forms of uncertainty have different impacts on the validity of a trust or power. The acid test is that 'there must be sufficient certainty for the trustees to execute the trust according to the settlor's intentions'. Let us take these four categories in order.

The issue of conceptual uncertainty is fundamental in the validity of a trust or a power. By 'conceptual uncertainty' we mean the precise definitions of words used in the trust or power. If a hopelessly vague term like 'nice people' is used to define the beneficial class then the trust or power will always be void because it is impossible to know what that term 'nice' means.[114] This does not mean that judges will be quick to rule that trusts or powers are conceptually uncertain. Instead, the courts will 'judge the degree of certainty with some measure of common sense and knowledge and without excessive astuteness to discover ambiguities'.[115] Since the decision in *Re Gulbenkian*[116] created the 'any given postulant' test, it would seem that they will not be too eager to validate unclear provisions. If it is impossible to render the concept certain, then the trust fails.[117]

The second category, 'evidential uncertainty', relates to the inability of the parties to prove that they do or do not fall within the beneficial class. The concepts used may be certain but it may be difficult to prove that the postulant does or does not fall within its scope. For example, a trust for the benefit of 'whoever sat in seat 3A on flight 323' on a given date would be conceptually certain but it might be difficult for someone to prove if they had discarded their boarding pass and if the airline would not release passenger information. Such a trust would be valid for certainty: the trust can be valid because it is conceptually certain even though one individual cannot prove that they fall within it. That a given postulant cannot prove they fall within the class does not mean that the class is necessarily void.[118]

The third category, 'ascertainability', will also not invalidate a trust necessarily. Ascertainability refers to the ability or inability of the trustees to track down all of the class of

---

110 [1972] Ch 256.
111 *Ibid*, 272.
112 *Schmidt v Rosewood Trust Ltd* [2003] 3 All ER 76.
113 (1982) 98 LQR 551.
114 *Re Sayer* [1957] Ch 423, 432, *per* Upjohn LJ.
115 See *Hillas & Co v Arcos Ltd* (1932) 147 LT 503, 514 *per* Lord Wright; and *Blathwayt v Baron Cawley* [1976] AC 397, 425, *per* Lord Wilberforce.
116 [1968] Ch 126.
117 *Re Baden (No 2)* [1973] Ch 9.
118 *Ibid*; and *Re Coxen* [1948] Ch 747, 760.

beneficiaries.[119] As Wynn-Parry J put it 'mere difficulty of ascertainment is not of itself fatal to the validity of the gift'. In practice the trustees will have to demonstrate that they have taken all reasonable steps to find and identify the members of that class. If it can be demonstrated that the trustees have taken suitable steps to identify the members of the class of objects then the court will order that the property be divided among the ascertained objects.[120]

The fourth category, 'administrative unworkability', refers to the feasibility of the trustees being able to carry out the settlor's wishes. If the trust or power is impossible to carry out then it may be held to be void. Lord Eldon held that if 'the execution of a trust shall be under the control of the court [then] it must be of such a nature that it can be under that control'.[121] If the trust required '£100,000 to be distributed among the inhabitants of Germany' then that would be too great a task for trustees to perform and for the court to assess. By contrast, if the trust required that the trustees of a pension fund should 'distribute £100,000 among the oldest 100 pensioners in that pension fund' then it would be possible for those particular trustees to conduct that task even though it would be impossible for you or I. When the requirements of the trust make it impossible for the trustees to perform their fiduciary obligations, this will invalidate the trust.[122] It should be noted that this principle applies to trust powers rather than to mere powers of appointment. It was held in *R v District Auditors ex p West Yorkshire CC*[123] that a trust for the benefit of the inhabitants of West Yorkshire would have covered 2.5 million people and therefore would be void for being administratively unworkable.

3.5.11 Answering problem questions on certainty of objects

It is suggested that this is the approach to take when answering problem questions in this area. First, identify the type of trust or power. Second, identify which test applies to that type of trust or power and apply it. Third, apply the means of eluding the main test which have been set out in later cases in the lower courts. Fourth, consider any exceptions to that test for that type of trust or power. That structure might look something like the following diagram.

	Fixed trust	*Discretionary trust*	*Fiduciary mere power*	*Personal power*
STAGE ONE: Identify the form of power	No discretion in the exercise of the trust	Obligation to exercise a discretion	No obligation to exercise discretion	Not intended to be exercised as a fiduciary
STAGE TWO: Identify the test appropriate to that power	*IRC v Broadway Cottages –* preparation of a complete list of beneficiaries	*McPhail v Doulton –* the 'is or is not' test	*Re Gulbenkian –* the 'is or is not' test	*Re Hay's ST –* 'nothing in the width of the power will invalidate the trust'

---

119 *Re Benjamin* [1902] 1 Ch 723; *McPhail v Doulton* [1970] 2 WLR 1110.
120 *Ibid.*
121 *Morice v Bishop of Durham* (1805) 10 Ves 522, 539.
122 *Ibid, per* Lord Wilberforce.
123 (1985) 26 RVR 24.

	Fixed trust	*Discretionary trust*	*Fiduciary mere power*	*Personal power*
STAGE THREE: Apply the means of eluding the strict test	None possible	*Baden (No 2)* – (1) reverse the onus of proof, or (2) a substantial number of certain beneficiaries is satisfactory	*Re Barlow* – construe the trust as a series of individual gifts	Not necessary – power cannot be invalid in any event
STAGE FOUR: Use an 'expert' to resolve uncertainty	*Re Tuck's ST* – unless irreconcilable conceptual uncertainty or administrative unworkability	*Re Tuck's ST* – unless irreconcilable conceptual uncertainty or administrative unworkability	*Re Tuck's ST* – unless irreconcilable conceptual uncertainty or administrative unworkability	Not necessary – power cannot be invalid in any event

Ordinarily, if a trust fails in part then the property in question is held according to any provision governing residuary property; or, if the trust as a whole is void, then that property is held on resulting trust for the settlor. In a complex trust with many different powers and trusts contained within it, it may be possible to invalidate some of those powers and to validate others. So, in *Re Leek*[124] it was accepted in principle that a trust made up of many different powers could continue to be valid if the one offending (or void) power contained in that trust were simply removed. In effect, that single power would be struck out and the trust given effect without it.

3.5.12 Answering problem questions in this area, and understanding the 'is or is not' test

Two different approaches to the 'is or is not' test in practice

Let us think about what the 'is or is not' test means for a trustee in practice. Imagine for a moment that you are a trustee. You will probably be one of a board of trustees; although it is possible that you will be the only trustee, in which case you will need to be even more careful. All trustees must be able to justify their decisions to avoid liability for breach of trust (as discussed in Chapter 18). Imagine that you are faced with a trust document in which clause 20 reads: 'the trustees shall have the power to pay £10,000 to any fine fellow'. Clearly this provision is vaguely drafted. What does 'fine' mean? It could mean well-dressed, sexually attractive, cool or almost anything else. In today's world, what is a 'fellow'? It could mean a man, or any person in modern usage, or it could mean a particular type of member of an Oxbridge university faculty. On one interpretation, the 'is or is not' test requires the trustees to ask themselves whether or not they can imagine any hypothetical person who might come in front of them about whom they could not be sure whether or not they were a 'fine fellow'. So, they would debate whether or not in theory they can know whether or not 'any given postulant' is or is not within the class of 'fine fellows' hypothetically. One hypothetical grey area would mean that the trust fails. The word 'fine' is so vague in describing a human being that there must be plenty of people we could imagine falling into a grey area between 'is' within the class or 'is not' within the class. Consequently, the power would fail for uncertainty.

Our assumption is that the test requires that the trustees will sit in a room together so as to decide hypothetically whether or not they can envisage any problems of certainty with the language used in the trust. Therefore, the trustees have to imagine whether or not they can dream up any types of person who might fall into an uncertain grey area. To use the colourful expression deployed by Harman J in *Re Gestetner*, they would be surveying the world from China to Peru in their minds. However, there is another possible approach. The other approach would simply be for the trustees to wait and see who turns up asking to be considered as a beneficiary. The trustees might advertise to all of the people who could possibly fall within the class that they would be meeting at a given place on a given date, and invite people to come forward to present their case for being treated as falling within the beneficial class, and give an email address for those who could not attend in person. Instead of treating the question as a hypothetical exercise, they would only ask whether or not any postulants who actually present themselves are or are not within the beneficial class. If the potential beneficiaries are required to come forward and make their case to the trustees as being 'fine fellows' or 'blue-eyed' or whatever then it is a somewhat simpler matter for the trustees simply to decide what they think about these applicants (or postulants). This second approach assumes real people coming before the trustees and being assessed, as opposed to hypothetical people. On this model, the trust would only be void if any real person came forward who could not be categorised as being inside or outside the class. Therefore, the second approach would be more likely to validate trusts.

This second approach to the interpretation of the trustees' practical task was suggested by Lord Wilberforce in *McPhail v Doulton*. This only requires that the trustees are able to say about anyone who actually comes forward as a potential object of the power whether they are or are not within the class. They do not have to consider hypothetical postulants. This is a very important point because it is far more likely that a trust will be validated if the trustees are only required to consider the people who actually come forward. Lord Wilberforce (depending on how you read his judgment) may well have widened the test massively by making this subtle adjustment to what it should be taken to mean.

There is a third approach to these questions in practice. Let us return to the provision which empowered the trustees to pay money to any 'fine fellow'. What Browne-Wilkinson J suggested in *Re Barlow* was that it would be possible to ask: what did the settlor personally mean by this otherwise vague expression? In that case, the settlor had died but it was suggested that *in relation to that specific settlor* it was possible to know what they meant by their 'friends'. Whereas, the term 'friends' might have been too vague in the abstract (as held by Megarry VC in *Brown v Gould*), it might be capable of definition if it could be known in relation to that specific settlor who their 'friends' were. So, if the settlor in our example had a group of golfing partners who were known to one another as 'The Fine Fellows', who had that expression etched onto their golf bags, and who were known as a group by that expression to their wives, then Browne-Wilkinson J might consider it possible to say in relation to that specific settlor that we know what is meant by a 'fine fellow' even if it may appear to be uncertain in other circumstances.

One final word of warning

One final word of warning. Law students are warm, positive human beings. I am sure, dear reader, that you are the same: kind to animals, open-hearted, wonderful. Consequently, law students like you often want to find a trust or a power to be valid if they possibly can. That is not your task. Your task is to judge dispassionately whether the provision you are given is void and to advise on any changes which you would make so that it would become valid. It is common for students to pay insufficient attention to the narrowness of the 'is or is not' test in examinations, and thus to fail to explain the likelihood of a trust provision failing on a strict application of that test in many circumstances. Instead, they tend to reach for cases like *Baden (No 2)* and *Re Barlow* (which are decisions of lower courts) at the outset as a means of validating trusts and powers which are hopelessly vague in their drafting. Some even do this without ever discussing the House of Lords cases in this area! That is a fatal mistake. The leading cases must clearly be analysed in detail first. Even judges like Sachs LJ in *Baden (No 2)* have made it clear that a conceptually uncertain term will be void, even while he was advancing a broader approach than the ordinary 'is or is not' test. Moreover, you should remember that a judge like Lord Upjohn would undoubtedly have invalidated that trust without any hesitation. So, you should take care to argue whether or not the provision in front of you is valid or void in light of all the decided cases, and not simply jump to a conclusion which validates the trust or power without first working your way through the arguments in order.

Chapter 4

The beneficiary principle

CAPSULE SUMMARY

A beneficiary acquires equitable proprietary rights in property held on an express trust. The beneficiary also acquires the right to require an account from the trustees and personal rights against the trustees in the event of a breach of trust. The principle in *Saunders v Vautier* provides that all of the beneficiaries acting together may direct the trustees how to deal with the trust property: this is taken to demonstrate the ultimate ownership of the trust property by the beneficiaries. The rights of the objects of discretionary trusts are more complex because they may have no vested rights until property has been appointed to them.

The 'beneficiary principle' requires that there be some person in whose favour the court is able to exercise the trust. If there is no beneficiary, then the trust will not be valid. Therefore, a trust which is created to achieve some abstract purpose, without any person entitled to take an equitable interest in the trust property as beneficiary, will be invalid. Therefore, it is necessary to distinguish between trusts for the benefit of people (which will be valid) and trusts for the achievement of abstract purposes (which will be invalid). The exception to this rule is the charitable trust, discussed in Chapter 23.

Transfers of property to unincorporated associations are particularly challenging for the beneficiary principle because those associations are not legal persons and therefore the property must be held for them by a legal person, and that may appear to be an abstract purpose trust (which would be invalid). There are a number of different ways of structuring such a transfer to make it valid: whether as a trust for the benefit of identified people, or as an accretion to the association's funds subject to contract, or as a transfer to the club's officers subject to a mandate to use that property in accordance with the association's purposes subject to contract, or as a gift to the members of the association. The case law analyses the distinctions between these various forms of transfer.

The Perpetuities and Accumulations Act 2009 now governs the maximum length of time for which a trust may exist. The statutory perpetuity period is now 125 years.

4.1 THE NATURE OF THE RIGHTS OF BENEFICIARIES IN THE TRUST FUND

4.1.1 The nature of the rights of beneficiaries as both proprietary rights and rights against the trustees *in personam*

A trust will only be valid under English trusts law if there is a beneficiary capable of enforcing the trustees' performance of their duties under the trust.[1] This principle is known as the 'beneficiary principle' and forms the principal focus of this chapter from section 4.2 onwards. However, that proposition does not necessarily tell us very much about the nature of the rights of the beneficiary. Indeed, some of the cases appear to be in conflict about what it means to be a beneficiary. Therefore, in section 4.1 we shall consider the nature of the rights of beneficiaries as the owners of the equitable interest under a trust. The rights of beneficiaries have two characteristics: first, a proprietary right in the trust fund and, secondly, personal rights against the trustees in relation to the proper management of the trust's affairs.[2] This means that the beneficiaries will be able to trace after any property which is taken in breach of trust (as discussed in Chapter 20) and they will be able to sue the trustees personally for breach of trust (as discussed in Chapter 18). In both cases it is equity which recognises the beneficiaries' claims against the trust property and against the trustees personally.

---

1 *Bowman v Secular Society Ltd* [1917] AC 406, 441, *per* Lord Parker.
2 See section 8.4.8.

The beneficiaries' rights are therefore rights which both attach to the trust property and protect the beneficiaries against the claims of third parties to that property. In consequence, the rights of the beneficiary should be understood both to be rights in the property comprising the trust fund as well as personal rights against the trustee. The following discussion considers the case of *Saunders v Vautier*,[3] which is generally taken, in English law, to establish the proposition that the beneficiaries' rights are rights in the trust property.

4.1.2 The principle in *Saunders v Vautier*

The principle in *Saunders v Vautier*[4] establishes that all of the beneficiaries, provided that they constitute 100% of the equitable interest in a trust fund and provided that they are all *sui juris*[5] and acting together, can direct the trustees how to deal with that trust fund. As Megarry J expressed this doctrine:[6]

> If under a trust every possible beneficiary was under no disability and concurred in the re-arrangement or termination of the trusts, then under the doctrine in *Saunders v Vautier* those beneficiaries could dispose of the trust property as they thought fit; for in equity the property was theirs.

This is a clear statement of the principle that the beneficiaries own the trust property in equity. That the beneficiaries can direct how the trustees deal with the trust fund (and even to dispose of it as they think fit) has two practical effects. First, it is taken to demonstrate that the beneficiaries are the ultimate owners of the trust property, as opposed to having merely personal rights against the trustees. Therefore, beneficiaries have proprietary rights in the trust fund. Second, it means that the beneficiaries (if they are acting together) can choose to disapply the settlor's intentions for the trust property and effectively take over control of the trust.

The case of *Saunders v Vautier*[7] itself is the best illustration of why this is important. It concerned a testator who bequeathed £2,000 worth of East India shares to Vautier on trust. The trust provided that the capital of the fund should be held intact until Vautier reached the age of 25 and that the dividends from the shares should be accumulated with the trust's capital. Vautier reached the age of adulthood (which was 21 years of age at that time) and sought delivery of the capital and dividends to him immediately rather than having to wait until he reached the age of 25. Lord Langdale MR held that 'the legatee, if he has an absolute indefeasible interest in the legacy, is not bound to wait until the expiration of that period, but may require payment the moment he is competent to give a valid discharge'. Therefore, Vautier did not have to wait until he was 25 to be able to order the trustee to hand over all of the trust property to him because he was the only beneficiary under this trust and therefore held the entirety of the equitable interest as soon as he had reached the age of 21. Consequently, it is possible for all of the beneficiaries acting together to override the terms of the trust and the wishes of the settlor. In other jurisdictions, such as the USA,

---

3 (1841) 4 Beav 115.
4 *Ibid.*
5 Where 'sui juris' means that they are adults and of full mental capacity.
6 In *Re Holt's Settlement* [1969] 1 Ch 100, 111.
7 (1841) 4 Beav 115.

the rule is that the settlor's instructions must be observed and therefore that a beneficiary like Vautier should have to wait until the age specified in the trust until he was entitled to receive the trust property.

A good example of this principle being used sensibly arose in the case of *Re Bowes*[8] in which a trust fund had been created over £5,000 (a very large sum of money at the time) for the express purpose of planting trees on a large estate. The beneficiaries appeared to have little money left under the fund and therefore all of the beneficiaries (representing all of the equitable interest and all being *sui juris*) applied to the court to have the trust property delivered to them and not kept to plant trees. North J held that the principle in *Saunders v Vautier* permitted the beneficiaries to demand delivery of the trust property to them. His lordship was encouraged by the fact that the trust's objective ultimately was to benefit those people. The Court of Appeal in *Re Nelson*[9] held that 'the principle [in *Saunders v Vautier*] is that where there is what amounts to an absolute gift it cannot be fettered by prescribing a mode of enjoyment'. In other words, when money is left to benefit people you cannot force them to use it for planting trees. They might prefer having food in their stomachs to having a beautiful view.

4.1.3 The effect of beneficiaries having proprietary rights in the trust fund

It is clear on the authorities that English trusts law considers beneficiaries to be the owners in equity of the trust property. Page Wood VC in *Gosling v Gosling*[10] and the Court of Appeal in *Re Nelson*[11] have recognised that ownership of the trust fund rests with the beneficiaries. Significantly, Lord Browne-Wilkinson in the House of Lords in *Westdeutsche Landesbank v Islington*[12] has held that the beneficiaries have proprietary rights in the trust fund as opposed merely to personal rights against the trustees. The consequence of beneficiaries having proprietary rights is that those rights will continue to exist after the trustees go into insolvency, that they can trace from rights in the original trust property into any substitute property, that beneficiaries may (unless tax law statute otherwise provides) be treated as the owner of the trust fund for tax purposes, and so forth.

4.1.4 Issues as to the nature of the rights of the objects of specific types of trust

If the trust is more complex than the examples given above then the principle in *Saunders v Vautier* may be more difficult to apply. The principle in *Saunders v Vautier* has become widely used, even in relation to complex trusts, where different parts of the trust fund are held for the benefit of different beneficiaries at different times. In *Re Smith*[13] Romer J held that the trustees of a discretionary trust were required to obey the directions given to them by all of the possible beneficiaries acting together even though the terms of the trust had given them a discretion to pass property to different beneficiaries in different contexts. It was important in that case that

---

8 [1896] 1 Ch 507.
9 [1928] Ch 920.
10 (1859) John 265.
11 [1928] Ch 920.
12 [1996] AC 669.
13 [1928] Ch 915.

all of the beneficiaries had agreed to this change in the treatment of the trust property. Taking that principle a step further, it was held in *Stephenson v Barclays Bank*[14] that one beneficiary could take delivery of their share of the trust fund (which the trust instrument provided was to be held separately for her) without needing to act together with the other beneficiaries. To take such an approach it is important that the applicant's share of the fund can be detached from the rest of the fund without causing loss or harm to the other beneficiaries. So, by way of contrast, in *Lloyds Bank v Duker*[15] a beneficiary also applied to be allowed to detach their portion of the trust fund from the rest of the fund. However, because their portion of the fund included shares which (taken together with other shares in the fund) gave the trust a majority shareholding in a company (and therefore the ability to control that company under UK company law) that beneficiary would not be permitted to detach their portion of the trust fund from the rest because it would have had an adverse impact on the rights of the other beneficiaries by reducing the trust's majority shareholding to a minority shareholding.

Another example where this principle is difficult to apply is in relation to discretionary trusts because the objects of that trust may never have any property appointed to them if the trustees never exercise their discretion in favour of some of them. However, the other beneficiaries who do receive property cannot claim to constitute the entirety of the beneficial interest under the discretionary trust without including those other objects who are left out. The analysis which has been taken by the Federal Court of Australia in *Richstar Enterprises Pty Ltd v Carey (No 6)*[16] is that the principle in *Saunders v Vautier* can only be used if the objects of the trust who are applying to take control of it from the trustees constitute 100% of all of the people who may possibly become objects of that trust in the future and if the trustees have the right to make a disposal of all of the property in the trust. If, however, there could possibly be other objects added to the trust (for example, if there is a trust for the settlor's children and the settlor might have more children in the future) or if the trustees are not permitted by the trust instrument to use all of the property held on trust, then the principle in *Saunders v Vautier* may not be used.

Previously in *Gartside v IRC*[17] the House of Lords suggested that the distinct nature of each object's claims to the trust property means that no object can be recognised as having a distinct interest in possession before any identified property has actually been appointed to her.[18] That does not prevent all of the possible objects from acting together, as in *Richstar*, because it is merely a restriction on individual objects of a discretionary trust dealing unilaterally with trust property before it is advanced to them by the trustees. Lord Wilberfore held in *Gartside* that an object of a discretionary trust does have an equitable interest under that trust (for example, an interest which entitles them to ensure that the trustees are obeying their duties under the trust instrument) but not a right which permits them to take property out of the trust before it is advanced them (and therefore that person would have no necessary obligation to pay tax on the trust's income, unless statute provides to the contrary).[19]

---

14   [1975] 1 All ER 625.
15   [1987] 3 All ER 193.
16   [2006] FCA 814.
17   *Gartside v IRC* [1968] AC 553, 606 *per* Lord Reid, 617 *per* Lord Wilberforce.
18   *Gartside v IRC* [1968] AC 553, 606 *per* Lord Reid, 617 *per* Lord Wilberforce.
19   [1968] AC 553, 617.

4.2 THE BENEFICIARY PRINCIPLE

4.2.1 The nature of the beneficiary principle

The basis of the beneficiary principle

Two ideas are fundamental to the law on express trusts. The first idea is that the consciences of the trustees can only be controlled if there are beneficiaries who can bring the trustees to court when the trustees have failed to perform their obligations under the trust adequately. Therefore, the courts insist on being able to take control of a trust in the event that there is some failure to perform the terms of the trust properly.[20] As Lord Grant MR put it in *Morice v Bishop of Durham*:[21]

> There can be no trust, over the exercise of which this court will not assume control . . . There must be somebody in whose favour the court can decree performance.[22]

There is no regulation of ordinary trusts and therefore trustees can only be controlled by the courts. The courts can only control the trustees if there is a beneficiary who can sue them. Therefore, trusts law requires that there must be an ascertainable beneficiary or beneficiaries for a trust to be valid.[23] This rule is known as the 'beneficiary principle'. In *Re Endacott*[24] it was said that 'no principle has greater sanction or authority' in the law of trusts. If there were nobody entitled to bring the trustees before the court by virtue of being a beneficiary, then the court would not be able to control the trustees. In the cases considered below, it will be seen that traditional judicial attitudes tended to invalidate trusts which did not satisfy the beneficiary principle on a very literal interpretation of their provisions.[25] By contrast, more recent cases have tended to validate trusts provided that there is some person or group of persons who could sensibly be said to be capable of controlling the trust by bringing matters to court.[26]

The second idea is that a trust requires that some property be held on trust for some person as beneficiary such that the beneficiary acquires a proprietary right in the trust property.[27] It is the beneficiary's proprietary right in the trust property which gives the beneficiary the *locus standi* to petition the court if the trustees fail to perform their duties.[28] In consequence, the so-called 'beneficiary principle' which we consider in detail in this chapter has become an essential feature of English trusts law.

People trusts are valid; purpose trusts are void

To distil all of the following discussion down to its essence we can state that 'people trusts' are valid but that 'purpose trusts' are void. A 'people trust' is a trust in which property is held on trust for the benefit of an ascertainable beneficiary or beneficiaries. The beneficiaries

---

20 *Morice v Bishop of Durham* (1804) 9 Ves 399; (1805) 10 Ves 522; *Bowman v Secular Society Ltd* [1917] AC 406.

21 (1804) 9 Ves 399; (1805) 10 Ves 522; *Bowman v Secular Society Ltd* [1917] AC 406, 441, *per* Lord Parker.

22 *Re Astor's ST* [1952] Ch 534; *Re Endacott* [1960] Ch 232.

23 *Leahy v Attorney-General for NSW* [1959] AC 457, as explained by Goff J in *Re Denley* [1969] 1 Ch 373.

24 [1960] Ch 232.

25 *Leahy v Attorney-General for NSW* [1959] AC 457.

26 *Re Denley* [1969] 1 Ch 373; *Re Lipinski* [1976] Ch 235.

27 *Saunders v Vautier* (1841) 4 Beav 115.

28 *Ibid.*

may be human beings or they may be companies: both of those categories are recognised by English law as being legal persons. A trust which is *not* for the benefit of ascertainable beneficiaries is described as being a trust for the pursuit of an abstract purpose. Trusts for abstract purposes are void under English trusts law precisely because there is no beneficiary who can enforce the trustees' obligations before the court.[29] If a trust could be created for an abstract purpose without any beneficiaries then there would not be anyone able to bring the trustees before the courts and there would be no one with ownership of the equitable interest in the trust property. The trustees would then be free to deal with the trust property exactly as they wished. Another problem would be that the trust could theoretically continue forever. The rule against perpetuities (considered in detail below) has held for many centuries that trusts may not exist in perpetuity because that would lock property into trusts when it ought to be allowed to circulate in the economy.

If it helps, you could think about the requirement for certainty of objects in Chapter 3 as linking with this requirement that there must be a beneficiary. Certainty of objects requires that we know the identity of the beneficiaries, whereas the beneficiary principle simply requires that there must be a beneficiary who is able to bring the trustees before the court.

In this section we shall identify two lines of cases. First, the traditional cases which take a narrow view of what it means to have a beneficiary under a trust sufficient to satisfy the beneficiary principle. Second, the more modern cases which take a more lenient approach to the beneficiary principle so that perfectly serviceable trusts are not invalidated due to sloppy drafting when the mischief of the beneficiary principle can otherwise be satisfied. We shall begin with two cases which show the nature of abstract purpose trusts and the ramification of them being invalidated.

4.2.2 The strict approach to the beneficiary principle

The approach based on the avoidance of trusts lasting in perpetuity

The traditional, strict approach to the beneficiary principle took a literal interpretation of the trust instrument and sought to decide whether or not there was any logical, possible risk of the trust fund failing to vest in a person as beneficiary within a reasonable period of time. In the quaint expression used by Viscount Simonds, any trust property which might vest outside such a time period would 'tend to a perpetuity' (i.e. the trust might continue forever) and therefore the trust would be void.[30] Consequently, the approach of the courts was to search for lapses in the drafting of trust instruments and to be astute in finding trusts void for bearing the risk of continuing in perpetuity and for propounding an abstract purpose. By way of example, in *Re Wood*[31] a trust had been created so that the profits from working gravel pits were to be held on trust for identified family members of the settlor. The trust instrument was poorly drafted and therefore, on the basis of the drafting, it was possible that these gravel pits might have been worked forever. It was held that the trust must be invalid because it could theoretically have continued forever. (The modern approach enshrined in the Perpetuities and Accumulations Act 2009 (discussed below) either waits for the trusts to come to a natural end or else imposes a perpetuity period.)

---

29 *Leahy v Attorney-General for NSW* [1959] AC 457.
30 *Leahy v Attorney-General for NSW* [1959] AC 457.
31 [1894] 3 Ch 381.

A good example of an abstract purpose trust was the purpose in *Re Endacott*[32] where a testator left money to erect 'some useful memorial to myself'. No identified person would take an identified benefit from that memorial and in that sense it existed to pursue an abstract purpose. It was therefore held to be void. In *Re Nottage*[33] a trust to provide a cup for a yachting competition was held to be void because that was a purely abstract purpose without a benefit to any identified beneficiary. It could have been said that the people who participated in the race (or even just the people who watched it) and the winner of the cup would have taken a benefit from it. However, the court wanted a clearer benefit than that. They wanted a benefit that involved proprietary rights over some property.

This same narrowness of view was evident in *Re Astor's Settlement Trusts*[34] when a trust was created with the objective of advancing 'the preservation of the independence and integrity of newspapers'. The particular objective was the preservation of *The Observer* newspaper which the Astor family had been instrumental in establishing. It could have been said that maintaining a newspaper would have been to the benefit of its readers or to a civilised, democratic society more generally. However, it was held that there was no beneficiary here in the sense of a person who would take ownership of any right, and furthermore that this purpose was in any event uncertain. Consequently, the purported trust was held to be void. Similarly, in *Re Shaw*,[35] the great socialist man of letters George Bernard Shaw had left money in his will to be applied in the creation of a new alphabet (with the ultimate objective of developing a new language which all of the peoples of the world could speak so as to increase understanding and peaceable relations between them). Again, it was held that this was a void purpose trust because there was no identifiable beneficiary.

These objectives were all held to be abstract purposes. What they lack is a property right for an identifiable beneficiary (or beneficiaries) and what they threaten is to last in perpetuity. In the following section we shall consider a small number of key cases which illustrate two different approaches to whether there will be a valid people trust or a void purpose trust. The traditional view (which tends to invalidate borderline cases) is exemplified by the judgments of Viscount Simonds in *Leahy v AG for New South Wales*[36] and Vinelott J in *Re Grant's WT*; whereas the alternative, modern view is represented by the judgments of Goff J in *Re Denley*[37] and Oliver J in *Re Lipinski*.

4.2.3 The distinction between 'people' and 'purpose' trusts

To recap, a 'people trust' is a trust the intention of which is to benefit identifiable people as beneficiaries,[38] as opposed to being focused on achieving some abstract purpose. If a trust qualifies as being a 'people trust', then it will satisfy the beneficiary principle and therefore be valid. By contrast, if a trust is a 'purpose trust' designed to pursue an abstract purpose without any identifiable beneficiaries then it will contravene the beneficiary principle and therefore will be void. Consequently, by way of example, a trust to provide sports facilities

---

32 [1960] Ch 232.
33 [1895] 2 Ch D 517.
34 [1952] Ch 534; [1952] 1 All ER 1067.
35 [1957] 1 WLR 729.
36 [1959] AC 457.
37 [1969] 1 Ch 373.
38 *Ibid.*

for employees of a particular company will be a people trust because it provides some benefit for identifiable beneficiaries,[39] whereas a trust to preserve gravestones will be a trust for an abstract purpose and will therefore be void.[40]

An example of the traditional, literalist approach: Leahy v Attorney-General for NSW

In the Privy Council in *Leahy v Attorney-General for NSW*[41] property was left:

> upon trust for such order of nuns of the Catholic Church . . . as my executors and trustees shall select.

The trustees selected the non-charitable order of Carmelite nuns. The property in question was farmland in New South Wales being a sheep station which stretched for 730 acres of grazing land and a single homestead comprising 20 rooms. Let us suppose, for the sake of argument, that the homestead could have accommodated at most two dozen nuns.[42] The question was whether this trust for 'such order of nuns' was an abstract purpose trust for the benefit of the order of nuns or whether it could be construed to be a people trust for the benefit of the individual nuns who belonged to the Carmelite order. The decision of the Privy Council was that this was a void purpose trust.

Viscount Simonds, delivering the leading opinion of the Privy Council, held that the trust was a void purpose trust for three principal reasons. First, most significantly, the trust was expressed as being made to the *order* of nuns, for the furtherance of their communal purpose, rather than to any specified, individual nuns. This is important. On a literal interpretation of the wording it was held that the settlor intended to benefit the purposes of the organisation that comprised the order of nuns as opposed to wanting to benefit any individual nuns. Therefore, the trust was deemed to have been intended for the abstract purposes of the order. Second, and building on the first point, it was held that because the terms of the trust provided that the property was being held for the order of nuns then that would mean that the trust would be used for people who would become nuns at some time in the future, rather than being limited to members of the order at the time of making the trust. This provision of property for nuns in the future was held by Viscount Simonds to 'tend to a perpetuity'. Therefore, his lordship would have held the trust void for perpetuities on that ground.[43]

Third, Viscount Simonds seems to have considered that to be a beneficiary under a trust required that you take 'immediate possession' of your rights under a trust.[44] His lordship held that as a matter of logic it could not have been intended that 'immediate possession' of the rights of beneficiaries could have been taken by all the nuns in the order over a small homestead on a sheep farm. On a purely common sense basis, his lordship was saying that a worldwide order of nuns made up of thousands of members could not be said to benefit as

---

39 *Re Denley* [1969] 1 Ch 373.
40 *Re Endacott* [1960] Ch 232.
41 [1959] AC 457.
42 *Ibid.*
43 *Ibid.*
44 This is not correct: the objects of a discretionary trust do not take their right immediately in possession and yet no one is suggesting that discretionary trusts are always void.

individual beneficiaries from a gift of land containing a sheep station which could accommodate only about two dozen of their number. This approach is clearly very narrow. The land making up the rest of the sheep farm could have been developed so as to accommodate large numbers of nuns on its 730 acres (approximately 700 football pitches in size). Viscount Simonds also referred to a lack of evidence as to whether or not the order of nuns would have been able to wind itself up so that the property could have passed to the nuns as individual beneficiaries, in line with the *Saunders v Vautier*[45] principle. Instead, his lordship required that for a person to be a beneficiary under a trust, that person must be intended to take 'immediate possession' of her rights in property, something which his lordship considered could not have been intended in relation to the Carmelite nuns.

Direct or indirect use or enjoyment of property: Re Denley

The decision of Goff J in *Re Denley*[46] took a different approach from *Leahy v Attorney-General for NSW*. In *Re Denley* a sports ground was left for the recreational purposes of a company's employees. The trust provided that: land should 'be maintained and used as and for the purpose of a recreation or sports ground primarily for the benefit of the employees of [a] company and secondarily for the benefit of such other person or persons (if any) as the trustees may allow to use the same'.[47] The question was whether this was a void purpose trust for the maintenance of a sports ground or a valid people trust for the benefit of the employees of the company. Goff J held that this was a valid trust for the benefit of the employees. Goff J found that this trust in favour of the employees of the company was very similar to an ordinary discretionary trust. Consequently, his lordship could see no problem with holding the trust to be valid. The facts of *Leahy v Attorney-General for NSW* were distinguished as creating a trust for abstract purposes, whereas *Denley* was a trust for the benefit of the beneficiaries. Goff J set out the following principle which is very different from the judgment in *Leahy*:

> Where, then, the trust, though expressed as a purpose, is directly or indirectly for the benefit of an individual or individuals, it seems to me that it is in general outside the mischief of the beneficiary principle.

So, even if the trust is drafted so that it appears to be an abstract purpose trust on its face, if the property is to be held directly or even indirectly for the benefit of an individual then that satisfies the beneficiary principle. Interestingly, Goff J held that what mattered was the 'mischief' of the beneficiary principle. Here his lordship referred back to *Morice v Bishop of Durham* (quoted at the start of this section 4.2) and the central principle that 'there must be someone in whose favour the court can decree performance'. On these facts, that there were employees of the company who could take a benefit meant that they could be the people who would take the matter to court in the event that the trustees breached their duties. However, that is not to suggest that Goff J was supposing that we can ignore the beneficiary principle in future cases – far from it. As the passage quoted above requires, where the benefit is so intangible that those purported beneficiaries would not be able to bring the matter to court to control the activities of the trustees, then the trust will nevertheless be found to be invalid.

---

45 (1841) 4 Beav 115.
46 [1969] 1 Ch 373.
47 *Ibid.*

What Goff J did do was to redraw the line at which trusts will be held valid or void – in effect making it easier to validate a trust than might have otherwise been possible. Another case which takes a similar approach is *Re Lipinski* which is considered in section 4.2.4 below.

A closer comparison of the cases of Leahy v Attorney-General for NSW *and* Re Denley

What is difficult to see is why there are different results in *Denley* and in *Leahy*. In the abstract, the facts of the two cases are very similar. In both cases there are large areas of land containing few buildings. In both cases it would be impossible for all of the potential class of people who might use the land to occupy it at the same time. In both cases it is possible to identify all of the human beings who will benefit from the property if you can get access to the necessary staff lists. So, those are the similarities. In *Leahy*, it was ascertainable who the members of the religious order would be. Therefore, it could have been said that the land in New South Wales would have been used for their benefit as an order, with different individuals taking turns to use the land at different times. After all there was no requirement in *Denley* that all of the employees would have been made to use the sports ground. Rather, groups of employees would use the sports ground from time to time in the manner made possible by the trustees, just as a few nuns at a time could have lived on the farm or used it as a religious retreat.

The more closely these two decisions are analysed, the more difficult it is to determine any substantive differences between them. The only way of understanding them is by understanding that the two judges had very different approaches to equity and trusts law. Viscount Simonds gave judgment in other key cases like *Grey v IRC* (see section 5.7.2) and *Gilmour v Coats* (see section 23.6.1) in which he always reached judgments based on narrowly-argued literal interpretations of the documents involved without any interest in the broader context. By contrast, Goff J became a leading light in the House of Lords and gave carefully progressive judgments in many cases. Goff J was concerned to maintain the validity of socially useful trusts (as was Oliver J below); whereas Viscount Simonds was concerned only with a close reading of words in a vacuum from their social context.

The continued use of the traditional approach

In spite of the foregoing discussion of *Re Denley*, it should not be thought that all decisions since *Leahy* have upheld trusts purposes as being valid. For example, in *Re Grant's Will Trusts*[48] Vinelott J considered a testamentary transfer which was expressed to be made 'to the Labour Party Property Committee for the benefit of the Chertsey HQ of the Chertsey . . . Constituency Labour Party'. The terms of the Labour Party's constitution laid down rigid rules as to the manner in which property of this sort was to be used for the purposes of the Labour Party nationally, as opposed to being used for the members of any local constituency party.[49] Vinelott J found that the rules of the Labour Party meant that the property could not be interpreted as being for the benefit of the individual members of the Chertsey Labour Party and instead that it could only be interpreted as being a permanent endowment for the

48   [1979] 3 All ER 359.
49   *Ibid.*

abstract purposes of the Labour Party. Therefore, it constituted an abstract purpose trust which was consequently void.

4.2.4 Where a transfer may be interpreted as constituting a gift rather than a trust

The discussion thus far has drawn a straightforward distinction between the people trust and the purpose trust. The decision in *Re Lipinski*[50] demonstrated both an agreement with the decision in *Re Denley* and also sufficient flexibility of thought to reinterpret a trust as constituting a gift so that the beneficiary principle in trusts law need not even apply. Here a testamentary bequest was left for the benefit of an association in a form which appeared, at first blush, to be a purpose trust. The precise terms of the bequest of the testator's residuary estate were as follows:

> as to one half thereof for the Hull Judeans (Maccabi) Association in memory of my late wife to be used solely in the work of constructing the new buildings for the association and/or improvements in the said buildings . . .

In particular, the words 'to be used solely in the work of constructing the new buildings' make that bequest appear to create a trust for an abstract purpose, and the words 'in memory of my late wife' were said by the claimants to create a permanent endowment. There appeared to be no doubt about this. A literal reading of the wording and the expression 'to be used solely' seemed to give no room for manoeuvre. Nevertheless, Oliver J held that, on the precise wording of the bequest, the testator intended that the association should take control of the capital completely. It was therefore possible for the association, if it considered it to be appropriate, to spend all of that capital at once in the construction and maintenance of the buildings. Oliver J held that granting the trustees control of the capital was equivalent to making a gift of that money to them. That was the incisive heart of the judgment: this was a case involving a gift, even if it was drafted to look like a trust, and therefore trusts law rules need not apply. His lordship held that the bequest could be interpreted as an outright gift rather than as a trust. Consequently, there was no problem with the beneficiary principle because the beneficiary principle does not apply to gifts. Perhaps his lordship was being disingenuous given that the document was so clearly drafted as a trust. Nevertheless, this route enabled him to come to the outcome he wanted: that is, to validate the bequest.

Oliver J took an even broader view of this area of law than *Re Denley*. Having considered the speech of Viscount Simonds in *Leahy*, Oliver J held that:

> There would seem to me to be, as a matter of common sense, a clear distinction between the case where a purpose is described which is clearly intended for the benefit of ascertained or ascertainable beneficiaries, particularly where those beneficiaries have the power to make the capital their own, and the case where no beneficiary at all is intended (for instance, a memorial to a favourite pet) or where the beneficiaries are unascertainable [as for instance in *Re Price*[51]].

---

50 [1976] Ch 235.
51 [1943] Ch 422.

In other words, a distinction is drawn between those cases in which, even though the trust power is drafted so as to seem like a purpose on its face, there is an intention to benefit people and those cases in which there is no intention at all to benefit people, for example where the trust is only intended to memorialise a pet. So, 'a trust for my friend Louey to help him recover from losing his phone' would be valid, whereas 'a trust to memorialise the beauty of my friend Louey's lost phone' would not be valid because there is only an abstract purpose in the latter example, whereas the former example had a human beneficiary (albeit that there was a collateral objective also specified). Where there are 'ascertained or ascertainable beneficiaries' that would be sufficient for Oliver J to find that the beneficiary principle would be satisfied. This is an approach which was very much in line with the approach taken by Goff J in *Re Denley* whereby only an indirect benefit for identified individuals would be necessary to satisfy the beneficiary principle.

It would not be correct to say that Oliver J simply distinguished the case in front of him on the basis that it concerned a gift rather than a purpose trust. After all, he also considered the approach in *Leahy*. This suggests that he was not completely confident of his gift analysis because there would have been no reason to discuss trusts law at all if he thought it really was just a gift. Alternatively, as a judge at first instance he might have been anticipating the likelihood of an appeal on the trusts law point if he did not analyse it.

4.2.5 Purpose trust or mere motive?

There a group of cases which some commentators consider raise a problem for the beneficiary principle. They are dealt with briefly here. It is suggested that in each case there are ascertained or ascertainable beneficiaries who will take a direct or an indirect interest in the trust property so that the mischief of the beneficiary principle is satisfied. Consequently, the approaches taken both in *Re Lipinski* and in *Re Denley* would have been satisfied. So, in *Re Osoba*[52] the testator made a bequest to his widow 'for the training of my daughter, Abiola, up to university grade'. The court accepted the argument that this bequest for the training of Abiola was not a purpose trust but was, rather, an absolute gift with a merely moral obligation expressed in the trust.[53] Clearly, Abiola was a human being taking a direct benefit under this trust; the objective of training her was collateral to that beneficial interest. Similarly, in *Re Andrew's Trust*[54] a trust had been created for the benefit of the seven children of a clergyman once their education had been completed. Kekewich J held that the intention had not been to create a purpose trust but rather to make an absolute gift to the children.

4.2.6 Anomalous purpose trusts which have been held to be valid

There are some anomalous cases in which abstract purpose trusts have been permitted in exceptional circumstances. In *Re Endacott*,[55] the Court of Appeal held that these anomalous cases could only be considered to be valid on their precise facts on the basis that no

---

52 [1979] 2 All ER 393.
53 Cf. section 3.3.2 above, where it was explained that a merely moral obligation will not constitute a trust.
54 [1905] 2 Ch 48. See also the discussion of *Re Grant's Will Trusts* below in section 4.3.3.
55 *Ibid.*

further anomalies will be permitted.[56] In that particular case, the Court of Appeal avoided a settlement of money for the purpose expressed by the settlor of 'providing some useful monument to myself' because that was an abstract purpose. Another feature of these anomalous cases is that they involved testamentary cases in which the settlor could not re-settle the property and their situations involved little property being used for narrowly-defined purposes.[57] The first category relates to trusts for the maintenance of specific animals.[58] The second category relates to trusts for the erection or maintenance of graves and sepulchral monuments, such as gravestones in churchyards.[59] The third category relates to trusts for the saying of Catholic masses in private (which would otherwise be non-charitable purposes because there is no public benefit derived from the activity).[60] The fourth category relates to trusts for the promotion and furtherance of fox-hunting, in particular a specific hunt from which no specific individuals could be said to derive direct, personal benefit.[61]

4.2.7 Perpetuities and accumulations

It has been a principle in the law of trusts for many centuries that no trust should be allowed to exist forever, or else property will be tied up in useless structures in perpetuity when that property should be used in the economy more generally. (The exceptions to this rule relate to charities, which are discussed in Chapter 23, and pension funds.) For trusts created before 1964, as explained by Joyce J in *Re Thompson*[62] every interest must vest within 21 years of the death of a person who had been alive when the trust was created. The Perpetuities and Accumulations Act 1964 governed trusts created after that time and before a new Act of 2009. The 1964 Act would validate trusts which were for the benefit of people not abstract purposes (as discussed above). The 1964 Act would 'wait and see' whether trusts without a termination clause in them actually terminated in good time, and if they did not terminate then the Act would close the class of people entitled to be beneficiaries and thus bring the trust to an end.

Section 5(1) of the Perpetuities and Accumulations Act 2009 creates a new perpetuities period of 125 years for trusts created after that Act came into effect. No other perpetuity period is now permitted, even if a different period is specified in the trust instrument, further to s 5(2). The question is: what happens if the trust may continue beyond that time? Very like the 1964 Act, s 7 creates a 'wait and see' provision in the sense that the trust is deemed not to be subject to the rule against perpetuities until the statutory period has expired and then any unused parts of the trust come to an end. Section 8 then introduces a 'class closing' rule to prevent any further beneficiaries acquiring rights after the statutory perpetuity period has been reached.

56   *Re Endacott* [1960] Ch 232.
57   *Re Hooper* [1932] 1 Ch 38.
58   *Pettingall v Pettingall* (1842) 11 LJ Ch 176; *Re Dean* (1889) 41 Ch D 552.
59   *Re Hooper* [1932] Ch 38.
60   *Bourne v Keane* [1919] AC 815.
61   *Re Thompson* [1934] Ch 342.
62   [1906] 2 Ch 199, 202.

4.2.8 Arguments suggesting that the beneficiary principle should be forgotten

International trusts law and the beneficiary principle

Chapter 21 discusses the important topic of commercial and international trusts. This topic is very important in practice. Many trusts law practitioners specialise in international trusts law and tax avoidance connected to trusts of that sort. There is no such area of law as 'international trusts law'. Instead, there are statutes in many different jurisdictions which have imported the trust concept into their law. Many practitioners who specialise in trusts would say that they practise international trusts law because they use the laws of different jurisdictions to achieve their clients' goals. Some of the most significant jurisdictions in this context are those which are used as 'tax havens' or so-called 'offshore jurisdictions' which charge little or no tax on income generated by trusts created in their jurisdiction: examples are the Cayman Islands, the British Virgins Islands, and the Cook Islands. Each of these jurisdictions have their own trusts law principles. Many of them follow English law except in very important particulars. One common exception used in these jurisdictions is the removal of the beneficiary principle by statute. So, in the Cayman Islands 'STAR trust' regime, for example, there is no requirement for a trust to have a beneficiary for it to be valid under the law of the Cayman Islands. Such a trust would be void under English law. The reason for these jurisdictions removing the beneficiary principle is that rich investors, for example from the UK and the USA, can invest in trusts in those islands without having any beneficial rights in those trusts. This means that an investor resident in the UK or the USA would not be liable for tax in their home jurisdiction, they hope, on any profit generated by that offshore trust because they are not a beneficiary under it. As it happens, the financial institution which will operate the trust on their behalf will nevertheless pay them profits in a tax-efficient way offshore.

There are two reasons for us to be concerned about this practice (which is discussed in much greater detail in section 21.2.4). First, these sorts of tax-avoidance structures are used by people who want to avoid any regulatory scrutiny. Consequently, among the people who use these structures are international criminal and terrorist organisations. Self-evidently, no change should be made to the law which would increase the impunity with which these sorts of organisations are able to use the international financial system to fund their activities. Second, there is a suggestion that English trusts law should dispense with the beneficiary principle so that tax avoidance can be conducted with impunity in the UK. It is suggested, quite simply, that this is a particularly bad reason for changing English trusts law. At a time of economic austerity in particular, it would be a ludicrous idea to excuse very wealthy people from their liability to tax in the UK, amounting to many billions of pounds, by allowing them to use that sort of trust. More generally, the trust grew out of an ideal of good conscience. There is no more conscionable act than contributing to the society in which you live by paying your taxes. Disingenuous tax avoidance achieved through these sorts of trusts structures is an unconscionable avoidance of one's moral responsibilities to one's fellow citizens.

The beneficiary principle is a political issue

What this short section should have made clear is that even the most apparently tedious areas of trusts law may have significant political dimensions. The utility of trusts to operate as 'property management vehicles' (that is, the sort of jargon term that is used by well-paid lawyers for trusts used to ensure better tax or other treatment for their clients' property) offers the means for all manner of purposes – good and bad – to be achieved with them. The study of trusts law involves us looking behind the veneer of the rules and principles to see what is really being done with trusts in the real world. In Chapter 5 we shall see several examples of trusts being used for tax-avoidance purposes; we considered sham trusts in the previous chapter. A survey of the politics of trusts law is set out in Chapter 17.

4.3 UNINCORPORATED ASSOCIATIONS

4.3.1 Introduction

This section considers the problem which is posed to the beneficiary principle when property is passed to social clubs and similar associations. This is a popular topic in examinations. The principal skill here is to be able to understand the different approaches which are taken in the various lines of cases, and then to show that you can apply those different analyses to the facts of problems. Usually examination questions in this area involve analysing a form of words which a settlor has purportedly used: you should identify the problem with the words they have used and you should advise on a better form of wording.

4.3.2 What is an 'unincorporated association'?

The juridical nature of an unincorporated association

If you are a law student then your law school will probably have a student 'law society' of some sort. That is an 'unincorporated association'. An association is any group of people which binds its members together by means of a contract between them. Usually that contract is in the form of a club constitution (i.e. the rules of the club: how its officers are elected, how subscriptions are collected, etc.) and members usually pay a subscription. Taken together, those rules and that payment constitute a contract. The association is 'unincorporated' in the sense that it has not been formed into a company (because companies are by definition 'incorporated'). A company is a separate legal person under UK company law and therefore can create contracts in its own name, it owns its own property and so forth. The company is a person recognised by law which is entirely separate from the human beings who staff it. By contrast, an unincorporated association is not a legal person. Therefore, an unincorporated association may not own its own property. Rather, some other person has to own that property on behalf of that unincorporated association.[63]

An issue is created every time someone tries to transfer property to an unincorporated association precisely because someone like the association's treasurer has to become the common law owner of that property on behalf of the association. At that moment it appears that the treasurer is acting as trustee of that property for the benefit of the unincorporated association's purposes. Remember what was discussed above: a trust for abstract purposes will be void. The case of *Leahy v AG New South Wales* (discussed in detail above) is a good example of this situation. The order of nuns in that case was an unincorporated association (because it was not an incorporated body and therefore could not own property in its own

---

63 *Conservative Association v Burrell* [1982] 1 WLR 522.

name). Therefore, when farmland was purportedly left to the association it was found to constitute a void, abstract purpose trust and was therefore void.

When purporting to transfer property to achieve the objectives of an unincorporated association it is essential to structure that transfer in such a way that it does not fall into the trap set by *Leahy* and by *Re Grant's WT*. The following sections consider the different possible analyses of such transfers on the basis of the decided cases.

4.3.3 Possible constructions of transfers to unincorporated associations

There are a number of possible analyses of transfers to unincorporated associations depending on the facts of each case. There are subtle differences between each one, so it is important to analyse the individual transfer closely to identify which interpretation applies in each case. While there are a number of different shades of interpretation on the decided cases, there appear to be seven analyses based on the cases which are considered below, some of which will be valid and others void:

(1) Trust for the abstract purposes of the unincorporated association: void.
(2) Outright gift, or assignment, to present members: valid.
(3) Trust for the people who are the present members: valid.
(4) Trust for the present *and future* members: may be void.
(5) Transfer to members as an accretion to the club's capital to be used in accordance with the club's constitution: valid.
(6) Transfer subject to a mandate to use the property in accordance with the club's constitution: valid.
(7) Trust for charitable purposes.

The skill which you are being asked to display in this context is an ability to analyse the problem question which is put in front of you and advise which of the following analyses best fits those facts (and how you would change the wording so as to achieve a different outcome). This involves you considering the wording you have been given and explaining why you think one analysis more than the others best fits that wording. Therefore, we will take each of these analyses in turn and explain how they operate. It should be borne in mind that many of these situations are problematic because the people who have drafted them have not made it plain which analysis they intend to use. So, we shall attempt to be clear.

(1) Trust for abstract, impersonal non-charitable purposes

The principal problem in cases of this sort is the risk of creating an abstract purpose trust which will be void, as in *Leahy v Att-Gen NSW* and *Re Grant's WT*. In those cases it was held that there were no human beings nor any companies (i.e. legal persons) who could take the property in question as beneficiaries, and therefore it was held that these purported transfers were void because they were trusts created for abstract purposes. For example, in *Leahy*, leaving property to the 'order of nuns', as opposed to leaving it to the nuns, was considered by Viscount Simonds to be a situation in which that property was being left to the abstract purposes of the Carmelite order of nuns, in a situation in which no people could be thought logically to go into 'immediate possession' of the trust property, and that that would 'tend to a perpetuity'. Consequently, when seeking to transfer property to an association, this is the structure to avoid.

As a further example, in *Re Grant's Will Trusts*,[64] a bequest was left to 'the Labour Party Property Committee for the benefit of the Chertsey HQ of the Chertsey & Walton Constituency Labour Party' or in default to the National Labour Party. Vinelott J held that the bequest should be interpreted as being intended to be held on trust for abstract purposes of the Labour Party as opposed to being held for any people. It was then held that the intention was to create an endowment (i.e. permanent capital) to generate income for the local or national Labour Party in perpetuity. Consequently, the bequest was held to be void for perpetuity, as well as being void as a purpose trust.

Clearly, this is the outcome we wish to avoid. Therefore, we should avoid wording which suggests that the organisation as opposed to identified people will benefit from the transfer, or that the transfer might continue in perpetuity, or that the people who will take a benefit will not have some sort of beneficial interest in the property itself.

(2) Outright gift, or assignment, to present members

The advantage of making a gift of property is that the trusts law concept of the beneficiary principle does not apply. Gifts are governed by common law and therefore no question of trusts needs to apply. However, it must be made clear that the absolute title in the property is being transferred from the donor to the members of the association as donees personally (and not being held on trust by any official on their behalf). A gift involves the transfer of all of the property rights in the property which is the subject of the gift. There is no trust because there is no equitable interest in a gift. By contrast, a trust passes the legal title in property to someone as trustee to hold it for the benefit of some person as beneficiary with an equitable interest in the property. It is a trust structure without a beneficiary which causes the problem here. An outright transfer of absolute title by way of a gift is not a problem.

If you are not sufficiently clear in your drafting then you will be reliant on finding a judge who is as benign as Oliver J in his interpretation of the facts. As was explained above, in *Re Lipinski*[65] Oliver J was prepared to read a trust which was drafted on its face as an abstract purpose trust – being a trust for the purpose of constructing new building for an association – as being a gift because the trustees were given complete control over the capital involved. That was a remarkable exercise by a very good judge indeed: to save the validity of that bequest, his lordship bent over backwards to come to the answer which he considered to be the most appropriate. His lordship was impatient with rules which would invalidate very communal, humane bequests like that intended by Mr Lipinski. A similar approach to *Lipinski* was taken in *Re Turkington*,[66] in which Luxmoore J held that where property had been left for the purposes of an unincorporated association to people who were both the trustees and also the sole beneficiaries, then effectively there had been a gift made to the association's members because they would own both the legal title in their capacity as trustees and also the equitable interest in their capacity as the only beneficiaries. In

---

64 [1979] 3 All ER 359; [1980] 1 WLR 360.
65 [1976] Ch 235; see section 4.2.3.
66 [1937] 4 All ER 501.

effect, those people owned the entirety of the property rights and therefore there was said to be a transfer of absolute ownership. Again, this judge was bending over backwards to validate a bequest.

A lot may depend on the nature of the property. Money is fungible and therefore a transfer of money can be interpreted in a number of different ways. By contrast, if a snooker table were left to a social club with 1,000 members then it would be difficult to analyse that as a gift of one snooker table to 1,000 people as its owners. Viscount Simonds would probably say that that was not property over which 1,000 people could simultaneously take immediate possession. His lordship would have held that that was property which was intended to be held for the abstract purposes of the club, and therefore that it would have been a void purpose trust. By contrast, if there were to be 1,000 snooker cues distributed among the members so that they acquired one cue each, then that could easily be analysed as a series of individual gifts to the members, and therefore as being valid. So, the nature of the property may assist the analysis of the circumstances.

(3) Trust for present members

A trust for the benefit of present members of the association would be a valid people trust, as in *Re Denley*. By being clear in the wording that it is restricted to present members, as opposed to future members, would remove any perpetuities problems and would probably convince even Viscount Simonds that a valid people trust is intended. Let us imagine a fund of £100,000 being settled on trust for the ten members of a social club who go on foreign holidays together. Using the exact form of wording (in italics) as was used in *Re Denley* – '£100,000 to be held on trust *for the benefit of* those 10 individual members of the travel club for a period of not more than fifty years' – would create a valid trust over the property for those current members as individuals.[67]

Therefore, structuring the transfer correctly can alter the proper analysis of the donor's intentions. An advantage for the donor of using a trust structure would be the availability of the remedies for breach of trust and to recover property if the trustee should fail to comply with the settlor's wishes. A clear advantage of a people trust over a gift is that the settlor retains some control over the use of the property by means of a well-drafted trust instrument. In a trust instrument it would be clear how the trustees were expected to use the trust property so as to give effect to the settlor's wishes. By contrast, once a gift has been made, then the donor has no legal control over the way in which the property is used because the property becomes absolutely the property of the donee. Everything will depend upon what your client wants from the situation: are they happy to let the donees do whatever they want or do they need trustees who can retain control? For example, if money is given to a club, how can the donor stop the club's members from voting to wind up the club and divide the money amongst themselves as soon as they receive the property? Therefore, there will be contexts in which a settlor will want to ensure that property is used in an appropriate, specified manner – in such contexts a trust is the best structure to employ. If a trust is to be used, then it must be structured appropriately so as to make it a valid people trust and not a void purpose trust.

---

67 As accepted in *Re Grant's WT* [1979] 3 All ER 359.

(4) Trust for present and future members

There is a subtle distinction between a trust for present members considered under (3) above and the endowment capital trust considered in this section. A trust which takes effect over endowment capital – that is, a trust which is intended to generate income in perpetuity from a large amount of capital – carries with it the problem that it will continue in perpetuity. This is something which would have prompted Viscount Simonds to find that it was a void trust. However, the 1964 Perpetuities and Accumulations Act came into effect subsequently and provided that such trusts would be validated and terminated at the end of the statutory perpetuity period. That situation is now governed in the same way by the Perpetuities and Accumulations Act 2009 with the insertion of a perpetuities period of 125 years.

(5) Transfer to members as an accretion to the club's capital to be used in accordance with the club's constitution

The foregoing analyses have already been set out in the discussion of the case law in section 4.3 of this chapter. This subsection and the subsection to follow consider cases which are new to this chapter. What is different about them is the replacement of trusts law and gift law analyses of transfers to unincorporated associations with contract law analyses of those transfers. In essence, the problem so far has been with trusts law. The problem specifically is with the abstract purpose trust. Consequently, some courts have accepted that the entire problem can be avoided if the transfer was governed by contract law. The cases considered here which use contract law are attempts by the judges to avoid the entire problem presented by trusts law in this area. In terms of your skills as a law student, this is a key part of you understanding how to use different legal techniques to reach propitious outcomes for your clients.

In *Re Recher's Will Trusts*,[68] a part of the residue of will trusts was to be held on trust for an anti-vivisection association which had ceased to exist. The issue arose as to the validity of the gift in any event, as if the association had still continued in existence. Briefly put, Brightman J held that this transfer could be interpreted to be an 'accretion to the club's fund' and that it would consequently fall to be administered in accordance with contract law under the terms of the association's constitution. His lordship held:[69]

> A trust for non-charitable purposes, as distinct from a trust for individuals, is clearly void because there is no beneficiary. It does not, however, follow that persons cannot band themselves together as an association or society, pay subscriptions and validly devote their funds in pursuit of some lawful non-charitable purpose. . . . Such an association of persons is bound, I would think, to have some sort of constitution; that is to say, the rights and liabilities of the members of the association will inevitably depend on some form of contract *inter se*, usually evidenced by a set of rules. In the present case it appears to me clear that the [members of the society] were bound together by a contract *inter se*. . . . In my judgment the legacy in the present case [to the association] ought to be construed as a legacy of that type, that is to say, a legacy to the members beneficially *as an accretion to the funds* subject to the contract which they had made *inter se*.

---

68 [1972] Ch 526; *Artistic Upholstery Ltd v Art Forma (Furniture) Ltd* [1999] 4 All ER 277.
69 *Ibid*, 538.

Brightman J is therefore suggesting that the beneficiary principle will not be an objection to the validity of a transfer of property to an unincorporated association if it is made under the law of contract as an accretion to the club's funds.[70]

What this analysis does not explain, however, is how the ownership of the property is to be explained. The association cannot *own* the property because it is not a legal person. Therefore, to say that the property is an accretion to its funds does not tell us anything about its ownership. The question is perhaps deliberately ignored by his lordship because it is difficult. The only sensible answer is that the property is held on trust by the association's officers. A second issue is that the donor has no control over the property once it is passed to the association because the membership can vote to wind up the association, or to change the rules governing the use of property, after that property has been received.

In deciding whether or not this *Re Recher* analysis is appropriate to any particular set of facts, we must consider the terms and the circumstances of the transfer closely. The donor should phrase his transfer as being 'an accretion to the association's general funds to be used in accordance with the terms of the association's constitution' for it to be held valid as in *Re Recher*. The donor should avoid using expressions such as 'the property is to be held on trust for the purposes of the association' because that would suggest the existence of a void purpose trust.

(6) Transfer subject to a mandate to use the property in accordance with the club's constitution as an agent of its members

In other cases there has been a drift away from trusts law in a way that is similar to (5) above. This model uses the idea of a 'mandate' to use property under a contract law analysis rather than a trusts law analysis. Where property is transferred into the control of one person to pursue the purposes of the association, that person may be held to be an agent of the other members of the club rather than a trustee of property for the purposes of that association. Thus, in *Neville Estates v Madden*,[71] Cross J held that such a transfer could be interpreted as 'a gift to the existing members not as joint tenants but subject to their respective contractual rights and liabilities towards one another as members' such that no individual member would be permitted to sever their share of that property.

This model was explained in *Conservative Association v Burrell* by Brightman LJ in the following way:[72]

> No legal problem arises if a contributor (as I will call him) hands to a friend (whom I will call the recipient) a sum of money to be applied by the recipient for political purposes indicated by the contributor, or to be chosen at the discretion of the recipient. That would be a simple case of mandate or agency. The recipient would have authority from the contributor to make use of the money, in the indicated way. So far as the money is used within the scope of the mandate, the recipient discharges himself vis-à-vis the contributor. . . . No trust arises, except the fiduciary relationship inherent in the relationship of principal and agent.

---

70 *Ibid.*
71 [1962] Ch 832, 849.
72 [1982] 2 All ER 1, 6.

A 'mandate' is a contractual direction which renders the person who is compelled to act on these instructions an agent of the person giving the direction. An example of a mandate would be an instruction given by a customer to her bank to make a regular payment by way of standing order out of her bank account: for example, monthly payments of rent to her landlord. In such a circumstance, the bank would be acting as an agent of its customer on the terms of the contract between them and not as a trustee. The fact that this arrangement takes effect under contract law means that there is no problem with trusts law nor with the beneficiary principle. Furthermore, the donor has some reassurance that their property will be used appropriately because the recipient's status as an agent means that they are bound by fiduciary duties in relation to that property.

That structure still does not explain the property law ownership of the property fully. If it was money in a bank account, then whose name would go on the signatory list? Everyone in the club? Might one thousand signatures be needed to pay a technician every time the coffee machine is repaired or the windows of the clubhouse cleaned? How are the signatories prevented from becoming trustees?

When answering a problem question, one must look at the circumstances of the case and decide whether or not this is the best explanation of the donor's intentions. Did the donor intend that the recipient should simply use the property in accordance with the terms of the club's constitution and not that the recipient was to be a trustee of that property for the abstract purposes of the association? A donor would be well-advised to draft the terms of the transfer as 'an outright transfer subject to a mandate that the treasurer use the property in accordance with the terms of the association's constitution'. The donor should avoid using expressions such as 'the property is to be held on trust by the treasurer' which would suggest a void purpose trust.

(7) Trust for charitable purposes

The final possible analysis would be that the purpose of the trust is charitable. Where the trust is for a charitable purpose, the beneficiary principle does not apply nor does the perpetuity rule. Charitable trusts are considered in Chapter 23.

Answering problems in this area

Students often find this a challenging topic because it is very different from anything which they have studied before. The key is to remember that the legal principles remain set in stone. It is only the facts of different problems or the factual circumstances of cases which change. So, you must analyse the facts of each different case and decide which of the different legal models they most closely resemble. Consider the words which the transferor used: which legal model do they most closely resemble? Is there anything about the nature of the property involved which leads you to one model rather than another?

The various advantages and disadvantages of these various analyses could be understood by reference to the following diagram. In essence this table records each of the five key analyses which have been described in this discussion and asks (a) whether or not each will be valid; and (b) whether or not each provides the donor with sufficient control over the use of the property once it has been transferred to its intended recipient. In essence, if a transferor transfers property to a person then she will want to know that that property will be used for the purpose for which she transferred it originally, whereas it is possible that when the officers of the unincorporated association receive the property they may decide that they want to use it for a purpose which would not meet with the approval of the transferor. Therefore, the fiduciary offices (like trustee and agent) offer protection to the transferor in that the fiduciary is bound by her fiduciary duties to use the property appropriately, whereas if the property is the subject of a gift then the recipient acquires 'complete control' over it and is free to do whatever she wants with the property.

Various analyses of transfer to unincorporated association	Abstract purpose trust	'People trust'	Gift passing 'complete control'	An accretion to funds	Taking property as agent subject to mandate
Leading case exhibiting this analysis	Leahy v Att-Gen NSW	Re Denley	Re Lipinski	Re Recher	Conservative Association v Burrell
Valid or Void?	Void	Valid	Valid	Valid	Valid
Does the transfer retain control of money after transfer?	Yes, but void	Yes, because governed by trustee's fiduciary duties	No, because all title passes	No, because governed only by terms of association's constitution	Yes, because governed by agent's fiduciary duties
Is it clear who owns the property?	Yes, but void	Yes, held on trust	Yes	No	No

On each set of facts, having analysed (as discussed already in this section) which analysis best fits the facts of the situation, it is then important to advise a transferor as to which of the various possible structures offers the transferor the best combination of valid transfer and suitable control over the property. For example, if the transferor is also one of the officers of the association who will receive the property on behalf of that association, then having little control over the property once received would not bother her particularly; whereas if she had no control over that body then she may require some control over the recipient once the property is transferred to the unincorporated association. A lawyer's role is to advise her client on the best structure for her goals. However, it is important to note that it is not a lawyer's (nor a student's) role simply to assume that the analysis which suits the client best is the one which necessarily applies. Instead one must look at the circumstances and recognise which analysis honestly fits the circumstances, and if one has the luxury of being able to restructure the circumstances before the property is transferred then one must ensure that the structure actually embodies the desired result. For example, if one wishes to seem most like *Re Denley* then one should use the precise formulation used in that case by Goff J.

4.3.4 Distributions on the winding up of an unincorporated association

Moribund associations – bona vacantia

If an association ceases to conduct any activities then it will be defined as being 'moribund'. At that point, a question arises as to the distribution of any property which was held for its objectives. Traditionally, equity would have ruled that the property should pass back on resulting trust to whoever contributed it (as considered below). However, when it is not possible for that property to be held on resulting trust (for example if there are no such people left alive) then that property passes *bona vacantia* to the Crown.[73] In practice that means the property passes to the Duchy of Cornwall (i.e. to Prince Charles currently).[74] This rule reflects the ancient logic of English property law that the monarch owns all property in the jurisdiction ultimately. You may find this remarkable in the 21st century.

For this principle to apply, there must be no members left in the association and no provisions in the association's rule specifying what should happen to the property. Consequently, when winding up an unincorporated association it was held by Lewison J in *Hanchett-Stamford v Attorney-General*[75] that if there was still one member left of an otherwise moribund association then the property attributed to that association would not pass *bona vacantia* to the Crown. Interestingly in *Air Jamaica v Charlton*[76] the Privy Council was faced with a Jamaican pension fund (which was treated as being an association for these purposes) which had surplus amounts in it which could not be returned to their contributors under the terms of the pension scheme. The court refused to apply the *bona vacantia* principle, preferring to return the property to its original contributors by means of resulting trust. It would have been awkward (to say the least) if Jamaican property had been redistributed to the English Queen.

Distributions among members on the winding up of an unincorporated association

A number of problems arise on the termination of an association to do with the means by which the property belonging to the association is to be distributed. There are three broad approaches discussed here. First, using a property lawyer's analysis, attempt to return the property to the people who provided it in the first place. This is the oldest method and used a resulting trust to return property to the original contributors. Second, using a contract lawyer's analysis, distribute the property in accordance with the contract between the parties in the form of the association's constitution. This is a more modern analysis in the case law. Third, use common sense to mix those various approaches. Let us take each approach in turn.

The first interpretation is that property should be returned to the person who transferred it to the association. The property is held on resulting trust if those subscribers can be identified. In *Re West Sussex Constabulary's Widows, Children and Benevolent (1930) Fund Trusts*[77] there were four principal methods in which property had been given to that unincorporated association: substantial donations and legacies, money donated via collecting boxes

---

73 *Westdeutsche Landesbank Girozentrale v Islington LBC* [1996] AC 669.
74 At present the income from the Duchy of Cornwall is paid directly to the Prince of Wales.
75 [2008] EWHC 330 (Ch), [2008] 4 All ER 323.
76 [1999] 1 WLR 1399.
77 [1971] Ch 1.

in the street, contributions from members, and entertainment such as raffles and sweepstakes. Goff J held as follows. First, where the makers of the donations were identifiable, then those legacies would be held on resulting trust for the donors. Goff J considered that the size of these donations meant that they were separately identifiable from the other property. Second, by contrast, smaller contributions were dropped anonymously into collection tins and as a result were not identifiable in the same way as the legacies. Third, contributions from members could be distributed in accordance with the rules of the association. Where the rules of the association were silent as to the redistribution of subscriptions to the membership, then those members would be taken to have received the services for which they had paid through their subscriptions so that they were entitled to nothing. Fourth, the proceeds of the entertainment were not capable of being returned to the people who participated on the basis that people who had contributed that money had received the entertainment for which they had paid (for example, the excitement of participating in the raffle).

The second interpretation, based on contract law, was suggested in *Re Bucks Constabulary Fund Friendly Society (No 2)*[78] by Walton J who held that resulting trusts ought not to apply because 'being a matter of pure contract, it is, in my judgment, as far as distribution is concerned, completely divorced from all questions of equitable doctrines'.[79] So, if the association's constitution contains rules as to the method of distributing property then the members are bound by those rules on the basis of contract law. The resulting trust approach has been preferred in relation to contributions to pension funds in cases such as *Davis v Richards and Wallington Industries Ltd*.[80] So, this development towards contract law might be limited to cases involving moribund associations and not to pension funds.

A problem arises when the association's constitution has no rules as to the distribution of property. In *Re Bucks Fund*, Walton J held that the proper approach in such a situation was to distribute the property rateably between the surviving members, according to their respective contributions, rather than passing it to the Crown as *bona vacantia*.

The third approach – using common sense – has appeared in fact in the first two approaches set out above. It was Megarry VC who held in *GKN Bolts & Nuts Ltd etc Works Sports and Social Club*[81] that the court should approach questions as to the winding up of unincorporated associations with 'the broad sword of common sense'. So, in *Re Sick and Funeral Society of St John's Sunday School, Golcar*[82] there were different categories of membership and so the question arose as to the respective property rights of those different types of owners. Megarry J held that the property should be divided rateably among the surviving members on the winding up of the association, such that the adult members would receive full shares and the children only half-shares in proportion to their subscriptions. The alternative approach which could have been taken would have been to say that all members had received what they had paid for and that they should have taken the property in equal shares.

It is often the case that clubs have different categories of members: some who use the full facilities; some who have only temporary access; some who have only limited voting rights in the affairs of the club and so forth. In *GKN Bolts & Nuts Ltd etc Works Sports and*

78   [1979] 1 WLR 936.
79   Followed in *Artistic Upholstery Ltd v Art Forma (Furniture) Ltd* [1999] 4 All ER 277.
80   [1990] 1 WLR 1511.
81   [1982] 1 WLR 774.
82   *Ibid.*

Social Club[83] the issue concerned the winding up of an unincorporated association when its constitution distinguished between full members and other sorts of members so that only full members could vote for a winding up of the association. It was held that only those full members should be deemed to be entitled to participate in a winding up of that association so as to be entitled to receive its property absolutely beneficially. Following that case in *Re Horley Town FC*[84] Lawrence Collins J had to consider the winding up of a club with full members, associate members, and temporary members who paid different amounts and received different access to the club's property. While his lordship was not required to rule on the parties' ultimate rights at that stage in the litigation, it was found under the club's constitution that the temporary members had no voting rights, and that the associate members did not have full voting rights, in relation to a winding up of the club. Therefore, it was considered that the temporary members should play no part in the winding up and that the associate members had insufficient contractual rights to participate either. This left the full members as the only people with a full right to participate in the club's property. However, in that case the issues were remitted for a full trial so no final decision was reached.

83   [1982] 1 WLR 774.
84   [2006] EWHC 2386.

Chapter 5

The constitution of trusts

CAPSULE SUMMARY

A valid declaration of trust over personal property will not require any formality, provided that it can be demonstrated that the settlor intended to create an immediate trust over the property. In relation to property to be made subject to a trust on death, in relation to trusts of land, and in relation to certain other property, there will be statutory formalities to be satisfied before a valid trust will be created.

The settlor must have had proprietary rights in the trust property at the time of purporting to create the trust; it will not be sufficient that the settlor acquires those property rights at some subsequent time. For the effective constitution of the trust, the legal title in the trust fund must be transferred to the trustee.

In cases of fraud, equity will not permit common law or statute to be used as an engine of fraud such that it may impose a trust even though there was no valid declaration of that trust.

The trust will not be used to perfect an imperfect gift, on the basis that equity will not assist a volunteer. Where the intention was to make a gift, whether or not a gift was validly made will be decisive of the matter.

Where a promise is made under covenant to the effect that the settlor will settle property which is to be acquired in the future, there will not be a valid trust. A valid trust will only be created if the settlor owned property rights in the trust property at the time of purporting to declare the trust. Otherwise, only the parties to that covenant will be entitled to enforce the covenant at common law for damages, or in equity by specific performance if they have given consideration for the promise. Trustees who are parties to a covenant may not enforce that covenant in trusts law, unless the benefit of the covenant itself has been settled on trust.

A disposition of an equitable interest must be effected by signed writing, unless both legal and equitable title pass together from the trust. Where a sub-trust is created, so that the beneficiary retains some office as sub-trustee, there is no disposition of the equitable interest – unless there is an outright assignment of that equitable interest. An agreement to transfer the equitable interest has been held to transfer the equitable interest automatically on the specific performance principle, without the need for signed writing.

5.1 SPECIFIC FORMALITIES IN THE CREATION OF TRUSTS

This chapter considers a range of issues to do with the creation (or, constitution) of trusts, and some of the key lines of cases which have grown out that process. First, there are some types of property which require specific formalities in the creation of trusts. Those contexts are considered at the outset. Second, we consider the particular problems associated with incompletely constituted trusts and failed gifts which the parties seek to effect as trusts. Third, we shall analyse the case law dealing with covenants to settle property in the future. Fourth, we shall explore the case law dealing with dispositions of equitable interests.

In this chapter we shall continue to develop the skills developed in Chapters 3 and 4 relating to the structuring and analysis of different ways of using trusts and other legal techniques to achieve a client's objectives in the real world. This is a core legal skill for those in practice. Whether or not you practise in this field, the skills which you will acquire here are vital in all areas of practice. This is one of the few parts of an undergraduate law degree in which you focus in such an intensive way on the ways in which altering the wording of documents can have such different legal outcomes. Therefore, the case law which we shall be considering turns on the desire of the parties to avoid a particular legal analysis because it would have an undesirable outcome (just as in the foregoing chapters we attempted to avoid a trust being void for uncertainty or for being an abstract purpose trust). In many contexts in this chapter the client is seeking to avoid liability to tax by using different legal structures (especially in section 5.5) which raises political questions about the role of trusts law in society (which is a debate which is continued in section 21.2.5).

5.1.1 Declaration of trust

The general rule: There are no specific formalities

As a general rule there are no specific formalities in relation to the creation of a trust, except for the situations which are identified in this chapter. The only pre-requisites for the creation of a trust over personalty are those discussed in Chapter 3 (that there must be certainty of intention to create a trust, certainty of objects and certainty of subject matter) and in Chapter 4 (that there must be a beneficiary in whose favour the court can decree performance). There is, however, no specific formality for the creation of a trust beyond satisfying those requirements. There is no magic form of words for the declaration of a trust. It is not necessary for there to be a written instrument creating a trust, as was clear from cases such as *Re Kayford* and *Paul v Constance* in Chapter 3. Of course, it is desirable for an express trust to have all of its terms contained in writing in a single document because then there should be no doubt about the settlor's intentions, the rights of the beneficiaries and the powers and duties of the trustees, unless that instrument is badly drafted. The following paragraphs of this section consider those circumstances in which statutes have created specific formalities governing the creation of trusts on death and in relation to land.

Declaration of trust on death

The Wills Act 1837 governs the formalities required for the creation of a valid will. It is common, as we have seen already in earlier chapters, for trusts to be contained in wills such that the executors hold the deceased's estate on trust for the identified legatees. Section 9 of the Wills Act 1837 provides that:

'No will shall be valid unless –

(a) it is in writing, and signed by the testator, or by some other person in his presence and by his direction; and

(b) it appears that the testator intended by his signature to give effect to the will; and

(c) the signature is made or acknowledged by the testator in the presence of two or more witnesses present at the same time; and

(d) each witness either –

(i) attests and signs the will; or

(ii) acknowledges his signature, in the presence of the testator (but not necessarily in the presence of any other witness),

but no form of attestation shall be necessary.'

Consequently a will (perhaps containing a trust) cannot be valid unless it is in writing, is signed by the testator, and is also attested by two or more witnesses. Failure to comply with these formalities will lead to a failure to create a valid will and therefore the testator will die intestate. Where these formalities are complied with then any trust in the will is valid.

Declaration of trust over land

When a trust is to be declared over land, s 53(1)(b) of the Law of Property Act 1925 ('LPA 1925') provides that:

(b) a declaration of trust respecting any land or any interest therein must be manifested and proved by some writing signed by some person who is able to declare such trust or by his will.

So, if a settlor wants to declare a trust over land, or indeed over any interest in land (such as a lease), then that declaration of trust must be evidenced in some written form and it must be signed by someone who has a suitable right in the property which is subject to the trust. This declaration of trust over land applies in relation to a trust created *inter vivos*; whereas if the trust was to be declared over land by means of a trust contained in a will then the formalities in the previous paragraph relating to wills must be satisfied. Section 53(2) of the LPA 1925 provides that there are no formalities in the creation of implied, constructive or resulting trusts over land or any other property.

5.1.2 A completely constituted trust cannot be undone

Once a trust has been validly declared then it cannot be undone by the settlor. This is a significant principle because it binds a settlor to the trust which they create. If they quickly regret transferring their property onto trust then it is impossible for them to recover their property. Consequently, a trust is not something to be created casually.

This idea needs some qualification: once a trust has been validly declared then it cannot be undone by the settlor in their capacity as settlor. However, the settlor's legal advisors might be able to build some escape hatches into the trust instrument. If the settlor is concerned about the trust property being used properly then the settlor might act as one of the trustees or the settlor might appoint trustees who are paid for their services and who are given a 'letter of wishes' by the settlor (outside the trust instrument) which explains how the trustees are expected to exercise their powers. It would be possible to grant the settlor a power (perhaps by making them one of the trustees) to cancel or revoke the trust but that might have tax consequences under statutory tax-avoidance rules such as the 'gifts with reservation of benefit' rules in inheritance tax law which are designed to stop settlors from hiding property in trust structures and then taking it back later when they think no one is watching. Alternatively, a trust may be terminated under the principle in *Saunders v Vautier* (discussed in detail in section 4.1) whereby all of the beneficiaries acting together can direct the trustees to deliver all of the trust property to them.

Otherwise, the settlor must think carefully about future contingencies and the various tax and other problems which might be created by building too many escape hatches into the trust instrument. The general principle remains, however: once a trust has been created then it cannot be undone. It might be helpful to think of the settlor as being like a boat builder who constructs a boat and sells it to a customer: once the customer sails the boat away from the shore, then the boat builder has no control over it. A good example of this principle is given by the case of *Paul v Paul*[1] in which a husband and wife had contributed property to a marriage settlement which was to have benefited both themselves and other people. Their marriage failed and so both husband and wife, *qua*[2] settlors, sought to unravel the settlement. However, it was held that the trust, once constituted, cannot be unwound. In that case it was significant that there were other people who stood to take rights from the trust. Nevertheless, the important central principle exists: once the trust has been created, the settlor cannot unpick it.

5.2 THE PROPER CONSTITUTION OF A TRUST

5.2.1 The general principle governing the constitution of trusts

A trust can only come into existence if the settlor is the owner of the property which is to be settled on trust and if the settlor manifests a clear intention to create a trust over it. In this section we shall consider a number of cases in which it was unclear what sort of property rights they had in an item of property when they purported to declare a trust over it – this was particularly important when the settlor tried to recover the property for themselves at a later date. As we shall see, the settlor must have had a property right in the property *at the time* they purported to declare the trust.

The settlor must then transfer the legal title in the trust property to the trustees so that they can hold the property on trust for the beneficiaries and discharge their duties under the terms of the trust. This part of the process was described by Turner LJ in *Milroy v Lord*[3] in the following way:

> in order to render a voluntary settlement valid and effectual, the settlor must have done everything which, according to the nature of the property comprised in the settlement, was necessary to be done in order to transfer the property [to the trustee] and render the settlement binding upon him. He may, of course, do this by actually transferring

---

1 (1882) 20 Ch D 742.

2 The word 'qua' is a useful word for trusts lawyers: it means 'acting in the capacity of'. So, here, we are talking about a human being acting in their capacity as settlor, even though they may also have other capacities in which they might be acting – such as a trustee or as a beneficiary.

3 (1862) 4 De GF & J 264.

the property to the persons for whom he intends to provide, and the provision will then be effectual and it will be equally effectual if he transfers the property to a trustee for the purposes of the settlement, or declares that he himself holds it in trust for those purposes . . . but in order to render the settlement binding, one or other of these modes must, as I understand the law of this court, be resorted to, for there is no equity in this court to perfect an imperfect gift.

This is a very important principle which governs most of the material in this chapter. First, the settlor is required to have done 'everything necessary' to create a trust over that type of property to make the settlement binding on the settlor. Note that the settlement here binds the settlor and not just the trustees because the settlor cannot recover the trust property once the trust is created. Second, the trust is constituted by transferring legal title in the trust property to the trustees. Third, significantly, it is not possible to re-label some other form of transfer as being a trust just to make it enforceable. So, as was discussed in relation to *Re Lipinski* in the previous chapter, if the defendant intended to make a gift of property (not a trust over it) then the claimant cannot try to enforce a failure to make a gift of the property by having it re-characterised as a trust. In that sense, the court will not complete (or, perfect) an incomplete (or, imperfect) gift.[4] We shall consider a number of cases in this chapter relating to the circumstances in which equity may intervene to support imperfect gifts and incompletely declared trusts (in section 5.4).

5.2.2 The constitution of trusts over personal property

In relation to trusts of personalty, there are no formalities to be complied with before the trust fund is transferred to the trustee.[5] For shares to be transferred validly under statute such that a trustee is vested with the legal title in those shares, it is necessary that the shares be registered in the name of the trustee. Company law has developed with the age of electronic registration of securities and so forth. However, at the time that many cases in this chapter were decided it was necessary to have a hard-copy register altered to acknowledge a change in share ownership. Some companies would have a rule placed in their constitution (known as the 'articles of association') to allow the company's directors or shareholders to decide whether or not they wanted to allow new people to become shareholders (so as to exclude business rivals and so forth). In older cases yet, holding a physical share certificate was evidence of ownership of shares. A so-called 'stock transfer form' would need to be completed to effect the transfer of shares at common law. In common with shares, copyrights and patents have their own particular formalities for the transfer of legal title in the property. This background may explain several of the cases to come, especially *Re Rose* below.

---

4 The word 'perfect' here comes from the Latin and means something that is complete. A thing is perfect if it is completed in this sense. We tend to think of 'perfection' as being aesthetic in its modern usage. It could be said that, because all human beings are always in the process of growing and developing (or at least ageing), no human being can ever be perfect in this Latin sense. Although, dear reader, I am sure you come as close to perfect as it is possible to be.

5 *Milroy v Lord* (1862) 4 De GF & J 264.

5.2.3 The constitution of trusts of land

As discussed above, declarations of express trusts in relation to land must comply with s 53(1)(b) of the LPA 1925 such that it must be manifested and proved by some signed writing. There are no formal requirements for constructive or resulting trusts over land under s 53(2) of the LPA 1925. Once a trust has been created over land then the provisions of the Trusts of Land and Appointment of Trustees Act 1996 govern the obligations of the trustees, the rights of the beneficiaries to occupy and otherwise deal with the land, and the circumstances in which a sale of the property can be ordered by the court. These provisions are considered in detail in Chapter 16.

5.2.4 The settlor must have a proprietary right in the trust property at the time of purporting to declare the trust

The settlor must have an appropriate interest in the trust property to create a valid trust

This section considers the very important principle that the settlor must own the property rights which are to be settled on trust at the time of purporting to declare that trust. If the settlor did not own the property rights at the time of purporting to declare that trust then there would be no valid trust. If there is no valid trust then the beneficiary does not acquire any rights over that property unless the settlor declares the trust again at a time when they do own the requisite property rights. Two cases illustrate this principle very clearly: *Re Brooks' Settlement Trusts* and *Re Ralli's Will Trusts*. We shall consider them in turn.

First, we will consider a case in which the settlor did not own the property rights which were to form the subject matter of the trust at the time he purported to declare the trust. Importantly, even though he became the owner of that property at a later date, he was not bound by his purported trust because it had never come validly into existence. So, in *Re Brooks' ST*,[6] there were two settlements over which a bank was trustee simultaneously. The beneficiary under one settlement, Arthur, had promised that any money he might receive from the first trust, over which his mother had a broad personal power of appointment, would be passed to the second trust. It is important to note that Arthur did not have any beneficial interest in the first settlement. Instead his mother held a mere power that she could advance money, if she chose to do so, from that trust. Consequently, Arthur had a mere hope (or, a mere *spes*; or, a mere 'expectancy' as it is referred to in the case) that his mother would decide to exercise her wide power of appointment to pay money to him at some time in the future. Significantly, he did not have beneficial rights which would have enabled him to sue his mother to enforce the transfer of money to him. At the time when Arthur purported to declare this second settlement he had no property rights in any money from his mother's power of appointment. Some time after purporting to declare that trust, Arthur's mother did appoint money to him from the first trust. When that money did reach Arthur's bank account, the bank was very efficient and effected an automatic transfer of that money onto the second settlement in accordance with the promise which Arthur had made. In the meantime, Arthur

---

6 *Ibid.*

had changed his mind and decided to keep the money for himself. Therefore, Arthur sued the bank for the return of the money.

The issue arose whether or not Arthur had created a valid trust over the money. At the time of promising the money to the second trust, he had had no rights in the money. Moreover, he had not sanctioned the transfer of the money onto the terms of the second settlement such that he could not be said to have declared that settlement at a later date. Therefore, because Arthur had had no proprietary rights *at the time of purporting to settle that money* on the terms of the second settlement, there was no valid trust ever created by Arthur. Consequently, Arthur was entitled to recover the money from the bank because there had never been a valid trust created which would have bound Arthur.

The second case is *Re Ralli's WT*,[7] in which the facts were superficially similar to those in *Re Brooks' ST*. In *Ralli,* Helen was the remainder beneficiary under a trust. This meant that she did own a property right in the trust fund but that she would not acquire rights to the income from the trust until the life tenant died. Helen purported to settle any property that she might receive under the trust in the future on trust. In time, money did come to Helen from the first trust and the trustees (who acted for both settlements) transferred that property onto the terms of the second settlement immediately in accordance with Helen's original declaration of trust. In the meantime, Helen had changed her mind and wanted to keep the money for herself. It was held that because Helen had had a proprietary right in the property comprised in the first trust (albeit that her rights were only the rights of a remainder beneficiary) then she had created a valid trust at that time and therefore she was bound by her declaration of trust.

The subtle difference between these two cases turns on the nature of the right which the settlor had *at the time of the purported declaration of trust* to decide whether or not there had been a valid declaration of trust. There was no property right in *Re Brook's ST*; whereas there was a property right in *Ralli* which compelled the trust to be carried out. Therefore, in accordance with *Paul v Paul*[8] Helen was obliged in *Re Ralli* to pass the property to the second settlement.

This same principle has been upheld in cases such as *Re Ellenborough*,[9] *Re Bowden*,[10] *Re Adlard*[11] and *Re Burton's Settlements*.[12] There is the exceptional decision of in *Re Antis*[13] in which Buckley J held that a term providing that all the property falling within a covenant 'shall become in equity subject to the settlement hereby covenanted' would be treated as having been settled on trust before any proprietary right was received by the settlor because the covenant constituted a contractual undertaking to settle that property on trust. The presence of that contractual obligation between the parties creates a different context, however, from *Ralli* and *Brooks* it is suggested. The particular problem with covenants (a form of contractual obligation created by means of a deed) is considered below, and can probably be considered to be a different situation.

---

7   [1964] 1 Ch 288.
8   (1882) 20 Ch D 742.
9   [1903] 1 Ch 697.
10   [1936] Ch 71.
11   [1954] Ch 29.
12   [1955] Ch 82.
13   (1886) 31 Ch D 596.

5.3 EXCEPTIONS TO THE RULES OF FORMALITY

5.3.1 The operation of implied, resulting and constructive trusts

This section considers situations in which formalities are not required to invoke equitable doctrines akin to a trust. Section 53(2) of the LPA 1925 provides that there are no formalities in the creation of an implied, resulting or constructive trust.

5.3.2 Fraud and unconscionability

We were reminded by Lord Browne-Wilkinson in *Westdeutsche Landesbank v Islington*[14] that all trusts arise on the basis of the conscience of the person who is made trustee over property. Therefore, as is discussed in detail in Chapter 12 in relation to *Constructive Trusts*, in cases of fraud and unconscionability there will be a trust imposed. The discussion in Chapter 1 of this book explored the roots of equity in seeking to achieve conscionable and creative outcomes so as to reach fair results in litigation. A good example of a court responding (perhaps a little contrary to doctrine) to deal with unconscionability arose in *Hodgson v Marks*[15] where a shyster convinced his landlady, an elderly woman called Mrs Hodgson, to transfer the title in her house into his sole name. Mrs Hodgson had felt sorry for him and had ignored other people's warnings about him. As soon as possible, he sold the house to Mr Marks while Mrs Hodgson was still living in it. Marks had bought it in good faith. Consequently, there was litigation between Hodgson and Marks as to who owned the house. Mrs Hodgson had been the victim of a shyster who had preyed on her good nature but it had not been Mr Marks who had done this to her. So, while there had been unconscionability, that had not been committed by either of the parties to the litigation. The court held that when Hodgson had transferred the property to the shyster that had been done on the understanding that she could live in the property for the rest of her life. Therefore, it was said that she should have an equitable interest in the house (on resulting trust, it was said) sufficient to protect her right of occupation during her lifetime, with unencumbered title passing to Marks on her death. This was a creative use of equity which did not require any formality, thanks to s 53(2) of the LPA 1925 which provides that there is no formality necessary for a constructive or resulting trust. Significantly, there had been unconscionability but not on the part of the litigants. So, the trust came into existence without the need for formality but so as to achieve a fair outcome between the parties (as we discussed in Chapter 1).

A straightforward example of equity responding to fraud arose in *Rochefoucauld v Boustead*[16] where the court upheld the ancient equitable principle that statute may not be used as an engine of fraud. There is real poetry in that expression. The defendant had borrowed money by way of mortgage secured over land but, because the agreement was only created verbally, the defendant sold the land to a third party. It was held that this was a fraud on the claimant mortgagee. It was held that 'it is a fraud on the part of the person to whom land is conveyed as a trustee, and who knows it was so conveyed, to deny the trust and claim the land himself'. Similarly in *Lyus v Prowsa Developments*[17] the claimant had

---

14   [1996] AC 669.
15   [1971] 2 WLR 1263.
16   [1897] 1 Ch 196.
17   [1982] 1 WLR 1044.

failed to register their rights and so the defendant took the opportunity to sell the land to a third party. Again, this was held to be a use of statute as an engine of fraud in the sense that the defendant was relying on the claimant having failed to protect their rights in the way that statute required.

5.4 IMPROPERLY CONSTITUTED TRUSTS AND IMPERFECT GIFTS

5.4.1 Introduction

Life is a river of disappointment. At times, one miserable experience follows on from another with such rapid succession that it appears to be a constant flood. Claimants who seek to enforce imperfect gifts as trusts are often motivated by disappointment. Imagine a person who has been promised a gift. Imogen travels to Martina's house on the train in such a state of excitement at the diamond ring which she has been promised that she almost draws blood by pressing her nails into the palms of her hand. She knows that Martina has bought the ring after they spotted it together in a small shop in Brighton's North Laine; she knows that it is sitting in a jewellery box in the dining-room, and that after dinner is eaten she will be presented with it. But then there is a terrible argument and the ring is never handed over. The gift is 'imperfect' (that is, incomplete). There is nothing that Imogen can do under the law of gift because Martina changed her intention before there was any transfer of possession or of title in the ring. Imogen may then argue that this is unconscionable and therefore she might try to argue that Martina should be treated as having created a trust over the ring in Imogen's favour. However, as we shall explore, the principle in *Milroy v Lord* prevents such an incomplete gift from being re-characterised as a trust. After litigation, Imogen's disappointment can only deepen.

5.4.2 Trusts and imperfect gifts

A trust can only be imposed if the settlor intended to create a trust as opposed to intending to make a gift; and then the trust must be properly constituted, as was established by Turner LJ in *Milroy v Lord*.[18] This section considers the problem that is caused when a gift fails for some reason and the mooted recipient seeks to prove that there should be a trust created over that property instead. Therefore, a claimant cannot rely on the law of trusts to effectuate an incomplete gift. We begin with that principle.

5.4.3 The rule that equity will not assist a volunteer and its impact on imperfect gifts

The ancient principle is that 'equity will not assist a volunteer'. A 'volunteer' is a person who has not given consideration for property. Anyone who receives a gift (without having paid for it) is therefore a volunteer. The one obvious exception to this principle is that beneficiaries are usually volunteers (unless they have created a trust as part of a contribution to a pension fund, a unit trust, or something of that sort) and yet equity protects them. Equity protects

18 (1862) 4 De GF & J 264.

beneficiaries because their settlors intended to create a trust and will have satisfied the principles in the first five chapters of this book. Otherwise, volunteers do not receive support in equity. Our concern for the moment is whether or not a failure to make a perfect gift can be saved by construing it instead to have been an intention to create a trust.

In the leading case in this area, *Milroy v Lord*,[19] Milroy purported to assign 50 shares to Lord by way of a deed. Contrary to company law at the time, no transfer of the shares was registered in the company's books. Consequently, Milroy remained the legal owner of those shares and Lord acquired no legal title in them. The claimant tried to show that a trust should have been created over those shares on these facts so that he in turn could take an equitable interest in them. It was held by the Court of Appeal that this ineffective transfer could not be taken to constitute a declaration of trust because there was no clear intention to create such a trust. One cannot try to argue for an express trust on the general basis of good conscience or failed gift if the settlor failed to vest legal title in the property in the trustee. As Turner LJ put it[20] 'the court will not hold the intended transfer to operate as a declaration of trust, for then every imperfect instrument would be made effectual by being converted into a perfect trust'.

5.4.4 'Doing everything necessary', not an incompletely constituted trust

The principle in Re Rose

In the foregoing section 5.4.3 we established a clear rule that equity will not assist a volunteer by perfecting an imperfect gift. In this section 5.4.4 we shall set out the first exception to that clear rule. In your studies you should be becoming used to the idea that any common law system no sooner creates a simple rule than the universe presents the courts with an inconvenient set of facts which compel them to create an exception to that rule. The principle in *Re Rose* relies on a very precise reading of the dicta of Turner LJ in *Milroy v Lord*, quoted above in section 5.2.1, so as to justify departing from the rule.

The Court of Appeal in *Re Rose* held that if a donor had done 'everything necessary' for them to do to transfer property, then equity would deem that property to have been transferred automatically. Because equity was deeming the transfer to take place, it would be a transfer of an equitable interest. The expression 'doing everything necessary' is taken from *Milroy v Lord*.

The facts of *Re Rose* (1952)[21] involved a question of tax law. Under inheritance tax law at the time, if a transfer of property took effect more than seven years before death then no inheritance tax would be payable. On these facts it was important that a transfer had taken place before a statutory cut-off. Mr Rose promised his wife that he would transfer some shares to her. To effect an outright transfer of those shares it was necessary to complete a share transfer form, to send it to the company, and for the company to register the new owner in its register. Mr Rose had completed the form and posted it before the relevant time in the tax law timetable. Unfortunately, the company did not re-register the ownership of the shares until some time later. Importantly, therefore, Mr Rose had done everything necessary for him to

---

19   (1862) 4 De GF & J 264.
20   *Ibid.*
21   [1952] Ch 499.

do to transfer the shares, but the company had not completed its part. It was held by Lord Evershed MR that because Mr Rose had done everything necessary for him to do then the equitable interest in the shares would be deemed to have passed at that time. His lordship's reasoning that was that it would have been inequitable for Mr Rose to have reneged on that gift and therefore that it was equitable to deem that the equitable interest in those shares passed at the time that Mr Rose completed his part of the procedure (i.e. when he posted the share transfer form).

The same principle was reached in *Re Rose* (1949) by Jenkins J where an intended outright transfer of shares was also held to have transferred the equitable interest automatically.[22] Mr Rose intended to make a transfer of shares to Hook but the transfer was not complete until the company approved the transfer after it had received the transfer form. Jenkins J held that, because Mr Rose 'had done everything in his power to divest himself of the shares in question', the equitable interest in the shares should be treated as having been passed to Hook by the transfer form and the transfer only perfected by registration. Jenkins J distinguished an earlier decision in *Re Fry*.[23] In *Re Fry* an American had sought to declare a trust over shares. He had completed a share transfer form but during wartime a transfer of shares in that company required the consent of the Treasury. The American was found not to have transferred the legal title in those shares because the Treasury did not give its consent in time. Jenkins J considered that the American in *Fry* had not done everything necessary to divest himself of the shares. However, it is difficult to see exactly which element remained outstanding in *Fry* which similarly had not been completed in *Rose*. The better point of distinction was the fact that the court in *Fry* wanted to uphold the spirit of the wartime limitation on foreigners dealing in company shares, whereas the court in *Rose* was predisposed to save the Rose family the cost of the inheritance tax.

Subsequent, problematic applications of the Re Rose principle

Re Rose has been followed in numerous other cases.[24] In *T Choithram International SA v Pagarani*,[25] a man lying on his deathbed sought to declare an *inter vivos* trust over his property. The settlor's intention was that he would be one of nine trustees over that property. However, the dead man failed to transfer legal title in the property to all nine trustees and, as a consequence, under the ordinary law of trusts, the trust would not have been validly constituted. Nevertheless, it was held that a valid trust was created over that property even though the deceased person had not transferred the legal title in the trust property to all nine trustees. The rationale given by the court was that the *Rose* principle could be applied so that the settlor could be taken to have done all that was necessary to create a trust and therefore that the equitable interest in his property should be taken to have passed automatically. Of course, the settlor had not done everything necessary for him to do to establish the trust he had intended to create.

The Court of Appeal in *Pennington v Waine*[26] followed *Choithram* when perfecting a gift of shares in circumstances in which the donor had neither effected a declaration of trust

---

22 [1949] Ch 78.
23 [1946] Ch 312.
24 *Vandervell v IRC* [1967] 2 AC 291.
25 *Choithram International SA v Pagarani* [2001] 1 WLR 1.
26 *Pennington v Waine* [2002] 1 WLR 2075.

over the shares nor done everything which was necessary for her to do to effect a transfer of the shares. Clearly, the principle had now stretched far beyond the original decision in *Re Rose*. In *Pennington v Waine*, Ada wanted to transfer 400 shares in a company to her nephew, Harold, and she also wanted Harold to be appointed a director of that company. Ada completed a share transfer form which she sent to her accountant, Pennington. However, Pennington failed to forward this form to the company or to Harold. Consequently, due to the failure to deliver the form, no transfer of the shares was made to Harold. Ada subsequently signed a form consenting to Harold becoming a director of the company but by her will she transferred him insufficient shares for Harold to have a controlling shareholding in the company. It was held by Arden LJ that an equitable interest in those 400 shares should be deemed to have passed to Harold because it was considered that it would have been unconscionable for Ada to have refused to transfer those shares to Harold. The Court of Appeal considered that it had remained Ada's intention throughout her life to transfer these 400 shares to Harold and this influenced their lordships' decision. The decision in *Pennington v Waine* extends the *Re Rose* principle beyond its former boundaries because the donor had not done everything necessary for her to have done to complete the transfer.

Two cases have put this area of law back in line with the original decision in *Re Rose*. In *Kaye v Zeital*[27] the Court of Appeal refused to accept a finding at first instance that a transfer had taken effect even though the purported transferor had failed to do everything necessary for him to do to transfer the property. In that case the purported transferor had not provided the purported transferee with the share certificate nor any other documentation which, in relation to that company, was required to demonstrate that a valid transfer had been made.

In *Curtis v Pulbrook*,[28] Briggs J took the sensible approach that where a man had failed to transfer shares to his wife and daughter because he had not completed the transfer process, then the *Re Rose* principle could not be relied upon. On those facts, his intention had been to make a gift of the shares, and yet he had neither completed a share transfer form nor sent the share certificates to the intended recipients. He then deposited documents which related to the shares in this company with his solicitors before leaving the UK to live with his new partner in Thailand: those documents did not contain a completed share transfer form either. Therefore, at no stage had he done everything necessary for him to do to effect a transfer of the property. Furthermore, he had not been authorised to effect a transfer of this sort to his wife and daughter in any event. Consequently, it was held that the principle in *Re Rose* had not been satisfied on these facts.[29] Briggs J considered that the decisions in *Pagarini* and *Pennington* established no clearly identifiable nor rational policy objective.[30] In other words, his lordship considered that the recent case law had not seemed to follow any clear principle. Briggs J summarised the decisions in the recent *Re Rose* cases as generating three bases on which the *Rose* principle would arise:[31]

---

27   [2010] EWCA Civ 159, [2010] 2 BCLC 1.
28   [2011] EWHC 167 (Ch), [2011] 1 BCLC 638.
29   *Pennington v Waine* [2002] 2 BCLC 448; and *Kaye v Zeital* [2010] 2 BCLC 1 applied.
30   [2011] EWHC 167 (Ch), [2011] 1 BCLC 638, [47].
31   *Ibid*, [43].

The first is where the donor has done everything necessary to enable the donee to enforce a beneficial claim without further assistance from the donor . . . [32] The second is where some detrimental reliance by the donee upon an apparent although ineffective gift may so bind the conscience of the donor to justify the imposition of a constructive trust . . . [33] The third is where by a benevolent construction an effective gift or implied declaration of trust may be teased out of the words used.[34]

What is interesting about this summary is that it does not reflect the precise rationale which Lord Evershed MR used in *Re Rose* itself, on the basis of unconscionability in reneging on the promise to make a transfer, as considered above. That aside, the first principle is the principle which can be divined from *Re Rose*, albeit not adopting the generally equitable approach in that case. While the *Re Rose* decision itself is used as authority for the 'constructive trust' argument, that idea is not broached at all in *Re Rose* itself. The third principle is not really a principle at all, but rather is a judicial determination to validate testamentary gifts wherever possible.

5.5 PERFECTING IMPERFECT GIFTS

The general principle is that equity will not assist a volunteer (such as the recipient of a gift) if their gift fails. There are two general exceptions to that rule which are considered in this section: *donatio mortis causa* and the rule in *Strong v Bird*.[35] The doctrine of proprietary estoppel may offer another exception where there is a representation made in reliance on which the claimant acts to their detriment: that area is discussed in Chapter 13.

5.5.1 *Donatio mortis causa*

The doctrine of *donatio mortis causa* was intended to be very narrow when it was created. Such a gift has been permitted to be exempt from the principle that equity will not assist a volunteer provided that the gift was made in the imminent expectation of death when it was unreasonable to expect someone to comply with legal formalities. A good example of the sort of situation which might give rise to a *donatio mortis causa* – literally, a gift made because of death – would be the victim of a terrific road accident being lifted into the ambulance and clutching the arm of a loved one, in the expectation that they might not live for much longer, and telling them how they want their property to be distributed. The Court of Appeal in *Sen v Headley*[36] considered the case of a couple who had lived together for ten years but had separated more than 25 years before the material time. One of the couple was dying of a terminal illness. Before his death he told his former partner (the plaintiff) that the house (with unregistered title) was hers and that 'You have the keys. The deeds are in the steel box.' It was held that the plaintiff could take the house as *donatio mortis causa*. Importantly, this did not require any of the formalities for the transfer of land.

---

32 *Pennington v Waine* [2002] 2 BCLC 448 at [55]–[56] and *Re Rose (decd), Rose v IRC* [1952] Ch 499
33 *Ibid*, [59].
34 *Ibid*, [60]–[61].
35 (1874) LR 18 Eq 315.
36 [1991] Ch 425.

5.5.2 The rule in *Strong v Bird*

The rule in *Strong v Bird*[37] provides that if I owe you a debt but you name me as the executor of your will, then the debt is discharged. The principle rests on the idea that the testator must be making a gift to the executor of a release from the debt. Otherwise the executor would have to sue herself for repayment of the debt after the testator's death. The obvious objection to this principle is that the testator might still have wanted the debt to be repaid (and the money distributed to her relatives after her death) and that the executor should not be forgiven the entire amount.

It is important that the testator must continue to benefit the executor. In *Re Gonin*,[38] a mother wished to pass her house to her illegitimate daughter on death but had formed the (incorrect) notion that she could not do so because her daughter had been born out of wedlock. Therefore, the mother wrote a cheque for £33,000 in her daughter's favour. When her daughter was subsequently appointed administratrix of her mother's estate, it was held that she could not claim title to the house because her mother had indicated an intention to replace the gift of the house with a gift of money instead. This decision seems a little harsh given that the mother had changed her mind on the basis of a mistake.

5.6 COVENANTS AND PROMISES TO CREATE A SETTLEMENT OVER AFTER-ACQUIRED PROPERTY

5.6.1 The problem of after-acquired property

The problem of covenants to settle relates to situations in which people promise that they will create trusts at some time in the future when they expect to receive property, then they change their minds in the meantime, before finally receiving the property after all. The people who were promised that property would be settled on trust for them usually sue to try to enforce that promise. This issue clearly follows on from the discussion of incompletely constituted trusts above in relation to *Re Brook's ST* and *Re Ralli's WT* in which it was held that there could only be a binding trust over property if the settlor owned property rights at the time of purporting to declare that trust. Therefore, if property was acquired after the purported declaration of trust then there would be no trust. This is known as the problem of 'after-acquired property': that is, property acquired after a trust had supposedly been declared. This discussion also follows on from the discussion of imperfect gifts whereby trusts law (and equity generally) will not complete an incomplete gift by calling it a trust because equity will not assist a volunteer.

In this section we shall consider how covenants have come to interact with that problem. A 'covenant' is a contract that is created by means of a document that is signed and delivered as a deed: therefore, a covenant is a contract but it is a contract which does not require consideration to be valid in itself simply because it is contained in a deed. It should be remembered that someone who does not give consideration for a contract is known as a 'volunteer' and that 'equity will not assist a volunteer' (as discussed above). Therefore, the covenant may be valid because it is made by deed but its parties will still be volunteers in equity's eyes if they have not given consideration for it. So, covenants will not entitle the

---

37 (1874) LR 18 Eq 315.
38 *Ibid.*

parties to the equitable remedy of specific performance of the contractual obligation unless consideration has passed. In relation to covenants which promise to settle property there will not be specific performance unless the parties to the covenant have given consideration (in the contract law sense) nor will there be a trust unless the property rights were owned by the settlor at the time of creating the covenant. Let us take a hypothetical example to illustrate what is happening in these situations:

> Colonel Brandon was an English soldier in his late 40s. He had served overseas for several years and fought in several wars. He had settled himself to a future as a solitary bachelor. He knew that he was entitled to receive a large amount of money and the right to occupy a large country house in Sussex (known as Lindfield House) under the terms of the Brandon family settlement. Colonel Brandon would only become entitled to these items of property if his uncle predeceased him.
>
> It seemed to Colonel Brandon that all of this property would be of no use to a soldier like him who was overseas most of the time and who had no real need for money when on active service. His brother was younger and was trying to start a large family with his wife. Therefore, in January, Colonel Brandon decided to enter into a covenant with his younger brother, John, his sister-in-law, Joanna, and his adult niece, Poppy. The covenant provided that half of any money received from the Brandon family settlement should be held on trust by Mr Flight and Ms Golightly, the family solicitors and trustees of the family settlement, and that if title to Lindfield House should pass to him then he wanted his interest to be passed to John and Joanna during his lifetime. There was some documentation which the Colonel and his relatives signed at the time which had been prepared by the solicitors Flight and Golightly.
>
> In April something unexpected happened. Colonel Brandon realised that he had begun to fall in love with a nurse, Florence. Over the ensuing months, the couple began a tentative romance until Colonel Brandon finally proposed marriage to Florence inside the field hospital while Florence was removing shrapnel from his fundament. When they returned to England in December they found that John, Lisa and Poppy were not pleased with the news of the proposed marriage. Their uncle had died in late November and all of the property under the family settlement was due to pass to the Colonel. The trustees of the family settlement (prompted by Lisa Brandon) proposed to hold the money on trust for Poppy and the house for the occupation of John and Lisa and their children from that time. Lisa was relying on the Colonel's promise in January. However, the Colonel had now decided that he wanted to keep the house and the money so that he and Florence could start a family together. He intended to retire to Sussex and keep bees.
>
> The family solicitors Flight and Golightly were a hare-brained lot who tended to answer their clients' questions about the Brandon family settlement without consulting the terms of the settlement itself. Like hare-brained undergraduate law students they preferred to pretend to be able to do everything from memory while talking enthusiastically. As every good lawyer knows, you must always analyse the terms of the documentation carefully. Therefore, as we go through the various possible analyses we shall see that the solicitors keep changing their minds about what the settlement and the January documentation actually provided.

This section will follow through this hypothetical example, fleshing out the facts as we go, to explain how the different case law analyses would apply to a case like the present. Because students sometimes find this area of law a little complex (with its many different cases presenting different analyses and coiling over one another like snakes in a basket), I have presented this discussion in the form of a narrative. You are asked to imagine that the parties in the example above are asking their incompetent solicitors to explain their rights and that the solicitors keep discovering new facts when they bother to read the documents properly. You can assume that the barrister whom they consult is an expert in trusts law who gets the law correct. It is hoped that this fictional narrative – which gives you a full explanation of the real decided cases as it goes – will be a helpful guide through this area of law.

5.6.2 To establish a trust the settlor must own the relevant property at the time of purporting to declare the trust

When the solicitors are first asked about the settlements in November (by Lisa Brandon), the solicitors tell her two facts: first, that the house and money pass to the Colonel under the Brandon family settlement and, second, that the settlement identifies the Colonel as being the remainder beneficiary under the Brandon family settlement.

The solicitors told Lisa Brandon that the Colonel was identified as a remainder beneficiary who took priority over his younger brother John under the Brandon family settlement. The solicitors had discovered the case of *Re Ralli's WT*.[39] In that case, Helen had been a remainder beneficiary and therefore had been found to have had property rights in the trust property when she promised to settle any property paid to her in the future. Because she had had property rights at the time of purporting to declare the trust then she had created a valid settlement which bound her when she did receive money in the future. Consequently, Mr Flight told Lisa with a self-satisfied smile, the Colonel had had property rights under the family settlement in January when he promised to settle any property acquired in the future on John, Lisa and Poppy. This meant that the promise had created a binding trust back in January. Lisa Brandon left their offices elated. She had never liked her gruff brother-in-law and believed that such a fine house would be wasted on him and a 'mere nurse'.

What had pleased Lisa Brandon particularly was that everything was so final. The solicitors had explained the case of *Paul v Paul*[40] to her: that case provided that once a settlement had been made then it could not be undone by the settlor simply because the settlor had changed their mind about the arrangement. She was happy now that everything was set in stone.

A few days passed and the solicitors contacted Lisa Brandon again, asking her to attend them in their offices in the town. Somewhat shame-faced they led her into their wood-panelled conference room, closed the door with a reassuring click and shuffled paper nervously until Lisa Brandon snapped at them and demanded to know what was happening. They told her that they had consulted the Brandon family settlement in the meantime and had discovered, much to their surprise, that under the terms of the family settlement Colonel Brandon had actually been the object of a mere power of appointment and not a remainder beneficiary. This meant that the Colonel had had no property rights when he had purported to pass any after-acquired property in January. The property only came to him months later in November when his uncle had died. The solicitors told Joanna that there was a letter of wishes from the settlor

39   [1964] 1 Ch 288.
40   (1882) 20 Ch D 742.

which instructed them to exercise their power of appointment in favour of the oldest male relative and that that was what they were compelled to do.

The solicitors had consulted counsel and had been referred to another authority: *Re Brook's ST*.[41] The decision in *Re Brook's ST* had also related to the object of a mere power of appointment who had purported to settle property on trust for his relatives before any property had been paid to him under the power. The court had held that, because he had had no property rights at the time of purporting to create that trust, then no trust was ever created and therefore when he had received money under the power of appointment there had been no legal basis for compelling him to transfer the property onto trust. Consequently, on these facts, the solicitors told Lisa Brandon that the Colonel was not bound by his promise in January because he had had no property rights under the power of appointment at that time either. He had only had a mere spes. Therefore, John, Lisa and Poppy had no rights under trusts law.

5.6.3 The enforceability of a promise under covenant

Lisa Brandon had left the solicitors' offices in a high temper, screaming the word 'negligence' over her shoulder as she went. This prompted the solicitors to take counsel's advice again (with another long trip to Lincoln's Inn in London as a result) to see if there was anything they could do to placate Mrs Brandon. Counsel reminded them that the promise which Colonel Brandon had made in January had been contained in a covenant. That is, a contract contained in a formal document known as a deed. That covenant had been signed in January by the Colonel, John, Joanna, and Poppy (who was 22 years old at the time), and also by Mr Flight and Ms Golightly in their capacity as trustees. Counsel advised that there were three lines of authority in contract law that would be important.

First, none of the parties had given consideration for the covenant. For example, none of the parties had paid any money in consideration for the Colonel executing the covenant. If they had done then ordinary contract law might have applied. However, because no one had given consideration then the equitable principle in *Pullan v Koe*[42] would apply such that equity will not assist a volunteer. That equity will not assist a volunteer means that no equitable remedy like specific performance will be available. Therefore no trust would be found, and no right to specific performance would apply because rights to specific performance are available only to those who have given consideration.[43] In *Pullan v Koe*[44] it was held that the claimant had been entitled to claim a right in contract law where she had given consideration as part of a marriage settlement, and in consequence was entitled to specific performance of the defendant's promise to settle after-acquired property on trust for her. If the claimant had not given consideration for the promise, it had been held, then her only claim would be based on an entitlement to damages at common law if she were a party to the covenant.

Second, precisely because they were parties to the covenant, the parties to the covenant would be entitled to common law damages for breach of covenant if the Colonel refused to be bound by the covenant. In the case of *Cannon v Hartley*[45] a father entered into a covenant

---

41 [1939] 1 Ch 993.
42 [1913] 1 Ch 9.
43 *Pullan v Koe* [1913] 1 Ch 9.
44 [1913] 1 Ch 9.
45 [1949] Ch 213.

to settle after-acquired property on his daughter and other people. His daughter had given no consideration for this covenant, but she was held to be entitled to damages at common law for breach of covenant when her father refused to transfer the property onto trust. She had this right because she had been a party to the covenant. Therefore, counsel confirmed that Poppy would be entitled to damages in relation to the promise of the money because she had been a party to the covenant, and that John and Lisa would also be entitled to damages in relation to the promise of the house for the same reason. As Lisa Brandon pointed out later, a right to damages would be less useful to them than ownership of Lindfield House outright because that grand house was likely to increase greatly in value in the future. In relation to young Poppy, she conceded that damages would be as good as a trust over money.

As counsel pointed out, there was the exceptional decision in *Tailby v Official Receiver*[46] which had held that an equitable interest in property should pass even if the covenanted promise was made only at a time when the promisor had had no rights in the property because it was held under a mere power of appointment. That decision had been reached on the basis of contract law and on the equitable principle that 'equity looks upon as done that which ought to have been done'. It was, however, significant in *Tailby* that the claimant had given consideration to the defendant and therefore that the claimant was not a volunteer.[47] So, while this case appears to decide differently from *Re Brook's ST* on its face, it was a decision based on contract law principles of specific performance being ordered because consideration had been paid for the contract. Therefore, counsel accepted that that decision would not apply to John, Lisa or Poppy here because they had not given consideration.

Third, the Contracts (Rights of Third Parties) Act 1999 has created rights for people to sue under contracts to which they were not parties if the contract was for their benefit. In relation to the issue of after-acquired property, the purported beneficiary will be able to enforce the contract if she is identified in the contract either personally or as part of a class of persons for whose benefit the contract has been created.[48] The claimant is entitled to rely on all of the rights accorded by contract law, including damages and specific performance – therefore, the contract takes effect at common law and in equity.[49] The creation of a trust is not a contractual remedy, however. It is unclear in the absence of clear authority whether this Act would create proprietary rights through specific performance. The problem would be that, on one analysis, if the purported settlor had had no property rights then there was no trust to be enforced by the Act, and therefore the claimant ought only to receive damages for breach of contract. Moreover, the third party would be a mere volunteer and therefore the principle that equity will not assist a volunteer (whether by granting specific performance or creating a trust) would apply. On another analysis, following *Tailby*, the Act could be interpreted as displacing the need for consideration by granting the third party rights under the contract for the first time with the result that the equitable interest will pass automatically. At present, it is suggested, the principle that equity will not assist a volunteer will continue to apply.

Lisa Brandon was dissatisfied with merely receiving damages from the Colonel because she wanted to live in Lindfield House and to become a person of note in local society. She wanted her husband to receive all of the future income from the trust and for Poppy to have enough money to pursue her interests in modern art. Lisa felt that her brother-in-law should

---

46 (1888) 13 App Cas 523.
47 See also *Re Lind* [1915] 2 Ch 345.
48 Contracts (Rights of Third Parties) Act 1999, s 1.
49 *Ibid.*

be held to his promise. She knew that that meant holding his feet to the fire in the company of expensive lawyers. Therefore, she decided to insist that the solicitors took her to meet their barrister in Lincoln's Inn so that she could decide for herself whether there was any way under trusts law of enforcing the Colonel's original promise.

5.6.4 Trustees seeking to enforce a promise to settle after-acquired property

Lisa Brandon had long since realised that the real problem had been the solicitors. On arrival at the splendid chambers in Old Buildings, Lincoln's Inn she had been astonished to learn that the solicitors had never shown the Brandon family settlement nor the covenant which had been signed in January to the barrister. After reading the documents over his reading glasses and hopping up to consult his copy of Thomas and Hudson on *The Law of Trusts*, the barrister had settled himself back into his leather desk chair with a smile of satisfaction. He said that new possibilities had opened up to him now that he had read the documents in full. For the benefit of Mrs Brandon, he said, he would work through the possibilities in order.

Trustee not permitted to enforce the promise

If there had been a trust created when Colonel Brandon had signed the covenant in January then that would have removed most of the problems. However, as was discussed above, because Colonel Brandon had merely been the object of a power of appointment in January then there had been no trust through *Re Ralli's WT*. Lisa Brandon interrupted the barrister's calm explanation and asked why the trustees could not enforce the covenant.

The barrister replied that that was an excellent point. The problem was that the trustees of the trust that the Colonel had promised to create in January (i.e. Flight and Golightly) would be prevented from suing to enforce the covenant. Lisa wanted to know why. The barrister replied that the answer could only be understood if you thought through what would happen next in logical stages. If the trustees were to sue on the terms of the covenant to force the Colonel to transfer the money and the house to them as trustees then there would be a problem as to the terms of the trust that would bind them. After all, there had never been a trust created in January precisely because the Colonel had not had any property rights at that time which could be settled on trust. Therefore, the trustees would be left holding property which they were not entitled to take beneficially for themselves (because they were only to be trustees of it) but which they could not hold on express trust because no trust had been created. Consequently, the trustees would be required to hold that property on resulting trust for the Colonel because there was no one else who could be a beneficiary of it. In plain English, the trustees would be required to give the property straight back to the Colonel even if they went to the trouble of getting it off him through the courts. There were three cases which were clear about this analysis: *Re Pryce*,[50] *Re Kay*[51] and *Re Cook*.[52] This last case, *Re Cook*, went further than the other two cases and held that the trustees should be prevented by the court from wasting the court's time by bringing proceedings when they would be obliged to pass the property back to the Colonel in any event.

---

50 [1917] 1 Ch 234.
51 [1939] Ch 329.
52 [1965] Ch 902.

In general terms, English law will not permit a person to sue for property in circumstances in which the claimant would be required to hold that property on resulting trust for the defendant in any event.[53] So, in *Re Kay's Settlement,*[54] a woman created a conveyance of property to herself for life and in remainder to other people. She did this while she was unmarried. The conveyance contained a covenant to settle after-acquired property. Subsequently, the woman married and had children. In later years she received property which fell within the terms of the covenant but to which she had had no entitlement at the time of creating the covenant. The woman refused to settle the property on trust in accordance with the covenant. It was held that none of the beneficiaries under the conveyance could establish any rights in the after-acquired property. The question arose whether or not the trustees, as parties to the covenant, could force the woman to settle the after-acquired property. In line with the earlier decision in *Re Pryce,*[55] it was held that the trustees should not be permitted to sue the woman under the terms of the covenant because the trust which they were seeking to enforce did not exist precisely because the woman had had no rights in the property at the time she had purported to create that trust. In the later case of *Re Cook*[56] this idea hardened into a strict principle that the trustees ought not to be permitted to commence such litigation because it would be vexatious and wasteful.

A trust of the covenant itself

The barrister saw how despondent Lisa Brandon now looked. He pointed out a sentence in the January covenant to her with a small smile. The solicitors had copied the text of the covenant out of a book of precedents and so they had never read it before either. The sentence read:

> I, Colonel Arthur Brandon, hereby covenant that any money and land I shall receive under the Brandon family settlement shall be settled on trust for John, Lisa and Poppy Brandon in accordance with clause 4 below such that the benefit of this covenant shall be deemed to be held on trust immediately.

With a barrister's typical sense of theatre, counsel waited for all three faces to look up at him for an explanation. The key words, said the barrister, are 'the benefit of this covenant shall be deemed to be held on trust immediately'. When a covenant is clear that the benefit of the covenant itself is to be held on trust then a trust will take effect over that benefit. The benefit of the covenant is itself an item of property – it is a chose in action created by the covenant. Therefore, it was possible for the Colonel to create a trust over the benefit of the covenant in January. The benefit of the covenant would be the trust property. Therefore, a trust had come into existence after all. Even if it was only a trust over the benefit of the covenant (and not over the money and the house initially) that was enough to create an equitable obligation over the Colonel. And therefore, finally, when the money and the house passed to him from the power of appointment, the Colonel was bound by this pre-existing trust over the benefit

---

53 *Hirachand Punanchand v Temple* [1911] 2 KB 330.
54 [1939] Ch 329.
55 [1917] 1 Ch 234.
56 [1965] Ch 902.

of the covenant to pass the money and the house into this settlement which had been created in January.

The authority on which the barrister relied was the decision in *Fletcher v Fletcher*.[57] In that case, a father had covenanted with his trustee to settle an after-acquired sum of £66,000 (which was an enormous sum of money in 1844) on his sons, Jacob and John. The property was passed to the trustee on the father's death. In reliance on the principles set out in the line of cases culminating in *Re Cook*,[58] the trustee contended that there had been no valid trust and that the trustee ought therefore to be absolutely entitled to the money. The court held, however, that the surviving beneficiary, Jacob, was entitled to sue under the terms of the trust on the basis that there had been property which could have been settled on the purported trust. The property identified by the court in *Fletcher v Fletcher* was the benefit of the covenant itself.

That a chose in action (like the benefit to be drawn from a contract or covenant) can be the subject matter of a trust is a well-established principle. In *Don King v Warren*[59] two boxing promoters entered into a series of partnership agreements whereby they undertook to treat any promotion agreements entered into with boxers as being part of the partnership property. It was held by Lightman J (and subsequently the Court of Appeal) that this disclosed an intention to settle the benefit of those promotion agreements on trust for the members of the partnership. Further examples of the benefits of contracts or statutory licences being capable of being the subject matter of trusts are *Swift v Dairywise Farms*[60] and *Re Celtic Extraction*.[61] Therefore, the point made in *Fletcher v Fletcher*,[62] that a trust can be declared over a chose in action, is one with modern support.

Therefore, Lisa Brandon left Lincoln's Inn exultant. She left her solicitors at the gates of that famous Inn and made her way across High Holborn to consult a firm of lawyers which specialised in suing negligent legal advisors. Colonel Brandon and Florence were disappointed at first but they had soon become bored of Sussex in any event. It was too quiet after their love had blossomed in the heat of battle. This being England, there was soon another war to fight and so they left their new home, never to return, and lived happily ever after.

5.7 DISPOSITIONS OF EQUITABLE INTERESTS

5.7.1 The rule in s 53(1)(c) of the Law of Property Act 1925

The purpose of s 53(1)(c) of the Law of Property Act 1925 was twofold: first, to prevent hidden oral transactions in equitable interests defrauding those entitled to property; and, secondly, to enable trustees to know where the equitable interests are at any one time. Section 53(1)(c) provides that:

> a disposition of an equitable interest or trust subsisting at the time of the disposition must be in writing signed by the person disposing of the same, or by his agent thereunto lawfully authorised in writing or by will.

---

57 (1844) 4 Hare 67.
58 [1965] Ch 902.
59 [1998] 2 All ER 608, *per* Lightman J; affirmed [2000] Ch 291.
60 [2000] 1 All ER 320.
61 *Re Celtic Extraction Ltd (In Liquidation), Re Bluestone Chemicals Ltd (In Liquidation)* [1999] 4 All ER 684.
62 (1844) 4 Hare 67.

Therefore, for a disposition of an equitable interest to take effect, the person who is making the disposition is required to make that disposition by signed writing. The term 'disposition' is a wide one which incorporates a range of methods for transferring an equitable interest which will include gifts and sales of equitable interests but does not necessarily require that the equitable interest has been destroyed.[63] Notably, a *declaration* of trust does not constitute a *disposition* of an equitable interest because a declaration of a trust effects the *creation* of an equitable interest rather than a disposition of a pre-existing equitable interest. Therefore, s 53(1)(c) does not apply to declarations of trusts.

The most important context in which s 53(1)(c) has operated in the reported cases is in relation to stamp duty. Stamp duty is a tax which is imposed on documents which effect transfers of certain types of property. Therefore, the requirement that there be writing for a disposition of an equitable interest has the effect of requiring that there be a document, which in turn may create a liability to stamp duty. Consequently, it became important for taxpayers in a number of situations to attempt to demonstrate that the transfer of their property took effect without the need for a written document. This means it is sometimes important to avoid s 53(1)(c) so as to avoid tax. The case law which has been spawned by this desperation to avoid tax is pleasantly intricate.

Understanding how legal practice often requires the development of legal techniques so as to 'structure' ways of avoiding tax or otherwise achieving your clients' objectives is a key part of developing your skills as a legal practitioner. So, the case law discussed in this section is a key part of developing those skills and a key part of your personal journey towards understanding whether or not you want to be the sort of legal practitioner who is involved in structuring complex arrangements for commercial, tax avoidance or other purposes.

5.7.2 Whether or not a transaction will fall within s 53(1)(c)

The decision of the House of Lords in *Grey v IRC*[64] establishes the analysis which all of the practitioners in Lincoln's Inn in the subsequent cases in this section were trying very hard to avoid. In *Grey v IRC* there was a scheme to avoid a type of tax known as 'stamp duty' on a transfer of valuable shares. Stamp duty would have been payable if the shares were transferred by means of a document. Therefore, professional advisors created a scheme to avoid using a document to transfer ownership of the shares – with disastrous results. Simply put, the plan was for the taxpayer, Hunter, to transfer shares to his grandchildren without paying stamp duty by settling those shares on trust and then moving the equitable interest in those shares verbally so as to avoid liability to tax. Let us explore that plan in more detail.

Hunter, created six settlements in 1949 for his five living grandchildren and one for grandchildren yet to be born ('the 1949 settlements'). These were six entirely separate settlements with different beneficiaries, but with the same trustees. On 1 February 1955, Hunter transferred 18,000 shares to those same people who acted as trustees of the 1949 settlements to hold them on bare trust for Hunter himself ('the 1955 settlement'). Then, on 18 February 1955, Hunter irrevocably directed his trustees to hold those shares on the terms of the 1949

63   *Newlon Housing Trust v Alsulaimen* [1999] 1 AC 313.
64   *Ibid.*

settlements as to 3,000 shares each. Subsequently, on 25 March 1955, Hunter and the trustees together executed six written declarations of trusts in respect of the shares which, they contended, merely confirmed the oral direction of 18 February in written terms. Hunter's plan was to argue that the oral direction, rather than the documents, effected the transfer and therefore that no stamp duty should be payable.[65]

The question for the court was whether the oral direction of 18 February was sufficient to transfer Hunter's interest in the shares, or whether that transfer only took effect when the documents were executed. The House of Lords, in the leading speech of Viscount Simonds, held that Hunter had made a disposition of his equitable interest because the equitable interest only passed on 25 March when the documents were executed. Therefore, the satisfaction of s 53(1)(c) was found to be a pre-requisite for any disposition taking place. As to the meaning of a 'disposition' Viscount Simonds considered that that word should be given its 'natural meaning'. So, on these facts, when the equitable interest started in one trust and then ended up in another trust, that was a disposition.

(The irony is that, if you look up the word 'disposition' in a dictionary you will see that it refers to somebody's mood or to the way in which chattels are laid out (for example when a dinner table is set). The natural meaning of the word 'disposition' was not the same as 'disposal'. The sense of a 'disposal' was a very recent meaning of the word 'disposition'. It was an odd word for the Parliamentary draftsperson to have chosen in this context.)

Following Viscount Simonds' judgment, the feature of this case which you should identify in later cases is the following: where the legal title stays in the same place, so that only the equitable interest moves between different beneficiaries, then there has been a disposition of the equitable interest requiring signed writing under s 53(1)(c). You might think of this like a pendulum in a clock: the fixed point at the top is the legal title remaining in the same place with the same trustees, and the swinging lower end of the pendulum is the equitable interest moving from one beneficiary to another. That is a disposition requiring signed writing.

Another point should be made about this judgment. Viscount Simonds was a judge who took very literal readings of cases (in the previous chapter we considered his judgment in *Leahy v AG New South Wales*). This is a very short judgment in *Grey v IRC*. His lordship considered this to be a very plain question. It is unlikely that Viscount Simonds would have validated this tax-avoidance scheme even if he had thought it was possible. The cases which we consider in the remainder of this section are mainly comprised of clever tax-avoidance schemes which different judges from a different generation were often prepared to permit.

5.7.3 Transactions not within s 53(1)(c)

This section considers a range of tax-avoidance schemes which have generated different ways of analysing or structuring ways of making dispositions of equitable interests without the need for signed writing under s 53(1)(c). We begin with litigation which established the perimeters of the rule in s 53(1)(c) concerning a successful man with a philanthropic

---

65 A similar argument was attempted in *Cohen & Moore v IRC* [1933] 2 KB 126.

streak that cost him a lot in tax because he was badly advised. Reader, meet Mr Anthony Vandervell – a man who laid down his estate so that law students could learn about dispositions of equitable interests.

Transfer of equitable interest together with legal interest

In *Vandervell v IRC*,[66] Mr Vandervell had begun with the philanthropic intention to benefit the Royal College of Surgeons ('RCS') and presumably ended with a profound dislike of tax-avoidance specialists. His philanthropic motives were pure. In this instance, he wanted to endow a Professorship in Pharmacology at the RCS – something which would require a large amount of money. (To this day there is a Vandervell Lecture Theatre in the RCS premises in Lincoln's Inn fields in London.) The means by which Vandervell was advised to benefit the RCS was complicated. Given the high rates of tax at the time, it would not have been efficient for him to have made a gift of cash to the RCS after having paid tax on that cash. Therefore, he decided to transfer some valuable shares to the RCS, so that when the annual dividend was paid out to the shareholders then that dividend would be paid in cash to the RCS directly by the company. The shares themselves had originally been held on trust for Vandervell himself as sole beneficiary. The trustees of this settlement were a bank and the Vandervell Trustee Co Ltd, a company which was wholly owned by Vandervell and used to manage his assets under this trust.

Therefore, when the arrangement began, Vandervell was seeking to benefit the RCS with shares in which he had only an equitable interest. Vandervell's trustees organised for the shares to pass to the RCS. To ensure that Vandervell could recover his shares once the dividend had been paid, the trustees reserved an option to repurchase those shares on payment of £5,000. The dividend was then paid.

The Inland Revenue argued that when the shares passed to the RCS then that was a disposition of the equitable interest which Vandervell had owned. Therefore, it was argued that signed writing was required under s 53(1)(c) to make the transfer effective. The House of Lords rejected this argument. It was held that when the shares transferred from Vandervell's settlement to the RCS then *both* the legal title and the equitable interest in the shares passed simultaneously. It was held that because both interests (legal and equitable) passed together then it was not necessary to fulfil a separate formality for the transfer of the equitable interest. Therefore, it was held that there was no need to have signed writing under s 53(1)(c).

The principle to take from this case is that there is no need for signed writing under s 53(1)(c) if the legal title and the equitable interest are passed together out of the trust to a different legal and equitable owner of that property. If it helps, imagine two trusts in the form of two buckets – one of them red and one of them blue – with handles on their tops. The equitable interest is contained in the red bucket in the form of white-coloured sand and the legal title is in the same bucket in the form of black-coloured sand. The different coloured sands are in two layers in the red bucket: the black sand is underneath the white sand. The red trustee is holding the handle of the red bucket. If both the white sand and the black sand are poured into the empty

---

66 [1967] 2 AC 291, HL.

blue bucket then, because both legal and equitable interests would be passing together, there would be no need for signed writing under s 53(1)(c) after the decision in *Vandervell v IRC*. If all that happened was that the white sand – the equitable interest – moved out of the red bucket on its own then that would be a disposition of the equitable interest alone and that would require signed writing under s 53(1)(c).

So, our first means of eluding s 53(1)(c) is to transfer the legal title and the equitable interest together from one trust to another trust. The property must pass from one trustee and from one beneficiary to an entirely different trust with different trustees (or at least the same people acting in a different capacity) and different beneficiaries in different capacities.

It is noticeable that in *Grey v IRC* Viscount Simonds did not discuss any of these nice-ties. It is suggested that Viscount Simonds would simply have been uninterested in this sort of approach. The court in *Vandervell v IRC* was prepared to support this argument on the s 53(1)(c) point. Vandervell lost this case on another, important point: when the shares were transferred to the RCS, the option to repurchase those shares was held to constitute an equitable interest in those shares which had not been allocated. That an option to purchase property (e.g. land) is an equitable interest in that property is a well-established point of law. That the ownership of the option had not been specified in these arrangements was regrettable and it may well have been a deliberate tax plan to give flexibility after the event. Nevertheless, failing to identify the owner of the option meant (as is discussed in Chapter 11) that that equitable interest passed back on resulting trust to its previous owner. Therefore, that equitable interest was held to pass back to Vandervell's settlement on resulting trust, which had disastrous tax consequences for him under tax law at the time.

5.7.4 Declaration of a new trust by trustees or third party with dispositive powers

The *Vandervell* litigation gave rise to many cases (two decisions of the House of Lords; three of the Court of Appeal). In the difficult decision of the Court of Appeal in *Vandervell (No 2)*[67] Lord Denning held that it may be open to the trustees to decide who should become the owner of the equitable interest under a trust. That case related to the attempt to return the equitable interest constituted by the option to repurchase the shares which saw Mr Vandervell's advi-sors attempt to pass the shares to an entirely different trust held for Mr Vandervell's children. At this point, Mr Vandervell has died and the children were claiming ownership of the shares while their stepmother (as Vandervell's principal legatee) sought ownership of those shares for herself. The correct analysis should have been the shares passed into Mr Vandervell's set-tlement because that settlement was where the equitable interest belonged. However, because £5,000 had been taken from the children's settlement to exercise the option, Lord Denning held that the shares should be deemed to have passed directly into that settlement (even though the option had never belonged there) on the basis either of promissory estoppel, or (remark-ably) that when the option was exercised then it simply ceased to exist and the ownership of the shares was unknown.

---

67 [1974] Ch 269.

5.7.5 Were *Grey v IRC* and *Vandervell v IRC* decided correctly?

There is an interesting article written by Brian Green which argues that *Grey v IRC* and *Vandervell v IRC* could have been decided the other way around.[68] In *Grey* it should be remembered that there were six pre-existing settlements before Hunter created his new, seventh settlement. While the trustees were the same human beings, they should have been considered to be acting in seven different capacities. So, even though the trustees were the same human beings throughout, there should have been a transfer of both the legal and the equitable interests out of Hunter's seventh settlement into the six pre-existing settlements, and not merely a transfer of the equitable interest alone. Therefore, *Grey* should have been decided like *Vandervell*, except for the fact that it was decided before *Vandervell* came up with that clever wheeze (and, moreover, Viscount Simonds would not have validated such a clever-clever tax-avoidance scheme).

As to *Vandervell v IRC*, there was a bank acting as co-trustee throughout in relation to the Vandervell settlement. The bank retained possession of the shares throughout the transaction. Its role was overlooked in the courts. However, it could be said that the constant presence of the bank in possession of the shares meant that it was a trustee throughout the transaction and therefore that the only thing which moved from the Vandervell settlement to the Royal College of Surgeons was the equitable interest in the shares. Consequently, there was a disposition of the equitable interest alone (and not a movement of legal and equitable interests together because the bank retained possession of the shares throughout). Therefore, if the bank's position was taken into account, the case of *Vandervell v IRC* could have been decided like *Grey*.

5.7.6 Sub-trusts

In the law of leases it is possible to create a sub-lease whereby the tenant under the head lease becomes the lessor under the sub-lease. Similarly, it is possible to create sub-trusts in which the beneficiary under the head trust becomes trustee over the sub-trust in favour of a sub-beneficiary. So, if a trust was declared over £10,000 then the trustee would hold that money on trust for the beneficiary. The beneficiary in turn would agree to hold the equitable interest in the £10,000 on sub-trust for a sub-beneficiary. The terms of the sub-trust, by definition, could not grant greater rights than the head trust. The question is whether the creation of a sub-trust constitutes a disposition of an equitable interest. In short, if the beneficiary under the head trust transfers *all* of their rights to the sub-beneficiary under the sub-trust then that will be deemed to be a disposition of the beneficiary's rights under the head trust. The metaphor used in *Re Lashmar*[69] is that we can 'look through' a bare trust so that a 'sub-trustee' effectively drops out of the picture because they have disposed of her equitable interest in favour of the sub-beneficiary so that the head trustee would be holding the property for the sub-beneficiary directly. That would be a disposition of the head beneficiary's equitable interest. By contrast, to avoid making a disposition, the beneficiary under the head trust should retain some rights or some meaningful role as trustee so that there would not be a complete disposition of the

68 (1984) 47 MLR 388.
69 (1891) 1 Ch D 258.

equitable interest. The sort of rights or role which might be retained would be a discretion as to the proportion of the income from the head trust that is to be paid to the sub-beneficiary or something of that sort.

5.7.7 Declaration of new trust

Another technique for avoiding s 53(1)(c) was attempted (unsuccessfully) in *Cohen & Moore v IRC*.[70] The idea is simply to terminate an existing trust so that the settlor becomes absolute owner of the trust property and to declare a brand new trust. So, in *Grey v IRC* Hunter could have terminated his settlement and re-settled the property, instead of transferring the equitable interest in that property so as to create a s 53(1)(c) disposition of it. Similarly, a variation of a trust under the Variation of Trusts Act 1958[71] will not constitute a disposition of an equitable interest within s 53(1)(c) requiring signed writing,[72] as in *Re Holt's Settlement*.[73]

5.7.8 Contractual transfer of equitable interest

It is a long-standing principle of equity that a contract to transfer property has the effect of transferring the equitable interest in that property automatically. This principle was upheld in the land law case of *Walsh v Lonsdale*[74] in which a contract to grant a lease was held to have created an equitable lease: that is, equity created a proprietary right automatically. The equitable interest was created because the contract created a right to specific performance and, because 'equity looks upon as done that which ought to have been done', equity deems that the proprietary right in the property has been transferred because contract law requires that it should be transferred. Hence an equitable interest transfers automatically. In terms of s 53(1)(c), this technique offers very exciting possibilities. So, in the House of Lords in *Oughtred v IRC*[75] a mother and son sought to swap the equitable interests in two parcels of shares which were held on the terms of two separate trusts, one for each of them. However, to have executed such a transfer in writing would have meant that the mother and son would have been subject to stamp duty. Therefore, they entered into an oral contract under which they sought to argue the equitable interest had passed before signed writing being effected. While the judgments are less than clear on the point, it appears to be accepted that the equitable principle set out in *Walsh v Lonsdale* has the effect of transferring the equitable interest automatically. In the subsequent decision of the House of Lords in *Chinn v Collins*,[76] Lord Wilberforce expressly approved the suggestion that the formation of a binding contract to transfer property would have the effect of passing the equitable interest in that property automatically.

---

70 [1933] All ER 950.
71 Considered below in Chapter 10.
72 In *Re Holt's Settlement* [1969] 1 Ch 100.
73 [1969] 1 Ch 100.
74 (1882) 21 Ch D 9.
75 [1960] AC 206.
76 [1981] AC 533.

5.7.9 Dispositions effected by trusts implied by law

When a contract to transfer an equitable interest has the effect of transferring that equitable interest automatically, the modern explanation of the means by which that takes effect is a constructive trust. Section 53(2) of the Law of Property Act 1925 provides that there are no formalities in relation to a constructive trust. The Court of Appeal in *Neville v Wilson*[77] approved a transfer of an equitable interest automatically on the creation of a contract between the transferor and transferee. This was done on the basis that a constructive trust arose on creation of the contract which compelled the transfer of that equitable interest without the need for further formality.

77 [1997] Ch 144.

Chapter 6

Secret trusts

CAPSULE SUMMARY

A secret trust arises when a testator wishes to benefit some person who, for some reason, cannot be named in a will. Typically, the testator leaves property to a trusted confidant by will on the understanding that that confidant will hold the property for third parties who are not named in the will. Equity will enforce this arrangement as a secret trust so that the confidant cannot claim to be beneficially entitled to the property left in the will. This secret trust operates in contravention of the provisions of the Wills Act 1837 and therefore illustrates equity's determination to prevent statute being used as an engine of fraud.[1]

Secret trusts fall into two main categories: fully secret trusts and half-secret trusts. Fully secret trusts arise in circumstances where neither the existence nor the terms of the trust are disclosed in the terms of the will. Oral evidence of the agreement between the testator and trustee is generally satisfactory. The settlor must have intended to create such a trust. That intention must have been communicated to the intended trustee. The trustee must have accepted the office and the terms of the trust explicitly or impliedly.[2]

For a valid half-secret trust, the settlor must intend to create such a trust. Further, the existence and terms of the trust must be communicated to the intended trustee before

---

1 Cf. *Rochefoucauld v Boustead* [1897] 1 Ch 196.
2 *Ottaway v Norman* [1972] 2 WLR 50.

the execution of the will. The intended trustee must then accept the office of trustee and acquiesce to the terms of the trust.[3]

6.1 INTRODUCTION

6.1.1 The background

There is something deliciously seedy about secret trusts. Stereotypically, in secret trusts cases, a man has a secret which he wishes to keep from his wife.[4] (As the singer Morrissey put it: 'All men have secrets'.) That secret, in these sorts of cases, is usually a mistress and an illegitimate child which is raised clandestinely by the mistress with money from the man. When the time comes for the man to write his will, he needs to provide for the maintenance of his 'love-child'[5] and so he purports to leave a large amount of property to someone he trusts: a close personal friend or a solicitor perhaps. The reason for leaving the property to that person is so that they can pass it to the man's mistress after his death in such a way that his wife and his family will never learn his secret. The problems are twofold. First, the friend may well purport to keep the property beneficially after the man's death. Second, s 9 of the Wills Act 1837 provides that no verbal evidence may be used to contradict the written terms of the will. So, the mistress will have the double-barrelled problem of proving that the friend was supposed to hold the property on trust for the love-child and also that the will should be ignored to the extent that it was silent about this. This is a classically equitable doctrine. Where it can be proved that the friend was supposed to hold the property on trust for the love-child, in this example, then equity will hold that a so-called 'secret trust' has come into existence and the friend will be required to hold the property on trust for the love-child as the testator had bid him to do. Equity is therefore ignoring the terms of the Wills Act so as to achieve justice on the facts, and to stop the dastardly friend from taking property beneficially when he was not supposed to have it beneficially at all. Aristotle would have approved. Aristotle, as discussed in section 1.1, would have said that the draftsman of the Wills Act made an 'error' in creating a rule that all of the terms must be included in the will or else they will be ignored because that failed to anticipate the injustice that would be caused in secret trusts situations. Therefore, equity is achieving its Aristotelian purpose in ensuring that the property goes to the right person.

The key feature of the secret trust is that it operates beyond the terms of the will. It is that feature which puts secret trusts in contravention of the Wills Act 1837 because s 9 of that Act provides that no will is valid unless it is in writing and signed by the testator, and witnessed. Moreover, no verbal evidence as to any other terms outside a will which were purportedly to be included in that will can be effective.[6] This principle has been a long-standing principle of English law since the 17th century which was intended to prevent frauds by ensuring that all of the terms of a will are included in a properly created document. As a result of the 1837

---

3 *Blackwell v Blackwell* [1929] AC 318.

4 There is no reason that it needs to be a husband cheating on his wife. Instead, it is just that many cases in practice involve that fact pattern. It could just as easily be a woman cheating on a woman, or it being some other sort of family secret.

5 Such a lovely euphemism: 'love-child'. A child born out of love; not out of Chardonnay, poor judgment and a dingy hotel room.

6 See recently on this rule: *Royal Society for the Prevention of Cruelty to Animals v Sharp* [2010] EWCA Civ 1474.

Act, only those people who are identified in a properly executed will as having rights against the testator's property shall be entitled to receive such property on the testator's death. Therefore, a secret trust (being an arrangement for the organisation of title in property after the testator's death outside the terms of the will) will be strictly invalid under the terms of the Wills Act 1837. The self-evident problem here is that the person named in the will might not be the person whom the testator wished to take the benefit of the bequest.

6.1.2 Distinguishing between types of secret trust

It is important to distinguish between the two primary forms of secret trust. The distinction is important because the case law attributes different rules to each form of secret trust in different situations. The distinction between the two types of secret is often a matter of degree, as will emerge from the following subsections.

Fully secret trust

The first kind is the 'fully secret trust' – that is, a trust which is not referred to at all in the terms of the will. In such a situation the testator will have communicated the terms of the arrangement to the intended secret trustee. The property intended to pass to the beneficiary of the arrangement will then be left to the secret trustee without any mention being made in the will as to the reason why the property is being left to that secret trustee. As will emerge from the discussion to follow, it is often very difficult to prove the existence of a fully secret trust, unless the testator had mentioned the detail of the arrangement to someone else, or has written emails or letters referring to it, or something of that sort which can be brought before a court.

Half-secret trust

The second kind of secret trust is the 'half-secret trust' – that is, a trust which is mentioned in some form in the will. This may be a mere hint that the secret trust exists or a more explicit mention of it. Importantly, the *existence* of the trust but *not its terms* are disclosed in the will. If all of the terms of the secret trust were disclosed in the will then it would be a testamentary trust and not a secret trust at all. The manner in which the half-secret trust is disclosed in the terms of the will differs from case to case. The borderline between a fully secret and a half-secret trust may be difficult to identify in some cases. It may be that the testator provides: 'I leave the sum of £1,000 to Ben for purposes which he knows all about.' That expression may be said to disclose a half-secret trust by hinting at 'purposes which he knows all about'; or it may thought to indicate that the testator is simply grateful to Ben for some particular kindness which he had performed in the past. Alternatively, the expression 'I leave the sum of £1,000 to Ben to carry out my particular wishes as set out in my letter to him of 15 December 2014' is more definite and would indicate a half-secret trust. Alternatively, it may be that such an explicit mention of another document may bring into play the probate doctrine of 'incorporation by reference' which would require that that letter be construed as forming a part of the will (as opposed to being a secret trust outside the will).[7] The point about a half-

---

7 *In the Goods of Smart* [1902] P 238; *Re Jones* [1942] Ch 238; as interpreted by *Re Edwards' WT* [1948] Ch 440.

secret trust is that there is some hint of its existence in the will, but that hint will fall short of setting out the terms of the trust.

Distinguishing between fully secret and half-secret trusts

Given that so much turns on the division made between a fully secret trust and a half-secret trust, it is important to note that in many circumstances it will be difficult to know whether a trust is fully secret or half-secret. In relation to the example cited above – that 'I leave the sum of £1,000 to my dear friend Ben for reasons which he knows all about' – it could be said that that trust is fully secret if no one understands the significance of what Ben knows. Suppose that, when the will is read to the beneficiaries by a solicitor, everyone turns and asks Ben: 'What did he mean by that?' If Ben explains away those words on the basis that he and the testator had a love affair at university and that this is just a remembrance of that relationship, then the sensation caused by that revelation might divert people's attention away from the true purpose of the bequest. It would only be if the surrounding circumstances, or something said by the testator to another person, put them on notice of the existence (but not the terms) of the trust that it could be said to be a half-secret trust. Therefore, we should acknowledge the trite point that words used by the testator may be susceptible to more than one interpretation. The point is that, in the real world in practice, it will typically be important to know what surrounding evidence there is to indicate the real purpose of the testator's words. For example, were there any emails or conversations indicating the existence of the secret trust? Did the mistress come forward after the testator's death asking if she was entitled to anything? And so forth. When creating strict divisions between categories of secret trusts that should be borne in mind.

Secret trusts on intestacy

There is potentially a third class of secret trust altogether. It is possible that a secret trust may arise to circumvent the Intestacy Rules. In a situation where a dying person was encouraged not to make a will and thereby to leave property so that it passes on intestacy, the dying person might agree with the person who would take title in his property as next of kin under the Intestacy Rules not to make a will on the basis that the next of kin would give effect to the dying person's wishes by way of secret trust. In such a situation, if the next of kin had induced the dying person not to make a will in reliance on his promise to give effect to the dying person's wishes, that next of kin would be required to hold the property received on trust for the intended beneficiaries.[8] This doctrine similarly prevents the recipient of property from perpetrating a fraud. There is one danger in this area. The Inheritance (Provision for Family and Dependants) Act 1975 does give the courts powers to provide for relatives and dependants who are not otherwise benefited in a person's will. Therefore, as we shall see with the case of *Rowstrom v Freud* in the next section, the arrangement must be very carefully structured so that it is not disturbed by the court, and even then there is always the chance that the court will interpret the

---

8 *Sellack v Harris* (1708) 2 Eq Ca Ab 46.

testator's silence in the wrong way (in the way that the defendant had argued unsuccessfully in that case).

6.1.3 An example of a secret trust

A hypothetical example of a secret trust

A 'secret trust' is almost as exciting as its name suggests. A testator creates a secret arrangement which ostensibly benefits person X but with the real intention of benefiting person Y. Suppose the following situation:[9]

> Charles was a successful partner in a law firm, married tediously and living in Sussex. He had an affair with a trainee, Mary, many years ago and Mary gave birth to Timmy as a result. Secretly, Charles has paid money to Mary to pay for Timmy's upbringing for 18 years. Charles organised this through his old school-friend Ben who managed Charles's tax affairs from his office in the British Virgin Islands. Charles left money in his will to Ben with the odd expression that it was 'for reasons that he knows all about'. Charles had told Ben that he was to pay this money to Mary so that it could be used to pay for Timmy's university education. Charles also told Mary about this arrangement. Nothing was written down. It was done in secret so that no upset would be caused to Charles's wife nor his four daughters. After Charles died, Ben purported to keep all the money for himself. Mary sued Ben but it was difficult to prove the existence of the secret arrangement because there was no written evidence. If all the facts were known, then Timmy would have been the beneficiary of a secret trust held for him by his mother, Mary.

This is indeed a 'secret' trust because the arrangement is something known only to Ben and to Mary. Its purpose is to benefit Timmy without having to identify him in the terms of the will. The purpose of a secret trust, however, is to prevent Ben from asserting beneficial ownership of this property. The case of *Rawstron v Freud*, discussed next, demonstrates how complex these situations can become.

An example of the practical complexities of a secret trust

An interesting example of a secret trust has arisen in relation to the estate of the famous painter Lucien Freud, in *Rawstron v Freud*.[10] Freud left his residuary estate to two women – one of whom was his solicitor to whom he spoke every day for about 20 years. Clause 6 of the will (drafted by Freud's solicitors) suggested that his residuary estate was being left to them absolutely. It provided:

> I GIVE all the residue of my estate (out of which shall be paid my funeral and testamentary expenses and my debts) and any property over which I have a general power of appointment to the said Diana Mary Rawstron and the said Rose Pearce jointly.

---

9 This hypothetical example has been expanded into a short story on my website, and will be part of *Equity and Trusts in Eighteen Tales*.

10 *Rawstron v Freud* [2014] EWHC 2577 (Ch).

The two women, however, claimed that they had been told to hold the property on trust for purposes which they were not allowed to reveal to the defendant. The defendant was Freud's son. The judge (Spearman QC) took the view that this was a fully secret trust because the will itself did not make the existence of any such trust clear and because this will had replaced an earlier will which had created a half-secret trust (thus suggesting that the solicitor and Freud had intended to move from a half-secret to a fully secret trust). Clause 6 of this will transferred the entire residuary estate to the named women, albeit jointly.[11] The secret trust arrangement only came to light because the women made the fact public. Therefore, it was held to be a fully secret trust.

Freud's son wanted to get his hands on the money left in Freud's estate. Lucien Freud was a very famous painter whose work sold for very large sums of money and whose residuary estate would be worth a huge amount of money. As Freud's son, he would have been able to claim rights to any property left intestate in Freud's residuary estate under the Inheritance (Provision for Family and Dependants) Act 1975. Therefore, Freud's son contested whether this was a secret trust at all, or whether Freud had been intestate as to his residuary estate on the basis that it was left to the two women apparently on trust but without any terms of that trust being included in the will. This was a poor argument because, as we know, the terms of a secret trust do not need to be disclosed in the will. It had already been explained to Freud's son by the solicitor that this arrangement was not intended to benefit him in any way and that he was not to be told of the objective behind the secret trust. It was held that this was a fully secret trust. By finding that the will created a bequest to the two named women (which they would presumably operate as a fully secret trust in practice) it was held to be impossible to make any finding for Freud's son because Freud had not died intestate as to this part of his estate. After all, he had made clear arrangements with his solicitor's advice. The judge was clearly influenced by the fact that one of these two women was Freud's solicitor with whom he was very close; that the will had been drafted by this solicitors' firm; that this will replaced another will which had disclosed a half-secret trust;[12] and that this arrangement had clearly been created after much thought. Consequently, reading the will exactly as it was drafted, and not interpreting it as creating a half-secret trust, appeared the most appropriate outcome on these particular facts.

6.1.4 Explaining the role of the secret trust

The original purpose of the doctrine of secret trusts in the early case law was to prevent statute (in the form of the Wills Act) or common law being used as an instrument of fraud.[13] As Lord Westbury put it in *McCormick v Grogan*:[14]

> The court has, from a very early period, decided that even an Act of Parliament shall not be used as an instrument of fraud; and that equity will fasten on the individual who gets

---

11 That use of the word 'jointly' is an interesting, possible indication of the existence of a half-secret trust because why else would these two women receive a gift of property jointly as opposed to, for example, in equal shares?

12 That earlier will had provided in clause 6.2 that: 'MY Trustees shall hold the Trust Fund on the trusts and with and subject to the same powers and provisions communicated before the execution of this Will to the persons named in clause 1 and set out in a deed already executed by me and them (which is not to form part of this Will)'. The reference to powers which have been communicated to the two women discloses the existence, but not the terms, of the trust. Therefore, the earlier will had created a half-secret trust.

13 *McCormick v Grogan* (1869) LR 4 HL 82; *Jones v Badley* (1868) 3 Ch App 362, 364; and *Blackwell v Blackwell* [1929] AC 318.

14 (1869) LR 4 HL 82, 97.

a title under that Act, and impose upon him a personal obligation, because he applies the Act as an instrument for accomplishing a fraud. In this way a court of equity has dealt with the Statute of Frauds, and in this manner, also, it deals with the Statute of Wills.

Thus, the legal owner of property may be made subject to a 'personal obligation' (akin to equity acting *in personam* against the conscience of the defendant) to act as trustee.

6.2 FULLY SECRET TRUSTS

6.2.1 Creating a valid, fully secret trust

As set out above, the term 'fully secret trust' refers to those trusts under which only the trustees and the settlor are aware of the existence of the trust and of the terms of the trust. In the leading case of *Ottaway v Norman*,[15] Ottaway devised his bungalow, half his residuary estate and a sum of money to Miss Hodges for her to use during her lifetime, provided always that she was, in turn, to bequeath this property to the claimant after her death. Hodges failed to do this in her will. Rather, she left the property by her own will to Mr and Mrs Norman. After Hodges's death the plaintiff brought an action against Hodges's executors claiming entitlement under secret trust principles to the property which had been left in Ottaway's will. Brightman J held that there were three requirements for proof of the existence of a fully secret trust: first, an intention to benefit the claimant-beneficiary; second, communication of that intention to the intended secret trustee; and, third, acceptance by the secret trustee of that obligation. It was found on the facts of *Ottaway v Norman* that Hodges had known of Ottaway's intention and had acquiesced in it. Therefore, it was held that the bungalow and residuary estate should pass to the claimant. However, the money was not subject to the same obligation because the court found it difficult to see how this could have been done if Hodges was entitled to use and spend the money during her lifetime.

Perhaps the easiest conceptualisation of what the court is really looking for, behind the three-stage test set out in *Ottaway*, appears in *Wallgrave v Tebbs*,[16] where it was held by Wood VC that where the secret trustee-legatee 'expressly promises' or 'by silence implies' that she is accepting the obligation requested of her by the testator then she will be bound by that obligation. These distinct components of the test (intention, communication and acceptance) are considered separately below.

6.2.2 Intention to benefit

Akin to the need for evidence of sufficient intention to create an express trust, the settlor of a secret trust must intend that the legal titleholder of property under a will (or intestacy) be trustee of that property for another.[17] If the deceased only intended to impose a moral obligation on the legatee as to the use of property, that will not be sufficient to create a secret trust.[18] In *Re Snowden*,[19] an elderly woman was unsure how to deal with her property

---

15 [1972] 2 WLR 50.
16 (1855) 25 LJ Ch 241.
17 *Ottaway v Norman* [1972] 2 WLR 50, *per* Brightman J.
18 *Re Snowden* [1979] 2 All ER 172.
19 *Ibid.*

on death. Therefore, she left the property to her elder brother with the words 'he shall know what to do'. It happened that her brother died only days later. The issue arose whether the brother had been subject to a secret trust in favour of the woman's niece and nephew. It was held by Megarry VC that the deceased woman had only intended to impose a moral obligation on him – an intention which could not be interpreted as imposing a positive trust obligation on her brother. Therefore, the property passed beneficially on the terms of her brother's will.

Another example is the decision of the House of Lords in *McCormick v Grogan*.[20] The facts are rather melodramatic. A testator executed a very short will in 1851 in which all of his estate was to pass to Mr Grogan. In 1854, the testator had contracted cholera and, knowing that he did not have long to live, he sent for Grogan. When Grogan arrived he was told by the testator that his will was in a desk drawer together with a letter instructing Grogan as to certain intended bequests. The letter contained the following, very important words: 'I do not require you to act strictly in accordance with the foregoing instructions, but rather I leave it entirely to your own good judgment to do as you think I would do if I was still living, and as the parties are deserving.' The claimant sought a declaration that there should be a secret trust held in his favour. The House of Lords held that the testator had not intended to impose a trust obligation on Grogan, particularly in the light of the sentence in the letter to him quoted above which explicitly absolved Grogan of any trusteeship. Therefore, it was held that Grogan held the property subject only to a moral obligation to provide for the people mentioned in the letter. Consequently, there was no secret trust under which the plaintiff could claim a benefit.

6.2.3 Communication of the secret trust

The basic principles in relation to the communication and creation of fully secret trusts can be briefly stated. Where the settlor intends to create a secret trust, it is important that this intention is communicated to the trustee and that the terms of the secret trust are similarly communicated to her. Without such communication of the trust to the secret trustee there can be no trust.[21] Communication and acceptance can be effectuated at any time during the life of the testator. Under fully secret trusts there need be communication only before death.

In *Re Boyes*[22] it was held that it was not sufficient to communicate the terms of a secret trust that the testator left two unattested documents in a drawer. In that case, the intended secret trustee had been told that there was to be a secret trustee but he was never told the terms of the trust. The rationale which Kay J used was that the trustee had not been given any opportunity to refuse to act under the trust (which was for the benefit of an undisclosed mistress and illegitimate child). There are cases, however, where secret trustees accept their duty without knowing the terms of their office: typically, this is done by telling the trustee that there is a letter in a drawer containing their duties which they must not read until the testator is dead.[23] Moreover, in *Re Colin Cooper*,[24] the testator communicated his intention to create a secret trust over a fund of £5,000 but then he sought to add more money to that

---

20   (1869) LR 4 HL 82.
21   *Ottaway v Norman* [1972] 2 WLR 50.
22   (1884) 26 Ch D 531.
23   *Re Keen* [1937] Ch 236.
24   [1939] Ch 811.

fund at a later date without telling the trustee. It was held that this addition of property was invalid on the basis that the identity of the property must be communicated to the trustee.

However, in *Re Keen*,[25] the court took the view that a trustee who knew of the intention to create a secret trust but not the terms of that trust was in the same situation as a ship's captain sailing under sealed orders. In such a situation, the captain of the ship sets sail but is not permitted to know his orders until the time at which he is allowed to open the envelope which contains a document setting out his precise instructions. Therefore, it can be valid for a trustee to accept the obligations of a secret trust without knowing the detailed terms of the trust.

6.2.4 Acceptance of the office of trustee

It was held by Wood VC in *Wallgrave v Tebbs* that a person accepts the office of secret trustee where that person 'either expressly promises, or by silence implied, that he will carry the testator's intention into effect' and that the property 'is left to him on the faith of that promise or understanding'.[26] In that case, a testator had left £12,000 'unto and to the use of Tebbs and Martin, their heirs and assigns, for ever, as joint tenants'. Oral and written evidence was presented to the court which demonstrated both that the testator had intended Tebbs and Martin to hold the property on secret trust. At no time had the testator's true intentions been communicated to Tebbs or to Martin. In consequence, Tebbs and Martin sought an order from the court that they were entitled to take beneficial ownership of the property left to them by will. Wood VC held that they could indeed take beneficial ownership and were not required to act as trustees, because there had been 'no such promise or undertaking on the part of the devisees [Tebbs and Martin]' which could have constituted acceptance of the office. However, on the authority of *Re Keen* (as considered immediately above), communication can also be given by means of a sealed envelope given to the trustee before the testator's death with instructions not to open it until after death, and the defendant may be taken to have accepted that office.[27]

6.3 HALF-SECRET TRUSTS

6.3.1 Creating a valid half-secret trust

A half-secret trust is a trust under which the *existence* of the trust is disclosed in a document, such as a will, but the *terms* of the trust remain secret. The requirements for a valid half-secret trust were set out in *Blackwell v Blackwell*[28] by Lord Sumner in the following terms:

> The necessary elements, on which the question turns, are intention, communication and acquiescence. The testator intends his absolute gift to be employed as he and not as the donee desires; he tells the proposed donee of this intention and, either by express

---

25   [1937] Ch 236.
26   (1855) 25 LJ Ch 241.
27   *Re Keen* [1937] Ch 236.
28   [1929] AC 318.

promise or by the tacit promise, which is satisfied by acquiescence, the proposed donee encourages him to bequeath the money on the faith that his intentions will be carried out.

Therefore, the test for a half-secret trust is very similar to that for a fully secret trust.[29] Those three elements are considered in turn in the sections to follow.

6.3.2 Communication

Communication must be before or at the time of the execution of the will.[30] Lord Sumner held in *Blackwell v Blackwell* that a 'testator cannot reserve to himself a power of making future unwitnessed dispositions by merely naming a trustee and leaving the purposes of the trust to be supplied afterwards'.[31] The rationale for this rule is that the trustee must know of the terms of the trust and be able to disclaim the obligations of trusteeship. Similarly, the testator is not entitled to use the secret trust as a means of delaying the point in time at which he will finally decide the terms on which he wishes his estate to be left. Where communication occurs after the will, the trust will fail and the legatee will hold on resulting trust for the residuary estate.[32] Therefore, there is a distinction between half-secret trusts and fully secret trusts in that the settlor must communicate before the execution of the will in the former, but need not communicate the existence or terms of the trust until the time of death in the latter.[33]

6.3.3 Acceptance

The rules relating to acceptance of the obligations contained in half-secret trusts are similar to those for fully secret trusts. Lord Sumner held in *Blackwell v Blackwell*[34] that there is acceptance if the 'proposed donee . . . either by express promise or by the tacit promise . . . encourages [the testator] to bequeath the money on the faith that his intentions will be carried out'.

6.3.4 Clash of doctrines – beneficiary attesting to the will

In *Re Young*[35] it was held that a prohibition in s 15 of the Wills Act 1837 against a witness taking beneficially under a will would not prevent a chauffeur, who witnessed his employer's will, from taking as a beneficiary under a secret trust. Dankwerts J considered that the purpose of the doctrine of secret trusts was to elude the terms of that Act and therefore that it should not be an obstacle in this instance.

---

29 *Ottaway v Norman* [1972] 2 WLR 50.
30 *Blackwell v Blackwell* [1929] AC 318.
31 *Ibid*, 339.
32 *Re Keen* [1937] Ch 236; *Re Bateman's WT* [1970] 1 WLR 1463.
33 *Re Spence* [1949] WN 237.
34 [1929] AC 318.
35 [1951] Ch 344.

Chapter 7

Essay: The paradox in express trusts

7.1 THE OSTENSIBLE PARADOX AT THE HEART OF EXPRESS TRUSTS LAW

This chapter reflects on the principles of express trusts law which have been considered in Part 2 of this book. It serves as a revision of some of the key principles of the leading cases. It also identifies the key paradox at the heart of express trusts, which is this: while trusts law is said to be based on general principles of equity, most of the cases which we have analysed so far have been based on rigid legal principles and clear tests which resemble the common law more than anything. So, while equity was said to be flexible and open-textured in Chapter 1, most of the leading cases on express trusts law have been concerned to create clear rules. How do we account for this?

When we analyse the cases a little more closely, it becomes clear that for every rule we established, there was at least one case which qualified that rule or established a different approach to the same question. So, for every *Grey v IRC*[1] there was a *Vandervell v IRC*[2] taking a different approach to a very similar question. For every *Re Gulbenkian*,[3] there was a

---

1   [1960] AC 1.
2   [1967] 2 AC 291.
3   [1968] Ch 785.

Re Barlow[4] or a *Re Baden (No 2)*[5] using a different approach to reach an outcome which the judge considered to be appropriate on the facts. This is true for every principal rule which was discussed in Chapters 2 through 5 of this book. Therefore, there has been some flexibility in those judgments but it has not been the sort of morally-centred flexibility you might have been expecting. On the other hand, there have been courts which have used general principles of equity to reach their decisions; a good example appeared in *Rochefoucauld v Boustead*.[6]

This essay will create a map through those cases and ask whether trusts law is really comprised of strict rules or whether it is built on general equitable principles. We shall also ask whether or not there is really a paradox at the heart of express trusts law at all, or whether these sorts of confusions are simply part and parcel of the development of laws in any jurisdiction. In short, the argument here is that the cases divide between those which established strict rules and those which sought, for a variety of reasons, to elude those strict rules. At root, the trust is so important in our society that some judges were eager to create strict rules so as to guide ordinary people and their lawyers. Yet, situations have arisen where fairness prompted other judges to reach different outcomes.

It might be tempting to pass over a chapter like this because it may seem like 'just more reading'. That would be to miss an opportunity. This chapter is intended to act as revision of the law we have studied so far. If there are points of detail from the cases which you do not remember, then you should go back the relevant discussions in the relevant earlier chapters. Consequently, it will help your learning by trying to put the law into perspective. It may also give you ideas about how you could approach your coursework if it is set in the area of express trusts law.

7.2 THE THESIS BEHIND THIS ESSAY

7.2.1 The two lines of cases

The most important cases on the law of express trusts can be divided into two, opposing halves. That is the central thesis behind this essay. In one camp we have the cases which have created the clear rules on which express trusts function. They were organised into the form which we have discussed in Chapters 3 through 5 primarily in the Victorian era. Good examples of these sorts of cases are *Morice v Bishop of Durham* and *Knight v Knight* which led in time to judgements like *Milroy v Lord*, *Re Gulbenkian*, *McPhail v Doulton*, *Leahy v AG for New South Wales*, *Re Grant's WT*, *Grey v IRC*, *Re Goldcorp* and so on. These were cases which created strict rules, or which created clear tests, or which applied older rules in a strict manner which would influence their later use.

In the other camp there are the cases in which the court was presented with unusual sets of facts or with sets of facts which made the literal application of the strict rule appear to be unfair or undesirable for the parties (e.g. *Re Baden (No 2)*), or which would have enabled the defendant to take unconscionable advantage of the claimant (e.g. *Rochefoucauld v*

---

4 [1979] 1 WLR 278.
5 [1973] Ch 9.
6 [1897] 1 Ch 196.

Boustead), or which was undesirable for some other reason (e.g. *Lehman Brothers v CRC*). It is this group of cases which have made the study of these areas of law so much longer! Good examples of these cases are *Re Rose, Re Barlow, Re Baden (No 2), Re Denley, Re Lipinski, Rochefoucauld v Boustead, Vandervell v IRC, Neville v Wilson,* and *Hunter v Moss*. If you compare this list of cases with the list of cases in the previous paragraph, you will see that they are mirror (i.e. opposite) images of the cases in the previous list. For example, *Hunter v Moss* takes a diametrically opposed view of the law on certainty of subject matter to *Re Goldcorp*; *Re Denley* and *Re Lipinski* are consciously diametrically opposed to *Leahy* and *Re Grant's WT*; *Vandervell v IRC* is opposed to *Grey v IRC*, and so on. On each occasion when a rule has been created then circumstances have created a set of circumstances which a later court has felt obliged to confront in a different way than the literal application of the clear, strict rule in the earlier case. At one level, this is simply the way in which common law systems operate. For example, the law of torts is arguably much more confused than the law of trusts. At another level, in the context of trusts law specifically, using different approaches to reach just outcomes is exactly what Aristotle had in mind in his *Ethics*.

7.2.2 The features of the two groups of cases

The strict cases

The first group of cases shares a common feature: those cases tend to generate strict tests, like contract law seeks to do, and they make a feature of applying that test strictly on the facts in front of them (just as in *Re Goldcorp*[7] a real focus is placed on Mr Leggatt not getting title in any gold coins). These cases are *literalist* in the sense that they apply their tests literally without much discernible interest in moral questions or taking a purposive or mischief-based approach to their rules. These cases are also primarily *rules-based* as opposed to being based on high-level, moral principles. The purpose behind their rules was to introduce certainty to the law.

In terms of the morality in these cases, it can only be discerned in the sense that these cases are *consequentialist*: that is, they follow the decisions made in earlier cases. Therefore, while all trusts are said to be based on the conscience of the legal owner of the property (i.e. the trustee) there are no questions of conscience in these particular cases because their rules are either taken from earlier cases or they are set out clearly by the court in that instance. The judges may have had a moral view that what was needed more than anything was order in the law, especially in cases involving the insolvency of large financial institutions (as in *Re Goldcorp*) in which large numbers of different creditors were all seeking to recover their losses at once.

The open-textured cases

The second group of cases demonstrates different characteristics. Their common character-istic is that they do not follow the clear rule set out by the appropriate case in the first line of cases. Importantly, however, they do not follow those rules for a variety of reasons. Some cases are concerned to be *pragmatic*. So, in *Lehman Brothers v CRC*,[8] the Supreme Court was concerned that it needed to ensure an orderly liquidation of the failed investment bank,

---

7 [1995] 1 AC 74.
8 [2012] UKSC 6.

Lehman Brothers, and that that could only be done by avoiding the strict test in *Re Goldcorp* which would have benefited some claimants and caused harm to others, when spreading the pain evenly was thought to be the pragmatically sensible approach. *Re Barlow* is another case which is pragmatic in relation to certainty of objects, as discussed below.

Many of these cases are *open-textured* in that their judgments are comprised of moral approaches (whether spoken or unspoken) in that the courts seek to achieve just outcomes. So, in *Rochefoucauld v Boustead* and in *Hunter v Moss* (the former more explicit than the latter) the judges are concerned to prevent an injustice regardless of the letter of the law. The particular injustices there would have involved one party taking an unconscionable benefit at the expense of the other party in a way that the judges considered to be wrong, having heard all the evidence. In cases like *Re Lipinski, Neville v Wilson* and *Re Baden (No 2)* (by way of example) the judges felt that the outcome would be unfair in a different way: they were concerned that the claimants would have been subjected to delay, or to an overly-pedantic application of the strict rule so that their trusts would be invalid even though there was nothing intrinsically harmful about their situation.

7.3 ANALYSING THE KEY CASES

This section considers the leading cases and their opposites in a few key areas of express trusts law. These two lists of cases present the strict rule and its mirror opposite. What we shall see here, from subject area to subject area, is the way in which leading cases are sometimes subverted by open-textured decisions and sometimes improved by them (in a way that would have appealed to Aristotle). This is the way in which law develops in our system. A leading case establishes a rule or states a principle, and then interesting cases emerge over time to test the edges and the limits of that rule or principle.

7.3.1 Certainty of objects

The clearest example of different analyses being taken between different courts over the same subject matter emerged in our study of certainty of objects.[9] In that area, for example, the decision of the House of Lords in *Re Gulbenkian* required that for there to be sufficient certainty for the creation of a valid fiduciary power it must be possible to say whether any given postulant is or is not within the class of beneficiaries. There were, of course, differences of view among the judges in *McPhail v Doulton* as to what Lord Upjohn had meant by this concept. We considered whether this test requires that it must be possible merely to say of anyone who actually comes forward asking to be considered as an object of that power that they are or are not within the class, or whether there must be certainty as to anyone in the world who could hypothetically come forward. Nevertheless, the wording of the test was clear: it is the 'is or is not' test.

In *Re Baden (No 2)*, however, Sachs LJ was so annoyed by the fact that the litigation had already lasted for 12 years before it reached his Court of Appeal that he was concerned to end the dispute once and for all. Sachs LJ took the view that, in applying the 'is or is not' test, the burden should fall on anyone who was claiming to fall within the class to prove that they did fall within the class. If they could not prove it, then Sachs LJ was prepared to find that

---

9   Section 3.4.

they did not fall within the class. Therefore, the literal logic of the 'is or is not' test would be followed. So, his lordship was prepared to adapt the law so as to reach a propitious outcome. Of course in that same case Megaw LJ was similarly motivated by the need to resolve the litigation that he returned to an earlier, overruled line of cases (including *Re Allen*) to find that all that was required was that there was a sufficiently significant number of people who would clearly fall within the class for it to be valid. That, it is suggested, is simply a lack of due respect for the doctrine of precedent and does not follow the 'is or is not' test. Stamp LJ avoided all of the jurisprudential disputes by finding that the specific word which was causing problems ('relatives') could be rendered certain.

It is suggested, however, that this is not a problem with equity. Rather, these different judicial approaches could have arisen in any branch of the common law. There is no reference to 'conscience' here. Instead, the judges are trying to solve a practical problem in *Baden (No 2)* and therefore they were creative in their approach to the law.

In *Re Barlow*, Browne-Wilkinson J took a very interesting, practical approach to the case in front of him (a dispute about the certainty of the term 'old friends') by finding both that the bequest was a gift as opposed to a trust, and by finding that on the specific facts of that case that it was clear whom the testatrix must have meant when she referred to her friends (because she presumably had a small, close-knit circle of friends). This is an example of the way in which the Chancery Division of the High Court has to dispose of cases in practice on many occasions: that is, the parties ask for an order as to how the trustees should proceed in their particular circumstances (so that the trustees cannot be sued for breach of trust later). The judge's responsibility is then to decide how best the trustees can effect the settlor's wishes. Interestingly, this particular decision failed to observe that Lord Upjohn had stated in *Re Gulbenkian* that a fiduciary power for the benefit of 'friends' would be a clear example of a class that must be void.

Again, the problem is not a problem of the inherent confusions created by equity being based on 'conscience' and ethics, but rather emerges from a judge's desire to achieve the best result on the facts before them. Here, his lordship could see that there was nothing intrinsically wrong with the bequest (and was convinced after listening to the evidence that the intended 'friends' could be identified in that particular instance) and that the scheme which the trustees had proposed should be allowed to proceed, even if there might be some jurisprudential concerns lurking in the background. Therefore, the open-textured approaches here were directed at achieving pragmatic, sensible outcomes on the facts before the court.

7.3.2 The beneficiary principle

The beneficiary principle, as described in *Morice v Bishop of Durham*,[10] required that there must be someone in whose favour the court can decree performance of a trust. This means that if there is no-one who can clearly take the trust property as a beneficiary (and who can therefore approach the court in the event that the trustees are thought to have breached their duties) then the trust will be void. This principle was fashioned into a strict rule at the very latest by the decisions in *Leahy v AG for New South Wales*[11] and *Re Grant's Will Trusts*.[12] Viscount Simonds took the view in *Leahy* that for there to be a beneficiary then there must be

10   (1805) 10 Ves 522.
11   [1959] AC 457.
12   [1980] 1 WLR 360.

people who would go into immediate possession of the property (such that an order of nuns with thousands of members could not logically go into possession of a single farmhouse), there must be a trust for individuals and not for an abstract organisation (such that a trust for an 'order of nuns' would not have a beneficiary), and there must not be a trust which would appear to continue in perpetuity.

By contrast, in *Re Denley*,[13] Goff J took a very different approach. He looked at the 'mischief' of the beneficiary principle and found that it was only intended to ensure that there was someone in whose favour the court could decree performance, and nothing more. None of those requirements about being able to go into immediate possession of the property and so forth. Therefore, on the facts in front of him there were beneficiaries enough in the form of the employees of a company who were entitled to have a sports ground made available for their use to satisfy the beneficiary principle. In *Re Lipinski*,[14] Oliver J took the view that there was only intended to be a distinction between cases where trusts were purportedly created for the benefit of a favourite pet where there would not be an ascertained or ascertainable group of people who would be beneficiaries (which would be void) and cases where there were ascertainable beneficiaries (which would be valid).

In these two lines of cases we have different approaches to the same legal question. The principal difference of view centres on the meaning of the traditional test. What is particularly interesting is the distaste which Oliver J displays in *Lipinski* for the *Leahy* approach in holding trusts to be invalid when there is nothing immoral nor illegal nor distasteful about the things which the parties were seeking to do. In *Lipinski*, after all, some perfectly nice Jewish people were proposing to build a social centre for themselves. There are few things more wholesome than groups of people coming together for social activities. So why, asked his lordship, was the law so eager to find their activities to be legally unenforceable? In this sense, there is a different form of pragmatism at play: one which looks to the social utility of the law instead of its jurisprudential niceties.

7.3.3 Certainty of subject matter

The age-old principle that there cannot be a valid trust unless there is certainty as to the subject matter of that trust was confirmed in *Re Goldcorp*. Importantly, the court in *Re Goldcorp* showed that the traditional rule would be strictly applied so as to ensure the orderly liquidation of a failed financial institution. *Lehman Brothers v CRC* in front of the Supreme Court was also a case concerning the orderly liquidation of a failed institution, but one in which the court appeared to consider that there could only be a proper liquidation if all of the many customers were entitled to proportionate shares in the assets held by Lehman Brothers, instead of attempting to differentiate between those who had had assets set aside for them and those who had not. Lord Walker complained in a dissenting judgment in that case that the Supreme Court was causing harm to the traditional principles of trusts law by holding that assets held in a large pool could be deemed to held on trust (under the terms of the appropriate financial regulations) for all of the clients of Lehman Brothers who had contributed to that pool. It appears that the liquidators of that bank must have considered that that was the best way to organise the distribution of those assets. What this means for the future of trusts

---

13   [1969] 1 Ch 373.
14   [1976] Ch 235.

law is unclear: will that decision be limited to cases involving those financial regulations or will it apply to trusts more generally?

It must be remembered that the collapse of Lehman Brothers in September 2008 almost caused the collapse of the entire global financial system. The International Monetary Fund has estimated that the crisis would cost the world economy US$ 12 trillion. Therefore, the pragmatism that underpinned Lord Dyson's leading judgment is plain: his lordship felt that finding a valid trust for all of the clients who had contributed to this fund would be beneficial to the entire economy. Lehman Brothers was like a tall building dangerously on the point of collapse. It needed to be dismantled carefully, piece by piece, instead of being allowed to fall on everyone. There was clearly pragmatism on a macro-economic scale at work here.

The decision in *Hunter v Moss*[15] was very different. Dillon LJ appeared to be motivated by the need to prevent an injustice being perpetrated by an employer against an employee by using a legal technicality to avoid paying a part of his emoluments. This was a simple dispute between two men in which one man appeared to be using a technicality to avoid paying (in the form of shares) another man what he was owed. I say 'appeared to be' because his lordship did not verbalise his real reasons for deciding as he did; instead, he just distinguished the earlier case law unsatisfactorily. It might have been preferable if Dillon LJ had linked his judgment to equitable ideas of unconscionability because his moral concerns would then have fitted more clearly with general equitable principles. What emerged nevertheless was a determination to circumvent the strict principle in cases like *Goldcorp*.

So, these cases show that a court may be motivated to avoid a strict legal rule – like the one in *Re Goldcorp* and *Re London Wine* – so as to achieve other goals, either doing justice between two men or resolving a threat to the stability of the global financial system. Again, this is not to demonstrate any weakness in the law. Rather, the courts are using those rules and competing analyses to reach the best outcomes in individual cases.

7.3.4 Dispositions of equitable interests

The decision in *Grey v IRC* is a classic piece of Viscount Simonds' thinking. His judgment is very short and he considers the questions to be straightforward. He asks us to look for the natural meaning of the word 'disposition' and in so doing he fails to notice that 'disposal' was not a natural meaning of that word. The *Oxford English Dictionary* refers primarily to a person's mood or to the way in which objects are laid out when defining the word 'disposition'. His lordship was clearly unimpressed by the attempt to avoid liability to tax in that case. That is the root of his decision.

By contrast, the court in *Vandervell v IRC* was prepared to accept precisely such clever thinking which enabled a well-meaning man to avoid tax when seeking to leave money to the Royal College of Surgeons. The attitudinal difference is striking. Viscount Simonds was so blunt that his approach was almost unintellectual. By contrast, clever judges in *Vandervell* (used to clever schemes in their former legal practices as clever barristers) were prepared to accept clever arguments which provided a route-map for tax lawyers who wanted to avoid stamp duty and other taxes for their clients in the future.

The word 'clever', I would suggest, is a word we use of children and dogs. It is not necessarily the case that a clever argument is a morally good argument nor is it necessarily an

---

15 [1994] 1 WLR 452.

argument which produces a good outcome. So, all of the cases on s 53(1)(c) of the Law of Property Act 1925 were concerned with avoiding tax, and that area of law continues to be used by tax-avoidance specialists on the look-out for clever ideas. Here again, the confusion is not being caused by equity but rather by other factors.

7.4 CONCLUSION: IS THERE A PARADOX AT THE HEART OF TRUSTS LAW?

The answer to the question 'is there a paradox in trusts law?', it is suggested, is that trusts law has sought to develop clear rules so that the socially significant field of trusts law is predictable, but that circumstances have required equitable approaches to emerge on the facts of particular cases which enable judges to reach just conclusions on particular sets of facts. Most of the judgments in the open-textured group of cases were not based on principles of equity. These are not cases in which – for the most part – discretionary equity is ruining the seamless fabric of the law, as Lord Eldon might have worried. Instead, these are cases in which the judges are simply trying to reach the correct outcome, in their eyes, on the facts in front of them having heard the evidence.

There are some cases – such as *Rochefoucauld v Boustead* and *Neville v Wilson* – which do use well-known equitable principles (either of equity not being used as an engine of fraud, or of constructive trusts) to justify the outcomes which they reach. The most obvious thing about those two judgments is that they are easy to correlate with the general principles of conscience-based equity because they make explicit reference to them. The difficult cases are the ones, like *Hunter v Moss*, in which the judges do not make it clear which moral or other factors are causing them to take a particularly obscure approach to the principles. Hence, *Hunter v Moss* is much-criticised because its reasoning is difficult to understand; and so we have to assume that the court did not like the employer taking advantage of the employee. At least when a judge says 'this person is a liar and to allow them to keep that property would be unconscionable' then their judgment is clear, even if it may feel a little overly emotional. So, when Sachs LJ reflected in *Re Baden (No 2)* that he may have seemed emotional early in his judgment, it made it easier for us to understand why the Court of Appeal went to such lengths to come to the outcome they did: they were concerned about the waste of money and the number of people waiting for 12 years to get their hands on the property which was clearly intended to be available to them as objects of a discretionary trust.

Part 3

The role of the trustees

Chapter 8

The duties of trustees

CAPSULE SUMMARY

The manner in which trustees are obliged to carry out their fiduciary duties is the core of the trust – the trustees owe those duties to the beneficiaries in relation to the trust fund. Statute provides for limited situations in which trustees who are incapable of performing their duties can be removed from office and other trustees appointed in their place.[1]

The duties of the trustees in any particular trust are to be identified from the terms of its trust instrument. The principal 13 duties contained in the case law are as follows.

(1) The duties on acceptance of office relating to the need to familiarise oneself with the terms, conditions and history of the management of the trust. (2) The duty to obey the terms of the trust unless directed to do otherwise by the court. (3) The duty to safeguard the trust assets, including duties to maintain the trust property, as well as to ensure that it is applied in accordance with the directions set out in the trust instrument. (4) The duty to act 'even-handedly' between beneficiaries, which means that the trustees are required to act impartially between beneficiaries and to avoid conflicts of interest. (5) The duty to act with reasonable care, meaning generally a duty to act as though a prudent person of business acting on behalf of someone for whom one feels morally bound to provide. (6) Duties in relation to trust expenses. (7) The duties of investment, requiring prudence and the acquisition of the highest possible rate of return in the context. (8) The duty to distribute the trust property correctly. (9) The duty to avoid conflicts of interest, not to earn unauthorised profits from the fiduciary office, not to deal on one's own behalf with trust property on pain of such transactions being voidable, and the obligation to deal fairly with the trust property. (10) The duty to preserve the confidence of the beneficiaries, especially in relation to Chinese wall arrangements. (11) The duty to act gratuitously, without any right to payment not permitted by the trust instrument or by the general law. (12) The duty to account and to provide information. (13) The duty to take

---

1   Section 8.2.

into account relevant considerations and to overlook irrelevant considerations, failure to do so coupled with a breach of trust may lead to the court setting aside an exercise of the trustees' powers if they have committed a breach of trust in so doing.[2] The trustees' liabilities for breach of trust are considered in Chapter 18.

The trustees bear only a limited obligation to give information to beneficiaries in relation to the administration and management of the trust fund and in relation only to that part of a trust fund in which they have a proprietary interest. Recent case law has emphasised the court's inherent discretion to make orders relating to the administration of trusts and therefore the access of beneficiaries to information may be enlarged in the future or alternatively it may continue to be exercised in accordance with traditional principles. Trustees are not obliged to disclose to beneficiaries any matter in relation to any exercise of their fiduciary discretion, nor are they obliged to disclose any confidential matter. The court reserves discretion as to the manner in which trustees exercise their powers, but not as to the content of any such decision unless there has been palpable wrongdoing.[3]

Trustees are entitled to have their liabilities for breach of trust and for negligence limited by the terms of the trust instrument. Such liability exclusion clauses are equitable devices and not contractual provisions. Trustees can limit their liability for negligence and gross negligence, but they may not limit their liability for dishonesty or fraud. There is a division in the authorities between a permissive approach to such exclusion clauses and an approach which prefers to limit them.[4]

The trustees may be controlled by the beneficiaries by means of an application to the court. The court has an inherent jurisdiction to make orders in relation to the administration of a trust. The court may make orders by way variously of (a) giving directions, (b) assuming administrative control, (c) judicial review (in a private law sense) of the trustees' actions, or (d) setting aside any decision of a trustee made by taking into account irrelevant considerations or failing to take into account relevant considerations.[5]

8.1 INTRODUCTION

8.1.1 The context of the law on the management of trusts

This Part 3 of this book explains the law governing the operation of trusts. This chapter analyses the duties of trustees of express trusts; Chapter 9 considers the law governing the investment of trust funds; and Chapter 10 considers the powers of trustees when managing trust funds. So far in this book we have considered the creation and nature of trusts. The rules and principles in these three chapters relate to the day-to-day, practical management of trusts.

The bulk of the law in this chapter is contained in case law. Necessarily those cases turn on the specific facts before the court and on the terms of the trust instrument created by the settlor (and her professional advisors). There is some statute in this area: the Trustee Act 1925 ('TA 1925') is the principal statute governing the office of trustee of express trusts and the Trustee Act 2000 ('TA 2000') is the principal statute governing the investment of trust

---

2 Section 8.3.
3 Section 8.4.
4 Section 8.5.
5 Section 8.6.

and related matters. Both of these statutes can be excluded by an express provision in the trust instrument in most circumstances, and their effect in particular circumstances is often governed by the case law in any event. Of course, there will be situations in which there is no trust instrument created by the settlor (as in cases like *Paul v Constance* where the parties did not realise they were creating an express trust). Therefore, the case law and the statutes (where applicable) will supply all of the trustees' obligations in those situations.

This means that there is no central statement of the duties of trustees. That may strike you as being remarkable. Instead, a practising trusts lawyer needs to be familiar with the many authorities governing the detail of the trustees' obligations. A company law practitioner, by contrast, can rely primarily on the exhaustive Companies Act 2006 to explain the duties of company directors, the rights of their shareholders and so forth. By contrast, a trusts lawyer needs to rely on a good textbook, lots of research, their own knowledge, and a deep reservoir of common sense in finding answers to practical problems which often arise between the competing interests of different classes of beneficiaries. This means that a large amount of trusts law practice involves giving advice on the day-to-day operation of trusts.

In practice, a well-drafted trust instrument will contain most of the answers to the questions which a trusts law practitioner will wish to answer: especially about the trustees' powers and their duties, the rights of the beneficiaries in different contexts, and it will regularise the tax position of the trust. A badly-drafted trust instrument will create a number of headaches but, for the specialist practitioner, it may also prove to be an endless source of fees in giving advice on its interpretation! There is no greater friend to the Chancery practitioners of Lincoln's Inn than a rich lay person who writes their own trust or will without legal advice: it commonly proves to be a source of sustenance for Chancery barristers for several years. Entire careers can be made on a single piece of bad drafting. Remember all of the trusts drafted for Gulbenkian, Baden, Gestetner, Vandervell and the other rich men in Chapters 3 and 4 of this book which generated expensive litigation that lasted for many years. Early in your legal career in the Admiralty field you will want to get involved in a good collision between two very expensive tankers at sea; in the construction law field you will want to get involved in a complex arbitration dispute about a large office block; and in the Chancery field you want a homemade trust instrument which involves plenty of money and which has intertwining, contradictory provisions which resemble a spaghetti dinner. Each of these sorts of case will begin your career deliciously. That is why anyone drafting a trust is well-advised to have a good, specialist practitioner draft it for them.

8.1.2 The principal duties incumbent on trustees

This section outlines the 13 principal duties which are incumbent on trustees of express trusts. Each of these duties is considered in greater detail below, with some of them receiving particularly detailed consideration (those are the issues which are most likely to form the focus of a university trusts law course). Those principles are outlined here and then considered in greater detail in the chapter to follow. They are known to my undergraduate students as 'the glorious 13'. Each states a principle of the general law of trusts which is incumbent on a trustee of an express trust unless it is excluded or adapted by the terms of a trust instrument.

(1) The duties on acceptance of office relating to the need for the trustees to familiarise themselves with the terms, conditions and history of the management of the trust.
(2) The duty to obey the terms of the trust unless directed to do otherwise by the court.

(3)   The duty to safeguard the trust assets, including duties to maintain the trust property, as well as to ensure that it is applied in accordance with the directions set out in the trust instrument.

(4)   The duty to act even-handedly between beneficiaries, which means that the trustees are required to act impartially between beneficiaries and to avoid conflicts of interest.

(5)   The duty to act with reasonable care, meaning generally a duty to act as though 'a prudent person of business acting on behalf of someone for whom one feels morally bound to provide'.

(6)   A series of duties in relation to trust expenses.

(7)   The duties of investment, requiring prudence and the acquisition of the highest possible rate of return in the context (which are considered in detail in Chapter 9).

(8)   The duty to distribute the trust property correctly.

(9)   The duty to avoid conflicts of interest, not to earn unauthorised profits from the fiduciary office, not to deal on one's own behalf with trust property on pain of such transactions being voidable, and the obligation to deal fairly with the trust property.

(10) The duty to preserve the confidence of the beneficiaries, especially in relation to Chinese wall arrangements.

(11) The duty to act gratuitously, without any right to payment not permitted by the trust instrument or by the general law.

(12) The duty to account and to provide information.

(13) The duty to take into account relevant considerations and to overlook irrelevant considerations, failure to do so may lead to the court setting aside an exercise of the trustees' powers.

These 13 duties are considered in section 8.3 of this chapter in turn. Section 8.2 sets out some general principles which underpin the duties of trustees generally before we come to those principles. Finally, at the end of the chapter, there is a discussion of the controversial principles governing the ability of trustees to exclude their liabilities for breach of trust.

8.2 THE OFFICE OF TRUSTEE

8.2.1 Some practicalities about the establishment of trusts

This chapter is concerned with the duties of the trustees of express trusts. As is considered below, the obligations of any trustee are fiduciary in nature and they are governed by the principle of good conscience which is set out in *Westdeutsche Landesbank v Islington*.[6] We discussed that core principle in Chapter 2: a trust takes effect over property in relation to a trustee's conscience. That is the high-level principle which remains behind all of the detailed rules and principles of trusts law. Therefore, overriding principles of good faith and good conscience, as explained in section 8.2.4, underpin all of the more detailed rules which govern the behaviour of trustees. Breach of these duties will impose a personal liability on the trustee to compensate the trust for any loss caused by that breach of trust (as discussed in Chapter 18).[7] We shall focus in this chapter primarily on the basic duties of trustees and leave those other issues about what happens when things go wrong until later chapters.

---

6 [1996] AC 669.
7 *Target Holdings v Redferns* [1996] 1 AC 421.

There are a number of basic questions which always confuse or intrigue students. Some of them can get in the way of understanding how a trustee's duties work in practice, and so I will try to answer some of them here. The first question is usually: how does someone become trustee? In a well-organised situation, with professional advisors overseeing the affairs of a wealthy client or a corporation, then a trust instrument will be signed and it will specify the trustees, when the trust begins, and what the trustees' duties are (and are not) in some detail. The law on the appointment, removal and retirement of trustees is considered in section 8.2.2. If there is no trust instrument, then (in cases like *Paul v Constance*) the court will look at the factors discussed in Chapter 5 about the constitution of a trust and decide when it seems most sensible to say that the trust came into existence: usually when the legal title of the trust property became vested in the trustees. It may be important to know for tax purposes exactly when the trust came into existence, for example when there were different tax rates applicable in different tax years it would be important to know in which year the trust came legally into existence.

Once a trustee has accepted the office of trustee, she is then bound by all of the terms of the trust instrument and, where applicable, by the requirements of the general law of trusts. So, what happens if the trustee does not want to act as trustee? A person may refuse to act as a trustee and is perfectly entitled to refuse the office from the outset.[8] Equally, it is open to a trustee to limit her liabilities as a trustee, which is best done by means of a provision in the trust instrument which makes that limitation of liability clear.[9] Agreement to act as trustee will be demonstrated if the trustee signs the trust instrument[10] or gives an explicit declaration of assent (such as writing a letter to that effect).[11]

If the intended trustee does not know that she has been appointed to a trust, then she is not bound until she knows of the appointment and accepts it. If she refuses to act as trustee, then another trustee will be appointed in accordance with TA 1925 (as discussed below) to take her place. Otherwise, it may be that the trustee is treated as being a bare trustee (albeit refusing to accept any onerous duties such as investment of the trust) if the property comes to be lodged in her possession. For example, if a wedge of banknotes and a signed trust instrument were thrust into her hands by the settlor at the airport before the settlor bounded through the boarding gate and onto a plane, then that person might be considered to be a bare trustee of that money (so that she could not claim to keep it beneficially, knowing that it was meant to be held on trust, but so that she had no onerous fiduciary duties) or she could be treated as being bailee of that money (meaning that she would be required simply to hold it, without any fiduciary obligations to safeguard or invest it, until it could be returned to its original owner). If no one can be found who will act as trustee (for example if the property involved is onerous or undesirable: like being made trustee of the computer equipment of someone who has just been convicted of online pornography offences) then the best analysis is probably that the property will return on resulting trust to the settlor.

Where there is more than one trustee, those trustees are expected to act jointly.[12] Therefore, as a general rule, the trust property is required to be vested in the name of all of the trustees

---

8 *Robinson v Pett* (1734) 3 Peere Wms 249, *per* Lord Talbot.
9 *Armitage v Nurse* [1998] Ch 241.
10 *Jones v Higgins* (1866) LR 2 Eq 538.
11 *Vickers v Bell* (1864) 4 De GJ & S 274.
12 *Luke v South Kensington Hotel Co* (1879) 11 Ch D 121; *Re Butlin's Settlement Trust* [1976] Ch 251.

jointly, all of the trustees must receive any trust income, all of the trustees must give a receipt, and so forth. However, the trust instrument may permit some other means of proceeding without unanimity[13] or necessity may require that assets be registered in the name of only one of the trustees at a given time.[14] In such situations, however, the property must not be left in the hands of one or only a few of the trustees for longer than is necessary.[15]

8.2.2 Appointment, retirement and removal of trustees

A trust instrument can create its own terms to govern the powers and duties of its trustees. A well-drafted trust instrument will do exactly that. Most specialist trusts law practitioners have their own precedents for different types of trust instrument, or other, basic trust instruments can be bought commercially in books of precedents or specialist practitioner texts. In the absence of any such provisions, then the TA 1925 will apply. It is possible for a settlor to exclude the terms of the 1925 Act in whole or in part.[16]

It is possible for new or additional trustees to be appointed under s 36 of the TA 1925. Section 36(1) provides that it is possible to appoint new trustees when an existing trustee falls dead; or remains outside the UK for a continuous period of more than 12 months; or wants to be discharged; or refuses to act as a trustee; or is unfit to act as a trustee; or is incapable of acting as a trustee; or is an infant. The remaining trustees (or anyone who is nominated in the trust instrument to have such a power) may appoint one or more people to replace the existing trustee in writing. Whether these trustees are acting reasonably in replacing that trustee under s 36 was held by Millett J in *Richards v Mackay*[17] to require merely that there is nothing so inappropriate about the proposed replacement that no reasonable trustee would entertain it. However, where a trustee is found to be incapable within the terms of the Mental Health Act 1983, then no new trustee may be appointed without an order to that effect being made under the Mental Health Act 1983.[18] Any appointees put into office under this s 36 are treated as having the same powers as if they had been originally appointed trustee.[19]

As a corollary to the appointment of new trustees, trustees may be removed from office on the basis of the same categories of event in s 36 of the TA 1925. Clearly, one can only replace a trustee if it is possible to remove the existing trustee as well as appointing a new trustee. However, it is possible to remove a trustee under s 36 without appointing a new trustee. Courts are likely to agree to remove a trustee whose personal interests conflict with the interests of the trust, as in *Moore v M'Glynn*[20] where removal of a trustee was approved in circumstances in which one of the trustees had set up in business in direct competition with the business interests of the trust.

Over and above these statutory provisions, the court retains a power to appoint new trustees under s 41 of the TA 1925 wherever it is 'expedient' to do so. This may arise, for example,

---

13 TA 2000, s 11.
14 *Consterdine v Consterdine* (1862) 31 Beav 330.
15 *Brice v Stokes* (1805) 11 Ves 319; *Re Munton* [1927] 1 Ch 262.
16 TA 1925, s 69.
17 [1990] 1 OTPR 1.
18 *Ibid*, s 36(9).
19 *Ibid*, s 36(7).
20 (1894) 1 IR 74.

when one trustee is obstructing the business of the trust by refusing to sign any documents necessary for the transfer of property. It is also possible under s 37 of the TA 1925 to increase the number of trustees (to a maximum of four) to hold a particular sub-fund within the trust. Further to s 40(1) of the TA 1925, this vesting of the trust fund in the newly appointed trustees takes place automatically, provided that the appointment of the new trustees was effected by deed. That is so unless the property is a mortgage over land, or a lease with a prohibition on assignment, or securities held on an electronic register, because each of them requires re-registration to pass ownership of the legal title.

8.2.3 Principles governing dealings with the trust property

The powers of trustees to deal with the trust property are considered in Chapter 10.

8.2.4 The manner in which the trustees are obliged to act in general terms

At the most basic level, trustees are required to act in good conscience.[21] This concept of acting in good conscience, and avoiding unconscionable activity, includes the avoidance of any conflicts between the trustees' personal interests and their fiduciary obligations to the beneficiaries.[22] The general law of trusts has always required that a trustee acts with prudence and care.[23] The precise concept, discussed in Chapter 10 in relation to the investment of the trust property, is that the trustee should act as a person acting on behalf of someone for whom they felt morally bound to provide. An example of someone whom we might feel morally bound to provide would be our children.[24] In *Armitage v Nurse*, Millett LJ doubted that there was such a general principle in English trusts law when considering the ability of trustees to have their liabilities for breach of trust excluded by the trust instrument.[25] However, latterly, the Trustee Act 2000 has provided that the trustees do owe a duty of care to exercise reasonable skill and care to the beneficiaries, as discussed in Chapter 10. It is suggested that it would be surprising if trustees, who are required to act as fiduciaries, did not owe a duty to act with some level of reasonable skill and care. The principle in *Armitage v Nurse* is unfortunate because it seems to undermine the idea that trustees must act in good conscience because they can apparently be grossly negligent without any recourse on the part of the beneficiaries if their trust instrument absolves them of such liability. The Privy Council in *Spread Trustee v Hutcheson* has doubted this approach because of the injustice it causes to beneficiaries who are the objects of the negligence of trustees.[26] The significance of exclusion of liability clauses and the *Armitage* case are considered in section 8.5 below.

---

21 *Westdeutsche Landesbank v Islington LBC* [1996] AC 669.
22 See section 8.3.9 below.
23 See, e.g., *Speight v Gaunt* (1883) 9 App Cas 1; *Learoyd v Whiteley* (1887) 12 App Cas 727.
24 The closest concept in French law is a person required to act 'en bon père de famille': that is, like a good father looking after his family.
25 [1998] Ch 241.
26 [2011] UKPC 13.

8.2.5 The nature of the trustees' liability for breach of trust

The corollary to a trustee having obligations is that that trustee will be personally liable for breach of trust, as discussed in Chapter 18. The trustees' principal obligation is to account to the beneficiaries both in the sense of rendering accounts as to the value of the trust fund and also to account in the sense of making good any loss caused to the trust by some breach of the trustee's obligations. In the event of a breach of trust, the beneficiaries must proceed first against the trustees. The leading case of *Target Holdings v Redferns*[27] held that the trustees will only be liable if the trust suffers a loss as a result of their breach of trust. There will not be any liability if the trust suffers a loss as a result of some other factor, even if the trustees have coincidentally committed a breach of trust at the same time. Lord Browne-Wilkinson explained that there are three remedies available to the beneficiaries as a result of a breach of trust. First, the trustees must recover the specific property which has been lost to the trust. Second, if that property cannot be recovered then the trustees are personally liable to reconstitute the value of the trust fund in cash terms. Third, the trustees must compensate the trust for any other loss resulting from the breach of trust. It is also possible for the beneficiaries to obtain an order to require the trustees to observe the terms of their obligations: for example, by selling unauthorised investments and acquiring authorised investments in their place.[28]

8.2.6 Right to remuneration

The trustee is entitled to be remunerated for any service to the trust even if that service could have been performed by a lay trustee (that is, someone not professionally qualified to carry out that task).[29] A trustee acting in a professional capacity is entitled to receive such remuneration as is reasonable in the circumstances.[30] Similarly, delegates may be remunerated on a basis that is reasonable in the circumstances.[31] The provisions as to remuneration of trustees apply only where they have not been expressly excluded by a trust instrument.[32]

8.2.7 Right to reimbursement and indemnity

Trusts operate through the trustees. That is, the trustees hold the legal title to the property, they must transfer property, give receipts, and so forth. Nothing can happen without the trustees. This opens the trustees up to potential liabilities. Therefore, the trustees will have rights to be reimbursed when they incur expenses on trust business[33] and to be indemnified against contractual obligations which they incur for the trust (as opposed to incurring them in their personal capacity).[34] As was outlined above, ordinarily the trustees will bear personal responsibilities only for breaches of trust which cause loss to the trust. In *Revenue & Customs Commissioners v Trustees of the Peter Clay Discretionary Trust*,[35] Lindsay J upheld the principle that general trust

---

27 [1996] 1 AC 421.
28 *Re Massingberd* (1890) 63 LT 296.
29 TA 2000, s 28(2).
30 *Ibid*, s 29(2), (3).
31 *Ibid*, s 32.
32 *Ibid*, s 28(1).
33 *Ibid*, s 31(1).
34 *Dowse v Gorton* [1891] AC 190.
35 [2008] 2 WLR 1052, Lindsay J.

expenses are met out of the capital of the trust fund, as opposed to those expenses being met out of trust income. This principle may not apply if those expenses clearly relate to one part of the trust only. The principle is based on the idea advanced in *Re Bennett*[36] that if expenses were borne for the benefit of the entire trust estate then they were attributable to capital. This will be important in the short-term to the life tenant who will want to maximise their income; however, a reduction in capital will reduce future income in ordinary circumstances because it reduces the amount of capital available to earn a profit.

8.2.8 Delegation of trustees' powers

Trustees are able to delegate their responsibilities in accordance with the principles of the TA 2000, as considered in section 10.2.

8.3 THE GENERAL DUTIES OF TRUSTEES

This section considers the 13 principal trustees' duties which were set out above in section 8.1, following the same numbering and taking each of them one at a time.

8.3.1 Duties on acceptance of office

Once a trustee accepts the office of trustee, that trustee is bound by all of the obligations in the trust instrument.[37] The trustee only has the powers expressed in the trust instrument;[38] unless the trust instrument is silent about something which has the effect that a provision of the TA 1925 or the TA 2000 comes into effect. These principles are amplified in section 8.3.2 below.

The general responsibilities of the trustee are to familiarise herself with the terms of trust, the nature of the property involved, the range of objects within the contemplation of the trust, the identity of the other trustees, to consult all of the documentation connected to the trust (including the trust instrument, any documents relating to the exercise of any discretionary power or power of appointment, trust accounts, the scope of investments made by the trust, statements of investment criteria and so forth) and to familiarise herself with any other information pertinent to the management of the trust which is not recorded in documentary fashion.[39] A trustee will be liable for any matters of which she had, or should have been expected to have had, knowledge.[40] Therefore, the trustee is obliged to find out information about her trusteeship and not simply to fail to investigate matters over which she is expected to exert control.[41]

The specific responsibilities of any trustee will come from two sources: first, any specific provisions of the trust instrument and, secondly, any duties arising out of the context of the trust or the nature of the trust property. For example, the trustee is required to consider the

---

36 [1896] 1 Ch 778; *Revenue & Customs Commissioners v Trustees of the Peter Clay Discretionary Trust* [2008] 2 WLR 1052, 1062.
37 *Clough v Bond* (1838) 3 My & Cr 490.
38 *Ibid.*
39 *Mond v Hyde* [1999] QB 1097.
40 *Young v Cloud* (1874) LR 18 Eq 634.
41 *Mond v Hyde* [1999] QB 1097.

nature of the trust property. The first duty is to ensure that the property is properly vested in the trustees.[42] Secondary duties will depend on the nature of that property. For example, if the property is money, then the trustees will be required to consider the manner in which that money should be invested;[43] or to sell any property in a reasonable time which the trust requires her to sell;[44] or to distribute income and capital at appropriate times;[45] or to collect rents from land.[46] If the property requires maintenance (such as building work on land or taking legal proceedings to collect income owing to it)[47] or insurance[48] or other, similar actions in relation to it, then the trustee must perform those duties in good order. If the trust property is a valuable racing stallion then the trustees must ensure the horse is cared for, that its stud fees are properly negotiated, that it is kept in training if it is to be raced, and so forth. Much of the trustees' business is governed by common sense.

8.3.2 Duty to obey directions of the trust

Each trustee is bound by all of the obligations in the trust instrument.[49] Failure to obey the terms of the trust will constitute a breach of trust.[50] If there is no trust instrument then the TA 1925 or the TA 2000, or some principle set out the case law will govern the duties of those trustees. Those principles emerge during this chapter and the two following chapters of this book. The liabilities of trustees for losses caused by any breach of trust may be limited by exclusion of liability clauses in the trust instrument.[51] Where the trustees are bound by other legislative codes, for example, in relation to unit trusts or pension funds or more generally as to investment under the Financial Services and Markets Act 2000 and the Pensions Act 1995 respectively, then those statutory obligations may supplement or even override any terms of the trust instrument.

8.3.3 Duty to safeguard trust property

The trustees are responsible for the safeguarding of the trust property. Quite what that means will differ from trust to trust and will depend, in common sense terms, on the nature of the trust property and the terms of the trust instrument. For example, a trust obliging the trustees to make a specific house available for the beneficiaries' occupation will require that house to be maintained and to be held in a condition which is suitable for those beneficiaries. If one of the beneficiaries suffered from a physical disability, then the trustees would be required to have the bathroom equipped with rails and so forth so that it would appropriate for that person's use. If the trust obliges the trustees to seek a sale of that property in certain circumstances, then the duties of the trustees would include an obligation to maintain the property in a condition in which it could be sold. In that sense, the nature of the trustees' duties may

---

42 *Lewis v Nobbs* (1878) 8 Ch D 591.
43 *Moyle v Moyle* (1831) 2 Russ & M 710.
44 *Wentworth v Wentworth* [1900] AC 163.
45 *Hawkesley v May* [1956] 1 QB 304.
46 *Tebbs v Carpenter* (1816) 1 Madd 290.
47 *Re England's Settlement Trusts* [1918] 1 Ch 24.
48 *Re Godwin's Settlement* (1918) 87 LJ Ch 645.
49 *Clough v Bond* (1838) 3 My & Cr 490.
50 *Ibid.*
51 *Armitage v Nurse* [1998] Ch 241.

depend on the property and the circumstances. The trustees must also act impartially between different groups of beneficiaries in doing this, as considered in the next section.

8.3.4 Duty to act impartially between beneficiaries

In general terms, a trustee is obliged to act impartially as between all of the beneficiaries.[52] At one level this requires the trustee to exercise fairness as between each beneficiary, showing no favour to any one; and at another level, this requires the beneficiary to act even-handedly as between different classes of beneficiaries. The expression many judges have preferred is that the trustees must act with an 'even hand'.[53] That does not mean that each beneficiary must be treated equally, particularly in situations in which the trustees are required to prefer one beneficiary over the others. For example, in a discretionary trust which requires the trustees to identify one person out of the class of potential objects who is to receive a payment of £10,000 in each year, by definition one person will feel pleased while the others might feel aggrieved when the trustees make the decision they are required to make which prioritises one beneficiary over the others. In such a situation, the trustees' obligation is to treat everyone impartially when making that decision. This principle was explained by Chadwick LJ in *Edge v Pensions Ombudsman* in the following way:[54]

> The so-called duty to act impartially . . . is no more than the ordinary duty which the law imposes on a person who is entrusted with the exercise of a discretionary power: that he exercises the power for the purpose for which it is given, giving proper consideration to the matters which are relevant and excluding from consideration matters which are irrelevant. If pension fund trustees do that, they cannot be criticized if they reach a decision which appears to prefer the claims of one interest – whether that of employers, current employers or pensioners – over others. The preference will be the result of a proper exercise of the discretionary power.[55]

One way of thinking about this obligation is that the trustees must be able to justify their decision as a fiduciary decision. As a fiduciary, the trustee is required to act in relation to each of the beneficiaries without any grace or favour, in the same way that the trustee must not take any personal advantage from the trust. Therefore, there must be impartiality in relation to the trustees' treatment of everyone involved with the trust.

Clearly, this duty will apply unless there a specific provision in the trust instrument which requires the trustees to prioritise one particular group of beneficiaries: for example, where a testator requires that the trustees prioritise the needs of his widow above the other beneficiaries.[56] One of the perennial problems facing trustees is the need to act impartially between life tenants (whose interest is in the income generated by the trust) and remaindermen (whose interest is in the preservation of the trust capital until the life tenant dies). Any action which seeks to increase income is likely to involve greater expense or to put the capital at greater risk. Therefore, the trustees will be required to justify any policy which prioritises income over capital, or vice

---

52 *Cowan v Scargill* [1985] Ch 270.
53 *Re Tempest* (1866) 1 Ch App 485, 487, *per* Turner LJ; *Re Lepine* [1892] 1 Ch 210, 219, *per* Fry LJ.
54 [2000] Ch 602, 627.
55 See also *Edge v Pensions Ombudsman* [1998] Ch 512, Scott VC.
56 *Ibid.*

versa. For example, when the financial markets and the general economy are depressed, it will require greater risks being taken with the capital to generate the same level of short-term invest-ment return for the life tenant. The remaindermen will be unhappy with the capital being risked in this way; while the life tenant will advocate this change. Similarly, the life tenant would be unhappy if the trustees decided not to take any greater risks so that they could protect the capital for the longer term. In either case, the trustees must be able to justify whichever decision they take. (The specific questions raised by investment decisions are considered in Chapter 10.)

8.3.5 Duty to exercise reasonable care

The trustee's obligation has always been stated in the case law as being to act as a prudent person of business would act if acting on behalf of someone for whom she felt morally bound to provide. Originally, it was held in *Learoyd v Whiteley*[57] and in *Speight v Gaunt* that a trustee must act as a businessperson of ordinary prudence acting for someone for whom they felt morally bound to provide. This approach was modified in *Bartlett v Barclays Bank*[58] in which it was held that trustees are permitted to take a 'prudent' degree of risk but must avoid anything which amounts to 'hazard'. That means that trustees can take a small amount of risk, but not too much. This more modern approach recognises, especially in relation to the investment of the trust property, that all investment involves some risk and therefore that trustees should be allowed to take some level of risk and not simply to act cautiously in avoiding all risk. The principles in relation to investment, and the change brought about by the TA 2000 in this context (by permitting the trustees to act 'reasonably' as opposed to 'cautiously' or 'prudently'), are considered in Chapter 9.

In the context of delegating authority to invest to some other person, the classic statement of the trustee's obligation was set out in the following terms in *Speight v Gaunt* in the decision of Lord Jessel MR:[59]

> It seems to me that on general trust principles a trustee ought to conduct the business of the trust in the same manner that an ordinary prudent man of business would conduct his own, and that beyond that there is no liability or obligation on the trustee.

Clearly, this may be a difficult test for a trustee to observe – particularly if that trustee is not acting in a professional capacity. The trustee will be judged by the standards of a prudent person experienced in business. As this concept was put by Megarry VC in *Cowan v Scargill*, the trustees are required to:

> take such care as an ordinary prudent man would take if he were minded to make an invest-ment for the benefit of other people for whom he feels morally bound to provide. This duty includes the duty to seek advice on matters which the trustee does not understand, such as the making of investments, and, on receiving that advice, to act with the same degree of prudence. Although a trustee who takes advice on investments is not bound to accept and

---

57 (1887) 12 App Cas 727.
58 [1980] Ch 515.
59 *Speight v Gaunt* (1883) 9 App Cas 1.

act on that advice, he is not entitled to reject it merely because he sincerely disagrees with it, unless in addition he is acting as an ordinary prudent man would act.[60]

Interestingly, this formulation does not assume that the trustee is a businessperson, but rather only a 'man'. The approach taken here is that the trustees are to focus primarily on the protection and maintenance of the trust fund, whilst also allowing it to grow steadily.[61] The focus of these dicta, although an encapsulation of the general principle, is on the subject of investment which we consider in detail in the next chapter. By contrast, Millett LJ in *Armitage v Nurse* suggested that he did *not* consider that there was a general duty on trustees to act with skill and care (as considered at 8.3.13 below). Nevertheless, it is respectfully suggested that Millett LJ cannot be correct in this regard because the case law has long contained a requirement of prudence, and subsequently because the Trustee Act 2000 now contains a general duty of skill and care, as is considered immediately below.

8.3.6 Duties in relation to trust expenses

The trustee is entitled to be reimbursed for any expense and to be indemnified against trust expenses generally, as considered in section 8.2.7 above. There are complex questions, however, as to the allocation of expenses between different parts of the same trust fund. Put crudely, if the trustees buy an ice cream when on business for the life tenant, can the cost of that ice cream be recovered only from trust income or can it also be recovered from trust capital? Who has to pay for trust expenses in the end: all the beneficiaries, or only beneficiaries who are affected? In *HMRC v Peter Clay Discretionary Trust*[62] an issue arose, in essence, as to whether or not the trustees of a discretionary trust could charge a part of their expenses relating to the capital portion of a trust fund to the income portion of that fund. There was thought to be a tax advantage in setting part of the expense against income. HMRC objected to this charge being made against the income from the trust for tax purposes. It was held, in line with traditional principle, that charges incurred 'for the benefit of the entire estate' should be charged to capital.[63] The issue was whether or not there could also be a charge to income in this case. In the earlier authorities,[64] Sir John Chadwick considered, deciding whether or not an expense was for the benefit of the whole estate depended on whether or not it benefited the entire estate: i.e. both the life tenant (the income beneficiary) and the remainderman (the capital beneficiary) in traditional settlements. Sir John Chadwick upheld the principle that if the work had been done for the benefit of the whole estate, both income and capital, then it would be chargeable to capital alone; however, because a part of the work which the trustees had done in this instance had been conducted exclusively for the income portion of the trust fund, then those expenses would properly be chargeable to the income portion of the fund alone because only the income portion of the fund had taken that benefit.[65]

---

60 *Cowan v Scargill* [1985] Ch 270, 289.
61 See *Nestlé v National Westminster Bank plc* [1993] 1 WLR 1260.
62 [2009] 2 WLR 1353.
63 See *In re Bennett* [1896] 1 Ch 778 and *Carver v Duncan* [1985] AC 1082.
64 *Ibid.*
65 See now Law Commission, *Capital and Income in Trusts: Classification and Apportionment*, Law Com No 315, 2009, in particular as to the treatment of distributions from companies as constituting capital when received by a trust.

8.3.7 Duty to invest the trust property

The duties in relation to the investment of the trust property are considered in detail in Chapter 9. This section presents a very brief summary of those principles. The case law principles on the investment of trusts is caught between an obligation on the trustees to secure the best performing investments available in accordance with the terms of the trust,[66] while balancing that quest for a high return with the general obligation to act prudently.[67] The tension between taking care and yet seeking the highest available return has developed into a modern requirement that trustees maintain a portfolio of investments.[68] A portfolio investment strategy requires that the trustees maintain a breadth of investments so as to balance out the risks associated with any individual investment which may generate a loss while still making a profit on the other investments.

If there is no trust instrument, then the TA 2000 has supplied a range of powers and duties for trustees when investing the trust property. The most significant statutory power is a general investment power for trustees whereby trustees have the investment powers of an absolute owner of the trust property.[69] The TA 2000 also requires trustees consciously to create standard investment criteria in the form of a set of principles by reference to which they will make their investments.[70] In making investment decisions, the trustees are also obliged to take professional advice.[71] When making investment decisions, the trustees are still governed by the general statutory duty of care to exercise reasonable skill and care.[72]

8.3.8 Duty to distribute the trust property correctly

Further to the trustee's duty to obey the terms of the trust[73] and the concomitant duty to avoid breaches of trust, the trustee must obey any instructions as to the distribution of the trust property set out by the settlor. Any failure to obey the terms of the trust will constitute a breach of trust, no matter what inducement there might have been to commit that breach, although the beneficiaries will only be entitled to recover any property lost to the trust fund or to recover the value of any loss suffered as a result of the breach of trust.[74] Breach of trust is discussed in Chapter 18.

8.3.9 Duty to avoid conflicts of interest

The general duty to avoid conflicts of interest

The trustee has an obligation not to permit conflicts of interest either between two competing fiduciary duties, or between the trustee's own personal interests and their fiduciary duties.[75] At one level, therefore, a trustee is not permitted to refrain from any action as trustee which

---

66 *Cowan v Scargill* [1985] Ch 270.
67 *Speight v Gaunt* (1883) 9 App Cas 1.
68 *Bartlett v Barclays Bank Trust Co Ltd.* [1980] Ch 515.
69 TA 2000, s 6(1).
70 *Ibid*, s 4(1).
71 *Ibid*, s 5(1).
72 *Ibid*, Sched 1, para 1(b).
73 *Clough v Bond* (1838) 3 My & Cr 490.
74 *Target Holdings v Redferns* [1996] 1 AC 421.
75 *Tito v Waddell (No 2)* [1977] 3 All ER 129.

would otherwise have been carried out, nor to take any action which would otherwise not have been performed, on the basis that the trustee's behaviour was motivated by a conflict between her personal interests and her countervailing fiduciary obligations.[76] If trustees (or any other type of fiduciary) acquire any personal profit from such a conflict of interest then that profit is held on constructive trust for their beneficiaries.[77] It is not just deliberate abuses of office which are treated in this way, however, because the courts are concerned to remove even the possibility that there might be any such abuse of fiduciary position by imposing a duty to avoid all potential, as well as actual, conflicts of interest. Therefore, fiduciaries are obliged to refrain from any potential conflicts of interest.

Trustee making unauthorised profits from the trust

If a trustee or any other form of fiduciary (whether a company director, a partner, an agent or any other form fiduciary) takes an unauthorised profit from their fiduciary office, then that profit is held on constructive trust for the beneficiaries of their fiduciary office. That the profit is held on trust means that any property which is acquired with that profit is also held on constructive trust. The principles underpinning this sort of constructive trust are considered in detail in Chapter 12.[78] In the law of trusts, the trustee must be able to show that they have received authorisation from the beneficiaries to absolve themselves of liability. If the trust instrument authorises the trustees taking such a profit, then there will not be a constructive trust over it. The Companies Act 2006 has provided a particular regime in relation to companies such that company directors can acquire authorisation from a vote of the other directors. It is suggested that it is more difficult in general terms to show that in family trusts the beneficiaries have given informed consent to the trustees taking such a profit.

This rule is a rule of long-standing at least since the decision in *Keech v Sandford*.[79] Lord Herschell held in *Bray v Ford* that this principle is 'an inflexible rule of equity' that no conflict of interest may be permitted and no unauthorised profit taken by the trustees. Significantly, it is not just that there must not be any profit taken from a conflict of interest but rather, as Lord Herschell put it, the fiduciary is 'not allowed to put himself in a position where his interest and duty conflict'. So, the possibility of a conflict is not permitted, let alone the earning of a profit from such a conflict. In the leading case of *Boardman v Phipps*,[80] a solicitor was in a fiduciary position in relation to a family trust. The solicitor realised, after conducting a large amount of research into a company in which the trust held a large shareholding, that a large profit could be made if a majority shareholding was acquired (by the acquisition of further shares) and the company's business activities reorganised. The solicitor only had access to this information because he was acting on behalf of the trust. The solicitor invested his own money together with the trust so as to acquire a majority shareholding in the company. His plan for the reorganisation of the company was a success and both he personally and the trust earned a large profit. However, when one of the beneficiaries learned of the solicitor's personal profit, the solicitor was sued to account

---

76 *Nocton v Lord Ashburton* [1914] AC 932.
77 *Boardman v Phipps* [1967] 2 AC 46.
78 Section 12.5.
79 (1726) Sel Cas Ch 61.
80 *Boardman v Phipps* [1967] 2 AC 46.

for that profit. It was held that this inflexible rule of equity that no fiduciary should benefit from a conflict of interest should be maintained. Therefore, the majority of the House of Lords held that the solicitor must hold his profit on constructive trust for the beneficiaries of the family trust, subject to an 'equitable accounting' to reward him for his work in earning that profit. This judgment demonstrates how strictly this principle is viewed.

The principle against self-dealing transactions

The so-called 'self-dealing' principle provides that, in a situation in which a trustee purports to deal on her own account with the trust property and especially if she takes a profit from such a transaction, then not only will the trustee be required to hold that profit on constructive trust for the beneficiaries of the trust but also the transaction itself may be set aside.[81] Such a transaction is voidable at the instance of the beneficiaries, rather than being automatically void.[82] The purpose of this rule is to prevent conflicts of interest.[83] As Lord Eldon put it in *Ex p James*,[84] 'the purchase [of trust property by the trustee on his own account] is not permitted in any case, however honest the circumstances'. That is a clear prohibition on any self-dealing. Similarly, Megarry VC in *Tito v Waddell (No 2)*[85] framed the self-dealing principle in the following terms: 'if a trustee purchases trust property from himself, any beneficiary may have the sale set aside *ex debito justitiae*, however fair the transaction'. Therefore, the fiduciary may not protest that they were acting in good faith. It is a matter of policy that this principle is strictly observed.[86] The right of the beneficiary is therefore to set aside the transaction. Further to *Boardman v Phipps*, above, any profit which is taken by the fiduciary in these circumstances will be held on constructive trust. By way of illustration, in *Wright v Morgan*[87] a fiduciary sought to buy trust property from a fellow fiduciary at a price which had been ascertained by an independent, open market valuation. A sale was permitted by the terms of the will trust in question. Nevertheless, it was held that this transaction was voidable on behalf of the beneficiaries because the fiduciary was dealing on his own behalf.

The fair dealing principle

Where a trustee deals with a beneficiary's interest in the trust, or acquires that beneficiary's interest, there will be an obligation on the trustee to demonstrate fair dealing. Thus, in *Tito v Waddell (No 2)*, Megarry VC held[88] that:

> if a trustee purchases the beneficial interest of any of his beneficiaries, the transaction is not voidable *ex debito justitiae*, but can be set aside unless the trustee can show that he has not taken advantage of his position and has made full disclosure to the beneficiary, and that the transaction is fair and honest.

---

81 *Tito v Waddell (No 2)* [1977] 3 All ER 129, 141, *per* Megarry VC.
82 *Parker v McKenna* (1874) 10 Ch App 96, 124, *per* James LJ.
83 *Re Brooke Bond & Co Ltd's Trust Deed* [1963] Ch 357.
84 (1803) 8 Ves 337, 345.
85 [1977] Ch 106.
86 *British Coal Corp v British Coal Staff Superannuation Scheme Trustees Ltd* [1993] PLR 303, 312, *per* Vinelott J.
87 [1926] AC 788.
88 [1977] 3 All ER 129.

Therefore, there is a burden of proof on the trustee to demonstrate both that no advantage was taken of the beneficiary and also that the beneficiary was made fully aware of the nature and the circumstances of the transaction. Where there is no disclosure to the beneficiary, therefore, the transaction will be set aside.[89]

8.3.10 Duties of confidence

One of the core duties of a fiduciary is a duty of confidence, which is coupled with the duty of loyalty.[90] A fiduciary is required to protect the confidential information of their beneficiaries, as well as maintaining any property held on trust (as considered above), as was made clear in *Reading v R*[91] by Asquith LJ. Loyalty is one of the principal duties of the fiduciary.[92] A trustee will be liable to account to the beneficiaries for any loss caused by a breach of these duties of confidence and to hold any profit taken from such a breach on constructive trust for those beneficiaries, as considered in Chapter 12. The general principles surrounding the equitable doctrine of confidences is considered in Chapter 24. The particular context of so-called 'Chinese wall' arrangements, which have spawned a large amount of litigation, and fiduciary confidentiality are considered in section 8.4.9 below.

8.3.11 Duty to act gratuitously

In general trusts law, it is assumed that the trustee accepts her office voluntarily and it is assumed equally that she will not permit any conflicts of interest between the beneficiaries' interests and her own personal interests. Consequently, it is assumed by the case law that the trustee will act without payment.[93] It is suggested, however, in the modern context that this duty is of reduced value for two reasons. First, in commercial trusts practice, the trustees will be entitled to remuneration by the terms of the trust instrument. Secondly, as considered above, there are rights to remuneration and reimbursement of expenses in general terms. Therefore, the main context in which this principle might be said to bite – that is, denying the trustees any sort of wage or emolument from their office – is circumscribed by the trust instrument in most cases in which the duties are so onerous as to require such remuneration. Therefore, the significance of this principle in modern practice is as a recognition of the trustee's obligations to act loyally in the service of the beneficiaries in the manner required by their fiduciary office. In that sense, beyond questions of authorised remuneration, the trustee continues to act gratuitously.

8.3.12 Duty to account and to provide information

The trustees' obligations to account to the beneficiaries and the extent of the trustees' obligations to provide information to the beneficiaries are considered in section 8.4 below.

---

89   *Hill v Langley* (1988) *The Times*, 28 January.
90   *Bristol & West Building Society v Mothew* [1998] Ch 1.
91   [1949] 2 KB 232 at 236.
92   *Bristol & West Building Society v Mothew* [1998] Ch 1 at 18, *per* Millett LJ.
93   *Robinson v Pett* (1734) 3 P Wms 249, 251.

8.3.13 Duty to take into account relevant considerations: The principle in *Pitt v Holt*

Introduction

Imagine for a moment how wonderful your life would be if you had a magic wand, Harry Potter-style, with which you could wipe out all of your poor choices in life, before going back and making those choices again. In the law of trusts, the 'principle in *Hastings-Bass*'[94] once seemed to offer trustees and their advisors just such a magic wand in that they could ask the court to set aside any inappropriate exercise of their powers or discretions so that they could make their choices again. By 'setting aside' the trustees' decision, that decision is erased and a magic wand waved over the situation so that the parties are transported back in time before the decision was made. That principle has been altered by the decision of the Supreme Court in *Pitt v Holt*.

The concept was this: if the trustees had made a decision in relation to a discretionary trust or under a power then that decision could be set aside (so that the parties went back to the position before that decision was made) if the trustees had relied on irrelevant considerations when making that decision or if they had failed to take into account relevant considerations when making that decision. Suppose, by way of example, that there was a discretionary trust which required the trustees to pay £3,000 per annum to any of the class of beneficiaries whom they considered to be 'in poverty and deserving of help' on Christmas Day, where 'in poverty' was defined in the trust to mean anyone in the class with less than £100 in their bank account or in cash. Suppose that £3,000 was paid to one of the beneficiaries 'on the basis of their big feet'. If the trustees had taken into account the beneficiaries' shoe sizes when deciding which of them was in poverty then that would be irrelevant and their decision should be set aside. If the trustees had failed to consider the beneficiaries' bank account balances when deciding which of them was in poverty then they would have failed to take into account something relevant. By setting aside the trustees' decision, the money would be restored to the trust fund and the trustees would be required to make their decision again.

In practice, this doctrine meant that if the trustees made a mistake which had tax consequences, then they could erase their error and make their decision again. However, the UK tax authority, HMRC, did not like this approach and so decided to participate in this area of litigation for the first time. Therefore, in the case of *Pitt v Holt*, the Court of Appeal and the Supreme Court considered this principle again. In essence, the principle now requires not only that the trustees had failed to take into account a relevant consideration, or that they had taken into account an irrelevant consideration, before it would be set aside; but rather the trustees must also have committed a breach of trust. In other words, it is not enough simply to take into account something irrelevant or to fail to take into account something relevant if the trustees were acting within the terms of their trusteeship. If the trustees make a poor decision within the terms of their trusteeship, then that decision will not now be set aside. Before the court will set aside the trustees' decision, it must be shown that the trustees were also in breach of their obligations such that they were committing a breach of trust. Equally, it is not enough that the trustees took professional advice which turned out to be incorrect. There must be a breach of trust. This principle is explained in greater detail in the next section.

94 *Re Hastings-Bass* [1975] Ch 25.

Taking into account relevant considerations and ignoring irrelevant considerations:
The principle in Pitt v Holt

Beneficiaries may be able to have the exercise of a power or a discretion by the trustees set aside if the trustees have taken into account irrelevant considerations or have not taken into account relevant considerations in so acting;[95] and provided that there has also been some breach of duty by the trustees.[96] The exercise of the trustees' power in such a situation is voidable at the instance of the court but not automatically void.[97] The principles were set out in detail by Lloyd LJ (as explained next) and then approved by Lord Walker in the Supreme Court.[98] Therefore, we shall begin with the Court of Appeal decision.

In the joined appeals of *Pitt v Holt* and *Futter v Futter*, the Supreme Court considered the so-called doctrine in *Re Hastings-Bass* and the (separate) doctrine of mistake (which is considered below in section 8.3.14). The decision of Lloyd LJ in *Pitt v Holt*, with which the other members of the Court of Appeal agreed and which the Supreme Court approved, had narrowed the *Mettoy* principle considerably by returning to the decision of Buckley LJ in the Court of Appeal in *Hastings-Bass* itself and subjecting it to a close re-reading. Lloyd LJ was careful to note that he was bound by the decision in *Hastings-Bass* but that the intervening decisions had all been decisions of the High Court alone. Lloyd LJ held in *Pitt v Holt*[99] that the duty to take into account relevant considerations is a fiduciary duty and therefore a trustee's decision could only be set aside if it was in breach of that fiduciary duty. Therefore, there must be a breach of trust before this doctrine may be activated. Moreover, the decision is not automatically void; but rather it can only be found to be void if the beneficiaries seek to have it declared to be void. Therefore, such decisions are merely voidable until the beneficiaries succeed in such an application. Furthermore, a matter is not irrelevant, nor has something relevant been overlooked, just because a professional's advice was incorrect. This approach was approved by the Supreme Court.

The case of *Pitt v Holt* itself concerned a man who had suffered brain damage in an accident. A receiver was appointed by the Court of Protection to act for him. The receiver created a discretionary trust as part of her scheme to care for him. However, she failed to appreciate the inheritance tax consequences of that scheme when she made her decisions. The joined appeal in *Futter v Futter* concerned a discretionary trust scheme: the trustees failed to appreciate that there would be a capital gains tax charge if they took the decision they wanted to take, even though they had taken professional advice as to their best course of action. None of the trustees had acted in breach of trust. In both cases, the trustees sought a court order to set aside their exercise of their powers so that they could take decision with a different tax effect. It was held on the facts in *Pitt v Holt* and in *Futter v Futter*[100] by Lord Walker that the actions of the trustees would not be set aside in either appeal because neither set of trustees had acted in breach of trust, even though they had failed to appreciate their respective tax law positions.

95 *Ibid.*
96 *Abacus Trust Company (Isle of Man) v Barr* [2003] 2 WLR 1362, 1370, para 24.
97 *Pitt v Holt, Futter v Futter* [2011] EWCA Civ 197, [2011] 3 WLR 19.
98 [2013] UKSC 26.
99 [2011] EWCA Civ 197, [127].
100 [2013] UKSC 26.

The nature of the relevant and irrelevant considerations which have been considered to be significant

The key question, therefore, is how does one identify a factor, whether considered or ignored by the trustees, as being of sufficient relevance for the objects of the power to commence an action? The relevant and irrelevant considerations will differ from case to case depending upon the objectives and terms of any given trust, the nature and identities of the beneficiaries, the nature of the trust property and so forth. So, the considerations in relation to a single beneficiary may differ from the considerations applicable in relation to a power over a large class of potential beneficiaries.[101] It is also difficult to know whether or not the interests of other users of the trust or others who may take an interest in remainder ought to be taken into account.[102] Examples of considerations taken into account or not taken into account include a failure to take an up-to-date valuation of assets held in a pension fund before transferring assets between funds,[103] failing to take into account the fiscal consequences of a decision,[104] or failing to take the settlor's wishes into account correctly.[105]

Failure to exercise a discretionary power will render any act of the trustees a nullity

It has been held that a failure to exercise a discretionary power will render any act of the trustees of a discretionary trust a nullity. In *Betafence v Veys*[106] Lightman J held that it would be a nullity if trustees with a discretion failed to realise that they had such a discretion and so failed to exercise their discretion. In this regard Lightman J followed *Turner v Turner*,[107] a case in which trustees of a discretionary trust simply followed the directions of the settlor without appreciating that they had a discretion and so without exercising their discretion. Consequently, their actions were held to be a nullity and they were therefore required to exercise their discretionary power conscious of that power and in a manner appropriate to fiduciaries. The error which gives rise to the doctrine in *Pitt v Holt* must be an error made by the trustees, not an error made by the settlor such as a mistake in the drafting of the trust instrument (for example, the scheme rules for a pension fund) nor an error made by some other person involved in the trust at a distance (such as the employer in relation to an occupational pension scheme).[108] Therefore, it was held in *Smithson v Hamilton*[109] that if a scheme rule in a pension trust fund failed to account for proper actuarial calculations, then that was not the fault of the trustees.[110] In such circumstances the proper remedy would not be to set aside the entire scheme under the *Pitt v Holt* principle, but rather to seek a rectification of the trust instrument.[111]

101 *Green v Cobham* [2002] STC 820.
102 *Stannard v Fisons Pension Trust Ltd* [1991] PLR 225.
103 *Ibid.*
104 *Green v Cobham* [2002] STC 820; *Burrell v Burrell* [2005] EWHC 245.
105 *Abacus Trust Company (Isle of Man) v Barr* [2003] 2 WLR 1362.
106 [2006] EWHC 999 (Ch), para [72].
107 [1984] Ch 100.
108 *Smithson v Hamilton* [2008] 1 All ER 1216, Park J.
109 *Ibid.*
110 *Ibid.*
111 *Ibid.*

8.3.14 Mistake in the exercise of a trustee's powers

A trustee's decision may be set aside on grounds of mistake. Lord Walker restated the principles relating to mistake in the Supreme Court in *Pitt v Holt* (and so as to disagree, on this point alone, with the judgment of Lloyd LJ in the Court of Appeal in *Pitt v Holt*). Lord Walker held that the exercise of a power will be set aside on grounds of mistake if it would be unconscionable to leave that mistake uncorrected, and if the nature and significance of the mistake required that form of action. As his lordship held:

> The court cannot decide the issue of what is unconscionable by an elaborate set of rules. It must consider in the round the existence of a distinct mistake (as compared with total ignorance or disappointed expectations), its degree of centrality to the transaction in question and the seriousness of its consequences, and make an evaluative judgment whether it would be unconscionable, or unjust, to leave the mistake uncorrected.

A mistake of this sort would be something different from inadvertence, misprediction of future facts, or mere ignorance. However, forgetfulness, inadvertence and ignorance could of course lead to such a state of mind that a significant mistake could occur.

8.4 THE TRUSTEES' DUTY TO PROVIDE INFORMATION AND TO ACCOUNT TO THE BENEFICIARIES

8.4.1 Introduction

An obsession with secrecy is a very English trait; particularly when it relates to an individual's financial affairs. This applies in relation to trusts. Trustees are required to maintain the confidentiality of their beneficiaries. The traditional English view is that access to information is limited to those with proprietary rights in the trust property to information relating specifically to the property in which they have rights.[112] Importantly, and perhaps surprisingly, there is no general obligation for the trustees to give full information to anyone who considers themselves to be entitled to an equitable interest under the trust.[113] An alternative approach has been mooted by the Privy Council which suggests that the court has a general discretion to supervise trusts and consequently to order access to information in favour of an applicant whenever it sees fit.[114] This alternative approach does not necessarily mean that trustees will be required to make information generally available to the beneficiaries because that could be interpreted so as to maintain the traditional, restrictive approach.

Even between beneficiaries of the same trust there may be confidentiality. For example, the affairs of the life tenant may not be disclosed to the remainder beneficiaries. The life tenant may want to keep their financial affairs secret from other beneficiaries (who might be members of their extended family or strangers). If the trust is the life tenant's only source of income, for example, then they may not want the other beneficiaries to know how much money they have. This also means that those other beneficiaries will not know how much income is being generated for that life tenant. They may also not be informed as to the precise investment strategies which the trustees are following, whether they are risky or safe, and so forth. What that

---

112 *O'Rourke v Darbishire* [1920] AC 581; *Re Londonderry* [1965] Ch 918.
113 *Re Londonderry* [1965] Ch 918; although see now *Schmidt v Rosewood Trust Ltd* [2003] 2 WLR 1442.
114 *Schmidt v Rosewood Trust Ltd* [2003] 2 WLR 1442.

means in practice is that it is very difficult for the remainder beneficiaries to know whether or not there has been any breach of trust in relation to the management of their arrangements. A core part of any trustee's duties is the obligation to account to the beneficiaries. Moreover, the entire logic of express trusts law – as expressed in the beneficiary principle in Chapter 4 – is that the trustees are ultimately held to account by there being beneficiaries who can sue them if there is any suspected breach of trust. However, the beneficiaries will not be able to sue the trustees if they are not entitled to receive any information about the operation of some parts of the trust. The rules of civil procedure in England and Wales will prevent the beneficiaries from going on 'fishing expeditions', i.e. starting litigation in the hope that they might find out something which would sustain a claim against the trustees. The beneficiaries are required to have sufficient information to begin such an action. If the trustees are not obliged to give them any information then there is little chance of litigation being commended.

There is, therefore, clearly a tension between the need for confidentiality about some aspects of the trust's operation and the ability of the beneficiaries to hold the trustees to account. This chapter considers the general duties of the trustees to give information and their power to withhold information, the duty to account for their actions as trustees, and the extent of their duties to account for the day-to-day management of the trust.

8.4.2 The limited duty to give general information as to the existence and nature of the trust

The trustees are required to inform the beneficiaries (assuming they are of sound mind and over the age of 18) that there is a trust in existence and they are required to inform the beneficiaries of the terms of a trust.[115] The trustees are not necessarily required to explain to the beneficiaries what those interests mean.[116] So, from the outset, the beneficiaries may be required to take legal advice just to understand the terms of their trust. Consequently, from the outset, the position of the beneficiaries and the position of the trustees may be set in opposition to one another. The trustees may take the view that they do not want the burden or the legal responsibility for explaining the meaning of the trust to the beneficiaries: any mistake might give rise to an obligation to compensate the beneficiaries.[117] If some beneficiaries cannot be found, then the trustees are only obliged to make reasonable efforts to locate and inform them.[118]

8.4.3 The limited duty to disclose trust documents to those with a proprietary interest under the trust

No right of access to trust documents if the trust instrument precludes such access

The beneficiaries will have no right to see or to possess copies of trust documents if the trust instrument expressly precludes such access.[119] The Privy Council in *Schmidt v Rosewood*[120] held that the court has an inherent discretion to order access to information, so it

---

115 *Hawkesley v May* [1956] 1 QB 304.
116 *Hamar v Pensions Ombudsman* [1996] PLR 1, 10–11.
117 *Miller v Stapleton* [1996] 2 All ER 449, 463.
118 *Re Hay's Settlement Trusts* [1982] 1 WLR 202.
119 *Tierney v King* [1983] 2 Qd R 580; *Hartigan Nominees v Rydge* (1992) 29 NSWLR 405, 446.
120 [2003] 2 WLR 1442.

unclear whether or not access to information might be ordered in the future where the trust instrument precludes it. It is suggested that in ordinary circumstances the courts are likely to uphold the settlor's wishes, unless they are creating intractable problems in the operation of the trust. If there were intractable problems then the parties may seek a variation of the terms of the trust as discussed in Chapter 10.

The traditional approach under English law: Access is based on ownership

Let us assume that there is no provision in the trust instrument dealing with the rights of beneficiaries to access information. The general duty of trustees to disclose trust documents to beneficiaries was expressed by Lord Wrenbury in *O'Rourke v Darbishire* in the following terms:[121]

> [A beneficiary] is entitled to see all the trust documents because they are trust documents and because he is a beneficiary. They are in a sense his own. Action or no action, he is entitled to access to them.

Therefore, at first blush, a beneficiary is entitled to see trust documents because the beneficiary has an equitable proprietary interest in the trust property and because the trust documents are part of the trust property. However, there are three problems in the application of this principle. First, it is not clear who will be a beneficiary in this context. For example, the objects of a class of objects of a discretionary trust may not be considered to be 'beneficiaries' in this context because they do not own any property until it has been appointed to them, as considered in section 8.4.5 below. Second, the remainder beneficiaries do not have property rights in the life tenant's income from the trust and therefore access to documents relating specifically to the income portion of the trust may not be available to them. Where the trust is more complex even than that, and the beneficial class is divided between many different people, then there may be several different 'cells' within the trust property where information is available only to beneficiaries with a right in that cell and not to beneficiaries with interests in any other. Third, it is not clear what will constitute 'trust documents' as opposed to other types of document in this context, as considered at 8.4.4 below.

The secretive approach to the provision of information prompted North J to hold that it may be the case then that one beneficiary's desire for information may be disadvantageous to the other beneficiaries.[122] This is the opposite of transparency. It becomes impossible for beneficiaries to know whether they are being treated well or badly if they have no information. That information is made available to other beneficiaries does not mean that the trustees are obliged to change their minds. If the trustees did change their minds after information became generally available then that would suggest that their first decision was incorrect.

The trustees are not required to give reasons for their discretionary decisions

While beneficiaries are entitled to see trust documents, there are many documents which are significant to the rights of beneficiaries which they may not access. Documents prepared by

---

121 *O'Rourke v Darbishire* [1920] AC 581, 626.
122 *Re Cowin* (1886) 33 Ch D 179, 197, *per* North J.

the trustees when making their decisions (for example, in discretionary trusts or relating to the exercise of powers) are not ordinarily considered to be trust documents and therefore are not ordinarily disclosed to the beneficiaries. The beneficiaries do not own these documents. Nevertheless they are important. Consequently, we can see how the *O'Rourke* approach can lead to restrictive applications of the law.

In the important decision of the Court of Appeal in *Re Londonderry*[123] the claimant sought copies of documents from the trustees in relation to a trust. The claimant was one of a class of beneficiaries who were the objects of a power of appointment over the trust's income. The trust capital had been exhausted in appointing property to the defendant. The claimant wanted this information so that he could find out why the power of appointment had been exercised in favour of the defendant such that there was no capital left. The Court of Appeal (in particular Harman LJ) held that trustees were not obliged to give reasons for their decisions. Following on from the idea in *O'Rourke v Derbyshire* that a beneficiary is entitled to documents relating to a part of the trust over which one has property rights, Harman LJ held:[124]

> If the [beneficiary] is allowed to examine [the minutes and agendas of trustees meetings], she will know at once the very matters which the trustees are not bound to disclose to her, namely, their motives and reasons. Trustees who wish to preserve their rights in this respect must either commit nothing to paper or destroy everything from meeting to meeting. . . .

Therefore, his lordship's opinion was based on the idea that trustees would need to destroy minutes of meetings and so forth so as to protect themselves from actions for breach of trust. (The other approach would be that the trustees should be required to make their reasoning plain and not to perform unjustifiable acts which are in breach of trust. However, that is not the English way.) Harman LJ continued, and it should be remembered that after *O'Rourke* it would ordinarily be the case that beneficiaries are entitled to see trust documents because they are the owners of those documents:[125]

> I would hold that, even if documents of this type [e.g. minutes of trustees' decisions as to their decisions] ought properly to be described as trust documents, they are protected for the special reason which protects the trustees' deliberations on a discretionary matter from disclosure. If necessary, I hold that this principle overrides the ordinary rule [i.e. in *O'Rourke*]. This is in my judgment no less in the true interest of the beneficiary than of the trustees. Again, if one of the trustees commits to paper his suggestions and circulates them among his co-trustees, or if inquiries are made in writing as to the circumstances of a member of the class, I decline to hold that such documents are trust documents the property of the beneficiaries. In my opinion such documents are not trust documents in the proper sense at all. On the other hand, if the solicitor advising the trustees commits to paper an aide-mémoire summarising the state of the fund or of the family and reminding the trustees of past distributions and future possibilities, I think that must be a document which any beneficiary must be at liberty to inspect . . . I cannot think that

---

123 [1964] 3 All ER 855.
124 *Ibid* at 860.
125 *Ibid* at 860.

communications passing between individual trustees and appointors are documents in which beneficiaries have a proprietary right.

The legal position after *Re Londonderry* is that the trustees are entitled to have the reasons for their decisions – especially in relation to discretionary trusts and powers – withheld from the beneficiaries. All documents recording their views (for example, the minutes or recording of meetings) should be withheld from the beneficiaries. The beneficiaries are entitled to information about the performance of the trust (e.g. in the form of annual accounts) but not about the reasons why the trustees acted as they did. It is different, however, if a solicitor prepares a document explaining the rights of the parties. The only distinction between a trustee's written reasons for making a decision circulated to the other trustees and a solicitor's explanation of the legal position of the trust, is that the trustee is not necessarily a professional expressing a professional view, but rather a fiduciary explaining her own thinking to her fellow trustees. That is a narrow distinction without any clear difference. After all, the solicitor and the trustee both owe fiduciary duties to all of the trustees to be able to justify their decisions and so forth.

The particular focus which Harman LJ has is on the ability of the trustees to think freely without having their ideas held against them. This is true of every university committee meeting I have ever attended. It is always said at the start of such meetings that all discussion is confidential. The reason is so that people can speak freely without any fear of comeback. However, it has always occurred to me that people should not voice opinions which are so outrageous or unacceptable if they think they will lead to them being sued successfully after the event. The reason for confidentiality here is that some people may stay silent because they wish to avoid the embarrassment of their views being generally known to people outside the meeting (especially to the students).[126] It is difficult to see why the feelings of trustees should be protected in the same way, given that they bear fiduciary duties to reach justifiable, conscionable decisions in the interests of the beneficiaries.

So, if a trustee were to voice an unacceptable opinion – such as 'I don't think we should advance any money to Jenkins because I hate his wife: she belongs to the wrong religion' – then that would be an inappropriate ground for denying Jenkins property from the trust and the trustee's inappropriate opinion and reasoning ought to be held against them. Their bigotry ought not to be protected behind a cloak of silence; they ought not to hold those views, and they ought not to base their fiduciary decisions on them. If another trustee were to voice a potentially unpopular opinion but one which was genuinely held – such as 'I think we should give money to Blenkinsopp because she is a young woman and she requires greater support in her career than a well-educated, wealthy man like Jenkins' – then that would not open that trustee up to a successful legal action for breach of trust because that is a rational point of view, even if other trustees and Jenkins may disagree with it. There is no reason to keep the second trustee's views confidential because there is nothing unlawful or actionable in them. That trustee should be required to stand by their view of the proper management of the trust. The first trustee should clearly be ashamed of themselves and it is difficult to see why their

---

126 It is usually when someone wants to say something outrageous that student representatives are asked to leave the room. Occasionally it is because there is something genuinely confidential about the content of exams or the affairs of individual university employees.

appalling views should be protected from the gaze of the beneficiaries. The beneficiaries would have a right to know that the trustees were making their decisions on the basis of bigotry not rationality.

There is a metaphor for granting transparency to these sorts of meetings which I rather like: it is referred to as 'the disinfectant properties of daylight'. That means, if things are made visible then everyone tends to behave themselves better. If people prefer to misbehave in the darkness then, especially when they are acting as trustees, we might ask why they should be allowed to misbehave at all.[127]

A different analysis: Schmidt v Rosewood Trust Ltd

The Privy Council in *Schmidt v Rosewood Trust Ltd*[128] suggested an alternative approach to understanding which beneficiaries are entitled to access to the trust documents. Rather than consider the beneficiary as being entitled on the basis of a proprietary interest, it was suggested instead that the power to order access to information is based on the court's inherent jurisdiction to assume control of a trust and to supervise the actions of the trustees. Therefore, the court should be permitted to order access to information wherever appropriate. What this approach does not help with is in telling us which beneficiaries are entitled to access to which sorts of information and which beneficiaries are not so entitled. All the *Schmidt v Rosewood Trust Ltd* approach suggests is that one can apply to the court for an order seeking disclosure and that the court has a discretion as to which beneficiaries will be entitled to disclosure and which will not. It does not tell us which types of beneficiary have an entitlement to peruse trust documents as of right.

By contrast with the decision in *O'Rourke v Darbishire*, the more recent decision of the Privy Council in *Schmidt v Rosewood Trust Ltd*[129] has suggested that there is no inherent right to disclosure of trust documents. As Lord Walker expressed this approach:

> no beneficiary . . . has any entitlement as of right to disclosure of anything which can plausibly be described as a trust document. Especially when there are issues as to personal or commercial confidentiality, the court may have to balance the competing interests of different beneficiaries, the trustees themselves, and third parties. Disclosure may have to be limited and safeguards may have to be put in place.[130]

So, Lord Walker was taking both a progressive and a regressive approach. This approach is progressive in the sense that a court has the power to order access to any document, whether or not the applicant owns it through their beneficial interest in the trust. This could be a relief for the objects of discretionary trusts and mere powers, for example. However, this approach may be regressive in the sense that no beneficiaries now have any *right* to trust documents at all. Instead, they must apply to the court and hope for the best.

---

127 There is a time and a place for misbehaving in the darkness, of course: the future of the human race literally depends upon it.
128 [2003] 2 WLR 1442.
129 [2003] 2 WLR 1442.
130 *Ibid*, 1463.

8.4.4 Which documents constitute trust documents?

Lord Wrenbury took the approach in *O'Rourke v Darbishire*, as was outlined above, that a beneficiary 'has a right of access to the documents which he desires to inspect upon what has been called in the judgments in this case a proprietary right'.[131] The reason for permitting beneficiaries access to documents is 'because they are trust documents, and because he is a beneficiary. They are, in this sense, his own.'[132] Two questions arise. First, who will be a beneficiary in this context? Second, what constitutes a 'trust document' in this context?

As discussed above in relation to *Re Londonderry*, the trust documents in a discretionary trust do not include documents relating to the basis on which the trustees have made their decisions as to the use of their discretion.[133] Otherwise, the beneficiaries are entitled to see documents relating to the day-to-day management of the trust (but not reasons for making decisions): thus, a beneficiary is entitled to see all documents held by the trustee which relate to the creation of the trust,[134] receipts as to payments made by the trustees or on their behalf,[135] or advice received from counsel.[136] So, the beneficiaries can know how much money is in the trust and what money has been spent on ordinary expenses, but not the reasons why appointments have been made to Blenkinsopp but not Jenkins.

8.4.5 Who constitutes a 'beneficiary' with a right to access to information?

If access to information about the trust comes as a right for the beneficiaries, then that raises a question about who will constitute a 'beneficiary'. Under discretionary trusts, the class of objects do not acquire vested property rights in any trust property until the trustees decide to appoint that property to them. Should that be the moment when that person acquires rights to trust property and thus access to information? What would that mean for the other members of the class of objects: would they never have property rights, on this model, and would they consequently never acquire rights to information? Alternatively, it was said in Chapter 4, that the objects of a discretionary trust can combine under the principle in *Saunders v Vautier* so as to direct the trustees how to deal with the trust property, but only if they constitute the only possible objects of that class and if the trust instrument requires that all of the property is distributed among that class (and not used for any other purpose). In such a situation, could we say that the objects of such a discretionary trust do have property rights under *Saunders v Vautier*? By extension, would no other objects or no objects of a mere power ever acquire rights to such information? If not, how could they ever enforce their rights against the trustees? If the purpose of this area of law is to ensure that the trustees are held to account, then it would appear to be preferable for a wide range of people to have a right to access information. The logic of trusts law threatens to collapse unless the beneficiaries have access to the necessary information. This idea is pursued below in section 8.4.7 in relation to *Breakspear v Ackland*.[137]

---

131 [1920] AC 581.
132 *Ibid.*
133 *Re Londonderry* [1965] Ch 918, *per* Danckwerts LJ.
134 *Ex p Houldsworth* (1838) 4 Bing NC 386.
135 *Clarke v Ormonde* (1821) Jac 108.
136 *Devaynes v Robinson* (1855) 20 Beav 42.
137 [2008] 3 WLR 698.

8.4.6 No obligation on trustees to give reasons for their decisions

As was made clear in *Re Londonderry*,[138] trustees are required to give accounts and to provide details about the outcomes of their decisions about the management of the trust. So, the beneficiaries are entitled to be informed of the outcome of a decision but not the reasons for that decision.[139] Consequently, the trustees may be required to disclose the material on which they based their decision (such as the accounts and the terms of the trust), but they are not obliged to divulge their reasoning in reaching the decision that they did. As a result, the trustees may not be obliged to disclose any material on which they based their decision if that would reveal the reasoning behind their decision.[140] If reasons are given then the court will consider their adequacy.[141] There are occasions on which the courts have set aside the trustees' decision or have required reasons to be given.[142] For example, in *Re Beloved Wilkes Charity*[143] the trustees selected a person to be benefited under a trust who did not fall within the terms of the class (because he lived in the wrong parish). It emerged that the reason for their choice was that a minister had asked them to advance money to his brother, and so they had done so. Lord Truro set aside the trustees' selection on the basis that it was done solely to benefit a person who had a nexus to the trustee and therefore was not a proper exercise of that power.

8.4.7 No obligation to disclose confidential information

It is common for settlors to prepare a letter of wishes which instructs the trustees (outside the terms of the trust instrument) how they would like the trustees to exercise their powers in practice. It may be, for example, that the settlor cannot put particular terms in the trust instrument for tax reasons, and therefore his lawyers would draft the trust appropriately but allow the settlor to write a letter which tells the trustees how to behave in practice. The question arises: should the beneficiaries be entitled to see these sorts of documents? In New South Wales, the majority of the court followed the decision in *Re Londonderry's Settlement*[144] in holding that the memorandum itself need not be shown to the beneficiary because it related to the exercise of the trustees' discretion.[145] Consequently, there is an implied obligation of confidentiality between trustee and settlor which would prevent the trustees from being obliged to disclose any such information. The rationale given by the Court of Appeal in *Re Londonderry* is that an obligation to make disclosure to the members of a family, for example, might cause irreparable harm to family relations if the settlor had sought to benefit some family members at the expense of others.[146] Similarly, correspondence between the trustees and one or more of the beneficiaries may be considered to be confidential and so not to be capable of disclosure.[147] Lord Walker recognised in *Schmidt v Rosewood* that 'no beneficiary (least of all a discretionary object) has any entitlement as of right to disclosure of anything which

---

138 [1965] 2 WLR 229.
139 *Hartigan v Rydge* (1992) 29 NSWLR 405.
140 *Ibid*, 445, *per* Sheller JA.
141 *Klug v Klug* [1918] 2 Ch 67.
142 *Re Beloved Wilkes Charity* (1851) 3 Mac & G 440.
143 *Ibid*.
144 [1965] 2 WLR 229.
145 *Hartigan v Rydge* (1992) 29 NSWLR 405.
146 [1956] Ch 928, *per* Salmon LJ.
147 *Re Londonderry's Settlement* [1965] Ch 918.

can plausibly be described as a trust document . . . [e]specially when there are issues as to personal or commercial confidentiality'.[148] Therefore, English law is set against the disclosure of these sorts of documents.

The question of a beneficiary's right to disclosure of information arose again in *Breakspear v Ackland*[149] when a beneficiary sought disclosure of a settlor's 'letter of wishes'. Briggs J ordered disclosure of the letter of wishes on the facts of the case before him but, fascinatingly, he did so only after reading the letter of wishes for himself and without telling us what the letter of wishes said. So, it is difficult to know what exactly convinced his lordship that that was the correct thing to do in this instance. His lordship followed the principle in *Re Londonderry* to the effect that the exercise of a trustee's 'discretionary dispositive powers' remained 'inherently confidential'.[150] That means, the reasoning behind the trustees' decisions remains confidential, and therefore a letter of wishes which guided those decisions was similarly confidential. However, Briggs J did accept that there might be circumstances in which it would be in the best interests of the beneficiaries to make disclosure. Briggs J did identify the potential problem of beneficiaries wishing to bring actions against the trustees but being unable to do so without sufficient information. In particular, his lordship identified the weakness in the old idea that the beneficiaries can bring actions questioning the actions of the trustees given that litigation is so expensive. He did accept the benefits of confidentiality in cases where there are family illnesses and similarly personal circumstances at play, 'regardless of my own opinion'[151] that openness is otherwise preferable.[152] The point remains, as his lordship acknowledged, that unless the beneficiaries can know what is in these documents then it is impossible to know whether or not the trustees have performed their duties properly.

8.4.8 The duty to render accounts

One of the trustees' most significant duties is the duty to render accounts to the beneficiaries as to their management of the trust's affairs. The accounts are required to give an accurate record of the trustees' management of the trust together with supporting documentation such as receipts.[153] This information must include, at the beneficiary's request, a valuation of the trust fund.[154] The beneficiaries are also entitled to have such trusts accounts and documents provided to their accountants[155] or legal advisors,[156] except for those sorts of documents to which those beneficiaries have no entitlement. This duty cannot be excluded by the trust instrument because it is one of the core obligations of trusteeship.[157]

---

148 *Ibid*, 1463–64.
149 [2008] 3 WLR 698.
150 *Ibid*, 707.
151 [2008] 3 WLR 698, 717.
152 *Ibid*, 717.
153 *Springett v Dashwood* (1860) 2 Giff 521.
154 *Armitage v Nurse* [1998] Ch 241, 261.
155 *Schmidt v Rosewood Trust Ltd* [2003] 2 WLR 1442.
156 *Hawkesley v May* [1956] 1 QB 304.
157 *Armitage v Nurse* [1998] Ch 241, 253, *per* Millett LJ.

8.4.9 Fiduciary duties in relation to Chinese walls and confidential information

One particular context in which this issue of the handling of confidential information by fiduciaries has become particularly important is in relation to so-called 'Chinese wall' arrangements. To give an example, where a merger or takeover is due to take place between two companies, there will be a period when the parties are involved in delicate negotiations in which their professional advisors (solicitors, accountants and so forth) will have sensitive information about their clients' businesses, negotiating position and so forth. Clearly, that information needs to be kept confidential. Oddly, there is no restriction on one law firm, for example, advising both parties to such a transaction. However, what that law firm needs to do is to put arrangements in place so that the lawyers advising one party to the transaction do not transfer confidential information to lawyers in the same firm working for the other side. The teams of lawyers advising each side will be divided into two. The firm will usually put the two teams of lawyers in different buildings, they will program their electronic keys so that each of them cannot enter the office space, photocopiers, printers, computer servers or other facilities of the other team. This is known as a 'Chinese wall' arrangement. In *Bolkiah v KPMG*[158] an accountancy firm failed to put appropriate systems in place, and some junior personnel moved between teams and the control of information was insufficiently secure. Lord Millett held that the duty of a fiduciary (as with an accountancy firm in such a transaction) in a Chinese wall arrangement is not to do their best to maintain their clients' confidential information but rather it is an absolute duty to maintain that confidence. Therefore, any failure in their systems, as here, automatically led to the fiduciary being liable to account to the beneficiary for their loss.

8.5 LIMITATION OF THE TRUSTEES' DUTIES

8.5.1 The validity of exclusion of liability clauses under case law

Introduction

In general terms, the trustees of an express trust may limit, or even exclude completely, their liability for breach of trust by means of a provision to that effect in the trust instrument. Strictly, it is the settlor who limits their liability in the trust instrument; although in practice it is the settlor's advisors (who will often be the trustees) who will insist upon, and also draft, this clause. The settlor's intention to limit the trustee's liability must be clear. In *Wight v Olswang (No 2)*[159] there were contradictory provisions in the trust instrument and therefore there was no clear intention to exclude the trustees' liability and therefore the trustees were held to be liable for a loss caused by their breach of trust. Such a provision is known as a 'limitation of liability' clause if it reduces the trustees' potential liability, or as an 'exclusion of liability' clause if it provides that the trustees bear no liabilities at all. English trusts law will not permit trustees to exclude their liabilities for dishonesty. However, as was held in the Court of Appeal in *Armitage v Nurse*,[160] the trustees may have their liabilities excluded for

---

158 [1999] 2 AC 222.
159 (1999/2000) 2 ITELR 689.
160 [1998] Ch 241.

everything including 'gross negligence'. The desirability of this rule has been doubted more recently by the Privy Council in *Spread Trustee v Hutcheson*.[161]

The debate about the desirability of the ability to exclude liability

In practice, it is the trustees who will want to have exclusion of liability clauses inserted into the trust instrument because it is the trustees who benefit from them. It is very undesirable for the beneficiaries because an effective exclusion of liability clause means that the beneficiaries may not sue the trustees for any loss caused by a breach of trust which they commit, provided that their breach of trust was not dishonest. There is a clear dividing line of opinion here. On the one hand, it is said that professional people will only agree to act as trustees if they can know that their liabilities for breach of trust are limited. This is said to make the law of trusts as commercially attractive as contract law by limiting the liabilities of professional trustees. (Such exclusion of liability provisions in trust instruments, however, take effect as equitable provisions and not as contractual provisions.[162]) Professional trustees would say that they only agree to act as trustees on the basis that they can limit their liabilities in this way, and that otherwise they would simply refuse to act in the first place.

On the other hand, it is said that to be a trustee involves a greater level of responsibility than an ordinary party to an ordinary contract because trustees are fiduciaries who are required to act in good conscience. Moreover, it is said that the beneficiaries do not have recourse to compensation in the presence of an exclusion of liability clause if the trustees are careless or negligent, even though cases like *Speight v Gaunt* and the Trustee Act 2000 impose duties of care and skill on trustees. There is clearly an irony in the fact that these professional trustees are charging fees for their professional skill, when at the same time they refuse to accept liability for being grossly negligent. By contrast, an inexpert trustee who has no professional expertise and who would not know to insist on a limitation of liability clause in her trust instrument, would be liable in full for even an act of mild carelessness when a professional would not be liable at all. A professional trustee would also be insured against actions of this sort and therefore the beneficiaries could recover their loss that way. It could be said that a professional trustee should be held to a higher standard than an inexpert trustee. To require merely that the trustee must be honest is to place the bar very low indeed on the standard of behaviour which a professional should attain when acting as a trustee. This area of law appears to undercut completely the purpose of basing trusts law on good conscience. In other areas of law related to trusts – such as trustees of pension funds and trustees of unit trusts (a very important kind of mutual investment fund in the UK) – statute prohibits trustees from excluding their legal and regulatory liabilities at all. Therefore, mainstream trusts law appears to be a little old-fashioned in this regard.

There is an ugly paradox in this area of law. A professional trustee, who purports to have expertise in this field and who will charge fees for their work, will know to insist that an exclusion of liability clause is inserted in the trust instrument so that, if she can only prevent herself from actually being dishonest, she will bear no liability even for grossly negligent breaches of trust. By contrast, a person without any professional expertise at all, who knows nothing of exclusion of liability clauses and who does their diligent best to serve the interests

---

161 [2011] UKPC 13.

162 *Re Duke of Norfolk Settlement Trusts* [1982] Ch 61, 77.

of the trust, may face financial ruin if they commit a technical breach of trust by accident and thus cause a loss to the trust. This area of the law appears to be iniquitous in that context. Perhaps the approach of the Privy Council in *Spread Trustee v Hutcheson* indicates the future for this area of law, as is discussed below.

The decision in Armitage v Nurse

The most significant case in this area is the decision of the Court of Appeal in *Armitage v Nurse*.[163] It was held that a clause excluding a trustee's personal liability even for gross negligence would be valid. Therefore, the trustee could be grossly negligent when causing a loss to the beneficiary and yet the trustee would not be liable for the loss caused by that breach of trust because of the exclusion of liability clause. The only type of exclusion of liability clause that would not be valid would be a clause which purported to exclude the trustee's liability for losses caused by her own dishonesty. Therefore, if a trustee acted dishonestly and thereby caused a loss to the beneficiaries, then that trustee would not be permitted to rely on an exclusion of liability clause to escape liability. In that case, the beneficiary was a 17-year-old girl who relied upon the income from the farm which was held on trust by the trustees.

The trustees were grossly negligent in their operation of the farm and caused extensive loss to that beneficiary. It was held that, because the trust instrument contained a clause which purported to exclude the trustees' liability for any loss caused by their gross negligence, then the trustees were not liable for the loss which they had caused to this girl. More specifically, the exclusion of liability clause in that settlement provided that the trustees would not be liable for any loss or damage caused to the trust fund unless it was caused by any trustee's 'own actual fraud'. In the words of Millett LJ,[164] a trustee will not be liable for breach of trust if there is an exclusion of liability clause 'no matter how indolent, imprudent, lacking in diligence, negligent or wilful he may have been, so long as he had not acted dishonestly'. It must be said that this appears on its face to be an unattractive rule which may promote carelessness among professional trustees. Nevertheless, it was held in *Armitage v Nurse* that the older case of *Wilkins v Hogg*[165] had established the principle that a settlor was able to limit the liabilities of her trustees if she so wished and provided that such an intention to exclude the trustees' liabilities was set out in the trust instrument.[166] An exclusion of liability clause will be interpreted so as to give that clause its natural meaning, but the settlor's intention to exclude the trustees' liabilities must nevertheless be plain.[167]

There is a spectrum of culpability starting from mere carelessness, progressing upwards in turn through negligence, gross negligence, recklessness and into dishonesty and fraud. What we know for sure is that trustees can escape liability for being grossly negligent, but that they cannot escape liability for being dishonest or fraudulent. That leaves the category of 'recklessness' in between as an unknown quantity on the basis of this decision (although there are other decisions, below, which assume it can be excluded too). Because the category of recklessness is unaccounted for by Millett LJ, many of my examination papers include trust instruments which purport to exclude liability for recklessness: that is, fault lying

---

163 [1998] Ch 241.
164 Followed in *Barraclough v Mell* [2005] EWHC 3387 (Ch), [90].
165 (1861) 31 LJ Ch 41.
166 *Armitage v Nurse* [1998] Ch 241, 255.
167 *Ibid.*

between gross negligence and dishonesty. Students are expected to discuss the desirability or undesirability of extending the *Armitage* principle to cases of recklessness. In *Barraclough v Mell*[168] there was a clause in a will trust which provided that the trustee's liability for breach of trust was to be excluded even when the trustee was 'not caring whether or not [his act] was wrongful', a provision that was close to recklessness. It was accepted that this provision would be enforceable without considering whether or not it fell outside *Armitage v Nurse*.

What Millett LJ did hold was that 'wilful default' on the part of the trustee, including a 'reckless indifference' to a risk of loss, might not be capable of being excluded by an exclusion of liability clause. What is important here is that there must be something about the trustee's actions which are 'wilful', deliberate or intentional. However, that is not the end of the matter because, as Millett LJ held, 'if [the trustee] consciously takes the risk in good faith and with the best intentions, honestly believing that the risk is one which ought to be taken in the interests of the beneficiaries, there is no reason why he should not be protected by an exemption clause which excludes liability for wilful default'. Consequently, even wilful default will not cause liability to be incurred if the foolish trustee thought they were acting in the best interests of the beneficiaries. By contrast, Lord Clarke considered in the Privy Council in *Spread Trustee Company Ltd v Hutcheson* that a trustee may not exclude their liability for wilful default.[169]

Practical implementations of the Armitage v Nurse *principle*

A surprising outcome of the principle in *Armitage v Nurse* is that a trustee will not be liable for breach of trust if she committed that breach of trust intentionally but not dishonestly. So, if a trustee, for example, chose to invest in Greek company shares when the trust instrument expressly forbade such an investment, and if that investment caused loss to the trust, then the trustee would not be liable for breach of trust if there was an exclusion of liability clause in the trust instrument. That would be the case provided that the trustee honestly believed that investment in those Greek shares would have been for the benefit of the trust (perhaps because they promised a higher return than other shares). This analysis is supported by the decision in *Woodland-Ferrari v UCL Group Retirement Benefits Scheme*[170] where two trustees of a pension fund committed breaches of trust causing a shortfall in that fund (between the amount of money held and the amount needed to meet the pensioners' entitlements) of approximately £870,000. The trustees claimed to be entitled to rely on an exclusion of liability clause contained in the trust instrument. It was held that no dishonesty had been proven even though the trustees had invested in shares in which they themselves had personal interests. (That conflict of interest could have been considered to be a reason for refusing to permit the exclusion of liability.)

Significantly, the trustee may rely on an exclusion of liability clause even if the trustee is the solicitor who drafted that clause. So, in *Bogg v Raper*[171] the Court of Appeal upheld a clause which excluded the trustees' liability for 'any loss' provided that they acted in good faith. The Court of Appeal rejected the argument that the trustees were the solicitors and accountants to the trust and as such that they should not be allowed to rely on a clause in the trust instrument which they had drafted and inserted themselves. (The rationale is that the trust is notionally created by the settlor, even if it is drafted by the lawyers.) Even

---

168 [2005] EWHC 3387 (Ch).
169 [2011] UKPC 13, [2012] 1 All ER 251 at [55].
170 [2003] Ch 115.
171 (1998/99) 1 ITELR 267.

where the exclusion of liability clause purports to exclude liability for anything, ostensibly even dishonesty, then in *Baker v JE Clark & Co (Transport) UK Ltd*[172] that clause was upheld because, on those facts, no bad faith or dishonesty could be proved.

Gross negligence in Spread Trustee Company Ltd v Hutcheson

The Privy Council has considered the law relating to the exclusion of liability of trustees in an appeal from Guernsey in *Spread Trustee Company Ltd v Hutcheson*[173] which related to a specific Guernsey statute. However, Lord Clarke did acknowledge that in English law liability could be excluded for gross negligence.[174] The Privy Council did acknowledge (as is the case) that English law does differentiate between the different categories of 'negligence' and 'gross negligence' in some contexts; whereas Millett LJ had considered gross negligence to be simply a type of negligence which was more than ordinarily negligent, and therefore merely a matter of degree but not a separate category of behaviour.

Interestingly, in an excellent dissenting judgment, Lady Hale observed that the Supreme Court has yet to consider *Armitage v Nurse*. She doubted that the law in England and Wales had always been clear about the treatment of grossly negligent breaches of trust, making the point that important earlier cases such as *Re City Fire and Equitable Insurance*[175] and *Re Trusts of Leeds City Brewery Debenture*[176] did not in fact consider the point whether or not trustees were entitled to exclude their liabilities. Therefore, *Armitage v Nurse* was treated by Lady Hale as being a decision which should be considered to be based on slighter authority than some people have thought. In a similarly forthright judgment, Lord Kerr held that if the aim of the concept of trusteeship is to appoint someone 'responsible' to manage trust property then holding them liable for gross negligence is 'entirely in keeping with that essential aim'.[177] This is, of course, entirely sensible. Lord Kerr reminded us that the claimant in *Armitage v Nurse* was a 17-year-old girl. He even reminds us that she is not simply a claimant but rather that she was a 17-year-old girl called Paula who suffered great loss as a result of the incompetence of the people in whom she was supposed to repose great faith that they would see to her well-being. Put like that, the decision in *Armitage v Nurse* does appear to be an opiate on the professionalism of trustees and consequently to be an undesirable decision which was too concerned with the commercial position of people who act as trustees in many trusts.

8.5.2 Disclaimer, release and extinguishment of powers

A trustee may disclaim their office.[178] That trustee will be prevented from acting once they have disclaimed their powers. Alternatively, the beneficiaries may agree to release the trustee from their obligations so that they are not liable for any subsequent breach of trust.[179]

---

172 [2006] EWCA Civ 464.
173 [2011] UKPC 13, [2012] 1 All ER 251.
174 Cf. Matthews, 1989 and *Midland Bank Trust Co (Jersey) Ltd v Federated Pension Services* [1995] JLR 352.
175 [1925] Ch 407.
176 [1925] Ch 532n.
177 *Ibid*, [180].
178 *Re Lord and Fullerton's Contract* [1986] 1 Ch 228, 233.
179 *Turner v Turner* (1880) 14 Ch D 829.

8.6 CONTROL OF THE TRUSTEES

8.6.1 Control of the trustees by the beneficiaries

The control of the trustees ordinarily takes place, further to the beneficiary principle discussed in Chapter 4,[180] by means of the beneficiaries bringing the trustees to court alleging a breach of trust, compelling the trustees to obey the terms of the trust by doing an act or refraining from an act. The court's ability to control the trustees will depend upon the precise nature of their obligation: whether it is a trust or a power, and whether it is a personal power or a fiduciary power. Trustees are required to consider the exercise of trust powers: they cannot exercise them entirely capriciously, unlike personal powers where those concerns do not apply.[181]

8.6.2 Judicial review of the trustees by the court

There is a private law doctrine of judicial review of trustees' actions (which has nothing to do with the public law doctrine of judicial review). In limited circumstances, the court will consider the manner in which a decision (for example under a discretionary trust or a power of appointment) was reached by trustees and will decide whether or not it is enforceable. The court will not make the trustees' decision for them. That is, the court will not tell the trustees what to do; instead, it will assess whether or not the trustees have arrived at their decision in an appropriate way with integrity, fairness and honesty. Lord Truro set out the basis of this doctrine in *Re Beloved Wilkes's Charity*[182] to the effect that: 'the duty of supervision on the part of the Court will thus be confined to the question of the honesty, integrity, and fairness with which the deliberation has been conducted, and will not be extended to the accuracy of the conclusion arrived at, except in particular cases'. Therefore, the form of judicial review at issue here is concerned with the honesty, integrity and fairness of the trustees' decisions or actions, but the court will not change the trustees' decision.[183] If these elements are lacking, then the decision will be set aside and the trustees will be decide again in a more appropriate manner. It seems that the courts are more inclined to set aside trustees' actions where the beneficiaries are children and the powers being exercised are for the maintenance of those children, particularly where the trustees have acted capriciously in the exercise of their powers,[184] or have acted on the basis of manifestly improper reasons.[185] More generally, courts have interfered with a trustees' discretions in circumstances in which the trustees have failed to examine the contents of deeds before signing them,[186] or have acted in a way which was so unreasonable as to appear vexatious.[187]

8.6.3 Setting aside trustees' decisions and relevant considerations

The decision in *Pitt v Holt* relating to controlling trustees' decisions in relation to the relevance of their decisions was considered above in section 8.3.13 above.

180 *Morice v Bishop of Durham* (1805) 10 Ves 522.
181 *Re Hay's ST* [1981] 3 All ER 786.
182 (1851) 3 Mac & G 440, 448.
183 *Gisborne v Gisborne* (1877) 2 App Cas 300, 305, *per* Lord Cairns.
184 *Re Hodges* (1878) 7 Ch D 754.
185 *Klug v Klug* [1918] 2 Ch 67.
186 *Turner v Turner* (1978) 122 SJ 696.
187 *Re Chapman* (1895) 72 LT 66.

Chapter 9

The investment of trusts

CAPSULE SUMMARY

When a trust instrument is silent about a trustee's investment obligations, the Trustee Act 2000 creates a statutory code to supply those obligations. It replaced a very narrow statutory code which had existed previously. The Trustee Act 2000 empowers the trustees to invest as though they were the absolute owners of the trust fund (i.e. they are not to be considered to be constrained in their investment decisions). To balance out this principle, however, the trustees owe a statutory duty of care to the beneficiaries. Significantly, the trustees' duty is to act 'reasonably', which is a change from the ancient case law principle of acting 'prudently'. The trustees must balance several statutory obligations when making investment decisions: the duty to act with skill and care, the duty to act reasonably, the duty to take proper advice, and the duty to observe the two 'standard investment criteria' that the trustees must invest 'suitably' and that they must diversify the trust's investments.

The trustee's general duties of investment under the case law can be summarised in the following principles: to act prudently; to act fairly between beneficiaries; to achieve the best financial return for the beneficiaries. The best interests of the beneficiaries are generally taken to be their financial interests. Recent cases have held that the trustees should observe 'portfolio investment theory' in the form of diversifying their risks. Importantly, it has emerged that the trustees will be unlikely to be held liable for breach of trust if their investment decisions were in line with the investment decisions being taken by the trustees of similar trusts in the marketplace.

Regulation by the Financial Conduct Authority and money laundering regulation are important in relation to trustees who are investing in a professional capacity. The trustees of ordinary private trusts will generally avoid this form of statutory oversight. Other forms of trustees of investment funds – such as the trustees of pension funds and the trustees of unit trusts – are subject to their own statutory regulatory codes.

9.1 THE USE OF TRUSTS AS INVESTMENT VEHICLES

9.1.1 The scope of this chapter

The law on the investment of trusts is a fascinating field in its own right. It is comprised, for the law student, of a series of interesting puzzles. More generally, as part of the general study of equity and trusts law within a modern legal system, it raises questions about the way in which practical, economic activity like investment is regulated by a formal statutory regulator (through financial regulation) while also being overseen by a system of case law principles developed over the centuries (through trusts law). The attraction of a trust for an investor is that all of the hard work of making investment decisions and managing the trust property is left to the trustees, who may be professional investment advisors. The trustees are bound by the fiduciary and other duties which were considered in Chapter 8 and the potential liabilities for breach of trust which are considered in Chapters 18–20. The beneficiaries then have only to take the income made from these investments secure in the knowledge that trusts law will enable them to proceed against their trustees for any losses that are suffered. Trusts, principally in the form of pensions funds and unit trusts, remain the principal institutional investors in the UK stock market today. Consequently, these principles have great significance for the UK economy.

The law on the investment of trusts is comprised of four parts. First, the terms of the trust instrument (if there is one) will govern the obligations of the trustees when making investments. The answer to any question about the duties of the trustees is answered first by consulting the terms of the trust instrument. Second, if the trust instrument is silent about the trustees' obligations when making investments, then the Trustee Act 2000 supplies those obligations. The provisions of the Trustee Act 2000 can be displaced, however, by the terms of the trust. Third, the ancient case law principles (including the requirement that trustees must act 'prudently') may still be significant in interpreting the duties of the trustees, and they remain significant in practice (especially in pensions contexts) as governing the behaviour of professional trustees when making investment decisions. Fourth, there is a vast regulatory architecture governing investment activity by professional trustees, governing the investment of pension funds and governing the powers of the state to investigate money laundering. While these regulations are usually overlooked in trusts law courses, they are very important in practice and offer an interesting comparison with the approaches of trusts law in this area.

This chapter begins with an analysis of the Trustee Act 2000. The discussion then moves on to consider the case law principles governing the investment of trusts beyond the scope of the Act, and in particular the case law requirement that trustees act 'prudently' when making investments. The principal issue is when trustees may be held to be liable for breach of trust as a result of their investment decisions on behalf of the trust. In the modern world of risk-taking investment activity, the old standard of prudence is considered to be too cautious by many. Consequently, the Trustee Act 2000 was passed to modernise the powers of trustees when making investment decisions (where the trust instrument is silent on the matter) and to re-orientate their obligations around a standard of 'reasonableness' as opposed to 'prudence'. That a trustee is required to invest 'reasonably' in the circumstances may permit a more aggressive investment strategy than one who is required to be cautious. Much will depend on the nature of the trust. An analysis of the Trustee Act 2000 then occupies much of this chapter.

9.1.2 The significance of trusts as investment vehicles

The trust has been a very important vehicle for investment in England over the centuries. As was discussed in Chapter 2, the trust was the means by which rich English families passed their land, their chattels and their investments down through the generations. That entire social class from the upper middle classes through the aristocracy were reliant on trusts (and therefore on trusts law) to protect their wealth. In the modern world, trusts remain very important in this respect. Pension funds, which have replaced the state pension for large swathes of the population, are organised on trusts law principles (albeit with a statutory regulatory mechanism created to oversee them). Unit trusts, which are collective investment vehicles used by many private citizens to invest their capital, operate on trusts law principles and are regulated by a statutory regulator. Those two forms of trust remain two of the most significant types of investor in the UK economy (especially in London financial markets). Consequently, the trust is very important to our wealth in the 21st century and now covers a much wider range of people than even the traditional family trust did in its 18th and 19th century heyday.

The role of the trustees in traditional family trusts, who would have been professionals employed for this task, was to invest the trust property so as to maximise the return for the trust while also doing so in a way that was safe. The word which governed this process was 'prudence'. The trustees were required by the case law to act as a 'prudent person of business would act for someone for whom they felt morally bound to provide'. Prudence requires that investments are made safely but also that they are made wisely and with a view to profit. Therefore, the trustee has to balance out the need to make a profit with the need to be careful. This standard of prudence is still interpreted by most trustees today as requiring caution before everything else. The result is that trustees tend to invest cautiously.

9.1.3 The structure of finance law in the UK and its overlap with trusts law

It is not really possible to consider the law on investment of trusts without considering, at least in outline, the regulatory structure which governs all investment activity in the UK today. Finance law in the UK is a complex patchwork of regulation by the statutory Financial Conduct Authority ('FCA'), the Prudential Regulation Authority and the Financial Policy Committee within the Bank of England. Many trustees will fall to be regulated by the FCA (and may possibly be regulated by the other bodies also). Principally, it will be professionals who are acting as trustees as part of their professional activities who will fall within the regulatory net. The *FCA Handbook* (that is, its regulatory rulebooks and their guidance notes) provides many protections for investors beyond the scope of ordinary trusts law. There is the very important context of money laundering regulation which imposes onerous obligations on specified types of professional person to be careful about the source of funds deposited with them (for example into trust funds), and which may impose criminal liability on them if they fail to report suspicious transactions. As mentioned above, pension funds have their own regulatory scheme beyond the FCA regulatory net. (The detail of financial regulation of this sort is discussed in my book *The Law of Finance*.[1])

9.2 INTRODUCTION TO THE PRINCIPLES OF THE TRUSTEE ACT 2000

9.2.1 The scope of the Trustee Act 2000

The Trustee Act 2000 ('TA 2000') created two principal sets of rules: one relating to the appointment of agents, nominees and custodians by trustees, and the other relating to the investment of trust funds.[2] (The TA 2000 does not apply generally to pension funds[3] nor to authorised unit trusts,[4] both of which have statutory and regulatory regimes of their own.) The TA 2000 provides a form of statutory default setting for trusts which have no terms governing the responsibilities of their trustees when making investments. However, the TA 2000 does not create mandatory rules for all trusts; rather, the provisions of the Act can be excluded by an express provision in the trust instrument or by inference from the construction of any trust provisions.[5] To this effect, the TA 2000 provides that 'the duty of care [imposed on trustees by the Act][6] does not apply if or in so far as it appears from the

---

1 Hudson, 2013.
2 See generally Hicks, 2001.
3 TA 2000, s 36.
4 *Ibid*, s 37.
5 See eg *ibid*, Sched 1, para 7 and other provisions referred to in the text to follow.
6 Considered below at section 9.2.2.

trust instrument that the duty is not meant to apply'.[7] Thus, settlors have the freedom to create whatever arrangements they wish without the interference of mandatory, legal rules which might prohibit certain forms of action. The role of the TA 2000 is therefore to supply trusts provisions where otherwise there would be a gap in the trusts provisions.

9.2.2 Approaching a question on the investment of trusts

This section summarises the best approach to problem questions (and practical legal questions) relating to the investment of trusts. The first thing is to understand that there is a hierarchy of rules relating to trustees' investment duties: first, the terms of the trust instrument; second, the provisions of the TA 2000; third, the case law principles as aids to interpretation of the TA 2000; and, fourth, any regulatory obligations imposed on the trustees.[8] The trust instrument can provide for almost any investment obligations for the trustees, provided they are not illegal (such as 'the trustees shall buy and sell Class A narcotics'). We shall not consider that first element in this chapter very much because it is dependent entirely on the specific wording of any individual trust. However, if a problem question provides you with a quotation from a trust instrument, then you should begin by asking whether or not the terms of that particular trust provision have been breached and whether or not that should open up the trustees to liability for breach of trust. If the trust instrument is silent on the matter of investment, or if there is no trust instrument at all (as in *Paul v Constance*) then the TA 2000 supplies the necessary investment provisions. This chapter considers the provisions of the TA 2000 in detail, and any breach of those statutory provisions will open the trustees to liability for breach of trust. The old case law principles will still be important in interpreting those investment provisions. So, this chapter considers the case law principles and the scope for liability for breach of trust. After considering whether or not there has been a breach of trust under any of these grounds (trust instrument, TA 2000, or the case law), then the second thing to consider is whether or not the trustees have breached any of these obligations such that they can be liable for breach of trust (which is considered in detail in Chapter 18).

9.3 THE GENERAL POWER OF INVESTMENT UNDER THE TRUSTEE ACT 2000

9.3.1 The scope of the general power of investment

The provisions of the trust instrument take priority over any principles of the general law when interpreting the investment powers and duties of trustees. If the trust instrument is silent about trustee investment powers (perhaps because the people drafting the trust did not consider investment, or because their provisions failed to deal with a particular investment problem), or if there is no trust instrument at all (because the trust was declared verbally), then the TA 2000 supplies the investment powers and obligations of the trustees. This section considers the trustees' powers of investment under the TA 2000. These provisions apply

---

7 TA 2000, Sched 1, para 7.
8 If your course does not cover financial regulation, then you can overlook this element.

to trustees' powers of investment provided that there is nothing to the contrary in the trust instrument.[9] The Act provides that:[10]

> a trustee may make any kind of investment that he could make if he were absolutely entitled to the assets of the trust.

This provision means that the trustee can make any investment as if she was the outright owner of the property in the trust fund. Consequently, the trustee has no limitations, at this point, on the investment which she may choose to make. This power is referred to in the legislation as the 'general power of investment'.[11] This provision marked a great change in the law in this area because it liberated trustees to make whatever investment they consider reasonable, provided that they comply with the other provisions of the Act considered below. There do remain some restrictions in the Act on the power of trustees to make investments in land unless by way of loans secured on land (such as mortgages)[12] but otherwise the Act is much more permissive than the previous law.

9.3.2 The meaning of 'investment'

The term 'investment' is not defined for the purposes of the TA 2000 and the approach of trusts law to investment remains fairly primitive. Its meaning in the general law of trusts has changed over time from simply earning income[13] into increasing the value of capital assets[14] and also into the use of diversified investment portfolios (where risks are spread by investing in several different types of asset through investment managers).[15] In relation to financial regulation, however, the Financial Services and Markets Act 2000 ('FSMA 2000') defines 'investment' in much more complex terms by identifying the sorts of financial market activities which are regulated by the Financial Conduct Authority. There is no link between the TA 2000 and the FSMA 2000 for our purposes, although many trustees will be regulated by the FCA and other regulators (such as the Pensions Regulator in relation to pension trust funds) in practice. Therefore, the practice of investment trusts law involves expertise in financial regulation as well as general trusts law.

9.4 THE TRUSTEES' STANDARD OF CARE WHEN MAKING INVESTMENTS

9.4.1 The statutory duty of care

The TA 2000 provides for a statutory duty of care in s 1 which imposes a duty of 'such skill and care as is reasonable in the circumstances' in the following terms:[16]

---

9   *Ibid*, s 6(1).
10 TA 2000, s 3(1).
11 TA 2000, s 3(1).
12 TA 2000, s 3(3).
13 *Re Somerset* [1894] 1 Ch 231, 247.
14 *Cowan v Scargill* [1985] Ch 270, 287; *Harries v Church Commissioners* [1992] 1 WLR 1241, 1246.
15 See discussion below at section 9.6.4.
16 TA 2000, s 1(1).

(1) Whenever the duty under this subsection applied to a trustee, he must exercise such care and skill as is reasonable in the circumstances, having regard in particular –
   (a) to any special knowledge or experience that he has or holds himself out as having, and
   (b) if he acts as trustee in the course of a business or profession, to any special knowledge or experience that it is reasonable to expect of a person acting in the course of that kind of business or profession.
(2) In this Act the duty under subsection (1) is called 'the duty of care'.

The most significant change which is introduced to the law by this provision is the shift from the old standard of 'prudence' to this new standard of 'reasonable skill and care'. As to the precise nature of this 'duty of care',[17] its application and meaning are relative to the context in which the trustee is acting. Interestingly, then, the trustee does bear a duty of acting with skill and care, even though Millett LJ had held in *Armitage v Nurse* in 1998 that there was no such general duty imposed on trustees under the case law. That skill and care must be exercised in a way that 'reasonable in the circumstances'. This standard is considered in the next section.

When assessing what it is reasonable for the trustee to do in the circumstances, the court must consider the trustee's level of experience and any experience which the trustee claimed to have had. In subs (1) it should be noted that the courts are not limited to the matters set out in paras (a) and (b) when deciding the extent of the trustees' liabilities; instead they simply must have regard to those factors. In circumstances in which the trustee has, or holds herself out as having, any particular 'special knowledge or experience', then the trustee's duty of care will be interpreted in the light of those factors.[18] If the trustee pretends to have experience which she does not have, then she will be treated as though she did have that level of experience. If the duties of trustee are performed 'in the course of a business of profession', then the duty of care is applied in the context of any special knowledge or experience which such a professional could be expected to have.[19]

So, a trustee who is inexperienced in investment matters, or in the activities of the trust more generally, will only be held to the standard of competence which could be expected of someone with her level of experience. Suppose that I personally acted as trustee of a family trust (being a barrister, a former investment banker with experience of the corporate finance and derivatives markets, and a professor of law) with my uncle as my co-trustee. Let us suppose that my uncle was a former professional footballer and retired fireman with no experience of investment or legal matters. Suppose then that we invested the entire trust fund in very risky financial instruments which were linked to the price of oil in Iraq, the Greek currency and so forth, and that those investments suffered large losses. In assessing our level of reasonableness, it would clearly be appropriate to hold me to a higher standard than my uncle because I have a large amount of experience in financial and related matters, whereas my uncle has none. If it emerged in evidence that I had urged my uncle to invest in these investments because I thought 'the massive profits we might make are well worth the risk' and that I badgered him for several months to agree with me, then it would be even more appropriate to say that I had acted unreasonably by taking some of the riskiest investments in the world

17 *Ibid*, s 1(2).
18 *Ibid*, s 1(1)(a).
19 *Ibid*, s 1(1)(b).

and by coercing my fellow trustee into agreeing with my proposed course of action. It would be appropriate, it is suggested, to say that what is reasonable for a former footballer and fireman would be to expect no investment expertise from him, except perhaps a little common sense. If he had been the only trustee then we might have said that it was unreasonable for him to take such risky investments himself; but because he was being advised by his co-trustee, who claimed to have great professional experience, to make those investments then it would have been reasonable for him to defer to the trustee who had that experience. So, it is suggested, everything will depend on the context in this area. A lot will also depend upon common sense. (In many circumstances, legal expertise is simply a combination of knowing the appropriate legal principles and applying common sense.)

9.4.2 The possible meanings of 'reasonable' care in this context

The TA 2000 requires trustees to act reasonably. The word 'prudent' has been used in the case law since the 19th century[20] to govern the activities of trustees in this area and it is generally interpreted in practice as requiring caution when making investments. Therefore, the TA 2000 transforms the key standard from caution and prudence into a standard of reasonableness. By requiring simply that trustees must act reasonably it becomes possible for trustees to be assessed against the circumstances of their particular trust (i.e. the amount of money in the trust, the investment objectives of the settlor, the terms of the trust and so forth). The TA 2000 liberated trustees from the overriding need to be prudent in their investment activities. Importantly, however, in practice many trustees and their legal advisors still tend towards prudence (in the sense of being cautious) when investing trusts because they are concerned about being sued for taking too much risk and causing loss to the trust.

Everything will now depend upon the context, it is suggested. For example, a trustee who is investing the only savings of a widow, and who is required to generate the only income on which that widow can live for the rest of her life, would only be acting reasonably if she did not risk the entire capital of the trust fund and if she only followed investment strategies which would generate the level of income required by the widow. Investing in high-risk, high-return investments like derivatives, or in volatile countries, might make a large income for the widow in the good times but it would risk losing her only source of income if those risky investments turned bad. The latter strategy would not be reasonable in that context because of the risk of loss. By contrast, a professional trustee who is employed by a flamboyant billionaire who has created a trust explicitly to 'take big risks' and to generate 'as large a return as possible' would be entitled to risk the loss of part of the trust fund by investing in risky derivatives which promised a larger profit than other investments while still being reasonable in that context. As Lord Nicholls reminded us in *Royal Brunei Airlines v Tan*, 'all investment involves risk'.[21] If all investment involves risk then the question is not whether the trustees should avoid risk but rather (because some level of risk is inevitable) the trustees must assess what level of risk is appropriate for the trust they are managing. The lesson we must all learn from the financial crisis of 2008 is that there are no safe investments: even famous investment banks like Lehman Brothers can go into bankruptcy. Therefore, all that trustees can be required to do is to assess what is a reasonable level of risk for their trust.

---

20 *Learoyd v Whiteley* (1887) 12 App Cas 727.
21 [1995] AC 379.

9.5 THE PROCESS OF MAKING INVESTMENT DECISIONS

9.5.1 The statutory duty of care in the process of making investment decisions

The TA 2000 creates a statutory duty of care to which trustees are subject when making investment decisions. The trustees must have regard to the two standard investment criteria when making investments under s 4 of the TA 2000. The first standard investment criterion is the need to ensure that the proposed investments are *suitable* for a trust of the type that the trustees are managing. The second standard investment criterion is the need to ensure that the trust's investment are sufficiently well *diversified* for a trust of that type. The duties which those trustees bear in the investment-making process are always subject to the statutory duty of care (unless the trust instrument provides to the contrary).[22]

9.5.2 Standard investment criteria

The trustees are required, under s 4(2) of the TA 2000, to consider:

(a) the suitability to the trust of investments of the same kind as any particular investment proposed to be made or retained and of that particular investment as an investment of that kind, and
(b) the need for diversification of investments of the trust, in so far as is appropriate to the circumstances of the trust.[23]

The term 'suitability' is one familiar to financial regulation specialists[24] which requires that, in general terms, investment managers are required to consider whether or not the risk associated with a given investment is appropriate for the client proposing to make that investment. In consequence, the investment manager could not sell, for example, complex financial derivatives products to inexpert members of the general public who could not understand the precise nature of the risks associated with such a transaction. Much will depend on the nature of the trust. If the trust is a small family trust with a comparatively weak risk appetite, the investments should be safe and should involve little risk. By contrast, if the trust fund is created by two financial institutions for the purpose of generating a large speculative return, then the trustees would be expected to be considerably more adventurous, and what would be suitable for that trust would be much riskier.

Secondly, the trustees must pay heed to 'the need for diversification of investments of the trust, in so far as is appropriate to the circumstances of the trust'.[25] Two points arise from this provision. First, the question as to the amount of diversification necessary is dependent on the nature of the trust. For example, a trust which requires the trustees to hold a single house on trust for the occupation of a named beneficiary does not require that the trustees diversify their investments. By contrast, a trust of £1 million created to invest in shares would be required to invest in shares in many different industries and in many different jurisdictions so as to construct a portfolio of different investments. It may require consideration of

---

22 TA 2000, Sched 1, para 1(b).
23 *Ibid*, s 4(2).
24 Hudson, *The Law of Finance*, 2009, paras 10–46 *et seq.*
25 TA 2000, s 4(2)(b).

investment in markets beyond ordinary share markets to guard against a general downturn in share markets (for example, by buying derivatives which would increase in value if shares fell).

9.5.3 The obligation to take professional advice

Trustees are under a positive obligation to take professional advice on the investments which they propose to make on behalf of the trust.[26] This obligation is set out in s 5 of the TA 2000 in the following terms:

(1) Before exercising any power of investment, whether arising under this Part or otherwise, a trustee must (unless the exception applies) obtain and consider proper advice about the way in which, having regard to the standard investment criteria [set out in the preceding section], the power should be exercised.

(2) When reviewing the investments of the trust, a trustee must (unless the exception applies) obtain and consider proper advice about whether, having regard to the standard investment criteria, the investments should be varied.

Under subs (1), before the trustees make any investment they are required to seek 'proper advice'. This advice must be taken before the exercise of any investment power.[27] Similarly, under subs (2), when considering whether or not to vary the investments which the trust has made, the trustees are also required to take qualified investment advice,[28] unless it appears reasonable to the trustees in the circumstances to dispense with such advice.[29] The type of advice which the trustee must acquire is 'proper advice': that is, advice from someone whom the trustee reasonably believes is qualified to give such advice.[30]

Once the advice has been obtained, the trustees are required to consider it and its bearing on the manner in which their investment power should be exercised.[31] There is no statutory obligation on the trustees to follow the advice which they receive and so it is open to them to follow whichever path they consider appropriate, provided they have received professional advice and considered it first. Consequently, trustees may well seek advice from different professionals before making up their own minds as to which course of action they consider to be most appropriate for the trust. Different stockbrokers might, for example, suggest different courses of action for a trust seeking to invest its cash. Thus, the trustees may reject advice given to them by one firm of stockbrokers in favour of another firm which fits with the trust's general ethos. Megarry VC held the following in relation to the trustees' obligations in relation to the advice they receive:[32]

Although a trustee who takes advice on investments is not bound to accept and act on that advice, he is not entitled to reject it merely because he sincerely disagrees with it, unless in addition he is acting as an ordinary prudent man would act.

26 TA 2000, s 5(1).
27 TA 2000, s 5(4).
28 *Ibid*, s 5(2).
29 *Ibid*, s 5(3).
30 *Ibid*, s 5(4).
31 *Ibid*.
32 *Cowan v Scargill* [1985] Ch 270, 289.

These dicta appear to be in line with the statutory approach. There is nothing in the statute to preclude trustees from taking advice from a number of sources, or to take advice from one source as to a range of different investment decisions which could be taken, before then selecting the strategy which most appeals to them in the context of their fiduciary responsibilities.

9.6 CASE LAW ON THE TRUSTEES' DUTIES IN THE INVESTMENT OF TRUSTS

9.6.1 The interaction of the Trustee Act 2000 and the old case law

The trustee's general duties of investment can be summarised as being bound up in the following three obligations: to act prudently and safely;[33] to act fairly between beneficiaries;[34] and to do the best for the beneficiaries.[35] Otherwise the law is concerned with negative duties on the trustees to refrain from making unauthorised personal profits[36] and from committing breaches of trust more generally.[37] Therefore, there is a mixture of negative obligations dealing with the prevention of breach of trust and positive obligations in relation to the investment of trusts requiring the trustee to generate the best available return on the property in the circumstances.

9.6.2 The duty to make the best available return

The issue arises as to the level of return which the trustee is expected to earn from their investments. This issue arose in the case of *Cowan v Scargill*,[38] in which the defendant was one of the trustees of the miners' pension fund and also President of the National Union of Mineworkers. The board of trustees was divided between executives of the trade union and executives from the Coal Board. The most profitable investments identified by the trustees were in companies working in oil and also in South Africa. The defendant refused to make such investments on the grounds that it was ethically wrong for the fund to invest in apartheid South Africa and also contrary to the interests of the beneficiaries to invest in an industry which competed with the coal industry, in which all the beneficiaries worked or had worked previously. Importantly, Megarry VC held that:

> When the purpose of the trust is to provide financial benefits for the beneficiaries then the best interests of the beneficiaries are their best financial interests.

Therefore, in relation to a pension fund (which exists to earn income for the beneficiaries) the trustees are required to prioritise earning the highest available income, instead of considering other factors. That is so even if the trustees are thereby required to act contrary to their ethics and even contrary to the best interests of the communities in which most of the beneficiaries

---

33 *Ibid.*
34 *Nestlé v National Westminster Bank plc* [1994] 1 All ER 118.
35 *Cowan v Scargill* [1985] Ch 270.
36 *Boardman v Phipps* [1967] 2 AC 46; see section 12.5 below.
37 *Target Holdings v Redferns* [1996] 1 AC 421; see section 18.1 below.
38 [1984] 3 WLR 501.

live: here, in the 1980s, coal miners tended to live in tightly knit communities, in competition with the oil industry for the market for supplying energy to power stations and so forth.

Nevertheless, his lordship focused on the objections which the defendant trustee had raised in respect of the particular form of investment which had been suggested. He held that while 'the trustees must put on one side their own personal interests and views', and later that 'if investments of this type would be more beneficial to the beneficiaries than other investments, the trustees must not refrain from making the investments by reasons of the views that they hold'. The irony is that, in relation to the moral nature of the obligations on the trustee to deal equitably with the trust fund, the trustee is not permitted to bring decisions of an ethical nature to bear on the scope of the investment powers. As his lordship put it: 'Trustees may even have to act dishonourably (though not illegally) if the interests of their beneficiaries require it.'

Thus, there is a positive duty to invest regardless of ethics. And yet Megarry VC was expressly prepared to accept that a *sui juris* set of beneficiaries with strict views on moral matters (for example, condemnation of alcohol) would be entitled to prevent the trustees from investing in companies involved in the production of alcohol: thus suggesting that ethics can control investment powers. The question which comes to mind is whether Megarry VC simply did not agree with the particular form of political belief advanced by an avowedly Marxist leader of the trade union, in this case Arthur Scargill. (Scargill appeared in person in court.) For example, why should refusing to invest in apartheid-controlled South Africa not be considered as valid an exercise of a trustee's discretion as a decision in favour of beneficiaries who all formed part of a Methodist temperance movement to refrain from investing in a whisky distillery? What is not clear from the judgment is what the court's approach would have been if the trust had expressly excluded investment in South Africa. It must be the case that such an express provision would have had to be enforced. It is worth bearing in mind that the coal industry was wound down by a Conservative government in the UK before most readers of this book were born. However, in the 1980s there had been a bitter coal strike in which the mineworkers were perceived as trying to bring down the Conservative government, and in which paramilitary policing tactics were used against trade unionists for the first time. Consequently, this particular piece of litigation was very highly charged indeed.

9.6.3 The standard of care of the prudent businessperson

*The duty to invest as though a prudent businessperson acting for
someone for whom one feels morally bound to provide*

Having established that there is an obligation on the trustee to generate the best possible return from the trust property in the circumstances, there is a counter-balancing duty in the old case law to act prudently. Evidently, there is a contradiction between acting prudently and making the maximum possible return on the property because the latter obligation requires the taking of risk while the former obligation suggests a level of caution. Under the old authority of *Learoyd v Whiteley*[39] it was held that the trustee must act as a businessperson of ordinary prudence would act when investing for someone for whom she felt morally bound

---

39 *Ibid.*

to provide. Another way of thinking about this standard is that the trustee is required to act a little like a father investing for the benefit of his own child. In *Bartlett v Barclays Bank*[40] it was held that the trustee must also avoid all investments of a hazardous nature. A distinction was drawn between taking a prudent degree of risk and something which amounted to 'hazard'. The former, prudently taken risk, would be acceptable, whereas to put the trust fund in hazard would be unacceptable.

Megarry VC summarised these principles in the following passage:[41]

> [The trustees are required to] take such care as an ordinary prudent man would take if he were minded to make an investment for the benefit of other people for whom he feels morally bound to provide. This duty includes the duty to seek advice on matters which the trustee does not understand, such as the making of investments, and, on receiving that advice, to act with the same degree of prudence.

One particular understanding of the word 'prudence' has bedevilled this area of law for some time. It has caused particular problems in practice because it has prompted trustees to behave very cautiously when discharging their duties. The term 'prudence' is commonly taken by trustees – especially the trustees of pension funds – to require that they act with *caution* and great care. It is thought that 'caution' is the natural meaning of the word 'prudence'. However, the dictionary definition of 'prudence' is broader than that. The dictionary definitions include concepts of 'wisdom' and also 'earning a profit'. Significantly, a prudent person is a person who has the wisdom to earn a profit and not simply a person who avoids all risks. More specifically, however, the standard of prudence in the case law is a concept which requires that a trustee act 'as a prudent man of business acting for someone for whom he feels morally bound to provide'.[42] The idea that one acts for someone for whom one feels 'morally bound to provide' means that one must *provide* for those people, and therefore there is an obligation to make a profit bound up in that duty. This suggests we are moving away from an understanding of prudence meaning only caution. It is not just a standard of protecting property. Rather, it must involve earning income for the trust. All investment involves some risk. The question is how much risk can be taken. It may mean 'taking an appropriate level of risk, without incurring too much hazard'.[43] Therefore, the idea of prudence is one which can be brought easily into the modern age in which investment managers are expected to manage risks – that is, to prevent losses being taken by reason of taking too much risk, and also to earn profits by taking suitable risks.

The duty to act fairly between beneficiaries

The trustees bear a duty to act fairly between the beneficiaries. This does not mean that the trustees are required to pay the same income to each beneficiary but rather that the trustees must be able to justify their decisions as being fair in the context. For example, under old family settlements it was common for there to be a life tenant (who was entitled to income) and a remainderman (whose interest was in the preservation of the capital until the life tenant

---

40   [1980] Ch 515.
41   [1985] Ch 270, 289.
42   *Ibid.*
43   Cf. *Bartlett v Barclays Bank Trust Co Ltd.* [1980] Ch 515.

died). Acting fairly between the beneficiaries required that the trustees must deal fairly in the sense of ensuring a balance between the generation of income in the short-term and also the protection and growth of capital for the long-term.

Being fair is not the same as being equal. In support of that point, Hoffmann J held the following in *Nestlé v National Westminster Bank plc*:[44]

> A trustee must act fairly in making investment decisions which may have different consequences for differing classes of beneficiaries . . . The trustees have a wide discretion. They are, for example, entitled to take into account the income needs of the tenant for life or the fact that the tenant for life was a person known to the settlor and a primary object of the trust whereas the remainderman is a remoter relative or stranger . . . It would be an inhuman rule which required trustees to adhere to some mechanical rule for preserving the real value of capital when the tenant for life was the testator's widow who had fallen upon hard times and the remainderman was young and well-off.[45]

What this meant was that the trustees must be able to look at the purpose of the trust and at the broader context. If the trust was created precisely to provide for the settlor's widow, then the trustees would be justified in prioritising the need to generate income for her over any other beneficiary wanting the capital to be protected. The remainder beneficiary might prefer to have the capital maintained, whereas the widow would want the capital to be spent by investing it in investments which would generate a short-term gain for her. If the remainder beneficiary was young and rich, whereas the widow was entirely reliant on the trust for her income, then the trustee would be justified in prioritising the needs of the widow over the comparative lack of need of the remainder beneficiary.

9.6.4 The management of risk through portfolio investment strategies

The last turn in the case law was to impose a duty on trustees to invest in accordance with portfolio theory. Portfolio theory is the investment theory which advocates the diversification of investment risk by holding a large number of different types of investment so that any losses in one asset class would be offset by gains in the other investments. This is thought to be preferable to investing in a small number of investments because it removes the risk that that small range of investments will crash. (The real skill is in choosing the investments which should go into that portfolio, of course.) In this vein, Hoffmann J held in *Nestlé v National Westminster Bank plc* that:[46]

> Modern trustees acting within their investment powers are entitled to be judged by the standards of current portfolio theory, which emphasises the risk level of the entire portfolio rather than the risk attaching to each investment taken in isolation.[47]

---

44   (1988): [2000] WTLR 795, *per* Hoffmann J; [1994] 1 All ER 118, CA. (This case was reported at first instance only some years after it was heard.)

45   *Nestlé v National Westminster Bank plc* [2000] WTLR 795, 802.

46   [2000] WTLR 795, approved at [1993] 1 WLR 1260.

47   A discretionary portfolio manager is someone who is given freedom to decide what investments are made and what risks are taken – see generally Hudson, 1999:1.

This need to diversify investments is now encapsulated in s 4 of the TA 2000, as discussed above. In a contradiction of the old requirement of prudence, it has been held that a failure to diversify a holding of government bonds into shares would itself be a breach of trust which would make the trustees liable to pay equitable compensation to the beneficiaries.[48] Identifying the level of compensation payable would be a difficult matter. It has also been suggested that one might look to the average return which would have been obtained by a reasonable investment professional over the same period of time.[49]

9.6.5 Liability in accordance with standard market practice

There is much in the law of trust investment which is anachronistic. There are many very long-standing family settlements still in existence. Trustees of these long-standing family settlements have tended to be very careful when investing their funds so that the capital of the fund is not lost. In that sense they were seeking to be 'prudent'. However, such an investment strategy tends to generate only a small income. The question which is raised in this context is the following: what if the trustees avoid making a loss but instead make a profit that is unacceptably small?

This was the case in *Nestlé v National Westminster Bank plc*,[50] where the beneficiaries alleged that the trustees who had managed the investment of a family trust between 1922 and 1986 had failed to generate sufficient profit. It was alleged that while the trust amounted to £269,203 in 1986, if properly invested over that same period it should have amounted to over £1 million. It was said that even if the size of the trust fund had only risen in line with the cost of living (a very conservative measurement of growth) then it would have amounted to £400,000. Consequently, the trust fund had clearly been invested very cautiously indeed. The beneficiaries argued that it had been invested over-cautiously. The trustee bank defended its management of the trust on the basis that it had generated a broadly similar return on capital for its clients as other banks investing large family trusts had generated for theirs. On these facts, Hoffmann J found that the bank had done no less than what had been expected of a trustee in managing such a fund. It was held that the trustees had not committed a breach of trust because they had invested in the same way as the trustees of similar trust funds had invested. On appeal, the Court of Appeal held that there was no default committed by the trustees; rather, the plaintiff was contending that there had been a failure to do better, which is not the same thing. If the plaintiff could have demonstrated some misfeasance in the management of the trust, then liability would have been easier to demonstrate. However, the trustee could not be shown to have acted wrongly in a manner which caused loss, only to have acted less profitably, which did not cause loss so much as it failed to generate a larger return. Therefore, at present, there has never been liability proved against trustees for failing to generate a sufficiently large investment return.

Similarly in *Galmerrow Securities Ltd v National Westminster Bank plc*,[51] trustees had invested in the UK property market in relation to an investment fund created specifically to

48 *Guerin v The Queen* [1984] 2 SCR 335; (1984) 13 DLR (4th) 321; cited with approval in *Nestlé v National Westminster Bank plc* [1993] 1 WLR 1260, 1268, *per* Dillon LJ.

49 *Nestlé v National Westminster Bank plc* [1993] 1 WLR 1260, at 1268, *per* Dillon LJ and at 1280, *per* Staughton LJ.

50 [1993] 1 WLR 1260.

51 [2002] WTLR 125.

invest in that market. That market fell in value causing a loss to the trust. The beneficiaries sued the trustees for breach of trust. It was held, *inter alia*, that the trustees would not be liable for breach of trust because all participants in the marketplace had lost money and because the investments for which the trust had been set up were simply a type of investment which had the risk of loss inherent in them.[52]

9.7 BREACH OF TRUST AND INVESTMENT

9.7.1 The concept of 'loss' and breach of trust

Breach of trust in general terms

The law on breach of trust is considered in Chapter 18 in detail. For the purposes of the investment of trusts, there are three contexts in which there might be a breach of trust: where a specific provision of a trust instrument is breached; where a relevant provision of the TA 2000 is breached; or where a relevant principle of the case law is breached. For liability for breach of trust to arise, the beneficiaries must have suffered a loss. It is not enough that there has been some technical breach of trust unless that breach of trust has caused a loss. The leading case of *Target Holdings v Redferns*[53] identifies three categories of liability for trustees who commit a breach of trust: a liability to recover the original trust property at their own cost; a liability to restore the value of the trust fund where is has been reduced by their breach of trust; and a liability to provide equitable compensation to the beneficiaries for any loss caused by their breach of trust.[54]

Investment in unauthorised investments

When a trustee invests in an asset class which is outside the assets in which she is empowered to invest by the trust instrument, then there is an issue as to what the trustee should do with those investments if they are profitable. The answer suggested by the case of *Re Massingberd*[55] is that the trustees should replace the unauthorised asset with an authorised investment. The trustee will bear the cost of doing so because it was the trustee's fault that incorrect investments were contained in the trust. If the unauthorised assets were unprofitable, then the trustee would also be liable for the beneficiaries' loss under ordinary principles of breach of trust.

9.7.2 The validity of exclusion clauses under case law

The general principles relating to the use of exclusion clauses in trusts law was considered in Chapter 8. In essence, it was held by the Court of Appeal in *Armitage v Nurse*,[56] before the enactment of the TA 2000, that a clause excluding a trustee's personal liability would be valid even where it purported to limit that trustee's liability for gross negligence.

---

52 See section 9.9.3 for further discussion of this case.
53 [1996] 1 AC 421.
54 *Ibid.*
55 (1890) 63 LT 296.
56 *Ibid.*

The enforceability of an exclusion of liability clause in an investment contract was considered in *Galmerrow Securities Ltd v National Westminster Bank plc*.[57] There, the fiduciaries in a unit trust scheme had expressly excluded their liability for the exercise of their investment obligations except in cases of negligence or fraud. The beneficiaries contended that the scheme managers had been negligent in their investment of the bulk of the fund in the real property market. The scheme managers contended that it would have been impossible to have amended their investment powers so as to have avoided the investment objectives of the unit trust and to have extracted the fund's investments from the real property market before it collapsed. The court held that:

> The venture was a speculation and like all speculations carried with it the risk of failure. It would not be right to visit the consequences of that misjudgment of the market upon NatWest which is not shown to have had any power open to it which would remedy or mitigate the consequence . . . it is not negligent to fail to act where no alternative course of conduct to the continuance of the present arrangement is proved to have been available to the person who has a power to act.

Therefore, it was held that the trustees should not be liable for breach of trust in these circumstances because there was no other course of action open to them on the terms of their trust. The trust's objective of speculating on the property market was, quite simply, a speculation which failed. The trustees were supposed to invest in that market due to the intractability of the terms of the trust. Those terms had been required to be that limited by the fund's regulators. An alternative view might be that the trustees could have identified the risk of loss and either liquidated the investment fund, or transformed it into cash until the property market improved, or have sought an alteration in the terms of the trust. That alternative view would have justified holding the trustees liable for a breach of trust by dint of failing to protect the trust's investment fund.

---

57 [2002] WTLR 125, at 155.

Chapter 10

The management of trusts

10.1 GENERAL POWERS OF TRUSTEES

Trustees are managers, stewards and fiduciaries: they act on behalf of the beneficiaries in the beneficiaries' interests. Therefore, they need to have powers to carry out their duties. We have already considered investment powers in the previous chapter, and powers to appoint and advanced property in Chapter 3 *Certainties*. This chapter considers the general management powers of trustees, including their ability to delegate their responsibilities, their ability to seek a variation of the terms of the trust, and their powers to cope with beneficiaries getting into difficulties by maintaining them. In Chapter 8 we treated trustees as people who are hemmed in by duties and obligations so as to protect their beneficiaries. In this chapter we consider them as actors with powers.

    The most important power of the trustees is bound up in the following principle: the trustee is the owner of the legal title in the trust property and as such must have a number of powers to use that property. In the first place, the trustees have any powers which the trust instrument grants them. Beyond that, general powers granted by the law of trusts supplement the powers in the trust instrument,[1] provided that those powers are neither expressly excluded by the trust instrument nor inconsistent with the terms of that instrument.[2] Self-evidently, unless the trustees had powers they could not perform any of their duties.

10.2 POWERS OF MAINTENANCE AND ADVANCEMENT

10.2.1 Powers of maintenance in relation to infant beneficiaries

Where trustees have powers to maintain the beneficiaries of a trust, they need to be able to act in the best interests of those beneficiaries as circumstances change. The basis of this area of law is that the terms of a trust may prove to be too narrow over time. Therefore, statute and case law have created means for trustees to be able to react to the circumstances without needing to change the terms of the trust. In particular circumstances, then, statute provides the trustees with extra powers which the court can grant to them.

Trusts created for the maintenance of particular types of beneficiary attract a specific statutory regime. Sections 31 and 32 of the TA 1925 give trustees wide powers to use income and capital for the maintenance of infant beneficiaries and for the advancement and benefit of all beneficiaries. These principles apply provided that there are no terms in the trust instrument to the contrary. The following discussion divides between beneficiaries with a general entitlement to income, an entitlement to income in particular situations, and an entitlement to capital. The issue of the variation of trusts to protect vulnerable beneficiaries is considered in section 10.4 below.

Income under a trust held for infant beneficiaries

The court has a power under s 31 of the Trustee Act 1925 ('TA 1925') to order that income is paid for the 'maintenance, education or benefit' of an infant beneficiary who has an interest under the trust. (Alternatively, such an order may be made under the court's inherent jurisdiction, as considered below.) Section 31 enables the trustees to pay the whole or part of the trust's income as 'may be reasonable' to the infant's parent or guardian. Self-evidently, the trustees must be able to show that it is reasonable to make this payment. Moreover, the trustees must be able to square their decision to make a maintenance payment with their obligations to treat all beneficiaries impartially. That is, the beneficiaries need not be treated equally, but their treatment must be justifiable where it is unequal. The trustees are empowered to make that payment after the infant has reached the age of 18 if that person does not have a vested interest in the income of the trust either until they die or until they acquire such a vested interest.[3] In general terms, 'the trustees shall have regard to the age of the infant and his requirements and generally to the circumstances of the case'.[4] Where there is more than

---

1 TA 1925, s 69(2).
2 *IRC v Bernstein* [1961] Ch 399, 412, *per* Lord Evershed MR.
3 TA 1925, s 31(1)(ii).
4 *Ibid*, s 31(1)(i).

one fund which can be used for the maintenance of the infant then those funds should be used proportionately and together.[5] The principal function of s 31 has been described as being:

> to supply a code of rules governing the disposal of income, especially during a minority, in cases where a settlor or testator has made dispositions of capital and either (a) being an unskilled draftsman has not thought about income, or (b) being a skilled draftsman, has been content to let the statutory code apply.[6]

Section 31 can be ousted where there is an express or implied contrary intention in the trust instrument to that effect. Such provisions are generally interpreted strictly, and therefore such a provision will not be effected where that would be inconsistent with the general objectives of the trust instrument.[7]

It is provided in s 31(2) of the TA 1925 that during a beneficiary's infancy any residue from the income of the trust is to be accumulated (i.e. saved). That accumulated income is to be held for that infant on reaching 18 or marrying. To the extent that it is not so used, the income must be accumulated and added to the capital of the trust fund.[8] If the infant dies before reaching the age of 18 or marrying, her estate will not be entitled to these accumulations even if her interest is vested.[9] At the age of 18, or if there is a marriage at an earlier age, the income (but not the accumulated income) will be paid to the beneficiary.[10] The beneficiary becomes entitled to the accumulation when she becomes entitled to the capital.

It is necessary to make a time apportionment when there is an alteration in the class of income beneficiaries. The case of *Re Joel*[11] concerned a fund which was held upon trust for the testator's grandchildren contingent on their attaining 21, and where the gift carried the intermediate income, which could be applied for the benefit of the grandchildren. Goff J held that each time a member of the class died under the age of 21, or a new grandchild was born, the income of the trust ought to be apportioned so that each member of the class enjoyed only that part of the income attributable to the period for which she was alive.

'Maintenance, education or benefit'

The meaning of the terms 'maintenance, education or benefit' are generally interpreted broadly.[12] It has been held that the trust's income may be applied directly to the benefit of the beneficiary or held on trust for that beneficiary absolutely,[13] or held contingently on the beneficiary reaching adulthood.[14] When deciding whether to use the income for such purposes, the trustees must consider the age and requirements of the infant, whether other income is available for her maintenance, and the general circumstances of the case. If the discretion is

---

5   *Ibid*, s 31(1).
6   *Re Delamere's ST* [1984] 1 WLR 813.
7   *Ibid*.
8   TA 1925, s 31(2).
9   *Re Delamere's ST* [1984] 1 WLR 813.
10 *Ibid*.
11 [1943] Ch 311.
12 *Re Heyworth's Contingent Reversionary Interest* [1956] Ch 364, 370.
13 *Re Vestey's Settlement* [1951] Ch 209.
14 *Pilkington v IRC* [1964] AC 612.

exercised in good faith, the court will not interfere.[15] The trustee is required to identify a use of the property which would be in the best interests of the beneficiary. This will often include a consideration of the circumstances of the infant's parents. As Cotton LJ held, in describing the sorts of issues which the courts should bear in mind when considering the meaning of the benefit of a female infant and the position, in that case, of the child's father as her source of maintenance:

> they should take into account that the father is not of sufficient ability properly to maintain his child, and that it is for her benefit not merely to allow him enough to pay her actual expenses, but to enable him to give her a better education and a better home. They must not be deterred from doing what is for her benefit because it is also a benefit to the father, though, on the other hand, they must not act with a view to his benefit apart from her.[16]

Therefore, the courts are required to consider the benefit to the infant even if it may have a collateral benefit for a parent who is unable to look after the child properly. The key factor is that the infant takes a genuine benefit. Of course, the trustees will also face complaints from other beneficiaries that the father ought to be caring for his own child and that their rights under the trust should not be subjugated to his inadequacies as a parent who cannot provide for his own child. The balance which the trustees must strike in cases of this sort is clearly very difficult indeed. On reaching the age of majority, any accumulated, unapplied income then passes to that beneficiary.[17]

The court's inherent jurisdiction

Beyond the statute, the courts have accepted that they are empowered to infer an intention on the settlor's part when preparing the trust instrument to provide for the maintenance of children.[18] This is the only situation in which a court will interfere with a testator's intention as set out in her will.[19] So, under the court's inherent jurisdiction, a court order may allow income to be used for an infant's maintenance.[20] The court's inherent jurisdiction can also be used to enable the trustees to provide for a person's maintenance even when the beneficiary is not an infant, where the court considers that to be just.[21]

10.2.2 Powers of advancement

In the absence of any express power, trust capital can be used for the benefit of a beneficiary who is not yet entitled to such capital. The trustees have a power to advance amounts out of capital under s 32 of the TA 1925, instead of holding them back to generate future income. Where the trust contains an express power permitting the trustees to advance the capital of the trust fund to specified beneficiaries, that express power will be decisive of the matter. In the absence of an express power, s 32 of the TA 1925 makes provision for

---

15 *Bryant v Hickley* [1894] 1 Ch 324.
16 *Re Lofthouse* (1885) 29 Ch D 921, 932, *per* Cotton LJ.
17 *Stanley v IRC* [1944] 1 KB 255, 261, *per* Lord Greene MR.
18 *Re Collins* (1886) 32 Ch D 229, 232, *per* Pearson J.
19 *Chapman v Chapman* [1954] AC 429, 456, *per* Lord Morton.
20 *Wellesly v Wellesly* (1828) 2 Bli (NS) 124.
21 *Revel v Watkinson* (1748) 27 ER 912.

powers of advancement so that the trustees may at any time pay capital for the 'advance-ment or benefit' of anyone who is entitled to the capital in the trust fund either absolutely or contingently.

The reference to applying money for the 'advancement or benefit' of the beneficiaries has been explained by the courts as involving 'setting up the beneficiary in life'.[22] Within the scope of 'setting up the beneficiary in life' falls the discharge of the beneficiary's debts and a resettlement of capital to avoid tax. The trustees must ensure that the advancements are applied for the purposes for which they are made.[23] There are restrictions on the power of advancement set out in s 32 of the TA 1925. The restrictions are as follows. First, the trustees must not advance more than half of the beneficiary's presumptive or vested share or interest.[24] Second, when the beneficiary becomes absolutely entitled to their interest then the advancement must be taken into account.[25] Third, an advancement must not be made if it prejudices a prior interest unless the person with such an interest gives consent to the advancement. If the life tenant under a protective trust gives consent, the protective trust will not be determined under s 33 of the TA 1925.[26]

In *Re Pauling's ST*,[27] the bankers Coutts & Co were trustees of a fund which was held on trust for a wife for her life, with the remainder passing on her death to her children. The trust instrument contained an express power for the trustees to advance to the children up to one-half of their share, with the consent of their mother. The husband of the life tenant, who was the father of the children, lived beyond his means and sought to obtain part of the trust moneys under cover of them being paid as advancements supposedly to his children. A series of advancements were made, nominally to the children, but the money was used for the benefit of their father or generally for the family. The Court of Appeal held that:

> the power of advancement can be exercised only if it is for the benefit of the child or remoter issue to be advanced or, as was said during argument, it is thought to be a 'good thing' for the advanced person to have a share of capital before his or her due time . . . [A] power of advancement [can] be exercised only if there was some good reason for it. That good reason must be beneficial to the person to be advanced; the power cannot be exercised capriciously or with some other benefit in view.

Therefore, to obtain advancements other than for the benefit of the beneficiaries would not be a proper advancement. Acquiring money solely for the use of a parent would not fall within this principle. Obtaining advancements so that the beneficiaries' parent could spend them on wild living would not be a good reason for using them. There is also a need to distinguish between a beneficiary seeking an advancement and a trustee stipulating the form of the advancement. To leave the payee free to decide how it should be applied may lead to a misap-plication of trust property. Unless the terms of the trust stipulate the objective for which the money must be used once it has been advanced to the beneficiary, then it may be difficult to

---

22 *Pilkington v IRC* [1964] AC 612.
23 *Re Pauling's ST* [1964] 3 WLR 742.
24 TA 1925, s 32(1)(a).
25 *Ibid*, s 32(1)(b).
26 *Ibid*, s 32(1)(c).
27 [1964] 3 WLR 742.

prevent such a misuse in practice. *Pauling* was an interesting case because a pattern of such misuse could be demonstrated.

10.3 DELEGATION OF TRUSTEES' DUTIES

10.3.1 The appointment of agents, custodians and nominees by the trustees

Trustees may well want to appoint professionals to act on their behalf. A non-professional trustee charged with investing a trust fund will want to delegate her responsibilities to a finance professional. Clearly this raises a conceptual problem that the trustees would not be performing their fiduciary duties themselves if they have engaged someone else to perform those duties in their place. As we shall see, statute deals with that problem in the following ways. The trustees can only appoint[28] agents, nominees or custodians if those appointees carry on business in that capacity, or if the appointee is a body corporate (such as an ordinary company) controlled by the trustees themselves, or if the delegates are a body corporate recognised under s 9 of the Administration of Justice Act 1985.[29] It is open to the trustees to decide on the remuneration of such delegates.[30] The terms of the trust instrument may expand or limit these provisions.

10.3.2 Agents

An agent is a form of fiduciary officer who acts, subject to the principles of contract law, on behalf of a principal. The Trustee Act 2000 ('TA 2000') provides that the trustees are permitted to 'authorise any person to exercise any or all of their delegable functions as their agent'.[31] The functions which are capable of being delegated to an agent are expressed as being any trustee functions except:[32] a decision as to the distribution of trust assets; the power to decide whether fees should be payable out of income or capital; any power to appoint some person to be a trustee; or any power to delegate the trustees' responsibilities. The agent is to be subject to the same duties as the trustees when the agent is exercising those powers.[33] The trustees can appoint one of the trustees to act on their behalf.[34] The trustees are not entitled to authorise a beneficiary to act as their agent.[35]

10.3.3 Nominees and custodians

Trustees may appoint a nominee to hold the trust assets[36] or a custodian to take custody of any trust assets.[37]

---

28 TA 2000, s 19(1).
29 TA 2000, s 19(2).
30 *Ibid*, s 20.
31 *Ibid*, s 11(1).
32 *Ibid*, s 11(2).
33 TA 2000, s 13.
34 *Ibid*, s 12(1).
35 *Ibid*, s 12(3).
36 *Ibid*, s 16(1).
37 *Ibid*, s 17(1).

10.3.4 Powers of attorney

Trustees are empowered to delegate their powers by means of a power of attorney.[38] The donor of the power (for example, the trustee transferring the power) is liable for acts of the donee (that is, the attorney acting on behalf of the trustee) as though they were his own acts.[39]

10.3.5 Liability for the acts of delegates

The key question in relation to the appointment of delegates is as to the extent of any liability which the trustees have for the acts or omissions of those delegates. In general terms, the trustee is not liable for any breach of duty carried out by the delegate, unless the trustee failed to comply with his duty of care in relation to the appointment of suitable agents.[40] The TA 2000 provides that the trustees are required to 'keep under review' the arrangements under which the delegate acts and to consider any 'power of intervention' which they may have,[41] including whether to revoke that delegate's authorisation or to give directions to the delegate.[42] If the trustees decide that there is a need to intervene, then they are required to intervene.[43] A trustee will not be liable for 'any act or default of the agent, nominee or custodian unless he has failed to comply with the duty of care applicable to him'.

10.3.6 The applicable standard of care for trustees under the case law

Under the case law, it was held in *Speight v Gaunt*[44] that 'a trustee ought to conduct the business of the trust in the same manner that an ordinary prudent man of business would conduct his own, and that beyond that there is no liability or obligation on the trustee'. In that case a broker who had been engaged by the trustees misappropriated trust funds and absconded with them. The trustee escaped liability by demonstrating that using a broker in this way was in the ordinary course of business.

10.3.7 An alternative approach

A different approach was adopted in *Re Vickery*.[45] Here a solicitor absconded with trust money after it had been lodged with him by the trustees. It was held that the appropriate test for the presence or absence of good faith was found to have been whether or not there had been 'wilful default' on the part of the trustee. This sets the test high, so that it is only possible to hold a trustee liable where they have acted wilfully in breach of their obligations. No such wilful default could be shown on the facts of this case.

---

38 Trustee Delegation Act 1999, s 5; by amendment to the TA 1925, s 25.
39 Trustee Delegation Act 1999, s 5(7).
40 *Ibid*, s 23(1).
41 TA 2000, s 22(1).
42 *Ibid*, s 22(4).
43 *Ibid*, s 22(1).
44 (1883) 9 App Cas 1.
45 [1931] 1 Ch 572.

10.4 VARIATION OF TRUSTS

10.4.1 Variation of trusts

Trust instruments may become restrictive when the trustees need to act in an unexpected way to support a beneficiary who has fallen on hard times, or to avoid a change in tax law, or to cope with other unexpected circumstances. Therefore, the Variation of Trusts Act 1958 provides for a means of applying to the court to vary the terms of the trust if the trust instrument does not have that flexibility built into it.[46] However, there is an important line to be drawn between mere variations of the trust and changes which are so substantial that they constitute a complete re-settlement of that trust.[47]

10.4.2 Duty not to deviate from the terms of the trust

The fundamental duty of the trustees is to observe the terms of the trust and not to deviate from those terms. Deviation from the terms of the trust will constitute a breach of trust. Nevertheless, the court has an inherent power to permit a departure from the precise terms of the trust[48] where that is necessary to cope with 'emergencies'[49] in the administration of the trust. This ability to sanction deviation from the terms of the trust is based on four situations identified in the decision of the Court of Appeal in *Chapman v Chapman*[50] in which the trustees do not need to obey the terms of the trust. Those four situations are as follows. First, cases in which the court has effected changes in the nature of an infant's property. Second, cases in which the court has allowed the trustees of settled property to enter into some business transaction which was not authorised by the settlement. Third, cases in which the court has allowed maintenance out of income which the settlor or testator directed to be accumulated. Fourth, cases in which the court has approved a compromise on behalf of infants and possible after-born beneficiaries.

So, in *Allen v Distillers Co (Biochemicals) Ltd*[51] it was ordered that there would be a postponement of a payment to a beneficiary suffering from a disability even though that beneficiary had reached the age of majority because a compromise had been reached between all the potential beneficiaries as to the manner in which the indisposed beneficiary ought best to be treated. Similarly, compromise has been achieved in relation to pension funds which have sought wider investment powers to enable a substantial capital fund to provide greater benefits for its members.[52] A good example of an emergency use of a power arose in *Re Jackson*[53] where buildings were on the brink of collapse. The court ordered a variation so that trust property could be applied to save the buildings from final collapse.

---

46 *Paul v Paul* (1882) 20 Ch D 742.
47 *Vandervell v IRC* [1967] 2 WLR 87.
48 *Re New* [1901] 2 Ch 534.
49 *Ibid, per* Romer LJ.
50 [1954] AC 429.
51 [1974] QB 384.
52 *Mason v Fairbrother* [1983] 2 All ER 1078.
53 (1882) 21 Ch D 786.

10.4.3 The Variation of Trusts Act 1958

The most significant power to vary trusts is contained in the Variation of Trusts Act 1958. The purpose of that Act is to permit variations of trusts in relation to specific types of beneficiaries.[54] The court's jurisdiction is then limited to variations and revocations to the extent that they interact with those categories of beneficiary. A variation may only be permitted if it would be for the 'benefit' of the beneficiaries, under s 1(1) of the 1958 Act. The term 'benefit' has been given a broad meaning beyond simply financial benefit, to include moral and social benefit too.[55]

The scope of people covered by the 1958 Act is set out in s 1(1) in relation to any trust, will, settlement or other disposition are the following:

(a) any person having, directly or indirectly, an interest, whether vested or contingent, under the trusts who by reason of infancy or other incapacity is incapable of assenting, or

(b) any person (whether ascertained or not) who may become entitled, directly or indirectly, to an interest under the trusts as being at a future date or on the happening of a future event . . ., or

(c) any person unborn, or

(d) any person in respect of any discretionary interest of his under protective trusts where the interest of the principal beneficiary has not failed or been determined. . .

Therefore, the focus of the legislation is on infants and incapacitated persons (for example, those suffering from mental health problems, as considered below). It also includes those people who might yet become beneficially entitled under the trust fund (either because their interest has not yet been awarded to them under some fiduciary discretion, or because they have not yet been born).

10.4.4 The general principle governing identification of a variation as opposed to a re-settlement

There is a distinction to be drawn between a major 're-settlement' of a trust and a mere 'variation' of that trust. The former is taken to be in effect a different trust, whereas the latter keeps the original trust in existence with a mere tinkering with its terms. The principal limitation on the courts' powers in this context is that all they may permit is 'an arrangement' in the sense of a mere variation of an existing trust, but not a wholesale re-settlement. As Wilberforce J held in *Re T's Settlement Trusts*[56] the courts may not permit a substantial re-settlement of the trust property which goes beyond a mere variation of its terms. In describing where the line is between a variation and a resettlement, Megarry J held that:

> if an arrangement, while leaving the substratum [i.e. the underlying substance of the trust], effectuates the purpose of the original trust by other means, it may still be possible to regard that arrangement as merely varying the original trusts, even though the means employed are wholly different, and even though the form is completely changed.[57]

---

54 *D (A Child) v O* [2004] 3 All ER 780.
55 *Re Holt's ST* [1969] 1 Ch 100, *per* Megarry J.
56 [1964] Ch 158, 162.
57 *Re Holt's ST* [1969] 1 Ch 100, 111.

Therefore, it will clearly be necessary to examine the true purpose of the trust (or its 'substratum') and identify whether or not that is changed to such an extent as to constitute a resettlement on new terms. Thus, in *Goulding v James*,[58] a proposal to re-effect trusts such that the great-grandchildren who took interests only in remainder ought to be entitled to a settlement of 10% of the capital was considered to be contrary to the stated intention of the settlor at the time of the creation of the settlement. Changing that amount of the capital and the grandchildren's interests was too great a re-settlement. By contrast, it was held in *Wyndham v Egremont*[59] that an alteration to the perpetuity period in a trust did not constitute a resettlement of that trust; nor did alterations to the line of future beneficiaries. In that case, Blackburne J considered that a change to ensure that the trust property pass with the male heir was not a complete resettlement of the trust, but rather only a variation of that trust.

10.4.5 There must be a benefit in the variation

The court must be satisfied that the proposal will be beneficial to the beneficiaries. This benefit may not be apparent at first but it must be demonstrable that there will be some benefit eventually. In complex settlements there will often be different groups of beneficiaries who will be benefited and harmed by any variation in the terms of the trust. In *Re RGST Settlement Trust*[60] it was argued that a proposed variation which would provide for a life interest for one beneficiary would be to the detriment of other beneficiaries who were children at the time and whose interests would therefore be delayed. However, the court considered that this variation would give the trustees more flexibility to advance property to the children, to minimise the trust's liability to tax and to acquire cheaper life assurance products. While the 'benefit' which is ordinarily sought is a direct pecuniary benefit,[61] a reduction in the trust's tax bill also falls within this sort of benefit.[62]

In *Wright v Gater*[63] Norris J provided us with an insight into the court's thought processes. First, the judge should approach the task with what Megarry J in *Re Wallace's Settlements*[64] described as 'a fair cautious and enquiring mind'. Then, the judge should remember that they are 'not redistributing property according to some wise scheme of which I approve', rather the judge is supplying the beneficiary's consent to that scheme[65] and therefore the judge must be satisfied that it is for their benefit. Third, the term 'benefit' is 'generally financial in nature' and consequently the court must involve itself in 'a practical and business-like consideration of the arrangement, including the total amounts of the advantages which the various parties obtain, and their bargaining strength'. Norris J held that ultimately, following *Re Irving*,[66] that the question must be: 'would a prudent adult, motivated by intelligent self-interest, and after sustained consideration of the proposed trusts and powers and the circumstances in which they may fall to be implemented,

---

58   [1997] 2 All ER 239, *per* Mummery LJ.
59   [2009] EWHC 2076 (Ch).
60   *Re RGST Settlement Trust* [2007] EWHC 2666 (Ch).
61   *Re Drewe's Settlement* [1966] 1 WLR 1518 at 1520.
62   *Re Weston's Settlement* [1969] 1 Ch 223 at 232, *per* Stamp LJ.
63   [2011] EWHC 2881 (Ch).
64   [1968] 1 WLR 711 at 718 H.
65   [2006] WTLR 1461, at para [16].
66   (1975) 66 DLR (3d) 387.

be likely to accept the proposal?' It was held that the court is acting in the best financial interests of a child beneficiary when it ensures that the variation will lead to a saving in tax of £89,000.

10.4.6 Variation of trusts as part of divorce proceedings

One significant context in which trusts may need to be varied is in relation to divorce. The parties may have created a marriage settlement which will need to be unpacked once the married couple divorce, or trusts may have been created during the marriage in relation to which one partner or both partners may have had interests, or trusts may have been created before the marriage in which only one partner has an interest. On divorce it will be important to consider whether those trusts should be considered to be part of the 'matrimonial property' which the court should take into account when settling the terms of the divorce. In this sense it is important to consider whether or not the settlement which is to be varied is a 'nuptial' settlement or a 'non-nuptial' settlement in divorce proceedings. In essence, where the settlement is a nuptial settlement then the property will be considered to be matrimonial property which is capable of being dealt with by way of a variation of the settlement as part of the divorce settlement under the broad powers of the court under the Matrimonial Causes Act 1973. Waite LJ considered that the powers of the court under the 1973 Act were almost 'limitless' in *Thomas v Thomas*.[67] In such circumstances, as for example in *Charman v Charman*[68] and in *Whaley v Whaley*,[69] the court will embark on a detailed examination of the situation of the parties, of the role which the trusts play as part of the parties' matrimonial property, and of the comparative justice between parties of making a variation of the sort suggested by the applicant. The trust must have continued in existence at the time of making the order.[70] So, in *BJ v MJ (Financial Remedy: Overseas Trust)*[71] Mostyn J considered two trusts in relation to divorce proceedings in the light of the dispositive powers of the court under the 1973 Act, and declared those powers to be 'unfettered and, in theory, unlimited'.[72]

10.4.7 Disagreement between different beneficiaries

What is more difficult to know is how to deal with an application in which not all of the beneficiaries are in agreement. Section 57 of the 1958 Act is important in this context because it allows the court to order trusts to be operated appropriately in the best interests of the beneficiaries. Trustees will suggest transactions or arrangements to the court, where the beneficiaries cannot agree about them, and the court will judge their suitability. In *Southgate v Sutton*[73] Mummery LJ explained s 57 as requiring that the proposed transaction is 'expedient'. The notion of the power being 'expedient' must be read in the context of the management of the trust as a whole. In *Southgate v Sutton* the application was unopposed, which in itself

---

67   [1995] 2 FLR 668.
68   [2007] EWCA Civ 503.
69   [2011] EWCA Civ 617.
70   *C v C* [2004] EWHC 742 (Fam).
71   [2011] EWHC 2708 (Fam).
72   *Ben Hashem v Al Shayif* [2009] 1 FLR 115, *per* Munby J at [290].
73   [2011] EWCA Civ 637.

made Mummery LJ 'nervous' because the court prefers in such situations to hear from both sides about whether or not the application is indeed expedient and proper. In that case the proposal was to 'appropriate and partition' the trust fund so that, in effect, one group of beneficiaries would in the future only enjoy income from a part of the trust fund as opposed to enjoying income from the entire trust fund. The court was concerned that this would effectively change the beneficial interests, even though the position in cash terms was expected to remain much the same. Nevertheless, the Court of Appeal was prepared to make the order to permit the change after it had heard evidence about the problems which the trustees were facing otherwise with the management of the trust. These kinds of applications are necessarily decided on their facts.

Part 4

Trusts implied by law

Resulting trusts

CAPSULE SUMMARY

Resulting trusts arise in favour of Y beneficially in the following situations: where Y has purported to create an express trust but has failed to identify the person for whom that property is to be held;[1] where Y has provided part of the purchase price of property with an intention to take an equitable interest in that property;[2] or where X has acquired property intended beneficially for Y using money provided by Y.[3]

There are other situations in which presumptions of advancement operate to deem that rights in property have passed by way of gift between husband and wife, and between

---

1 *Vandervell v IRC* [1967] 2 AC 291.
2 *Dyer v Dyer* (1788) 2 Cox Eq Cas 92.
3 *Ibid.*

father and child.[4] A resulting trust will arise in favour of the donor where that presumption of advancement can be rebutted on the facts.[5]

No resulting trust will arise over property in favour of a person who has committed an illegal act in relation to that property.[6] However, a person who has committed an illegal act can nevertheless take beneficially under a resulting trust where she does not have to rely on the illegal act itself to assert beneficial title in the property.[7]

11.1 INTRODUCTION – WHAT IS A RESULTING TRUST?

11.1.1 Defining the resulting trust

A resulting trust is a form of trust which is imposed 'by operation of law': that is to say, a resulting trust is imposed automatically by equity and recognised by the courts without the need for the parties to have intended to create a trust. The resulting trust is best understood as a sort of residuary category of trust which is created when otherwise it would be unclear who is to take beneficial ownership of property. Lord Browne-Wilkinson held, in the leading case of *Westdeutsche Landesbank v Islington*, that resulting trusts arise in two circumstances.[8] First, in circumstances in which two or more people acquire property with the intention that they are all intended to be the equitable owners of that property. In that context, the property is said to be held on resulting trust for those contributors to the purchase price in proportion to the size of their contributions to the property (so, someone who contributed one-third of the purchase price would acquire one-third of the equitable interest in that property, for example). Second, where an owner of property has attempted to transfer property outright, or has attempted to create a trust over it, but that intention has failed for some reason, then the equitable interest in that property is held on resulting trust for the original owner of that property.

In *Re Vandervell (No 2)*,[9] Megarry J set out a similar division between two types of resulting trust which is still significant in the case law. His lordship divided between 'automatic resulting trusts', where the resulting trust comes into existence automatically on the happening of an event as in *Vandervell v IRC*[10] where there is a failure to transfer property or to create a trust; and 'presumed resulting trusts', where property was bought by two or more people with the intention that they be equitable owners of it. This rather neat division between the categories governs the organisation of this chapter.

To explain the doctrine of resulting trusts we shall simply consider the case law for the bulk of this chapter. We shall leave the academic disputes about the nature of resulting trusts until the end of the chapter. Much of that commentary is concerned with what resulting trusts *ought* to be. Consequently, much of that academic discussion is unhelpful in deciding what the law on resulting trusts actually *is*.

---

4 *Bennet v Bennet* (1879) 10 Ch D 474.
5 *Fowkes v Pascoe* (1875) 10 Ch App Cas 343. See now *Stack v Dowden* [2007] UKHL 17.
6 *Tinsley v Milligan* [1994] 1 AC 340; *Tribe v Tribe* [1995] 3 WLR 913.
7 *Ibid.*
8 [1996] AC 669.
9 [1974] Ch 269.
10 [1967] 2 AC 291.

11.1.2 Resulting trusts in *Westdeutsche Landesbank v Islington LBC*

Two categories of resulting trust

Lord Browne-Wilkinson identified two categories of resulting trust in *Westdeutsche Landesbank Girozentrale v Islington LBC*.[11] This is the leading case on the definition of the different categories of trust under English law, and so we shall start with it before turning to the rest of the case law on resulting trusts.

Purchase price resulting trusts

The first category of 'purchase price resulting trusts' arises when two or more people contribute to the purchase price of property with the effect that each contributor acquires an equitable interest on resulting trust principles in that property in proportion to the size of her contribution to the purchase price. This principle has existed in English trusts law at least since the judgment in *Dyer v Dyer*.[12] Lord Browne-Wilkinson held as follows:

> (A) where A makes a voluntary payment to B or pays (wholly or in part) for the purchase of property which is vested either in B alone or in the joint names of A and B, there is a presumption that A did not intend to make a gift to B: the money or property is held on trust for A (if he is the sole provider of the money) or in the case of a joint purchase by A and B in shares proportionate to their contributions. It is important to stress that this is only a *presumption*, which presumption is easily rebutted either by the counter-presumption of advancement or by direct evidence of A's intention to make an outright transfer.

Equity will presume that all of the parties were intended to take an equitable interest on resulting trust unless it can be proved that the intention was different. Therefore, a resulting trust will be presumed to exist unless that presumption can be rebutted by clear evidence to that effect. The sort of evidence which might be important would be evidence that one of the parties was making a loan to the other person to acquire the property instead of there being an intention that they would be equitable co-owners of that property.

Two illustrations of purchase price resulting trusts

To give examples of these presumptions, let us suppose the following. Jack and Jill are an unmarried couple in their late 30s in a long-term sexual relationship. They move to a new town in a semi-rural setting so that they can afford to buy a house because they want to have children in a wholesome environment. Their new house costs £200,000 to buy, and so each of them contributes £100,000 in cash from their separate savings to the purchase price. They then contribute equally to the costs of furnishing and decorating their property, and they do all of the work together. (If it helps you to picture the scene, then imagine one of those montage scenes from the movies where the young couple are painting the walls of their new home – she has a diaphanous scarf tied round her head and he wears belt-less, ripped

---

11 [1996] 2 All ER 961; [1996] AC 669.
12 (1788) 2 Cox Eq Cas 92.

jeans hanging loosely from his hips – and they splash each other with paint, accidentally at first, before collapsing into a giggling heap on the old sheets that cover the floor.) Clearly, the intention here is that both people are intended to have a half share in the home because they are sharing it as a couple. Indeed the ancient land law principle of 'joint tenancy' would consider them to be owners of the property together as though they were one person, one flesh. The presumption here would be that the entire equitable interest in the property is held on resulting trust for Jack and Jill as beneficiaries. (The detail of the law on ownership of the home when things get complicated between the parties is discussed in Chapter 15 *Trusts of Homes*. In that chapter we shall see that simply focusing on the financial contributions made by the parties is no longer the modern way and therefore the resulting trust has waned in importance in that context.)

By contrast, let us imagine another situation entirely in which the position is more complex. Suppose that Bertie wants to start a publishing business so that she can publish cheap e-textbooks for law students. Bertie approaches her uncle Donald, who has experience in the publishing business, for advice, and in the hope that Donald might provide her with some capital for her new business. Donald gives her £10,000 and a lot of free advice. Donald and Bertie agree that the first things she must buy for the business are new computers and the appropriate editing software. This costs £20,000 in total. Bertie uses the £10,000 advanced by Donald and £10,000 of her own savings to buy the software and the computers. The business is a roaring success and is valued ten years later at £4 million. Donald writes to Bertie asking for his £2 million share of the business to be paid to him as quickly as possible. Bertie tells him he is being ridiculous, that he does not own any of the business, and instead sends him a cheque for £10,000 'in repayment of the loan you made me all those years ago'. Here there will be difficulties. Donald will argue that he should be entitled to a half share of the computers and the software, and consequently a half share of the business which grew out of them because he contributed half of the business's original capital. On resulting trust principles he will argue that he is entitled to half of the business and all of its assets. Bertie will argue that Donald was merely making her a loan (as opposed to acquiring a half-share of her business), that her only obligations arose under contract law to repay that loan, and that Donald acquired no rights under resulting trust or property law at all as a result.

This case is clearly less clear than the case involving Jack and Jill and it would be difficult to know what to presume. Let us suppose that nothing was written down and that there were no witnesses to their original conversations. In practice, everything would turn on the common understanding which Bertie and Donald formed when he paid her the original £10,000. However, in practice, both parties will remember the circumstances very differently, and both will swear in their affidavits[13] and in the witness box in court that their different recollections of what was said were correct. The judge will therefore have to infer an answer from the circumstances because the only relevant witnesses (Bertie and Donald) will be in flat disagreement with one another. On these facts, it would be surprising that Donald had said nothing for ten years if he truly thought that he was the half-owner of the business and similarly it would be surprising if he had played no part in the business (not even annual meetings as a part

---

13 An affidavit is a formal document prepared in the course of litigation (and otherwise) in which the parties and witnesses state their recollection of events.

owner) if he genuinely thought that he was an owner of half of it.[14] Therefore, on balance, a court would be likely to find that Donald could only have intended to make a loan to his niece.

Resulting trusts arise by operation of law. Therefore, it is a difficult question in many circumstances for the judge to know whether or not a resulting trust is appropriate. Judges will often be cautious of seeming to create property rights (for example, by way of a resulting trust) out of thin air in cases of this sort because to create property rights for Donald would rob property rights from Bertie.

Resulting trust where no adequate disposal of the equitable interest

The other form of resulting trust arises automatically so that there is no gap in the ownership of property. By way of illustration, in *Vandervell v IRC*[15] Tony Vandervell purported to transfer title in some shares from his first settlement to another trust but, fatally, there was an option to repurchase those shares which was unallocated: i.e. it was not made clear who was supposed to be the equitable owner of that option. An option to acquire property constitutes an equitable interest in that property. Ownership of the option to acquire these shares may have been unallocated deliberately for tax purposes, or it may have been out of carelessness. Nevertheless, it was held that because ownership of this equitable interest was unknown then that equitable interest should be deemed to bounce back to Tony Vandervell's first settlement on resulting trust. Thus, where ownership of an equitable interest is unknown because an attempt to transfer property onto a trust has failed, then a resulting trust will come into existence automatically so as to carry that equitable interest back to its last-known owner. Lord Browne-Wilkinson explained this second category of resulting trust as coming into existence in the following situation:

> (B) Where A transfers property to B *on express trusts*, but the trusts declared do not exhaust the whole beneficial interest.[16]

So, Lord Browne-Wilkinson drew this kind of resulting trust quite narrowly as arising in situations where there was an intention to create an express trust but for some reason those trusts do not explain the ownership of the whole of the equitable interest in the property. That might be because the trust failed completely (perhaps because there was some uncertainty of objects, as discussed in Chapter 3) or because there was some item of property left unallocated (such as the option to reacquire the shares in *Vandervell v IRC*).

Put crudely, this model of resulting trust is based on the common sense proposition that if the current owner of property is unknown then the law should assume that the last person who can be proved to have been the owner of the property should be deemed still to be the owner of that property. Imagine that the title property is one of those children's toys on which a little rubber ball is attached by a piece of elastic to a small wooden bat. When the ball is hit against the bat it bounces away until it reaches the full extent of the elastic, and then it bounces back to the bat again. An automatic resulting trust works in the same way. If

---

14   You might be wondering what sort of owner Donald could be. Donald would probably argue that his £10,000 contribution would have created a partnership with Bertie whereby each of the partners would be the owners of a half each of the business.

15   [1967] 2 AC 291.

16   [1996] AC 669.

the property owner tries to pass the property to someone else then the property will bounce back to that property owner if the transfer fails for some reason, or if the intended recipient is not identified clearly. So, if you fail to transfer property to someone else then that property bounces back to you on resulting trust.

11.2 AUTOMATIC RESULTING TRUSTS

11.2.1 No declaration of trust, by mistake

The clearest example of an automatic resulting trust was considered above. The decision of the House of Lords in *Vandervell v IRC*,[17] which was considered in detail in Chapter 5, is a good authority for this type of resulting trust. The trustees of Tony Vandervell's personal trust purported to transfer valuable shares to the Royal College of Surgeons temporarily, but a small part of the equitable interest was not transferred to the College. That small part of the equitable interest was an option to repurchase those shares. The issue arose as to who owned that small part of the equitable interest. That issue was very important for tax purposes. It was held that that small part of the equitable interest was held on resulting trust for Tony Vandervell's personal trust. So, the failure to identify the owner of that option meant that the equitable interest in the shares which was constituted by the option meant that that equitable interest was held for Tony Vandervell's personal trust on resulting trust principles.

The most common explanation of this sort of resulting trust is that the equitable interest 'jumps back' to its original owner. However, another analysis is possible. It might be said that Tony Vandervell's personal trust only transferred away a part of the equitable interest in the shares and instead retained the option throughout the transaction. After all, no other person became the owner of that option and therefore it is difficult to see how it could have passed away. Consequently, it could be said that the option did not 'jump back' to Tony Vandervell's personal trust because it never left it in the first place. As we consider the following cases on automatic resulting trusts, it is important to ask whether or not any property actually 'jumps back' or whether the better explanation is that the property remains with the settlor throughout.

11.2.2 Failure of trust

Where a trust fails then the property is held on resulting trust for the settlor. A trust may fail if its underlying objective fails.[18] In *Re Cochrane's Settlement Trusts*[19] both parties to a marriage brought property to a marriage settlement. The marriage came to an end and the question arose whether the former wife was entitled to the property which her former husband had contributed to the fund before he died. It was argued, on behalf of the former husband's legatees that the failure of the marriage should signal the failure of the trust, with the effect that the property which he had contributed to the marriage settlement should pass back to the former husband's estate on resulting trust. The terms of the marriage settlement provided that the wife would receive the income from the trust provided that she lived with him. It was held that the wife received the equitable interest in the property which she had

17 [1966] Ch 261; [1967] 2 AC 291.
18 *Vandervell v IRC* [1967] 2 AC 291.
19 [1955] Ch 309.

contributed to the marriage settlement on resulting trust, but that the property which the husband had contributed to the marriage settlement passed to his estate on resulting trust after his death. The basis for this decision was the failure of the purpose of the marriage settlement (that is, that they should stay together) giving rise to a return of the property to the original settlor on resulting trust. Similarly, in *Re Ames' Settlement*[20] a marriage was declared null and void: that means, the marriage had never existed. Given that the marriage had never existed it was held by Vaisey J that the marriage settlement failed, put crudely, on the basis that if there was no marriage then there was no marriage settlement. Consequently, any property purportedly settled on the terms of the marriage settlement passed back to its original owners on resulting trust.

11.2.3 Surplus property after performance of trust

What happens once the purpose of a trust or unincorporated association has been performed and there is still property left over? In *Re Gillingham Bus Disaster Fund*[21] there had been a subscription fund raised from the public in the wake of a bus crash for its victims. The public were clearly very generous. The victims of the crash did not require all of the money raised. The issue arose as to the proper treatment of the surplus money which had been raised from the public. The court held that the surplus should be held on resulting trust for the subscribers.[22] Harman J held that each resulting trust should arise *sub modo*, on its own terms and in a way that was appropriate to its own circumstances. This interesting idea, which is considered at the end of this chapter, would suggest that resulting trusts can operate like constructive trusts so that they come into existence in a variety of forms (not just the two identified by Lord Browne-Wilkinson) and on their own terms dependent on their circumstances (rather than existing only in some pre-packaged format).

Similarly, in *Re Trusts of the Abbott Fund*,[23] a trust fund was created in favour of two elderly ladies, and subscriptions were sought from the public. The aim underlying the trust was not fully performed before the two ladies died. It was held that the trust property remaining undistributed at the time of death should be held on resulting trust for the subscribers. It can be seen from these two cases that the resulting trust is the instinctive response of the English courts in these sorts of cases where there is excess property beyond the needs of the trust. Matters may be different in relation to unincorporated associations, as considered next.

11.2.4 Upon dissolution of unincorporated association

The context of the unincorporated association was considered in Chapter 4 in relation to purpose trusts. The traditional view, applied in *Re West Sussex, etc Fund Trusts*[24] was that a resulting trust would be imposed over property held by an unincorporated association (here, a benevolent fund for police officers' families) if that association ceased to exist. However,

---

20 [1964] Ch 217.
21 [1958] Ch 300.
22 *Re Hillier* [1954] 1 WLR 9.
23 [1900] Ch 326.
24 *Re West Sussex Constabulary's Widows, Children and Benevolent (1930) Fund Trusts* [1971] Ch 1.

the later decision in *Re Bucks Constabulary Fund*[25] is that the dissolution of a society and the distribution of property held for its purposes is a matter purely of contract: that is, the association's rules should govern the treatment of the property. Therefore, in relation specifically to unincorporated associations (which are based on the contract between their members, as discussed in Chapter 4) it appears that the prevailing view is that it is contract law which should govern their dissolution and not resulting trusts principles. However, if the contract governing the association is silent about the proper division of property on the termination of an association then that leaves the question at large as to the method by which the property used by the association should be divided.

11.3 *QUISTCLOSE* TRUSTS

Quistclose trusts arise specifically in relation to loan contracts in which the lender specifies that the borrower may only use the money for a specified purpose. That term of the contract imposes a trust over the loan moneys so that, if the borrower goes into insolvency, then the loan moneys are held on trust for the lender and are not distributed among the borrower's unsecured creditors. It is commonly accepted that *Quistclose* trusts constitute a form of resulting trust. However, *Quistclose* trusts create a number of complications and their classification as a type of resulting trust is controversial. Therefore, *Quistclose* trusts are discussed in Chapter 22 in a chapter on their own.

11.4 PRESUMED RESULTING TRUSTS

11.4.1 Introduction

Everyone lies. Sometimes people are just confused, and their confusion causes them to say things that otherwise would be lies. In the witness box, this is as true as anywhere. Over the time that it takes for cases to come to court, the truth will be forgotten or it will have been filtered through months and years of bitterness, conversations with lawyers, drafting affidavits asserting your case and reading pleadings (your claim, your defence and so forth) drafted by your counsel. Consequently, it is very difficult for the courts to find the truth. Each witness gives a partial account of what they claim happened, or even of what they honestly think (after all the time that has passed) did happen. The judge has to come to a decision as to what the facts are, and then as to the best outcome for the parties in the light of the law.

Precisely because it can be so difficult for a court to identify 'the truth' there are situations in which English law presumes that certain sets of facts give rise to certain legal outcomes. The presumptions are a default setting which the courts use in cases of uncertainty. Think of it as being a little like a computer which, when you exit all of the software packages, returns to its default setting at the log-on screen, or like pressing Ctrl+Alt+Del on a Windows computer. It is the result which the court plumps for when it cannot know on the evidence which is the correct result. In many circumstances, as we shall see, resulting trusts are the presumptive default setting used by property law. As Lord Upjohn held in *Vandervell v IRC*:[26] 'in reality the so-called presumption of a resulting trust is no more than a long-stop to provide an answer where the relevant facts and circumstances fail to reach a solution'.

---

25 [1979] 1 All ER 623.
26 [1967] 2 AC 291, 313.

Equity has generated a group of situations in which it presumes that a given analysis must be the case when the facts are otherwise unclear, possibly because documents have been lost or possibly because the parties' evidence is contradictory. So, we shall see that there are circumstances in which equity presumes that a gift has taken place because that is the law's best guess as to the likely analysis, and there are other circumstances in which equity presumes the existence of a resulting trust. The most obvious example of a presumed resulting trust is the situation in which two or more people contribute to the purchase price of property. In that situation, the law presumes that those people are intended to take equitable interests in that property in proportion to the size of their contribution to that purchase price. However, there are other presumptions which have developed over time. We shall begin with the so-called 'presumption of advancement'.

11.4.2 Presumption of advancement – special relationships

This section considers some of the specific relationships which the case law considers give effect to deemed outright transfers of property in the absence of evidence to the contrary, by way of presumption. The presumption of advancement is intended to be removed by statute for the future, and has been overruled in relation specifically to cases involving the home. In cases other than these two situations, the law presumes that a gift has been made by one person to the other when it is otherwise unclear what the correct analysis is.

Where a father transfers property to a child, in the absence of compelling evidence about the father's intention, it has been presumed that the father intends to make an outright gift of that property to that child.[27] This is referred to as 'the presumption of advancement'. It is a presumption that a gift is being made. The understanding behind the presumption of advancement was that fathers (but not mothers) were expected to take care of their children and therefore it could be presumed that when a father passed property to his child then that was intended to be a gift to that child.[28] A father can rebut this presumption with cogent evidence to demonstrate that no gift was intended. In such a situation, the property would be held on resulting trust by the child for the father. In the absence of any cogent evidence to rebut this presumption of advancement, no resulting trust would be imposed on the property in favour of the father.[29]

The same presumption applies in relation to transfers of property from husband to wife[30] (but not in the other direction historically).[31] So, when a husband transfers property to his wife then the presumption is that the husband intends to make a gift of that property to his wife because it is a husband's duty to 'maintain' his wife. (That expression always makes the wife sound like an old outbuilding.) It would only be if the husband could produce cogent evidence to rebut this presumption that the property would be held on resulting trust by the wife for the husband. The clearest modern application of the presumption of advancement between husband and wife arose in *Tinker v Tinker*.[32] Mr Tinker transferred land into the name of Mrs Tinker with the intention of putting the land beyond the reach of his business creditors.

---

27 *Bennet v Bennet* (1879) 10 Ch D 474; *Lavelle v Lavelle* [2004] EWCA Civ 223.
28 *Bennet v Bennet* (1879) 10 Ch D 474.
29 Rebuttal of the presumption is considered at section 11.4.5 below.
30 *Tinker v Tinker* [1970] P 136.
31 Historically these presumptions also applied to any transfer of property from master to servant. Perhaps that gives a taste of the era in which these ideas were created.
32 [1970] P 136.

His plan was that, if he went insolvent, then Mr Tinker could argue that Mrs Tinker was the owner of the land on which the business was conducted so that his creditors could not seize the land.[33] The Tinkers' marriage broke down subsequently and Mr Tinker sought to recover the land from his wife. Lord Denning held that Mr Tinker could not argue against his wife that the property was held on resulting trust for him while also arguing against his creditors that the property was vested in his wife. It was impossible to know which of Mr Tinker's contradictory arguments about the ownership of the property was the truth. Consequently, Lord Denning held that the presumption of advancement fell to be applied so that it was presumed that the transfer to Mrs Tinker was intended to be an outright transfer of the land to her.

Self-evidently, these presumptions are anachronistic in a modern society. Presuming that only fathers and only husbands owe any responsibility to care for other family members is a relic from another age. In *Pettitt v Pettitt*,[34] Lord Diplock held that it would be 'an abuse' to continue to apply these 'presumptions which are based upon inferences of fact which an earlier generation of judges drew as the most likely intentions of the earlier generations of spouses belonging to the propertied classes of a different social era'. Following the decision of the House of Lords in *Stack v Dowden*,[35] the Supreme Court in *Jones v Kernott*[36] has held that the presumption of advancement should not apply in the context of the equitable ownership of the home. Therefore, the presumptions of advancement can only apply today to property which is not the family home or related land. (The position relating to ownership of the home is considered in detail in Chapter 15.)

The Equality Act 2010 contains provisions which seek to abolish the presumption of advancement in the future. That legislation has yet to be brought fully into effect. Section 199 of that Act provides that 'the presumption of advancement is abolished' but that abolition applies only to 'anything done' after the Act comes into effect. Section 198 of the Act provided that '[t]he rule of common law that a husband must maintain his wife is abolished'.

11.4.3 Voluntary gift

The case law on making voluntary gifts is complex. The awkward decision in *Re Vinogradoff*[37] concerned a grandmother who transferred a war loan worth £800 into her name and her infant granddaughter's name. It was never made plain what the grandmother's intention was in doing this. After her death, Farwell J held that the property should be presumed to have been held on resulting trust the grandmother on the bases that she did not fall within the category of fathers presumptively making gifts to their children, and also because the grandmother kept all of the dividends paid on the war loan for herself (thus leading the court to believe that she had really intended to keep the war loan for herself beneficially). So, his lordship's reasoning was that she did not fall within the usual category of the presumptions because she was not the child's father but only her grandmother. In *Westdeutsche Landesbank Girozentrale v Islington LBC*,[38] Lord Browne-Wilkinson explained *Re Vinogradoff*[39] as being a case in which

---

33   Mr Tinker had a garage business in which, presumably, he used to tinker with cars.
34   [1970] AC 777.
35   [2007] 2 WLR 831.
36   [2011] 3 WLR 1121.
37   [1935] WN 68.
38   [1996] AC 669.
39   [1935] WN 68.

the grandmother demonstrated no intention to make an immediate gift such that a resulting trust was appropriate to carry the equitable interest in that property back to her.[40]

In *Hodgson v Marks*[41] an unconscionable swine by the name of Evans convinced an elderly woman to sign her house over to him. She did this because Evans had convinced her that he would be destitute after her death and that her nephew would evict him from her house (where he had been a lodger). As soon as Evans received the transfer of the property, he sold it to Marks. Marks sought vacant possession of the property. Mrs Hodgson successfully relied on a promise made to her by Evans that she would be able to live in the house for the rest of her life so that she would be able to remain in the property. While this might seem to disclose a right to proprietary estoppel (discussed in Chapter 13, whereby she had relied on this promise to her detriment), it was held that Mrs Hodgson acquired rights in the property on resulting trust principles. The only explanation for this being a resulting trust is that it arose *sub modo* in the way suggested by Harman J in *Re Gillingham Bus Disaster Fund* on its own terms, or else that the court was seduced by the metaphor of property passing away from Mrs Hodgson and then passing back to her by way of a resulting trust. The Court of Appeal held that Mrs Hodgson had a right under 'a resulting trust of the beneficial interest to the plaintiff, which would not, of course, be affected by section 53(1)'.[42] It is suggested that the court must have assumed that these were property rights which bounced back to Mrs Hodgson when she transferred the property to Evans.

11.4.4 Contribution to purchase price

The clearest form of presumed resulting trust, accepted both by Lord Browne-Wilkinson in *Westdeutsche Landesbank Girozentrale v Islington LBC*[43] and by Megarry J in *Vandervell (No 2)*,[44] is the situation in which a person contributes to the acquisition price of property and is therefore presumed to take a corresponding equitable interest in that property. It is only in relation to ownership of the home (as discussed in Chapter 15) that different principles have been developed so that ownership of the home is not dependent entirely on who paid for the purchase price, but rather 'takes into account the entire course of dealing' between the members of the cohabiting unit or family.[45]

It is a pre-requisite for the establishment of such a resulting trust that the claimant demonstrates that the contribution to the purchase price is not made for any purpose other than acquisition of a right in the property. So, in *Elithorn v Poulter*[46] the court held that a woman intended to make a loan to her partner so that he could acquire a half-share in their house, and not that she was intended to be the sole equitable owner of that house. This was odd given that in practice she paid for the entirety of the purchase price of that house. Nevertheless, she was found on the facts to have intended, when she wrote her cheque for the entire purchase price of the house, to make a loan to her partner so that he could acquire a half-share in that house with her. Consequently, it was held that her partner had acquired a half-share in the property together with a common law

---

40   Martin, 1997, 246.
41   [1971] Ch 892.
42   *Ibid*, 933, *per* Russell LJ.
43   [1996] AC 669.
44   [1974] Ch 269.
45   *Jones v Kernott* [2011] 3 WLR 1121.
46   [2008] EWCA Civ 1364.

debt to repay the loan to her. The evidence for finding that there was such a loan was obscure and it did mean that the woman had (in practice, before any repayments of the so-called loan were made to her) paid for the whole purchase price but only received half of the equity in the house. To add insult to injury, Rimer LJ referred to her as 'Madeline' throughout the case but referred to her partner as 'Dr Elithorn', which suggests that he was being accorded somewhat more respect than her unconsciously in this case for reasons which are equally baffling. Why was she being called by her first name when he was being called by his highest university degree?

11.4.5 Rebutting the presumption

The defendant can rebut the presumption of advancement by adducing cogent evidence that they intended something else by the transfer of property to their spouse or child. In the old case of *Finch v Finch*,[47] Lord Eldon suggested that the court should not accept a rebuttal of the presumption of advancement unless there was a sufficient weight of evidence to justify such a rebuttal. The more modern approach, indicated by cases like *McGrath v Wallis*,[48] is to accept a rebuttal of the presumption of advancement in family cases on the basis of comparatively slight evidence – even in a situation where an unexecuted deed of trust was the only direct evidence indicating the fact that a father intended a division of the equitable interest rather than an outright transfer when conveying land into his son's name.[49] The clearest general statement of principle surrounding rebuttals of the presumption was made in *Fowkes v Pascoe*[50] when James LJ held that the principle governing the rebuttal of the presumption was as follows:

> Where the Court of Chancery is asked, as an equitable assumption of presumption, to take away from a man that which by the common law of the land he is entitled to, he surely has a right to say: 'Listen to my story as to how I came to have it, and judge that story with reference to all the surrounding facts and circumstances.'[51]

There is perhaps no clearer statement of any equitable principle: a court of equity is required to listen to the parties' stories as to how they have come into the position they occupy, and then to use good conscience to craft the appropriate response. It is central to the human condition in the modern world that we want to be valued as an autonomous human being and we want to be heard.

Where bank accounts are held jointly between husband and wife, the courts have not tended to presume that any money paid into that joint account is intended to be a gift to the wife. So, where property was paid into a bank account by a husband with the intention that that property should be held on a joint tenancy basis by himself and his wife, the account was found to have been held on joint tenancy for them and furthermore passed absolutely to the survivor of the two; it was not intended to be a gift to the wife.[52] Similarly, property acquired with funds

---

47 (1808) 15 Ves Jr 43.
48 [1995] 2 FLR 114.
49 *Ibid.*
50 (1875) 10 Ch App Cas 343.
51 *Ibid*, 349.
52 *Marshall v Crutwell* (1875) LR 20 Eq 328; *Re Figgis* [1969] Ch 123.

taken from that joint bank account would belong to both husband and wife as joint tenants,[53] unless that property was expressly intended to be taken in the name of one or other of them.[54] If, however, the husband continues to use the purportedly joint bank account as though it was entirely his own account, then the presumption of advancement might be rebutted.[55]

Difficult questions of fact have arisen in cases in which parents have passed property to their children so as to avoid liability to tax. In *Sekhon v Alissa*,[56] a mother transferred property into her daughter's name with the intention to avoid liability to capital gains tax. It was held that this was a suitable rebuttal of any presumption that might have been argued in favour of the daughter. However, demonstrating that each case must be taken on its own facts (listening to the witnesses carefully), in *Shephard v Cartwright*[57] it was held by Viscount Simonds that a father should be presumed to have intended a gift of shares to his three children, even though evidence was advanced that he had intended to minimise his liability to tax by doing this before he died. While fact patterns can look the same in the abstract (in both of these two cases we have parents who are trying to minimise their liability to tax) that does not mean that the judges who hear the evidence and see the witnesses believe each person's intentions to have been the same. So, in *Warren v Gurney*[58] while a father conveyed land into his daughter's name, it was held that his retention of the title deeds in relation to that land should negative a presumption that he had intended to make a gift of the land to her. In that case, the retention of title deeds was found by the judge to disclose an intention in that man's mind that he did not want to part with his land outright; whereas in *Shephard v Cartwright* it was argued that that father had similarly intended to retain control of the land because he told his children what to do with the land and instructed them to sign documents governing the land when he presented those documents to them. Yet, in the latter case, the court found that the father's intention was to part with the land, such that the presumption of advancement was justified, and (having listened to all of the witnesses and the evidence) that the other factors did not negative that intention.

Studying case law solely from books can be a frustrating business because it is often difficult to get a sense of the witnesses and of the parties to the litigation. Several property law professors (including myself) attended a famous case before the Supreme Court in which reading the law reports one might have garnered the impression that a father had abandoned his family, when in truth it was clear from watching the parties in the cafeteria that he was still very close to his children. Very astutely, the mother's solicitors ensured that the children sat next to her in court. Similarly, it is often difficult to know why one case is decided one way, when a seemingly identical case is decided another way by another judge. One explanation of this difference might be that the judges simply take different views on how the law should operate. A more likely explanation is that the evidence brought by the witnesses and their performance in the witness box in front of the judge at first instance might have created a particular impression on that judge which led to a different outcome. So, in the cases just discussed, the different judges simply formed different views of what the people in those cases really intended.

53 *Jones v Maynard* [1951] Ch 572.
54 *Re Bishop* [1965] Ch 450.
55 *Young v Sealey* [1949] Ch 278.
56 [1989] 2 FLR 94.
57 [1955] AC 431.
58 [1944] 2 All ER 472.

11.4.6 Illegality and resulting trust

The problem in outline

A particularly significant issue has arisen with respect to resulting trusts concerning people who have acted illegally in relation to property but who are seeking to impose a resulting trust over that property so as to assert their ownership of it. Let us begin by outlining the problem which is at issue. If a person has contributed to the purchase price of property, or if that person falls within one of the classes of person in whose favour a resulting trust is usually presumed, then should they be able to assert the existence of a resulting trust if they had been acting illegally beforehand? It is a long-established principle of equity that she who comes to equity must come with clean hands. In other words, if a person wants to claim a resulting trust then they must not have committed an unconscionable act themselves to establish that resulting trust. So, in cases like *Tinker v Tinker*[59] (discussed above) the claimant had acted illegally by trying to put his assets beyond the reach of his creditors when he was insolvent. It was held that the claimant would not be able to rely on equitable, resulting trust principles because of his illegal act. This principle can be traced back into older cases such as *Holman v Johnson* where in the words of Lord Mansfield:

> No court will lend its aid to a man who founds his cause of action upon an immoral or an illegal act.[60]

By contrast, in *Tinsley v Milligan*[61] (which is discussed next) the claimant had acquired a property with her partner but she had committed the criminal offence of claiming housing benefits when she knew she had property rights in a home. Nevertheless, the majority of the House of Lords held that she was entitled to a resulting trust over that property because she had contributed entirely lawfully to its purchase price, and therefore she did not need to rely on her subsequent illegal act to establish her right to the property. After all, she had not stolen the house; she had simply lied about her ownership of it when claiming benefits. Lord Browne-Wilkinson was careful to ignore the backdrop of illegality in that case and to focus forensically on the fact that the claimant had acquired her property rights perfectly lawfully at the outset.

These cases and several others are considered in detail below. What is important is that equity will traditionally prevent you from relying on an equitable doctrine when you have been involved in illegal behaviour; but that the recent cases have tended to make forensic distinctions between the claimant's illegal behaviour and the lawful acts which acquired rights in property in some of the cases in the first place. It is this sort of moral question which we consider in this chapter: do we deny rights to people who have acted unconscionably or illegally in general terms, or do we examine the precise source of their rights and thereby ignore their unconscionable behaviour if it was not the source of those rights?

---

59 [1970] P 136.
60 (1775) 1 Cowp 341, 343, *per* Lord Mansfield CJ; as applied by Lord Goff in *Tinsley v Milligan* [1994] 1 AC 340.
61 [1994] 1 AC 340.

The presumptions, resulting trusts and illegality

The law in this area is a little knotted. Let us remind ourselves of the long-standing principles on presumed resulting trusts, which were discussed above, before considering the more recent case law which has considered those principles in the context of illegal acts. First, if a person contributes to the purchase price of property then they will acquire an equitable interest in that property on resulting trust principles in proportion to the size of their contribution. Second, if a father advances property rights to his son or daughter then it is presumed that he intends to make a gift of that property to his son or daughter. Third, the father can rebut that presumption of a gift by bringing forward evidence that he did not intend to make a gift. If the father is successful in rebutting this presumption of a gift to the satisfaction of the court, then the equitable interest in that property will be held on resulting trust for him. Fourth, there will be a problem with the father's argument if the evidence he uses to rebut the presumption requires him to admit that he intended to commit an illegal act (for example, trying to put property beyond the reach of his insolvency creditors by passing it to his son or daughter). Traditionally, a court of equity would not permit a person to have a resulting trust if they had committed an illegal act to get it. The question in the more recent cases has been whether or not the illegal act was actually the device which acquired that person their property rights. We shall begin by dissecting the important case of *Tinsley v Milligan*, and then we shall analyse the difficult case of *Tribe v Tribe* which involved almost exactly the pattern of facts just used in this hypothetical example of the father and his children.

The decision of the House of Lords in Tinsley v Milligan

In the case of *Tinsley v Milligan*[62] Stella Tinsley and Kathleen Milligan were in a long-term lesbian relationship. They acquired a house together which they intended to run jointly in business as a lodging-house. Importantly, both Stella and Kathleen contributed to the purchase price of that property. However, they hatched a criminal conspiracy such that Kathleen would claim social security benefits to pay for her 'rent' in occupying this property. The property was placed in Stella's sole name at the Land Registry so that Kathleen (who did not share a surname with Stella and whose relationship with Stella (they hoped) would be invisible to the authorities) could claim benefits. This meant that Kathleen was committing a criminal offence because she knew that she had rights in the property. Kathleen was convicted of that criminal offence. The question arose whether Kathleen could claim an equitable interest in the property in a dispute with Stella. Kathleen argued that her contribution to the purchase price should have given her a resulting trust right in the property; whereas Stella argued that Kathleen had to rely on evidence of her criminal activity to prove that resulting trust and therefore that equity should not assist her due to her unclean hands. It was held by the majority of the House of Lords that Kathleen had acquired her property rights through the parties' common intention that her contribution to the purchase price meant that she was to have an equitable interest in the property. That purchase of the property at the outset had been perfectly lawful and that entitled her to a right under resulting trust principles in the property. Her subsequent criminal activity did

62 [1994] 1 AC 340.

not affect the property law analysis that she had had an equitable proprietary right in the property from the outset.

The majority in Tinsley v Milligan

Lord Browne-Wilkinson held, in essence, that Kathleen did not have to rely on her own illegality because she had been entitled to an equitable share in the property from the moment that she had contributed to its purchase price. The illegality was therefore not the *source* of her equitable rights; rather, it was her contribution to the purchase price that was the source of her rights.

Lord Browne-Wilkinson identified three principles. First, property rights in chattels and land can pass under a contract which is illegal and therefore would have been unenforceable as a contract. So, here, property rights could pass in this house even though there was a criminal conspiracy. Second, at law a claimant can enforce any property rights acquired through that arrangement provided that she does not need to rely on the illegal contract for any purpose other than providing the basis of his claim to a property right. So, it is acceptable to say 'I paid for half of the house but I was not registered on the legal title because Stella and I were hiding my ownership rights for criminal purposes' but it would not have been acceptable to say 'I acquired my rights in the house by fraud'. In the former situation, the property rights were acquired lawfully and therefore should be protected; whereas in the latter situation, the property rights were acquired unlawfully (by virtue of being acquired fraudulently) and therefore equity ought not to help. Third, it is irrelevant that the illegality of the underlying agreement was either pleaded or emerged in evidence. Lord Goff (as is considered next) was concerned about the idea that property rights in equity could be created from such an illegal agreement.

The preferable approach, it is suggested, is to say that the rights were sourced lawfully, even if the property was used unlawfully later. Let us take the example of Tony Soprano (from the television programme *The Sopranos* – it does not matter if you have not seen it). Tony is the boss of a criminal gang which earns a lot of money from illegal activities. Tony also owns a legitimate delicatessen business operated from a shop on a busy high street. Suppose that Tony buys a car with the legitimate profits from his delicatessen. His shiny Jaguar XJ cost £75,000 in cash. All of that money can be traced into lawful sales of expensive food products to high-class caterers. The Jaguar XJ (in indigo blue, with a barley corn, cream leather interior, and walnut dashboard trim) is undoubtedly his absolutely. Suppose then that this car is used as a getaway car when Tony has to collect one of his gang in an emergency from an attempted 'hit' which goes wrong. Does that car cease to belong to Tony because it was used in a crime? The answer must be that the car continues to be owned outright by Tony throughout. His lawful acquisition of the car is not brought into question simply because he uses it for a criminal purpose subsequently.

If a different car, a Mercedes E-Class, had been bought by Tony using proceeds from criminal activities (such as the sale of drugs) then the Proceeds of Crime Act 2002 would define that as the proceeds of a criminal lifestyle and therefore there would be justification under that Act for the state's assets recovery agency, created under that Act, to seize the car as a product of that criminal lifestyle. In this example, the car would have been bought with criminal money. The source of Tony's ownership of it would be an illegal act. In the previous example, the Jaguar XJ was bought with money that had been legitimately earned from a legitimate business. In the same way, when Kathleen acquired her rights in the lodging-house she did so entirely lawfully. It was the purpose to which she put her property rights subsequently that was unlawful. Lord Browne-Wilkinson focused on the original source of those property rights – honestly-earned money and a mortgage – as opposed to Kathleen's subsequent activities. If Kathleen had stolen the money which she used to acquire her share in the property then that would have been different.

The minority in Tinsley v Milligan

Lord Goff dissented, and approved the general approach (if not the precise detail) of the judgments in the Court of Appeal. Lord Goff cited a number of authorities including *Tinker v Tinker* [63] and *Re Emery* [64] as establishing the proposition that equity will not assist someone who transfers property to another in furtherance of a fraudulent or illegal design to establish an interest in property. This approach is founded primarily on the ancient equitable maxim that 'he who comes to equity must come with clean hands'[65] and the fear that an extension of the principle propounded by Lord Browne-Wilkinson would 'open the door to far more unmeritorious cases'. For Lord Goff, the question was simple at its root: Kathleen had committed a criminal offence and was now seeking equity's help in recovering an equitable interest in the property. Lord Goff considered that she should not be entitled to any equitable assistance.

The judgment of Nicholls LJ in the Court of Appeal in *Tinsley v Milligan* was particularly interesting in considering the nature of equity.[66] It was argued by Nicholls LJ that there ought to be a 'public conscience' test in cases such as *Tinsley v Milligan*. A public conscience test would mean that the judge could decide whether, in all the circumstances, they thought that the defendant's behaviour was sufficiently unconscionable to justify denying the award of property. This conscience would be equity in its purest sense: without reference to precedent or statute, the judge would be able to balance, in the words of Nicholls LJ, 'the adverse consequences of granting relief against the adverse consequences of refusing relief'.[67] Lord Goff was not prepared to condone such a broad discretion for judges, even if he was in agreement with the general outcome of the case.

There are two uncomfortable ironies with Lord Goff's argument. First, if Kathleen had been denied rights in the property then Stella would have been the only beneficial owner of the property. Stella had been a party to the criminal conspiracy which led to Kathleen claiming those benefits but Stella would nevertheless be entitled to absolute beneficial ownership of the property because she was not the one who filled in the social security forms. By default, if Kathleen was denied rights in the property then Stella would own them all. Stella was no more worthy of equity's assistance than Kathleen. Second, the only reason that Kathleen had been convicted of a criminal offence was that she had had property rights in a home that was available for her occupation. If she had not had property rights and an entitlement to occupy the property rent-free then she would not have committed a criminal offence

63 [1970] 2 WLR 331.
64 [1959] Ch 410.
65 Following *Groves v Groves* (1829) 3 Y&J 163, 174, *per* Lord Chief Baron Alexander; *Tinker v Tinker* [1970] P 136, 143, *per* Salmon LJ.
66 [1992] Ch 310.
67 *Ibid*, 319.

by claiming housing benefit. Therefore, if the House of Lords was to deny her rights in the property then that would call into question the very basis on which she had been convicted, and therefore she might not have committed any criminal activities which would have called into question her property rights under a resulting trust.

Tribe v Tribe – *the end of ethics?*

The decision of the Court of Appeal in *Tribe v Tribe*[68] posed a similar ethical problem to that in *Tinsley v Milligan*. Here, a father sought to conceal his ownership of a large shareholding in the family company by transferring the legal title in those shares to his son. That was an illegal act because Tribe Senior (i.e. the father) effected the transfer in the expectation that he would be forced into bankruptcy and therefore his creditors would seek possession of those shares. The shares were transferred at an undervalue (and the son did not pay for them in the end). The reason for Tribe Senior thinking that he was going into bankruptcy was that the lease over the business premises included a 'dilapidations clause' which meant that Tribe Senior would be responsible for a huge bill for repairs to the property. In the end, the landlord agreed to excuse Tribe Senior from paying that bill in return for a surrender of the lease. Therefore, Tribe Senior did not go into bankruptcy. So, he went to his son and asked for a return of the shares. Tribe Junior (i.e. the son) refused to return the shares. Tribe Junior argued:[69] this was a transfer from father to son and therefore there must be a presumption that you, father, intended to make a gift of those shares to me. Tribe Senior argued in return: no, son, I only transferred those shares to you so that I could put them beyond the reach of my creditors, but now I am not going bankrupt I want the shares back. Clearly, I did not intend to make a gift of them to you – instead, you must hold them on resulting trust for me. Tribe Junior then responded: so, father, you have to admit that you committed a criminal act by putting property beyond the reach of your creditors, but in equity you cannot rely on your illegality to rebut the presumption of gift and prove a resulting trust. So, the presumption of gift remains and I am now the owner of the family company. Tribe Senior, presumably, muttered an oath at this point and called his solicitors.

Millett LJ held that the shares should be returned to Tribe Senior on resulting trust because there was a flaw in Tribe Junior's logic: his father had not actually committed a criminal act because he had not been forced into bankruptcy and therefore there were no insolvency creditors who could have been defrauded by this transfer of the shareholding. This is a novel turn in the law in this area. Millett LJ is pushing the coldly logical approach taken by Lord Browne-Wilkinson in *Tinsley v Milligan* to its limit. (This judgment has been followed in later cases,[70] so that is not to doubt that it is good law.) Tribe Senior clearly intended to commit an unlawful act and he committed the actus reus: he was fortunate (or a skilful negotiator) in that he did not actually go into insolvency. It could have been said that Tribe Senior intended to carry the illegal act into effect when he transferred the shares to his son and therefore that he had had unclean hands at that moment. However, we might also reflect that his son was aware of the situation and therefore the son was in no greater ethical position than his father to pray equitable doctrines in aid. In cases such as this, the judges are not always put in a situation in which it is easy to decide between 'the good guys' and 'the bad guys'.

---

68   [1995] 4 All ER 236.
69   I have fabricated the dialogue so as to bring the arguments to life.
70   E.g. *Lowson v Coombes* [1999] Ch 373; *Collier v Collier* [2002] EWCA Civ 1095.

Instead, it is often the case that whoever wins, that person was involved in the unethical behaviour at some point. Therefore, *Tribe v Tribe* shows that the court simply has to identify the key principles and choose what it considers to be the better answer. Here, in spite of the sin that was in Tribe Senior's heart, because he did not have to carry his illegal purpose into effect (because he did not actually go into bankruptcy and therefore did not actually have to deceive his creditors) he was entitled to a resulting trust over his shares.

As Millett LJ put it, in a series of numbered propositions:

> (1) Title to property passes both at law and in equity even if the transfer is made for an illegal purpose . . . (2) The transferor's action will fail if it would be illegal for him to retain any interest in the property. (3) Subject to (2) the transferor can recover the property if he can do so without relying on the illegal purpose . . . (5) The transferor can lead evidence of the illegal purpose whenever it is necessary for him to do so provided that he has withdrawn from the transaction before the illegal purpose has been wholly or partly carried in to effect.

What we can know for sure is that every family celebration in the Tribe household must have been ruined in perpetuity by this litigation.

The *Tribe v Tribe* approach has been followed in several cases subsequently. In *Lowson v Coombes* an unmarried couple put their home in the woman's sole name in an effort to hide the man's equitable interest from his wife in matrimonial proceedings: but it was held that this was an illegal act and that equity required that the man could not purport to dispose of this property.[71] In *Patel v Mirza*,[72] the Court of Appeal was required to consider a situation in which two people had formed a putative agreement to use inside information in relation to a company. The use of 'inside information' in relation to corporate securities within the ambit of the Criminal Justice Act 1993 is a criminal offence. In this instance a payment of £620,000 was made from one person to another in furtherance of their intended agreement. In the end, the agreement was not performed and therefore no illegal act was actually committed. The question was whether or not the payer could recover the £620,000 that had been paid in expectation of that agreement. It was argued by the payer that the money could be recovered on the basis of a resulting trust; and it was counter-argued by the recipient that the illegal purpose prevented a resulting trust being used. The judgment in *Tribe v Tribe* was relied upon by Rimer LJ. On the basis that the illegal purpose had not been carried out, they could be no objection to a resulting trust applying in the circumstances in accordance with the judgment of Millett LJ in *Tribe v Tribe*.[73]

11.4.7 Illegality, the Insolvency Act 1986 and resulting trust

As has emerged from the previous discussion, illegality often arises when insolvency looms up on the horizon. Whether it is an individual facing bankruptcy or a company facing liquidation, it is common for people to try illegally to hide their assets so that, if

---

71 [1999] Ch 373.
72 [2015] 2 WLR 405.
73 Gloster LJ decided that this was a 'Quistclose-type trust'. The problem with that analysis is that a *Quistclose* trust only arises in relation to loans, and that her ladyship was supposing that it described a sort of general-purpose trust (which we know from Chapter 4 would have been void in any event under the beneficiary principle).

insolvency does strike, then they can use those assets after the insolvency proceedings have been wound up. This is an illegal act because it is a fraud on the creditors in the insolvency. Section 423 of the Insolvency Act 1986 empowers the court to reverse trans-actions in which sales of assets are made at an under-value (typically where the insolvent sells their property at a very low price to a friend or associated company with a view to recovering the property later) or where assets are simply given to a third party by means of a transfer for 'no consideration' (typically for the same nefarious reasons). The court's powers are then to make 'such order as the court sees fit'[74] to restore the *status quo ante*.[75] In practice, this provision is commonly used as an extra dimension to cases like *Tribe v Tribe* above.

A good example of this phenomenon in action was *Midland Bank v Wyatt*.[76] Mr Wyatt set up a textiles business. This was a new venture for him. Therefore, with the assistance of his solicitors, he decided to settle his half-share of the matrimonial home on trust for his wife and daughters. His intention was that, if he or his business should go into insolvency, then the house would be protected from his creditors. However, Mr Wyatt did not tell his wife nor his daughters about this settlement. Indeed, Mr Wyatt continued to borrow money against his half-share in the house as though it had not been settled on trust. Moreover, even when the Wyatts' marriage ended in divorce a few years later, Mrs Wyatt was never told of the settlement (which should have meant that she owned nearly all of the equitable interest in the house even before the divorce was settled). Subsequently, the textiles business did go into insolvency. Mr Wyatt claimed that his creditors could not claim his share in his house because it was held on trust for his wife and daughters. The court held, first, that the trust had been a sham and could therefore be ignored. A sham is any situation in which the parties' documentation and other devices are a 'pretence'[77] so as to give 'the appearance of creating between the parties legal rights and obligations different from the actual legal rights and obligations (if any) which the parties intended to create'.[78] That Mr Wyatt had not mentioned the supposed trust to its beneficiaries, that it had not been mentioned in the Wyatts' divorce proceedings and that Mr Wyatt continued to treat that share as though it was his own, demon-strated that it had been a sham. Second, it was held that s 423 could be relied upon to reverse the trust in any event because it had been a transfer for no consideration. The resulting trust analysis is that Mr Wyatt purported to transfer property on trust to his wife and daughters but that purported transfer failed because the trust was a sham, and therefore those property rights returned to Mr Wyatt on resulting trust. Because those property rights were held on resulting trust for Mr Wyatt, they formed a part of his estate and therefore could be taken by his insolvency creditors to satisfy the debts owed to them.

11.5 ISSUES WITH RESULTING TRUSTS

The term '*resulting* trust' is said to come from the Latin term 'resalire' meaning to 'go back' or to 'jump back'. So, in an automatic resulting trust it is said that when the owner of property fails to transfer property to another person, then the property bounces back to its original

---

74   Insolvency Act 1986, s 423(2).
75   I.e. to restore the parties to the position they had occupied before the transfer at an under-value.
76   [1995] 1 FLR 697.
77   *National Westminster Bank plc v Jones* [2001] 1 BCLC 98, para [36], *per* Neuberger J.
78   *Snook v London & West Riding Investments Ltd* [1967] 2 QB 786, 802, *per* Diplock LJ.

owner. However, there are types of resulting trust in which it is unclear whether any property leaves the original owner, let alone 'bouncing back' to her. For example, the discussion of *Re Ames Settlement* and *Vandervell v IRC* above raised the question whether any property passed away or whether that property should be considered as having remained with its owner throughout the transaction because there was never a transfer of property to any third party or no allocation of the new beneficial owner of that property respectively. Nor does this explanation of 'bouncing back' explain presumed resulting trusts. Instead, a contribution to the purchase price acquires equitable rights in the property, nothing jumps *back* because those rights are being acquired for the first time.

There is a suggestion by Harman J in *Re Gillingham Bus Disaster Fund*[79] that resulting trusts should be considered as arising in their own way in each circumstance. His lordship suggested that resulting trusts should arise '*sub modo*': that is, each resulting trust should arise on its own terms in its own circumstances. This would make resulting trusts more akin to the flexible model of constructive trusts as considered in the next chapter.

The other key debate surrounding resulting trusts, before the decision of the House of Lords in *Westdeutsche Landesbank v Islington* rejected this suggestion, was that resulting trusts should be expanded so that they provided the remedy for all situations in which there had been an unjust enrichment of a defendant by the acquisition of property. This theory is discussed in Chapter 25. Professor Birks took the view[80] that when a defendant was found to have acquired property by means of some unjust factor (such as duress or exploiting a mistake made by the claimant) so that the defendant was enriched, then the court should create a resulting trust so as to 'subtract' that enrichment from the defendant. In essence, Lord Browne-Wilkinson rejected this idea because resulting trusts arise in only two, narrowly-defined circumstances and because it would not provide an explanation as to why resulting trusts apply in cases of insolvency by arising automatically as opposed to arising only when the court gives judgment after a finding of an unjust enrichment.

---

79   [1958] Ch 300.
80   Birks, 1992.

Chapter 12

Constructive trusts

CAPSULE SUMMARY

Constructive trusts arise by operation of law, which means that they arise automatically and their existence is recognised retrospectively by the courts. In general terms, a proprietary constructive trust will be imposed on a person who has knowledge that her dealings with an item of property have been unconscionable.[1] All constructive trusts can be understood as arising on the basis of this central principle, even though there are many different sub-species of constructive trust which may appear to be superficially different.

The most significant categories of constructive trust are the following. A fiduciary will be constructive trustee of any unauthorised profits made from her fiduciary office, even where she has otherwise acted in good faith, so as to prevent the possibility of a conflict of interest.[2] If the property cannot be located or identified, then the fiduciary will be liable to account for its equivalent amount. No liability will arise if the profit was authorised. The Companies Act 2006 permits company directors to receive authorisation from other directors in specific circumstances.

A fiduciary who receives a bribe will be required to hold that bribe or any substitute property acquired with that bribe on constructive trust. That fiduciary will also be required to hold any profits derived from that bribe on constructive trust. The same approach is taken in relation to any person who acquires property as a result of an illegal act such as killing or theft. Constructive trusts have also arisen in relation to contracts for the sale of land, in relation to some agreements to develop land, in relation to mutual wills, and in relation to specific equitable doctrines, as detailed in this chapter.

There are also personal liabilities to account as a constructive trustee – meaning that no property is held on trust but rather the defendant must compensate the beneficiaries – where a person has dishonestly assisted in a breach of trust or knowingly received property unconscionably as a result of a breach of trust. These heads of liability for so-called 'strangers' are considered in Chapter 19.

Constructive trusts over the home are considered in detail in Chapter 15 *Trusts of Homes*.

---

1 *Westdeutsche Landesbank Girozentrale v Islington LBC* [1996] AC 669.
2 *Boardman v Phipps* [1967] 2 AC 46. See section 12.5 below.

12.1 INTRODUCTION

12.1.1 Fundamentals of constructive trusts

Defining the 'constructive trust'

Constructive trusts arise by operation of law. That means that constructive trusts are imposed by the courts when a defendant deals with property in a way which they know is unconscionable. As Lord Browne-Wilkinson described this process in the leading case of *Westdeutsche Landesbank v Islington*:[3]

> (i) Equity operates on the conscience of the owner of the legal interest. In the case of a trust, the conscience of the legal owner requires him to carry out the purposes for which the property was vested in him (express or implied trust) or which the law imposes on him by reason of his unconscionable conduct. (constructive trust)

Therefore, the doctrine of conscience is at the heart of all trusts, including constructive trusts. When a person acts unconscionably in relation to property, provided that they realise they are acting unconscionably, then they will hold that property on constructive trust. The key requirement is that the defendant must have had knowledge of some factor which should have affected their conscience. As Lord Browne-Wilkinson put it:

> (ii) Since the equitable jurisdiction to enforce trusts depends upon the conscience of the holder of the legal interest being affected, he cannot be a trustee of the property if and so long as he is ignorant of the facts alleged to affect his conscience, ie until he is aware . . . in the case of a constructive trust, of the factors which are alleged to affect his conscience.

Therefore, the defendant's conscience is only affected if they have knowledge of the thing that is said to be unconscionable about their treatment of property. For example, if Alfred transferred property to Bertha on the basis of a mistake that a contract between them was valid then it would be unconscionable for Bertha to keep that property. However, if neither party realised that they had made a mistake then the constructive trust would not be imposed over Bertha until Bertha became aware of that mistake. Only at the moment of that realisation would Bertha be subject to a constructive trust. In essence, that was the factual situation in *Westdeutsche Landesbank v Islington* itself. In that case a bank transferred money to a local authority on the basis of a contract which it transpired had been void throughout. The local authority had spent all of the money before either party became aware that the contract was void (as the result of another decision of the House of Lords).[4] It was held that the local authority could not be considered to have held that money on constructive trust because they had spent all of the money before they had had knowledge of the mistake. Consequently, there was no constructive trust because the defendant had not known of the mistake until after it was too late.

In *Paragon Finance plc v DB Thakerar & Co*,[5] Millett LJ provided a very similar general definition of a constructive trust:

---

3   [1996] AC 669.
4   *Hazell v Hammersmith & Fulham LBC* [1991] 1 AC 1.
5   [1999] 1 All ER 400.

A constructive trust arises by operation of law whenever the circumstances are such that it would be unconscionable for the owner of property (usually but not necessarily the legal estate) to assert his own beneficial interest in the property and deny the beneficial interest of another.[6]

Two important points emerge from both of these definitions of the constructive trust. First, a constructive trust is recognised by the court as coming into existence automatically, and so it is not created by a settlor. Second, a constructive trust is brought into being by the defendant's awareness of their own unconscionable conduct.

The doctrine of constructive trusts is so creative that some judges have suggested that it cannot be defined. Edmund-Davies LJ in *Carl Zeiss Stiftung v Herbert Smith & Co* held that:

> English law provides no clear and all-embracing definition of a constructive trust. Its boundaries have been left perhaps deliberately vague so as not to restrict the court by technicalities in deciding what the justice of a particular case might demand.[7]

This remark does the field of constructive trusts a disservice. It is perhaps unfair to say that constructive trusts are 'vague'. Rather, judges appreciate the flexibility which this doctrine gives them to reach what they consider to be the correct conclusion in cases in which someone has acted unconscionably. Notably, his lordship held that it is only *at the boundaries* that any vagueness exists. As we shall see in this chapter, there are several established categories of constructive trust which have become predictable and clear over the centuries. It is at the edges that the judges are able to create new types of constructive trust as circumstances require. The constructive trust is the principal doctrine through which judges in England and Wales are able to achieve moral outcomes to individual cases (in company with proprietary estoppel and injunctions) in line with the foundational principles of equity which were considered in Chapter 1.

12.1.2 Placing the constructive trust within equity more generally

The trust is a creature of equity which has developed specific principles of its own beyond the general principles of equity. That much is historical fact. As was discussed in Chapter 1, the core purpose of equity was established by Lord Ellesmere in the *Earl of Oxford's Case*[8] to be 'to correct men's consciences'.[9] In this sense, the constructive trust operates so as to prevent a benefit being taken from unconscionable conduct and to protect the rights of other people in property.

The general principle on which constructive trusts operate is clear: a constructive trust prevents a defendant from taking unconscionable advantage of the claimant's property. The cases on constructive trusts are divided between different categories of unconscionable behaviour. Thus, by way of example, a person who steals property will be considered to have

---

6 Similarly in *James v Williams* [1999] 3 WLR 451, 458, *per* Aldous LJ: 'As a general rule a constructive trust attaches by law to property which is held by a person in circumstances where it would be inequitable to allow him to assert full beneficial ownership of the property.'

7 [1969] 2 Ch 276, 300.

8 (1615) 1 Ch Rep 1.

9 As discussed in section 1.1 of this book.

dealt unconscionably with it;[10] a person who receives a bribe in the conduct of a fiduciary office will have dealt unconscionably with that bribe;[11] a person who takes property by means of fraud will have dealt unconscionably with it;[12] and so on. In each of these categories of case, and in many others considered in this chapter, the defendant is held to be a constructive trustee of that property because she has knowingly dealt with that property in an unconscionable manner. We know what equity considers unconscionable conduct to involve in this context by reference to these decided cases on the categories of constructive trust.

The case law on constructive trusts sees equity confronting some of the worst excesses of society. Most of the categories of constructive trust and unconscionability are self-evident: these are stories of theft, bribery and murder. There are some more esoteric categories of unconscionability in there too, such as fiduciaries taking a benefit from their office as a result of a conflict of interest between their personal and their fiduciary capacities. So, we shall see that constructive trusts arise when public prosecutors take bribes not to prosecute organised criminal kingpins; when a jealous doctor murders his wife for her money; and also when a hard-working solicitor spent some extra hours making profits for a trust which he advised but then was found to have acted wrongfully when he took a little something for himself.

12.1.3 The English 'institutional' constructive trust

Constructive trusts in English equity are said to be 'institutional'. In essence, that means that constructive trusts come into existence automatically at the time when the defendant knowingly committed their unconscionable act. When a dispute reaches court many months or years later, what the court does is to recognise that the constructive trust came into existence retrospectively at the time when the defendant knowingly committed their unconscionable act. This means that if the knowing and unconscionable act was performed on Monday, if the defendant went bankrupt on Tuesday and if the court only gave judgment on Wednesday, then the constructive trust is deemed to have arisen automatically on Monday when the knowing and unconscionable act was committed. Therefore, the claimant will have their rights recognised at the trial on Wednesday in such a way that they are deemed to have existed since Monday. Consequently, the claimant's rights under the constructive trust will pre-date the defendant's insolvency. If, as happens in other jurisdictions, those rights only came into existence on Wednesday when the judge made their order then that would be a 'remedial' doctrine which would post-date the insolvency. Australia and the USA have remedial constructive trusts of this sort which have the benefit that they give the courts' some leeway in the form of the constructive trust that they impose, but they do not provide automatic property rights on the English model. In this way, English constructive trusts provide good title in the event of the defendant's insolvency.

There is an ongoing debate about whether or not English constructive trusts should be remedial. In essence, it is suggested in this book that the doctrine of proprietary estoppel (discussed in Chapter 13) provides a remedial doctrine of exactly this sort which overlaps with constructive trusts in many circumstances and therefore the English constructive trust need not change.

---

10 *Westdeutsche Landesbank v Islington* [1996] AC 669.
11 *Attorney-General for Hong Kong v Reid* [1994] 1 AC 324.
12 *Westdeutsche Landesbank v Islington* [1996] AC 669.

12.2 CONSTRUCTIVE TRUSTS IN GENERAL TERMS

12.2.1 The general potential application of the constructive trust

All forms of constructive trust can be understood as operating on the basis of the central principle that is restated in *Westdeutsche Landesbank v Islington* to the effect that all trusts arise when the conscience of the legal owner of property is affected, and that constructive trusts arise by operation of law when the defendant knows of something which affects their conscience. Section 53(2) of the Law of Property Act 1925 provides that 'implied resulting or constructive trusts' do not require formalities in their creation. This section will focus on the explanation given of the constructive trust in *Westdeutsche Landesbank v Islington*. This case was by no means the first to link the trust (and indeed all of equity) to the concept of conscience, as was discussed in Chapter 1. It is, however, the most recent statement of the principles underpinning this area of the law by the Supreme Court in this jurisdiction.

12.2.2 Rights in property and merely personal claims

It is important to distinguish at the outset between personal rights and proprietary rights. That distinction is one which will be familiar to all students of property law and has been explored in this book already.[13] Nevertheless, it bears repeating. A proprietary right attaches to specific property. Lord Browne-Wilkinson held in *Westdeutsche Landesbank Girozentrale v Islington LBC* that 'in order to establish a trust there must be identifiable trust property' and 'from the date of [the trust's] establishment the beneficiary has, in equity, a proprietary interest in the trust property'.[14] These principles apply to constructive trusts as well as to express trusts. Therefore, the proprietary constructive trusts which are discussed in this chapter attach to identified property. The advantages of a proprietary constructive trust are that they grant the beneficial owner protection against the trustee's insolvency and all of the other benefits that flow from proprietary rights.

These proprietary constructive trusts are different from a personal right such as a right to force another person to pay compensation. There are two situations considered in section 12.9 below in which a person who interferes with trust property will only be personally liable to account to beneficiaries in the event of a breach of trust. Those two situations – known as 'dishonest assistance' and 'unconscionable receipt' – do not grant any proprietary rights. Nevertheless, they are referred to as imposing 'constructive trusteeship' on the defendants because those people are 'construed' (or, deemed) to be trustees even though there is no express trust in existence. This is what the word 'constructive' means: equity is *construing* the situation as being one which should create a trust automatically. Otherwise, all of the doctrines considered in this chapter are concerned with proprietary rights.

12.2.3 The leading case of *Westdeutsche Landesbank v Islington*

The facts of the case of *Westdeutsche Landesbank v Islington*[15] are a perfect illustration of the principles underpinning the constructive trust. A bank and a local authority thought that they were entering into a valid interest rate swap contract (a complex financial

---

13 See section 2.5.
14 *Chase Manhattan v Israel-British Bank* [1980] 2 WLR 202.
15 [1996] AC 669.

instrument intended to manipulate the level of interest which the local authority would have to pay on its debt). The contract was supposed to have lasted for ten years. The bank paid £1.5 million to the local authority at the beginning of the contract which the local authority promptly spent on its general expenses. However, after only five years had elapsed there was a decision of the House of Lords in *Hazell v Hammersmith & Fulham*[16] which told the parties for the first time that the local authority did not have the legal capacity to enter into such a contract. Therefore, the contract was void *ab initio*: i.e. the contract was void as if it had never existed. The question arose whether the local authority should be deemed to hold any property on constructive trust for the bank. It was held that there were two reasons for not finding a constructive trust. First, all of the money had been already spent and therefore there was no money over which the constructive trust could take effect. Second, most importantly, at the time when the local authority had received the money and spent it, the local authority had not known that the purported contract was void. Consequently, Lord Browne-Wilkinson explained that because the local authority had not known that the contract was void then its conscience was not affected before it spent the money and therefore no constructive trust ever came into existence. The bank was entitled to recover the amount of money which it had paid to the local authority by means of the personal remedy of 'money had and received' (which means that the local authority had to pay the bank an amount equal to £1.5 million under a personal claim at common law), but not by way of constructive trust. That the bank was only entitled to receive a personal claim for money had and received (as opposed to a proprietary constructive trust) meant that it did not receive the higher rate of compound interest to which it would have been entitled on constructive trust principles on the law at the time: that was a difference of approximately £1 million by the end of the litigation.

12.2.4 Illustrations of constructive trusts

Lord Browne-Wilkinson explained the operation of the concept of conscience and knowledge in constructive trusts by explaining how another case, the decision of Goulding J in *Chase Manhattan v Israel-British Bank*,[17] should have been decided. In that case, a payment was made by Chase Manhattan to Israel-British Bank, and then that same payment was mistakenly made a second time. After receiving the second, mistaken payment, Israel-British Bank went into insolvency. The question arose whether or not Chase Manhattan was entitled to have that second payment held on constructive trust for it. Goulding J found a trust on the basis of a mixture of equitable principles and restitution of unjust enrichment. This decision was overruled by Lord Browne-Wilkinson who explained if it could have been shown that Israel-British Bank had had knowledge of the mistake before its own insolvency, then it would be bound in good conscience to hold that payment on constructive trust for Chase Manhattan from the moment it had realised the mistake. However, if Israel-British Bank had not realised its mistake before going into insolvency then no constructive trust would have arisen. Here the unconscionability would be taking advantage of another person knowing that they were acting under a mistake: the mistake here was keeping a second, mistaken payment if they knew that they had already been paid what they were owed. By contrast, if they

---

16   [1992] 2 AC 1.
17   [1980] 2 WLR 202.

had not realised that they had been paid twice then there would have been no unconscionable activity because they would not have been knowingly taking advantage of another person's misunderstanding.

If banking seems a little dry, then let us take the example of a gruesome murder to illustrate how constructive trusts combat unconscionable activity. The case of *In re Crippen*, the infamous Dr Hawley Crippen was convicted of the murder of his wife Cora Crippen. She was a vivacious musical performer who flaunted her many affairs in front of her insignificant, mousey husband. Dr Crippen began an affair of his own with Ethel and was found to have conceived a plan to murder his wife before concealing her remains in the basement of their house. Cora Crippen's will named her husband as her principal legatee. The question which arose in *Re Crippen* was whether or not Cora's estate should pass to Hawley under the terms of her will. It was argued on behalf of the people who would have inherited from Hawley Crippen that he would have acquired all of the property on Cora's death in any event (whether due to a murder or some other, natural event later in life) and therefore all that had happened was that the transfer of the property took effect sooner than might otherwise have been anticipated. Of course, this argument did not account for Cora changing her will, for Hawley predeceasing her if he had not murdered her, and for the distastefulness of allowing a murderer to take a profit from his crime. It was held that Hawley Crippen could not be allowed to benefit from his unconscionable act of murdering his wife. Instead, the property which passed to him under the will would be held on constructive trust for the benefit of those people who would have taken the property (after Hawley Crippen) if Cora had died intestate. Therefore, equity prevented any benefit flowing from the unconscionable act of killing someone unlawfully.

What the law on constructive trusts achieves, therefore, is a means of combating unconscionable behaviour in a broad variety of contexts, from banks' trading floors to doctors' surgeries (or basements). There are clear categories of constructive trust but also the possibility of new ones emerging in line with the central principle set out in *Westdeutsche Landesbank v Islington*.

12.3 PROFITS FROM UNLAWFUL ACTS

This large category of constructive trusts considers the effect of acts which are unlawful either in the sense that they constitute criminal offences or that they are not lawful under some other rule of law. Among the unlawful acts considered in this section are killing, bribery and theft. Since *Bridgman v Green*[18] it has been held that the profits of crime will be held on constructive trust. This is a core equitable principle: no one can benefit from an unconscionable act. The core principle in *Westdeutsche Landesbank v Islington* that a constructive trust will be imposed over property when the defendant has knowingly acted unconscionably in relation to that property, clearly applies here. When a defendant steals property, or receives property by way of a bribe, or kills so as to access property, then that property will be held on constructive trust. Clearly, the central principle of conscience in *Westdeutsche Landesbank v Islington* binds all of these sub-categories of constructive trust together.

---

18 (1755) 24 Beav 382.

12.3.1 Profits from bribery

Introduction

The legal treatment of bribery became very interesting again for a couple of years when the Court of Appeal in *Sinclair v Versailles*[19] changed the law back to its condition in the late 19th century that bribery was merely a common law matter. Since then, the Supreme Court in *FHR European Ventures v Cedar Capital*[20] has re-imposed the idea that when a fiduciary receives a bribe then that person will hold that bribe and any property acquired with that bribe on constructive trust for the beneficiary of their fiduciary duties. Consequently, as a result of the Supreme Court's decision, the unconscionable act of receiving a bribe (which was described by one judge in a Privy Council case as being 'evil') returned bribery to the list of unconscionable acts which would give rise to a constructive trust. Indeed, when the Court of Appeal in *Sinclair v Versailles* had briefly removed it from that list, it had made the area of bribery an anomaly in the area of unconscionable acts, as was acknowledged by the Federal Court of Australia in *Grimaldi v Chameleon Mining*.[21] This issue has caused a furious debate in the academic journals as well as between the judges.

There is a great focus on combating bribery in the 21st century. It is recognised as a great enemy of international trade as well as being an enemy of proper behaviour in our societies more generally. The Bribery Acts of 2010 and 2012 criminalised areas of bribery which had not necessarily been criminal before. Therefore, bribery has become a focus of public policy in recent years in a way that it had not been before. The Court of Appeal had briefly shown itself to be entirely out of step with the rest of society when they downgraded bribery from being a constructive trust to being merely a common law matter (which would allow the person receiving the bribe to keep their profits, as we shall see). The Supreme Court has restored the position but there remain some concerns about the way in which they have done that. This section will begin by describing the law as it is now, before considering the debate that led to the Supreme Court's decision (because it is good material for coursework essays).

Illustrations of the traditional principle

Let us begin with the simplicity of the traditional equitable approach to the receipt of bribes. The judgment of the Court of Appeal in *Reading v Attorney-General*[22] related to a British Army sergeant who was stationed in Cairo after the 1939–45 war who received bribes to ride in uniform in civilian lorries which were carrying contraband. The presence of a British soldier of a sergeant's rank in uniform in the cab of those lorries meant that they would not be stopped at army checkpoints. It was held by the Court of Appeal that the sergeant occupied a fiduciary position in relation to the Crown in respect of the misuse of his uniform and in respect of his position as a soldier in the British Army. Therefore, it was held that any money paid to him for riding in the lorry in breach of his fiduciary duty was held on constructive trust for the Crown by way of an account of his profits.

---

19 [2012] Ch 453.
20 [2014] UKSC 45, [2014] 3 WLR 535.
21 [2012] FCAFC 6, 287 ALR 22.
22 [1951] 1 All ER 617.

This case demonstrates two things. First, that the categories of fiduciary office are elastic. If the court considers that the defendant should be treated as a fiduciary then they are able to create entirely new categories of fiduciary duty to accommodate that defendant. Indeed, it is suggested that it is likely that anyone who receives a bribe will be held to be a fiduciary because, by definition, anyone who is worth bribing must occupy some sort of office which is sensitive in that context. Such a sensitive office is likely to be treated as being a fiduciary office, even if it is only fiduciary in a very narrow context. For example, in *Brinks Mat Ltd v Abu-Saleh (No 3)*[23] it was held that a security guard occupied a fiduciary position. If we think about the status of security guards in corporate organisations, they are usually treated as occupying the lowest rung on the ladder alongside the cleaners. (I write as one who has worked both as a security guard and as a cleaner during my undergraduate years.) The security guard was nevertheless treated as being a fiduciary (in common with the board of directors of that company!) because he accepted a bribe to allow armed robbers access to the company's premises so that they could commit a robbery. Despite his lowly position in the company's organisation chart, he occupied a very sensitive role when it came to admitting people to the company's secure premises. Therefore, it is suggested that anyone worth bribing is probably a fiduciary in that particular context.

Second, this case demonstrates that a bribe is held on constructive trust from the moment that it is received. The employer (as the beneficiary of this particular fiduciary relationship) acquires an equitable interest in the property that is held on the terms of this constructive trust. This approach was followed in *Attorney-General for Hong Kong v Reid*,[24] as explained below. The conceptual problem with this approach is that profits made from bribes will not have been the property of the beneficiary before they were received by the fiduciary. Therefore, the court is imposing a constructive trust solely in response to the defendant's wrongdoing and not to compensate any loss suffered by the beneficiary.

The 19th century authorities on bribes took the view that if a fiduciary (such as an employee operating a weigh-bridge) received a bribe (for example, to allow third parties to cross the weigh-bridge fraudulently) then that fiduciary would owe a debt to their employer equal to the amount of the bribe that they had received. They held that there was no constructive trust here. The problem with this analysis is that if the employee was able to invest their bribe then they would be able to profit from their wrongdoing, even if they had to account for the amount of the bribe which they had received. The alternative analysis would be to say that the recipient of a bribe must hold it on constructive trust from the moment of its receipt so that anything bought with the bribe would also be considered to be held on constructive trust. The advantage of this second analysis is that the recipient cannot benefit from their bribe because any benefit is held on constructive trust. This second analysis was concretised in England and Wales by the decision of the Privy Council in *Attorney General for Hong Kong v Reid* which we shall consider first.

Bribes are held on a conscience-based constructive trust:
Attorney-General for Hong Kong v Reid

The leading case in this area used to be the decisions of the Privy Council in *Attorney-General for Hong Kong v Reid*.[25] The leading speech of Lord Templeman speaks for the traditional equitable view of a constructive trust which is based on conscience. In that

---

23 [1996] CLC 133.
24 [1994] 1 AC 324.
25 [1994] 1 AC 324.

case, the former Director of Public Prosecutions for Hong Kong had accepted bribes not to prosecute certain individuals accused of having committed crimes within his jurisdiction. The bribes which he had received had been very profitably invested in New Zealand. The question arose whether or not the property bought with the bribes and the increase in value of those investments should be held on constructive trust for the Director of Public Prosecutions's employer, or whether the Director of Public Prosecutions owed only an amount of cash equal to the bribes paid to him originally. Lord Templeman, giving the leading judgment (with which Lord Goff agreed), overruled the 19th century case of *Lister v Stubbs*. He held that a proprietary constructive trust is imposed as soon as the bribe is accepted by its recipient. As he put it:

> Equity . . . which acts *in personam* insists that it is unconscionable for a fiduciary to obtain and retain a benefit in breach of duty.[26]

Therefore, in common with the judgment in *Westdeutsche Landesbank v Islington*, Lord Templeman founded this area on the idea that constructive trusts arise in response to the unconscionable act of the defendant. His lordship also relied on the ancient equitable principle that equity looks upon as done that which ought to have been done: therefore, because good conscience requires that the bribe is passed to the beneficiary, then equity will deem that that has already happened by declaring that it is held on constructive trust for that beneficiary. Later cases have identified the reason for imposing a constructive trust on the recipient of a bribe in *Reid* was that it would have been 'as a fiduciary unconscionable for him to retain the benefit of it'.[27]

The form of the constructive trust is important. From the moment that the bribe is received by the defendant, the bribe is held on constructive trust. Consequently, anything which is acquired with the bribe is also held on constructive trust. (To use the jargon, the property acquired with the bribe is the 'traceable substitute' for the bribe.) This means that the employer is entitled in equity to any profit generated by the cash bribe received from the moment of its receipt because anything acquired with the bribe is held on constructive trust. There is a further limb to this trust, however. Lord Templeman held that the constructive trustee is also liable to account to the beneficiary for any *decrease* in value in the investments acquired with the bribe, as well as for any increase in value in such investments. So, if the recipient of the bribe were to invest that money unwisely and lose money, then they would *both* have to hold the bribe on constructive trust and also have to account to beneficiary for the fall in the value of the property (for example, by writing a cheque equal to that difference in value).

We should be in no doubt that Lord Templeman was motivated by moral sentiment. He described bribery as being 'an evil practice'. Self-evidently, it is a particularly evil practice when it is the leading state prosecutor who is taking bribes so that dangerous criminals can continue to be at liberty. As Lord Templeman held, it might be possible to put a figure on the bribe which has been received but it may not be possible to put a figure on the harm that is done to a society by bribery of this sort.

---

26   [1993] 1 All ER 1, 4.
27   *Yugraneft v Abramovich* [2008] EWHC 2613 (Comm), para [373], *per* Clarke J.

This constructive trust in operation

The approach of the Privy Council in *Attorney-General for Hong Kong v Reid*[28] was applied in a number of High Court cases.[29] In *Tesco Stores v Pook*,[30] a bribe was paid to Mr Pook, who was employed in Tesco's e-commerce business in South Korea. Smith J applied the decision in *Reid*[31] to the effect that this bribe should be held on constructive trust.[32] He approved the idea both that the bribe is held on constructive trust and also that when there is any decrease in the value of any property acquired with the bribe then the fiduciary 'is required to make up the difference'.[33] In *Daraydan Holdings Ltd v Solland International Ltd*,[34] the Sollands, who were directors of a property development company, organised for the payment of a secret commission to Khalid by increasing the budget payable by their client for a refurbishment project by 10% and then diverting that extra 10% to Khalid. Lawrence Collins J also followed *Reid* in the treatment of the bribe. He also held that a fiduciary should not put himself into a situation in which his duty and his personal interest would conflict, as had happened when the Sollands breached their duties to their client by corruptly increasing the price of the development work to pay for Khalid's secret commission. Therefore, the constructive trust here was based on avoidance of conflict of interest[35] as well as the need to deal with the 'evil practice' of bribery.

The decision of the Supreme Court in FHR European Ventures v *Cedar Capital Partners LLC*

FHR European Ventures v Cedar Capital[36] involved an agency arrangement. In particular, the payment of the commission relating to the sale of a hotel. The defendant failed to notify the claimant that they were receiving a commission for brokering the sale of the hotel. The question was whether or not this secret commission should give rise to a constructive trust or merely give rise to an obligation to pay equitable compensation to the agent's principal. It is interesting that Lord Neuberger describes this claim as being a choice between constructive trust on the one hand and equitable compensation on the other hand. The case of *Lister v Stubbs* had treated this as being a question of common law debt and not one of equitable compensation. By focusing on equitable compensation, Lord Neuberger keeps the entire question within equity as opposed to common law. The outcome of the decision in the Supreme Court is that a secret commission gives rise to a proprietary constructive trust, which returned to the law (on its surface) to the position under *Reid*.

The difficulty is the winding road which Lord Neuberger felt compelled to follow in reaching that conclusion. A large amount of academic commentary is cited and, rather than return to first principles, his lordship surveyed a large amount of the old case law. The

---

28 [1994] 1 AC 324.

29 Culminating in *Daraydan Holdings Ltd v Solland International Ltd* [2004] EWHC 622 (Ch).

30 [2003] EWHC 823 (Ch).

31 [1994] 1 AC 324.

32 [2003] EWHC 823 (Ch), para [45] and [69].

33 *Ibid*, para [69].

34 [2005] Ch 1.

35 Considered below in section 12.5 in relation to *Boardman v Phipps* [1967] 2 AC 46, the liability for fiduciaries earning unauthorised profits.

36 [2014] UKSC 45, [2014] 3 WLR 535.

preponderance of the case law dealing with bribes, as opposed to secret commissions, has always taken the view that there should be a proprietary right imposed over any profit that is received by a fiduciary. The old case law which supports a proprietary right derives from the principle that equity operates *in personam* against the defendant's conscience. What is significant is that Lord Neuberger does not mention the concept of conscience anywhere. What is clear is that the old case law makes sense if it is understood as being based on conscience; whereas if the conscience is overlooked in that discussion then those cases can seem to be arbitrary.

Ultimately, Lord Neuberger reached his judgement based on what he called 'principle and practicality'. The main argument against the imposition of a constructive trust was that in situations in which the defendant was insolvent that would be to grant a proprietary right to the claimant which would advance them ahead of any other unsecured creditors. The basis of the principle that a constructive trust should be imposed is predicated on the idea that a fiduciary should not accept a bribe nor a secret commission because it puts that person in a conflict between their duties and their personal interests. As Lord Neuberger acknowledged, if an agent has accepted a bribe then it is likely that the principal will have done business at a disadvantageous price because the person paying the bribe would probably otherwise have had to pay a higher price to the principal. So, the principal is losing out in some way: probably financially and otherwise.

The real problem which is not discussed by Lord Neuberger is that if the recipient of a bribe is entitled to keep their bribe and invest it profitably without the imposition of a constructive trust then that will mean that the false fiduciary who received the bribe will be able to take a benefit from their wrongdoing. That is simply wrong by any measure. Bribery is immoral because it causes financial and ethical harm to the parties and to society at large. It is only by recognising the moral underpinnings to the argument advanced by Lord Templeman in his judgement in *Reid* that we can understand why a constructive trust is necessary. By imposing a constructive trust over a bribe from the moment that it is received by the fiduciary, then it becomes impossible for that fiduciary to take any personal benefit from the bribe or any profits which flow from that bribe. In a world in which the international commercial community and governments of various jurisdictions have begun to bear down on bribery in commercial activity, it would be an unwelcome development for English law to allow fiduciaries receiving bribes to take any sort of benefit from that activity. As Lord Herschell put it in *Bray v Ford*, it is 'an inflexible rule of equity' that no fiduciary should be entitled to keep any such profit.

The debate about the treatment of bribes: Sinclair Investment v Versailles Trading

The earlier Court of Appeal in *Sinclair Investments (UK) Ltd v Versailles Trading Ltd*[37] had refused to follow *Reid*. This judgment (ironically delivered by Lord Neuberger when in the Court of Appeal) has now been overruled. However, it is only possible to understand the debate in this area if we consider the counter-arguments to the form which the law takes now. (This may also be useful for writing coursework essays in this area.) The Versailles Trading companies, run by Cushnie, took investments from 'traders' and borrowed huge amounts of money from banks on the promise that they would be invested in identified

---

37 [2011] 3 WLR 1153.

financial markets and then share the profits with their investors. Unfortunately, this was a fraud perpetrated by Cushnie to make it look as though he was conducting investment business when in truth he was living off the investors' money and simply paying them some of their capital in the pretence that it was profit he had earned. In particular, Cushnie bought a very expensive house in Kensington, London. When the companies went into insolvency, the Kensington house was the only valuable asset remaining. The claimant sought to establish a constructive trust over the property which had been used to buy the Kensington house. It was held that that there should not be such a constructive trust in this case.[38] There were several cases arising out of these facts. To simplify, this particular case was treated as one in which a bribe had been paid in breach of a duty owed to the claimant and then used to acquire the Kensington house.

In essence the reason for that decision was to maximise the assets available to the unsecured creditors in general. The Versailles companies had several creditors and the Kensington house was the principal remaining asset. Lord Neuberger considered it significant that if a proprietary constructive trust were to be imposed in favour of the claimant then the assets which were held on trust would not be available to be distributed among the other creditors. Lord Neuberger considered that *Reid* should not be followed unless trust property had been used to acquire the Kensington house: if trust property had been used to acquire the Kensington house then that would justify the imposition of a constructive trust. Otherwise, if the defendant had acquired the property with a bribe then that would not justify the imposition of a constructive trust. Instead, all that would be owed would be a debt. In reaching this conclusion, Lord Neuberger was following the older case of *Lister v Stubbs*.

The argument in favour of *Lister v Stubbs* which is presented separately by Professor Graham Virgo[39] and Professor Roy Goode[40] was dominated by the law of insolvency. Both asked the question: why should there be a proprietary right? The reason why they both ask that question is that they fear for the unsecured creditors of the recipient of the bribe. If the recipient of the bribe is required to hold that bribe on constructive trust for the beneficiary of their fiduciary duties, then that bribe will not be available to be passed among her unsecured creditors when she goes into insolvency. Of course, one could also ask the question: what if the recipient of the bribe does *not* go into insolvency? If the recipient of the bribe does not go into insolvency, then she will have to account for an amount of cash equal to the bribe, but she will be able to keep any profits which she has made on investing that bribe and any valuable property bought with that bribe. Therefore, the Virgo and Goode argument only holds water at all if there has been an insolvency.

If the insolvency situation is thought to be such a significant exception to the general principle underpinning constructive trusts in policy terms, then there should simply be a legislative carve-out for insolvent recipients of property in situations such as bribes, just as there is a carve-out under s 423 of the Insolvency Act 1986 which prevents sales at an under-value transferring property beyond the reach of insolvency creditors. There is no need to allow insolvency law to prevent the imposition of a perfectly principled constructive trust in other circumstances.

---

38 Followed in *Cadogan Petroleum plc v Tolly* [2011] EWHC 2286.
39 G Virgo, 'Profits obtained in breach of fiduciary duty: personal or proprietary claim?' (2011) 70 CLJ 502.
40 R Goode, 'Proprietary liability for secret profits – a reply' (2011) 127 LQR 493. The reply is to the article by Hayton J below.

The other argument which Professor Goode raises is that there is no basis for a proprietary right in any event, other than some hand-wringing about morality. That, however, is completely to overlook that the conscience-based trust is predicated on a moral base, and that the immorality of the defendant is all that is required to trigger a proprietary obligation which the recipient of the bribe owes to the beneficiary of their relationship. The rationale for the proprietary base is that it is wrong for the recipient to keep either the bribe or any property which flows from the bribe. This is an entirely appropriate situation in which a constructive trust should be imposed to prevent the recipient from taking an unconscionable benefit from their breach of their fiduciary duties.

The equity traditionalists resisted the *Sinclair* decision. Hayton J[41] (formerly Professor Hayton, author of *Underhill and Hayton on Trusts and Trustees*) and Sir Peter Millett[42] (formerly Lord Millett) have both written articles in support of the approach in *Attorney-General for Hong Kong v Reid*. Hayton focused on whether or not the Court of Appeal had been bound to follow the earlier Court of Appeal decision in *Lister v Stubbs* as opposed to the Privy Council decision in *Reid*. From the perspective of trusts law, Hayton identified the old principle that the beneficiaries are entitled to argue that the trustee was bound to invest on behalf of the trust and therefore that when the trustee took a bribe and invested it then the trustee should be deemed to have made that investment on behalf of the trust, with the result that the bribe and the profits should be added to the trust property.[43] As Kekewich J put it, the court 'treats the trustee as having received such a bribe not on his own behalf but on behalf of and as agent for the trust'.[44] This creates a link between the bribe and the trust property, which Hayton wants to do so as to justify the imposition of a constructive trust.

Hayton criticised the distinction that is made in *Sinclair v Versailles* 'between profit made from exploitation of *property* and profit made from exploitation of *office*, a proprietary remedy being available in the former instance but not the latter'.[45] In many circumstances, the use of the office and of trust 'property' may overlap: as where an army officer uses his uniform to enable contraband or drugs to cross a checkpoint, given that the uniform is army property and the officer's rank attaches to the office. By way of a final word, Hayton points out that the Federal Court of Australia in *Grimaldi v Chameleon Mining NL (No 2)*[46] rejected the analysis in *Sinclair v Versailles* in favour of the decision in *Reid*, albeit that the Australian constructive trust is a discretionary remedy unlike the English institutional trust. Importantly, the Federal Court of Australia found that *Lister* had placed an 'anomalous' limitation on the extent of the English constructive trust. After all, bribery is unconscionable, so why would it be treated differently from other unconscionable acts?

Millett takes a very different, and more direct, tack. Millett argues that the Court of Appeal in *Sinclair* was 'incorrect' and that:[47]

---

41 D Hayton, 'The extent of equitable remedies: Privy Council versus Court of Appeal' (2012) 33 *Company Lawyer* 161.

42 P Millett, 'Bribes and secret commissions again' (2012) 71 CLJ 583.

43 This point was made originally by P. Millett, 'Bribes and secret commissions' [1993] Restitution Law Review 7, 20.

44 [1896] 1 Ch 71, 77.

45 D Hayton, *op cit.*, 163.

46 [2012] FCAFC 6.

47 P Millett, 'Bribes and secret commissions again' (2012) 71 CLJ 583. This quotation, which summarises the pith of Millett's excellent article, is taken from the Abstract.

The duty of the trustee is to serve the interest of the principal to the exclusion of his own interest. A fiduciary who keeps a profit for himself abuses the trust and confidence placed in him by the principal. He is bound to hand it over to his principal the moment he receives it. Equity's response to a breach of this duty is to enforce the duty by means of the constructive trust.

What is interesting is that Hayton and Millett are both reluctant equity specialists in that they refuse to allow themselves to take Aristotle's approach: i.e. to use equity to achieve a just outcome.[48] Instead, they are careful to find a proprietary base on which their constructive trusts can be erected. Lord Templeman was bolder than that. Lord Templeman was prepared to identify bribery as an evil practice, to focus on the unconscionability of someone taking a profit from such an evil practice, and to impose a constructive trust as a result. It is breath-taking in its simplicity. And unlike much of our modern law-making, it deals simply with right and wrong.

The obligations of company directors in relation to bribes under statute

The Companies Act 2006 introduced a statutory code of directors' general duties for the first time.[49] The directors' duties in the Act are 'based on certain common law rules and equitable principles'[50] and moreover those statutory duties 'shall be interpreted and applied in the same way as common law rules or equitable principles'.[51] The statutory duties are then to be interpreted in the future in accordance with the development of those case law principles.[52] The principles in relation to bribes are predicated on the equitable doctrines relating to bribes (as in *Attorney-General for Hong Kong v Reid*).[53] Section 176(1) of the Companies Act 2006 provides that:

> a director of a company must not accept a benefit from a third party conferred by reason of (a) his being a director, or (b) his doing (or not doing) anything as director.

Section 176(3) provides that '[b]enefits received by a director from a person by whom his services (as a director or otherwise) are provided to the company are not regarded as conferred by a third party.' Section 176(4) provides, however, that 'this duty is not infringed if the acceptance of the benefit cannot reasonably be regarded as likely to give rise to a conflict of interest'. In effect, both of these provisions grant defences to directors for actions which otherwise have attracted liability in equity.

12.3.2 Profits from killing

Perhaps the clearest example of unconscionable activity is the unlawful killing of another human being. It is a feature of many movies and detective novels that people commit murder so as to acquire the victim's property. It may be that a husband murders his wife because he

---

48 More accurately, of course, Aristotle's approach involved circumventing statute when the legislator had failed to anticipate a specific factual scenario and had thus made an 'error', as was discussed in Ch.1.

49 Companies Act 2006, s 170 *et seq*.

50 *Ibid*, s 170(3).

51 *Ibid*, s 170(4).

52 *Ibid*, s 170(4).

53 *Ibid*, s 178.

knows that he will inherit his wife's property. In such a situation, the killer will become a constructive trustee of any property acquired as a result of that killing. This principle applies in general terms to all forms of killing which constitute a criminal offence.[54] In consequence, a person guilty of murder will fall within the principle,[55] as will a person convicted of inciting others to murder her husband.[56] It has been held that the principle will not cover involuntary manslaughter where there was no intention to kill.[57]

The best-known example of this principle arose in the case of *In the Estate of Crippen*,[58] which was a particularly well-known murder which has been dramatised for television on many occasions (and which was outlined at the start of this chapter). Dr Hawley Harvey Crippen was an insignificant little man with an outgoing wife, Cora. Cora (whose real name was Kunigunde Mackamotski) was a successful music hall performer. Hawley was a homeopath rather than a medical doctor, with a mere diploma rather than a degree. In Hawley Crippen's trial for his wife's murder, it emerged that the Crippens had had an odd marriage. It seemed that Cora Crippen had taken many lovers during their marriage and it was said that she had somewhat flaunted this fact in front of her husband. It was memorably said of Cora Crippen during the trial that she was a woman 'the path to whose affections was both easy of access and well-trodden'. In other words, it was easy to become her lover and many people had done so. Hawley Crippen had begun an adulterous relationship of his own, with Ethel Le Neve, and began to plot to kill his wife so that he could get her money and be with Ethel. Cora disappeared. Hawley Crippen was found guilty of having murdered her and dismembered her body, burying parts of it under their house at 39 Hilldrop Crescent, Camden, London.[59] After Hawley Crippen had murdered Cora, he escaped on a ship bound for Canada with Ethel. However, the new technology of wireless telegraphy meant that his description could be sent to the ship and it was confirmed that they were aboard (albeit in disguise). This is one of the most intense parts of any dramatisation of this affair.

One of the issues which arose after these events was whether Hawley Crippen could inherit his wife's estate. Hawley Crippen had known that he was the principal legatee under his wife's will. Therefore, it was argued that by killing her he was merely bringing forward the time at which he would acquire her money. It was said that Dr Crippen was the rightful owner of his wife's estate because he was named as such in her will. Clearly, however, Hawley Crippen had acted unconscionably. Consequently, it was held any property which he acquired from his unconscionable act would be held on constructive trust so that he could not take a benefit from it for himself. In those circumstances, Hawley Crippen (or rather, his estate) held the property that came to him under his wife's will on constructive trust for the people who would otherwise have acquired Cora Crippen's estate under the intestacy rules if Hawley Crippen had not been alive. Consequently, the killer's unconscionable act prevents them from acquiring unencumbered ownership of the victim's property by imposing a constructive trust over any property acquired as a result of the killing.

Consequently, the principle is that the murderer becomes constructive trustee of all rights and interests in property which would otherwise have vested in them under the deceased's

---

54 *Gray v Barr* [1971] 2 QB 554.
55 *In the Estate of Crippen* [1911] P 108.
56 *Evans v Evans* [1989] 1 FLR 351.
57 *Re K (Deceased)* [1986] Ch 180.
58 [1911] P 108.
59 Recent news reports have suggested that modern DNA techniques can prove that the remains found under the house were not the remains of Cora Crippen after all.

will,[60] or even as next-of-kin in a case of intestacy.[61] The criminal will not acquire rights under any life assurance policy which has been taken out over the life of the deceased.[62] Similarly, a murderer will not be entitled to take a beneficial interest under the widow's pension entitlements of his murdered wife.[63]

Exceptionally, in the case of *Re K (Deceased)*, a wife, who had been the victim of domestic violence, accidentally killed her husband with a shotgun during a physical attack on her. The court exercised its discretion under the Forfeiture Act 1982 to make an order not to oblige the wife to hold property received as a result of her husband's death on constructive trust. The court's reasoning was that there had not been an intention to kill the husband and therefore the mischief of the principle did not apply here.

12.3.3 Profits from theft

Lord Browne-Wilkinson held in *Westdeutsche Landesbank v Islington*[64] that stolen property must be held on constructive trust by the thief for the benefit of its true owner. In consequence, the victim of the crime acquires an equitable interest against the thief and therefore is able to establish an equitable tracing claim into any substitute property acquired by the thief with the stolen property (for example, after selling the stolen property),[65] as considered in Chapter 20. Imposing a constructive trust on the thief has the ostensibly odd result of seeming to confer legal title in the stolen property on her as constructive trustee. One can see why judges might be uncomfortable at the suggestion that a thief acquires any type of property right. However, the *Westdeutsche* approach merely requires that the thief must hold the stolen property on a bare constructive trust for the victim of the crime and, as will often be the case, to hold any property acquired by disposing of the stolen property on constructive trust too. A different approach was taken in *Shalson v Russo*[66] by Rimer J who held that a thief cannot acquire any proprietary interests in stolen property and therefore cannot be a constructive trustee. Nevertheless, his lordship held that a victim of crime should be permitted to trace into the property taken from him as part of the fraudulent scheme.

12.3.4 Profits from fraud

Lord Browne-Wilkinson held in *Westdeutsche Landesbank v Islington*:[67] 'when property is obtained by fraud, equity places a constructive trust on the fraudulent recipient'. So, in *Bank of Ireland v Pexxnet Ltd*[68] the defendants presented forged instruments at a branch of the claimant bank which caused the bank to credit the defendants' accounts with approximately 2.4 million euro before the forgery was discovered. It was held that this constituted an unconscionable act which, further to *Westdeutsche Landesbank v Islington*, meant that that money was to be held on constructive trust by the accountholders for the bank.[69] This was held to

---

60 *Re Sigsworth* [1935] 1 Ch 89.
61 *In the Estate of Crippen* [1911] P 108.
62 *Cleaver v Mutual Reserve Fund Life Association* [1892] 1 QB 147.
63 *R v Chief National Insurance Commissioner ex p Connor* [1981] 1 QB 758.
64 [1996] AC 669.
65 *Bishopsgate v Homan* [1995] 1 WLR 31.
66 *Shalson v Russo* [2003] EWHC 1637 (Ch), [110].
67 [1996] AC 669, 716.
68 [2010] EWHC 1872.
69 [2010] EWHC 1872, [55]-[57].

be a 'classic case' of the constructive trust in *Westdeutsche Landesbank v Islington*. Those defendants who could be proved to have known of the fraud would therefore be required to hold property on constructive trust.

Examples of fraud giving rise to constructive trusts abound. In *Collings v Lee*[70] an estate agent defrauded clients by transferring land to himself acting under an alias. There had been no intention to transfer the property to the agent and in consequence the agent had been in breach of his fiduciary duties. Therefore, the agent was required to hold the land on constructive trust for his clients. In *JJ Harrison (Properties) Ltd v Harrison*[71] a director of a company was held to be a constructive trustee of property which he had fraudulently obtained from the company.[72] Similarly, in *Glen Dimplex Home Appliances Ltd v Smith*[73] the first defendant committed a straightforwardly fraudulent act by diverting £2.8 million from her employer into bank accounts in her husband's name. It was held that the money was impressed with a constructive trust. Following *Royal Brunei Airlines v Tan*[74] it was held that it would be dishonest to fail to ask questions about the money in the account and to close one's eyes. Consequently it was held that her husband had been dishonest on this basis and was also subject to the constructive trust.

There is a line of authority which held that the acquisition of property by means of a fraudulent misrepresentation does not lead to a constructive trust.[75] The reason for this principle, as set out in *Lonrho v Al Fayed (No 2)*[76] by Millett J, is that 'a contract obtained by fraudulent misrepresentation is voidable, not void, even in equity'. Consequently, it was held that a constructive trust could not come into effect because the contract might be affirmed by the claimant. Oddly, Millett LJ held in *Paragon Finance v Thakerar*[77] that 'equity has always given relief against fraud by making any person sufficiently implicated in the fraud accountable in equity' as a constructive trustee. While the two types of fraud in these cases were subtly different, it is suggested that the better general principle would be to find that any kind of fraud will give rise to a constructive trust *sub modo* so that it may be disapplied if the claimant elects to enforce the contract which was the basis of the fraud.

12.4 FIDUCIARY MAKING UNAUTHORISED PROFITS

12.4.1 The development of the principle that a fiduciary may not make unauthorised profits

The principle in its essence

Fiduciaries are not allowed to make 'secret profits'. That means, no fiduciary may make personal profits which are not authorised by the terms of their office. If a fiduciary does make unauthorised personal profits from their fiduciary office then a constructive trust will be placed over those profits from the moment that they are received, and in

---

70 (2001) 82 P & CR 27.
71 [2002] 1 BCLC 162.
72 See also *Russell v Wakefield Waterworks Co* (1875) LR 20 Eq 474, 479, *per* Lord Jessel MR.
73 [2011] EWHC 3392 (Ch).
74 [1995] 3 All ER 97.
75 *Daly v Sydney Stock Exchange Ltd* (1986) 160 CLR 371, 387.
76 [1992] 1 WLR 1.
77 [1999] 1 All ER 400, 408.

consequence that constructive trust will take effect over any property which is acquired with those unauthorised profits.[78] If, for some reason, the unauthorised profits or any property acquired with those profits cannot be identified (perhaps because it has been moved out of the jurisdiction or has been concealed in some way) then the fiduciary will be required to account personally for the amount of their profits, which means that they will be required to pay money or money's worth to the beneficiaries from their own pockets.[79]

A clash of moralities

This is possibly one of the most significant aspects of being a fiduciary. As we shall see, this rule is applied strictly in relation to trusts and in relation to all other forms of fiduciary office (including partnerships, agency arrangements and company directorships). Most of the cases have related to company directors in the last 50 years because that is the situation in which it is most likely that individuals will be able to make personal profits for themselves by exploiting commercial opportunities which they diverted away from the company towards themselves. The Companies Act 2006 has now made the position of company directors clearer, although even that legislation expressly aligns itself with the case law principles.

What is important about the liability of fiduciaries for unauthorised profits is that much of the law appears to belong to another era: a better time when fiduciaries were expected to work selflessly and loyally for their beneficiaries. In many of the leading cases – including *Boardman v Phipps* in the House of Lords – it is common for people to feel sorry for the defendant who was a fiduciary but who demonstrated a large amount of initiative in making a profit for himself and for the trust he was advising. Nevertheless, the court held that he must account for his personal profits because they were unauthorised. The point is that being a fiduciary compels you to act for other people and to take no account of your personal interests while doing so. In practice, many professional fiduciaries (such as solicitors, accountants and bankers acting in fiduciary capacities) insist on the terms of their office being drafted so that they can take personal profits in particular circumstances.[80] Therefore, it is not as though fiduciaries cannot protect themselves if they act decently, as we shall see. This issue is similar to the debate in section 8.5 about the rights of trustees to have their liability for negligence in the conduct of their office excluded by the terms of the trust instrument. What is significant in the cases which we shall discuss is that those fiduciaries are not protected by exclusion of liability language. Moreover, the traditional morality that a fiduciary must act faithfully in the service of another person clashes with the attitudes of some of the commercially-minded judges in the early 21st century who have tried to broaden some of the principles in recent years, only to see the law returned to its earlier condition latterly.

---

78 *Boardman v Phipps* [1967] 2 AC 46; *CMS Dolphin Ltd v Simonet* [2001] 2 BCLC 704; *Sinclair Investment Holdings SA v Versailles Trade Finance Ltd (No 3)* [2007] EWHC 915.

79 *Sinclair Investment Holdings SA v Versailles Trade Finance Ltd (No 3)* [2007] EWHC 915.

80 It is not necessary for the defendant to occupy one of the traditional fiduciary categories for this principle to apply. Rather, categories of office which may be defined by the courts are being 'fiduciary' is open-ended: *Cobbetts LLP v Hodge* [2010] 1 BCLC 30.

The emergence of the core principle

The rule that a fiduciary cannot take an unauthorised, personal benefit from her fiduciary office can be traced to the decision of Lord Chancellor King in *Keech v Sandford*[81] in 1726. A lease was held on trust for an infant beneficiary. The lease expired and the trustee sought to renew it. Under the law at the time, it was impossible to renew the lease in the name of the infant beneficiary. Therefore, the trustee sought to renew the lease in his own name. An issue arose as to whether this was a breach of the trustee's duties. It was held by Lord King that the lease must be held on trust by the trustee for the infant. There had been no allegation of fraud but nevertheless the Lord Chancellor considered that the principle that a trustee must not take an unauthorised profit from a trust should be 'strictly pursued' because there were risks of fraud in allowing trustees to take property in their own name.

The concern in the case law has not simply been with actual fraud or with trustees actually taking personal profits. Instead, the courts have been concerned to prevent even the possibility of a conflict of interest between the trustee's personal interests and their fiduciary obligations. This is important. The courts are seeking to prevent conflicts of interest in general, and not only the taking of unauthorised profits. The rationale for this approach is explained by Lord Herschell in *Bray v Ford*:[82]

> It is an inflexible rule of the court of equity that a person in a fiduciary position . . . is not, unless otherwise expressly provided, entitled to make a profit; he is not allowed to put himself in a position where his interest and duty conflict. It does not appear to me that this rule is, as had been said, founded upon principles of morality.[83] I regard it rather as based on the consideration that, human nature being what it is, there is danger, in such circumstances, of the person holding a fiduciary position being swayed by interest rather than by duty, and thus prejudicing those whom he was bound to protect. It has, therefore, been deemed expedient to lay down this positive rule.

The defendant may not put themselves in a position where their personal interests and their fiduciary duties conflict. Otherwise, given human nature, at some point human beings are likely to take advantage of this position. Therefore, we have an odd idea: there is an *inflexible rule* of equity here, even though (as we discussed in Chapter 1) equity is usually characterised as being comprised of flexible principles.

12.4.2 The application of this principle: *Boardman v Phipps*

The leading case in this area is the decision of the House of Lords in *Boardman v Phipps*.[84] The respondent, Boardman, was a solicitor who advised the trustees of a trust (the 'Phipps family trust'). While he was not a trustee, Mr Boardman was treated as being a fiduciary because he was so important in the management of the trust. The trust fund included a minority shareholding in a private company. While working on trust business, and because

---

81 (1726) 2 Eq Cas Abr 741.
82 [1896] AC 44 at 51.
83 Although see, e.g., Parker LJ in *Bhullar v Bhullar* [2003] 2 BCLC 241, para [17] referring to the 'ethic' in these cases.
84 [1967] 2 AC 46, 67.

he was representing the trust, Boardman was permitted to have access to the management accounts of that company: that is, Boardman was given access to information which was not publicly available. Boardman formulated a plan that the company could sell its Australian operations and refocus its British business so as to make a large profit. To achieve this goal, Boardman needed to have control of the company. Therefore, Boardman agreed with one of the trustees, Mr Fox, that they would acquire shares together with the trust so that, acting together, they would hold a majority shareholding. Once they acquired this majority shareholding, Boardman's plan was successful and the Phipps family trust, Boardman and Fox personally all made large profits. Importantly, Boardman had not acquired authorisation from all of the trustees because one of them was very ill and otherwise only Fox was engaged in the management of the trust. Therefore, Boardman had come, in effect, to direct the trust's affairs. Boardman did not acquire authorisation from the beneficiaries either. The claimant was one of the beneficiaries who learned of Boardman's personal profits from this activity and therefore sued him for an account of Boardman's personal profits. It was held by the majority of the House of Lords that Boardman should hold his profits on constructive trust for beneficiaries of the Phipps family trust. The rationales of their Lordships are important.

Boardman had argued that he had risked his own money and used his own expertise to make profits for everyone involved. He had argued that he had acted in good faith throughout. Lord Upjohn and Viscount Dilhorne held that because Mr Boardman had not acted in bad faith, he should not be required to hold his profits on constructive trust. They were in the minority, even though the majority had sympathy with their view. The majority preferred to uphold the view in *Bray v Ford* that this should be a strict rule which prevented the possibility of any profit being taken by a fiduciary from a conflict of interest. Lord Cohen and Lord Hodson wondered whether the constructive trust could be justified on the basis that Boardman had effectively been using trust property because it was only due to the fact that he had been working on trust business that he was given access to the company's management accounts in the first place. Moreover, it was argued, that accounting information was a form of confidential information which could be taken to have belonged to the trust. If Boardman had misused trust property to make a personal profit then there would have been no doubt that he would have had to hold those profits on constructive trust. In this instance, their lordships were undecided whether or not this sort of information should be treated as being property.

The key statement of the principles in this area was set out by Lord Upjohn (even though he was in the minority as to the outcome) in the following form:

> Rules of equity have to be applied to such a great diversity of circumstances that they can be stated only in the most general terms and applied with particular attention to the exact circumstances of each case. The relevant rule for the decision of this case is the fundamental rule of equity that a person in a fiduciary capacity must not make a profit out of his trust which is part of the wider rule that a trustee must not place himself in a position where his duty and his interest may conflict.

In support of this contention, Lord Upjohn then quoted the passage from *Bray v Ford* which was quoted in the previous section. These *dicta* contained the central statement of principle which can be found in the speeches of all of their Lordships to the effect that the constructive trust in this case is predicated on the need to prevent conflicts of interest.

It is clear that the basis of this doctrine is the possibility that fiduciaries may benefit from conflicts of interest. The Court of Appeal in *Bhullar v Bhullar*[85] upheld the principle on the basis that it is not dependent on any interference with trust property, but rather is based on the avoidance of conflicts of interest.[86] As Lord Cohen also held in *Boardman v Phipps*, 'an agent is, in my opinion, liable to account for profits which he makes out of the trust property if there is a possibility of conflict between his interest and his duty to his principal'. The objective here is to ensure that the wrongdoing fiduciary is not permitted to retain their unauthorised profit.[87]

Three further issues arise: how can authorisation be acquired? To whom are the fiduciary's duties owed? And what is the nature of the remedy? Each issue is considered in turn in the subsections to follow.

12.4.3 When the fiduciary will have acquired authorisation

The 'defence' of authorisation

It might be useful to think of this area of law in the following way. First, if a fiduciary has acquired a personal profit which is not expressly permitted by the terms of their fiduciary office (in the trust instrument, for example) then they will be prima facie liable to hold that profit on constructive trust for the beneficiaries of the trust. Second, the fiduciary may try to demonstrate that they should be deemed to have received authorisation if the circumstances are appropriate. This could be thought of as being a type of defence to their prima facie liability. The cases which are considered in this section demonstrate the circumstances in which a defendant will and will not be deemed to have received authorisation. (If you are answering a problem question in this area, then you should begin with the liability considered above in *Boardman v Phipps*, but the bulk of your answer will probably revolve around trying to prove whether or not the defendant should be deemed to have received authorisation for their actions.)

The question is then: what will constitute authorisation and what will not? When answering problem questions, I recommend the following system: think of the cases as saying 'yes' and the cases saying 'no' as being on a spectrum. You should identify the features of the decided cases which led to 'yes' and the features which led to 'no', and then identify which of those features are shared by the facts in the problem in front of you. Thus, you can decide whether your case is closer to one end of the spectrum or the other. That is what we shall do in this instance, beginning with the cases which have found authorisation, of which there are very few. It is worth noticing that these cases relate primarily to limited companies. One important difference between trading companies and family trusts is that trading companies involve people who are professionals and who are more likely to be able to give informed consent to a fiduciary to take a personal profit because they understand the issues, whereas beneficiaries in a family trust may have no professional experience at all and therefore may not be taken to have given authorisation in that context as easily.

---

85 [2003] 2 BCLC 241, para [27], *per* Parker LJ.
86 *Chan v Zacharia* (1984) 154 CLR 178.
87 *United Pan-Europe Communications NV v Deutsche Bank* [2000] 2 BCLC 461, para [47].

In the Privy Council decision in *Queensland Mines v Hudson*,[88] the defendant, Hudson, had been managing director of a mining company. He had therefore been in a fiduciary relationship with that company. He learned of the opportunity to pursue some potentially profitable mining contracts and decided to propose that the company should pursue that opportunity. He presented his view to the board of directors of the company. The board was comprised of representatives of the majority shareholders and executives with experience in the mining industry. The board of directors listened to Mr Hudson and then decided not to pursue this opportunity. (It is the fate of Hudsons across the world that they have magnificent ideas which are not appreciated by anyone else.) Hudson then took his own advice, pursued this opportunity on his own account after leaving the company, and made a large profit. The company sued Hudson for earning profits from his fiduciary office for which he should account to the company. It was held by the Privy Council that Hudson should be deemed to have had authorisation from the company to do what he did because he had presented the opportunities entirely honestly to the board of directors, the board of directors had then made an informed decision as professional people that the company should not pursue that opportunity, and consequently that there was no objection to Hudson having pursued the opportunity on his own account subsequently as a result.

This decision caused some concern among purists because it appears to weaken the principle in *Bray v Ford*. It is suggested that the finding that there had been informed consent on the part of the company's directors, and that there had been complete openness on Hudson's part, was significant. Matters might have been different if, for example, Hudson had been the trustee of a family trust and if he had sought to conceal his intention to pursue an opportunity on his own account by presenting inexpert beneficiaries with a complicated set of documents which they could not possibly have understood; then it would have been appropriate to say that he had not acquired authorisation from them. If, like Boardman, the fiduciary failed to consult the beneficiaries at all and only mentioned the plan to one of the trustees, then that would not lead to a finding of authorisation. However, in *Queensland Mines v Hudson* the situation was different: the other fiduciaries were professionals who decided not to participate in a context in which they could be understood to be experts and to have had all the information put at their disposal in a comprehensible form. These are the factors which are important when answering a problem question.

The decision of the House of Lords in *Regal v Gulliver*[89] was significant in this regard. *Regal* held that there was no authorisation when the four directors of a company purported to give themselves permission to divert a corporate opportunity from the company towards themselves personally. Not entirely surprisingly, the House of Lords held that it would be unacceptable for the fiduciaries to purport to excuse themselves from their duties and allow themselves to become personally very rich when they should have been exploiting that opportunity on behalf of the company. In company law cases the courts have focused on the idea of a corporate opportunity as being something which belongs to a trading company and which the directors may not divert from the company because the profits are ultimately earned for the company and are to be divided among the shareholders (where they are

88 (1977) 18 ALR 1.
89 [1942] 1 All ER 378.

distributable). The specific context of company law after the 2006 Companies Act is considered below at section 12.4.5.

Similarly, in *Industrial Development Consultants Ltd v Cooley*[90] Mr Cooley had been the managing director of a consultancy before a client of the business approached him and suggested that they would like to work with him personally (but not with the business). Cooley resigned from the company, citing ill-health as his reason for leaving. After he had left, Cooley exploited this opportunity on his own behalf. His former employers sued him on the basis that he had diverted a commercial opportunity to himself which ought to have been earned for the business to which he owed fiduciary duties. Cooley argued that the offer had been personal to him. It was held, however, that his fiduciary duties meant that he owed this opportunity to the business and that his fault had only been made worse by the fact that he had deceived his employers about his reason for leaving. Cooley's lack of openness can be contrasted with Hudson's behaviour in relation to his company.

To whom are the fiduciary's duties owed?

It is important to know to whom these duties are owed. If Boardman owed his duties to the trustees, then he would only need to seek authorisation from them. However, if Boardman owed his duties to the beneficiaries then they would be the people who would need to grant him authorisation. This is left unclear by the House of Lords because Boardman did neither successfully. Given that the beneficiaries own the trust property beneficially and given that they have the right to sue the fiduciaries for breach of trust, it could be said that it would be better to seek authorisation and indemnity from the beneficiaries.[91] Alternatively, if the trustees have the management of the trust delegated to them then it could be said that the should make this decision as a management decision, provided that the trustees who make the decision do not also stand to take a personal benefit, as in *Regal v Gulliver*. In relation to companies, it is the company as a separate person which is the beneficiary of the directors' obligations, not the shareholders (because the shareholders do not own a company's property unless there is a winding up of the company). Section 170 of the Companies Act 2006 provides that directors owe their duties to the company (on which see below).

12.4.4 The equitable response to unauthorised profits

The proper approach to the nature of the remedy when a fiduciary acquires an unauthorised profit was set out by Rimer J in *Sinclair Investment Holdings SA v Versailles Trade Finance Ltd (No 3)*[92] and by Lawrence Collins J in *CMS Dolphin Ltd v Simonet*.[93] In essence, the remedies operate as follows. First, the unauthorised profit is held on constructive trust from the moment that the defendant receives it. Because that profit is held on constructive trust from that moment, anything which is acquired with that profit is also held on the same constructive trust from the moment of its acquisition. It is a simple matter of the law on constructive trusts that the beneficiaries can trace their proprietary rights

90 [1972] 2 All ER 162.
91 Hayton, 1996.
92 [2007] EWHC 915.
93 [2001] 2 BCLC 704.

into any property that is substituted for the profits (for example, by being acquired with those profits). Second, in the alternative, if the profits or their traceable substitute cannot be identified so as to be subjected to a constructive trust (for example, if the fiduciary moves the assets out of the jurisdiction or they are destroyed somehow) then the fiduciary is personally liable to account for the value of the profits and any substitute property to the beneficiaries.

12.4.5 The corporate opportunity doctrine in company law

The traditional corporate opportunity doctrine

Company law takes a subtly different approach to these questions from trusts law. In the company law context, it is misuse of a corporate opportunity which will be sufficient in triggering a liability to hold profits on constructive trust. For trading companies, their corporate opportunities (a putative deal with a customer, or a chance to expand into a new business) are central to their profitability. When shareholders invest in a company, they do so in the expectation that the company's expected business activities will turn a profit in accordance with the company's strategy. Consequently, the courts traditionally took a dim view of a company director spotting an opportunity while retained by a company, then leaving the company, and subsequently pursuing that opportunity for herself. In such a situation, the company director would be required to hold any profits taken from that opportunity on constructive trust for the company. To do otherwise would have made it very difficult to bind directors to work in the interests of the company instead of working in their own interests. There may be factual problems in any given case as to whether the company could have exploited the opportunity or whether the opportunity had matured sufficiently to be meaningful when the director was working for the company: this would be especially so if the director was careful not to let the opportunity mature until after they had left the company.

We have considered the position of Hudson in *Queensland Mines v Hudson* and the different position of Cooley in *IDC v Cooley* above: Hudson made a full exposition of the opportunity which was rejected by the board of directors, after which Hudson exploited the opportunity in his own name; whereas Cooley deceived his employers as to his reasons for leaving, while hiding the opportunity, and then exploited an opportunity in his own name thereafter. The leading case must remain *Regal v Gulliver* in which the directors of a company that operated cinemas decided to keep a new opportunity to open cinemas to themselves by creating a new company into which they diverted the chance to exploit the new cinema opportunities. A strict line was taken by the House of Lords as to the duties of loyalty which the directors owed to their company. The House of Lords was concerned, amongst other things, to prevent the management from perpetrating a fraud on the shareholders by diverting a business opportunity to themselves which ought properly to have been exploited on behalf of the company.

Another rare (but straightforward) example of a director being allowed to keep a profit for themselves arose in *Island Export Finance Ltd v Umunna*.[94] The company had a contract with the government of Cameroon to supply them with post boxes. Mr Umunna was responsible for this contract. He resigned from the company after the contract had been completed. In time, the company got out of this line of business. After his resignation, Umunna

---

94 [1986] BCC 460.

entered into a similar contract on his own behalf. The company sued him for the personal profits which he made for himself under this second contract. The court held that, while Umunna's fiduciary obligations towards the company did not cease once he resigned from its employment, nevertheless there was no evidence that the company had intended to pursue a business opportunity of this sort for itself when Umunna had developed this opportunity for himself after leaving the company. It was important that there had not been a clear link between Umunna leaving the company and there being a maturing business opportunity in existence (as had been the case in *Cooley*). As Falconer J made clear in *Balston v Headline Filters Ltd*,[95] there is no harm in a director resigning from a company and then beginning to exploit a new business opportunity afterwards. Provided that the opportunity had not been maturing and had not caused the director to leave the company so as to keep the opportunity for herself, then there would be no requirement to account for any profits taken.

The retreat from the traditional approach

There are some more difficult recent cases which have found that a director should be permitted to take an opportunity for themselves without having to account to the company for the profits which they took. The common thread which runs through these cases is that the director had effectively been excluded from the management of the company when they had begun to exploit the opportunity for themselves, albeit that they were still in post as directors when they had begun to do so. In the case of *In Plus Group Ltd v Pyke*[96] Mr Pyke was a director of a company, which we shall call 'Plus Ltd'; but he had 'fallen out with his co-director' and in consequence he had been 'effectively excluded from the management of the company'. Mr Pyke decided to set up a new company while he was still a director of Plus Ltd. The new company entered into contracts on its own behalf with a major customer of Plus Ltd: a clear example, one might have thought, of diverting the original company's opportunities to oneself (through a new corporate vehicle). Nevertheless, the Court of Appeal held that Mr Pyke was not in breach of his fiduciary duties to Plus Ltd because he had not used any property belonging to Plus Ltd to obtain this business and also because he had not made any use of any confidential information which he had acquired while he was a director of Plus Ltd. Sedley LJ described this decision as having been reached 'quite exceptionally'.

A similar approach was taken in *Foster v Bryant*[97] where the defendant director had been effectively excluded from the business by his co-director. Eventually, the defendant resigned from the company after his co-director (who was also the majority shareholder) 'truculently' made the defendant's wife redundant. We can imagine the breakdown in the relationship in this company with two directors, one of whom is squeezing the other one out. The defendant was found to have been excluded from the operation of the business, just like the defendant in *In Plus* above. One of the company's principal clients wanted to retain the services of both directors. Before the defendant's resignation came into effect (that is, while he was still technically a director but after he had tendered his resignation) the client began to talk to the defendant about the way in which the defendant could work with this client. Importantly, the defendant had tendered his resignation at this stage. When the defendant's notice period finished, he began to work for the client. The company sued the defendant on the basis that

95 [1990] FSR 385.
96 [2002] 2 BCLC 201.
97 [2007] Bus LR 1565.

he had been a director of the company when the business opportunity came to light and therefore it was argued that any profits earned from that opportunity should be subject to an account in favour of the company. While it was the company which brought the action, in practice it was the majority shareholder (who was also the defendant's co-director) who was driving the litigation. It was the same person who had driven the defendant to resign. The Court of Appeal held for the defendant.

The sympathy of Rix LJ was evidently with the defendant in *Foster v Bryant*. He sought to distinguish the decided cases on the basis severally that they concerned a misuse of the company's property or a 'faithless fiduciaries' taking advantage of their employers (as in *Cooley*), whereas the defendant here was blameless at that level. Rix LJ did not doubt the general principle that a director must deal in good faith with the company, nor that a fiduciary could not earn profits in secret from her office from an opportunity which belonged to the company or for which the company was negotiating. However, his lordship considered that the facts in this instance were such that the defendant should be excused from liability because the director had effectively not been playing any part in the running of the company and therefore for him to work with a client (after resigning) did not interfere with his obligations in any meaningful way. It was considered important that we should deal with these principles in a 'fact-sensitive' way: that idea suggests a dilution of the central principle in *Bray v Ford* to the effect that this was 'an inflexible rule of equity'.

The return to the traditional approach

More recent cases have reverted to the traditional approach after *Foster v Bryant* and *In Plus Ltd*. A comparatively straightforward case of diverting business opportunities away from a company arose in *Berryland Books Ltd v BK Books Ltd*.[98] Significantly, this case also involved a remarkable misuse of the company's assets. The defendant director managed the UK operation of an international publishing company. The defendant realised that he could be earning profits for himself rather than for the company. So, he established a new company which exploited the publisher's business opportunities. This would be easy to do in publishing: deals for exciting new books could be diverted to the new company. The defendant also solicited the publisher's staff to work for his new company. Again, this would be important if those staff had contacts with writers or if they knew about the production and marketing processes. The defendant even used the publisher's equipment and online materials to create websites, to set up stands at book fairs and to exploit other marketing opportunities to push his new venture. It was held that the defendant had breached the 'fundamental duty of loyalty' bound up with being a director. The court returned to the core principle in this area. However, given the brazen nature of the defendant's breach of duty it would have been impossible to have done otherwise.

Similarly, the Court of Appeal in *Re Allied Business and Financial Consultants Ltd*[99] returned to the traditional 'no conflict' principle set out in *Aberdeen Railway v Blaikie Bros*[100] and *Regal v Gulliver* to the effect that company directors owe an undivided loyalty to the company akin to the obligations of a trustee. Here a director had diverted a business opportunity to an undertaking under his control when it had been difficult to interest any

---

98 [2009] 2 BCLC 709.
99 [2009] 2 BCLC 666.
100 (1854) 2 Eq Rep 1281.

of the company's clients in investing in the opportunity. The strictness of the traditional principle was nevertheless upheld. In *PNC Telecom plc v Thomas (No 2)*[101] a problem arose about the control of a company and whether or not the defendant director should remain as a director of it. It was found, clearly, that there would be a conflict of interest if the defendant was permitted to cast a vote in the meeting which considered his own directorship. It was held that the conflict of interest principle still applied, even though this was clearly the sort of case on exclusion from participation in the management of the business which had so moved Rix LJ in *Foster v Bryant*.

The duties of directors under the Companies Act 2006

The Companies Act 2006 introduced a statutory code of directors' general duties for the first time.[102] In essence, s 175 provides that company directors will be absolved from liability for taking personal profits from their fiduciary office if a majority of the other directors vote to permit them to do so. Section 175(1) provides that 'a director of a company must avoid a situation in which he has, or can have, a direct or indirect interest that conflicts, or possibly may conflict, with the interests of the company'.[103] The principal change is in s 175(4) which provides that there is no breach of this principle if either the profit is authorised or 'if the situation cannot reasonably be regarded as likely to give rise to a conflict of interest'. Significantly, s 175(5) provides that authorisation will be deemed to have taken place if the company's constitutional arrangements for approving such a situation have been followed: this is usually satisfied by a majority vote of the directors to that effect. Therefore, directors may explicitly now rely on authorisation being given by the board of directors, provided that the meeting which does so is quorate and that the votes of any directors with such a conflict of interest are discounted.[104]

12.4.6 Equitable accounting

Importantly, it was found that Mr Boardman should be entitled to some compensation (known as 'equitable accounting') on a liberal scale for his work, in spite of the imposition of the constructive trust.[105] This strikes me as being remarkable. Boardman was a qualified and experienced solicitor, and yet he did not take the effort to acquire proper authorisation to take these personal profits (under a rule which had been a key part of English law since the early 18th century). Moreover, he was paid for his work as a solicitor. Therefore, it is surprising that everyone is concerned to salve Boardman's wounds. The claimant's somewhat jealous greed in bringing this litigation might make one feel less affinity for his case given that he had already made a profit from this transaction as a beneficiary under the trust. Nevertheless, equity has always required the utmost good faith from fiduciaries (including solicitors). Consequently, the House of Lords, it is suggested, was right in the conclusion it reached.

---

101 [2008] 2 BCLC 95.
102 Companies Act 2006, s 170 *et seq.*
103 *Ibid*, s 177 provides also that: 'If a director of a company is in any way, directly or indirectly, interested in a proposed transaction or arrangement with the company, he must declare the nature and extent of that interest to the other directors.'
104 *Ibid*, s 175(6).
105 As considered at section 12.5.3 below.

Nevertheless, Boardman was considered to have been deserving of equitable compensation. By way of contrast, in *Guinness v Saunders*,[106] a director of Guinness Plc, Ernest Saunders, had made personal profits from criminal insider dealing in connection with a takeover bid for the company in breach of his fiduciary duty. The company sought to recover those profits. Saunders argued that he should receive an accounting in light of his hard work for the company. Lord Templeman was not prepared to allow Saunders to take any personal benefit in the light of his criminal activity on the basis that Saunders had come to equity with unclean hands. Similarly, the defendant in *Cobbetts LLP v Hodge*[107] had sought an accounting (an 'equitable allowance'[108]) for the work he had done for the firm, while acquiring a private placement of shares for himself in breach of his fiduciary duties. This was not allowed because the defendant had misled the firm and therefore would not receive equitable assistance. His failure to make a disclosure constituted unclean hands.

12.5 UNCONSCIONABLE DEALINGS WITH PROPERTY

12.5.1 Understanding the concept of unconscionability

The doctrines which are discussed in this section derive from the general principle of unconscionability which was illustrated most clearly in the judgment of Lord Browne-Wilkinson in *Westdeutsche Landesbank Girozentrale v Islington LBC*.[109] What is interesting about the doctrines considered in this section is that they contain very specific and technical ideas of what constitutes unconscionability as opposed to the more obvious categories of unconscionability which were considered in section 12.3 above because they related to clearly unconscionable activities such as killing, theft and bribery. This demonstrates that our understanding of what it means to act unconscionably will be formed by studying the situations in which decided cases have found particular types of behaviour to fall within that category or to fall outside it. We shall begin by considering a range of situations in which dealings with land have led to findings of constructive trust.

12.5.2 Constructive trusts in relation to land

Constructive trusts in relation to land in general terms

Constructive trusts may arise in relation to land in three principal ways. First, in relation to the ownership of the domestic home by means of a common intention constructive trust.[110] This category is considered in detail in Chapter 15. Second, by entering into a contract for the transfer of rights in land, there is an automatic transfer of the equitable interest in that land as soon as there is a binding contract in effect.[111] That contract would have to be in writing in one document signed by the parties which contained all the terms of the contract.[112] However, proprietary estop-

---

106 [1990] 2 AC 663.
107 [2010] 1 BCLC 30.
108 *Ibid*, [113].
109 [1996] AC 669.
110 *Lloyds Bank v Rosset* [1990] 1 All ER 1111.
111 *Lysaght v Edwards* (1876) 2 Ch D 499; *Jerome v Kelly* [2004] 2 All ER 835.
112 Law of Property (Miscellaneous Provisions) Act 1989, s 2.

pel will now offer a means of evading this statutory requirement in circumstances in which the transferor made assurances to the transferee that the transferee would receive title in this land and where that transferee acted to her detriment in reliance on those assurances.[113] This category is considered below at section 12.6.2. Third, in relation to joint ventures over land.

Joint ventures in relation to land

There has been a lot of case law relating to the situation in which parties agree to develop land together or to pursue some other commercial venture of that sort. Often the parties fall out with one another before the work is complete. This raises a question as to the parties' respective property rights in that land. A good example of the traditional approach appeared in *Banner Homes Group plc v Luff Development Ltd*[114] where two commercial parties entered into a joint venture to develop land in Berkshire. No binding contract had been formed between the parties by the time that the defendant sought to exploit the site alone without the involvement of the claimant. There had previously been extensive negotiations between claimant and defendant and their respective lawyers. It was held that the defendant could establish a constructive trust even though the parties had never signed a binding contract to cover their venture. It was held that there had been sufficient agreement between the parties for the claimant to have relied on the arrangement with the result that it was unconscionable for the defendant to renege on their putative deal. It was enough that there had been extensive negotiations so that the claimant could reasonably have relied on the parties' common intention to enter into a joint venture agreement.

Importantly, however, the subsequent decision of the House of Lords in *Cobbe v Yeoman's Row*[115] took the opposite view. In that case, the claimant and the defendant had entered into negotiations to develop property. The claimant even took the step of spending a large amount of money to secure planning permission to develop the land. Nevertheless, the parties had not created a binding contract between them. Subsequently, the defendant decided to exploit the property without the claimant. The claimant sued in an effort to establish rights in the property. In the High Court and in the Court of Appeal it was held that the claimant had acted to his detriment in reasonable reliance on the understanding that the property would be developed together. Lord Scott took the opposite view for the majority in the House of Lords. His lordship was clearly impatient with the rash of cases which had involved commercial parties who were aware that they had not completed a contract between them but who nevertheless sought to rely on proprietary estoppel and constructive trust to protect them when they rashly took the risk of spending money on the property in the absence of the protection of a contract. Therefore, it was held that in the absence of a contract, the claimant should not acquire any rights in the property.

The alternative approach would have found that it was unconscionable for the defendant knowingly to permit the claimant to spend such a large amount of money without acquiring any rights. The subsequent decision of the House of Lords in *Thorner v Major*[116] reversed the position in *Cobbe* in relation to proprietary estoppel by allowing the claimant to acquire rights in farmland as a result of working unpaid for seven days per week (often for 16 hours per day) on that land for its owner. Interestingly, in that case, no clear spoken or written

---

113 *Yaxley v Gotts* [2000] Ch 162.
114 [2000] Ch 372.
115 [2008] 1 WLR 1752.
116 [2009] 1 WLR 776.

representation had been made between the parties but rather the claimant was considered to have acquired the impression that the land would be left to him entirely reasonably. While that is not exactly the same point as the constructive trust over land as a result of a joint venture, in the absence of Lord Scott the House of Lords in *Thorner v Major* was clearly taking a different approach to that type of situation generally.

12.5.3 Constructive trusts to 'keep out of the market'

The so-called 'equity in *Pallant v Morgan*' arises in situations in which the claimant has refrained from exercising a commercial opportunity due to an agreement with the defendant who then exploits that opportunity.[117] One of the oldest examples would be a situation in which two people attend an auction and then agree that only one of them will bid for an item of property (something which is referred to as 'keeping out of the market') so that they can both benefit from acquiring the property at a lower price than if they competed with one another.[118] When the defendant takes their advantage then the benefit is held on constructive trust for the parties together because the claimant will have suffered detriment by failing to exploit a commercial opportunity.

12.5.4 Statute cannot be used as an engine of fraud: *Rochefoucauld v Boustead*

The decision in *Rochefoucauld v Boustead*[119] held that the defendant could not use statutory formalities as a pretext for failing to transfer property to the claimant as was required under an agreement between them. This was considered to be an example of statute being used as 'an engine of fraud'. Millett LJ held in *Paragon Finance v Thakerar*[120] that the decision in *Rochefoucauld v Boustead* was an example of a constructive trust. Similarly, in *Lyus v Prowsa*,[121] a mortgagor sought to deal with property in contravention of the mortgage on the basis that the mortgagee had failed to register the mortgage. It was held that the mortgagor held the property on constructive trust for the mortgagee nevertheless, because the mortgagor had undertaken in the mortgage contract to respect the rights of the mortgagee.[122] These cases were considered in detail in section 5.2.

12.5.5 'Doing everything necessary': *Re Rose*

The doctrine in *Re Rose*[123] provides that the equitable interest in property which was intended to be passed from a transferor to a transferee would pass automatically provided that the transferor had done everything necessary for them to do to effect that transfer. This doctrine was discussed in detail in section 5.4.3 above where is was understood as an exception to the principle that equity will not perfect an imperfect gift. In *Re Rose* itself, Mr Rose had

---

117 [1952] 2 All ER 951.
118 *Chattock v Miller* (1878) 8 Ch D 177; *Pallant v Morgan* [1952] 2 All ER 951.
119 [1897] 1 Ch 196.
120 *Paragon Finance plc v Thakerar & Co* [1999] 1 All ER 400.
121 [1982] 1 WLR 1044.
122 See also *IDC Group v Clark* (1992) 65 P & CR 179.
123 [1952] Ch 499, considered at section 5.4.3 above.

intended to transfer shares to his wife. To have completed the transfer he needed to complete a share transfer form and the company needed to register the change in ownership. In fact, Mr Rose had completed that form and posted it off to the company, but the share ownership had not been re-registered in time. It was held by Lord Evershed MR that because Mr Rose had done everything necessary for him to do to effect the transfer then it would have been inequitable for him to have reneged on the transfer, and therefore the equitable interest would be deemed to have taken place automatically. Modern explanations of this doctrine have identified it as being a species of constructive trust whereby the dictates of conscience transfer the equitable interest in the property automatically.[124]

12.6 CONSTRUCTIVE TRUSTS AND AGREEMENTS RELATING TO PROPERTY

This section considers the situations in which constructive trusts come into existence in relation to land, especially in relation to contracts and other forms of agreement to transfer rights in land.

12.6.1 Common intention constructive trusts and the home

The law on ownership of the home is considered in detail in Chapter 15 *Trusts of homes*. In that context there is a particular form of constructive trust known as the 'common intention constructive trust' which comes into existence supposedly to give effect to the common intention of cohabitants as to their rights in their home. This form of constructive trust is best understood as being a different sort of constructive trust which is specific to the context of the home. It was the House of Lords in *Gissing v Gissing*[125] which held, when deciding which members of a household should have which equitable interests in the home, that the court should consider the common intention of the parties. The leading case in that area is now the decision of the Supreme Court in *Jones v Kernott* which held the court should presume that if only one person was entered on the legal title as proprietor of the home that that person was intended to be the sole equitable owner of the property; or if there were two or more legal owners of the property then those people should be presumed to be equitable co-owners of the property. If that presumption was found not to reflect the parties' true intention then the court should consider the entire course of dealing between the parties to try to identify objectively the common intention of the parties. If such a common intention could not be identified, that the court should decide what is fair. Consequently, that type of constructive trust is considered separately from the other constructive trusts considered in this chapter because it operates on different principles from the conscience and knowledge model in *Westdeutsche Landesbank v Islington*.

12.6.2 On conveyance of property

As a general rule, when a contract is created for the sale of any property, that contract will have the effect of transferring the equitable interest in that property to the purchaser automatically when the contract becomes legally binding.[126] The transfer of the equitable interest

---

124 Oakley, 1997.
125 [1971] AC 886.
126 *Neville v Wilson* [1997] Ch 144.

takes effect by means of a constructive trust.[127] The rationale for this constructive trust is that the creation of a binding contract entitles the purchaser to specific performance of the contract (an equitable remedy), and because the ancient principle provides that 'equity looks upon as done that which ought to have been done' then equity pretends that the equitable interest passed automatically when the contract was enforceable.[128] Alternatively, it might be said (in modern parlance) that the constructive trust arises because it would be unconscionable for the vendor to renege on their specifically enforceable obligations to transfer title to the purchaser on the terms of the contract.[129] *Neville v Wilson* upheld the proposition that a contract for the transfer of personal property has the effect of transferring the equitable interest in that property automatically when the contract is legally enforceable. It was held that this automatic transfer of the equitable interest took effect by way of a constructive trust over the property which was the subject matter of the contract in favour of the purchaser.

This rule that a contract for the sale of property transfers an equitable interest in that property applies to land in the same way that it applies to other items of property,[130] provided that the contract is in writing containing all of the terms of the agreement in one document which is signed by all the parties.[131] Once that contract has been created, the equitable interest in the land is deemed to have transferred automatically to the purchaser of that interest.[132] The vendor holds the property on constructive trust for the purchaser until completion of the sale or transfer.

There are competing authorities as to whether this trust comes into existence on execution of the contract of sale[133] or on completion of the contract of sale:[134] that is, does the constructive trust come into existence when the parties effect their contract or when the purchaser goes into possession of the land? The problem in the real world is that vendors and purchasers are often in a combative relationship with one another. As is well known, purchasers will often try to reduce the purchase price of a domestic home late in the negotiations when they know that the vendor is emotionally committed to the sale; by the same token the vendor may be hoping that purchaser never changes their mind based on the musty smell in the bedrooms or the ghost in the attic. Therefore, if the purchaser seeks, for example, to change the price and if the vendor is supposed to act as constructive trustee for the purchaser, then that would seem to require the vendor to act in the purchaser's interests and reduce the price. That could not be sensible. Therefore, it was suggested in *Jerome v Kelly*[135] the existence or the terms of such a constructive trust should depend upon the situation. It was held by Lord Walker that such a constructive trust should arise '*sub modo*' (i.e. on its own terms dependent on the circumstances) and should not be assumed to come into existence automatically such that it operates in the same way in all circumstances.

---

127 *Chinn v Collins* [1981] AC 533; *Neville v Wilson* [1997] Ch 144.
128 *Ibid.*
129 *Neville v Wilson* [1997] Ch 144.
130 *Lysaght v Edwards* (1876) 2 Ch D 499.
131 Law of Property (Miscellaneous Provisions) Act 1989, s 2.
132 *Lysaght v Edwards* (1876) 2 Ch D 499.
133 *Paine v Meller* (1801) 6 Ves 349; 31 ER 1088, *per* Lord Eldon.
134 *Shaw v Foster* (1872) LR 5 HL 321.
135 [2004] 2 All ER 835.

The older case of *Lysaght v Edwards*[136] held that the equitable interest passed automatically when the contract was executed. The various practical problems which might affect the purchaser were discussed by Mason J in *Chang v Registrar of Titles*, for example as to the nature of the vendor's title or whether the purchaser had sufficient money to pay for the property.[137] Consequently, it was accepted by Lord Walker in *Jerome v Kelly*[138] that the trustee is not a constructive trustee under an ordinary bare trust but rather must be accepted as having a very particular kind of trusteeship which will differ from circumstance to circumstance. The obligations of the constructive trustee will depend upon the circumstances. In the ordinary situation, the vendor would simply hold the property on bare trust for the purchaser. However, there may be situations (like the complex transaction in *Jerome v Kelly*) in which the vendor may be required to assume more complicated obligations in relation to the property, in which case that situation would govern the terms of their trusteeship.

The fact that the nature of these trusts depends on their circumstances was suggested by *Lloyds Bank v Carrick*.[139] The claimant entered into a contract with her brother-in-law, the defendant, to lease a home to her. The defendant took out a charge over the property which led to the mortgagee seeking repossession of the property. The claimant sought to defend her entitlement to remain in possession. It was held that property rights passed to the claimant automatically when she began to perform her obligations under the contract by way of paying rent and so forth. Consequently, the claimant acquired an equitable proprietary right in the property further to the contract.

12.7 VOLUNTARY ASSUMPTION OF LIABILITY

The categories of constructive trust assembled in this section are said to arise on the basis of voluntary assumption of liability, where a person is deemed to be a constructive trustee because of some relationship or some course of dealing into which she entered voluntarily.

12.7.1 Secret trusts

Secret trusts were the subject of Chapter 6. One of the explanations which was advanced for the operation of secret trusts was that they impose constructive trusts on defendants who have unconscionably sought to take title in property which was intended to be passed beneficially to a third party. The classic example of a secret trust arises when a testator has a child by someone other than their spouse and then wants to pass property to that person without their spouse learning of their secret family. To this end, property is passed to a trusted friend who is charged with the responsibility of passing that property in turn to the child's mother. That trusted friend is then named in the will as being a legatee of that property. The

---

136 (1876) 2 Ch D 499, 506, *per* Sir George Jessel MR.
137 (1976) 137 CLR 177, 184.
138 [2004] UKHL 25, para [31].
139 [1996] 4 All ER 630.

Wills Act 1837 does not permit any person not named in the will to take that property. If the friend was to purport to keep the property beneficially for themselves then that would clearly be unconscionable. Therefore, equity requires that the property is held on trust for the child as the testator had really intended. Secret trusts could be understood as being constructive trusts which operate so as to prevent statute from being used as an engine of fraud, and thus as being constructive trusts.[140]

12.7.2 Mutual wills

The doctrine of mutual wills applies to wills created by two or more people with the intention that the provisions of all of those wills shall be irrevocably binding. Imagine an elderly couple who have been together but unmarried for a very long time. Afraid that the law might not protect them because they are unmarried, they decide to write their wills on the same day. In those wills, they leave all of their property to one another. Their intention is that those wills are intended to be interlinked: 'I leave you all of my property on the basis that you promise to leave me all of your property, but the surviving party must leave all of the property to the Battersea Dogs Home.' These wills are said to be 'mutual wills'. The mutual wills doctrine prevents one of those parties from changing their will in contravention of this pact. Ordinarily, the law on wills allows a testator to change their will at any time and nothing outside the will would be permitted to affect the application of their last, properly constituted will under the Wills Act 1837. An exception is the doctrine of mutual wills. Lord Camden held in *Dufour v Pereira* that the first person to die is carrying the agreement into effect and therefore it would be a 'fraud' for the other party to the agreement to change their will so as to achieve a different purpose.[141]

A mutual will arrangement requires that there must be clear and satisfactory evidence of an agreement between two testators to the effect that each would make wills in a particular form and that neither party would revoke that will without informing the other testator.[142] Those wills must be irrevocable[143] and they must be intended to bind both parties after one of them dies.[144] The doctrine of mutual wills operates in such a way that 'the conscience of the survivor's executor' is bound by a trust which arises out of 'the agreement between the two testators not to revoke their wills'.[145] That trust comes into effect when the first of the two dies without having revoked her will.[146] This is a constructive trust, as was made clear by Deane J in *Birmingham v Renfrew*,[147] in the sense that the surviving party to the arrangement is bound by a constructive trust to leave the property covered by their arrangement in accordance with their agreement.

---

140 See section 12.3.4 above.
141 (1769) 1 Dick 419.
142 *Olins v Walters* [2009] 2 WLR 1.
143 *Re Green* [1951] Ch 158; *Re Cleaver* [1981] 1 WLR 939.
144 *Re Goodchild (Deceased)* [1996] 1 WLR 694.
145 *Thomas and Agnes Carvel Foundation v Carvel* [2007] 4 All ER 81; and *Olins v Walters* [2009] 2 WLR 1, 10, *per* Mummery LJ.
146 *Ibid.*
147 (1937) 57 CLR 666, 683.

The Court of Appeal in *Olins v Walters*[148] was confronted by a mutual wills arrangement effected between an elderly couple whose relationship had deteriorated by the time that the wife died. The husband no longer wanted to be bound by the arrangement and even claimed that he had no recollection of it. Their grandson, who was a solicitor, had advised them about the arrangement. The trial judge,[149] Norris J, found on the facts that the couple had formed a mutual wills arrangement, not least on the basis of their grandson's recollections and on documents created by the couple. The Court of Appeal held that this doctrine was an equitable doctrine (not a contract law doctrine) and that it took effect by way of constructive trust which governed the conscience of the surviving testator so as to prevent him from altering his will without the agreement of the other party to the mutual will.

This sort of refusal to be bound by the mutual will is the sort of dispute which tends to arise in this area. It might be difficult for third parties (who might be the ultimate beneficiaries of the will) to prove its terms. They would have to rely on the evidence of witnesses at the time or of legal advisors who drew up paperwork for the parties. It may be that the surviving party to the arrangement falls in love again or simply changes their mind about how they wish to deal with the remaining property. The effect of a mutual will arrangement is that they are bound by an agreement they formed in life even after their partner's death. It may be difficult, if no solicitors are approached, to prove that a mutual will arrangement was intended. In *Re Hagger*,[150] a husband and wife made separate wills, but both of their wills contained terms that the parties had agreed to the disposal of their property in accordance with each other's wills and that they intended their wills to be irrevocable. It was held that this constituted sufficient intention to create mutual wills. By contrast in *Re Oldham*[151] a husband and wife created substantially similar wills with identical treatment of their property, but those wills were not expressed as being irrevocable and there was no clear evidence of an intention to create mutual wills: it was held that the parties had probably not intended to create mutual wills as a result. So, it is important that the parties make it plain that their wills are intended to be irrevocable (i.e. that they cannot write new wills at a later date without the permission of the other party)[152] and that their wills are intended to be binding even after the death of the first party.[153] There may be issues as to whether both parties had the requisite intention to make a will, let alone a mutual will arrangement. In *Baker v Baker*[154] medical evidence led to the conclusion that one of the parties did not have the necessary capacity to make a will as they lay terminally ill in hospital.

Assuming that the parties have the necessary capacity, then the mutual will arrangement becomes binding once one of the parties dies: otherwise it would be open to both parties to agree to terminate their arrangement at an earlier date.[155] The obligations of the survivor depend on the terms of their arrangement. It may be that the parties agree to leave their house to their grandchildren, or that they will leave their money to a specified charity – in such a

---

148 [2009] 2 WLR 1.
149 [2007] EWHC 3060.
150 [1930] 2 Ch 190.
151 [1925] Ch 75.
152 *Re Green* [1951] Ch 158; *Re Cleaver* [1981] 1 WLR 939.
153 *Re Goodchild (Deceased)* [1996] 1 WLR 694.
154 [2008] 2 FLR 767.
155 *Stone v Hoskins* [1905] P 194.

situation the survivor would be bound to do that. Clearly, the survivor may prefer not to do so if they have remarried or if they have fallen out with their grandchildren. There may also be problems after property which the survivor only acquires after the first party's death: the agreement may or may not have covered it. Clearly, each arrangement may therefore have their own terms. It is generally assumed that the survivor is to be treated as the absolute owner of the property during their lifetime, subject to a fiduciary duty to settle the property by will in accordance with the arrangement after death.[156] It would be an inhuman rule which prevented the surviving party from using the money left over, for example, to repair their house if it was ruined by a flood. The surviving party is unlikely to be treated as being required to keep all of the property in the same condition as when the first party died because the surviving party may live for decades thereafter. The critical point is that the relevant property must be left by will in the way that was specified in the mutual will arrangement.

12.8 TRUSTEES *DE SON TORT* AND INTERMEDDLERS AS CONSTRUCTIVE TRUSTEES

If someone who is not an express trustee interferes (or intermeddles) with a trust, for example by taking over its management, then that person will be construed to be a trustee of that trust. Smith LJ described such as a person as being 'a trustee *de son tort*' (that is, a trustee as a result of their own wrong by interfering with the trust) and as being a 'constructive trustee' as a result.[157] By way of example, in *Blyth v Fladgate*[158] a trustee had transferred securities from a trust fund into the possession of a firm of solicitors. In the meantime, the trustee died. The solicitors sold the securities and acquired a mortgage with them. The solicitors were held to be trustees *de son tort* because they had taken it upon themselves to sell the securities and to acquire a mortgage which lost money. Consequently, as trustees *de son tort*, the solicitors were required to account to the beneficiaries of the trust for the loss which they suffered. Similarly, in *Lyell v Kennedy*,[159] where a manager of land continued to collect rents in respect of that land after the death of the landlord, but without informing the tenants of their landlord's death, then that manager was held to be a constructive trustee of those profits due to his intermeddling with the property.

12.9 PERSONAL LIABILITY TO ACCOUNT AS A CONSTRUCTIVE TRUSTEE

There are two principal doctrines in which personal constructive trusteeship will be imposed on defendants. Those two doctrines are considered in Chapter 19 *Strangers*. That liability applies to 'strangers' to a trust: i.e. people who are not trustees. Where such a stranger dishonestly assists a breach of trust, then that person will be personally liable to account to the beneficiaries of the trust for the loss caused by the breach of trust.[160] Alternatively, where

---

156 *Re Cleaver* [1981] 1 WLR 939; *Goodchild v Goodchild* [1996] 1 WLR 694.
157 *Mara v Browne* [1896] 1 Ch 199, 209.
158 [1891] 1 Ch 337.
159 (1889) 14 App Cas 437.
160 [1995] 2 AC 378.

such a stranger receives trust property with knowledge of a breach of trust in a way that is unconscionable, then that person will be liable to account to the beneficiaries for the loss caused by the breach of trust.[161] No property is held on constructive trust under either head of liability: instead, the defendant is personally liable to account for the breach of trust *as if* there was property held on trust. The case law relating to those two doctrines is too detailed to consider in this chapter. Instead, the liability of strangers is considered in Part 8 as part of the law relating to breach of trust.

12.10 IS THE DOCTRINE OF CONSTRUCTIVE TRUST COHERENT?

There is one specific issue about the way in which constructive trusts operate which divides the academic commentators. It is said by some commentators that constructive trusts are hopelessly incoherent because there is no central principle binding them together.[162] Instead, they are said to arise higgledy-piggledy as judges choose to impose them. It is said that calling them a 'constructive' trust does not help us to define how they come into existence. The contrary viewpoint is that constructive trusts are all bound together by the idea of good conscience just as an egg binds together a cake mix. Illustrations of what that word 'conscience' (and its technical corollary 'unconscionable') means in this context are provided by the centuries of case law on constructive trusts. We know that it is deemed to be unconscionable for a fiduciary to receive a bribe or to take unauthorised profits, it is unconscionable to acquire profit from someone who was acting under a mistake and so on.

If we recall our discussion in Chapter 1, the law on constructive trusts both sets out a central moral (i.e. 'deontological') principle of unconscionability and then it develops 'consequentialist' illustrations of how that central principle works in practice. A deontological approach is one which relies on abstract, philosophical discussion of a concept; whereas a consequentialist approach is one which builds an understanding of a moral principle by observing how that principle is applied in practice. The law on constructive trusts does both. We come to understand what 'conscience' means both by discussions of the concept in leading cases like *Westdeutsche Landesbank v Islington* and by worked applications of that concept in the case law.

So, the central principle is that the constructive trust arises whenever the defendant acts in a way that is unconscionable, as was set out by Lord Browne-Wilkinson in *Westdeutsche Landesbank v Islington*. All of the cases on constructive trusts can be understood as applying that central principle, even if not all of the cases use the precise language of 'conscience' throughout. The law on constructive trusts is divided into pre-existing (i.e. consequentialist) categories in which the courts have found the defendant has acted in an unconscionable way in previous cases. Therefore, much of our definition of what 'unconscionable' means in this context is provided by looking at the categories of what equity has taken that term to mean in the decided cases. The following categories of activity are unconscionable, with the result that the commission of any of them will lead to any property acquired from them being held on constructive trust: theft, murder, fraud, taking a bribe, profiting as a fiduciary

---

161 *Polly Peck International v Nadir (No 2)* [1992] 4 All ER 769, 777, *per* Scott LJ.
162 P Birks, 'Trusts raised to avoid unjust enrichment', (1996) *Restitution Law Review* 3.

from a conflict of interest, and so forth. Therefore, a person who steals property and sells it will then be required to hold the sale proceeds earned from the stolen property on constructive trust. The authorities tell us that these types of behaviour are taken by the courts to be unconscionable and therefore they will lead to the imposition of a constructive trust in appropriate circumstances. In this way we can assemble an understanding of what it means to act unconscionably.

Chapter 13

Proprietary estoppel

CAPSULE SUMMARY

The doctrine of proprietary estoppel is a very powerful, remedial doctrine. That it is a 'remedial' doctrine means that the courts are empowered to award a wide range of proprietary or personal remedies dependent on the circumstances such that those remedies take effect from the date of the court judgment forwards. There are two stages to making a proprietary estoppel claim: first, proving the three elements of the estoppel and, second, identifying the appropriate remedy on the facts. (There are other forms of estoppel in English law but this chapter will focus on proprietary estoppel.)

First, the elements of the estoppel. Proprietary estoppel arises in circumstances in which the defendant has made a representation to the claimant on which the claimant has relied to their detriment. Therefore, the three elements of proving the estoppel are: representation, reliance and detriment. In the decided cases, a representation may involve the making of a specific promise on one particular day or, frequently, it involves the making of a series of representations over time which when taken together create an understanding in the claimant's mind which it was reasonable for them to have formed. Remarkably, in *Thorner v Major*, just such an understanding was formed by the claimant from the circumstances even though the parties had never actually discussed the question at issue. Reliance is a question of fact requiring a link between the representation and the actions which the claimant took as a response. The concept of detriment has been treated differently in different cases: spending money is the clearest example of suffering detriment, but in some cases even agreeing to move house with one's children in reliance on a promise that you will all have a new home if you do so has been held to be detriment. So, there are differences on the authorities as to the meaning of detriment.

Second, the remedies. Once the court has accepted that entitlement to the estoppel has been demonstrated then the court will identify the appropriate remedy. The courts have awarded a wide range of remedies spanning a spectrum from outright ownership of the property in question, through to a mere award of money in compensation for the detriment suffered. Given that different cases have based their remedies on compensation for detriment, the fulfilment of a promise that had been made, or more general response to unconscionability, the doctrine of proprietary estoppel appears to be an equitable doctrine in the most discretionary sense. By way of example, in *Jennings v Rice* the claimant received £200,000 in cash, whereas in *Pascoe v Turner* the claimant was awarded the fee simple over the home which was the subject of the representation. In other cases such as *Gillett v Holt* the claimant has been awarded a combination of property rights and money.

Proprietary estoppel is said to be a remedial doctrine because the nature of the remedy is not known until the end of the case. This makes proprietary estoppel the opposite of constructive trusts. Whereas constructive trusts, considered in Chapter 12, were said to arise on an institutional basis (that is, retrospectively from the time of the unconscionable act and automatically without any discretion on the part of the court), proprietary estoppel arises on a remedial basis (that is, prospectively from the date of the court order with the precise nature of the remedy being at the court's discretion).[1]

13.1 INTRODUCTION

Proprietary estoppel is one of the several types of estoppel which exist in English equity and even at common law.[2] The modern doctrine of proprietary estoppel is based on the idea that a defendant has made a representation to the claimant on which the claimant relied to their detriment. Each of these elements – representation, reliance and detriment – is considered in detail below. Once those three elements have been proved, the court can fashion a remedy to suit the circumstances. Proprietary estoppel is a 'remedial' doctrine, which means that the claimant's rights come into existence from the time of the court's judgment and take effect prospectively (i.e. forwards in time). The courts are able to award a broad range of remedies. The courts have awarded full ownership of property at one end of the spectrum[3] right through to the other end of the spectrum where they have awarded a mere amount of money to compensate the claimant for the detriment which they have suffered or to prevent them from being treated

---

1   *Gillett v Holt* [2001] Ch 210, 235; *Jennings v Rice* [2003] 1 P & CR 100.
2   *Jorden v Money* (1854) 5 HLC 185; (1854) 10 ER 868: a doctrine recognised both by common law and by equity.
3   *Re Basham* [1986] 1 WLR 1498; *Pascoe v Turner* [1979] 2 All ER 945.

unconscionably.[4] Some courts have awarded combinations of proprietary rights and personal rights to money where the circumstances have suggested that that is appropriate.[5]

In the House of Lords in *Canadian and Dominion Sugar Company v Canadian National (West Indies) Steamships*, Lord Wright approved the words of Sir Frederick Pollock to the effect that 'the law of estoppel' in its many forms is 'perhaps the most powerful and flexible instrument to be found in any system of court jurisprudence'.[6] That is quite a claim and it will take us the rest of this chapter to justify. Proprietary estoppel is one of the purest forms of equity in the sense that, once the three elements have been demonstrated, the courts have a very wide discretion to act as they think appropriate when framing the appropriate remedy. There have been judgments and commentary[7] which have suggested that proprietary estoppel is best understood as arising so as to prevent unconscionability. As Lord Goff put it, talking about the many forms of estoppel which exist in equity:

> In the end, I am inclined to think that the many circumstances capable of giving rise to an estoppel cannot be accommodated within a single formula, and that it is unconscionability which provides the link between them.[8]

Similarly two judgments of Walker LJ in *Jennings v Rice*[9] and in *Gillett v Holt*[10] have explained the principle of proprietary estoppel as being based on preventing the claimant from suffering unconscionable behaviour where she had relied to her detriment on an assurance given to her by the defendant. While there have been cases in which proprietary estoppel has been identified as arising on the basis of unconscionability,[11] there has also been a much-criticised decision of the House of Lords in *Cobbe v Yeoman's Row*[12] which presented a different, narrower understanding of proprietary estoppel. That approach in *Cobbe* was not, however, followed by the subsequent decision of the House of Lords in *Thorner v Major*[13] which returned proprietary estoppel to the general, equitable form which has been outlined so far.

Proprietary estoppel is presented in this chapter as a cousin of constructive trusts and resulting trusts in that the remedies which flow from the finding of the estoppel come into existence at the discretion of the court and not by the intention of the parties. As a result of this range of potential remedies, proprietary estoppel can only be a remedial doctrine (unlike the institutional English constructive trust discussed in Chapter 12 which takes effect automatically and retrospectively) because the parties cannot know what their rights are until the court has given judgment. It is clear that proprietary estoppel is a very flexible doctrine and one which appears to be most akin to the traditional forms of equity that were discussed in Chapter 1 in that the court has wide discretion to make awards which meet the justice of the

---

4   *Campbell v Griffin* [2001] EWCA Civ 990; *Jennings v Rice* [2003] 1 P & CR 100.
5   *Gillett v Holt* [2001] Ch 210.
6   *Canada and Dominion Sugar Company Ltd v Canadian National (West Indies) Steamships Ltd* [1947] AC 46, 56.
7   See in particular the excellent E Cooke, *The Modern Law of Estoppel*, 2000.
8   *Johnson v Gore Wood & Co (No 1)* [2002] 2 AC 1.
9   [2003] 1 P & CR 100.
10   [2000] 2 All ER 289.
11   *Jennings v Rice* [2003] 1 P & CR 100.
12   [2008] 1 WLR 1752.
13   [2009] 1 WLR 776.

case. These issues arise in the discussion to follow and the theoretical debates about estoppel are considered again in the final section of this chapter.

13.2 DEBATES ABOUT THE NATURE OF EQUITABLE ESTOPPEL

The nature of estoppel in equity is a matter for some debate. It is worth spending a little while describing the shape of that debate at the outset. There are academics who seek to limit and organise proprietary estoppel;[14] whereas there are academics with greater sensitivity to the history of equity who consider that all equitable estoppel arises as a single doctrine based on the principle of unconscionability.[15] The same division of opinion exists between the judges. On the one hand, Lord Scott in *Cobbe v Yeoman's Row*[16] sought to limit the doctrine of proprietary estoppel (as in the old case of *Wilmot v Barber*)[17] to circumstances in which there had been a mistake exploited by one party at the expense of another. In *Cobbe* itself this approach meant that a claimant, who was aware that he did not have the benefit of a binding contract when he spent money acquiring planning permission for a mooted property development, could not say that he was operating under a mistake (because he knew he did not have a binding contract) and therefore could not rely on proprietary estoppel. Lord Scott was particularly keen to stop commercial people from taking risks (such as investing in planning permission without having a binding contract to develop property in partnership with the defendant) and then seeking to rely on proprietary estoppel after the event when their risk went wrong. In that case, the defendant had simply decided to develop the property by herself.

By contrast, Lord Walker and Lord Rodger took the view in the later House of Lords decision in *Thorner v Major*[18] that proprietary estoppel remains a broad doctrine based on representation, reliance and detriment, with a broad range of potential remedies. The claimant in *Cobbe* had won before the High Court and the Court of Appeal because he could show that the defendant had made a representation to him that they would develop the property together, on which he relied to his detriment in spending money acquiring planning permission. The defendant was found in the lower courts to have acted unconscionably in taking advantage of the claimant in this way. However, Lord Scott had chosen to exhume the old approach to the estoppel which required that there had been a mistake. It was Lord Scott's conviction that proprietary estoppel had simply grown too large.

By contrast, Lord Walker had taken the view when he was a judge in the Court of Appeal in *Jennings v Rice*[19] that proprietary estoppel is based on resolving 'unconscionability' and, importantly, in the House of Lords in *Thorner v Major* he disavowed the general approach taken in *Cobbe*. As a result of the decision in *Thorner v Major*, the law at present is based on the model of which requires representation, reliance and detriment to be shown. What is evident, however, is that this debate about the nature of proprietary estoppel (as with all equitable doctrines) divides the judges and academics between those who support the breadth of this characteristically equitable doctrine and those who would prefer to limit it.

---

14 B McFarlane, *The Law of Proprietary Estoppel*, 2014.
15 E Cooke, *The Modern Law of Estoppel*, 2000.
16 [2008] 1 WLR 1752.
17 (1880) 15 Ch D 96.
18 [2009] 1 WLR 776.
19 [2002] EWCA Civ 159.

There is, however, another question about the nature of estoppel: is there one doctrine or are there several doctrines? Professor Cooke takes the view that estoppel can be understood as being one doctrine which operates around a standard of unconscionability and, as mentioned above, there are judges like Lord Goff and Walker LJ who have been explicit in finding that proprietary estoppel operates on the basis of unconscionability. By contrast, Wilken and Villiers have taken the approach that, as a matter of reading through the many cases on the many different types of estoppel, there have been several different types of estoppel in existence over the centuries.[20] In theory, both approaches are correct: there are judicial statements that equitable estoppel is governed by unconscionability, but that is not the approach taken in all of the cases and therefore it is possible to divide the case law into different sub-categories. This is a common feature of debates about equitable doctrines: on the one hand there appears to be a central principle being used in the cases, while on the other hand it is possible to subdivide the precise uses to which different judges have put the doctrine across all of the case law. What we shall attempt to do primarily in the discussion to follow is to describe what the law *is*, as opposed to what different people think the law *ought to be*.

13.3 THE BASIS OF PROPRIETARY ESTOPPEL

13.3.1 Proprietary estoppel and mistake

The early form of proprietary estoppel was based on mistake, as was set out in the decision of the House of Lords in *Ramsden v Dyson*.[21] Lord Cranworth held that proprietary estoppel required that there must be a mistake which was induced in the claimant's mind by the defendant with the result that the claimant acted detrimentally in reliance on it.[22] So, in *Wilmot v Barber*[23] Fry J developed 'five probanda' necessary to be able to rely on proprietary estoppel whereby it had to be shown that the claimant had made a mistake as to their rights and that the claimant had acted in reliance on this mistake, while the defendant must have known that they had a right which was inconsistent with the claimant's purported right and the defendant must also have known of the claimant's mistake before encouraging the defendant to act to their detriment. In essence, the basis of this model of the doctrine was to prevent a fraud being exerted over the claimant by the defendant. As outlined above, this model of proprietary estoppel was exhumed somewhat controversially by Lord Scott in *Yeoman's Row v Cobbe*.[24] So, in that case it was held that, because the claimant had not been mistaken about his rights when he spent money acquiring rights over development land, the claimant could not rely on proprietary estoppel in spite of the defendant's representation to the claimant that they would exploit the land together. In modern estoppel cases the courts do not require that there has been a mistake of this sort, as was illustrated by the subsequent House of Lords decision in *Thorner v Major*;[25] although *Cobbe* may remain a good authority for commercial situations in which property is being developed on the basis of a supposed partnership.

---

20 This was the approach that S Wilken and T Villiers, 1999, have taken since the first edition of that book.
21 (1866) LR 1 HL 129.
22 *Ibid*, 140.
23 (1880) 15 Ch D 96.
24 [2008] 1 WLR 1752.
25 [2009] 1 WLR 776.

13.3.2 The various approaches in modern proprietary estoppel

Having identified the unexpected return of an old form of proprietary estoppel in the judgment of Lord Scott in *Cobbe* in the previous section, we shall turn to examine the mainstream approach to proprietary estoppel which was approved by the House of Lords in *Thorner v Major*. This model of proprietary estoppel is based on demonstrating that there was a representation on which the claimant relied to their detriment, as outlined above. We shall take each of those three elements in turn.

13.3.3 The three elements of the modern test for proprietary estoppel

The three elements of proprietary estoppel

The modern form of proprietary estoppel is comprised of three elements which the claimant must prove: that there has been a representation (or assurance) made by the defendant to the claimant, in reliance on which the claimant has acted (or refrained from taking some action), and as a result of which the claimant has suffered some detriment.[26] Each of those elements is considered in the sections which follow.

(1) What will constitute a representation?

The first requirement of proprietary estoppel is that there has been a representation made by the defendant to the claimant. It is important that the assurances made by the defendant were intended to lead the claimant to believe that she would acquire rights in property. So, for example, it would not be sufficient if the defendant was merely toying with the claimant without either party forming a reasonable belief that the claimant would acquire any property rights. For example, as Walker LJ put it in *Jennings v Rice*, 'it is notorious that some elderly persons of means derive enjoyment from the possession of testamentary power, and from dropping hints as to their intentions, without any question of any estoppel arising'.[27]

It will clearly be sufficient for demonstrating proprietary estoppel if the defendant makes an express representation to the defendant,[28] but it would also be sufficient to establish an estoppel if some implied assurance were made in circumstances in which the defendant knew that the claimant was relying on the understanding which she had formed.[29] It has been suggested that there need not be a clear representation at all provided that a common understanding arose between the parties that one of them would acquire rights of some kind if the other acted to her detriment.[30] What is important is that the defendant intended the claimant to rely on the representation, assurance or understanding, and that the defendant knew that the claimant was so relying.[31]

---

26 *Taylor Fashions Ltd v Liverpool Victoria Trustees Co Ltd* [1982] 1 QB 133.
27 *Gillett v Holt* [2000] 2 All ER 289, 304.
28 *Taylor Fashions Ltd v Liverpool Victoria Trustees Co Ltd* [1982] 1 QB 133; *Re Basham (Deceased)* [1986] 1 WLR 1498.
29 *Crabb v Arun DC* [1976] Ch 179.
30 *Gillett v Holt* [2001] Ch 210.
31 *Crabb v Arun DC* [1976] Ch 179, 188, *per* Lord Denning; *JT Developments v Quinn* (1990) 62 P & CR 33, 46, *per* Ralph Gibson LJ; *Barclays Bank v Zaroovabli* [1997] Ch 321, 330, *per* Scott VC.

Therefore, while the clearest example of a representation would be a single promise made by one party to another which can be proven in court, it is not necessary for there to have been a single promise made on a specific day by the defendant. Instead, it is possible for the 'representation' to be created incrementally over time, as was demonstrated by the Court of Appeal in *Gillett v Holt*.[32] It might be best to think of this sort of representation as being the development of an understanding on the claimant's part that a representation was being made.

The important decision of the Court of Appeal in *Gillett v Holt*[33] was concerned with a friendship between a farmer, Holt, and a young boy of 12, Gillett, which lasted for 40 years, during which time the boy worked for the farmer. Gillett left his real parents and moved in with Holt when aged 15; there was even a suggestion that the farmer would adopt the boy at one stage. On numerous occasions, the claimant, Gillett, was assured by Holt that he would inherit Holt's farm. Gillett worked hard on the farm, renovating a farmhouse and working on the drainage problems in a particular field. Gillett began a relationship with a young woman, which caused a coolness in his friendship with Holt, but over time they became a perfectly happy family. Gillett's wife and family were described as being a form of surrogate family for the farmer. In time a third person, a trainee solicitor called Wood, turned Holt against Gillett. The result was that Gillett was removed from Holt's will.[34] The question, for present purposes, was whether or not there had been a representation made. It was argued on behalf of Holt that there was never a clear representation made on which Gillett could rely. For Gillett it was shown in evidence that Holt had tended to intimate or to promise at family occasions (birthdays and so forth) that the farm would be left to Gillett. It was held that these statements and suggestions made over time, when taken together, were sufficient to constitute a representation on which Gillett could rely to found the estoppel. This is particularly so when it should have been clear to Holt that Gillett was relying on those settlements in relation to the work he did on the farm working for little money, renovating a disused cottage on the land, and so forth. On the facts of *Gillett v Holt*[35] it was clear that these assurances had been repeated frequently and were sincerely meant when they had been made. Consequently, the courts will infer a representation from the circumstances, even over a long period of time, without the need for there necessarily to have been a single representation made.

Another example was the case of *Re Basham*[36] in which the claimant was promised by an elderly relative for whom she was caring that she would be left that relative's house in their will. Those promises were made regularly over time and the claimant did a number of acts in reliance on them (including solving a boundary dispute at the property), and also turned down an offer of alternative accommodation which came with her husband's job. These factors were taken in the aggregate to have constituted a representation on which the claimant could rely when seeking proprietary estoppel. She was awarded the house by the judge, Edward Nugee QC, as is discussed below.

The decision of the Court of Appeal in *Jennings v Rice*[37] demonstrates, in tandem with *Gillett v Holt*, that there need not be a clear representation made at any particular time nor that

---

32 [2000] 2 All ER 289.
33 [2001] Ch 210.
34 The nature of their relationship is a fascinating matter for conjecture.
35 *Ibid.*
36 [1986] 1 WLR 1498.
37 [2002] EWCA Civ 159.

the representor be proved to have understood that she was making a binding representation; rather, it is sufficient that a 'representation' appears to emerge over time. In that case, Mr Jennings worked for low or no wages for 20 years as an odd-job man for a rich lady, Mrs Royle. In time, after she had been burgled, Mrs Royle asked Mr Jennings to start to sleep over at her house to make her feel more secure. This was something which upset Mrs Jennings. In time, however, even Mrs Jennings began to help her husband at Mrs Royle's house. When Mrs Royle died, the Jennings' would have been upset to learn that they had not been left the house. Walker LJ held that this situation would have been enough to have created a reasonable understanding in the mind of Mr and Mrs Jennings that they would have acquired something in return for their years of detrimental reliance on whatever it was they hoped to receive. Significantly, Walker LJ held that it would have been 'unconscionable' for the Jennings couple to have received nothing in these circumstances. However, as we shall see below, Walker LJ held that a cash payment of £200,000 was sufficient to compensate them in these circumstances.

The concept of a representation was extended remarkably in *Thorner v Major*.[38] The claimant contended that a representation had been made to him over time by the deceased to the effect that the claimant would become the owner of the deceased's farm after the deceased's death. In the event, the deceased had died without leaving the farm by will to the claimant. What is remarkable is that the two men never discussed the assertion that the farm would be left to the claimant, David. The facts were these. Jimmy and Peter were cousins, and David was Jimmy's adult son. David worked for no pay for 29 years on Peter's farm in Somerset, as well as working for no pay on Jimmy's farm. David's lifestyle was one of hard physical work for about 16 hours a day for seven days a week. It is worth pausing for a moment here: for no pay, David worked for up to 16 hours per day for seven days per week. It is unremarkable, perhaps, that this background would influence the court to find that David should be deemed to be entitled to something. It was held that what is required under proprietary estoppel principles is a representation which suggests a promise of ownership of that property together with clear identification of the property involved.[39] In this case, however, the evidence was unclear because the two men had never discussed the situation. Their Lordships, especially Lords Walker and Rodger, made much of the fact that was found by the trial judge that farmers in this part of Somerset could be naturally taciturn, that these two men in particular spoke very few words to one another about anything (including the work that needed to be done on the farm), and therefore that the absence of any more explicit representation should not necessarily be read as negating the presence of a suitable understanding between these parties that the claimant's work was being done (to his evident detriment because he received no pay) in reliance on that understanding. Much emphasis was placed on the fact that on one particular day in 1990, Peter left a document for David to read which related to insurance policies over Peter's life. David had taken this as an indication that he was intended to become the future owner of Peter's property, including the farm, after Peter's death because there was no reason to have shown him this document otherwise. That incident apart, the pair did not tend to say much to one another about anything despite working together for so much time.

---

38 [2009] 1 WLR 776.
39 [2009] 1 WLR 776, para [61] *et seq*, *per* Lord Walker.

It was held on these facts that these circumstances were sufficient to demonstrate that there had been a representation made to David that he could expect to become the owner of the farm after Peter's death. It was found that there had been a sufficient assurance made by Peter to David on the basis of which it was reasonable for David to have formed the impression in these circumstances that he would become the owner of Peter's farm after his death, in reliance on which he had worked to his detriment on Peter's farm. Ironically, then, the court in *Thorner v Major* found that a representation was impliedly made even though nothing was actually said between two parties too taciturn to discuss their respective rights. As Lord Rodger put it, there does not need to be a 'signature event' on which a clear representation was made.[40] Instead it is sufficient, for Lord Rodger[41] and Lord Walker,[42] that the 'relevant assurance' which was made was 'clear enough' in the context. Lord Hoffmann and Lord Neuberger concurred in general terms with Lord Walker. So, if the representor was 'standing by in silence' aware that the claimant was acting to his detriment on the belief that he was thus acquiring a right in the property, then that would be enough to grant him rights on the basis of proprietary estoppel.[43] It is suggested that *Cobbe* is to be understood as being limited to commercial joint ventures as a result of *Thorner v Major*.

What will not constitute a representation

The leading cases discussed in the previous paragraph may have given the impression that the courts will find a representation on the slenderest of evidence. However, that is not true. While the courts may infer representations from the facts of many cases, they will not accept anything as constituting a representation. If the circumstances are too slight to suggest representation then no representation will be found.

A good illustration of this point arose in *Lissimore v Downing*[44] in which a very rich rock musician, Kenneth Downing, started a relationship 'on the rebound' with a woman, Sarah Lissimore, after they had met in a pub one evening. She was married and worked in a chemist's shop in Wolverhampton some distance from Kenneth's home in Shropshire. He was something of a heavy metal cliché having made an enormous amount of money as part of Judas Priest, one of the definitive 1970s heavy metal bands from the English Midlands, and then bought himself an exquisite manor house on 380 acres of prime farmland in the Shropshire countryside.[45] It was worth millions of pounds, and Kenneth had plans to transform it into a country hotel as well as maintaining the large farm. It is worth trying to form a picture of the scene in your mind to understand the arguments that were being made about proprietary estoppel. One evening, Kenneth went to a pub some way from his home and ran into Sarah for the first time, the woman who would become his lover. He was 41 and she was 25 at that time. The couple began a very casual, sexual relationship in which it might usefully be recalled that she was cheating on her husband. At the outset, Kenneth was clear that this was just 'fun'. By contrast, later in court, Sarah relied on the fact that he had told her that he

40 *Ibid*, para [24].
41 *Ibid*, para [26].
42 *Ibid*, para [56].
43 *Ibid*, para [55], *per* Lord Walker.
44 *Ibid*.
45 If it helps to paint a picture, PG Wodehouse set his idyllic Blandings Castle stories in the Shropshire countryside and presented it as a sort of Eden in Albion.

had always taken care of his girlfriends, which she argued was suggestive of a representation that she would acquire some rights in his property.

Their relationship eventually lasted for eight years in total. However, the very start of their relationship is interesting.[46] Matters changed when he first took her to his beautiful home. We can suppose that instead of being the random, ordinary-looking guy she had met in a pub, he suddenly swam into focus as a successful musician with a lot of money when she saw his property. Seeking to impress his new lover, he had taken her to a gate at the edge of his estate, pointed back across his beautiful land, and said to her something like 'I bet you never thought all this could be yours in a million years'. Over time he took to calling her 'the lady of the manor'. He asked her to live with him and she claimed that she had decided not to put in an offer on a flat in Wolverhampton when she was offered the chance to live in this manor house in Shropshire. In essence, she claimed that this pattern of behaviour – these specific words and the general circumstances of them living together for nearly eight years – constituted a representation that she was to acquire property rights in his manor house and land. In effect, Sarah argued that she had thought his words to her leaning over that gate at the edge of his land was a promise to make her 'lady of the estate' that should be taken to grant her property rights in that estate. Kenneth argued that he was merely trying to impress her in the sense of saying 'I bet you would love to live somewhere fantastic like this, wouldn't you?' At the end of the relationship she argued that this should entitle her to an equitable interest in his multi-million pound property. (There is a suggestion in that case that the litigation may have begun because the musician had a particular sexual fetish[47] (about which she obviously had knowledge) which he did not want to be leaked to the press, and therefore that the litigation might have been an attempt to leverage money from him given his reluctance to risk publicity.)

Norris QC, sitting as a judge, began his judgment with the idea from Millett J in *Windeler v Whitehall* that 'a husband has a legal obligation to support his wife even if they are living apart. A man has no legal obligation to support his mistress even if they are living together.'[48] We should think about why it is that such primacy is appointed to married couples over unmarried couples in long-term relationships; and more particularly why married women are accorded much greater legal rights than women in unmarried relationships. For Sarah, this meant that she would have to be able to demonstrate a cogent representation to establish rights in this multi-million pound home. The judge noted several factors which suggested that Sarah could not have genuinely believed that she was being offered part ownership of this property: the fact that she had continued living with her husband after this supposed representation had been made, that she had maintained her job working in a chemist's shop, and the fact that it was simply unlikely that the musician would have intended to give her such a large share of his hard-earned country estate on such a short acquaintance. It was held that her argument was simply not credible in the circumstances. Taking all of these circumstances into account, the court held that no representation had been made to the effect that Sarah would acquire proprietary rights in Kenneth's country estate. So, common sense will be applied so that not everything that is said (especially in the heat of amour) will accidentally grant rights in property.

---

46 If you have seen the movie *French Film*, starring Eric Cantona, Anne-Marie Duff and Hugh Bonneville, then you will know how important the start of relationships can be.

47 No, I am not going to tell you what it is. I want you to read the case for yourself, so you are going to have to find out for yourself.

48 [1990] 2 FLR 505, 506.

There have been several cases in which representations have not been found on the facts of cases. A lot will turn on a common-sense evaluation of the circumstances. When an adult daughter had been told by her mother something like 'there, there, I will help you buy a house one day', that would not equate to a representation that the mother would leave her own house by will to her daughter. There was no other evidence in that case to suggest that the mother had intended to make such a representation to her daughter.[49] Mere belief that something will happen, especially when it is an unreasonable belief, will not be enough. By contrast, where a father promises his adult son that the son will acquire an equitable interest in a house which the father owned, and where the son acted in reliance on that promise (with his father's agreement) by selling his own house so that he could pay for renovation works on his father's house, then it was held that there had been sufficient representation, reliance and detriment to found a claim for proprietary estoppel.[50] Clearly, the extent of the son's detrimental reliance – selling his own house and paying for renovation works – is of a different order from mere disappointment that a mother never bought her daughter a house.

(2) Reliance on the representation or assurance

The court will look to the context to decide whether or not it was reasonable for the claimant to have relied on the particular representor in relation to that particular representation.[51] In one case this was expressed as requiring a 'mutual understanding' between the parties that the actions of the claimant were a reasonable response to the representation made by the defendant.[52] It is essential that the claimant be able to demonstrate a connection between the actions which were performed and the representations which were made. Therefore, where a claimant can demonstrate that she worked for lower wages than her trade would ordinarily have attracted with a view to acquiring rights in property, then she would be entitled to a remedy based on proprietary estoppel; whereas if she had accepted those lower wages out of love for her employer who was also her partner, then she would not.[53] The greater difficulty is those situations in which the claimant suffers only personal detriment, such as moving house, and therefore finds it difficult to demonstrate that the agreement to move house was based on the representation that she would acquire rights in property and was not simply based on love and affection.[54]

(3) Detriment suffered by the claimant

It is necessary that the claimant has suffered some detriment for there to be a proprietary estoppel because equity will not assist a mere volunteer who has neither given consideration nor suffered detriment.[55] The question is then as to the type of behaviour which will constitute detriment. The Court of Appeal in *Gillett v Holt*[56] explained the principle of proprietary

---

49 *Turner v Jacob* [2006] EWHC 1317 (Ch).
50 *S v R* [2008] EWHC 1874 (Fam).
51 *Gillett v Holt* [2000] 2 All ER 289, 306.
52 *Re Basham (Deceased)* [1986] 1 WLR 1498.
53 *Wayling v Jones* (1993) 69 P & CR 170.
54 *Coombes v Smith* [1986] 1 WLR 808; cf. *Grant v Edwards* [1986] Ch 638.
55 In *Re Basham (Deceased)* [1986] 1 WLR 1498, it was suggested that merely the existence of unconscionable behaviour, without a correlative suffering of detriment, would not make out the estoppel.
56 [2000] 2 All ER 289.

estoppel as being based on preventing unconscionable behaviour. The court refused to accept that proprietary estoppel should be seen as confined to narrow categories, preferring instead to recognise that it is based on that underlying concept of good conscience.[57] By reference to the facts of that case (which were discussed above) Walker LJ held that there had been sufficient detriment suffered by Gillett in the course of their relationship over 40 years evidenced by the following factors: working for Holt and not accepting other job offers; performing actions beyond what would ordinarily have been expected of an employee; taking no substantial steps to secure for his future by means of pension or otherwise; and spending money on a farmhouse (which he expected to inherit) which had been almost uninhabitable at the outset before he worked on it. The combination of these factors over such a long period of time was considered by the Court of Appeal to constitute ample evidence of detriment sufficient to found a proprietary estoppel.

Similarly, it was suggested that there was no requirement that detriment be considered in a narrow, technical fashion. Rather, different types of representation or assurance could connote different forms of detriment which would stretch beyond spending money.[58] Therefore, it had been suggested that in assessing detriment, one should look in the round at the circumstances of the parties. Lawrence Collins J held in *Van Laetham v Brooker* that:

> Detriment is not a narrow or technical concept. The detriment need not consist of the expenditure of money or other quantifiable financial detriment, so long as it is something substantial. The requirement must be approached as part of a broad inquiry as to whether repudiation of an assurance is or is not unconscionable in all the circumstances.[59]

Spending money will be a clear demonstration of detriment,[60] unless it is expenditure (relating to the acquisition of rights in the home) which is indirectly related to the property such as paying for household bills.[61] Also accepted as constituting detriment will be settling a boundary dispute relating to the property at issue,[62] giving up alternative accommodation in reliance on the availability of the property at issue,[63] working for reduced wages in reliance on the acquisition of some right in the property at issue,[64] providing unpaid services in the defendant's home in reliance on the acquisition of some rights in the property,[65] and continuing to work unpaid for someone who had previously made payment for gardening work in reliance on a promise that the gardener would inherit the property.[66] Paying for extensive building work on the property will constitute detriment,[67] although merely supervising building work will not.[68] In each of these instances it can be seen that the detriment suffered was connected in

---

57 See also *Jennings v Rice* [2002] EWCA Civ 159 in this regard.
58 *Grant v Edwards* [1986] Ch 638. Cf. *Coombes v Smith* [1986] 1 WLR 808.
59 [2005] EWHC 1478 (Ch), [74].
60 Even if it is not a large amount of money: *Pascoe v Turner* [1979] 2 All ER 945.
61 *Burns v Burns* [1984] Ch 317; *Lloyds Bank v Rosset* [1991] 1 AC 107.
62 *Re Basham* [1986] 1 WLR 1498.
63 *Ibid.*
64 *Wayling v Jones* (1995) 69 P & CR 170. Also where the duties were beyond the ordinary course of employment: *Gillett v Holt* [2001] Ch 210.
65 *Greasley v Cooke* [1980] 1 WLR 1306; *Re Basham* [1986] 1 WLR 1498.
66 *Jennings v Rice* [2003] 1 P & CR 100.
67 *Inwards v Baker* [1965] 2 QB 29.
68 *Lloyds Bank v Rosset* [1991] 1 AC 107.

some way to the acquisition of rights in the property, which some judges have considered to be significant.[69]

By contrast, there is the more difficult question as to whether suffering detriment which is purely personal – as opposed to financial – will constitute detriment sufficient to found proprietary estoppel. There are competing authorities, for example, on the question whether leaving one romantic relationship to begin another, on the basis that one might expect some property rights in the home established in that second relationship: some cases taking the view that this would not constitute detriment because it was purely personal,[70] whereas other cases have considered this to be detriment when there were children involved because the children also had to move home.[71]

13.4   REMEDIES IN PROPRIETARY ESTOPPEL

13.4.1   The ambit of remedies for proprietary estoppel

After the estoppel has been demonstrated (by means of representation, reliance and detriment), the separate question arises as to the form of remedy that is appropriate. Whereas constructive trusts are institutional (that is, they arise automatically when the defendant has knowledge which affects her conscience in relation to property, and they create property rights retrospectively from the time that conscience is affected), proprietary estoppel is remedial (that is, the courts decide only at the end of the trial what rights, if any, are appropriate (whether they are personal or proprietary) such that those rights can only come into existence from that moment prospectively). So, this section considers the sorts of rights which have been awarded in the decided cases by the courts.

Before starting into the detail of the case law, it is worth identifying that there are many different streams of authority which feed into the larger river of proprietary estoppel. There are three principal, competing motivations behind the award of remedies in this area which have arisen in the cases. The first is to prevent frustration of the expectation created by the representation and the court may therefore give effect to the promise made in the defendant's representation. Most of the modern cases are concerned with the frustration of the claimant's expectations after defendant's express representation or assurance had allowed the claimant to believe that she would acquire rights in property.[72] By way of example, in *Pascoe v Turner*[73] a woman had been promised that she would be entitled to live in a house for the rest of her life. In reliance on that promise, she spent money on decorating the property. It was found in the circumstances that the only appropriate remedy was a transfer of the freehold interest in the property to her because there was no other mechanism in land law for protecting her ability to remain in the property. The court's objective therefore appeared to be to give effect to the promise which had been made to her. So, if the claimant had been promised by a relative that they would have a home for the rest of their life and if they had worked for many years in that relative's home in caring for them in the expectation that the house would

---

69   *Re Basham* [1986] 1 WLR 1498.
70   *Coombes v Smith* [1986] 1 WLR 808.
71   *Grant v Edwards* [1986] Ch 638.
72   *Ramsden v Dyson* (1866) LR 1 HL 129, 170.
73   [1979] 2 All ER 945.

become theirs, then the court might be motivated by frustrated expectation which that person had formed into granting the claimant ownership of the house after the relative's death.[74]

Second, to compensate the claimant for suffering detriment in reliance on the representation which had been made to her. If the claimant has only suffered a small detriment then the award of property rights might appear to be inappropriate: so, if the claimant had merely spent £20 on a train ticket to visit property which had been promised to her, it might seem inappropriate to award that person the freehold in a house worth £500,000 when they have only spent £20 in reliance on the promise.[75] Compensation might be used instead to award them £20.

Third, to prevent unconscionable benefit being taken from the detrimental reliance of a person on a representation made to her.[76] In the Court of Appeal in *Jennings v Rice*,[77] it was held that 'the essence of the doctrine of proprietary estoppel is to do what is necessary to avoid an unconscionable result' and was 'to do justice' between the parties.[78] This approach was accepted by the Privy Council in *Knowles v Knowles*.[79] Similarly, the doctrine of proprietary estoppel was explained in *Taylor Fashions v Liverpool Victoria Trustees Co Ltd*[80] by Oliver J such that 'it would be unconscionable for a party to be permitted to deny that which, knowingly or unknowingly, he has allowed or encouraged another to assume to his detriment'.[81] This approach entitles the court to use any combination of proprietary and compensatory remedies to address that unconscionability, as in *Gillett v Holt*.

13.4.2 Proprietary remedies

The courts are able to award a range of proprietary remedies in proprietary estoppel claims. The court will have complete freedom to frame its remedy once it has found that an estoppel is both available and appropriate. Those remedies may be enforceable not only against the person who made the assurance but also against third parties.[82] So, in the cases discussed so far, there is a range of proprietary remedies available. In *Pascoe v Turner*, the claimant was awarded the entire fee simple in property in which she had been promised she could live for the rest of her life. In *Re Basham* similarly, the claimant was awarded the fee simple in property on the basis that she had been promised that property before she suffered detriment. In those cases, the award of outright ownership was considered appropriate to achieve the minimum equity necessary to respond to their detriment.[83] By contrast, acting in expectation of being left property by will, as in *Jennings v Rice*, may lead only to an award of money. The outcome depends upon the judge's assessment of the equities in the situation: for every case in which one relative is awarded the fee simple, there is another relative who loses their ability to occupy property which may ostensibly have been left to them in the will.

---

74 *Re Basham* [1986] 1 WLR 1498.
75 *Jennings v Rice* [2003] 1 P & CR 100.
76 *Sledmore v Dalby* (1996) 72 P & CR 196.
77 [2002] EWCA Civ 159.
78 *Jennings v Rice* [2002] EWCA Civ 159, para 36, *per* Aldous LJ.
79 [2008] UKPC 30, para [27], *per* Sir Henry Brooke (reading the judgment of the entire court).
80 [1982] QB 133.
81 *Ibid*, 151.
82 *Hopgood v Brown* [1955] 1 WLR 213.
83 *Crabb v Arun DC* [1976] Ch 179.

The type of property right which may be awarded can differ from case to case. So, in *Baker v Baker* the claimant would have been entitled to an equitable interest in a co-owned home on resulting trust principles (having contributed to its purchase price) but the court assessed his needs as requiring money to pay for nursing care for the rest of his life due to his old age.[84] Therefore, the property right was abandoned in favour of a better outcome for the claimant. By contrast, in *Gillett v Holt* the claimant's work on the defendant's farm for many years was held to entitle him to ownership of a previously disused cottage which he had renovated, a plot of land on which he had done much work, and a lump sum of cash. Thus, the claimant acquired some property rights which were linked to the detriment he had suffered, as well as acquiring personal rights to money. Proprietary estoppel is sufficiently flexible to create property rights out of thin air where the justice of the case demands it.

Perhaps most remarkably of all, in *Porntip Stallion v Albert Stallion (Holdings) Ltd*,[85] Porntip separated from her husband when he married another woman, Lilibeth. Porntip, her husband Albert, and Lilibeth cohabited for a while in Porntip's former matrimonial home, and they continued to cohabit up to the time of Albert's death. Albert had promised Porntip that she would be able to continue to occupy her matrimonial home even after Albert's remarriage to Lilibeth, provided that Porntip did not contest his divorce petition. In consequence, the judge (Judge Asplin QC) held that Porntip and Lilibeth should continue to cohabit in the matrimonial home. In this way, Porntip acquired a court order entitling her to remain in her home.

13.4.3 Personal remedies

As Lord Denning put it, 'equity is displayed at its most flexible' in relation to proprietary estoppel.[86] Thus, in *Gillett v Holt*, the claimant, who had worked on the defendant's farm and who had been promised to inherit the farm, was awarded the freehold in a farmhouse, 42 hectares of farmland and £100,000. In *Jennings v Rice*, it was suggested by Walker LJ that the appropriate methodology was 'to do what was necessary to avoid an unconscionable result' by means of a proportionate remedy and consequently the claimant was awarded £200,000 in response to about 27 years of casual labour and care for the deceased woman.[87] In *Campbell v Griffin*,[88] the claimant's detrimental reliance was held to entitle him to a payment of £35,000 instead of granting him a right in the property which would 'hold up the administration of the estate for a generation',[89] thus considering the needs and rights of all of the people involved in a case and not just the person who had suffered detriment. This general approach is similar to Sir Arthur Hobhouse's dicta to the effect that the court should 'look at the circumstances in each case to decide in what way the equity can be satisfied'.[90] It is suggested that the more that the cases come to focus on the detriment suffered by the

---

84 *Burrows & Burrows v Sharpe* (1991) 23 HLR 82.
85 [2009] EWHC 1950 (Ch).
86 *Crabb v Arun DC* [1976] Ch 179, 189F.
87 [2003] 1 P & CR 100, para 56.
88 [2001] EWCA Civ 990.
89 *Ibid*, 991, *per* Robert Walker LJ.
90 *Plimmer v Wellington Corporation* (1884) 9 App Cas 699, 714; approved by Walker LJ in *Gillett v Holt* [2001] Ch 210, 235.

claimant, the more likely it is that the courts will seek to compensate that detriment by payment of money.

13.5 AGREEMENTS TO DEVELOP PROPERTY

Proprietary estoppel underlines one of the key tenets of equity: that it can do justice between the parties. Proprietary estoppel may be able to set aside statutory principles. In *Yaxley v Gotts*,[91] a joint venture was formed for the acquisition of land. The joint venture did not comply with the requirement in s 2 of the Law of Property (Miscellaneous Provisions) Act 1989 that the terms of any purported contract for the transfer of any interest in land must be in writing. It was held that there had been a representation that there would be a joint venture between the parties in reliance on which the claimant had acted to its detriment. It was held by the Court of Appeal that a constructive trust had arisen between the parties on the basis of their common intention – and that this constructive trust was indistinguishable in this form from proprietary estoppel.[92] The doctrine of constructive trust is therefore outwith the ambit of s 2 of the 1989 Act.[93]

However, the House of Lords in *Cobbe v Yeoman's Row*[94] held that such agreements for the development of land will not be capable of being supported by proprietary estoppel if they are not formally effective. As discussed above, the claimant had spent money on acquiring planning permission for development land on the basis that the defendant would exploit that land with him. The defendant reneged on their understanding. Importantly, the parties had not created a binding contract for this joint venture. The claimant argued that there had been a representation, reliance and detriment. Lord Scott was clear that commercial parties should not be entitled to rely upon proprietary estoppel to supplement their failure to create binding contracts to cover their activities. Therefore, the approach taken in *Yaxley v Gotts* cannot now be considered to be applicable in all circumstances. The case law on constructive trusts and agreements to develop property are considered in Chapter 12.

13.6 ANALYSIS

Professor Elizabeth Cooke has explained how the entire doctrine of estoppel could be understood as being based on a single concept of unconscionability.[95] In general terms, Cooke considers the doctrine of estoppel to be a means of preventing a person from changing her mind in circumstances in which it would be unconscionable so to do.[96] This is an approach which has a long judicial pedigree in those judgments in which the judges have given consideration to the basis for proprietary estoppel. In the Court of Appeal in *Jennings v Rice*,[97] it was held that 'the essence of the doctrine of proprietary estoppel is to do what is necessary to avoid an unconscionable result' and was 'to do justice' between the parties,[98] as was accepted by

91 [2000] 1 All ER 711.
92 *Ibid*, 721 *et seq*, *per* Robert Walker LJ.
93 *Kilcarne Holdings Ltd v Targetfollow (Birmingham) Ltd* [2004] EWHC 2547 (Ch), para [219], *per* Lewison J.
94 [2008] 1 WLR 1752.
95 Cooke, 2000 generally.
96 E.g., *Amalgamated Investment and Property Co Ltd v Texas Commerce International Bank Ltd* [1982] 1 QB 84, 104, *per* Goff J.
97 [2002] EWCA Civ 159.
98 *Jennings v Rice* [2002] EWCA Civ 159, para 36, *per* Aldous LJ.

the Privy Council in *Knowles v Knowles*.[99] Similarly, the doctrine of proprietary estoppel was explained in *Taylor Fashions v Liverpool Victoria Trustees Co Ltd*[100] by Oliver J such that 'it would be unconscionable for a party to be permitted to deny that which, knowingly or unknowingly, he has allowed or encouraged another to assume to his detriment'.[101] Lord Goff, similarly, considered that: 'the many circumstances capable of giving rise to an estoppel cannot be accommodated within a single formula, and that it is unconscionability which provides the link between them'.[102]

The twin strengths of the doctrine of proprietary estoppel are that the potential remedies are broad and that the three requirements for establishing the doctrine are clear. If we put ourselves into the minds of counsel preparing to bring a case, for example to establish proprietary rights in a house, then we can understand that the principal problem facing counsel is how to demonstrate that the facts available to them will prove that their client has a right to property under a constructive trust or proprietary estoppel. Counsel may be nervous about proving such a broad doctrine, especially when they do not know which judge will hear the case when they draft their pleadings.[103] However, because proprietary estoppel is based on three clear elements, then counsel will be able to identify whether or not they have a representation, some reliance on that representation, and some detriment which has been suffered as a result, which can be proved clearly on the facts in front of them. If counsel does have those elements provable across the documents, emails, witness statements and so forth which are available to them, then it is preferable to argue proprietary estoppel rather than some other doctrine. Moreover, they might be able to convince the court to provide a general remedy which would meet their client's precise circumstances. By contrast, the generality of the constructive trust doctrine may sometimes be off-putting to counsel when bringing a case.

Moreover, the flexibility of the proprietary estoppel remedies may prevent the need for the creation of remedial constructive trust in English law. The only principal advantage which an institutional constructive trust has over proprietary estoppel is that it arises retrospectively and so can provide protection against an earlier insolvency in the right circumstances. By contrast, a remedial constructive trust would arise only at the date of the court order and therefore would not have that advantage over a proprietary estoppel remedy. The only difference would remain the need to prove representation, reliance and detriment which, as considered immediately above, might actually be an advantage in many cases.

---

99   [2008] UKPC 30, para [27], *per* Sir Henry Brooke.
100   [1982] QB 133.
101   *Ibid*, 151.
102   *Johnson v Gore Wood & Co (No 1)* [2002] 2 AC 1, [2001] BCC 820 at 842, *per* Lord Goff.
103   'Pleadings' are the documents which lawyers prepare during litigation which sets out the parties' clams, defences and so forth.

Chapter 14

Essay: Fiduciaries

14.1 INTRODUCTION

The purpose of this chapter is to draw together some of our considerations of the idea of fiduciary duties in this book. Fiduciary responsibility is open-textured (in that the categories of fiduciary responsibility are always capable of expansion) and yet it is supported by some inflexible legal rules (for example, relating to fiduciaries taking unauthorised profits and allowing conflicts of interest, preserving the confidence of their beneficiaries, and acting with unswerving loyalty to the terms of their duties). This combination ensures protection for the beneficiaries of a fiduciary relationship once they have been accepted into the categories of fiduciary duty. Nevertheless, there are differences of opinion as to the extent of the fiduciary concept. Some judges, such as Millett LJ (as he was) preferred a model of fiduciary duties that was commercially convenient. He achieved this by limiting the scope of those fiduciary duties for professional fiduciaries so that many commercial arrangements would fall outside the fiduciary category altogether. Other judges, such as Lord Browne-Wilkinson, preferred a broad model of fiduciary duties which covered many arrangements but with terms which were heavily dependent on their context. These differences of opinion will emerge from the discussion to follow.

14.2 THE FIDUCIARY CONCEPT

14.2.1 The strength of the fiduciary concept

The strength of the fiduciary concept, from the claimant's perspective, is that it presents a range of remedies which protect and support the beneficiary of any fiduciary relationship. As considered in Chapter 12, the fiduciary is prevented from taking any unauthorised profits from their fiduciary office and from self-dealing with the trust's property.[1] Similarly, anyone who receives a bribe will hold that bribe and any profits flowing from that bribe on constructive trust for the beneficiary of whatever arrangement caused them to be bribed in the first place.[2] Even if that person would not have been considered to be sufficiently senior within an organisation to have their ordinary duties described as being fiduciary – such as the work of a security guard sitting on reception in an office building – there will be contexts when that person does become a fiduciary, for example when that security guard accepts a bribe to admit armed criminals onto their employer's property.[3] A director of that company will always be a fiduciary in relation to that company but the security guard will only become a fiduciary when the circumstances require it.

In either circumstance, any profit taken will be held on constructive trust for the beneficiaries of the fiduciary arrangement. The moral underpinning of these rules is that no person who acts in a way which equity considers to be unconscionable (ranging from permitting conflicts of interest through to committing criminal offences) is allowed to benefit from their unconscionable conduct. The strength of the fiduciary concept is that its beneficiaries will be protected by its core principles (against conflicts of interest, against self-dealing, against taking unauthorised profits, and so forth) in all circumstances, unless the instrument governing their fiduciary duties provides differently.

14.2.2 Defining the fiduciary concept

The first question is to define what is meant by a fiduciary obligation. A dictionary definition of the term 'fiduciary' begins with the late 16th century meaning of that word derived from the Latin *fiduciarius* meaning '(holding) in a trust' and previously from *fides* meaning 'faith' and 'trust'.[4] In this sense the word 'trust' has a link in the Latin with 'faith: *fides*' which is also the root of the English word 'confide', literally to have faith in someone or to have confidence in someone. There is therefore a clear connection between the ordinary use of the word 'fiduciary' with notions of 'faith', 'belief', 'confidence' and 'trust'. In the modern trust, the beneficiary has faith in the trustee. In that sense the fiduciary is trusted. Lord Browne-Wilkinson described a fiduciary relationship as coming into existence by reference to the following, simple principle:

> The paradigm of the circumstances in which equity will find a fiduciary relationship is where one party, A, has assumed to act in relation to the property or affairs of another, B.[5]

While this definition of a fiduciary relationship does have the benefit of being concise, it is perhaps too elliptical to be comprehensive. Exactly what this concept means in practice has been the subject of some slight difference in the key cases decided in this area in the 1990s.[6] It is to that debate which we shall turn next.

---

1 *Boardman v Phipps* [1967] 2 AC 46.
2 *FHR European Ventures v Mankarious* [2014] 3 WLR 535.
3 *Brinks Mat Ltd v Abu-Saleh (No 3)* [1996] CLC 133.
4 *Encarta World Dictionary*, 1999.
5 *White v Jones* [1995] 2 AC 207 at 271.
6 The 1990s were a golden era for equity and trusts law (whether in a family or a commercial context) with a House of Lords comprised of the following expert Chancery judges: Browne-Wilkinson, Goff, Nicholls, Scott, and Millett, as well as the commercial chancery expertise of Hoffmann and Hobhouse.

14.2.3 The core principles of fiduciary relationships

The breadth of the category of fiduciary duties

One of the most significant points about the law on fiduciaries is that the categories of fiduciary relationship are entirely elastic. The courts will define a defendant as being a fiduciary whenever their duties exhibit an appropriate quality of confidence being place in them and loyalty being required of them. If we understand that the number of fiduciary offices is potentially infinite, and that the category of fiduciary relationships is therefore an elastic one, it should be recognised that the obligations befitting a fiduciary will differ from circumstance to circumstance. As Lord Browne-Wilkinson has held:

> the phrase 'fiduciary duties' is a dangerous one, giving rise to a mistaken assumption that all fiduciaries owe the same duties in all circumstances. That is not the case. Although so far as I am aware, every fiduciary is under a duty not to make a profit from his position (unless such profit is authorised), the fiduciary duties owed, for example, by an express trustee are not the same as those owed by an agent.[7]

So, the precise terms of any given fiduciary relationship will depend on the context and on the terms of any instrument governing that relationship.[8] As was made clear in Chapter 8, for example, the liabilities of trustees can be limited by an appropriate term in the trust instrument.

The contextual differences in the extents of different fiduciary duties are common-sensical. A trustee will be responsible for the investment of a trust fund and therefore duties will be owed to the beneficiaries. However, suppose that a trustee and a beneficiary leave a trust meeting and emerge into the open air. The beneficiary starts to cross the road unaware of the danger of oncoming traffic. At that point in time any obligation which the trustee owes to the beneficiary to pull her back onto the kerb is not a fiduciary duty. We may think that one human being owes another human being some indefinable, quasi-moral obligation to try to save her in such a situation, but whatever form that obligation may or may not take, it is not a fiduciary obligation. Similarly, a solicitor will typically owe fiduciary duties to a client in relation to the conduct of the client's legal affairs but not in relation to the client's choice of socks. It is all a matter of context.

The established categories of fiduciary duty

There are four established categories of fiduciary relationship: trustee and beneficiary; company directors; partners *inter se* (within the terms of the 1890 Partnership Act); and principal and agent.[9] Examples of other situations in which fiduciary relationships have been found are as follows:[10] where a solicitor acts on behalf of his client[11] when advising that client as to

---

7 *Henderson v Merrett Syndicates* [1995] 2 AC 145 at 206.

8 Whether under a resulting trust or a constructive trust.

9 The nature of fiduciary duties is considered in Thomas and Hudson, 2004, para 25.15 *et seq*.

10 These examples have arisen primarily in England and Wales, whereas other jurisdictions have accepted that a doctor may own fiduciary duties to his patient (*McInerney v MacDonald* (1992) 93 DLR (4th) 415) and that a parent who has abused his child is taken to have breached fiduciary duties to that child (*M(K) v M(H)* (1993) 96 DLR (4th) 449; *H v R* [1996] 1 NZLR 299).

11 *Nocton v Lord Ashburton* [1914] AC 932; *McMaster v Byrne* [1952] 1 All ER 1363; *Brown v IRC* [1965] AC 244; *Boardman v Phipps* [1967] 2 AC 46; *Maguire v Makaronis* (1997) 144 ALR 729. By contrast, the Law Society owes no fiduciary duties to the solicitors whom it represents: *Swain v Law Society* [1983] 1 AC 598.

the client's affairs within the scope of the solicitor's retainer;[12] in relation to senior employees holding sensitive positions with reference to their employers,[13] or where any employee exploits his office to generate a personal profit by way of a bribe;[14] between the promoter of a company and the company itself;[15] in relation to those who occupy public office whether as members of the secret service,[16] or as members of the armed forces using their rank to obtain passage for contraband through army roadblocks,[17] or as Director of Public Prosecutions in particular when taking a bribe not to prosecute an alleged criminal.[18]

The narrow model of fiduciary duties

Millett LJ favoured us with the following, often-quoted definition of a fiduciary in *Bristol and West Building Society v Mothew* which focuses on a narrow range of duties of loyalty and confidence and the need to avoid conflicts of interest:[19]

> A fiduciary is someone who has undertaken to act for or on behalf of another in a particular matter in circumstances which give rise to a relationship of trust and confidence. The distinguishing obligation of a fiduciary is the obligation of loyalty. The principal is entitled to the single-minded loyalty of his fiduciary. The core liability has several facets. A fiduciary must act in good faith; he must not make a profit out of his trust; he must not place himself in a position where his duty and his interest may conflict; he may not act for his own benefit or the benefit of a third person without the informed consent of his principal. This is not intended to be an exhaustive list, but it is sufficient to indicate the nature of fiduciary obligations. They are the defining characteristics of the fiduciary.

What emerges from this definition of the fiduciary concept is that the categories of fiduciary are open-ended. So, while there are four clear categories of fiduciary office, it is always possible to find that fiduciary duties exist in new contexts on a case-by-case basis. It is worth noting that Millett LJ set out a very narrow understanding of the duties of trustees in *Armitage v Nurse*[20] which refused to accept that there was even a responsibility imposed on trustees to act with reasonable skill and care (as was considered in section 8.4). All that Millett LJ would ascribe to trustees was an obligation not to act dishonestly. That is, after all, an obligation which ought to imposed on all citizens in all legal contexts

---

12 *Marks & Spencer plc v Freshfields Bruckhaus Deringer* [2004] 3 All ER 773, [2004] EWHC 1337; *Bolkiah (Prince Jefri) v KPMG* [1999] 2 AC 222.

13 *Canadian Aero-Services Ltd v O'Malley* (1973) 40 DLR (3d) 371 at 381, *per* Laskin J; *Sybron Corporation v Rochem Ltd* [1984] Ch 112 at 127, *per* Stephenson LJ; *Neary v Dean of Westminster* [1999] IRLR 288.

14 *Attorney-General for Hong Kong v Reid* [1994] 1 AC 324.

15 *Erlanger v New Sombrero Phosphate Company* (1878) 3 App Cas 1218.

16 *Attorney-General v Guardian Newspapers Ltd (No 2)* [1990] 1 AC 109. Cf. *Attorney-General v Blake* [1998] 1 All ER 833.

17 *Reading v Attorney-General* [1951] 1 All ER 617.

18 *Attorney-General for Hong Kong v Reid* [1994] 1 AC 324.

19 [1998] Ch 1 at 18.

20 [1998] Ch 241.

and, it is suggested, insufficient to mark out a fiduciary office as being different from any other.

The broad model of fiduciary duties

The beneficiary in a fiduciary relationship acquires a range of equitable claims against the fiduciary in equity. There are five principal obligations: first, the fiduciary may not permit any conflict between their personal capacity and their fiduciary obligations; secondly, the fiduciary may not take any unauthorised profit from their fiduciary obligations; thirdly, the fiduciary must maintain the confidentiality of their beneficiaries' affairs; fourthly, the fiduciary must act entirely in good faith in the interests of their beneficiaries; and, fifthly, that the fiduciary must act with care and skill. This last obligation is a significant one in relation to financial institutions acting on behalf of their customers. Lord Browne-Wilkinson held in *Henderson v Merrett Syndicates Ltd* that:[21]

> The liability of a fiduciary for the negligent transaction of his duties is a not a separate head of liability but the paradigm of the general duty to act with care imposed by law on those who take it upon themselves to act for or to advise others . . . It is the fact that they have all assumed responsibility for the property or affairs of another which renders them liable for the careless performance of what they have undertaken to do, not the description of the trade or position which they hold.

This model of fiduciary duties imposes more obligations on fiduciaries than that of Millett LJ above. It is suggested that this model recognises the significance of the fiduciary duty, that beneficiaries are dependent on the behaviour of their fiduciaries (whether a trustee investing pension funds, an agent negotiating commercial contracts for a client, or a director advocating the acceptance of a company merger) and therefore it is desirable to impose obligations of reasonable care and skill on fiduciaries in the discharge of their duties. Moreover, Millett LJ upheld the exclusion of liability clause used in *Armitage v Nurse* which excluded the liability of fiduciaries for gross negligence in the discharge of their duties which, it is suggested, is contrary to the approach taken by Lord Browne-Wilkinson in *Henderson v Merrett Syndicate*.

14.2.4 The basis of fiduciary principles

The responsibilities of the fiduciary are based on a standard of utmost good faith. The older case law took the straightforward attitude that if there were any loss suffered by a beneficiary then the fiduciary would be strictly liable for that loss.[22] This attitude has been promulgated by the decisions in *Regal v Gulliver*[23] (concerning directors of a company) and *Boardman v*

---

21   [1995] 2 AC 145, 205.
22   *Keech v Sandford* (1726) Sel Cas Ch 61.
23   [1967] 2 AC 46, 134n.

Phipps[24] (concerning a solicitor advising trustees), which imposed strict liability for all unauthorised gains made by the fiduciaries deriving, however obliquely, from their fiduciary duty.

The case of *Attorney-General for Hong Kong v Reid*[25] demonstrates two important facets of fiduciary responsibility. First, liability as a fiduciary can be imposed in entirely novel circumstances; there is no need to demonstrate a close analogy with any existing category of fiduciary. That constructive trust was founded on equity's determination that that which ought to have been done is looked upon as having been done and to prevent the unconscionable ('evil') activity of receiving bribes in a public office.

The liability imposed on a trustee is not necessarily linked to any pre-existing relationship but may arise in relation to some subsequent act and relate only to that act. The liability imposed on the defendant in *Reid* was imposed not only in relation to property used in breach of the fiduciary duty, but also in relation to an obligation to make good any loss on the investment of such property. The strict nature of fiduciary liability was observed once again. Beyond any precise contractual obligations owed by the Director of Public Prosecutions to the government which employed him, there were the fiduciary obligations of a constructive trust in the receipt of the bribes alone – that action of receipt of a bribe generated fiduciary obligations (to hold the bribes on constructive trust) from that moment onwards.[26]

The beneficiary rides in an equitable sedan chair borne by the fiduciary, cushioned against every bump in the road. Hence the difficulty in reaching any precise definition of the term 'fiduciary' – it is a deliberately fluid concept permitting of addition and adaptation. As such it is at one with the underlying theory advanced in this book of equity as constituting a means of ensuring fairness in individual cases in mitigation of potential injustices that would otherwise be caused by literal application of the common law.

14.3 THE DEVELOPMENT OF NEW CATEGORIES

14.3.1 How do my fiduciaries grow?

So much for the established categories of fiduciary: what of the future? The utility for the beneficiary of the fiduciary concept means that there will always be pressure in a common law system for further categories of fiduciary to be added, or for other relationships to be accepted as being closely analogous to fiduciary duties. Claimants will continue to press for new forms of relationship to be accepted as giving rise to fiduciary duties. The advantages of fiduciary status for the beneficiary have been set out above.

14.3.2 Mortgagee–mortgagor

A mortgagee acquires extensive powers of repossession and sale of mortgaged property. The right of repossession is said to exist 'even before the ink is dry on the mortgage contract',[27] whereas the statutory power of sale does not obtain until the mortgagor has been in breach

---

24 *Ibid.*
25 *Ibid.*
26 Cf. *Attorney-General v Blake* [2000] 4 All ER 385.
27 *Four Maids v Dudley Marshall* [1957] Ch 317.

of the mortgage agreement or is in arrears for at least two months on payments of interest.[28] The question which arises in the cases is the precise nature of the obligations, if any, which are imposed on the mortgagee when exercising the statutory power of sale. The common law has long accepted that the mortgagee owes no fiduciary obligations to the mortgagor in exercising this power of sale.[29] The only fiduciary obligation arises when the property has been sold, when the mortgagee is deemed to hold the sale proceeds as trustee to discharge the expenses of the sale and the mortgage debt, and finally to transfer any surplus to the mortgagor.

Interestingly, however, a departure from this line of authority was accepted in *Palk v Mortgage Securities*[30] by Nicholls VC that the mortgagee owes duties which are 'analogous to fiduciary duties' when both refusing to sell the property and dealing with that property prior to any future sale in a manner which is oppressive of the mortgagor. In *Palk*, the mortgagee refused to consent to a sale at a time of low property prices until the value of the property rose to match the amount owing to the mortgagee. In consequence the debt owed by the mortgagor, who was unable to repay the mortgage, rose by about £30,000 annually, with no end then in sight given the depressed state of the housing market at the time. His lordship considered this situation to be oppressive of the mortgagor and so ordered a sale of the property. What the mortgagee would have been obliged to do as a fiduciary would have been to act in the best interests of the mortgagor: that is, to prevent the debt escalating year on year while both parties waited for the property market to improve. Here the obligation on the quasi-fiduciary is focused solely on avoiding taking action that would have been oppressive of the beneficiary of that duty.

14.3.3 Doctor–patient

The relationship of doctor and patient (in circumstances in which the doctor is treating the patient for some medical complaint) is one of particular sensitivity. The clearest disparity in power between the two is that the doctor has all the knowledge of medicine which most patients will not. Consequently, the patient is particularly dependent on the doctor.[31] In English law the doctor–patient relationship is not a fiduciary one.[32] This is so even in relation to confidentiality which would usually connote a fiduciary responsibility,[33] as has been accepted in Canada.[34] As Kennedy explains, these developments in the law relating to confidentiality in Canada are examples of equity seeking to provide a remedy where none would otherwise exist – that is, for example, in preventing the doctor from disclosing confidential patient information by injunction and by compensating the patient for any such disclosure.[35] Quoting Sopinka J in *International Corona Resources Ltd v LAC Minerals Ltd*,[36] 'fiduciary obligation must be reserved for situations that are truly in need of the special protection which equity

---

28 Law of Property Act 1925, s 103.
29 *Cuckmere Brick v Mutual Finance* [1971] Ch 949.
30 [1993] 2 WLR 415.
31 Kennedy, 1996.
32 *Sidaway v Governors of Bethlem Royal Hospital* [1984] 1 QB 515.
33 Kennedy, 1996, 123.
34 *McInerney v McDonald* (1992) 93 DLR (4th) 415; *Norberg v Wyrinb* (1992) 92 DLR (4th) 449.
35 Kennedy, 1996, 130.
36 (1989) 2 SCR 574, 596.

offers'. This is perhaps the acid test for future developments in the field of fiduciary liability: that is, whether there is a special need for patient to seek the protection of equity.

14.3.4 Abuser–abused

The question arises whether or not there is any remedy which the law can provide for the victim of sexual abuse against their abuser. It is not suggested here that we can 'compensate' the victim of such abuse as though money could somehow remove their pain. Rather, what is being suggested here is that compensation could fund the activities which the victim may need to undertake as part of the process of coping with a history of abuse, such as paying for therapeutic and other services. In *Sidaway v Governors of Bethlem Royal Hospital*[37] the Court of Appeal suggested that English law would only use fiduciary liability to protect the economic interests of claimants and not to protect them, for example, from sexual exploitation. The reluctance of English law to develop in this direction will result from the fact that this context is far from the paradigm case of the fiduciary: that is, the trustee holding property on the terms of an express trust.

The primary advantage of the creation of a fiduciary obligation in English law to cater for such situations would be that equity has a lower threshold of liability in such circumstances. The fiduciary becomes almost strictly liable for all loss flowing from his actions once fiduciary liability is accepted. The important corollary is the obligation on the fiduciary 'to do the best possible' for the beneficiary – which offers a broader range of liabilities than that contained within the narrowness of the duty of care.[38]

While vulnerability will not in itself found fiduciary liability,[39] it is suggested that a breach of a relationship of trust (in the vernacular sense of that term) should found such a liability. As such, in line with the dicta of Sopinka J in *International Corona Resources Ltd v LAC Minerals Ltd*[40] that 'fiduciary obligation must be reserved for situations that are truly in need of the special protection which equity offers'.

---

37   [1984] 1 QB 515, 519.
38   As considered generally in Chapter 8.
39   *Mabo v Queensland (No 2)* (1992) 175 CLR 1.
40   (1989) 2 SCR 574, 596.

Part 5

Trusts of land and of the home

Chapter 15

Trusts of homes

CAPSULE SUMMARY

The Supreme Court in *Jones v Kernott* did not deliver a single model for the law in this area. In consequence, this chapter is modelled on the joint judgment of Lady Hale and Lord Walker (with which Lord Kerr agreed for the most part). That judgment did not overrule much earlier case law. Instead, it retained the concept of 'common intention' and therefore much of the earlier case law will remain important. The approach which was taken in *Jones v Kernott* was the following (qualifying the earlier decision of the House of Lords in *Stack v Dowden*). The common intention must be identified using objective evidence where possible.

First, if only one person is entered on the legal title over the property then that person is presumed to be the sole equitable owner. Whereas, if two or more people have been entered on the legal title then those people are presumed to be joint owners in equity of the property. Second, these two presumptions can be rebutted by evidence that the parties' 'common intention' was something different. The concept of 'common intention' has been discussed in many cases and applied in several different ways. This chapter seeks to organise those different ways under five headings.

(1) The decision of the House of Lords in *Lloyds Bank v Rosset* in which a common intention constructive trusts is created either (a) when the parties form an agreement,

arrangement or understanding as to their rights in the property before the date of acquisition and in circumstances in which they suffer some detriment, or (b) when a party contributed to the purchase price or to the mortgage instalment such that it will be at least extremely doubtful whether anything less will do. This approach was ignored in most of the later cases. (2) Where, on resulting trust principles, the parties have contributed to the purchase price, including by way of a reduction in the value of the property by statutory discount. This is dubbed 'the balance sheet approach'. (3) The court will conduct a survey of the entire course of dealing between the parties and take into account many more factors than mere contribution to the purchase price. This is dubbed 'the family assets approach'. (4) Some courts have focused on avoiding 'unconscionability' being suffered by either one of the parties. This is dubbed the 'unconscionability approach'.

(5) The doctrine of proprietary estoppel will grant an equitable interest to a person who has been induced to suffer detriment in reliance on a representation that she would acquire some rights in the property as a result. Proprietary estoppel is a remedial doctrine whereby the court may award any one of a number of rights ranging from the entire freehold through to merely equitable compensation in money.

Jones v Kernott suggests that if the 'common intention' will not reveal an answer, then the court may have resort to what is 'fair'.

15.1 INTRODUCTION

15.1.1 Understanding the legal treatment of the home

The material covered in this chapter is perhaps the most fascinating on any trusts law course. In this chapter we shall be considering the ways in which the English and Welsh courts recognise who has property rights in their homes based on their relationships and their behaviour. This chapter will consider every sort of cohabiting relationship except married couples who are divorcing: the law on divorce is governed by statute and is outside the scope of this book. Much of the discussion in this chapter has the rapidly changing nature of the family in modern Britain as its backdrop. However, there are many other types of relationship which may involve co-ownership of property beyond families. Many sexual relationships begin as purely casual arrangements which harden out of carelessness or simply out of the passage of time into something else. Many of the cases which we shall discuss in this chapter are prompted by mortgagees seeking repossession of property and therefore the question about the nature of the cohabitants' relationship is not necessarily one which they have ever asked themselves: instead, it might be a question which is prompted by the fact that they cannot pay their mortgage.

The technical legal questions are equally fascinating, and this chapter operates as a closed discussion which is only tangentially related to the rest of this book. The reason for this difference in ideas is simply because the home is different from all other types of property. There is something quintessentially emotional about the connection to the home and the things that go on there between different people that seems to have necessitated its own legal treatment. Consequently, ideas of constructive trust, resulting trust and estoppel appear in these judgments but in very different forms from the way they were discussed in Chapters 11 through 13 of this book.

The leading case of *Jones v Kernott*[1] has deliberately left the way open for the case to continue to develop in the way it has since the decision of the House of Lords in *Pettitt v Pettitt* in 1970.[2] The Supreme Court in *Jones v Kernott* established some key principles but otherwise allowed the courts to judge individual cases on the basis of high-level principles about the common intention of the parties, about 'fairness' between the parties, and about conscience.

15.1.2 An exercise in difference

Given the number of cases in this field which take radically different approaches from one another and the fact that many High Court judgments simply ignored earlier House of Lords judgments, this chapter will lend a structure to the law to assist you in answering problem questions or writing essays. In creating a structure, this chapter will nevertheless ensure that the open-textured energy of the case law is not lost. It would be a mistake to try to make all of these cases reconcile with one another. The judges were simply in disagreement with one another. We shall see, for example, how the traditionalist approach of Lord Neuberger in *Stack v Dowden*[3] was ignored by the rest of the House of Lords; we shall see how almost every academic and judge refused to be bound by the strict test set out by the House of Lords in *Lloyds Bank v Rosset*;[4] and we shall see how some of the Supreme Court in *Jones v Kernott* tidied up their earlier judgments in *Stack v Dowden*, but that they could not come to a unanimous view about the law.

15.1.3 The social context of the law

The social context

The law on trusts of homes is all about people. Possibly more so than most legal fields. Land law is concerned with dealings with land; contract law is concerned with commerce; and criminal law is concerned with wrongs. The law relating to the home is concerned with the ways in which people behave when they are behind closed doors and living the most intimate aspects of their lives: making plans, cooking food, sharing beds. There is something different about two people negotiating the use of their shower from two people negotiating for the sale of a car. When people are discussing the use of their shower they are in a very different mindset from people discussing a formal purchase and sale of a vehicle on a forecourt. When someone is discussing what happens in their bedroom it is in a different tone of voice from someone contemplating robbing a high street bank. The home is a very different space emotionally for the human being. Their relationships with other people who live in that home with them are different from every other relationship in the outside world. Therefore, when the law intervenes in questions about the home, it must be sensitive to that context and it is unsurprising that a different range of considerations come to mind as a result.

This chapter relates to people owning their own home. It does not relate to rented accommodation (which is covered in land law courses under the law on leases). At the time of writing, approximately 65% of people live in owner-occupied homes in the UK, as opposed

---

1 [2011] UKSC 53.
2 [1970] AC 777.
3 [2007] UKHL 17; [2007] 2 AC 432.
4 [1991] 1 AC 107.

to people who rent their homes. The continued steep rise in house prices in the UK (due to a lack of common sense on the part of successive governments and a shortage of housing supply in the UK) mean that more and more people need to rent their homes. A semi-detached house that cost £4,000 in suburban London in 1970 would sell today for approximately £500,000. At a time when inflation is supposedly running at less than 2% per annum, house prices have apparently risen 20% in London in the previous year. The explosion in home ownership that occurred in the 1980s with the policies of the Thatcher administration altered the balance between rented and owner-occupied homes markedly. Homeowners tend to measure their wealth by the arbitrary increase in the value of their homes – unless you leave the UK or move into a caravan in the woods, selling your home will usually only provide you with enough money to buy another house almost exactly like it.

It is important to say a little about some of the social changes in England and Wales over the years which impact on these cases. The essay in Chapter 17 considers the sociology of trusts law and in particular the way in which trusts law has treated women over the centuries. Before the Married Women's Property Act 1882, the law of property used to provide that all of a woman's property passed to her husband when she married. (In Chapter 2 we discussed the importance of trusts in protecting wealthy women against their husbands. The poor had no effective protection.) Therefore, a woman could be left destitute if she was abandoned by her husband. It was not until the 1970s that England and Wales created a right to divorce through statute. Case law in 1970, as we shall see below, started the idea that a married woman could acquire rights in her home which were distinct from the rights of her husband. The idea of a couple having a 'common intention' as to the ownership of their home emerged from these cases. In the late 20th century there was great concern that the focus in the case law on allocating rights in the home to whoever had paid for it meant that heterosexual women were disadvantaged because they were less likely to be in work, or if they were in work they were likely to be paid less; and because it was women who would tend to care for children and for the home with the result that they were statistically less likely to have paid for the house than their male partners. By the time we come to the 21st century, however, we can see that it is Ms Stack in *Stack v Dowden* and Ms Jones in *Jones v Kernott* who were larger earners than their male partners and therefore an allocation of rights in proportion to the parties' financial contributions to the property advantaged them. Nevertheless, a more enlightened approach in equity (mirroring family law to some extent) to the sorts of activity which acquired rights in the home (beyond merely spending money) meant a different manner of allocating rights in the home became possible. This chapter follows the case law on common intention through chronologically not least because that allows a sense of the developing mores in our society and in the courts to become clear as time progresses.

Cohabitants – a neutral expression

The law discussed in this chapter relates to any people who cohabit in a home except for married people (straight or gay) who are divorcing (because divorce is governed by statute). Therefore, we need a catch-all term which will govern the types of people who are being discussed here. It must be a term which governs sexual couples and people who are sharing homes non-romantically, short-term couples and long-term relationships, gay and straight relationships, couples with and without children, and couples who are facing the repossession of their property by mortgagees. In *The Beiderbecke Affair*, an unmarried couple in a long-term sexual relationship described themselves as being 'spousal analogues': that is, people who are similar to spouses. I rather like that expression, but it does not cover non-romantic couples. So, in this chapter we shall use the term 'cohabitants' to cover people who are living together in whatever circumstances.

15.1.4   The principles set out in *Stack v Dowden* and in *Jones v Kernott*

This section summarises the key principles which are to follow as taken from the decision of the House of Lords in *Stack v Dowden*[5] and from the decision of the Supreme Court in *Jones v Kernott*.[6] This summary will make it easier to understand the structure of this chapter because this chapter follows the principles set out by Lady Hale and Lord Walker in *Jones v Kernott* and the way in which they had developed in earlier cases. What the Supreme Court did in *Jones v Kernott* was to set out a number of general principles. To understand how those general principles operate, we must look at the earlier cases in which they were forged, developed and put to work. As will emerge from the discussion to follow, the older authorities will continue to be important because *Stack* and *Kernott* overruled very little previous authority and because their broad principles still leave room for those earlier cases to apply.

The most important decision in this context is the decision of the Supreme Court in *Jones v Kernott*.[7] The most significant judgment was the joint judgment of Lady Hale and Lord Walker. Lord Kerr delivered a judgment which agreed with them about most points. Somewhat disappointingly, however, the Supreme Court could not come to a single judgment on this particularly important area of the law. The assumption made here is that the lower courts will follow the structure set out by Lady Hale and Lord Walker. This case is considered in detail in section 15.9.7 below. What is important to observe is that the bulk of this judgment considers the earlier judgment of Lady Hale in *Stack v Dowden* and deliberately avoids overruling a large amount of earlier case law. Therefore, this structure necessarily requires us to examine the earlier case law. The position after *Jones v Kernott* is as follows.

First, the court must examine the legal title held at the Land Registry. If the legal title is held in the name of one person alone then that person is presumed to be the sole owner of the equitable interest. If the legal title is held in the name of more than one person then those people are presumed to be owners in common of the equitable interest in that property. These are merely presumptions. One or other of the parties can rebut those presumptions by demonstrating that the parties had a common intention which was something different.

Second, if the presumptions can be rebutted, then the court must consider the parties' common intention in accordance with the earlier case law. There are many cases from *Gissing v Gissing* in 1971 through to the present day which take different views as to what is meant by 'common intention'. The House of Lords in *Lloyds Bank v Rosset*[8] held that it should be restricted to explicit agreements between the parties as to their ownership of the property or to contributions to the purchase price or mortgage repayments over the property. Nothing else would be considered. The Court of Appeal in *Midland Bank v Cooke*[9] took the view that the court should undertake a survey of the entire course of dealing between the parties and include matters like raising the children, paying utility bills, and so forth. These two

---

5   [2007] UKHL 17; [2007] 2 WLR 831.
6   [2011] UKSC 53, [2011] 3 WLR 1121.
7   [2011] UKSC 53, [2011] 3 WLR 1121, [2011] 3 FCR 495.
8   [1991] 1 AC 107.
9   [1995] 4 All ER 562.

approaches are radical opposites, as we shall explore below. The High Court in *Cox v Jones*[10] was concerned to ensure that the claimant was not treated unconscionably, and therefore took a very general view of the parties' interaction. Just these three examples illustrate the range of views that are taken in the cases. This chapter collects these different cases under five general headings for ease of reference. It is a difficult thing to prove the common intention of the parties to disputes of this kind because they may not have clear evidence, their accounts in the witness box are likely to be biased and unreliable in large part, and their intention may have changed over time (whether reasonably or unreasonably). Therefore, the court is supposed 'objectively [to] infer the intentions of the parties' by reference to the evidence that does exist.

Third, if the evidence is not conclusive as to the parties' common intention, then further to the judgment of Lord Walker and Lady Hale in *Jones v Kernott*, the court will consider what would be 'fair' between the parties in the light of the evidence. This concept of 'fairness' is left open-ended by the Supreme Court to be developed in subsequent cases. Thus, ultimately, the court will have to have recourse to what is 'fair' between the parties. This will require, it is suggested, that the courts will potentially have recourse to all of the earlier authorities considered in this chapter in deciding what constitutes fairness between the parties.

The concept of proprietary estoppel, which continues to decide many cases in this area (and which was discussed in Chapter 13) was not mentioned by the Supreme Court. Nevertheless, the important role played by proprietary estoppel is discussed below.

15.1.5 The approach taken in this chapter

This chapter will follow the structure laid out by Lady Hale and Lord Walker in *Jones v Kernott*. First, we consider the role played by express trusts and by the presumptions according to the legal title over the property. Second, we shall consider the development of the law on 'common intention' from its roots in the judgment of the House of Lords in *Gissing v Gissing*. This is the largest section of this chapter because 'common intention' has been taken to mean so many different things in the cases. We shall divide between five approaches to common intention and take each of them in the following, chronological order: the decision of the House of Lords in *Lloyds Bank v Rosset* which attempted to generate a strict test for common intention; the balance sheet cases based on resulting trust; the family assets cases which 'undertake a survey of the entire course of dealing between the parties'; the cases which focus on the avoidance of 'unconscionability'; and an analysis of the role of proprietary estoppel in this area. Third, we shall consider what 'fairness' might be taken to mean in future cases.

This order, it is suggested, is the best structure to use when approaching problem questions. At present, the courts ask us to look for the common intention of the parties. Apply each different approach to the facts in front of you one at a time and explain how each of them would come to a different outcome. Because there are so many different approaches to what 'common intention' means, it is suggested that taking the different analyses in turn will impose order on that otherwise slightly scattered range of authorities. This may also provide a good structure for an essay in this subject.

---

10 [2004] 3 FCR 693.

15.2 EXPRESS TRUSTS OF HOMES

If there is an express trust over a home then that will be decisive of the beneficial ownership of the property. So, in *Goodman v Gallant*[11] the deed of conveyance of a property included a declaration of an express trust which allocated the entire equitable interest between the parties. The parties had contributed different amounts to the purchase price of the property. Therefore, one of the parties sought to argue that the express trust should be ignored and their cash contribution used to decide their beneficial ownership of the property. The Court of Appeal held that the express trust in the deed of conveyance was decisive of all of the interests of the parties to land. This principle will apply even where the parties to the conveyance had neither read nor necessarily understood it, provided that the declaration was formally valid.[12]

It should be remembered that in order for there to be a valid declaration of trust over land, the declaration must comply with s 53(1)(b) of the Law of Property Act 1925: 'a declaration of trust respecting any land or any interest therein must be manifested and proved by some writing signed by some person who is able to declare such trust or by his will'. Failure to comply with that formality requirement will lead to a failure to create a valid express trust over land. Moreover, it should also be remembered that under s 53(2), there is no formality requirement in relation to constructive and resulting trusts.

15.3 RESULTING TRUSTS AND THE EMERGENCE OF COMMON INTENTION

15.3.1 Traditional resulting trust principles

The traditional resulting trust provides that a person who contributes to the purchase price of property is entitled to receive a proportionate share of the equitable interest in that property, provided that was the parties' intention. So, a contribution of one quarter of the purchase price would entitle that person to one quarter of the equitable interest in that property. This principle was clear by the time of the judgment of Eyre CB in *Dyer v Dyer*.[13] That principle was affirmed by Lord Browne-Wilkinson in *Westdeutsche Landesbank Girozentrale v Islington LBC*.[14] The shortcoming with this principle in the context of the home is that it takes no account of other contributions to a family's life, such as bringing up the children, making sacrifices for one's own career and life to accommodate one's partner, and so forth. Even the best-laid plans of a romantic couple will probably be thrown off course by illness or ill-luck over time. Therefore, the rigidity of a resulting trust is considered undesirable by many. The Supreme Court in *Jones v Kernott* held that resulting trusts should not now be used to decide cases relating to the home. As we shall see, the resulting trust formed the basis for many decisions on common intention and its basic rationale (that a contributor of money to the purchase price should receive a proportionate share in response) appears to mimic the outcome of the most recent cases, such as *Stack v Dowden* and *Jones v Kernott* where the claimants received shares of the equitable interest which mirrored their total cash contributions over the years.

---

11   [1986] FLR 513.
12   *Pink v Lawrence* (1978) 36 P & CR 98.
13   (1788) 2 Cox Eq Cas 92.
14   [1996] AC 669.

15.3.2 The birth of common intention

The use of resulting trusts since the time of *Dyer v Dyer* was displaced in the early 1970s by two decisions of the House of Lords. It was these judgments which gave rise to the important concept of 'common intention' in the law. It is important to understand that the UK had undergone significant social changes since the 1939–45 war with the creation of the welfare state and with the great change in attitudes that was heralded by the 1960s. If it helps to imagine the change, think about the young women in a Jane Austen period drama with their formal manners and then think about the screaming young women who greeted the Beatles in the 1960s every time they stepped off an aeroplane. As the poet Philip Larkin put it, sexual intercourse began in 1963. By the 1970s there were great changes in the air: race relations legislation, equal pay legislation and a modern law of divorce. So, the birth of the law on trusts of homes happened at the same time as other great social changes (even though some of the judges involved might have been born while Queen Victoria was still on the throne).

There was still no divorce legislation, however, when in 1970 the House of Lords gave judgment in *Pettitt v Pettitt*.[15] Therefore, the earliest cases in this field related to married couples. Mrs Pettitt had been bequeathed the entire beneficial interest in a cottage. Her husband performed renovation works on that cottage which cost him £730, and which were agreed to have increased the value of the property by about £1,000. Mr Pettitt contended that he had acquired some equitable interest in the cottage by virtue of those works, and sought an order to that effect. It was held that Mr Pettitt had not performed sufficiently important works to be entitled to an equitable interest in the property. Interestingly in the Court of Appeal, Diplock LJ had made mention of the idea of looking at the common intention of the parties. Some old voices did remain. For example, Lord Upjohn held in *Pettitt* in 1970 that the meaning of the Married Women's Property Act 1882 could not be taken to 'have changed merely by reason of a change in social outlook since the date of its enactment'.[16] Instead, his lordship considered that 'it must continue to bear the meaning which upon its true construction in the light of the relevant surrounding circumstances it bore at that time'.[17] This was Britain in the 1970s: half the population clinging to the old ways, and the other half of the population trying to start something new. Punk began in 1977. This was the era when David Bowie, heavy metal, reggae, ska and disco crashed into the mainstream. Everything was changing. In *Gissing v Gissing*[18] the House of Lords accepted that an agreement between a married couple would be enforceable in equity where it constituted a 'common intention' formed between them. It is that case which we consider next.

15.3.3 The central text

The decision of the House of Lords in *Gissing v Gissing* remains the central text in this field because it gave rise to the concept of common intention. Mrs Gissing found a job for her husband at the place where she worked at the end of the 1939–45 war. He did well. The couple bought a house in 1951 which was registered in the husband's name. The purchase price was provided predominantly by a mortgage in the husband's name together with a loan

---

15 [1970] AC 777.
16 *Ibid*, 813.
17 *Ibid*.
18 [1971] AC 886.

from the couple's employers. Mrs Gissing spent £220 on laying a lawn at the house and on furnishings for the house. Her husband left her in 1961 to live with another woman. It was held, unanimously, that Mrs Gissing acquired no beneficial interest in the property on the grounds that she had made no contribution to the purchase price of the property. Expending money on ephemeral items was not the same as contributing to the purchase price. So much for the facts of the case. As to the general principles, the House of Lords accepted that the common intention of the parties played an important part, but the court was concerned that such common intentions should not be too loosely defined. In particular, Lord Diplock held that the court should not impute a common intention in circumstances where there was no direct evidence of any express agreement between the parties.[19] Significantly, Lord Diplock acknowledged that any common intention 'is more likely to have been concerned with the economic realities of the transaction than with the unfamiliar technicalities of the English law of legal and equitable interests in land'.[20] It is important to recognise that in the real world, people do not necessarily talk about their legal rights in their home; instead they talk about who will pay for the mortgage, how they will afford the bills, and what colour to paint the bedroom walls. Consequently, the common intention may have to be inferred from these more general discussions.

15.4 CONSTRUCTIVE TRUSTS – ACQUISITION OF EQUITABLE INTERESTS BY CONDUCT OR AGREEMENT

15.4.1 Foundations of the common intention constructive trust

The emergence of the concept of common intention in *Gissing v Gissing* meant that the doctrine of constructive trust became the key concept in cases of ownership of the home instead of the resulting trust. This form of constructive trust would not be based on the same principles as *Westdeutsche Landesbank v Islington* and the concepts discussed in Chapter 12. Instead the cases divided between those which focused on the amount of money which the parties had contributed and those which focused on the size of the equitable interest which the parties had agreed to allocate to each of them. There were cases like *Grant v Edwards*[21] in which Browne-Wilkinson J, true to form, focused on the idea that neither party should be treated unconscionably in the allocation of rights in the home. To some judges, these differences of approach in the cases was unacceptably messy. In *Pettitt v Pettitt*, Lord Hodson suggested that total judicial discretion in this area would not be appropriate because that 'would be to substitute the uncertain and crooked cord of discretion for the golden and straight metwand of the law.'[22] (This obsession with metwands among some judges is discussed in section 26.1.2.) In other words, the law should always strive for certainty and principle as opposed to permitting judges to do as they thought fit in any case. With that approach in mind, Lord Bridge delivered one of the most rigid judgments in this field in *Lloyds Bank v Rosset* with a view to making the law more predictable and organised.

---

19   [1971] AC 886, 904.
20   *Ibid*, 906.
21   [1986] Ch 638.
22   *Pettitt v Pettitt* [1970] AC 777, 808.

15.4.2 *Lloyds Bank v Rosset* – the common intention constructive trust

The context of Lloyds Bank v Rosset

The House of Lords in *Lloyds Bank v Rosset*[23] considered a case in which Mr and Mrs Rosset decided to renovate a semi-derelict farmhouse as a joint venture. The house was registered in the husband's name. Mrs Rosset oversaw all of the building work. She had a flair for interior design and therefore this was her contribution to the project. Her husband acquired the property with a mortgage (without his wife's knowledge) but was unable to keep up with the repayments. Therefore, Lloyds Bank sought repossession. To resist repossession, it was important to show that Mrs Rosset had a substantial equitable interest in the property. It was held that Mrs Rosset had no equitable interest in the property because merely supervising renovation work was considered to be too insignificant to acquire an equitable interest. Lord Bridge identified two ways in which a so-called 'common intention constructive trust' could come into existence so as to create a right in the home, but Mrs Rosset had the benefit of neither. Either the constructive trust would be based on an agreement between the parties or it would be based on conduct. Each of these constructive trusts is considered in turn.

Common intention evidenced by agreement

The first form of common intention is constituted by the parties creating an express agreement, arrangement or understanding between them before the date of acquisition as to their respective rights in the property, provided that they suffer a detriment. In the words of Lord Bridge:[24]

> The first and fundamental question which must always be resolved is whether, independently of any inference to be drawn from the conduct of the parties in the course of sharing the house as their home and managing their joint affairs, there has at any time prior to acquisition, or exceptionally at some later date, been any agreement, arrangement or understanding reached between them that the property is to be shared beneficially.

This is the court's first inquiry.[25] This assumes that the parties do concentrate on the legal niceties sufficiently to reach a clear agreement before the property is acquired. In the words of Lord Bridge:[26]

> The finding of an agreement or arrangement to share in this sense can only, I think, be based on evidence of express discussions between the partners, however imperfectly remembered and however imprecise their terms.

This agreement certainly does not need to be a contract. However, it must be capable of proof. The problem in cases of this sort is that the parties rarely recall the events with perfect clarity and generally recall them in a way which contributes to their own argument. It is clear

---

23   [1991] 1 AC 107.
24   [1990] 1 All ER 1111, 1116.
25   *Savill v Goodall* [1993] 1 FLR 755.
26   [1990] 1 All ER 1111, 1117.

that *Rosset* requires that the parties come to an agreement specifically about their respective rights in the property and not about anything else. So, when a claimant sought an equitable interest in the defendant's home on the basis that she had lent money to the defendant's business, it was held that there had been no agreement, arrangement or understanding that the claimant would acquire any interest in the defendant's home and therefore the claimant acquired no such interest.[27] Where there is no evidence to substantiate the existence of an agreement, the court will not create one out of thin air.[28]

Common intention evidenced by conduct

The second form of common intention constructive trust arises in the absence of an express agreement or arrangement to share the beneficial ownership. This constructive trust depends on the parties' conduct. The only form of conduct which Lord Bridge was prepared to countenance was a contribution to the purchase price or to the mortgage instalments. In the words of Lord Bridge:[29]

> . . . direct contributions to the purchase price by the partner who is not the legal owner, whether initially or by payment of mortgage instalments, will readily justify the inference necessary to the creation of a constructive trust. But as I read the authorities it is at least extremely doubtful whether anything less will do.

Those final words are important: it is at least extremely doubtful whether anything less than contributing to the purchase price or to the mortgage will do. As we shall see, the law could take the view that caring for children or performing renovation work or agreeing to give up one's job to move with one's partner would constitute 'conduct' which ought to give rise to a right in the home. In *Rosset*, however, that is insufficient. Only payment towards the purchase price or the mortgage instalments will count.

The requirement for detriment in common intention constructive trust

It was held in *Lloyds Bank v Rosset* that the claimant must demonstrate that she has suffered detriment before being able to demonstrate a common intention constructive trust. The same point was made in *Midland Bank v Dobson*.[30] In *Grant v Edwards*,[31] it was held that detriment could constitute personal detriment. In *Coombes v Smith*[32] it was held that detriment would need to be something more than merely personal. The axiomatic example of this form of detriment would involve spending money. An example of personal detriment would involve moving home with the children from a former relationship on the promise that they would have a home or moving in with another person intending to have children with them.

---

27 *Koulias v Makris* [2005] All ER (D) 352.
28 *Churchill v Roach* [2002] EWHC 3230; [2004] 3 FCR 744.
29 [1990] 1 All ER 1111, 1117.
30 [1986] 1 FLR 171.
31 [1986] Ch 638.
32 [1986] 1 WLR 808.

15.4.3 Application of the common intention constructive trust concept

The decision of the Court of Appeal in *Ivin v Blake*[33] applied the decision of the House of Lords in *Rosset*. This is noteworthy because it is one of very few Court of Appeal cases to apply the *Rosset* test. In *Ivin v Blake*, it was held that a claimant could not acquire rights in the defendant's property because she had made it possible for the defendant to afford the mortgage by working in her pub. It was held that this satisfied neither limb of the *Rosset* test because there had not been an agreement between the parties to that effect and because this was not conduct appropriate to the acquisition of rights in the property.

One of the key findings in the cases ranging from *Gissing v Gissing*, through *Nixon v Nixon*[34] and the Court of Appeal in *Burns v Burns*,[35] and on to *Rosset* is that a mere contribution to household expenses will not acquire an interest in property. Later cases, such as *Midland Bank v Cooke*,[36] take a different approach and roll consideration of this issue into a general survey of the facts. Similarly, under *Rosset*, a temporary contribution to repayments of a mortgage will not, without more, found a right in property; nor will merely providing security for another person's acquisition of property.[37]

15.4.4 The difficulties with a strict application of the *Rosset* test

The principal advantage of the *Rosset* test was that it was clear and therefore legal practitioners would be able to give their clients clear advice as to their rights in their home. I have long advised students to begin an analysis of 'common intention' by applying Lord Bridge's tests literally to the facts in front of them: unlike the other doctrines discussed in this chapter, that tends to produce a clear answer which can be compared and contrasted with the other doctrines. The disadvantages with the *Rosset* test are that it contains no mechanism for achieving fairness or justice between the parties, particularly if their circumstances or their relationships have changed since they acquired their home in a way which might be thought to require a different allocation of the property rights.

There are two principal problems with the judgment in *Rosset*. First, technical issues. The concept of 'resulting trust' is not mentioned even though contributions to the purchase price would ordinarily be considered to be a resulting trust. Instead, Lord Bridge tended to run the terms 'constructive trust or proprietary estoppel' together as though those two doctrines were the same concept. A proprietary estoppel claim depends on there being a representation on which the claimant relied to their detriment; this is different from an institutional constructive trust predicated on an unconscionable act. Lord Bridge did not explain how they could run together. (It might be possible to run them together but only by changing one or other of them radically, and in any event Lord Bridge did not discuss that possibility.)

Second, more general issues of injustice. Lord Bridge envisages that only people who contribute to the purchase price can acquire a right in the property. This disadvantages people who do not have money. Historically, this has disadvantaged women because it is women who take career breaks to have children (thus reducing their personal wealth) and because

---

33 [1995] 1 FLR 70.
34 [1969] 1 WLR 1676.
35 [1984] Ch 317.
36 [1995] 4 All ER 562.
37 *Carlton v Goodman* [2002] 2 FLR 259.

women tend to be paid less than men in practice (even after 40 years of equal pay legislation). Moreover, if one partner pays for expenses other than the mortgage while their co-partner pays for the mortgage, then only the co-partner paying for the mortgage would acquire an equitable interest in the property under Lord Bridge's test. The very rigidity of this test is its principal shortcoming. It fails to accord value to things like childcare and it fails to recognise that a relationship may have values other than financial values. What Lord Bridge appeared to forget is that people fall in love. And that when they fall in love they sometimes move in together, or get married, or have children. Or sometimes they don't fall in love but they have children and so have to move in together. It is not possible to create a strict test like that in *Rosset* and expect either that people will always sit down calmly in those glorious early days of a relationship and decide who is to have what equitable interest in the home, or that people will be able to form a common intention at the start of their relationship which will work perfectly throughout it without anyone becoming ill, being made redundant, falling out of love, or whatever else. Life is just not like that. It is suggested that it is contrary to the very core of equity's flexible ability to do right on a case-by-case basis to use concepts like that in *Rosset* to attempt to fetter and bind the ability of the courts to see the right result in any particular case.

The inadequacies and inflexibilities of the *Rosset* test meant that it was largely ignored by the lower courts in later cases, in spite of the doctrine of precedent. In the sections to follow we shall consider four groups of cases which have taken different approaches: the balance sheet cases in section 15.5; the family assets cases in section 15.6; the unconscionability cases in section 15.7; and the proprietary estoppel cases in section 15.8. Then we consider *Stack v Dowden* and *Jones v Kernott* in detail.

15.5 THE BALANCE SHEET APPROACH

15.5.1 Introduction

One thing which the internet has revealed, by making available to us hundreds and hundreds of cases which would otherwise have faded into well-deserved obscurity, is that the doctrine of precedent seems to be ignored commonly in our legal system. This problem is probably becoming worse now that more and more lawyers rely on internet and database searches which tend to throw up the most recent case on a point, rather than identifying the older, leading case on a point. Consequently, this research method means that undesirable ideas made in a recent case are likely to be repeated in place of the dicta set out in the leading case some years before. Today, fewer litigators seem to settle down with a thick textbook and read their way into an area of law that way. That the doctrine of precedent was only weakly observed in some circumstances was demonstrated by the way in which the lower courts ignored *Lloyds Bank v Rosset*. As a judgment of the House of Lords it should have been applied strictly (as Lord Bridge clearly intended it to be) so as to remove the confusion in this area of law. Instead, the lower courts seemed to treat it as only one of a range of judgments which they might consider. Frequently, judges chose to return to the generalities in the House of Lords decision in *Gissing v Gissing* to justify whatever outcome they wished to reach.

In this section we shall consider a short line of cases which used the resulting trust as the principal means for allocating rights in the home. This is important because *Rosset* did not mention the resulting trust concept at all, and therefore by applying resulting trusts analyses these cases were ignoring Lord Bridge's judgment in *Rosset*. By using resulting trusts they did appear to create the problem of focusing solely on financial contributions. However, as we shall see, the Court of Appeal in this area did understand the resulting trust as being something which was capable of being adapted on a case-by-case basis so as to account for changes in the parties' circumstances. Indeed, in the House of Lords in *Stack v Dowden*, in his dissenting judgment, Lord Neuberger used a model of resulting trust which could be changed to account for appropriate factors which came to light after the purchase of the home. The other members of that court and the Supreme Court in *Jones v Kernott* considered that resulting trusts should not be used in the future.

The essence of the 'balance sheet approach' (which is my own jargon) is that the court draws up a list of financial contributions made by each party towards the property, akin to an accountant preparing a balance sheet, and calculates each party's proportionate equitable interest in the home according to those calculations. What will emerge from the following discussion is that the times at which these contributions are made need not comply with the requirements set out in *Rosset* that they be made before the acquisition and that they be directed solely at acquiring interests in property.

15.5.2 Calculating the size of the equitable interest

One of the earlier cases to exhibit the use of a balance sheet approach was a decision of the Court of Appeal in *Bernard v Josephs*.[38] The court calculated the total contribution made by each party across different items of property.[39] While *Rosset* focused on contributions to the purchase price and to the mortgage, there can be contributions made throughout the life of the property not just to the mortgage but to renovation and rebuilding work (although *Rosset* excluded mere supervision of that work). Many properties are acquired in the 21st century with a view to transforming them so as to increase their value – this is something which should be taken into account by the court. Some people add extensions or conservatories, and there are numerous television programmes devoted to showing Britons who are addicted to the property market how to increase the value of their property with only a little work. It is a difficult matter for the court to know whether it is the work which has increased the value of the property or whether steeply rising market values were responsible for that increase anyway. This is exactly the sort of issue which the courts tend to ignore, or leave to expert evidence before the court at first instance.

Ordinarily in cases of resulting trust, the size of each party's interest will be proportionate to their contribution to the total purchase price.[40] Interestingly, the balance sheet cases are more creative than that. The Court of Appeal in *Huntingford v Hobbs* was prepared to look behind the documentation signed by the parties which suggested that they held the equitable interest in the property in equal shares. It was held that to look behind such documents there must be 'cogent evidence' that any documentation signed by the parties was not intended to constitute the final statement as to their beneficial interests.

38 [1982] Ch 391.
39 *Ibid.*
40 *Huntingford v Hobbs* [1993] 1 FLR 736.

There is also the possibility of equitable accounting to take into account periods of rent-free occupation and so forth by one or other of the parties.[41] When a relationship terminates, it is common for one party to leave the property and live somewhere else. The partner left in the property may be occupying without having to pay anything (if the mortgage has been paid off, for example) while the other partner is renting a flat somewhere on their own. In such a situation, the court will often order that the party who remains must pay something to the other party.

15.5.3 What can be taken into account?

There have been interesting developments in what can be taken into account since *Rosset* was decided. In *Springette v Defoe*[42] Ms Springette was entitled to a discount on the purchase price of her property under the government's statutory scheme to encourage tenants of council housing to buy their own homes. This meant that she was entitled to a 41% discount on the market value of the property due to her lengthy occupation of it. Mr Defoe moved into the property and contributed a mere £180 in cash to the purchase price of approximately £25,000 (before the discount) before he left Ms Springette three years later. He had promised to make half of the mortgage repayments over the property. The Court of Appeal held that Mr Defoe was entitled to an account for his cash contribution and his agreement to pay half of the mortgage. Even though he only made mortgage repayments for three years he was treated as though he had paid for half the mortgage in full, which is a remarkably short-sighted approach. In practice, the parties usually agree (as they did in *Huntingford v Hobbs*) that the party who remains in the property will assume the mortgage repayments in the future, or else the property is sold. In this instance, Ms Springette was entitled to take into account her statutory discount rights as though they were cash: in this instance that was worth just over £10,000. What is clear is that the rigidity of *Rosset* is not being followed.

Discounts are an interesting issue. In *Cox v Jones*,[43] the claimant had acquired a flat on a private basis from a vendor whom she had known personally. It was held that this discount on the property (obtained purely through personal contact and not through a statutory right) was one of the many things which could be taken into account when assessing her rights and ensuring that she would not be treated unconscionably. Interestingly, it was not given a cash value as had been the case in *Springette v Dafoe*. In the case of *Evans v Hayward*[44] it had been held that mere haggling to reduce the purchase price of property would not entitle the person who had obtained the reduction to a larger equitable interest as a result. Perhaps we should think of Ms Springette as having acquired her specific right with a specific cash value on the basis that it was a statutory right to that precise reduction in the purchase price which could be considered to be akin to a sort of statutory voucher.

In *Huntingford v Hobbs*[45] the claimant and defendant acquired a house for £63,250. The defendant had sold her former matrimonial home (where her new partner had not wanted to live) and contributed £38,860 in cash to the new property. The remainder of the purchase price was provided by means of a mortgage for £25,000 in the claimant's name. The claimant

---

41   *Bernard v Josephs* [1982] Ch 391; *Huntingford v Hobbs* [1993] 1 FLR 736.
42   (1992) 24 HLR 552; [1992] 2 FLR 388.
43   [2004] 3 FCR 693.
44   [1995] 2 FLR 511.
45   [1993] 1 FLR 736.

had contributed approximately £5,000 in mortgage interest payments and £1,500 in capital repayments. He had also spent £2,000 constructing a conservatory after the couple had moved in. It was held that all of these amounts would be allocated between the parties in a sort of balance sheet so as to calculate the percentage of the total equitable interest they would acquire. Interestingly, the Court of Appeal treated all of these amounts as if they were immediate cash payments when, for example, the obligation to repay the mortgage was a future obligation which would not be completely performed until the mortgage was repaid many years in the future. Usually, the so-called 'time value of money' concept in finance would mean that making a cash payment now would be considered to be more valuable that making a payment in the same amount over a longer period of time. It was also found that the parties could change their obligations so that the defendant in this instance could assume responsibility for the mortgage in the future and thus 'buy the claimant out' of her share of the property. In practice, it is often the case that the parties will come to some agreement of this sort before trial to save themselves the expense of lengthy proceedings and the risk of losing.

Here the Court of Appeal used the resulting trust once again but by taking the money spent on the conservatory into account they used an item of expenditure which was made after acquisition. This offered new possibilities for the resulting trust by allowing it to be adjusted over time. Exactly that approach was taken by Lord Neuberger in *Stack v Dowden* in his dissenting judgment where his lordship suggested that the court should begin by establishing the financial contributions of the parties to the property (at the date of acquisition and thereafter), before then adjusting that resulting trust by using constructive trust principles to account for any relevant issues. This was not intended to allow the court to do what it considered to be 'fair' in general terms. As was mentioned above, the rest of the court and the Supreme Court in *Jones v Kernott* were against the use of resulting trusts in the future; although, as is discussed below, the outcomes of these leading cases came to the same conclusion as if they had simply used a resulting trust analysis and focused on the parties' financial contributions to the property.

In *McHardy v Warren*,[46] parents paid the deposit on their son's matrimonial home in the amount of £650. It was found by the court that this was intended to be a gift to both husband and wife. The remainder of the purchase price was provided by way of mortgage. The only cash contribution was the gift of the deposit. It was found that this meant that husband and wife each had a half share in the equitable interest over the property which was based on the intention that the payment for the deposit was intended to be a gift to both husband and wife. Therefore the wife had a sufficiently large interest to resist repossession proceedings brought by a mortgagee. Interestingly, this root of equitable title flowed from the couple's first home into two successive homes which were bought with the sale proceeds of the first house and with mortgages. Therefore, the wife's equitable interest which was based on her share in the gift of the deposit continued into the two successive home purchases, as opposed to the equitable interests necessarily being reset when a new house was purchased. It is to be assumed that if the parties had consciously decided to change their common intention on the acquisition of a new house then that would have held sway, but in this situation that had not been the case.

46 [1994] 2 FLR 338.

15.6 THE FAMILY ASSETS APPROACH

15.6.1 Explaining the approach

In the retreat from the decision in *Rosset*, one of the most important developments is the emergence of principles which will grant rights to the parties but which are not based solely on financial contributions to the purchase price. There has been talk in the case law of the development of different principles and yet few cases have produced outcomes which are different from the outcome the court would have reached if it had simply applied resulting trust thinking. One area in which there have been different outcomes is in relation to proprietary estoppel (as discussed in section 15.8 below). Another area has been developed by the decisions of Waite LJ in *Hammond v Mitchell* and in *Midland Bank v Cooke* in which a form of 'family assets' doctrine has emerged in which the home is treated as part of the family's life together. For Waite LJ a family emerges as being a unit in which people will share their lives and not simply their money. Consequently, there is a greater likelihood that the home will be shared equally between partners to a long-term relationship if this approach is taken. We consider these cases next.

15.6.2 Where equality is equity

In *Midland Bank v Cooke*,[47] for example, the Cookes were a married couple who shared all of life's challenges between them before Midland Bank sought repossession of their home when they could not meet the mortgage repayments. The Cookes needed to show that Mrs Cooke had a substantial right in the property so as to resist the mortgagee's claim for repossession. Waite LJ favours us with a detailed examination of their married life. They have lived together for several years and had children. Mrs Cooke played the role of mother and housewife for a large part of their marriage but, importantly, when Mr Cooke was unemployed or when they needed money then Mrs Cooke would find part-time work. She paid utility and other bills from time to time and she also paid the mortgage on occasion (although the details of how often that happened or how much money that involved are unclear). For Waite LJ, this married couple were in a true partnership and therefore, his lordship held, they should be taken to have equal shares in their matrimonial home. The rationale is very interesting. To avoid the strictures of *Rosset*, Waite LJ began his survey of the authorities with *Gissing v Gissing* and its vague statements about the nature of the common intention between the parties. This allowed Waite LJ to show that there was a large amount of contradictory authority on the case law (and thus to avoid the truth that he should have followed the House of Lords' decision in *Rosset*) and that he was therefore able to select the most appropriate path for himself. Very importantly, his lordship held that the court must 'undertake a survey of the entire course of dealing between the parties'. This expression became very important in later cases because it meant that *Rosset* was not to be followed. Instead, the court could (in theory) take into account anything that happened between the parties. On these facts, Waite LJ decided that he should have recourse to the ancient equitable principle that 'equality is equity' because it was not possible otherwise to identify the shares which each party should take in the property. Therefore, Mrs Cooke acquired a half share in the property without having to make a substantive cash contribution to the purchase price.

---

47 [1995] 4 All ER 562.

What is clear is that Mrs Cooke acquires a very different quality of right from the sort which Lord Bridge would have permitted. It is this judgment which offers a radically different outcome as a result of using the common intention concept from the earlier cases. In the more recent decisions (considered in the sections to follow) the parties tend to acquire rights in proportion to their cash contributions even though the judges were clear that they did not want to be limited to resulting trust principles. Nevertheless, it is only Waite LJ who has shown a clear intention to find a different type of right for the parties through using the common intention concept.

15.6.3 Communal undertakings in the judgments of Waite J

It might be thought that his lordship was particularly keen on these facts to unearth some sort of right for Mrs Cooke so that the family could remain in their home; if the couple had been squabbling between themselves then it would have been interesting to know whether the same outcome would have been reached. The decision in *Hammond v Mitchell* delivered by Waite J did involve an unmarried couple disputing ownership of the home between one another, and Waite J did show a very similar approach (although he did not find that the parties held their home in equal shares). The facts were as follows. They are remarkable facts and the judgment is remarkable. Indeed, I will go further. This is possibly my favourite case of the several thousand I have read over the last 30 years. This is the sort of case which makes the study of law worthwhile in itself. I urge you to read it in its original form and to think about what it means.

Tom Hammond was a used car salesman from Essex in the prime of life (by which I mean he was in his 40s). He was driving a Jaguar motor car through Epping Forest one day when he was flagged down by a hitchhiker. The hitchhiker was a woman in her early 20s who worked as a Bunny Girl at the Playboy nightclub in London's West End. She was called Vicki Mitchell. Pause for a moment. A middle-aged man is driving his large, executive saloon through the woods when a young woman who works in the glamour industry flags him down. This is Essex. That legendary county. Tom Hammond must have thought he was in heaven; Vicki Mitchell must have been glad of the lift. Possibly euphemistically, Waite J tells us that their relationship began shortly afterwards. Who knows whether that was in terms of hours, days or weeks. They appear to have been wonderfully matched. We are told that 'they both shared a zest for the good life'. They are both entrepreneurial and they begin to work together as a team very quickly in one another's businesses. Tom has several businesses – buying and selling cars and many other things. They run market stalls together (which makes me think of the long-running BBC TV programme *Eastenders*, set in east London) and Vicki makes clothes which she sells to the women with whom she works. Vicki also enters into a restaurant business in Valencia, Spain on her own account. Their relationship lasts for 11 years, there are two children, they work hard, they argue from time to time, and they seem to live as happily as anyone can in this cold and indifferent world. It seems that Tom promised to marry her when he was divorced and that he told her that the house was as much hers as it was his. They never did marry, however.

The soap opera begins when Vicki begins an affair in Spain. Tom's son warns his father that something is going on. Vicki travels backwards and forwards to Spain on her own to see to the restaurant and, it seems, to see her lover. Rather than discuss this with Vicki in the security of their home, Tom travels to Valencia to confront her. In a scene straight from a soap opera, Tom secretly buys himself a ticket on the plane which Vicki is taking back to the UK and organises that he is sitting in the seat next to her. He boards the plane early and is waiting for her when she arrives on-board, fresh (perhaps) from her lover. There is a tremendous argument between them on the plane and they are removed. On their return to the UK, Vicki leaves Tom with a large number of valuables crammed into a Jaguar XJS motor car (a classic sports car from that era). Tom begs her to return, which she does. Briefly. Then she leaves him again, this time with more valuables crammed into a Mercedes.

When this matter comes before Waite J, he reveals himself to be a great romantic. He tells us that this couple were too much in love to count the pennies or to ask who was providing them. When his lordship considers their ownership of their home and their many other items of property, this is important because it means that they could not have been expected to identify their equitable interests in that property from the outset. When couples are in love – especially after they meet remarkably in a forest one day – then they are unlikely to think about the legal niceties. (As we shall see below in relation to *Cox v Jones*, it may be that even practising barristers are incapable of identifying their property rights.) Therefore, Waite J takes an approach which is very different from *Rosset*, and which foreshadows his later judgment in *Midland Bank v Cooke*, when he considers the entire course of dealing between the parties. That course of dealing suggests that Tom Hammond should be taken to have intended to give property rights in the home to Vicki, even though it was his home at the outset. Vicki can be understood to have kept the Valencia restaurant for himself on these facts because Tom played no part in it. As to their many movables (many of which were sold in their market stall businesses and so forth) the way they worked together as a team suggested joint ownership of those items of property on the basis that 'equality is equity'.

There is something wonderfully humane about these judgments. Rather than the arid formalism of Lord Bridge's judgment or the cold mathematics of resulting trusts, the court is examining the way in which the parties lived their lives and identifying the best outcome for them. This is very like a family law court deciding an application for ancillary relief in divorce proceedings in which the courts use high-level principles (instead of hard-and-fast rules) to decide the problems in front of them. There is a greater focus on the needs of the parties in family law claims rather than on their formal, legal rights (as in most property law claims). As is discussed at the end of this chapter, one of the problems with the 'common intention' concept is that it tends to take an unrealistic approach to relationships.

15.7 THE UNCONSCIONABILITY APPROACH

15.7.1 The nature of the unconscionability approach

There is a line of cases which has been superseded now by the decision in *Jones v Kernott*: that line of cases seeks to avoid the claimant suffering unconscionability by being denied rights in the home. This line of cases goes back to the roots of equity, as discussed in Chapter 1, by focusing on the idea of conscience. An early landmark in this regard appears in the judgment of Browne-Wilkinson VC in *Grant v Edwards*.[48] It was held that the equitable interest would arise on principles which were more typically associated with constructive trusts. Browne-Wilkinson VC held that the claimant 'has to establish a constructive trust by showing that it would be inequitable for the legal owner to claim sole beneficial ownership'.

---

48 [1986] Ch 638.

His lordship required that there must be a common intention that both parties would have a beneficial interest (but that the court would decide the size of that interest) and both parties must have suffered some detriment. The focus on the word 'inequitable' here is in line with the idea of unconscionability: it must be inequitable for the defendant to have the entire beneficial interest and for the claimant to be denied rights.

The decision of Walker LJ in the Court of Appeal in *Jennings v Rice*[49] also revolved around the concept of 'unconscionability'. Here, Jennings worked unpaid or lowly paid for many years in the service of a wealthy widow. His role evolved from being a gardener and odd-job man to a permanent help-meet who even spent the night at her home after she was burgled. His wife began to help her too. She did not leave her house in her will in the way that Jennings and his wife had clearly come to anticipate. It was held that it would have been unconscionable for Mr and Mrs Jennings to be denied any rights in the property on the basis of proprietary estoppel (as discussed below). However, due to the flexible nature of the remedy which can be awarded in proprietary estoppel cases, the Court of Appeal ordered that the Jennings would receive a cash sum of £200,000 to prevent them being treated unconscionably instead of a property right in the house. This case is discussed in detail in section 15.7.3.

15.7.2 The consensual approach taken in *Oxley v Hiscock*

The decision of the Court of Appeal in *Oxley v Hiscock*[50] concerned a dispute between a woman and a man as to ownership of their home. He had contributed approximately 60% of the purchase price and she had contributed 40%. The equitable interest was divided in broadly those proportions. Chadwick LJ attempted to reconcile all of the authorities discussed so far, with little success. Relying particularly on *Grant v Edwards* as an explanation of *Pettitt v Pettitt* and *Gissing v Gissing*, the court held that the first question which a court must ask itself was whether or not there had been any common intention formed between the parties, either on the basis of direct evidence or inferred from the circumstances. Having identified such a common intention, it was held that one must then quantify the size of the right intended by that agreement. The conclusion to which Chadwick LJ came in *Oxley v Hiscock*[51] was that the role of the court 'is to supply or impute a common intention as to the parties' respective shares (in circumstances in which there was in fact no common intention) on the basis of that which, in the light of all the material circumstances (including the acts and conduct of the parties after the acquisition) is shown to be fair'. This approach is therefore shown to be based on fairness, which is in line with the unconscionability approach taken in the other cases considered in this section. Interestingly, the role of the court is said to be 'to supply' the parties' common intention: that is, the court will tell them what their common intention was, as opposed to it necessarily being the actual common intention formed by the parties themselves. The ideas of fairness and of the awkwardness of the court identifying the parties' common intention for them are considered again in *Jones v Kernott* below.

---

49 [2003] 1 P & CR 100.
50 [2004] EWCA Civ 546.
51 *Ibid*, para [66].

15.7.3 Proprietary estoppel and unconscionability: *Jennings v Rice*

Proprietary estoppel arises when there is a representation made to the claimant on which she relied to her detriment. This was discussed in more detail in Chapter 13. This section considers the way in which proprietary estoppel has been used in relation to the home, especially in relation to the emerging unconscionability approach. It was Walker LJ in *Jennings v Rice*[52] who expressed the view that proprietary estoppel is intended to prevent unconscionability. That idea had appeared in the case law before then. For example, the judgment of Oliver J in *Taylor Fashions v Liverpool Victoria Trustees Co Ltd*[53] provided that if an award of proprietary estoppel were not made in that case then 'it would be unconscionable for a party to be permitted to deny that which, knowingly or unknowingly, he has allowed or encouraged another to assume to his detriment'. So, in *Yaxley v Gotts*[54] it was held that both doctrines are 'concerned with equity's intervention to provide relief against unconscionable conduct'. Similarly in *Grant v Edwards*[55] it was suggested by Browne-Wilkinson VC that 'useful guidance may in future be obtained from the principles underlying the law of proprietary estoppel which in my judgment are closely akin to those laid down in *Gissing v Gissing*'.[56] This was one of the first judgments to suggest the idea that the law relating to the home should combine estoppel with constructive trust. In *Van Laetham v Brooker*, Lawrence Collins J held that the *remedies* provided in proprietary estoppel and constructive trust are effectively the same in that the courts award whatever rights they consider appropriate in good conscience.[57] Consequently, his lordship identified an amount of money which the claimant was entitled to receive in that case which reflected her financial and other contribution to the acquisition and development of various properties, while also taking into account the skilled and larger contributions of the defendant. Thus, instead of arguing that the two doctrines are identical, the courts tend to suggest that there are merely general similarities between them. The key similarity is that both doctrines – being equitable – are based on ideas of conscience.

15.7.4 Seeking fairness in all the circumstances: *Cox v Jones*

The case of *Cox v Jones*[58] is fascinating. Mann J focused on avoiding the claimant being treated unconscionably. In so doing, his lordship traversed doctrines with a lightness of tread that is remarkable or alarming, depending on your view. The approach which Mann J took was to pour all the facts into a pot, to stir it around, and then to decide what was the most conscionable outcome. Mr Jones and Ms Cox were barristers. Jones was older and senior to Cox, and richer. The couple bought a country house in Essex together in October 1999 but it was put in his sole name and he paid for it. Cox spent a large amount of time supervising renovation work at this house instead of trying to develop her fledgling legal practice in London. The couple also bought a flat in Islington in a building in which Cox had lived previously. She was able to negotiate a reduction in the purchase price on the property because

---

52   [2002] EWCA Civ 159.
53   [1981] 2 WLR 576, 593.
54   [2000] Ch 162, 176, *per* Walker LJ.
55   [1986] Ch 638, 656, *per* Browne-Wilkinson VC.
56   [1971] AC 886.
57   [2006] 2 FLR 495, para [263].
58   [2004] 3 FCR 693; [2004] EWHC 1486 (Ch).

she knew the vendor. The couple had previously lived in Lincoln's Inn where they had a tempestuous relationship in which they argued. Her boisterous Alsatian dog lived with them too. During one argument, Jones pretended to fling Cox's engagement ring out of the window. Ownership of these items of property was contested. It was held that the keynote was to avoid Cox being treated unconscionably by the land having been placed in Jones' name. Mann J commented that both parties – especially Jones – had proved unreliable and unconvincing witnesses in their own causes. His lordship held that Cox should acquire rights in the Essex house through supervising renovation work and the detriment involved in not concentrating on her Bar practice. Ironically, this was exactly the behaviour which failed to acquire Mrs Rosset any rights in her home. Nevertheless, Cox acquired a one quarter share in the equity. It is unclear precisely what constituted the unconscionability here, especially when Mann J also awarded Cox the entire ownership of the Islington flat. The engagement ring was found to have been a gift to Cox in the ordinary way and therefore her ownership of it continued in spite of their relationship ending. Mann J rehearses the facts at length, mentions the concept of unconscionability, and then uses the judgment of Solomon to dispense property rights between the parties. He looked for a solution which would be 'fair having regard to the whole course of dealing between them in relation to the property'.

15.7.5 A model of the general constructive trust combined with the common intention constructive trust

There have been very few cases in which traditional constructive trusts of the sort discussed in Chapter 12 have been used in relation to the law on trusts of homes. The reason for this is the legacy of the judgment in *Gissing v Gissing*. An exception arose in the judgment of Lawrence Collins J in *Van Laetham v Brooker*[59] in which his lordship applied the test from *Grant v Edwards* outlined above. The judgment was based on inequitability, together with common intention and detriment. The Court of Appeal in *Oates v Stimson*[60] looked for 'the minimum equity to do justice' between the parties,[61] in accordance with proprietary estoppel cases like *Crabb v Arun DC*. Following *Midland Bank v Cooke*, it was held that 'there is also an obligation to take into account all relevant circumstances including the conduct of the parties'.[62] Auld LJ held that the case turned detrimental reliance by the claimant giving rise to a constructive trust because it would be unconscionable not to enforce an agreement between the parties. This model explains situations in which there would be unconscionability – for example, where one party misled the other – but might not explain situations as well when the parties have acted properly and where, for example, it is a third party who is seeking to acquire rights over the property.

15.7.6 The 'excuses' cases: rights not based on common intention

It may be that the parties' purported agreement simply demonstrates that their common intention was something different if one of them was lying to the other one. There have been cases in which men have lied to women about their reasons for excluding the women from the legal

---

59 [2005] EWHC 1478 (Ch).
60 [2006] EWCA Civ 548.
61 *Ibid*, para [13].
62 *Ibid*, para [13].

title over the property. They were found to have done this so as to acquire the legal title for themselves. Therefore, the agreement between the parties appears to be that the man will be the sole owner of the property. However, the courts have held in these cases that the parties' true common intention must have been that the women would have had rights in the property but for the lies told to them by the men. Consequently, the women would be found to have had rights in the property on common intention principles. So, in *Eves v Eves*[63] the claimant was told by the defendant that her name could not be put on the legal title of the property until she was 21. It was held that because the defendant had led the claimant to believe that she would acquire a beneficial right in the property by using excuses, when in truth he intended to deny her any rights in the property, then the claimant was entitled to an equitable interest in the property. In *Grant v Edwards*[64] the defendant gave the claimant an excuse for not putting her on the legal title immediately but suggested that her name would be added to the legal title in the future. Consequently, it was held that the excuse amounted to a representation that she would acquire such a right in the future and therefore it would be unconscionable to deny her a right in the property. In *Van Laetham v Brooker*[65] the defendant provided an excuse for not putting the land in question in joint names, namely that the woman would have had to pay capital gains tax if the property had been put in her name. In each of these cases, the couple did have express discussions which led to the man purportedly taking the entire interest in the property. However, because those discussions were based on lies and excuses intended to prevent the woman from having rights which she otherwise could have had, then the true intention of the parties was found to be that the woman should have rights in the property.

15.8 PROPRIETARY ESTOPPEL

15.8.1 The test underlying the doctrine of proprietary estoppel

This section considers the doctrine of proprietary estoppel as it relates to the home. Chapter 13 considered the breadth and scope of equitable estoppel in greater detail. The reader is therefore also referred to that chapter for a more detailed discussion of these principles and of recent cases. This section operates as a reminder of the main principles in that discussion as they apply to ownership of the home. It should be remembered that proprietary estoppel has been treated in three different ways in the case law discussed in this chapter. First, proprietary estoppel has operated as an entirely distinct doctrine in many cases with no mention of common intention. Second, proprietary estoppel has been purportedly treated as though it was the same as the common intention constructive trust – as in *Lloyds Bank v Rosset* – but without any explanation as to how those two doctrines could be elided together (because one would need to change radically to accommodate the other). Lord Walker suggested in *Stack v Dowden* that proprietary estoppel should not be merged with constructive trusts. Third, proprietary estoppel has been ignored altogether when attempting to summarise the law in this area, for example in *Jones v Kernott*.

The modern understanding of the doctrine of proprietary estoppel was set out most clearly by Edward Nugee QC in *Re Basham*[66] to the effect that a claimant will make out the estoppel

---

63 [1975] 1 WLR 1338, 1342, *per* Lord Denning.
64 [1986] Ch 638.
65 [2005] EWHC 1478 (Ch).
66 [1986] 1 WLR 1498.

when a representation was made by the defendant on which the claimant reasonably relied to their detriment.[67] This is the first stage of the process: making out the estoppel. The second stage of the process (considered in detail below) is identifying the appropriate remedy. What is important is that proprietary estoppel is a remedial doctrine: that means the court is empowered to decide what outcome it wants to order to fit the circumstances at the end of the trial. It is clear on the authorities that the courts may order a transfer of the entire interest in the property to the claimant at one end of the spectrum, through to a mere order for an amount of money to compensate the detriment which the claimant has suffered.

The principal differences between proprietary estoppel and the common intention constructive trust are twofold. First, proprietary estoppel is a remedial doctrine because its remedy is imposed at the date of trial and takes effect prospectively from that date (unlike a constructive trust which recognises the existence of a right retrospectively).[68] The proof of this proposition is demonstrated by the fact that that remedy may range from the award of the freehold over property through to a mere award of monetary compensation. The claimant does not know what form of remedy she will receive and therefore that remedy only exists prospectively from the date of the judgment. Second, proprietary estoppel arises on the basis of three clear elements: representation, reliance and detriment. This makes this claim popular with some litigators because it can be easier to know whether or not you have a strong case because you ask whether or not you can prove those three elements from the outset. By contrast, the generalities of ordinary constructive trusts and their doctrine of good conscience seem to be vaguer than proprietary estoppel, and it may seem to litigators that their clients' claim is more speculative as a result. Of course, in relation to the concept of common intention, the judgments of Lady Hale and Lords Walker and Kerr in *Jones v Kernott* have clarified the test helpfully.

15.8.2 The nature of the representation

The principles in the case law governing representations have expanded in recent years. The most significant decision, in many senses, was the decision of the House of Lords in *Thorner v Major*[69] in which two Somerset farmers, who were described by the judge as being taciturn, untalkative men by nature, failed to discuss the prospects of a farm passing from one of them to the other when the first man died. Nevertheless, the court held that there had been enough in the circumstances for the claimant to argue that he had formed the reasonable impression that the farm would be left to him. The long, long hours he worked on that farm for many years in heavy manual labour must have influenced the court to find such a representation. The outcome for the doctrine of proprietary estoppel is that a 'representation' may be made without anything being said on the subject! There does not need to be a 'signature event' at which a clear representation is made:[70] which means that there does not need to be a single moment when the representation is made. It is enough that the 'relevant assurance' which was made was 'clear enough' in the context. So, if the representor was 'standing by in silence' aware that the claimant was acting to his detriment on the belief that he was thus

---

67 *Ibid; In Re Sharpe (A Bankrupt)* [1980] 1 WLR 219.
68 *In Re Sharpe (A Bankrupt)* [1980] 1 WLR 219.
69 [2009] 1 WLR 776.
70 *Ibid*, para [24], *per* Lord Rodger.

acquiring a right in the property, then that would be enough to grant him rights on the basis of proprietary estoppel because the representor would have understood the effect which his words were having on the claimant when the claimant began to suffer detriment.[71]

The Court of Appeal in *Gillett v Holt*[72] held that there need not be a single statement on a single day which constitutes the representation, but rather than an impression can be formed over time by a series of statements such as promises that 'one day this will be yours' at birthday celebrations and so forth. Therefore, a series of suggestions made at family gatherings over a number of years which caused the claimant to believe that doing work on land for low wages would lead to the acquisition of some interest in the land was sufficient to constitute a representation. It is important that the person making the representations must appreciate the effect which they are having in the mind of the claimant. The court will not find representations where it would be unreasonable to do so. For example, in *Lissimore v Downing*[73] a millionaire rock musician took a woman with whom he had begun a casual relationship back to his enormous country home, complete with farmland, and said something along the lines of 'I'll bet you would love to be the lady of this manor'. Their relationship continued for a while. Later, the woman claimed that these sorts of statements by the rock musician must be taken to constitute representations that she would acquire property rights in his extremely valuable estate. The court held that those sorts of statements could not have been intended to constitute binding representations from which she could derive property rights.

15.8.3 The nature of the remedies awarded under proprietary estoppel

Proprietary estoppel may arise so as to achieve a number of different objectives. The first objective identified in the cases is to avoid the claimant suffering uncompensated detriment. In *Walton Stores v Maher*,[74] Brennan J held that the objective of the estoppel is not to compel the defendant to perform their promise; but rather it is to avoid the detriment that will result from the representation not being performed. Lord Browne-Wilkinson held in *Lim v Ang*[75] that the purpose of proprietary estoppel is to provide a response where 'it is unconscionable for the representor to go back on the assumption that he permitted the representee to make', that is, to avoid the detriment caused from retreating from that representation and to prevent unconscionability.

There are cases like *Pascoe v Turner* in which the court passed the freehold in property to the claimant because she had been promised that she would be able to live in the property for the rest of her life. Oddly, her detriment had only been to pay for a small amount of work to be done on the property. Another way of dealing with the case of *Pascoe v Turner*[76] would have been to pay the claimant an amount of money equal to her expenditure and then to allow the freehold to pass where the freeholder had intended. Nevertheless, the award of the freehold appeared to be concerned with enforcing the promise rather than compensating detrimental reliance on any representation. Similarly, in *Re Basham*[77] the claimant was awarded

---

71 *Ibid*, para [55], *per* Lord Walker.
72 [2001] Ch 210.
73 [2003] 2 FLR 308.
74 (1988) 62 ALJR 110.
75 [1992] 1 WLR 113, 117.
76 [1979] 1 WLR 431.
77 [1986] 1 WLR 1498.

title over a house because she had nursed the freeholder, had solved a boundary dispute at the property and had passed up the opportunity offered to her by her husband's employers to live in a house which came with her husband's job. Again, her detriment could have been compensated by an amount of money just as Walker LJ held in *Jennings v Rice* that £200,000 would compensate decades of working unpaid for a wealthy woman before she died. In both cases, the house was left by will to another person. Yet in *Basham* it was held that the claimant should be entitled to the freehold, whereas in *Jennings v Rice* the claimant merely received money so as to prevent him being treated unconscionably by being denied anything at all. The same approach was taken in *Campbell v Griffin*.[78] The expression which was used in cases like *Crabb v Arun DC*[79] was that the court was looking to do 'the minimum equity necessary' between the parties. This general expression permits the court to decide what it thinks is an appropriate remedy. A combination of remedies can be made: in *Gillett v Holt* the claimant was awarded a freehold over a cottage on farmland which he had renovated, together with a field on which he had worked hard and a sum of money as well.

One of the most interesting cases in this area was the decision in *Baker v Baker*[80] in which the court ordered that an elderly man (who could have been awarded a share of the equitable interest in the home he had acquired with his relatives) would be paid an amount of money which was sufficient to buy an annuity which would generate enough income to pay for nursing care for that man for the rest of his life. The court used the flexibility of proprietary estoppel principles to cater for the man's needs rather than to provide him with property rights which in themselves would not care for him in his old age.

Another good example of the flexibility of the proprietary estoppel in action is *Porntip Stallion v Albert Stallion Holdings (Great Britain) Ltd*.[81] Porntip Stallion, who was from the Philippines, came to London to work for Albert Stallion in 1984 and later married him in June 1989. She lived at Stallion's property in London with him. The couple divorced in 1995. Albert promised Porntip that she could continue to live in the property provided that she did not contest the divorce petition. This was in Albert's interests and to Porntip's detriment because she could have acquired greater property rights if she had contested the divorce petition. In the meantime Albert married Lilibeth in the Philippines in 1996 before they moved to London together. Porntip had continued to occupy the property after the divorce. Interestingly, she occupied that property with Albert and Lilibeth. Albert Stallion died in 2004. Porntip argued that representations had been made to her that she would be able to live at the property rent-free for the rest of her life, and that she had suffered detriment in not contesting the divorce in reliance on those representations. Judge Asplin QC found[82] (following *Thorner v Major*[83]) that 'on the balance of probabilities' such representations had been made and that Porntip had relied upon those representations to her detriment. It was held that Porntip would be entitled to occupy the property rent-free for the remainder of her life. She would not be granted exclusive possession of the property, but rather she would be required

78 [2001] EWCA Civ 990.
79 [1976] Ch 179.
80 (1993) 25 HLR 408.
81 [2009] EWHC 1950 (Ch), [2010] 1 FCR 145.
82 [2010] 1 FCR 145, [110] *et seq*.
83 [2009] UKHL 18.

to occupy the property in common with Lilibeth (and her new husband and daughter).[84] On the facts it was found that the parties would be able to live together in tolerable harmony.

Proprietary estoppel will thus provide an entitlement to a broad range of remedies the application of which is at the discretion of the court. The court's discretion will be exercised so as to prevent the detriment potentially suffered by the claimant. What is less clear, then, is the basis on which proprietary estoppel arises. The role of estoppel is to prevent a legal owner from relying on common law rights where that would be detrimental to another. Alternatively, proprietary estoppel might be bundled up with the constructive trust notion of preventing unconscionable conduct more broadly, in particular if *Rosset* is taken to have elided the concepts. Some authorities would describe proprietary estoppel as raising a 'mere equity' which is binding only between the parties until the judgment is performed. Evidently, in many situations, proprietary estoppel is the only means by which a claimant can sue *and* be awarded rights in land. For example, the award made in *Pascoe* operates in the face of *Rosset*, which would not have awarded any proprietary rights to the claimant for mere decorative work on the building. Consequently, the doctrine has the hallmarks of a *de facto* claim made to preclude unconscionability rather than to deal with the claimant's pre-existing property rights.

15.9 THE PRINCIPLES IN *STACK V DOWDEN* AND *JONES V KERNOTT*

15.9.1 Introduction

This section considers the decision of the House of Lords in *Stack v Dowden*[85] and the later decision of the Supreme Court in *Jones v Kernott*.[86] The decision in *Jones v Kernott* is, in large part, a commentary on the decision in *Stack v Dowden*. Therefore, to make sense of the judgments in *Jones v Kernott* we need to begin with an analysis of *Stack v Dowden*. That is the approach we shall take here.

15.9.2 What the House of Lords decided in *Stack v Dowden*

Put simply, *Stack v Dowden* concerned an unmarried, heterosexual couple who bought a house together. She contributed the larger part of the cash contribution, approximately 65% of the total, because she earned more than he did. The House of Lords held that she should receive a 65% share of the equitable interest. Clearly, the outcome is not the most interesting aspect of this case. Rather, the rationales which were advanced by the court were more interesting. The most significant judgment was that delivered by Baroness Hale, with whom the majority agreed. It was held that if there is more than one person registered on the legal title of the home then those legal owners should be presumed to be the owners of the equitable interest in that home equally; whereas, if there is only one person registered on the legal title of the home then that sole legal owner should be presumed to be the sole owner of the equitable interest in that home. These presumptions were merely presumptions, and could therefore be rebutted by any evidence which suggested that the parties' common intention

---

84 [2010] 1 FCR 145, [137] and [138].
85 [2007] UKHL 17, [2007] 2 WLR 831.
86 [2011] UKSC 53, [2011] 3 WLR 1752.

was something different from the presumption. As Baroness Hale held: '[t]he search is to ascertain the parties' shared intentions, actual, inferred or imputed, with respect of the property in light of their whole course of conduct in relation to it'.[87] These principles were upheld in *Jones v Kernott*.

Baroness Hale approved the general drift in the law which was suggested by *Oxley v Hiscock* (and thus *Midland Bank v Cooke*), in particular taking into account the whole course of dealing between the parties and not simply their financial contributions to the purchase price of the property when assessing their common intention.[88] Significantly, unlike *Oxley v Hiscock*, the majority of the House of Lords did not agree that the court could simply identify what they considered to be fair. This is interesting because looking for what is fair (if no common intention can be identified) is the fall-back position which is identified in *Jones v Kernott*: there, Lady Hale and Lord Walker held that the court should look for what is fair when they cannot find a clear common intention.[89] The movement towards fairness in *Kernott* is a progressive step because it liberates the courts to identify the appropriate outcome in any given case. It is an equitable step away from the obscurity of the concept of a common intention.

15.9.3 The facts in *Stack v Dowden*

The precise facts in *Stack v Dowden* were as follows. Ms Dowden was a successful electrical engineer who contributed the majority of the family's finances. Mr Stack was a self-employed builder and decorator. The couple began a relationship in 1975. Ms Dowden bought a house in her sole name in 1983. Over time, they had four children. The couple sold their first house for three times its purchase price and then bought a second home in their joint names. Ms Dowden provided 65% of the purchase price of the second home, with the balance being provided by way of a mortgage. Ms Dowden paid off about 60% of the capital on the mortgage. Mr Stack paid for the mortgage interest instalments, and the parties separately paid the premiums on separate endowment insurance policies. The couple kept their bank accounts separate, in large part because Mr Stack operated his business accounts separately. The House of Lords upheld the judgment that the equitable interest in the property should be divided 65:35 in favour of Ms Dowden. Undertaking a survey of the entire course of dealing between the parties, including the extensive work which Mr Stack had performed on both properties, the equitable interests nevertheless closely reflected their financial contributions in fact, such that Ms Dowden received 65% of the equitable interest.

15.9.4 The individual judgments in *Stack v Dowden*

Simply put, Lords Hoffmann, Hope and Walker agreed with Baroness Hale. Lord Neuberger delivered a dissenting judgment. Nevertheless, each judge delivered a judgment. We shall consider each in turn. Lord Hope suggested that English law might become the same as Scots law in this area, even though Scots law does not have a concept of equity. Lord Walker – the trusts law specialist in the court – put aside his judgment so as to agree with Baroness Hale. Lord Walker did not persist with his support for the concept of unconscionability in earlier

87 [2007] 2 AC 432, para [60].
88 [2007] UKHL 17, [2007] 2 WLR 831, para [61] *et seq.*
89 See *Holman v Howes* [2007] EWCA Civ 877, para [29], *per* Lloyd LJ.

cases such as *Jennings v Rice*. Nevertheless, he did make three important arguments. First, that this area of law will not develop into unjust enrichment and instead will remain a part of equity. Second, that the concepts of constructive trust and proprietary estoppel should not be fused together. Third, that *Lloyds Bank v Rosset* had many features that opened it up to criticism, although it was not expressly overruled. Lord Walker explicitly decided not to consider the 'academic questions' which abound in this area. Lord Hoffmann raised an interesting idea in argument (but did not mention it in his judgment) to the effect that the law could develop so as to create an 'ambulatory constructive trust' which refers to a constructive trust which would change over time as the parties' circumstances change. The difficulty with such a concept is that it is unclear what would make it 'ambulate' and what are the poles between which it could ambulate.

The leading speech was delivered by Baroness Hale. Her Ladyship did not set out a clear test in the way that Lord Bridge did in *Rosset*, for example. Instead, she hoped that the Law Commission would generate clear proposals for legislation in this area. However, as this writer can attest from past experience advising politicians in Parliament in this area, no politician wants to promote legislation in this field because there are no 'goodies' and no 'baddies', which is the way politicians like things. The cases are so disparate and the relationships so different from one another that trying to produce a single model which will answer all cases is a fruitless exercise. Similarly, her Ladyship hoped that the use of TR1 land registration form would mean that solicitors would identify their clients' wishes as to ownership of the property. Unfortunately, many high street solicitors and conveyancing specialists do not seem to understand the detail of this area of law and many other cases (like *Hammond v Mitchell*) involve situations in which one person moves into a home that is already owned by the other person such that there is no acquisition using a TR1 land registration form.

Baroness Hale introduced the two presumptions set out above: that is, the entry on the legal title will govern the equitable interest presumptively. Importantly, because those presumptions can be rebutted by evidence of common intention it remains important to understand all of the preceding cases discussed in this chapter on the concept of common intention. Therefore, all of the law before *Stack v Dowden* will still be important to identify both those situations in which people other than the legal owners can acquire an equitable interest in that property, and also the circumstances in which the proportionate shares of the parties in the equitable interest can be greater or less than an equal share in that equitable interest. Significantly, Baroness Hale expressed approval for the approach which has been identified in this chapter as the 'family assets approach': that is, an approach which undertakes a survey of the entire course of dealing between the parties and which is not limited to the financial contributions of the parties. To that limited extent, *Oxley v Hiscock* is approved. However, her Ladyship did not approve (in this judgment, unlike *Jones v Kernott*) the use of the concept of fairness nor the attempt to reconcile all of the earlier cases.

As outlined above in relation to the balance sheet cases, Lord Neuberger delivered a dissenting judgment which advocated the use of resulting trusts to identify the initial rights of the parties prior to adjusting those rights when later circumstances justified such an adjustment. His lordship would not permit the use of a general idea of fairness to impute rights to the parties.[90]

---

90   [2007] UKHL 17, [2007] 2 WLR 831, para [125].

15.9.5 The key passages from the judgment of Baroness Hale in *Stack v Dowden*

Two ideas from the speech of Baroness Hale in *Stack v Dowden* have been accorded great significance in later cases. First, the question whether the courts should 'infer' the parties' common intention by deducing it from the evidence, or whether the courts should 'impute' the parties' common intention by means of supplying the parties' common intention for them. Baroness Hale held that:[91]

> The search is to ascertain the parties' shared intentions, actual, inferred or imputed, with respect to the property in the light of their whole course of conduct in relation to it.

In *Jones v Kernott* this issue was discussed in terms of the court needing to identify what the parties' common intention must have been as deduced from whatever objective evidence is available.

Second, the law is focused on 'undertaking a survey of the whole course of dealing' between the parties, but not simply looking for what the court considers to be 'fair'. A financial contribution could readily give rise to a finding of common intention. The question is then what else will give rise to a finding of common intention. As Chadwick LJ held in *Oxley v Hiscock*, 'in many such cases, the answer will be provided by evidence of what they said and did at the time of the acquisition'.[92] When considering what other factors may give rise to rights at a later time, Chadwick LJ held that the court should analyse 'the whole course of dealing between them in relation to the property which includes the arrangements which they make from time to time in order to meet the outgoings (for example, mortgage contributions, council tax and utilities, repairs, insurance and housekeeping) which have to be met if they are to live in the property as their home'.[93]

15.9.6 The development of the principles in *Stack v Dowden* in subsequent cases

The decision in *Stack v Dowden* was commonly considered to have been a missed opportunity to move the law out of the shadow of the previous decision of the House of Lords in *Lloyds Bank v Rosset* and to assert new principles. Instead, Baroness Hale put her faith in future legislation and in the continuation of general principles of common intention in the absence of a general concept of fairness. Subsequent judgments, prior to *Jones v Kernott*, seized on the idea generated by Baroness Hale that 'the search is to ascertain the parties' shared intentions, actual, inferred or imputed, with respect of the property in light of their whole course of conduct in relation to it'.[94]

The Court of Appeal in *Holman v Howes*[95] held that simply launching an inquiry into what is 'fair' between the parties would be 'impermissible'.[96] Sir John Chadwick in the Court

---

91 *Stack v Dowden* [2007] UKHL 17, [2007] 2 WLR 831, para [60].
92 [2007] UKHL 17, [2007] 2 WLR 831, para [61].
93 [2007] UKHL 17, [2007] 2 WLR 831, para [61].
94 [2007] UKHL 17, [2007] 2 AC 432, para [60]. See also *Bindra v Chopra* [2008] EWHC 1715 (Ch); and *Morris v Morris* [2008] EWCA Civ 257.
95 [2007] EWCA Civ 877, [2007] BPIR 1085, para [29] *et seq, per* Lloyd LJ.
96 *Ibid*, para [32].

of Appeal in *James v Thomas*[97] held that the common intention between the parties can be formed at any time (whether before, during or after acquisition of the property) and accepted that a judgment as to the fairness of the situation cannot be the sole criterion but rather must follow an inquiry into the parties' common intention. The decisions of the Court of Appeal in *James v Thomas*[98] and *Morris v Morris*[99] demonstrated that in the absence of an express agreement after the date of acquisition, the courts will generally be reluctant to infer an intention to vary the parties' pre-acquisition beneficial interests in the home based on their conduct alone. Exactly that point was made in *Mirza v Mirza*.[100] So, in *James v Thomas* it was found to be insufficient that the claimant performed extensive acts of physical labour on the property for her to acquire a right in the property to vary their previous understanding. In *Morris v Morris*,[101] Peter Gibson LJ explained that the fact that the claimant was starting a riding school business or that the claimant was participating in the farm business was insufficient to suggest that the defendant was representing (either for constructive trust or for proprietary estoppel purposes) that the claimant was intended to acquire any greater beneficial interest in the farm or other property.[102]

That the law remained confused was evident from the decision of the Court of Appeal in *Williams v Parris*[103] which proceeded primarily on the basis of *Lloyds Bank v Rosset* in finding that there was an agreement sufficient to constitute a common intention constructive trust between people who decided to acquire flats in their block and to let them out for their common benefit. It was held that all that was required beyond the express discussions which constituted the agreement that each person was to have an equitable interest in the property, was that the parties must have suffered some detriment. There was clearly a need for the Supreme Court to re-explain *Stack v Dowden*. The stage was set for *Jones v Kernott*.

15.9.7 The decision in *Jones v Kernott*

The decision on the facts

The decision in *Jones v Kernott* made the national news, even though it did not effect seismic change. The judgments given in that case are primarily discussions of the law in *Stack v Dowden*. The facts were easily resolved before the Supreme Court: in essence, Ms Jones had contributed approximately 90% of the cash put towards the property and Ms Jones received approximately 90% of the equitable interest. Therefore, the outcome appeared to be very similar to a resulting trust analysis, even though the court was keen to express a movement beyond legal principles based solely on financial contributions. In particular, the Supreme Court affirmed the idea of using presumptions to recognise that the equitable interest should mirror the legal title. However, those presumptions can be rebutted by evidence of a common intention to the contrary. The common intention is to be identified from objective evidence.

---

97 [2008] 1 FLR 1598.
98 [2007] EWCA Civ 1212, [2007] 3 FCR 696, [2008] 1 FLR 1598, at [36], *per* Sir John Chadwick.
99 [2008] EWCA Civ 257, at [36], *per* May LJ.
100 [2009] 2 FCR 12, 33.
101 [2008] EWCA Civ 257, at [36], *per* May LJ.
102 [2008] EWCA Civ 257, at [24]. Cf. *Thorner v Major* [2009] 1 WLR 776 where extensive physical labour on a farm was held to be suggestive of a representation that the claimant was to acquire rights under proprietary estoppel in the farm and other related property.
103 [2008] EWCA Civ 1147. In relation to the acquisition of other property, such as a boat, see *The 'Up Yaws'* [2007] EWHC 210 (Admlty), [2007] 2 FLR 444.

What is different in *Jones v Kernott* is that the court may turn to a general concept of fairness if the search for a common intention is fruitless.

Ms Jones was a mobile hairdresser; Mr Kernott was an ice cream salesman. In 1981, Jones bought a mobile home in her sole name and Kernott moved in with her in 1983. They had two children. In 1985, Jones sold her mobile home and the couple bought a property in on Badger Hall Avenue in Thundersley, Essex. The Badger Hall Avenue property was bought in their joint names. The purchase price of £30,000 was cheap because it had belonged to a relative of a client of Jones. Jones contributed £6,000 in cash by way of deposit on the property, with the remainder coming by way of an endowment mortgage in the parties' joint names. Kernott contributed £100 per week to household expenses, with Jones paying for everything else 'out of joint resources'.[104] The couple took out a joint loan to extend the property, with Kernott and friends doing the building work, with a 50% increase in the value of the property to £44,000. Kernott left in 1993 after a little over eight years of cohabitation. Thereafter, for over 14 years, Ms Jones met all the expenses associated with the property and Kernott made very little contribution to the maintenance of his two children. The parties later cashed in a joint insurance policy so that Kernott could put down a deposit on his own home, something he could afford to do in part because he was not contributing to the maintenance of his children. Jones sought to sell the property at Badger Hall Avenue and Kernott claimed that he had an equitable interest in the property. The judge at first instance found on the facts that the equitable interest in the property should be divided roughly in the proportions 90:10 in favour of Ms Jones, a division which broadly reflected their financial contributions over the nearly 23 years they had held the property and was in line with the evidence as the judge could find it in relation to the parties' intentions. The majority of the Court of Appeal, unaccountably given that Jones had paid for everything in relation to the property for 14 years, held that this was a joint tenancy which meant that Kernott was entitled to one half of the equitable interest. The Supreme Court restored the judgment at first instance. We shall turn to consider the significant, joint judgment of Lady Hale and Lord Walker.

The principles set out by Lord Walker and Lady Hale

Lord Walker and Lady Hale delivered a joint judgment in which they sought to clarify the principles which had been held in *Stack v Dowden*. Lord Walker and Lady Hale distinguished between homes in which the legal title is held in joint names and homes held in the name of only one party when they held that:[105]

'[51] . . . the following are the principles applicable in a case such as this, where a family home is bought in the joint names of a cohabiting couple who are both responsible for any mortgage, but without any express declaration of their beneficial interests:

(1) The starting point is that equity follows the law and they are joint tenants both in law and in equity.
(2) That presumption can be displaced by showing (a) that the parties had a different common intention at the time when they acquired the home, or (b) that they later formed the common intention that their respective shares would change.

---

104 [2011] 3 WLR 1121 at [38]
105 [2011] UKSC 53, [2011] 3 WLR 1121, [2011] 3 FCR 495 at [51].

As before, the court will apply the presumptions. Those presumptions can be rebutted by evidence of a common intention at the time of acquisition of the home or at a later date. The question then arises as to the manner in which the common intention is to be identified:

> (3) Their common intention is to be deduced objectively from their conduct: 'the relevant intention of each party is the intention which was reasonably understood by the other party to be manifested by that party's words or conduct notwithstanding that he did not consciously formulate that intention in his own mind or even acted with some different intention which he did not communicate to the other party' (Lord Diplock in *Gissing v Gissing*[106]). Examples of the sort of evidence which might be relevant to drawing such inferences are given in *Stack v Dowden*.[107]

This passage contains the difficult notion that the parties' own common intention is to be 'deduced objectively'. Logically, we might think that the parties' common intention would be proved by evidence of their subjective state of mind. However, there might be no evidence (such as a recording of a conversation they had) to prove what they thought. Instead, the court will have to rely on the evidence which is adduced by the parties in the witness box. In the witness box, as in *Cox v Jones*, the parties may be unreliable, biased in their own interests, and forgetful of details as a result of the passage of time. Therefore, all the court can do is to look to objective evidence and try to draw inferences from that evidence. For example, if the parties both contributed equal amounts to the bank account from which their mortgage was paid every month or if they told friends that they intended to hold the property together, then these might be the sorts of objective evidence which might indicate to the court that the property was intended to be held equally between them.

The question then is what the court should do if there is no clear evidence of the parties' common intention. It was held as follows that the court can look to what is 'fair' in the circumstances:[108]

> (4) In those cases where it is clear either (a) that the parties did not intend joint tenancy at the outset, or (b) had changed their original intention, but it is not possible to ascertain by direct evidence or by inference what their actual intention was as to the shares in which they would own the property, 'the answer is that each is entitled to that share which the court considers fair having regard to the whole course of dealing between them in relation to the property': Chadwick LJ in *Oxley v Hiscock*.[109] In our judgment, 'the whole course of dealing . . . in relation to the property' should be given a broad meaning, enabling a similar range of factors to be taken into account as may be relevant to ascertaining the parties' actual intentions.

Therefore, the court should analyse the whole course of dealing between the parties and ascertain what is fair in that context. The court is permitted to consider a full range of factors,

---

106 [1970] 2 All ER 780 at 790, [1971] AC 886 at 906.
107 [2007] 2 FCR 280 at [69], [2007] 2 All ER 929.
108 See *Graham-York v York* [2015] EWCA Civ 72 on the need to survey the entire course of dealing between the parties as a preface to considering fairness.
109 [2004] 2 FCR 295 at [69], [2004] 3 All ER 703.

unlike the narrowness in *Lloyds Bank v Rosset*. The concept of 'fairness' is not explained in any more detail. Instead, that concept is left to develop on the case law:

> (5) Each case will turn on its own facts. Financial contributions are relevant but there are many other factors which may enable the court to decide what shares were either intended (as in case (3)) or fair (as in case (4)).

The wheel has turned completely here from *Rosset*. Financial contributions matter but they are not decisive of the parties' rights. It remains to be seen how this observation will be used in future cases because *Oxley*, *Stack* and *Kernott* all came to conclusions which mirrored the parties' rough financial contributions. It was *Midland Bank v Cooke* and the proprietary estoppel cases which have demonstrated an ability to generate outcomes which are different from the parties' financial contributions to the property.

The other members of the Supreme Court did not adopt this list of five principles as being a correct statement of the law in this area, although Lord Kerr did prepare a list of principles which is very similar to the list set out above. Lord Collins agreed with the reasoning for allowing the appeal but did not express concurrence with the judgment. Lord Wilson disagreed about the desirability, in his view, of imputing a common intention to the parties, as opposed to finding the parties' subjective common intention.

The principal concept which was not mentioned in the Supreme Court in *Jones v Kernott* nor in the House of Lords in *Stack v Dowden* was 'unconscionability'. *Jones v Kernott* could have been decided on the basis that to have allowed Kernott a half share would have been unconscionable, as it would have been unconscionable to have left him with nothing. *Stack v Dowden* could have been decided on the basis that good conscience entitled Ms Dowden to a 65% share in the property in that case. The absence of the concept of unconscionability in these cases is all the more surprising given that Lord Walker had previously argued for the concept of unconscionability in judgments like *Jennings v Rice*. The law in Australia is built on exactly that concept: the court should make an order so as to ensure that neither party is treated unconscionably by denying them rights in the property. Such a principle – as opposed to the principle of fairness, which it resembles – would mirror the concept of good conscience that was outlined in Chapter 1 and is considered in Chapters 26 and 27 below.

15.10 PERSISTENT PROBLEMS WITH COMMON INTENTION

The concept of the common intention has been referred to as being a 'phantom'[110] because it usually does not exist between the parties in many of the decided cases. After all, what is a common intention? It is difficult to talk about the biggest issues in a relationship, assuming that the parties even know that they ought to be discussed. Take the relationship in *Hammond v Mitchell*. Vicki Mitchell moved into Tom Hammond's house. He already owned it (and was going through a divorce). Without a formal transfer of rights or declaration of trust, it would have required something great to form or alter their common intention. Baroness Hale's hope in *Stack v Dowden* that the TR1 land registration form would solve these issues would not deal with the situation in that case where the house was already owned by one party. How would that discussion work? 'I won't move in until you transfer me half the house. Now

---

110 *Pettkus v Becker* (1980) 117 DLR (3rd) 257.

pass the jam, please.' When two people are starting a relationship and they decide to move in together, or circumstances dictate that they must (one of them loses their home, or falls pregnant, or whatever), then when will they discuss the legal details? They are more likely to discuss the practicalities of who will pay for what, what colour they will paint the walls, and how this will affect their commute to work. The legal details will be left undiscussed. Why risk a new relationship in its most delicate, early stage by discussing who gets what share of the house? Moreover, before you read this chapter, how much of this area of law did you understand? Would you have thought to discuss all of these things?

The poet Philip Larkin expressed this problem best when he said that talking in bed ought to be easiest.[111] That word 'ought' is the problem. He does not say that talking in bed is easiest. He says that it ought to be. Lying there in the most intimate place in the home ought to be the place where anything can be discussed. Somehow, however, it becomes even more difficult to talk about the big issues for fear of causing hurt, for fear of embarrassment, or for fear of harming the relationship. In some long-term relationships it becomes more difficult to discuss things with the passage of time. When situations change (for example, when one person becomes ill or loses their job) then most people will cope with the practical problem rather than talking about its ramifications for their legal rights. People cope in a crisis because it is usually obvious what must be done, or it is obvious that there is nothing to do. The difficulty and the problem with talking about your problems comes later. Let's think about the things that matter to most people.

There is an episode of the TV show *Sex and the City* in which Carrie is trying to move her relationship with her lover, Big, to the next level. She wants to be able to leave property in his apartment as a symbol that she has a long-term place there. Just a hairdryer or a toothbrush will do it, she thinks. This causes an episode's worth of emotional turmoil as she sneaks chattels into his home, only for him to have them removed. What she cannot do is to talk to him about her problems because that would be embarrassing or it might jeopardise their relationship by bringing up difficult questions. Talking in bed ought to be easiest but it is not. At length, Big agrees to let her use one of the unused toothbrush heads from his electric toothbrush instead of leaving her own toothbrush at his apartment. She rejoices because this, to her, is a symbol of some permanence to their relationship. In property law terms it confirms that she has a mere licence to be in his apartment because she had to ask permission to use his chattels and has no freedom to introduce her own. If she did not need permission then she might have been on her way to acquiring proprietary rights like Vicki Mitchell. What this demonstrates is the difficulty of broaching the subject in the first place. 'Can I leave a toothbrush here? Some underwear maybe? Just for the nights when I stay over? It saves me bringing a bag every time.' Those simple questions mark a change in the relationship from mere casual sex to something slightly more permanent: at the very least, regular sex and breakfast. It begins to look like cohabitation. For many couples that requires discussion and careful timing. Talking in bed ought to be easiest, but often it isn't.

The common intention concept does not capture this subtlety. In relationships which start like Carrie and Big, and which progress painfully through 'the toothbrush phase', there is never a time when one could sensibly press pause and assess what the parties' common intention was. If she became pregnant then they might talk about how they could earn money, adapt their current home to accommodate a baby, or even talk about the ramifications of

---

111 Larkin, 'Talking in Bed', *The Whitsun Weddings*, Faber, 1964.

buying a new home to start a family. This is different from forming a common intention. This is reacting to circumstance. Typically, any discussions will be concerned with resolving the crisis: who will earn the money? Where will the baby sleep? Should we get married? What will I tell my wife? Those discussions will not necessarily involve any mention of the parties' property rights. So, it is more likely that the court will assess fragments of information like the parties' reaction to the news that they were about to become parents for the first time so as to create a mosaic of what the parties could reasonably be expected to have said if someone had asked them what their plans were for ownership of their home. Alternatively, the court could create a mosaic of what would be appropriate or conscionable for it to order in light of this sort of information. That is why the idea of fairness is so significant because it permits the court to assess objectively what it thinks would be appropriate when assessing the parties' respective rights in their home. The problem is that common intention is a myth because parties rarely formulate them consciously; and, even if they do, then they can go out of date very quickly as their circumstances change. When one person's perception of their common intention changes, the parties might not be able to point when the change happened nor to identify what their new intention is.

In summary, there are three significant difficulties with these cases. First, real relationships between homesharers are messier than the courts have accepted. The concept of common intention is often ill-suited to resolving those issues. The courts frequently have to 'supply' the parties' common intention (as in *Oxley v Hiscock*) because it is impossible to identify a clear, conscious common intention from the evidence. Second, the persistence of relying on financial contributions for all of the fine talk about the law having 'moved on'.[112] It is sociologically significant that *Stack v Dowden* and *Jones v Kernott* were cases in which it was the women who were the higher earners and who acquired the larger shares in the equitable interests over their homes, whereas previously it was always the men who had been the higher earners while their partners had raised the children and therefore acquired lesser rights under tests that were focused on financial contributions. And yet, the outcome of those recent cases has mirrored the effect of using a traditional resulting trust analysis. It is only the family asset cases and proprietary estoppel which have led to different outcomes. Third, the difficulties of differentiating between imputing or inferring a common intention have meant that the courts have finally had to recognise in *Jones v Kernott* the need to return to a concept of fairness, just as Lord Denning had done over 50 years ago – which only goes to show that there is nothing so new in human relationships that essential truths from years past remain relevant.

15.11 THINKING ABOUT FAIRNESS

The courts will be required to ask what is 'fair' in cases at first instance as a result of *Jones v Kernott* because evidence of the parties' true common intention will be difficult to isolate among the mass of evidence.[113] The higher courts have left us no indication as to what that might mean in recent cases. Therefore, the courts at first instance will have recourse to all of the preceding authority to decide what is fair. It is the last, and necessary, resort of the law in this area but courts at first instance require a little guidance as to how they should approach it, not least to minimise the number of likely appeals. In circumstances which involve 'intimate relationships'

---

112   [2007] 2 AC 432, at [60], *per* Baroness Hale.
113   [2011] UKSC 53, at [36].

it may be sensible to move lock, stock and barrel to adopting family law concepts which give the courts an ability to decide whatever they think is suitable for the parties. What makes judges nervous of doing this is that they do not wish to appear to be producing property law rights out of thin air.[114] Property law is easier for English judges because they appear to be giving effect to pre-existing rights and not to be fabricating them on an entirely discretionary basis.

Many of the philosophical models of fairness are built on the idea of equality. For example, John Rawls argued for fairness in his book *A Theory of Justice* (which was once a staple of university jurisprudence courses).[115] Rawls imagined how we would organise society if we began again. He asked us to imagine that society was being re-booted and that none of us would know what our role would be in the new society: millionaire, beggar or thief. Rawls proposed that in such a situation we would all agree to be equal in the new society because that would be the only fair allocation of resources. (What he was really trying to do was to make an argument for greater equality in society by imagining a utopia where we could start again.) This would be his model of fairness: equality. Just as Waite LJ relied on the equitable maxim 'equality is equity' in *Midland Bank v Cooke* to allocate Mrs Cooke a half-share in the matrimonial home, this could be one route through a decision about fairness. Family law cases have tended to start from an assumption of equality between the parties but then looked at the factors in any given case to see whether or not there is any justification for deviating from a finding of equality. This, it is suggested, could be the way in which courts of equity identify fairness on the facts of individual cases relating to ownership of the home.

114 See Rotherham, 2002, ch 10.
115 Rawls, 1971.

Chapter 16

Trusts of land

16.1 INTRODUCTION

There is a statutory scheme governing 'trusts of land' under the Trusts of Land and Appointment of Trustees Act 1996 ('TLATA 1996') dealing with trusts of land. That is the focus of this chapter. The previous chapter considered the creation of trusts over the home and disputes about whether or not parties had rights. This chapter considers trusts over land once they have been created and their operation thereafter, as governed by the Act.

16.2 TRUSTS OF LAND

16.2.1 Introduction to the treatment of trusts of land

Once a person has a right in land under some form of trust or further to a claim for proprietary estoppel, the question arises as to the operation and management of that trust. Before the enactment of the TLATA 1996, under the old s 30 of the LPA 1925, there was a presumption that the property would be sold (and so the term 'trust for sale' was used) unless some clear intention to the contrary was shown.[1] Section 30 of the LPA 1925 has since been replaced by s 14 of the TLATA 1996 with the creation of a new procedure. Similarly, the Settled Land Act 1925 was replaced by the 1996 Act. Otherwise, the general principles of trusteeship will apply to a trustee of a trust of land as to any other trustee of a trust implied by law, except as discussed below.[2]

16.2.2 The Trusts of Land and Appointment of Trustees Act 1996

Technical objectives of the Act

The TLATA 1996 was enacted further to the Law Commission Paper *Transfer of Land: Trusts of Land.*[3] The fundamental technical aim of the TLATA 1996 was to achieve the conversion of all settlements under the Settled Land Act 1925, all bare trusts, and all 'trusts for sale' under the LPA 1925 into a composite form of trust defined as a 'trust of land'. Alongside these objectives was the impetus to reform the rights of beneficiaries under trusts of land so that they could occupy the land (instead of being treated as an investment which should be sold) and to extend the categories of person whose rights should be taken into account when reaching decisions on applications for the sale of the home.

Importantly, s 3 of the TLATA 1996 abolished the doctrine of conversion. The doctrine of conversion had previously automatically converted any rights a beneficiary had in relation to a trust over land into rights in the proceeds of the sale of that land. This was because the old law treated a trust over land as being a trust to sell the land which obliged the trustees to seek a sale. This doctrine ran contrary to the intention of most people acquiring land for their own occupation, even if it did simplify the conveyancing of land held on trust by deeming that the trustees were supposed to sell the trust land. Given the automatic nature of this old doctrine, the case law had developed the notion of an implied 'collateral purpose' in trusts for sale under which the court would resist the obligation to sell the property in place of an alternative purpose which assumed that the trust land could be retained by the trustees, perhaps as a home for the beneficiaries.[4] The 1996 Act repealed all of this.

16.2.3 The meaning of 'trust of land'

For the purposes of the TLATA 1996, the term 'trust of land' means 'any trust of property which consists of or includes land'.[5] Therefore, any trust will become a trust of land if it includes a parcel of land within a more general portfolio of property, even if the remainder of the trust property is comprised of chattels and intangible property. Trusts of land include not only express trusts but also constructive trusts, resulting trusts, 'implied

---

1 *Jones v Challenger* [1961] 1 QB 176; *Re Citro* [1991] Ch 142.
2 As considered in Chapter 8.
3 Law Com No 181.
4 *Jones v Challenger* [1961] 1 QB 176; *Re Citro* [1991] Ch 142.
5 TLATA 1996, s 1(1)(a).

trusts', bare trusts and trusts for sale: indeed 'any description of trust'.[6] Trusts are caught within the scope of trusts of land whether they were created before or after the 1996 Act came into force.[7] In terms of trusts implied by law, the statute covers any trusts 'arising' before or after the coming into force of the Act, as well as any express trust consciously 'created' before or after the Act.[8] There are two forms of land which fall outwith the Act: land which was settled land under the Settled Land Act 1925 (before the TLATA 1996 came into force) or land to which the Universities and Colleges Estates Act 1925 applies.[9]

16.2.4 The functions of the trustees of land

The trustees have general powers to deal with the trust property as though they were the absolute owners of the trust property, as expressed in the following terms:[10]

> For the purposes of exercising their functions as trustees, the trustees of land have in relation to the land subject to the trust all the powers of an absolute owner.

Therefore, the trustees are entitled to deal with the property held under the trust as though they were its absolute owner. This has the benefit of reassuring third parties dealing with the trustees as to the trustees' capacity and of confirming to the trustees what their capacities are in that context. The reference to 'their functions as trustees' in s 6(1) is a reference to the powers and the obligations of the trustees considered in Chapters 8–10 of this book and the specific terms of the trust instrument dealing with the powers of the trustees.

Nevertheless, the trustees are required to act in the best interests of the beneficiaries and to avoid any conflict of interest between their personal and their fiduciary capacities. Within the TLATA 1996, there is also an express restriction to the effect that:[11]

> The powers conferred by [s6] shall not be exercised in contravention of, or of any order made in pursuance of, any other enactment or any rule of law or equity.

Within the reference to the 'rule of . . . equity' can be supposed to be a reference to the principles limiting the powers of trustees, as considered above in Part 3 of this book generally. In any event, the trustees are expressly required by statute to 'have regard to the rights of the beneficiaries'.[12] Furthermore, the TLATA 1996 provides that the generality of the power does not operate so as to override any restriction, limitation or condition placed on the trustees by any other 'enactment'.[13]

---

  6 *Ibid*, s 1(2)(a). The reference to 'trusts for sale' is to trusts falling under the LPA 1925, a code repealed by the 1996 Act.
  7 TLATA 1996, s 1(2)(b).
  8 *Ibid*, s 1(2)(b).
  9 TLATA 1996, s 1(3).
 10 TLATA 1996, s 6(1).
 11 TLATA 1996, s 6(6).
 12 *Ibid*, s 6(5).
 13 *Ibid*, s 6(8).

The TLATA 1996 contains two further express powers for trustees. First, provided that all of the beneficiaries under the trust of land are of full age and full capacity, the general powers of the trustees include a power 'to convey the land to the beneficiaries even though they have not required the trustees to do so'.[14] The beneficiaries are then required to do 'whatever is necessary' to ensure that the property vests in them as beneficiaries subject to the possibility that a court may order them so to do.[15] Secondly, the trustees have 'power to purchase a legal estate in any land in England or Wales'.[16] This power can be exercised by way of investment,[17] to provide land for the occupation of any of the beneficiaries[18] or for any other reason.[19]

16.2.5 The trustees' duty of care

Trustees owe a general duty to exercise reasonable skill and care towards the beneficiaries in the management of their obligations.[20] Under s 1 of the Trustee Act 2000, the trustee must 'exercise such care and skill as is reasonable in the circumstances'. That duty of care and skill is to be interpreted with regard to 'any special knowledge or experience that he has or holds himself out as having' and where the trustee is a professional with regard to 'any special knowledge or experience that it is reasonable to expect of a person acting in the course of that kind of business or profession'.[21] The effect of this provision is to enlarge the potential liabilities of trustees of land, particularly those acting in furtherance of a business or profession, by imposing an implied duty to exercise reasonable skill and care in the discharge of their fiduciary obligations. The duty of care under the 2000 Act is imposed on trustees of land by means of an amendment to s 6 of the 1996 Act.

16.2.6 Exclusion and restriction of the powers of trustees of land

Importantly, the provisions of the TLATA 1996 may be excluded by the terms of the trust instrument. It is provided that those powers:[22]

> do not apply in the case of a trust of land created by a disposition in so far as provision to the effect that they do not apply is made by the disposition.

Therefore, the powers of the trustees to deal with the land as absolute owner or to partition the land can be excluded by the trust instrument itself. Moreover, the terms of s 8(1) of the TLATA 1996 would appear to have the effect of enabling the settlor to postpone the trustees' right of sale of the property indefinitely. Furthermore, in general terms the trustees are prevented from exercising either of these powers without the consent of the beneficiaries if the consent of the beneficiaries is required.[23]

---

14 TLATA 1996, s 6(2).
15 *Ibid*, s 6(2)(a) and (b).
16 TLATA 1996, s 6(3).
17 *Ibid*, s 6(3)(a).
18 *Ibid*, s 6(3)(b).
19 *Ibid*, s 6(3)(c).
20 TA 2000, s 1(1).
21 *Ibid*.
22 *Ibid*, s 8(1).
23 TLATA 1996, s 8(2).

16.2.7 Delegation of the powers of trustees of land

The TLATA 1996 has given trustees of land much wider powers to delegate their responsibilities than was possible under the Trustee Act 1925. Section 9 provides that:[24]

> The trustees of land may, by power of attorney, delegate to any beneficiary or beneficiaries of full age and beneficially entitled to an interest in possession in land subject to the trust any of their functions as trustees which relate to the land.

Consequently, the trustees are entitled to delegate their functions in relation to the land only when acting collectively. The delegation under s 9 of the TLATA 1996, requiring the trustees to act as a body and not individually, must be agreed unanimously.[25] Purchasers of the land dealing with a delegate exercising the powers of the trustees are given protection by s 9.

16.2.8 The rights of beneficiaries under a trust of land

The meaning of 'beneficiary'

The term 'beneficiary', for the purposes of the TLATA 1996, means:

> a person who under the trust has an interest in property subject to the trust (including a person who has such an interest as a trustee or a personal representative).[26]

In consequence, the definition of 'beneficiary' encompasses express trusts, constructive trusts and resulting trusts over the land. That the definition includes any person with a proprietary interest in the land has the effect that mortgagees and trustees in bankruptcy constitute beneficiaries under the terms of the Act. Similarly, trustees and personal representatives are expressly defined as falling within the definition of 'beneficiary'. The purpose behind this extensive definition is to grant *locus standi* to this broad a range of people with interests in the property to be consulted as to dealings with the property or to commence proceedings to seek an order for the sale of that property or some other order from the court.

The beneficiaries' power of consent

Section 10 of the TLATA 1996 provides as follows:

> If a disposition creating a trust of land requires the consent of more than two persons to the exercise by the trustees of any function relating to the land, the consent of any two of them to the exercise of the function is sufficient in favour of a purchaser.[27]

In effect, the statute seeks to simplify the trustees' obligations in relation to obtaining consent from all of the people who might have been required to consent under the terms of the trust

---

24 *Ibid*, s 9(1).
25 *Ibid*, s 9(3).
26 TLATA 1996, s 22(1).
27 *Ibid*, s 10(1).

instrument. Section 14(2) of the TLATA 1996 permits the trustees to acquire an order from the court to relieve them of the requirement to obtain the consent of any person connected with the operation of the trustees' functions, which may be useful if some of the beneficiaries refuse to cooperate or even to respond to the trustees' requests.

The beneficiaries' rights to be consulted by the trustees

The TLATA 1996 provides for beneficiaries to be consulted by the trustees in relation to the carrying out of any of their powers.[28] Section 11 provides:[29]

> The trustees of land shall in the exercise of any function relating to land subject to the trust –
>
> (a)   so far as practicable, consult the beneficiaries of full age and beneficially entitled to an interest in possession in the land, and
> (b)   so far as consistent with the general interest of the trust, give effect to the wishes of those beneficiaries, or (in case of dispute) of the majority (according to the value of their combined interests).

The trustees are not obliged to obey the beneficiaries, merely to consult with them. Nevertheless, failure to consult the beneficiaries at all when required to do so will itself constitute a breach of trust.[30] Moreover, it might be that if the trustees failed to take into account some relevant consideration raised by the beneficiaries, then any decision made on that basis might be capable of being set aside.[31] Section 14(2) of the TLATA 1996 permits the trustees to acquire an order from the court to relieve them of the requirement either to consult any person or to obtain the consent of any person connected with the operation of the trustees' functions.

The beneficiaries' limited rights of occupation

One of the underlying aims of the changes introduced by the TLATA 1996 was to grant beneficiaries under trusts of land a qualified right to occupy land held on trust for them. The contexts in which this right of occupation was permitted will, in some circumstances, limit the rights of some beneficiaries to occupy the land at the expense of others. Section 12 of the TLATA 1996 provides that:

> A beneficiary who is beneficially entitled to an interest in possession in land subject to a trust of land is entitled by reason of his interest to occupy the land at any time if at that time –
>
> (a)   the purposes of the trust include making the land available for his occupation (or for the occupation of beneficiaries of a class of which he is a member or of beneficiaries in general), or
> (b)   the land is held by the trustees so as to be so available.

---

28   TLATA 1996, s 11(3).
29   TLATA 1996, s 11(1).
30   *Re Jones* [1931] 1 Ch 375; *Crawley Borough Council v Ure* [1996] QB 13; [1996] 1 All ER 724.
31   *Re Hastings-Bass* [1975] Ch 25.

Therefore, the 1996 Act provides for a right of occupation for any beneficiary whose interest is in possession at the material time. What is clear is that no beneficiary has a right to occupy the land simply by virtue of being a beneficiary under a trust of land.[32] Rather, the terms of the trust instrument must entitle the beneficiary to go into occupation and, therefore, the trust instrument must not contain provisions which exclude that possibility. The right of occupation, as expressed in s 12, can be exercised at any time and therefore need neither be permanent nor continuous.

The exclusion of beneficiaries from occupation of the property

The more contentious part of the legislation is that in s 13(1) whereby the trustees have the right to exclude beneficiaries in the following circumstances:

> Where two or more beneficiaries are entitled under s 12 to occupy land, the trustees of land may exclude or restrict the entitlement of any one or more (but not all) of them.

The limits placed on this power by the legislation are set out in s 13(2):

> Trustees may not under subsection (1) –
>
> (a) unreasonably exclude any beneficiary's entitlement to occupy land, or
> (b) restrict any such entitlement to an unreasonable extent.

Therefore, the trustees are restricted from excluding any beneficiary unreasonably. In deciding which of the beneficiaries to allow into occupation and which to exclude from occupation, the trustees are required to take into account 'the intentions of the person or persons . . . who created the trust'[33] and 'the purposes for which the land is held . . .'[34] and 'the circumstances and wishes of each of the beneficiaries . . .'.[35] Therefore, all that the s 13 power to exclude achieves is the application of the purposes of the trust, while recognising that the trustees do have the power to exclude beneficiaries.

The mechanics of the statutory trust in favour of a minor

A statutory trust is automatically created in any situation in which a legal estate is purportedly conveyed to a minor.[36] A question arises as to the operation of that trust when, for example, a lease (which is a legal estate) is purportedly granted to a minor. In *Hammersmith & Fulham LBC v Alexander-David*[37] a 16-year-old girl was granted a tenancy over a local authority flat which, further to Sch 1 of TLATA 1996,[38] the local authority held on trust for her. This raised the interesting problem that the local authority as her landlord could not serve her with a notice to quit for two reasons: first, such a notice to quit should be served on the trustee, not the beneficiary; and, second, the landlord was also trustee and therefore serving the notice to quit would appear to constitute a breach of trust because the trustee would be terminating the trust in so doing. The

---

32 *IRC v Eversden* [2002] STC 1109 at para 25.
33 TLATA 1996, s 13(4)(a).
34 *Ibid*, s 13(4)(b).
35 *Ibid*, s 13(4)(c).
36 Trusts of Land and Appointment of Trustees Act 1996, Sched 1, para 1.
37 [2009] EWCA Civ 259, [2010] Ch 272.
38 Trusts of Land and Appointment of Trustees Act 1996, Sched 1, para 1(1)(b).

local authority had nevertheless served a notice to quit on the girl. The Court of Appeal found for the young woman on the basis that the notice to quit had been served on the wrong person. It should have been served by the local authority as lessor on the local authority as trustee, and not on the tenant-beneficiary directly. Of course, this case does have the odd effect that if there is to be a valid notice to quit served then the lessor must serve that notice on itself.

16.2.9 The powers of the court to make orders, *inter alia*, for the sale of the land

The range of people entitled to petition the court

When there are disputes between the beneficiaries to a trust, or between trustees and some or all of the beneficiaries, then it is open to the parties to petition the court for an order as to how they should proceed. The parties will seek an order of the court further to s 14 of the TLATA 1996. A court which is apprised of an application under s 14 of the TLATA 1996 is free to make any order which it sees fit, except in relation to the appointment or removal of trustees.[39] Section 14(1) provides that:

> Any person who is a trustee of land or has an interest in property subject to a trust of land may make an application to the court for an order under this section.

Consequently, occupants of property can only make an application to the court if they have an 'interest in property': that is, if they have a proprietary right in the land held on trust. It is suggested that there are three categories of person with a sufficient interest in the property. First, the trustees may make an application as expressly envisaged by the statute. Second, the beneficiaries may make an application (as the archetypal person with 'an interest in property')[40] seeking an order to direct that the trustees deal with the property in a given way. The most common form of application in the decided cases relates to beneficiaries seeking a sale of the property, for example, in the event of a relationship breakdown, and thus seeking an order that the trustees effect such a sale. The respondent to such an application will typically seek either to resist the application in its entirety or to agree to such an order only on terms, for example, as to her right or the right of any children of the relationship to continue in occupation of the home. Third, an application may be made by any other person who has 'an interest in property'[41] such as a mortgagee or other secured creditors with a right secured over the home.

The powers of the court

The scope of any order which the court is entitled to make is set out in s 14(2) of the TLATA 1996 in the following terms:

> the court may make any such order –
>
> (a) relating to the exercise by the trustees of their functions (including an order relieving them of any obligation to obtain the consent of, or to consult, any person in connection with the exercise of any of their functions), or

---

39 TLATA 1996, s 14(3).
40 *Ibid*, s 14(1).
41 *Ibid*.

(b) declaring the nature or extent of a person's interest in property subject to the trust, as the court thinks fit.[42]

The principal question, then, is as to the matters which the courts are required to take into account when exercising their powers under s 14 of the TLATA 1996: s 15 sets out those matters. The four categories of persons whose interests and preferences are to be considered in relation to an exercise of a power under s 14 are as follows:[43]

(a) the intentions of the persons or persons (if any) who created the trust,
(b) the purposes for which the property subject to the trust is held,
(c) the welfare of any minor who occupies or might reasonably be expected to occupy any land subject to the trust as his home, and
(d) the interests of any secured creditor of any beneficiary.

There is a balancing act to be conducted by the court between these four potentially contradictory considerations. It does not appear that there is any significance in the ranking of these matters which the courts are required to take into account: that is, it does not seem to matter that the matters to be taken into account have been listed in this particular order.[44]

The rights of children in occupation of the property

The most contentious part of s 15 is para (1)(c), which imports into this area of trusts law the need to consider the rights of children in relation to their homes. Under ordinary principles of trusts law, children do not have rights in the home on the basis that they are unlikely to have made a financial contribution to the acquisition of the property. Consequently, ordinary trusts law would not consider the rights of children in deciding the allocation of rights in the home, as considered in Chapter 15. The inclusion of para (c), therefore, requires that the position of the children be taken into account for the first time.

The case law dealing with s 30 of the LPA 1925 did give peripheral consideration to the place of the children in making an order under that section. For example, in *Re Holliday*,[45] the needs of the children to finish their schooling were taken into account such that the order for sale of the property was made conditional on the children of the relationship reaching school-leaving age. What was obvious, however, was that the rights of a mortgagee[46] or a bankruptcy creditor[47] would always take priority over the needs of the children in those cases. In the case of *Re Citro*[48] it was held that it was no answer to an application for sale on behalf of the bankrupt's creditors that the loss of the home which was the subject of the trust would require the family to leave the area in which they lived and to uproot their children from their schooling. It was held that a sale of the property would not be refused unless the circumstances were exceptional and that this form of hardship was not exceptional.

---

42 TLATA 1996, s 14(2).
43 TLATA 1996, s 15(1).
44 *Av B* (unreported, Family Division, 23 May 1997), *per* Cazalet J.
45 [1981] 2 WLR 996.
46 *Lloyds Bank v Byrne* (1991) 23 HLR 472; [1993] 1 FLR 369.
47 *Re Citro* [1991] Ch 142.
48 [1991] Ch 142.

The significance of the introduction of s 15(1)(c) is that the needs of children might be elevated to being of equal significance to the rights of secured creditors and other people. The case of *Mortgage Corp v Shaire*[49] has suggested that the TLATA 1996 could be read as intending to alter the manner in which the old case law should be dealt with by the courts. The legislative intention might be taken to create equality between the rights of secured creditors such as mortgagees and the rights of occupants of the property and their families. This provision may lead to the importation of elements of child law and of the case law under the Children Act 1989 to this area, under which the welfare of the child is made paramount.[50]

16.2.10 The protection of purchasers of the land

Section 10 of the TLATA 1996 provides that where two or more people are to give their consent in advance of a valid sale, consent being given by any two of them is sufficient to transfer good title to the purchaser.[51]

---

49 [2001] Ch 743; [2001] 4 All ER 364. See also *Bank of Ireland Home Mortgages Ltd v Bell* [2001] 2 All ER (Comm) 920; *First National Bank plc v Achampong* [2004] 1 FCR 17.

50 *Bankers Trust Co v Namdar* [1997] EGCS 20; *Barclays Bank v Hendricks* [1996] 1 FLR 258; *Mortgage Corporation v Shaire* [2000] 1 FLR 973; *Grindal v Hooper* (2000) *The Times*, 8 February.

51 *Ibid*, s 10(1).

Chapter 17

Essay: A politics of trusts law

17.1 INTRODUCTION

In university law school courses, it is common to think of trusts law as being simply a technical subject, or even as being a bit boring. It becomes easy to think of the law you study as being 'just one thing after another' as your lecturers wheel out yet another topic in a new series of lectures. Many of the cases in Part 2 of this book in particular came from earlier centuries with distant people doing vague things which have caused obscure tests to balance on a knife edge. It is easy to see a lot of this as being irrelevant in the world.

Nothing could be further from the truth. Trusts law is of vital importance in the modern world. Trust funds are the largest investors in our stock markets (through pension funds and unit trusts, for example) and the law of trusts typically governs how our property passes after our deaths and how rights in co-owned homes are allocated. In an age of economic austerity – where a lack of public money has apparently necessitated cutting public services by 40% in each of the last two Parliaments – trusts are central to the international tax-avoidance industry which costs the British public purse many billions of pounds every year. International trusts are also central to the funding of international terrorism and serious organised crime. The beneficiary principle – that anodyne subject we studied in Chapter 4 – might be the last bulwark against an even greater flood of tax avoidance and an even greater amount of concealment of dirty money around the world.

These are political questions. In this chapter we shall consider a sociology of trusts law, and in particular the impact of trusts on women; and we shall consider how trusts law affects geopolitics.

17.2 A SOCIOLOGY OF TRUSTS LAW

17.2.1 Trusts and social class

There is an obvious point about trusts: they matter most for the richest in society. As the novelist EM Forster put it in *Howard's End*, trust is 'a luxury in which only the wealthy can indulge; the poor cannot afford it'. In the old family settlements – like those in the Jane Austen novels of the 18th century and the Dickens novels of the 19th century – it was only the landed families who owned property which needed to be left by way of trust. Therefore, all of the law which we studied in the first section of this book was based on the concerns of the rich.[1] So, the first sociological point to make here is that we are considering the law relating to the landed classes, or to commercial parties. Many cases discussed in Part 2 of this book involved litigants with noble titles and large estates, or wealthy industrialists like Gestetner and Gulbenkian. There are very few cases which relate to anyone outside those social groups. One exception was *Paul v Constance*[2] in which the parties were not rich. However, the lack of availability of legal aid now means that fewer and fewer cases will be brought before the courts based on trusts law principles. Therefore, your university law school curriculum is obliging you to study a part of express trusts law which is of very little direct relevance to the bulk of society. It is not that those people might not make use of trusts, it is just that creating and operating an express trust requires such expensive professional advice that ordinary people cannot access it.

What we have seen in Part 5 of this book, relating to ownership of the home (especially Chapter 15 *Trusts of Homes*) is that trusts law is relevant to ordinary people. When this area of law began in 1970 with the decision of the House of Lords in *Pettitt v Pettitt*[3] and then in *Gissing v Gissing*[4] the following year, the social classes which owned their own homes were the landed classes and the affluent middle class. To illustrate how different an age that was, the first credit card in Britain was only released by Barclays Bank in the 1970s.[5] When *Jones v Kernott*[6] was decided by the Supreme Court in 2011, the parties were a hairdresser and an ice-cream salesman. Noble callings, of course, but nevertheless symptomatic of a great shift in British society: many more people own their own homes in the 21st century than has ever been the case before. Consequently, trusts law has become important to a much broader range of society because their homes are worth so much more money relative to their incomes than ever before. Student readers of this book will struggle to get onto the bottom rung of the housing ladder precisely because prices have risen beyond all common sense: a house in suburban London worth £6,000 in 1970 may be worth £600,000 today. This is something which reflects a great unbalancing in the British economy, but it also makes litigation over the home seem worthwhile given the amount of money involved and the significance of the home to the parties.

1   That is, even more modern cases were using principles created in relation to the rich originally.
2   [1977] 1 WLR 527.
3   [1970] AC 777.
4   [1971] AC 886.
5   Interestingly, some husbands took the cards, which were distributed without request to many affluent customers of that bank, back to the bank because they considered the encouragement to their wives to spend money on credit to be immoral.
6   [2011] UKSC 53.

Land law is similarly locked into the concerns of the rich. Until this comparatively recent shift in home ownership patterns, the majority of the population rented their homes and many of them rented from the state. And yet most land law courses spend no time at all on public sector leases or public housing law, nor do they spend any time on agricultural law. Instead, a large amount of time is lavished on easements and covenants, instead of the more significant aspects of planning law and environmental law which apply more generally across the population. As a sociological question, our property law courses at university therefore do tend to focus on particular sections of society.

If we go back to the heroines of Jane Austen novels, they belong to the petit bourgeoisie: that is, people who expect (and are expected by society) to have servants but who worry about how they are going to pay for them. We are talking about the property rights of members of the landed classes, not about there being any property rights for their female servants. In Austen's novel, *Pride v Prejudice,* one of the heroines (Jane Bennet) rides to a neighbouring house (some miles away across the countryside). She is caught in heavy rain and contracts an illness sufficiently severe for her to be confined to bed at the neighbour's house.[7] Everyone is thrown into a panic as a result. No panic results, however, when a relay of servants carry messages and clothes backwards and forwards between the houses in the same weather. The class distinction is clear: the rich girl's sickness induces panic but the poor servants' well-being hardly matters. In the same way, trusts law was concerned entirely with the propertied classes because only those people have sufficient property to settle on trust and because only those people can afford the expensive lawyers who draft and maintain complex family settlements.

By the time we progress to the Victorian period, the protagonists in Dickens's novel *Bleak House*[8] – whose poverty is ensured by badly-drafted trusts – are in a different situation. All of the Jarndyce family in that novel come from the bourgeoisie, and many of them live in grand houses (or have relatives who can accommodate them in their grand houses); but they are often teetering on the brink of bankruptcy, like poor Miss Flite, whom we meet early in the novel and who lives in genteel poverty with her caged birds waiting for judgment from the Lord Chancellor's Court of Chancery. By the late 20th century – not least with cases like *Paul v Constance* – we can see that trusts are not always the preserve of the wealthy, although most cases in this book decided since 1990 have involved financial institutions like banks.

17.2.2 International trusts law and billionaire elites

One of the most significant aspects of modern trusts law is the use of the trust device in offshore 'tax havens' (that is, jurisdictions which charge little or no tax to investors) so that assets can be held and profits earned without regulatory oversight or without paying tax. This phenomenon is discussed in detail in Chapter 21. What it means in practice is that international terrorist and criminal organisations can hide their assets in trusts, or they can

---

7 This juxtaposition between life for the rich people above-stairs and life for the servants below-stairs is shown nicely by the use that is made of characters from the Jane Austen novel *Pride and Prejudice* (published in 1813) when it is seen from the perspective of the servants by Jo Baker in her modern novel *Longbourn* (published in 2013).

8 Published in serial form from 1852–3.

launder their assets through anonymous trusts in offshore jurisdictions around the world. Consequently, the trust is at the centre of the most important questions in global geopolitics. Recently, well-known banks like HSBC and Standard Chartered have been found to have allowed such organisations to launder their money through those banks' accounts and into the anonymity of the New York banking system from where that money can be passed anywhere in the world.[9]

17.2.3 Trusts and women

Equity was considered by judges like Lord Denning to be the potential saviour of women. When he created the 'married woman's equity' he was seeking to identify an area of equity which would protect wives from mistreatment by their husbands and being thrown out of their homes in an era before modern marriage law. At that time it was the men who owned the home and had the money to pay for it (in most circumstances) and therefore women were at a great disadvantage. It is worth noting that this equity was available to married women only, and not to unmarried women who might suffer similarly from being thrown out of their homes. Nevertheless, equity was available, in theory, to help women when the common law and Parliament would not.

In a different way, the trust was a great potential boon to women. If the paterfamilias within a family – that is, the person who ultimately owned beneficially the house and chattels which could be settled on trust – was sufficiently enlightened (or if his lawyers were) then he would create a settlement which protected his female relatives, as discussed in Chapter 2.[10] By allocating female relatives an equitable interest in property and an income from the trust, or a right to occupy identified property with an income, it was possible to maintain women who (being of that social class at that time) could not earn an income for themselves. As Cretney explains in his wonderful *Family Law in the Twentieth Century*[11] when women married before the Married Women's Property Act was passed in 1882, then their husbands became the owners of their property. The wife was said to become 'the shadow of her husband'. An awful idea. On marriage, the wife simply disappeared in a legal sense. This meant that if the wrong husband was chosen, then the wife's money would be spent and the wife herself effectively abandoned. So, an enlightened settlor would structure the family settlement so that the female relatives owned nothing outright under the trust. Instead, their rights to the trust property would be subject to discretionary trusts or powers to use the property for other people. The settlor and the trustees might have understood that the property would never be used for any other purpose but it meant that the female relatives would never become the sole equitable owners of any property with the result that their husbands could not take that property off them because it did not belong to their wives in the first place.

So, if Eleanor is entitled under a trust to occupy a cottage in Devon and to receive £2,000 per annum from an identified portion of a trust fund, it would be potentially disastrous for

---

9 http://www.hsgac.senate.gov/subcommittees/investigations/hearings/us-vulnerabilities-to-money-laundering-drugs-and-terrorist-financing-hsbc-case-history (accessed 14 March 2013). See Hudson, *The Law and Regulation of Finance*, 2013, paras 58–84 through 57–86.

10 Section 2.2.

11 Cretney, [2010].

her to be the sole beneficial owner of the cottage and to be entitled to the whole of the fund from which the £2,000 is drawn if she were to marry Mr D'astard, a secret drunk and physical bully, because D'astard could take the cottage and the money for himself when they married. Instead, it would be safer to give the trustees the power to decide which of a range of people could occupy the cottage and to give the trustees the power to appoint a maximum of £2,000 to a range of people. In that way, Eleanor would own nothing, and therefore if she was unwise enough to marry D'astard then D'astard could not take that property because it did not belong outright to Eleanor. Rather, the trustees would know that their duty was to provide for Eleanor before everyone else and therefore in practice they would decide annually to allow Eleanor to live in that cottage and to pay her £2,000, but D'astard would never be able to get his hands on any property until it was actually in Eleanor's hands. In this way a well-structured trust could protect a woman against the vagaries of the law at the time. Jane Austen's novel *Persuasion* is a great illustration of this phenomenon.

However, trusts were also the agents of poverty in women. Jane Austen gives us the best illustrations of this again. In Jane Austen's *Pride and Prejudice* the family's property was devised in the following way:[12]

> Mr Bennet's property consisted almost entirely in an estate of two thousand a year, which, unfortunately for his daughters, was entailed in default of heirs male [i.e. after his death it was left to the next male heir, or if there were none], on a distant relation; and their mother's fortune, though ample for her situation in life, could but ill supply the deficiency of his [i.e. her money was not enough to make up for the paucity of his].

Mr and Mrs Bennet had no boys, only girls. The nearest male relative was a distant cousin they hardly knew. This was unfortunate for the Bennet girls because once their father died, then their home and all of the chattels that went with it would pass to that distant relation. Consequently, they needed to contract good marriages before their father died. The settlor, another distant relative, who had created this settlement originally had clearly been caught up in the ubiquitous idea at the time that male relatives were to be preferred to female relatives. The tension in the book comes from the panic in Mrs Bennet, the mother, to marry her daughters off well, and their travails in finding good husbands.

In Jane Austen's *Sense and Sensibility*, the Dashwood girls are in the same position. They live a bourgeois life with servants but they have to worry constantly about how they can maintain their family life with a paltry income from a family settlement. When their father died, the family property passed to their brother and it was their sister-in-law who ensured that he would settle as little as possible on his sisters and mother. They too needed to contract good marriages before their sister-in-law's patience ran out. This genteel high-wire act with little money was a key feature of Austen's novels and of Georgian life in this social class. The trust was particularly important in this period because it dominated the fortunes of everyone in the propertied classes. Consequently, any change in trusts law had a direct effect on this social class as well.

---

12 J Austen, *Pride and Prejudice*, 1813, the opening paragraph to Chapter 7. If you are not familiar with Jane Austen's novels, then do read them. If you cannot bear reading them, then there are film adaptations and television boxsets which will do the hard work for you.

As we mentioned before, this sort of protection would only be available to the wealthy. Women from poor families did not have this sort of protection available to them. As the famous constitutional lawyer and historian, AV Dicey, put it

> the daughters of the rich enjoyed for the most part the consideration and protection of equity; the daughters of the poor suffered under the severity and injustice of the common law.[13]

So, it is important to start by noting that when we talk about 'women', until comparatively recently, we are talking about women from rich families.

17.3 LAW AND THE HOME

17.3.1 Intersections of the law and the home

There are many ways in which the law and the home intersect which include the following: trusts of cohabited homes, divorce law dividing homes, land law conveying private homes, the law on private leases renting homes, the law on public sector leases renting homes, the law on housing associations providing much social housing, the law and regulation of residential mortgages, and the law on homelessness governing the limited statutory rights to be advised and assisted to find a home if you are in priority need. In this book we have focused only on the ownership of private homes in cohabitation. That law covers all non-married couples seeking to divide their homes on the breakdown of their relationship; all couples seeking to establish their property rights against a mortgagee or other creditor; and non-romantic homesharers seeking to establish their rights. We have considered the rights of the straight and the gay, the romantic and the non-romantic, the traditional and the unusual. However, we have considered people who can own their own homes, or else find a mortgagee prepared to risk their ability to repay the purchase price of their property. We are therefore considering the modern landed classes – a much larger group than it was in the past: about 65% of the British population at present.

17.3.2 The limitations of common intention

The law made a great leap when the House of Lords in *Gissing v Gissing* accepted that cohabitees – particularly married couples at that time – could form a 'common intention' which would dominate their rights in their home. This was in 1971 before divorce law as we know it was created by the Matrimonial Causes Act 1973. However, that concept of 'common intention' never really made very much sense. It caused the Commonwealth nations to part from England and Wales in this area of law. Rightly, each jurisdiction – Canada, Australia and New Zealand – developed their own socio-cultural understandings of how ownership of the home should be identified. In Canada, the principles focused on the injustice of a man having a woman raise his children and look after his house without giving her property rights in that home. The man was taken to have been enriched unjustly at her expense. In Australia, the focus was on the unconscionability of denying property rights to such a person. In New

---

13   Dicey, *Law and Opinion in England*, quoted in Crane, 1965, 254.

Zealand, the courts looked to the claimant's legitimate expectations of rights in the property and sought to do what was fair.

In England and Wales, the courts played with a fiction. The fiction lay in purporting to identify the parties' common intention and to give effect to it, even though the parties may well have never formed a common intention, or that they may have changed it over time, or that they may have forgotten it, or that they may have chosen to lie about what they thought it was when they came to give evidence in court. As Chadwick LJ put it in *Oxley v Hiscock*,[14] the English courts will 'supply' the parties' common intention: that is, the court will fabricate the parties' common intention for them. Given that the court is fabricating the parties' common intention, it is only a fiction.

What the English courts forgot was that people fall in love, and that when they fall in love they fail to map out all the legal niceties of their relationships. The more common experience of falling in love is of being so infatuated, besotted and possessed by the other person that you cannot sleep (or you cannot sleep without them), or you cannot focus on any other task for more than a couple of minutes without being possessed by them again. Smells, tastes, images, moments caught in time forever. In this context, any common intention is hazy at best.

So, Lord Bridge sought in *Lloyds Bank v Rosset* to introduce clarity in this area of the law. There is no commentator who celebrates that judgment enthusiastically. And yet, to defend his lordship for a moment, Lord Bridge attempted to bring order to a chaotic area of the law, mindful presumably of its social importance. Unfortunately, his model set many of the worst aspects of the old law of resulting trusts in stone. By focusing, in relation to the common intention constructive trust by conduct, on contributions to the purchase price or to the mortgage instalments, Lord Bridge confirmed that the people with the money in a relationship – at that time, usually a man in the nuclear family model – acquired the property rights. Even the common intention constructive trust formed by agreement depended on there being some detriment suffered, such as spending money.

The rigidity of this test, and its many doctrinal problems (such as omitting the concept of resulting trust from what was clearly a resulting trust, and eliding constructive trusts with proprietary estoppel), was deaf to the reality of the lives of most unmarried and married cohabitees. In the real world, people react to circumstances. Illness requires treatment; redundancy requires someone to get work; pregnancy requires a crib. None of these events prompts ordinary people to take legal advice about its impact on their property rights. So, Lord Bridge's expectation that a common intention will be formed at the outset of a relationship and that it will continue intact throughout that relationship is simply unreasonable. People are too busy living their lives to get legal advice about them.

And what is this common intention formed at the outset of a relationship anyway? Who does form a conscious agreement about their rights at the beginning of their relationship? An example of someone who did exactly that is Dr Sheldon Cooper. Sheldon Cooper is a character in the television comedy *The Big Bang Theory*. Sheldon is the comic heart of that show because he appears to be at the extreme end of the Asperger's spectrum in that his brilliant scientific mind prevents him from understanding the attitudes and opinions of ordinary people. In one particular episode, Sheldon agrees to begin a form of relationship with Amy Farah Fowler. However, before doing so, he requires her to agree and sign a document called

'The Girlfriend Agreement' which details all of the parties' obligations in the event that the other falls ill, or needs a lift to the shops or whatever. The studio audience laughs like a drain at this aberrant behaviour. It is ridiculous for Sheldon to insist on this agreement at the start of a relationship. Yet that is exactly what Lord Bridge seems to expect that people will do.

The common intention constructive trust by agreement requires that the parties form an agreement, arrangement or understanding as to their rights in the property before the date of its acquisition, or exceptionally at some later date, in tandem with them suffering some detriment. Therefore, while the parties are going through the emotional terrain of deciding to live together in their first home – and negotiating through estate agents with the seller who is trying to squeeze every last penny out of the deal – they are expected to form this view in advance. Buying a home is important and it would be ideal if the parties thought about their common intention at the start: but they often do not. In *Stack v Dowden*[15] similarly, Lady Hale took the view that the solicitors should take the parties through the TR1 land registration form and ensure that the parties identify the rights that they intend each other to have in their home. Clearly, in practice many solicitors do not do this. In many cases, of course, the homes which the parties acquire are bought by one of them alone, or they are already owned by one of them when the relationship begins and the other person moves into the property.[16]

The other problems are in identifying exactly what a common intention is in any event. An intention as to what? As to the parties' intentions as a cohabiting unit? Let us assume we are talking about sexual couples, because non-sexual homesharers constitute an even broader range of possible motives. If the relationship begins as an ordinary romantic union of two people clinging to one another for security, warmth and orgasms, then when does the intention start? If one of them falls pregnant, then does the intention begin when they agree to have their child and how to fund their newly enlarged family? If one of them falls ill or loses their job, does the intention change at that moment? If they never speak out loud about their rights in their home, how do we tell what their common intention in relation to that home ever was? As was said in *Jones v Kernott*, do we infer objectively what their common intention must be? With reference to what information do we make that inference? Documents, emails, evidence from friends?

What of a common experience in many relationships where the parties, especially in the early stages, are afraid to tell each other what they are really thinking? In those early dates, you are prone to show the best side of yourself, to hide the bits of yourself you think will be unattractive. As time goes on, it becomes more and more difficult to reveal those parts of your inner life to the other person, until it is too late for them to do anything about it. I have a favourite postcard somewhere in which a perfect 1950s woman is smiling at us and saying: 'I think I know you well enough now to let you have a glimpse of the horrible monster I really am'. The joke is that people usually keep those parts of themselves hidden from their partner for as long as possible. In these sorts of circumstances, which elements are a part

---

15 [2007] 2 AC 432.

16 I have written in *Great Debates on Equity & Trusts*, for example, about the threat of the toothbrush. If you are the homeowner (and as the law student, it is likely that you will be the homeowner in time) then your new partner may very well want to move into your lovely home and to live in the shade of your income. The threat comes when that person starts to move their chattels into your home. Each tiny item is a flag staking claim to territory. In the vanguard of this land grab will be the toothbrush. The toothbrush is always the first thing they will leave: 'Oh it will be so much easier if I could just *leave* a toothbrush here'. Later they will leave toiletries and underwear. Then they will want a drawer of their own and later still they will want a half-share in your house.

of the parties' real individual intentions, let alone their common intention? How can we be expected to form common intentions if we are prone to conceal so much about ourselves anyway?

17.3.3 A brave new world?

The developments in the law between *Lloyds Bank v Rosset* and *Stack v Dowden* were great. After *Rosset*, most courts ignored the House of Lords authority and followed their own paths, as discussed in Chapter 15. Lady Hale made a telling observation in *Stack* to the effect that the law had 'moved on' since *Rosset*. Society had certainly moved on. Mrs Rosset was a woman who stayed at home and oversaw the development and decoration of the parties' home. Ms Stack was a successful woman who earned more than her partner and who therefore, from her separate bank account, contributed more to the purchase price of the property. As a result she received about 60% of the equity in the home for about 60% of the cash spent. In *Jones v Kernott*, Ms Jones earned more than her partner and so contributed about 90% of the money spent on the property over 14 years. Consequently, she received about 90% of the equity in the home.

For all the much-vaunted change in the law, the outcome was exactly the same as the resulting trust cases: the equitable interest was awarded in proportion to the cash contribution. It just happened that it was the women who were contributing more to some of these properties in the 21st century cases than in 1970, but the outcome was the same. So, the new law has not yet had any great effect on the outcomes in these cases.

The only authority, and the most progressive case, which has had a profound effect was *Midland Bank v Cooke*.[17] In that case, resisting a mortgagee's claim to possession, Mrs Cooke was found to have acquired a half-share in the property on the basis of the nature of her relationship with her husband more than her occasional contributions to the family's income, to meeting household expenses and so forth. In this judgment it was the unsung hero, Waite LJ, who developed the idea that the court should 'consider the entire course of dealing between the parties', and not simply the question as to whom had contributed how much to the initial purchase price. It was this concept which ushered in the possibility of taking into account a much wider range of factors than money alone. Together with developments in proprietary estoppel, it has been this conceptual development which has been central to the modernisation of the law in this area.

17.3.4 The technique of equity: family law is an equity

Modern equity is a technique. That technique is to begin with central, high-level principles of 'conscience' and 'unconscionability', and to develop meaning for those principles by means of theoretical discussion and particularly by putting those principles to work in individual cases. It is suggested that open-textured family approaches, like those used in *Midland Bank v Cooke*, are the answer to questions about ownership of the home precisely because the range of circumstances which will come before the courts are so varied that a rigid principle (like resulting trusts or *Rosset*) cannot answer them adequately.

---

17 [1995] 4 All ER 562.

Family law operates on the basis of very general principles which are applied on a case-by-case basis so that those general principles are applied in a way that is suitable for each individual case. Each divorcing couple, each child in need of a home life with its separate parents and each family unit, is different. Family law treats them as being different. In that way it seeks appropriate, principled outcomes which work on the facts of each case.

What marks family law out from other legal fields is its methodology. Let us take as an example section 1 of the Children Act 1989. That section provides that the welfare of the child is paramount. That is a very good example of a general principle. This principle sits at the heart of every decision about children: with whom shall they live? Who shall have the right to see them and when? When do those rights end? The court must always prioritise the welfare of the child. This raises questions, of course, about what is meant by 'welfare', which 'child' is to be considered first in a family with several children, and what does it mean to make it 'paramount'? Those principles have been coloured in by the courts in a succession of cases. This methodology is in line with equity: begin with a central, high-level principle and develop the application of that principle on a case-by-case basis. One future for equity in this area would be to adopt the approach of family law by establishing broadly-based, high-level principles so that they are applied consequentially on a case-by-case basis.

Part 6

Breach of trust and tracing

Chapter 18

Breach of trust

CAPSULE SUMMARY

A trustee will be liable for breach of trust if that breach of trust causes a loss to the beneficiaries. Such a trustee will be liable in the event of a breach of trust either to restore the trust property which was passed away in breach of trust or, if that is not possible, to reconstitute the value of the trust fund in cash to its level before the breach of trust, or to pay equitable compensation to the beneficiaries.[1] A trustee will be liable in the situation in which the breach of trust has caused some loss to the trust.[2] There will be no liability in respect of a breach of trust where that breach resulted in no loss to the trust.[3] The measurement of compensation will be the actual, demonstrable loss to the trust, rather than some intermediate value of the property lost to the trust.[4]

18.1 INTRODUCTION

18.1.1 The liability of trustees within the context of breach of trust more generally

This chapter considers the liabilities of the trustees of a trust for any breach of trust. That breach of trust may arise under the terms of the trust instrument specifically or under the law of trusts generally. There is a broader context to the law dealing with breach of trust, however, which it is useful to understand from the outset. The law of trusts offers litigants a uniquely broad range of remedies, which is part of the reason why some commercial people choose to use English trusts to organise their property management because they have so many remedies available to them.

The three chapters in this Part 6 of the book considers the range of doctrines dealing with breaches of trust. When there is a breach of trust (possibly where the trustees do something which is not permitted by the terms of the trust instrument or where the trustees do something which is in breach of any other rule of the general law of trusts) the beneficiaries are required to bring proceedings against the trustees in the first place. The trustees will then be obliged to recover any property lost to the trust, or to reconstitute the cash value of the trust fund out of their own pockets, and to compensate the beneficiaries for any other losses caused to the trust. In essence, once the beneficiaries bring such an action against the trustees, they can sit back because in practice the trustees will then either be required to pay up or the trustees will commence proceedings against anyone else who was involved in the breach of trust.

18.1.2 The nature of liability for breach of trust

Trustees will be personally liable for any breach of trust that causes a loss to the beneficiaries.[5] A breach of trust may be a breach of an express term of the trust instrument or it may be a breach of one of the obligations which are imposed on trustees (and which were discussed

---

1 *Nocton v Lord Ashburn* [1914] AC 932; *Target Holdings v Redferns* [1996] 1 AC 421.
2 *Target Holdings v Redferns* [1996] 1 AC 421.
3 *Ibid.*
4 *Ibid.*
5 *Target Holdings v Redferns* [1996] 1 AC 421.

in Chapters 8 through 10 of this book). The leading case in this area is the decision of the House of Lords in *Target Holdings v Redferns*.[6] The law on breach of trust has developed over the centuries from trustees being personally liable for any theoretical breach of trust to the current position where trustees are only liable if their breach has caused a loss to the trust. The remedies are threefold. First, a liability to recover any property which was lost to the trust as a result of that breach of trust. Second, a liability to reconstitute the monetary value of the trust if the original trust property cannot be recovered. Third, a liability to compensate the beneficiaries for any subsequent loss, for example if the trust fund needs to be changed or if a loss was caused by not having property in the trust fund.

No dishonesty, negligence or other mental element is required to fix a trustee with liability for breach of trust. Rather, for there to be a breach of trust, it is enough that there has been a breach of the terms of the trust or a breach of one of the duties of trustees in the general law.

18.1.3 What constitutes a breach of trust

In the leading case of *Target Holdings v Redferns*, Lord Browne-Wilkinson held that:[7]

> The basic right of a beneficiary is to have the trust duly administered in accordance with the provisions of the trust instrument, if any, and the general law.

Therefore, the most obvious example of a breach of trust would be a breach of the terms of the trust instrument.[8] If the trust instrument requires that the trustee must wear a red hat when making decisions, and if the trustee fails to do so and if that also causes loss to the trust, then the trustee will be personally liable for that loss. Alternatively, a trustee will be liable for any breach of the general law of trusts as discussed in the earlier chapters of this book. So, that might be a breach of the Trustee Act 2000 discussed in Chapter 9 (if that legislation has not been excluded by the terms of the trust instrument), or of the Trustee Act 1925, or of any of the case law discussed in earlier chapters. Among the significant case law rules in this context are the 13 general obligations incumbent on trustees which are discussed in Chapter 8, the investment obligations in Chapter 9, or the prohibitions on self-dealing and taking unauthorised profits which were discussed in Chapter 12. Any breach of any of these obligations, if it causes a loss to the trust, will lead to liability for breach of trust.

18.2 THE BASIS OF LIABILITY FOR BREACH OF TRUST

18.2.1 The development of liability for breach of trust

The law on breach of trust is now dominated by the decision of the House of Lords in *Target Holdings v Redferns*,[9] which modernised the law in this area markedly. Previously the law had imposed liability for loss on trustees for any technical breach of trust, even if it had not

---

6 *Ibid.*
7 *Target Holdings v Redferns* [1996] 1 AC 421, 434.
8 *Clough v Bond* (1838) 8 LJ Ch 51.
9 *Ibid.*

been the cause of a loss to the trust. That was reversed by *Target Holdings*. In that case, Lord Browne-Wilkinson made it plain that trustees would only be liable if their breach of trust had caused the loss suffered by the beneficiaries. Aside from that stipulation, none of the sorts of requirement about causation or foreseeability which are so significant in tort law apply in this context.

The background to breaches of trust

It is worth thinking about the background to trust administration so as to understand the sorts of problems which commonly arise in breach of trust claims. The trustees' obligations will depend on the terms of any trust instrument and on the circumstances of the particular trust. The easy cases are those in which the trustees breach the terms of the trust and cause a loss to the trust as a result. The more difficult cases are those in which the trustees think they are acting in the best interests of the trust by refusing to follow the terms of the trust. Equally, the trustees can easily become caught up in the busy work of managing the trust day to day without thinking about the terms of their trust. If the trust is comprised of a large investment fund, then the trustees will spend their time selecting the best available investment opportunities in accordance with the level of risk which the settlor was prepared to allow them to take.

Similarly, if the trust is comprised of a farm, then the trustees will be pre-occupied with questions of farm management and making the best return for the beneficiaries in the context of a market which is very difficult for farmers. Suppose a trust instrument required the trustees 'to operate the land as a milk-producing dairy farm'. With British supermarkets often paying less for milk than it costs farmers to produce that milk, the trustees may need to consider moving a dairy farm into different areas of agriculture or diversifying their dairy products into high-return products like artisan cheese or organic yoghurt. When making those sorts of decisions, the trustees may feel constrained by the terms of the trust instrument which was, by definition, drafted in the past. Sensible trustees would use the structures discussed in Chapter 10 to have the terms of the trust changed; however, less sensible trustees might start to commit technical breaches of their trust by doing things which they consider to be in the best interests of the trust, even if they breach the terms of the trust. So, if the trustees started to keep alpacas on the land for their wool, this would be in technical breach of trust but it might appear to be more profitable for the trust than maintaining a loss-making dairy herd. This may raise the question whether or not those technical breaches of trust should be actionable. If no loss is caused to the trust, then the modern law will not give the beneficiaries any right to claim compensation from the trustees, as we shall see.

Nevertheless, even if a breach of trust does not cause a loss to the trust, the trustees may still be required to administer the trust in accordance with the terms of the trust instrument. The trustees could be compelled to stop committing that breach of trust even if it is not causing a loss to the trust. For example, if the trust instrument requires investment only in Alpha Plc shares but the trustees have bought Beta Plc shares, then the beneficiaries can compel the trustees to sell the Beta Plc shares and to buy Alpha Plc shares instead. The costs of effecting the sale and the purchase would be borne by the trustees because their breach of trust would have required that expense.[10] The beneficiaries may have moral

---

10 *Re Massingberd's Settlement* (1890) 63 LT 296.

views about the business conducted about Beta Plc (perhaps it is a company that is known to pollute rivers) and therefore they may want the terms of the trust to be observed scrupulously. Alternatively, there may be situations in which the trustees will want to breach the literal terms of a trust if obeying the trust would cause a loss. For example, if the trust specified that the trustees must only acquire shares in British clearing banks at a time when there is a financial crisis (as in 2008 when the share price of banks fell catastrophically low), then the trustees would be acting in the best interests of the beneficiaries if they refused to buy shares in British clearing banks and bought shares in some other public companies instead. In such a situation, the trustees would be well-advised to seek an order from the court or an indemnity from the beneficiaries absolving them from liability in that circumstance, as well as seeking an alteration in the terms of the trust instrument as discussed in Chapter 10.

Older approaches to the law on breaches of trust

As was considered in detail in Chapter 8, the trustee owes a range of obligations under general trusts law to the beneficiaries beyond any obligations which may be included in any particular trust instrument. So, a breach of trust may arise either on the basis of a breach of an express term of the trust instrument or a breach of an obligation contained in the general law of trusts.

The trustee's principal duty is said to be to account to the trustees both in the sense of providing accounts as to the contents of the trust fund from time to time and also in the sense of justifying their actions to the beneficiaries. In the event that the trustees have breached their trust, then the beneficiaries may choose to 'surcharge and falsify the account' in the old expression, which means that they will refuse to accept it. They would then compel the trustees (possibly through litigation) to restore the trust fund.[11]

However, the language of 'surcharge and falsification' is not the language which has been used by the House of Lords in *Target Holdings v Redferns*. The modern approach to liability for breach of trust requires that the beneficiaries have suffered a loss and there must have been a causal link between the loss suffered and the trustees' actions. The older approach took a strict deterrent policy in relation to the trustees' liability for breach of trust[12] by making the trustee strictly liable for any loss which resulted from a breach of trust.[13]

18.2.2 The modern law on breach of trust: *Target Holdings v Redferns*

This section analyses the decision in the leading case of *Target Holdings v Redferns*.[14] Target wanted to lend money to people who transpired to be fraudsters. Target wanted to take a mortgage over an identified piece of land as security for the loan. The fraudsters organised for a valuer to give a fraudulently high valuation for that land so that Target would think that

---

11 Millett, 1998.
12 Hayton, 1995, 845.
13 *Clough v Bond* (1838) 8 LJ Ch 51.
14 [1996] 1 AC 421.

it was getting good security so that it would make the loan. Target did indeed make that loan but the land was worth much less than Target believed. The fraudsters took the loan moneys and disappeared. It was only then that Target realised it had been duped. Therefore, Target looked for someone to sue. Eventually, Target focused their attention on Redferns, a firm of solicitors who had acted for Target in the transaction. Redferns had been completely innocent of the fraud and had taken no part in it whatsoever. What Redferns had done, however, was to act as trustee for Target by holding the loan moneys on trust in one of its client accounts while waiting for the loan transaction to go ahead. In breach of that trust, Redferns had dipped into that trust account; but Redferns had replaced the money before the loan moneys had to be paid out. So, there had been a technical breach of trust by Redferns (in dipping into the trust account) but that had not caused any loss to Target or anyone else (because the loss had been caused by the fraudsters' over-valuation of the mortgaged land). Nevertheless, Target sued Redferns for breach of trust and sought to recover the whole amount which it had lost to the fraudsters.

It was held by the House of Lords that Redferns' breach of trust had not caused Target's loss and therefore Redferns bore no liability to account to Target. Lord Browne-Wilkinson refused to hold a trustee liable to account to the beneficiaries for a loss which had not been caused by any breach of trust which they had committed. Target had tried to argue that at the very moment that Redferns had dipped into the trust account then there had been a loss of money at that moment. This argument was rejected because Redferns had replaced the money in time for the loan to be made.[15] Lord Browne-Wilkinson was adamant: the loss that Target suffered was caused by the fraudsters and not by Redferns' breach of trust.

18.2.3 Loss as a foundation for the claim

The underpinning rationale for the decision in *Target Holdings v Redferns*[16] is that there must be a loss suffered as a direct result of the breach of trust, or else there would be beneficiaries who might seek to 'double up' on their damages by suing on a breach of trust even if that technical breach of trust actually benefited the beneficiaries. This development is contrary to the approach in the older cases which did not permit a trustee to plead some intervening act which allegedly caused the loss.[17]

The particular problem with the old approach – in which a trustee would face strict liability for any breach of trust even if there was no loss – which was identified by Lord Browne-Wilkinson in *Target Holdings v Redferns*[18] was with a 'carping beneficiary' who might benefit from the trustees acquiring shares not permitted by the trust instrument but which earned a large profit. Lord Browne-Wilkinson considered it undesirable for such a beneficiary to be able to recover compensation from the trustee for the breach of trust when she had suffered

---

15 Ironically, of course, it would have been to Target's benefit if Redferns had stopped the loan transaction from going ahead in these circumstances.
16 *Ibid.*
17 Cf. *Re Brogden* (1888) 38 Ch D 546.
18 [1996] 1 AC 421.

no loss. (However, the beneficiary would be able to require that the trustee replace the unauthorised shares with authorised shares.[19])

Re BA Peters plc, Moriarty v Atkinson shows that there must have been a trust in existence before any breach of trust can take place.[20] So, if a trustee acquires shares of an unauthorised kind before the trust comes into existence, the beneficiaries cannot claim any breach of trust. However, there may be situations in which the person who will become the trustee does some action which will poison the well for the future beneficiary of the future trust. Moreover, it is only a beneficiary who has actually suffered a loss who can sue for breach of trust. If it is a company which is the beneficiary under a trust, then shareholders of that company cannot claim that they will have suffered some loss indirectly through their shareholding.[21]

There are circumstances in which it might be difficult to identify whether or not there has been a loss caused to a trust. In Chapter 9 we considered the decision in *Nestlé v National Westminster Bank plc (No 2)*[22] in which the defendant had acted as trustee of a will trust for 60 years. The beneficiaries argued, in effect, that the low rate of return which the trustees had earned through their very cautious investment strategy was so low that it should be interpreted as being a loss when compared to the level of earnings which they should have made. The beneficiaries argued that even a rate of return equivalent to the cost of living index would have earned hundreds of thousands of pounds more for the trust. It was very difficult for the beneficiaries to prove the rate of earnings which the trustees should have made. The trustees were successful in resisting this claim in front of Hoffmann J and the Court of Appeal latterly on the basis that other trustees (mainly banks) acting for large family trusts of this sort were investing in similarly safe investments which generated similarly low returns. Therefore, it was held that there had been no actionable failure by the trustees in the discharge of their investment obligations. For our purposes, this resists a claim that a poor rate of profit will be equivalent to a loss. Therefore, beneficiaries will struggle to bring a claim for breach of trust if there has been some profit, particularly when it can be proved that comparable trustees managing comparable trusts were investing in the same way. This judgment, in effect, authorises herd behaviour as a defence to an action for breach of trust.

18.2.4 Allocating liability for breach of trust among a number of trustees

The trust property is required to be vested in the name of all of the trustees jointly, all of the trustees must receive any trust income, all of the trustees must give a receipt, and so forth. Liability for breach of trust to the beneficiaries attaches to the trustees jointly and severally. The reason for all of the trustees being held to be jointly and severally liable for the breach of trust is that to do otherwise would encourage trustees to take no responsibility for the decisions made in connection with their trusteeship. That is, it would be attractive to individual

---

19 *Re Massingberd's Settlement* (1890) 63 LT 296.
20 *Re BA Peters plc, Moriarty v Atkinson* [2008] EWCA Civ 1604.
21 *Shaker v Al-Bedrawi* [2003] Ch 350.
22 [1993] 1 WLR 1260; [1994] 1 All ER 118.

trustees to take no part in the management of the trust so that they could claim later not to have been responsible for any decision or action. It has been held that encouraging the trustees to act in this way would be an 'opiate on the consciences of the trustees', whereas it is in the interests of the beneficiaries to have all of the trustees taking an active part in the management of the trust so that they exercise control over one another.[23]

There are circumstances in which the trustees need not act jointly and in relation to which there is no requirement that all of the trustees should be jointly and severally liable. For example, the trust instrument may permit some other means of proceeding without unanimity[24] or necessity may require that assets be registered in the name of only one of the trustees at a given time.[25] If a trustee is also a beneficiary under that trust, then if the trustee has committed a breach of trust that person cannot take their beneficial interest until they have accounted for their breach of trust.[26]

The general position is that the trustees are jointly and severally liable for any breach of trust. However, it has been held that no individual trustee will be liable for any default which is the individual fault of another trustee.[27] The easiest way to understand this point is that, in essence, the trustees can apportion responsibility between themselves, provided that the beneficiaries are able to recoup their loss. Trustees may be liable to make contributions alongside the other trustees in situations in which they are liable for a breach of trust in common with those other trustees further to the Civil Liability (Contribution) Act 1978. The 1978 Act displaced the inherent power of the courts of equity to order a trustee to make such a contribution. The Act operates so that any trustee who is made liable to compensate the beneficiaries for any breach of trust is entitled to recover a contribution towards her liability from the other trustees who are also liable for that same breach.[28] The amount of the contribution to be made is such as the court considers to be just and equitable in the circumstances.[29] The courts will generally apportion liability evenly between the trustees[30] except in circumstances in which one trustee has acted fraudulently[31] or has demonstrated wilful default.[32]

It is possible for the settlor to structure the trust in the trust instrument (possibly at the insistence of professional trustees from the outset) so that different trustees will be liable only for defaults in relation to particular parts of the trust or in particular contexts. So, if a trust fund includes a dairy farm and a portfolio of shares, then the settlor may appoint a farm manager and a stockbroker to be trustees of that trust on the basis that the stockbroker will be the only trustee who will bear any responsibility for losses to the share portfolio.

---

23 *Bahin v Hughes* (1886) 31 Ch D 390, at 398, *per* Frey LJ.
24 TA 2000, s 11.
25 *Consterdine v Consterdine* (1862) 31 Beav 330.
26 *Re Dacre, Whitaker v Dacre* [1916] 1 Ch 344 at 346–347, *per* Lord Cozens-Hardy MR; *Brazzill v Willoughby* [2009] EWHC 1633 (Ch).
27 *Townley v Sherbourne* (1633) Bridg 35.
28 Civil Liability (Contribution) Act 1978, ss 1(1), 6(1).
29 *Ibid*, s 2(1).
30 *Ramskill v Edwards* (1885) 31 Ch D 100.
31 *Charitable Corporation v Sutton* (1742) 2 Atk 400.
32 *Scotney v Lomer* (1886) 29 Ch D 535.

18.3 REMEDIES FOR BREACH OF TRUST

18.3.1 The remedies for breach of trust in outline

There are three remedies which arise from *Target Holdings v Redferns* in relation to the loss suffered as a result of the breach of trust. As Lord Browne-Wilkinson held in *Target Holdings v Redferns*:[33]

> The equitable rules of compensation for breach of trust have been largely developed in relation to such traditional trusts, where the only way in which all the beneficiaries' rights can be protected is to restore to the trust fund what ought to be there. In such a case the basic rule is that a trustee in breach of trust must restore or pay to the trust estate either the assets which have been lost to the estate by reason of the breach or compensation for such loss.[34]

These dicta can be unpacked as disclosing three different remedies. First, that the trustee must restore the original property which formed part of the trust fund, referred to here as 'specific restitution of the trust property'. Second, if the original property cannot be recovered, that the trustee must reconstitute the value lost to the trust fund in money or money's worth. Third, that the trustee must pay equitable compensation to make good any further loss suffered by the trust. Even in situations in which the loss or breach of trust was caused by the dishonesty of a third party to the trust, the beneficiary is required to proceed first against the trustee for breach of trust in any event.[35]

18.3.2 Specific restitution of the original trust property

Specific restitution is a proprietary obligation on the trustee to recover the original trust assets which were lost to the trust as a result of the breach of trust. In the words of Lord Browne-Wilkinson that is restoring to the trust what ought to be there. The beneficiaries may prefer to recover the specific property that was lost to the trust for any one of a number of reasons: because it will grant a proprietary right as opposed merely to a personal right, because it had sentimental value, because it was expected to increase in value, or because it was intrinsically valuable. By receiving its mere cash equivalent from the trustee, under the second remedy, would not include any future profits which might be earned from that property and which would not reflect any value beyond its market value in cash. It was accepted in *Harris v Kent*[36] that specific restitution might not be appropriate if none of the parties want to keep the trust in existence, something which would have been achieved by recovering the original trust property. Therefore, it was considered that the better remedy would be

---

33   [1996] 1 AC 421.
34   *Nocton v Lord Ashburton* [1914] AC 932, at 952, 958, *per* Viscount Haldane LC.
35   *Target Holdings v Redferns* [1996] 1 AC 421.
36   [2007] EWHC 463 (Ch), Briggs J.

to compensate the beneficiary for the loss she would not have suffered but for the breach of trust.

18.3.3 The obligation to restore the value of the trust fund

If the specific property which comprised the trust fund cannot be recovered, then the following course of action arises from the speech of Lord Browne-Wilkinson:

> If specific restitution of the trust property is not possible, then the liability of the trustee is to pay sufficient compensation to the trust estate to put it back to what it would have been had the breach not been committed.[37]

The second course of action is then for restoration (confusingly rendered in the cases as 'restitution')[38] of an amount of money equal to the value of the property lost to the trust fund by the breach of trust. This approach was applied in *Lee v Futurist Developments Ltd.*[39] The issue of valuation is considered further at section 18.3.5 below, but in general terms the valuation will be an amount to return the trust to the position it had occupied before the transaction which constituted the breach of trust.[40]

18.3.4 Equitable compensation for losses to the trust in general

Equitable compensation is available to compensate any consequent loss in the wake of the breach of trust over and above the first two remedies for recovery of the original property or the reconstitution of the value of the fund. This would include an incidental costs or expenses which flowed from the breach subsequently.[41] Compensation is an equitable remedy which is purely personal in nature, giving no right to any specific property. In *Swindle v Harrison,*[42] the (wonderfully-named) solicitor Mr Swindle failed to disclose all the material facts to his client Mrs Harrison when acting for her in his fiduciary capacity in a purchase of property. Mrs Harrison lost money in the transaction as a result. She then sought compensation from Swindle for her loss. The Court of Appeal held that the amount of compensation to which she was entitled was restorative compensation only: that is, an amount of compensation to put the trust into the position which it had occupied before the transaction.

There is a question as to the amount of compensation which is to be paid. As Lord Browne-Wilkinson held in *Target Holdings v Redferns* in describing the remedy of equitable compensation:[43] 'the defendant is only liable for the consequences of the legal wrong he has done to the plaintiff and to make good the damage caused by his wrong or to pay by way of compensation more than the loss suffered from such wrong'. Compensation for breach is therefore based on fault, rather than on any strict liability of the trustee.

---

37   Cf. *Caffrey v Darby* (1801) 6 Ves 488; *Clough v Bond* (1838) 40 ER 1016.
38   *Swindle v Harrison* [1997] 4 All ER 705.
39   [2010] EWHC 2764 (Ch), [49].
40   *Swindle v Harrison* [1997] 4 All ER 705; *Bristol & West Building Society v Mothew* [1996] 4 All ER 698.
41   *Gwembe Valley Development Co Ltd v Koshy* [2003] EWCA Civ 1048; at [142].
42   [1997] 4 All ER 705.
43   [1996] 1 AC 421; [1995] 3 All ER 785, 792.

18.3.5 A comparison of common law damages and equitable compensation

There is no strict rule of foreseeability in an action for breach of trust, nor of remoteness of damage, in relation to a breach of trust. As Lord Browne-Wilkinson put it:

> the common law rules of remoteness of damage and causation do not apply. However, there does have to be some causal connection between the breach of trust and the loss to the trust estate for which compensation is recoverable, viz the fact that the loss would not have occurred but for the breach.[44]

Therefore, a trustee will be liable to compensate the beneficiaries for the loss caused by a breach of trust even though the loss may flow unexpectedly from the breach.

18.3.6 Valuation of the loss to the trust

A difficult question arises in relation to compensation for breach of trust: at what level should compensation be awarded in respect of property which fluctuates in value between the date of the breach and the date of judgment? In *Jaffray v Marshall*[45] the court adopted the 'highest intermediate balance' approach which required that the court identify the highest value for the trust property between the time of the breach and the date of the trial, and that that valuation should be used to identify the amount to be compensated. However in *Target Holdings v Redferns*, Lord Browne-Wilkinson held that that valuation might involve an impossible sale: just because the value of an item of property was theoretically at level *x* at a given time does not mean that the beneficiaries would have been able to sell the property for that price at that time. Therefore, his lordship overruled *Jaffray v Marshall* and preferred that the courts simply identify the amount that was actually lost by the beneficiaries and use that as the valuation. The claimant would have to prove what they had lost.

It has been held more generally by the courts that the measure of compensation for breach of trust would be 'fair compensation', that is to say, the difference between proper performance of the trust obligations and what the trustee actually achieved, not the least that could have been achieved.[46] It has been held that the trustee will not be liable for speculative or unliquidated losses: the beneficiary must be able to demonstrate that amounts have been lost.[47]

The trustees are not permitted to set off a profit in one transaction against a loss in another transaction.[48] So, in *Dimes v Scott*,[49] trustees breached their trust by paying the income of the trust to the testator's widow but their delay in the administration of the trust had permitted them to buy more securities for the trust than would otherwise have been the case: it was held that the commission of the breach of trust was actionable in itself regardless of any profit which the trustees had made in some collateral transaction.[50] The trustees were not allowed to reduce the amount lost by the widow by the amount they made on the securities transaction.

44 See also *Nestlé v National Westminster Bank plc* [1993] 1 WLR 1260.
45 [1993] 1 WLR 1285.
46 *Nestlé v National Westminster Bank plc* [1994] 1 All ER 118; [1993] 1 WLR 1260, CA.
47 *Palmer v Jones* (1862) 1 Vern 144.
48 *Dimes v Scott* (1828) 4 Russ 195, Lord Lyndhurst.
49 (1828) 4 Russ 195.
50 See also *Fletcher v Green* (1864) 33 Beav 426.

18.3.7 Breach of trust in relation to investment of the trust fund

For a detailed consideration of liability for breach of trust as it relates to the investment of the trust property, see section 9.9.1 above.

18.4 DEFENCES TO LIABILITY FOR BREACH OF TRUST

18.4.1 Lack of a causal link between breach and loss

The claimant is required to prove a causal link between the loss suffered and the breach of trust.[51] If there is no link between the breach of trust and the loss, then the trustee will not be liable for any loss that is suffered. The discussion of *Target Holdings v Redferns* in this chapter has demonstrated this principle.

18.4.2 Breach committed by another trustee

As considered above, a trustee may be able to claim an indemnity from another trustee who was individually at fault for the breach of trust, in section 18.2.4. It is possible that one trustee will not be held liable for the actions or omissions of another trustee in appropriate circumstances.[52]

18.4.3 Failure by the beneficiary to alleviate loss

Failure by the beneficiary to minimise her own loss does not constitute a full defence to a claim for breach of trust, but it may serve to reduce the trustee's liability. Where the beneficiary fails to take straightforward measures to protect herself against further loss, after due notice and opportunity to do so, then the trustee will not be liable for any further loss arising after the beneficiary could have taken action to protect herself.[53]

18.4.4 Release

Where the beneficiaries agree formally to release the trustee from any liability, the equitable doctrine of release will operate so as to protect that trustee from any liability arising from her breach of trust.[54]

18.4.5 Trustee exemption clause

Where the trust instrument contains a clause excluding or limiting the trustees' liabilities, that exemption of liability provision will generally be enforced.[55] This position was considered in great detail in section 8.5.1.[56]

---

51 *Nestlé v National Westminster Bank plc (No 2)* [1993] 1 WLR 1260.
52 *Townley v Sherborne* (1633) Bridg 35.
53 *Corporacion Nacional del Cobre de Chile v Sogemin Metals Ltd* [1997] 1 WLR 1396, 1403.
54 *Turner v Turner* (1880) 14 Ch D 829.
55 *Armitage v Nurse* [1998] Ch 241.
56 See section 8.5.1 above.

18.4.6 Excuses for breach of trust

There is a power for the court in s 61 of the TA 1925 to grant partial or total relief for breach of trust. That section provides that:

> If it appears to the court that a trustee . . . is or may be personally liable for any breach of trust . . . but has acted honestly and reasonably, and ought fairly to be excused for the breach of trust and for omitting to obtain the directions of the court in the matter in which he committed such breach, then the court may relieve him either wholly or partly from personal liability for the same.

Therefore, the question is whether or not a trustee has acted honestly such that the court considers it appropriate to relieve her of her liability. This provision was directed primarily at the perceived harshness of the case law on breach of trust, which tended to hold non-professional trustees liable for the whole of any loss suffered by beneficiaries in circumstances in which there was no reason to suppose that those trustees had held themselves out as having any particular competence to manage the trust to any particular standard.

So, in *Re Evans (Deceased)*,[57] a daughter acted as administrator in her deceased father's estate, holding that estate on trust for herself and her brother beneficially as next-of-kin under the intestacy rules. When she came to distribute the estate she assumed that her brother was dead because she had not heard from him for 30 years. The defendant bought an insurance policy to pay out half the value of the estate in the event that her brother re-appeared. Her brother did re-appear four years later and claimed that the defendant had breached her duties as trustee by taking all of the fund for herself beneficially, and claimed further that the insurance policy would be insufficient to meet his total loss. Clearly, it had not been unreasonable for the defendant to assume that her brother was no longer alive. Consequently, the judge concluded that the defendant ought to be granted partial relief. Her liability to account to her brother was limited to the amount which could be met from the sale of a house forming part of the estate.

The approach of the courts has been to take a case-by-case approach to relief under this provision, dependent usually on whether or not the trustee has acted reasonably[58] in the manner in which she might have handled her own property,[59] or whether the trustee acted unreasonably by leaving the trust property in the hands of a third party without good reason[60] or on an erroneous understanding of the law.[61] It has been held that if a trustee has acted grossly negligently in breaching her trust obligations then the relief under s 61 will not be available to the trustee.[62] On this basis, there may be a defence for the trustee where she can demonstrate that there was a good reason for her treatment of the trust property.[63]

---

57 [1999] 2 All ER 777.
58 *Chapman v Browne* [1902] 1 Ch 785.
59 *Re Stuart* [1897] 2 Ch 583.
60 *Wynne v Tempest* (1897) 13 TLR 360.
61 *Ward-Smith v Jebb* (1964) 108 SJ 919.
62 *Barraclough v Mell* [2005] EWHC B17 (Ch), [98], *per* Judge Behrens QC.
63 *Ibid.*

18.4.7 Action not in connection with fiduciary duties, or action permitted by the terms of the trust

A trustee will not be liable for breach of trust in circumstances in which either the terms of the trust permit the action complained of[64] or if the action complained of is not connected to the trustee's fiduciary duties.[65] For example, in *Ward v Brunt*,[66] a woman was held not to have breached her fiduciary duties as a partner in a farm business when she exercised a right which she had in a personal capacity as landlord to the farm business. It was held that there is no liability for breach of trust, even if the fiduciary is acting contrary to the interests of the beneficiaries, provided that the powers which the fiduciary is exercising accrue to her in a personal capacity, as was the case here.

18.4.8 Concurrence by a beneficiary in a breach of trust

If a beneficiary concurs or acquiesces in a breach of trust, then that beneficiary is estopped from seeking to recover compensation for that breach of trust from any trustees to whom that concurrence was proffered.[67]

18.4.9 Change of position

There is authority to suggest that the defence of change of position may potentially have been available for claims for breach of trust. This defence is considered in detail in Chapter 19. The only defence which would have been available in *Haugesund Kommune v Depfa ACS Bank*[68] was the defence of change of position.[69] It was held that this was a transaction in which the recipient of the payments knew that they would have to be repaid and therefore that the defence of change of position would not apply.[70]

18.5 ALLOCATING CLAIMS

18.5.1 Choice between remedies

The equitable doctrine of election arises when there is more than one remedy available to a claimant such that the claimant may elect between alternative remedies.[71] In *Tang v Capacious Investments*, the possibility of parallel remedies arose in relation to a breach of trust, for the plaintiff beneficiary to claim an account of profits from the malfeasant trustee or to claim damages representing the lost profits to the trust. It was held that these two remedies existed in the alternative and therefore that the plaintiff could claim both, not being required to elect between them until judgment was awarded in its favour. Clearly, the court would not

---

64   *Galmerrow Securities Ltd v National Westminster Bank plc* [2002] WTLR 125.
65   *Ward v Brunt* [2000] WTLR 731.
66   *Ibid.*
67   *White v White* (1798–1804) 5 Ves 554.
68   [2010] EWCA Civ 579.
69   Cf. *Goss v Chilcott* [1996] AC 788.
70   The approach of Pill LJ to change of position was cited with approval in *Ibrahim v Barclays Bank* [2011] EWHC 1897 (Ch).
71   *Tang v Capacious Investments Ltd* [1996] 1 All ER 193.

permit double recovery in respect of the same loss, thus requiring election between those remedies at the end of the proceedings. The defendants may then bring proceedings against one another under the Civil Liability (Contribution) Act 1978 as discussed above, to allocate responsibility for the amounts paid to the claimant.

18.5.2 Limitation period

One point which has arisen recently is whether there is any limitation period on an action for account. It has been held that the appropriate period is that for common law fraud, unless there has been a dishonest breach of fiduciary duty, in which case there is no period applicable.[72]

18.6 LITIGATION IN RELATION TO A BREACH OF TRUST

In litigation, the claimant sues the defendant. However, it is often the case that the first defendant will argue that third parties were responsible for the loss which the claimant is seeking to avenge, and therefore those third parties will be joined to the litigation by the first defendant. In breach of trust litigation, it is usually easy for the beneficiary to show that there has been a breach of trust, especially if there was an express term of the trust instrument which has been breached. If so, and if that breach has caused a loss to the trust, then the trustees will be prima facie liable. It is said that 'primary liability' attaches to the trustees.

What this means in breach of trust cases is that the trustees will be required to recover any property that was taken from the trust fund. So, if the trust fund had contained a yacht, then the trustees will be required to sue to recover that yacht and to bear the expenses of doing so themselves. Therefore, the trustees will add as third parties to the litigation anyone who became owner of that yacht after the breach of trust. This sort of claim is discussed in Chapter 20 *Tracing* in the form of 'following' actions to recover the original trust property. If the yacht was sold and its sale proceeds used to buy shares, then the trustees will trace the property rights that were originally vested in the yacht into the shares and seek to claim ownership of the shares for the trust. As discussed in Chapter 20, this is a 'tracing' action to assert a proprietary claim over that substitute property. There might also have been someone who received the yacht physically (perhaps a ship's captain who sailed the yacht to its new harbour) who could be held liable for 'unconscionable receipt' of the trust property, as discussed in Chapter 19, such that they would be personally liable to account to the beneficiaries for the loss caused to the trust by the breach. There might also have been someone who arranged the movement of the yacht, perhaps a harbourmaster, who did not come into contact with the yacht but who made all the arrangements for its transport. That harbourmaster would be potentially liable for 'dishonest assistance' in the breach of trust because they assisted the breach of trust by arranging the movement of the vessel, and therefore the harbourmaster could be personally liable for the loss caused to the trust by the breach (as is discussed in Chapter 19).

Therefore, the liability discussed in this Chapter 18 has considered the liability of the trustees for a breach of trust. The issues discussed in Chapter 20 *Tracing* consider the possibilities for the recovery of the trust property, or for tracing those property rights into substitute property in place of the original property (especially where the original property cannot be recovered). This is a proprietary doctrine which may give rise to proprietary remedies. Then,

---

72 *Coulthard v Disco Mix Club Ltd* [2000] 1 WLR 707.

in Chapter 19, we consider the possibility of suing third parties who have either received trust property with knowledge of the breach of trust or who have assisted the breach of trust in a way that was dishonest: in either case, the defendant would be personally liable to account to the beneficiaries for the loss caused to the trust by the breach. This is a personal doctrine which imposes merely personal liabilities against those third parties. (If the third parties did have trust property in their hands, then a tracing action would be brought against them.)

Taken together, these liabilities constitute a significant arsenal in the protection of beneficiaries against loss. Common law claims for losses caused by breach of contract or by tort only give rise to claims for damages against other contracting parties or against the tortfeasor personally. The law governing breach of trust across these three chapters (Chapters 18–20) throws the net much more broadly and permits proprietary claims as well as personal claims. In this way, the law of trusts is very attractive to commercial people as a way of protecting their property (through the fiduciary duties of the trustees and the protection that offers against the trustees' insolvency) and of recovering any loss if something should go wrong.

Chapter 19

Strangers: Dishonest assistance and unconscionable receipt

CAPSULE SUMMARY

A person who dishonestly assists in a breach of trust will be personally liable to account to the beneficiaries of that trust for the loss to the trust. The test for dishonesty is an objective test which requires that the court consider what an honest person would have done in the circumstances, albeit seen through the lens of the personal characteristics and knowledge of the defendant.[1] There is a line of authority (now discredited) which held that the test for dishonesty should also require that the defendant was aware that their behaviour would be considered to be dishonest by honest and reasonable people. 'Dishonesty' in this context encompasses fraud, lack of probity and reckless risk-taking.

A person who knowingly receives trust property in breach of trust will be personally liable to account to the beneficiaries for the loss to the trust, provided that she has acted unconscionably.[2] 'Knowledge' in this context includes actual knowledge, wilfully closing one's eyes to the obvious, or failing to make the inquiries which an honest and reasonable person would have made.[3]

19.1 INTRODUCTION

19.1.1 The liability of strangers to the trust in relation to a breach of trust

Trusts law is flexible and it protects its beneficiaries from breaches of trust in as many ways as it can. The previous chapter considered the liability of the trustees of an express trust for a breach of trust. This chapter considers the liability of third parties who are *not* trustees for their involvement in such a breach of trust. (Those third parties who are not trustees are referred to as 'strangers' to the trust.) There are two heads of claim against strangers, both of which are analysed in this chapter. First, 'dishonest assistance'. Under this head, anyone who *assists* a breach of trust in a way that is *dishonest* will be personally liable to compensate the beneficiaries for any loss caused by that breach of trust. Second, a claim known as 'knowing receipt' or as 'unconscionable receipt'. Under this head, anyone who *receives* trust property with *knowledge* of a breach of trust in a way that is *unconscionable* will be personally liable to compensate the beneficiaries for any loss caused by that breach of trust. In either case, the defendant is referred to as being a 'constructive trustee' because that person is treated as though they were a trustee – that is, they are 'construed' to be a trustee – and made liable for the loss caused to the beneficiaries *as if* they were an express trustee facing personal liability under *Target Holdings v Redferns*[4] as discussed in Chapter 18. The manner in which compensation is paid is known as 'an account': hence, the remedy is known as 'a personal liability to account' for the loss caused by the breach of trust.

---

1 *Royal Brunei Airlines v Tan* [1995] 2 AC 378; *Dubai Aluminium v Salaam* [2002] 3 WLR 1913; [2003] 1 All ER 97.
2 *Re Montagu* [1987] Ch 264; *Agip v Jackson* [1990] Ch 265, 286, *per* Millett J; [1991] Ch 547, CA; *Lipkin Gorman v Karpnale* [1991] 2 AC 548; *El Ajou v Dollar Land Holdings* [1993] 3 All ER 717, appealed [1994] 2 All ER 685.
3 *Re Montagu* [1987] Ch 264.
4 [1996] 1 AC 421.

In practice, the beneficiaries sue the trustees for breach of trust in the first place because the trustees bear the primary responsibility for any breach of trust (so that the trustee is the 'first defendant' in any litigation) and then it is the trustee who will sue the strangers to recover the loss from them by joining them as second and third defendants to the litigation. The usefulness of these different heads of claim is that if the trustee cannot compensate the loss suffered by the beneficiaries then the strangers may be able to make good that loss. In essence, the beneficiaries are seeking to recover their loss from their trustees and any strangers who have participated in the breach of trust by assisting it or by receiving property as a result of it. As was said at the outset: trusts law is flexible and it protects its beneficiaries.

19.1.2 Understanding the basis of each claim

The receipt claim and the assistance claim

This subject is straightforward. Nevertheless, sometimes students can allow themselves to be confused by the fact that different judges have advanced different approaches in some cases. This chapter takes care to explain the different approaches to the tests for dishonest assistance and knowing receipt in different courts, and to separate them out. You should understand these judges as having disagreed with one another about the proper form of the test, as is explained below. That different judges take different approaches is an opportunity for you to show off in examinations that you understand those differences. In answering problem questions in this area it is suggested that you should apply each different test one at a time to the facts of your problem and demonstrate that you understand how each approach might lead to a different outcome.

Before diving into the detail of each claim, this section will outline those differences of opinion. You should think of this section as being an outline map of the discussion to follow.

First, 'dishonest assistance'. A stranger to the trust will be personally liable to account for any loss suffered in a situation in which she dishonestly assists the commission of a breach of trust. She will not need to receive any proprietary right in that trust property herself.[5] The key issue is the test for 'dishonesty'. The leading case provided that the question is how an honest person would have acted in the circumstances. If the defendant failed to act as an honest person would have acted in the circumstances, then the defendant will be found to have been dishonest.[6] This is an objective test, which means that the court is seeking to identify what an honest person would have done in the circumstances and then to ask whether or not the defendant lived up to that standard. This notion of dishonesty extends beyond straightforward lying and fraud into activity such as reckless risk-taking with trust property.[7] Latterly, there have been cases which have tried to apply a subjective approach to dishonesty: which means that the court must also identify whether or not the defendant personally realised that her behaviour was dishonest.[8] The law has now settled on the objective approach. What has

5 *Royal Brunei Airlines v Tan* [1995] 2 AC 378.
6 *Ibid.*
7 *Ibid.*
8 *Twinsectra v Yardley* [2002] 2 AC 164.

become difficult in more recent cases, however, is that judges in the High Court have nevertheless sought to insert a small amount of subjectivity into the test by looking the defendant's level of intelligence and their education, as well as considering the circumstances in which they were acting. These different approaches in the case law require you to distinguish carefully between the different approaches and to show that you understand how each will apply to the facts of any problem.

Second, 'unconscionable receipt'. A stranger to the trust will be personally liable to account for any loss suffered in a situation in which she receives trust property with knowledge that the property has been passed to her in breach of trust in an unconscionable manner.[9] (This form of liability is referred to as 'knowing receipt' in most of the cases.) 'Knowledge' in this context includes actual knowledge, wilfully shutting one's eyes to the obvious, or failing to make the inquiries which a reasonable person would have made in the circumstances.[10] It is in more recent cases that it has been accepted that liability for receipt of property in breach of trust should be based on proof that the defendant has acted unconscionably as well as having knowledge of the breach of trust.[11] Acting unconscionably, it is suggested, would include having knowledge that there had been a breach of trust.

How dishonest assistance and unconscionable receipt combine with other claims relating to breach of trust

Claims for dishonest assistance and unconscionable receipt should be understood as combining with the claims brought against trustees for breach of trust (considered in Chapter 18) and actions brought to trace any substitute for any original property which was taken in breach of trust (considered in Chapter 20). Suppose the following.

> Arnold is a financial advisor employed by Wessex Bank to give investment advice to clients. He meets Sarita who is the trustee of the Hardy family trust. The trust instrument includes a provision that 'the trustees may only invest in shares quoted on the FTSE-100'. Nevertheless, Arnold advises Sarita that she should invest in interest rate swaps (which are not shares quoted on the FTSE-100) because they are expected to be more profitable that shares. Sarita relies on Arnold's advice and makes the investments in derivatives by purchasing them from Wessex Bank. To do this, Sarita transfers £300,000 to Wessex Bank.

Clearly, this is a breach of trust by Sarita and therefore she would face the primary liability under *Target Holdings v Redferns* (discussed in Chapter 18) as the trustee for her breach of trust. However, Arnold may be secondarily liable as someone who assisted the breach of trust. The question would be whether or not Arnold acted 'dishonestly' – we shall consider the tests for that below. The sorts of facts which we would need to know are whether Arnold was aware of the terms of the trust, whether Arnold encouraged Sarita to make the investment in full knowledge that it was a breach, whether Arnold stood to make some personal profit (e.g. by way of a commission) from the transaction, and so forth. Wessex Bank

---

9 *Re Montagu's Settlements* [1987] Ch 264.
10 *Ibid.*
11 *BCCI v Akindele* [2001] Ch 437; *Charter plc v City Index Ltd* [2008] 2 WLR 950.

receives the trust's property (because Sarita pays the money directly to Wessex Bank, not to Arnold) and therefore it is Wessex Bank which might be liable for unconscionable receipt of the property. As we shall see, the principal questions will be whether Wessex Bank can be said to have had knowledge of the breach of trust and whether the Bank can be said to have acted unconscionably. One of the key factors will be whether or not Arnold's knowledge can be attributed to the bank as a corporate entity (as discussed in section 19.5.1) so that it can be liable for unconscionable receipt. The beneficiaries of the Hardy family trust would bring all of these claims simultaneously against Sarita, Arnold, and Wessex. They would be first, second and third defendants to this action respectively. In practice, the trustee would join the other defendants to this action and would bear the costs of doing that. The Civil Liability (Contribution) Act 1970 allocates responsibility among the three defendants as to who would contribute to the final amounts owed to the beneficiaries. The beneficiaries would not be able to recover more than their loss.

19.2 DISHONEST ASSISTANCE

19.2.1 Introduction

It was Lord Selborne LC in the House of Lords in *Barnes v Addy* in 1874 who clarified the basis of the liability for dishonest assistance in a breach of trust[12] as resting on the stranger having knowledge that they were assisting in a 'dishonest and fraudulent design' on the part of the trustee. That approach was changed significantly in 1995 by Lord Nicholls in the Privy Council in *Royal Brunei Airlines v Tan*[13] in the sense that there was a movement away from 'knowledge' towards 'dishonesty' as the foundation for the claim, and in the sense that it was no longer a requirement that the trustee must be proved to have been acting dishonestly but instead that only the defendant needed to be acting dishonestly. Importantly, it was Lord Nicholls who established both that dishonesty was the foundation of the claim now and also that dishonesty must be objective in nature. Therefore, it is with that case which we shall begin.

19.2.2 The nature of dishonest assistance

There are three elements to a claim for dishonest assistance. First, there must have been a breach of trust. Second, the defendant must have assisted that breach of trust. Third, the defendant must have been dishonest in so doing. Each element is considered in turn.

The requirement that there has been a breach of trust

The defendant must have genuinely assisted the breach of trust in some way. The assistance must have had some link to the loss suffered by the claimant, as was held in *Brown v Bennett*.[14]

---

12 (1874) 9 Ch App 244, 251–52.
13 *Royal Brunei Airlines v Tan* [1995] 3 All ER 97, 102.
14 [1999] 1 BCLC 659.

The basis of the liability on proof of the stranger's dishonesty

The leading case on, and the clearest illustration of, the test for dishonest assistance is the decision of the Privy Council in *Royal Brunei Airlines v Tan*, which is considered next.[15] In *Dubai Aluminium v Salaam*[16] Lord Nicholls explained this form of liability as being a form of 'equitable wrong'.[17]

19.2.3 The objective test for 'dishonesty'

Dishonesty in Royal Brunei Airlines v Tan

In *Royal Brunei Airlines v Tan*[18] the appellant airline contracted an agency agreement with a travel agency, BLT. BLT was a company. Under that agreement, BLT was to sell tickets for the appellant. BLT held money received for the sale of these tickets on express trust for the appellant. BLT was therefore the trustee. BLT was contractually required to account to the appellant for these moneys within 30 days. The respondent, Mr Tan, was the managing director and principal shareholder of BLT. From time to time, amounts were paid out of the current account into deposit accounts controlled by Tan. The current account was used to defray some of BLT's expenses, such as salaries, and to reduce its overdraft. This was all in breach of trust. In time, BLT went into insolvency. Therefore, the appellant sought to proceed against Mr Tan personally for assisting a breach of trust. The Privy Council held that Tan was personal liable to account for assisting in the breach of trust.[19] Moreover, it was held that it was unnecessary for the trustee itself to have been dishonest; instead, it was sufficient that a stranger acted dishonestly if that stranger was to be fixed with liability for assisting the breach of trust.

The most important part of this decision was the test of 'dishonesty' that was set out in the judgment of Lord Nicholls. The concept of 'dishonesty' replaced the old test of 'knowledge'. The central point is this: Lord Nicholls held that the question whether or not the defendant was dishonest was one to be assessed by reference to what an honest, reasonable person would have done in the circumstances. Therefore, if you want to prove that a defendant is dishonest, then what you must do is to identify what an objectively honest person would have done in the circumstances, and ask whether or not the defendant lived up to that standard. If the defendant failed to live up to that standard then the defendant was dishonest.

In describing the nature of the test for dishonesty in this context in *Royal Brunei Airlines v Tan*, Lord Nicholls held that:[20]

> acting dishonestly, or with a lack of probity, which is synonymous, means simply not acting as an honest person would in the circumstance. This is an objective standard.

---

15 [1995] 2 AC 378.
16 [2002] 3 WLR 1913.
17 At para [9].
18 *Royal Brunei Airlines v Tan* [1995] 3 All ER 97, 102.
19 Applied in *Statek Corp v Alford* [2008] EWHC 32, Evans-Lombe J.
20 *Royal Brunei Airlines v Tan* [1995] 2 AC 378, 386.

This is the central statement of Lord Nicholls's approach in *Tan*: to find that someone is dishonest is to find that they failed to act as an honest person would have acted in those circumstances. If the defendant did not act in the way that an honest person would have acted in those circumstances, then the defendant is deemed to have been dishonest. The court will therefore be holding the defendant up to an objective idea of what constitutes honest behaviour.

The two possible readings of the test in Royal Brunei Airlines v Tan

Lord Nicholls's judgment repays close analysis. His lordship acknowledges that usually '[h]onesty has a connotation of subjectivity' and that:

> for the most part dishonesty is to be equated with conscious impropriety. However, these subjective characteristics of honesty do not mean that individuals are free to set their own standards of honesty in particular circumstances. The standard of what constitutes honest conduct is not subjective.

Therefore, it is clear that (in this part of his judgment) Lord Nicholls accepts that we might assume that dishonesty has some subjective elements but that in this particular legal context it is not subjective. Instead, the question is what would an honest person have done in the circumstances. Dishonesty means 'simply not acting as an honest person would in the circumstance' and as a result:

> This is an objective standard.

Consequently, it is an objective test. That much is clear from the face of the judgment. The one qualification to the purity of the objectivity in this section of the judgment is that we must look at 'the circumstances'. That could be read two ways. First, it could be read as meaning we must place the objectively honest person who is to be our benchmark in the circumstances in which the defendant found themselves, such as being a trader on a banking floor, or a managing director of a travel agency and so forth. Alternatively, this could be read as incorporating all of the defendant's personal circumstances such as their intelligence, their education, their level of personal experience in their job and so forth. The objectively honest person under the first reading does not need to have any of these personal characteristics of the defendant because those are subjective characteristics. If the second reading requires constructing the personality of the objectively 'honest person' so that it is the same in all material respects as the defendant then that is not really an objective standard. If we imbue the 'honest person' with all of the defendant's characteristics and history then we are really creating a subjective assessment of what the defendant personally should have done in those circumstances. That is not what Lord Nicholls meant when he said that this is an objective standard. Clearly, the question of the relevant circumstances to be taken into account requires a difficult question in each case concerned with deciding what are the relevant factors to take into account in assessing the 'honest person'.

What is difficult in this 15-page judgment is that his lordship held later that 'a court will look at all the circumstances known to the third party at the time' (which is the same as the passages quoted above) and also that the court 'will also have regard to personal attributes of the third party such as his experience and intelligence, and the reason why he acted as he did'. The first of these qualifications is unremarkable: one must consider what an honest person would have done in the circumstances in which the defendant found themselves (that is, whether they were traders in a bank, security guards at a security firm and so forth). The second is different. These 26 words qualify a judgment of nearly 7,000 words because they seem to introduce a note of subjectivity when the rest of the judgment was so keen to exclude it. When a judge starts to consider the defendant's experience, intelligence and so forth then that judge is beginning to stray into subjective factors which militate against the idea of a purely objective test. In particular, when we ask why the defendant personally did what she did then that is clearly a subjective factor; whereas asking what a honest person would have done does not require us to investigate the defendant's personal motivations (unless, for example, the chance of making a personal profit would suggest dishonesty). When the judgment is read as a whole, this subjectivity is a tiny part of the whole; nevertheless, the later High Court cases discussed below in section 19.2.5 have seized on this idea and have begun to use it to soften the objectivity of the law. They achieve this softening by saying that the court should consider both what an objectively honest person would have done in the circumstances and also what a person with the defendant's characteristics should have been expected to do.

Who is the 'honest person'?

Importantly, the objective test for dishonesty is not really a test of 'being dishonest' but rather it is a test of 'not being honest'. Colloquially, we might think that 'dishonesty' involves things like lying and being consciously deceitful, but nothing more than that. Failing to be honest might be quite a different test. If there is only one cake left on the table at the end of a tea party hidden under a napkin, you might think it is a little naughty to eat it while no-one is looking but you might not think it is deceitful or 'dishonest' in the ordinary sense of that term. The approach might be quite different if you ask what would an honest person do in that circumstance. Your eyes might spot Sarah across the room: perfect Sarah who never says a bad word about anyone, who works with the poor on her days off, and who never once told a lie even as a child. Is Sarah our standard for the honest person? How do we assess her as being honest? Is she brutally honest with other people when they ask: 'does this coat suit me?' Does Sarah always answer truthfully: 'no, it looks awful and everyone else will laugh behind your back'? An ordinary person might tell a 'little white lie' to be kind; but an *entirely* honest person probably would not. (If so, she might not have many friends; although you would probably trust her to feed your cat if you are away for the weekend.) If Sarah – an idealised human being – is our standard of absolute honesty then presumably we would have to say: Sarah would not have taken the last cake without asking everyone first, and so to fail to act as Sarah would have acted is to be 'dishonest' in the sense Lord Nicholls intends. Alternatively, should we interpret Lord Nicholls as meaning that our 'honest' person must be an average human being with the ordinary human frailties? The trouble is we need to identify which human frailties those are.

Very quickly it may appear that our objectively honest person is just a cypher for what the judge personally thinks – in which case we have actually created a test of the judge's subjectivity masquerading as objectivity. In practice, it is suggested, judges will seek to justify why they think that their model of objectivity is the correct one and not simply subjective. Perhaps this is why the judges often like to reflect on the defendant's personal characteristics when giving judgment because it justifies their judgments if the defendant can be proved to have been subjectively dishonest instead of objective judgment being imposed on an unwitting (if less than honest) defendant. This is a question which we explore in detail below. As will emerge below, some judges began to talk about 'ordinary standards' rather than the 'honest person'; other judges have focused on the defendant's characteristics. First, however, we must examine a case in the House of Lords which was more explicit in introducing subjectivity into the test of dishonesty.

19.2.4 Introducing subjectivity to the test of 'dishonesty'

Twinsectra v Yardley: *The hybrid objective–subjective approach*

The decision of the House of Lords in *Twinsectra v Yardley*[21] proposed a different direction for the test for 'dishonesty'. Lord Hutton, a criminal lawyer by experience, was uncomfortable with a purely objective test for dishonesty. From the perspective of a criminal lawyer a defendant is only found to be dishonest if that defendant was subjectively aware that their behaviour would be considered to be dishonest by other people (for example in the *Ghosh*[22] test for dishonesty in the law on theft). The *Tan* approach to dishonesty imposes liability whether or not the defendant realises what the popular attitude to their behaviour is. In *Twinsectra v Yardley* Yardley borrowed money from Twinsectra on the condition that the loan money was held by Yardley's solicitor, Sims, and that it was only to be used to acquire identified property. Sims was required to hold the money subject to a 'solicitor's undertaking' which made him a fiduciary. Subsequently, Yardley replaced Sims with another solicitor, Leach. At Yardley's instruction, Leach transferred the money directly to Yardley, and then Yardley misused the money. Twinsectra sued Leach for dishonest assistance. The question was whether or not Leach had been dishonest. The House of Lords was concerned that there was great stigma in finding a professional person, like a solicitor, guilty of dishonesty because that would have ruinous consequences for their career. Consequently, Lord Hutton suggested that the court should begin with Lord Nicholls's objective test but then that the court should also ask whether or not the defendant had realised that their behaviour would be considered to be dishonest by honest and reasonable people. If the defendant had not realised that honest and reasonable people would consider their behaviour to have been dishonest then they would not be found to have acted dishonestly in this context. As Lord Hutton put it:

> for liability as an accessory to arise the defendant must himself appreciate that what he was doing was dishonest by the standards of honest and reasonable men.

Therefore, Lord Hutton created a hybrid test comprised of a subjective and an objective approach. First, the court must ask (as Lord Nicholls did) whether the defendant acted in the way that an honest person would have acted in the circumstances and then, second, whether the defendant realised that honest and reasonable people would consider their behaviour to

21 [2002] 2 AC 164.
22 [1982] QB 1053.

have been dishonest. This means, in effect, that if the defendant's belief system was genuinely such that they had no idea what other people would think of them, or if they had a genuine code of morals that went against the popular point of view, then they would not be liable for dishonesty because they would not have realised that honest and reasonable people would have considered them to be dishonest. This was exactly the argument which defendants attempted to run in later cases. It is worth noting that Lord Hoffmann expressed agreement with Lord Hutton to the effect that 'a dishonest state of mind' is to be conceived of as 'consciousness that one is transgressing ordinary standards of honest behaviour', that is dishonesty requires that the defendant is aware that they are breaching society's standards. The weakness in this approach was displayed in *Barlow Clowes v Eurotrust*, as is discussed next.

The overlooked decision in Dubai Aluminium v Salaam

A subsequent decision of the House of Lords in *Dubai Aluminium v Salaam*[23] has re-established the test for dishonesty as being purely objective and has reaffirmed that personal liability to account as a dishonest assistant is an equitable wrong giving rise to 'constructive trusteeship'. Unfortunately, however, this important case is rarely cited in the discussions about dishonest assistance, seemingly because it relates to a case of assistance in a breach of a different kind of fiduciary duty (i.e. a partnership) and dealt with a number of other issues alongside dishonesty. Salaam had defrauded the claimants and the claimants were seeking (amongst other issues) to establish whether or not liability could be established against Amhurst who was a partner in a firm of solicitors. The claimant hoped that by imposing liability on Amhurst they would be able to fix the solicitors firm with liability in turn. Lord Nicholls gave a leading speech in *Dubai Aluminium v Salaam*[24] with which Lord Slynn concurred. Lord Millett gave a speech in slightly different terms. Lord Nicholls re-established the test for dishonesty as being the objective test set out in *Royal Brunei Airlines v Tan*. Lord Nicholls described liability for dishonest assistance as being the 'equitable wrong of dishonest assistance in a breach of trust or fiduciary duty',[25] and that the defendant would be a 'constructive trustee'[26] whose 'misconduct gives rise to a liability in equity to make good resulting loss'.[27] Interestingly, Lord Hutton did not repeat any of his arguments in *Twinsectra*. Instead, he simply concurred with Lord Nicholls and Lord Millett.

The change of direction in Barlow Clowes v Eurotrust

There were judgments which applied the *Twinsectra* test set out by Lord Hutton. For example, Lewison J held in *Ultraframe (UK) Ltd v Fielding*[28] that the test for dishonesty had changed as a result of *Twinsectra v Yardley* to the effect that the defendant must be shown to have understood that she had acted dishonestly and not simply that an honest person would not have acted as she had done.

---

23 [2002] 3 WLR 1913; [2003] 1 All ER 97.
24 [2002] 3 WLR 1913; [2003] 1 All ER 97.
25 *Ibid*, para 9.
26 *Ibid*, para 40.
27 *Ibid*.
28 [2005] EWHC 1638 (Ch), [2005] All ER (D) 397, para [1481].

The movement back towards a straightforwardly objective test for 'dishonesty' in this context is signalled by the decision of the Privy Council in *Barlow Clowes v Eurotrust*.[29] The Barlow Clowes group of investment entities went into insolvency. It was a complex collapse which involved large-scale fraud, which caused losses in relation to most of the £140 million which had been raised from ordinary British investors, and which made front page news. It took several years to track the payments out of the Barlow Clowes organisation through the various people and organisations who had come into contact with it. Clowes and his associate Cramer, who were fiduciaries in relation to the funds they managed, paid four sums totalling more than £8 million through a small financial institution in the Isle of Man called 'ITC'. One of the principal directors of ITC was a man called Henwood. Henwood became the defendant to the dishonest assistance claim because he had met with Cramer and, perhaps somewhat dazzled by the size of the entities which Clowes and Cramer ran, agreed to act for them. Cramer organised for the four sums to be paid through ITC and then passed on again so that they became untraceable. The question was whether Henwood was acting dishonestly when he assisted Cramer to breach his fiduciary duties in relation to these four payments. Henwood argued that his personal philosophy about treating clients meant that his customers were always to be treated as being right and that therefore he would not question them. Consequently, his lawyers argued that Henwood should not be considered to be dishonest under Lord Hutton's test in *Twinsectra v Yardley* because he had not realised that other people would consider him to be dishonest. It is possible that Henwood was simply being disingenuous by arguing this but the Privy Council decided that the law should be returned to an objective test so that this sort of argument could not be made.

Lord Hoffmann delivered the collective judgment of the Privy Council (a court which included Lord Nicholls). It was held that Henwood had been dishonest because by reference to 'ordinary standards' his behaviour had been dishonest. It was held that Henwood had had an 'exaggerated notion of dutiful service to clients' and that he had a 'warped moral approach'. Consequently, it would be inappropriate to use a subjective test which allowed that warped moral approach to excuse him from liability. As Lord Hoffmann put it, perhaps a little inelegantly, in paragraph [10]:

> Although a dishonest state of mind is a subjective mental state, the standard by which the law determines whether it is dishonest is objective. If by ordinary standards a defendant's mental state would be characterised as dishonest, it is irrelevant that the defendant judges by different standards.

This repeats Lord Nicholls' point in *Tan* to the effect that we might assume that dishonesty is subjective, but that the legal concept in this context required an objective test which was to be assessed (in Lord Hoffmann's words) by reference to 'ordinary standards'. What is not made clear is what those 'ordinary standards' would be and how they would be identified.

What was interesting in the judgment of the Privy Council (which, it should be remembered, could not overrule the House of Lords because its judgments are of merely persuasive authority) was that it attempted to re-explain the judgment of the House of Lords in

---

29 *Ibid.*

Twinsectra as not having intended to add an element of subjectivity into the law at all (in spite of the passages quoted above from Lord Hutton and Lord Hoffmann himself). As Lord Hoffmann put it in *Eurotrust*:

> knowledge of the transaction had to be such as to render his participation contrary to normally acceptable standards of conduct. It did not require that he should have had reflections about what those normally acceptable standards were.[30]

It might have been easier to acknowledge that the approach that was actually taken in *Twinsectra* was undesirable than to pretend that the judges did not say what they said. It was important to identify whether future cases would follow this approach in *Eurotrust* or whether it would follow the approach in *Twinsectra*.

The Court of Appeal in *Abou-Rahmah v Abacha*[31] purportedly followed the Privy Council in *Eurotrust*. Unfortunately, in that case Rix LJ held that the test should be objective but that the court should also consider the defendant's knowledge. Arden LJ held that the test is whether 'the defendant knows of the elements of the transaction which make it dishonest according to normally accepted standards of behaviour'. This is not the same as asking what would an honest person do in the circumstances, but rather it focuses on the defendant's knowledge and whether their actions ran contrary to ordinary standards of behaviour. Neither of these versions of the test were exactly the same as that set out by Lord Nicholls in *Tan*. This is the beginning of a series of different expressions of the test in cases after *Eurotrust*, each of which involved elements of subjectivity. Those cases are considered next.

19.2.5 The development of the law in subsequent cases

This section considers more recent cases which discuss the nature of the law after *Eurotrust*. Let us think about what it means to be a judge at first instance assessing the facts of a case involving a claim of dishonest assistance. The instinct of any judge at first instance is to identify the facts: it must be remembered that the hearing at first instance is the trial and that any appellate court will rely on the facts which the trial judge finds by reference to the evidence submitted in court. Ordinarily, it is only the trial judge who hears the witnesses and who sees examination and cross-examination of their evidence. Therefore, a trial judge will tend to devote a large amount of their judgment to a finding of fact. In dishonest assistance cases a large amount of attention tends to be lavished on evidence as to the subjective motivations, beliefs, intelligence, experience and actual knowledge of the defendant. In relation to a strictly objective test, where all that one should consider is what an honest person would have done and not at all what the defendant subjectively thought or knew, this is largely irrelevant. Nevertheless, because the trial judge is both the finder of fact and is also someone concerned to do justice between the parties according to the law, it seems to be difficult for them to exclude a lot of these seemingly subjective materials from their judgments because they want to include all of the facts that they have found in their judgments.

A good example of this tendency to focus on subjective matters arose in *Markel International Insurance Co Ltd v Surety Guarantee Consultants Ltd*.[32] The case concerned a

---

30   *Barlow Clowes v Eurotrust* [2006] 1 WLR 1476, [15].
31   *Abou-Rahmah v Abacha* [2006] EWCA Civ 1492, CA.
32   [2008] EWHC 1135 (Comm).

complex financial transaction in which the inexpert defendant was accused of dishonest assistance. The defendant contended that he had taken advice from experts in bond trading and that he had acted in accordance with it. It was held by Tearse J that the defendant appeared in consequence to have acted as an honest person would have acted by following professional advice as to his course of action in the transaction. That much appears to be an entirely sensible approach. What is interesting is that Tearse J also devoted many pages of his judgment to setting out descriptions of the defendant's personal circumstances, experience and so forth. Judgment could have been reached without this subjective information but his lordship nevertheless felt obliged to record it.

The decision in *Markel* was based in large part on an earlier judgment of Smith J in *AG Zambia v Meer Care & Desai* where his lordship had held that the 'test is an objective one, but an objective one which takes account of the individual in question's characteristics, experience, knowledge' and so forth. In that case, the defendants had been held to have been dishonest when passing money which had been obtained fraudulently by the former President of Zambia through accounts which they controlled. The court should therefore 'take account of what the individual knew, his experience, intelligence and reasons for acting as he did' even though whether 'the individual was aware that his conduct fell below the objective standard is not part of the test'. Therefore, this model of the test ignores whether the defendant knew the views of honest and reasonable people and instead focuses on the defendant's personal characteristics when deciding what objective honesty would involve in those circumstances. This, it is suggested, is to dilute the objective test with too much subjectivity.

Starglade Properties Ltd v Nash[33] is an important case because it illustrates the difficulty that is faced by judges at first instance with identifying the law that they are supposed to follow. After a negligently prepared report into development land had caused loss to the claimant, a settlement was reached between the various parties. That settlement provided that money received in satisfaction of the negligence claim would be held on trust for all of the injured parties. In breach of the agreement, money was paid to some injured parties (including Nash) but not to Starglade. Starglade sued Mr Nash for dishonest assistance in the breach of trust which had led to payments being made to some injured parties but not to others. Mr Nash had seen the terms of the settlement agreement but it was found by the judge that he was not an educated man, that he had not understood what a trust was, that he had thought that a company was entitled to use its money to pay its creditors in any way that it wished, and that therefore he had not known that there was a trust. Clearly, the judge here was using a large number of subjective factors to reach his judgment about Nash's honesty.

This matter was appealed to the Court of Appeal where it was held that:[34]

> There is a single standard of honesty objectively determined by the court. That standard is applied to specific conduct of a specific individual possessing the knowledge and qualities he actually enjoyed.

This clearly appears to adopt the objective standard, and yet it renders it subjective by limiting the objectively 'honest person' to someone who has the same subjective characteristics

---

33 [2009] EWHC 148 (Ch), [2010] WTLR 1267.
34 [2010] EWCA Civ 1314, [25].

as the defendant. The Chancellor considered the test to be objective[35] in the sense that the relevant standard is 'the ordinary standard of honest behaviour' and significantly held that 'the subjective understanding' of the defendant is 'irrelevant'. Significantly, then, the Court of Appeal corrected the tendency of this trial judge to focus on subjective qualities.

There are other cases which have downplayed this use of a subjective measurement of the defendant's behaviour. In *Otkritie International Investment Management Ltd and others v Urumov*[36] Eder J held:[37]

> Although it has been suggested that the subjective element of the test requires that the third party realised that by the standards of reasonable and honest people his conduct was dishonest, Mr Berry [of counsel] submitted (and I accept) that the better view is that there is no such requirement.[38]

Morgan J set out a summary of the principles in *Aerostar Maintenance v International Ltd v Wilson* which suggests a hybrid concoction of subjectivity and objectivity, in the following terms:[39]

> Dishonesty is synonymous with a lack of probity. It means not acting as an honest person would in the circumstances. The standard is an objective one. The application of the standard requires one to put oneself in the shoes of the defendant to the extent that his conduct is to be assessed in the light of what he knew at the relevant time, as distinct from what a reasonable person would have known or appreciated. For the most part dishonesty is to be equated with conscious impropriety. But a person is not free to set his own standard of honesty. This is what is meant by saying that the standard is objective. If by ordinary objective standards, the defendant's mental state would be judged to be dishonest, it is irrelevant that the defendant has adopted a different standard or can see nothing wrong in his behaviour.

In that case the defendant had admitted in emails that he was 'doing the dirty' on a woman because she had 'done the dirty' on someone else. The defendant therefore considered his behaviour to have been justifiable. Nevertheless, it was held that his behaviour had been objectively dishonest and therefore his actions, even if justifiable subjectively in his own mind, were dishonest.[40] The outcome of the case therefore appears to be unobjectionable in that a *Twinsectra* defence (of subjective ignorance of the views of the majority of the population) failed. What is difficult is this idea of 'putting oneself in the shoes of the defendant' because it connotes subjectivity. If that means looking at the circumstances in which the case arose, then that merely situates the objective measurement; however, if that means seeing everything through the defendant's eyes then that is subjective.

---

35 *Ibid*, [32]
36 [2014] EWHC 191 (Comm).
37 *Ibid*, para [75].
38 His lordship based that principle on the following authorities: *Twinsectra Ltd v Yardley* [2002] UKHL 12, [2002] 2 AC 164 at 27 and 36, *per* Lord Hutton; *Barlow Clowes International Ltd v Eurotrust International Ltd* [2006] 1 WLR 1476 at para 15–16, *per* Lord Hoffmann; *Starglade Properties Ltd v Nash* [2010] EWCA Civ 1314 at para 23–31, *per* the Chancellor of the High Court; *Bank of Ireland v Jaffery* [2012] EWHC 1377 (Ch) at para 289, *per* Vos J.
39 [2010] EWHC 2032 (Ch), at [184]. This approach was followed in *Electrosteel Castings (UK) Ltd v Metalpol Ltd* [2014] EWHC 2017 (Ch).
40 [2010] EWHC 2032 (Ch), [185].

19.2.6 A summary of the cases on the test for dishonesty

The three main approaches

Sometimes students allow themselves to become confused by the fact that different judges have taken different approaches to the same legal principles. The law is in fact quite simple. All of the difficulty revolves around the meaning of the term 'dishonesty' in relation to dishonest assistance. There are three possibilities on the case law. First, the objective approach which requires the court to ask 'what would an honest person have done in these circumstances?' If the defendant failed to do what an honest person would have done in those circumstances then the defendant is held to have been dishonest. Second, the 'hybrid subjective' approach in which, for a defendant to have been dishonest, it must be shown *both* that the defendant did not act as an honest person would have acted *and also* that the defendant realised that their behaviour would have been considered to be dishonest by reasonable people. Third, as has been held in recent cases, a purportedly objective approach (which asks what an honest person would have done in the circumstances) has been taken, but this approach nevertheless takes into account some subjective factors (such as the individual defendant's education, experience and so forth when considering what an honest person would have done). This third approach really just demonstrates a judicial queasiness with finding people to be dishonest entirely on the basis of an objective concept of what would be honest. So, judges using the third approach are really finding a pretext for not holding an individual defendant to be dishonest where they are poorly educated or inexperienced or something similar. This dilutes the objective test, in effect.

Thinking about subjectivity and objectivity

Lord Hutton took the view in *Twinsectra v Yardley* that a finding of dishonesty must be based on some understanding by the defendant that what they were doing was wrong. It would not be enough to find a person liable for dishonesty that they had transgressed some objective idea of what a person ought to have done in their circumstances. This is the approach of a criminal lawyer: guilt can only attach to someone who knows subjectively that they have done wrong. The problem with that approach is that it enables a person to claim that they did not realise that what they were doing was wrong, and it also enables a person with a warped personal morality to escape liability if they genuinely did not understand that what they were doing was wrong.

In the psychology literature, the terms 'sociopath' and 'psychopath' refer to someone who fails to understand the ordinary mores of the society in which they live with the result that they are able to manipulate the people around them without a qualm. A sociopath is someone who simply fails to understand other people's feelings or value systems, and who acts entirely in their own interests and in accordance with their own belief systems as a result. A subjective approach to the test of dishonesty allows sociopaths to escape liability simply by saying 'I didn't realise everyone else would think that what I was doing was wrong'. Therefore, the problem with a subjective test in this context is that it will tend to relieve people with sociopathic tendencies (i.e. people who simply do not understand the moral views held by the rest of society) from liability, but it will tend to hold liable sensitive people who do understand society's mores.

The television series *Breaking Bad* is a good example of these sorts of tensions between subjectivity and objectivity. (There are some spoilers in this text if you have not seen it.) Walter White is a high school chemistry teacher in New Mexico, USA who learns that he has cancer. By chance he encounters one of his former pupils, Jesse Pinkman, who is a low-level crystal meth 'cook' and dealer.[41] Desperate to earn some money to support his family after his likely death, Walter decides to cook crystal meth himself. This is a moral question in itself. Should Walter deal in illegal drugs at all, knowing the harm that they will do? He decides that the needs of his family are greater than any moral qualms about causing harm to other people or the demands of the criminal law. This is a subjective approach which is at odds with the standards which law must require of its citizens. The various series of *Breaking Bad* present several examples of Walter using entirely subjective salves to his conscience. Walter is a monster, only he cannot see it. As the various series progress, Walter must confront his conscience, the needs of his family, and his growing love for the thrill of being a drug dealer. He lies to his family, he kills people, and his drug is so cruelly addictive that it ruins many lives. In one odd episode, one of Walter's low-level street dealers, Badger, is arrested. The concern is that Badger will tell the police about Walter's operation. His lawyer, the wonderfully sleazy Saul Goodman, suggests two alternatives: either having Badger killed in prison or paying someone else to go to prison in Badger's place. Walter would say that his conscience is assuaged because he refuses to let someone stab Badger in prison. He thinks he is being moral because he decides to pay someone to go to prison in Badger's place. It takes a warped moral approach to think of yourself as acting in good conscience simply because you pay a stool pigeon to go to prison instead of having someone else stabbed to death, especially when that is against a backdrop of killing, drug-dealing and so forth. Walter clearly thinks he is making the conscionable choice in accordance with his peculiarly subjective worldview. As Saul Goodman says, while sorting out the cash that is needed to pay their stool pigeon: 'conscience does cost, doesn't it?' It is a very odd kind of conscience. This is why objective approaches to questions of conscience and honesty are more satisfying.

19.2.7 Dishonesty and professionals

In *Twinsectra v Yardley* the House of Lords excused Leach, a solicitor, from liability in large part because they were concerned about the effect on his career if he was found to have been dishonest. Another approach to this question would be to say that Leach was a solicitor and that he should have understood the nature of his obligation to Twinsectra such that passing the money to Yardley was self-evidently a breach of his obligations. Moreover, there is clearly an argument that professionals should be held to a higher standard of behaviour than non-professionals, instead of holding Leach to a lower standard.

19.2.8 Investment, risk-taking and dishonesty

One of the principal contexts in which dishonest assistance arises is in relation to investment transactions, typically where the defendant is advising an investment fund. As Lord Nicholls held:[42] '[a]ll investment involves risk'. This is the central belief of investment transactions: the greater the risk, the greater the return that must be paid to the investor for taking that risk. The question is the point at which a defendant has taken so much risk that it might be considered to be dishonest. As his lordship put it, being imprudent is not being dishonest 'although

---

41 'Crystal meth' (or, more properly, 'methamphetamine') is a highly addictive drug which has ruined many, many lives in the USA and elsewhere.

42 *Royal Brunei Airlines v Tan* [1995] 2 AC 378, 387.

imprudence may be carried recklessly to lengths which call into question the honesty of the person making the decision'.[43] This means that reckless risk-taking in the investment arena may be treated as being dishonesty. A person is more likely to be treated as being dishonest 'if the transaction serves another purpose in which that person has an interest of his own', for example when the defendant earns a commission from that transaction.

19.2.9 The nature of the remedy

The defendant will be personally liable to account as a constructive trustee to the beneficiaries for any loss suffered by the breach of trust. This liability is based on the defendant's dishonesty in assisting the breach of trust. It is based on compensating the beneficiaries' loss. It is not concerned to subtract an unjust enrichment from the defendant. The nature of the remedy is considered in further detail below at section 19.7.1.

It has been held possible for the defendant to provide an account of profits in relation to a claim for dishonest assistance. So, in *Novoship (UK) Ltd v Mihaylyuk*[44] there was a claim brought on the basis of dishonest assistance when the defendant had arranged the charter of ships for the claimant in return for bribes. (Clearly this point could have been argued on the basis of the decision of the Supreme Court in *FHR European Ventures v Cedar*, as discussed in Chapter 12. Nevertheless it was argued on the basis of dishonest assistance.) Interestingly, the Court of Appeal considered a remedy of account of profits in this instance. It was held that they must be a causal connection between the dishonest assistance and the profit which the defendant acquires. The Court of Appeal took the view on the basis of *Royal Brunei Airlines* that a dishonest assistant is to be treated as having 'the responsibility of an express trustee',[45] which includes 'a liability to account for profits'. Of course, a dishonest assistant is not required to be an express trustee. Ordinarily, liability for dishonest assistance is a personal liability to account for the loss which is suffered by the claimant (i.e. a form of compensation for the harm caused) and not to account for any profit that is earned by the defendant (i.e. an amount equal to the profit which the defendant took from the transaction).

19.3 UNCONSCIONABLE RECEIPT

19.3.1 Introduction

The doctrine of 'knowing receipt' imposed liability on a person who receives property in breach of trust to compensate the beneficiaries for any loss so caused. The cases before 2001 simply required that the defendant must have had knowledge of the breach of trust when receiving trust property. In 2001, a decision of the Court of Appeal in *BCCI v Akindele* held that the defendant must not only have had knowledge but that she must also have acted unconscionably. Hence this chapter referring to 'unconscionable receipt' even though most of the cases use the term 'knowing receipt'.

Liability for unconscionable receipt arises when a person knowingly receives trust property which has been transferred away from the trust or otherwise misapplied, and where that

---

43 *Ibid.*
44 [2015] 2 WLR 526.
45 *Ibid*, para [82].

person has acted unconscionably, then that person will incur a personal liability to account as a constructive trustee to the beneficiaries of that trust for the amount of their loss. As Morritt VC put it, a claim for unconscionable receipt is 'parasitic on a claim for breach of trust in the sense that it cannot exist in the absence of the breach of trust from which the receipt originated'.[46] In other words, a claim for unconscionable receipt can arise only after there has been a breach of trust. Once a breach of trust has been proved, then the claimant bears the burden of proving that the defendant received the property, that the defendant had the requisite knowledge,[47] and that the defendant acted unconscionably.[48] This section is organised on the following simple scheme: first, the meaning of 'receipt'; second, the concept of 'knowledge'; and, third, the meaning of 'unconscionable' in this context.

As the Supreme Court in *Williams v Central Bank of Nigeria*[49] accepted, there is no trust here in the ordinary sense of that term: that is, the defendant does not hold property on trust for the claimant.[50] Instead, the defendant is liable to compensate the beneficiaries of a trust for any loss that they suffered as a result of a breach of trust which caused property to pass knowingly to the defendant. This form of liability has always been described in the past as being a personal liability to account to the beneficiaries on the basis of constructive trustee*ship*. That means that the defendant is construed to be liable *as if* they were a trustee.

19.3.2 The nature of 'receipt'

The first question is what actions will constitute 'receipt' under this category. There are two models in the case law. The first model suggests that receipt is satisfied if someone takes property into their possession or has it under their control. That does not require that the recipient becomes the owner of the property. The second model suggests that the recipient acquires some ownership rights in the property and that the property need not simply be trust property but that it could be some other property which was acquired with trust property. (I must express a personal preference for the first model.)

So, let us begin with the first model. In the decision of Millett J in *Agip v Jackson*,[51] it was held that 'there is receipt of trust property when a company's funds are misapplied by any person whose fiduciary position gave him control of them or enabled him to misapply them'. Therefore, a person receives trust property if she takes that property under her control or is able to misuse it. Neither of those requirements equates to ownership. Seemingly, it is enough that the property passes through the stranger's hands, even if the stranger never had the rights of an equitable or common law owner of the property. There must be some meaningful control over the property, however. Lack of proof of receipt will prevent a claim for knowing receipt being commenced with the result that a claim will be struck out.[52] For example, a bank through which payments are made appears to be capable of being accountable for knowing receipt of money paid in breach of trust, even though it did not have any

---

46 *Charter plc and another v City Index Ltd* [2007] 1 WLR 26.
47 *Polly Peck International v Nadir (No 2)* [1992] 4 All ER 769, 777, *per* Scott LJ.
48 *Charter plc and another v City Index Ltd* [2007] 1 WLR 26.
49 [2014] UKSC 10.
50 In that case it was important to know whether or not there was a 'trust' in the ordinary sense to decide whether the claim was time-barred under s 21 of the Limitation Act 1980.
51 *Agip v Jackson* [1990] Ch 265, 286, *per* Millett J; [1991] Ch 547, CA.
52 *Fraser v Oystertec* [2004] EWHC 2225 (Ch); see also *Compagnie Noga D'Importation et D'Exportation v Abacha* [2004] EWHC 2601 (Comm).

rights of ownership over that money.[53] Once money is paid into a person's bank account, then the owner of that bank account will have received that money.[54] Equally, using another person's property to pay off one's own debts constitutes receipt of that other person's property.[55] More evidently, where consignments of hazelnuts, which had been appropriated in breach of trust, were delivered to the defendant and placed knowingly in storage by the defendant, that would constitute receipt.[56] That the hazelnuts were in the defendant's possession in storage was sufficient to constitute receipt.

Let us move to the second model. A test for what constitutes 'receipt' in this context which is often cited in subsequent cases is the one set out by Hoffmann LJ in *El Ajou v Dollar Land Holdings*:[57] 'the plaintiff must show . . . beneficial receipt by the defendant of assets which are traceable as representing the assets of the plaintiff'. Hoffmann LJ seems to be more concerned with ownership of the property than mere possession or control over it. In this context 'beneficial receipt' by the defendant sounds like the acquisition of some sort of ownership of the property.

A number of problems arise with this formulation. First, it is problematic that there must be 'beneficial receipt' of the property because that would be to suggest that the recipient must become the owner of the property in equity; whereas the formulation by Millett J in *Agip v Jackson* is founded on the basis that the defendant need only take the property under her control or into her possession. Acquiring control or possession or property does not make a person the owner of that property necessarily. This latter approach has the advantage of broadening the scope of liability to include people who knowingly pass property between themselves but in a way that ensures that they never acquire property rights in it. Secondly, interestingly, on Hoffmann LJ's formulation the defendant does not need to receive the original trust property but rather may receive other property which constitutes the traceable proceeds of the trust property (as discussed in Chapter 20). So, for example, if a painting was held on trust and that painting was sold in breach of trust, then receipt of the sale proceeds would constitute receipt of the traceable proceeds of the breach of trust because that money was derived from the original painting.

It is suggested that Millett J correctly extended the ambit of liability to any person who commits the equitable wrong of taking property into her possession, for example as part of a money laundering scheme where property is put beyond the reach of its true beneficial owner. Liability should be predicated on knowing contact with the property which was more than a merely fleeting contact, which constituted intermeddling with trust property and involvement in a breach of trust. It should not require that the defendant owned the trust property. It is only under Millett J's formulation that *all* persons 'knowingly' and 'unconscionably' involved in the breach of trust can be held liable for knowing receipt. A number of other problems arise. Strictly, if property were stolen from a trust and passed to the defendant, then the defendant could not become *beneficially* entitled to the stolen trust property and so on Hoffmann LJ's formulation could never strictly found liability for knowing receipt of that property, which cannot be correct.

---

53 *Polly Peck International v Nadir (No 2)* [1992] 3 All ER 769.
54 *Ibid*; *Versailles Trade Finance Ltd v Artagent Ltd* [2004] All ER (D) 318.
55 *MT Realisations Ltd v Digital Equipment Co Ltd* [2003] 2 BCLC 117.
56 *Bank of Tokyo-Mitsubishi Ltd v Baskan Gida* [2004] EWHC 945 (Ch).
57 [1994] 2 All ER 685, 700.

19.3.3 The nature of 'unconscionability' in unconscionable receipt

The evolution of the doctrine of 'knowing receipt' into a doctrine which involved both 'knowledge' and 'unconscionability' happened in the decision of the Court of Appeal in *Bank of Credit and Commerce International v Akindele*[58] in which it was held that, for a defendant to be liable for unconscionable receipt, it is enough to establish that she knew or ought to have known of the breach of trust or fiduciary duty as well as having acted unconscionably. Nourse LJ held the purpose of the test of knowledge was to establish whether or not it was unconscionable for the defendant to retain the money.[59] In this regard, Nourse LJ was following dicta of Buckley LJ in *Belmont Finance Corpn Ltd v Williams Furniture Ltd (No 2)*[60] and of Megarry VC in *In re Montagu's Settlement Trusts*[61] to the effect that there is a requirement that the defendant's 'conscience is sufficiently affected for it to be right to bind him by the obligations of a constructive trustee' having received the trust property. In consequence, it was held, this doctrine should also require that the defendant could be shown to have acted unconscionably. That the defendant had the necessary knowledge would be a part of demonstrating unconscionability but it would not constitute the entire test. Therefore, the defendant is taken to have acted unconscionably if her knowledge was such that it would be unconscionable for her to retain any benefit taken from the receipt of the property. It has been accepted by the Supreme Court in *Williams v Central Bank of Nigeria*[62] that liability now involves unconscionability.

In *Bank of Credit and Commerce International v Akindele*[63] itself Chief Akindele, the defendant, was a client of a bank, BCCI, which later collapsed amid systematic fraud among many of that bank's officers. The defendant had been promised a very high return on his investments by the bank's officers. He was an important client. His investments under-performed and those bank officers were concerned about admitting this to him. Therefore, the bank officers acted in breach of their fiduciary duties to the bank by paying the defendant the return on his investments which they had promised him. The defendant was sued for knowing receipt on the basis that he had received money from the bank which had been paid to him in breach of fiduciary duty. The question was whether or not he had knowledge of that breach on the basis that he had known the terms of his investment contract and therefore that he should have been put on inquiry when he received such a healthy return from the bank. Nourse LJ held that the defendant could not be held liable because he had not acted unconscionably. In essence, he might have been liable on a literal application of the categories of knowledge but because he was not acting unconscionably otherwise he would escape liability.

In the Court of Appeal in *Charter plc v City Index Ltd*,[64] Carnwath LJ (with whom Mummery LJ agreed) took the view that the test of unconscionability in *BCCI v Akindele* is now to form part of the appropriate test in cases of receipt of property in breach of trust.[65] As his lordship put it:

58 [2000] 4 All ER 221.
59 *Ibid*, 455.
60 [1980] 1 All ER 393, 405.
61 [1987] Ch 264, 273.
62 [2014] UKSC 10.
63 [2000] 4 All ER 221.
64 *Charter plc v City Index Ltd* [2008] 2 WLR 950.
65 *Ibid*, [31].

liability for 'knowing receipt' depends on the defendant having sufficient knowledge of the circumstances of the payment to make it 'unconscionable' for him to retain the benefit or pay it away for his own purposes.

The notion of unconscionability is therefore linked to the requirement of knowledge. The concept of knowledge is discussed in section 19.3.4.

Hart J and the Court of Appeal in *Criterion Properties Ltd v Stratford UK Properties*[66] applied the unconscionability test in relation to an interlocutory motion relating to the ability of a company to enter into a joint venture agreement so as to fend off a takeover. (It was held in the House of Lords that those facts did not disclose a case of knowing receipt and that that issue need not arise when the matter went to trial. There was no adverse comment made concerning the concept of knowing receipt nor any rejection of the unconscionability concept in that case.[67]) In *Criterion Properties plc v Stratford UK Properties LLC*[68] the Court of Appeal had approved the flexibility of the notion of 'conscionability'[69] in relation to a claim brought on behalf of shareholders to the effect that the directors of a company had knowingly committed breaches of duty by entering into arrangements which would prevent a takeover of that company by third parties. The Court of Appeal in *Niru Battery Manufacturing Co v Milestone Trading Ltd*[70] expressed its support for the test of unconscionability.

19.3.4 The nature of 'knowledge'

The fundamental question is what constitutes 'knowledge' in this context. As Lord Browne-Wilkinson held in *Westdeutsche Landesbank Girozentrale v Islington LBC*:

> If X has the necessary degree of knowledge, X may himself become a constructive trustee for B on the basis of knowing receipt.[71] But unless he has the requisite degree of knowledge he is not personally liable to account as trustee.[72] Therefore, innocent receipt of property by X subject to an existing equitable interest does not by itself make X a trustee despite the severance of the legal and equitable titles.[73]

The most significant judicial explanation of the various categories of knowledge was that set out by Peter Gibson J in *Baden v Société Générale*,[74] based on the categories of knowledge that had been suggested to his lordship in argument, as follows:

(1) actual knowledge;
(2) wilfully shutting one's eyes to the obvious;
(3) wilfully and recklessly failing to make inquiries which an honest person would have made;

---

66 [2003] 1 WLR 218, CA.
67 [2004] UKHL 28.
68 [2003] 2 BCLC 129.
69 *Ibid*, [38].
70 [2004] 2 WLR 1415, [188], *per* Sedley LJ.
71 [1996] AC 669.
72 *Re Diplock* [1948] Ch 465 and *Re Montagu's Settlement Trusts* [1987] Ch 264.
73 [1996] 2 All ER 961, 990.
74 *Baden v Société Générale* [1993] 1 WLR 509.

(4) knowledge of circumstances which would indicate the facts to an honest and reasonable man;

(5) knowledge of circumstances which would put an honest and reasonable man on inquiry.

As we shall see, the court in *Re Montagu* was keen to limit the categories to only the first three. These categories were rendered slightly more memorably by counsel in *Baden* as follows: the first category is referred to as 'actual knowledge'; then the second category of 'wilfully shutting one's eyes to the obvious' was referred to as being 'Nelsonian knowledge' (a reference to the Admiral Nelson who, in an act of bravery, put a telescope to his blind eye so that he could not see the enemy's fleet and gave the order to continue bravely in that direction); and the third category of wilfully failing to make inquiries as being 'naughty knowledge'.[75] (These terms are often used in the literature because they are a useful shorthand. However, in answering problem questions it is important to unpack and apply them in full.) In answering a problem question, you will have to examine in detail whether or not the defendant exhibited any of these types of knowledge in the light of the precise models set out above.

The first category – actual knowledge – requires proof that the defendant actually, consciously knew of the breach of trust and of the source of the property which she received. If there is no such proof then the claimant will have to rely on the second and third categories which are constructive forms of knowledge in which the defendant is deemed to have had knowledge of the breach even if actual knowledge cannot be proved definitively.

The second category – Nelsonian knowledge – requires that there was something obvious about the circumstances which should have indicated there had been a breach of trust which the defendant ignored. Suppose the defendant was standing in a restaurant car park at noon while by the entrance door there was a person shouting 'Where are the trust's diamonds? I have lost a big bag of diamonds belonging to a trust!' If a shifty looking person (who was a second trustee) hurried up to the defendant and said 'Here, mate, wanna buy a bag of diamonds really cheap?', then the defendant would be shutting his eyes to the obvious if he paid £200 for the bag of diamonds and claimed not to have known what was going on. The defendant would be treated as having had knowledge of the breach of trust. Was it obvious that he was being offered the diamonds which he knew had just gone missing? Was he being wilfully blind (i.e. deliberately blind) to that fact? Or was there some other circumstance which justified his behaviour?

The third category – naughty knowledge – requires us to ask what are the inquiries which an honest and reasonable person would have made in the circumstances? For example, if a jeweller had seen the television news and its dramatic reporting of a daring robbery of rare 'chocolate diamonds' (diamonds with an appealing brown hue) from a nearby stately home the previous day, and if the defendant was offered a chocolate diamond in his shop the following morning, then the inquiries we would expect from the defendant would have been to identify the provenance and source of the diamond. If the defendant simply bought the chocolate diamond for a suspiciously low price without asking any questions then the defendant would be treated as having had naughty knowledge of the theft. What are the inquiries which

---

75 Hayton, 1995:2, 412.

an honest and reasonable person would have made in the circumstances? Did the defendant make those inquiries? Was he wilful in failing to make those inquiries?

The fourth and fifth categories are the most interesting, given that they are potentially the broadest: the fourth and fifth categories do not require that the defendant had acted 'wilfully' or intentionally, merely that there were 'circumstances' which might have put them on inquiry. This is important because, as we shall see, the judges in later cases (such as *Re Montagu*, discussed below) have preferred that the defendant must have shown some wilfulness or unconscionability.

The following section considers some important applications of these concepts in the case law. The appropriate structure in answering a problem question, it is suggested, is to begin by asking whether or not the defendant has received trust property in breach of trust; second, is to ask whether the defendant had any of the first three categories of knowledge; and, finally, is to ask whether the defendant was also acting unconscionably.

19.3.5 The concept of knowledge in context

Introduction

This section considers the concept of knowledge as it has been applied in particular cases. First, we shall see how the *Baden* categories of knowledge were narrowed down to only three. Second, we shall see how this concept has been applied in the numerous cases relating to bankers.

Knowledge is subjective and therefore knowledge can be forgotten

The decision of Megarry VC in *Re Montagu's Settlement*[76] is fascinating. The 10th Duke of Manchester was a life tenant under a settlement created by the 9th Duke. On the terms of the settlement, the trustees considered themselves to have a power to transfer good title in the trust's property to the 10th Duke. This was actually in breach of trust but the trustees were in the habit of acceding to the Duke's wishes. The Duke had seen the terms of the settlement and had had them explained to him at some earlier point in time. Nevertheless, the trustees allowed the Duke to take several very valuable, antique chattels from the trust, including a painting by the Dutch master Van Dyck and a travelling trunk which had belonged to one of Henry VIII's wives, Catherine of Aragon. These chattels were sold at auction at the family's castle and at the premises of the London auctioneers Christie's. After the 10th Duke's death, the issue arose whether or not the 10th Duke's estate should have been held liable for knowing receipt of these chattels in breach of trust. (Interestingly, no one seems to have confronted the Duke about this during his lifetime.)

The question was whether or not there had been knowledge of the breach of trust when the Duke received the trust property before selling it at auction. Megarry VC took the view that there had been 'an honest muddle' in this case. It was found as a fact that the 10th Duke had undoubtedly had actual knowledge of the terms of the trust at one stage in the past, in part because explicit references were made to the relevant provisions of the settlement in correspondence between the parties. Therefore, it could have been said that the Duke, at

---

76 [1987] Ch 264.

the very least, had knowledge of circumstances which should have put him on inquiry as to whether or not he could sell these items. Megarry VC disagreed and accepted that the Duke might have forgotten the detailed terms of the settlement over time. Consequently, it was held that a defendant does not have the requisite knowledge on which to base a claim for knowing receipt if the defendant has genuinely forgotten the relevant factors.[77] In light of this, no liability for knowing receipt attached to the 10th Duke nor to his estate. Because the three categories of knowledge applied in *Re Montagu* were all predicated on wilful behaviour or actual knowledge, having forgotten information would absolve a person from having acted 'wilfully'. Therefore, it was important for Megarry VC to limit the concept of 'knowledge' to the first three *Baden* categories.

Interestingly, during his lifetime, Vice-Chancellor Megarry had himself been embroiled in litigation with the Inland Revenue over unpaid tax. His defence was that he had become muddled about his tax affairs and therefore that he had simply made an innocent mistake. In consequence, we might think it unsurprising that Megarry VC would be moved by the argument advanced on behalf of the Duke here.

Knowledge in the banking context

The case of *Polly Peck v Nadir (No 2)*[78] is a useful illustration of knowing receipt in more complex cases. The facts related to the actions of Asil Nadir in respect of the insolvency of the Polly Peck group of companies. This particular litigation referred to an action brought by the administrators of the plaintiff company against a bank, IBK, which was controlled by Nadir, and the Central Bank of Northern Cyprus. It was alleged that Nadir had been responsible for bleeding money out of the Polly Peck companies and passing them in breach of his fiduciary duties into Northern Cyprus. This was achieved by converting the sterling amounts taken from Polly Peck into lire by entering into a large foreign exchange transaction with the Central Bank of Northern Cyprus. The plaintiff claimed that the Central Bank should be liable for knowing receipt on the basis that it received the sterling during the foreign exchange transaction and that it should be treated as having constructive knowledge of the breaches of duty to Polly Peck. Scott LJ held that the Central Bank would not be liable for knowing receipt. The acid test which Scott LJ advanced was whether or not the recipient of the property 'ought to have been suspicious' that the property had been acquired in breach of fiduciary duty.[79] In the context of a central bank, his lordship considered, transactions of a large size would be a regular occurrence and there would have been nothing about this transaction which should have made the bank suspicious. The test in banking cases was what an 'honest and reasonable banker' would do in the circumstances.[80] Even though the transaction was for £45 million, that was not considered to be exceptional for a central bank.

The alternative argument would have been that money laundering and similar regulations oblige bankers to investigate the source of payments. Even counter staff in high street branches are trained to be suspicious of regular cash deposits by particular customers in case

---

77 Followed in *MCP Pension Trustees Ltd v AON Pension Trustees Ltd* [2010] EWCA Civ 377, at [14], *per* Elias LJ.
78 [1992] 4 All ER 769.
79 *Eagle Trust v SBC (No 2)* [1996] 1 BCLC 121; *Hillsdown plc v Pensions Ombudsman* [1997] 1 All ER 862.
80 *Ibid*, 778–80.

they are the products of drug dealing, and so forth. Even when I am attempting to pay in my miserly small royalty cheques from writing textbooks, my high street branch questions the source of the money and asks me to produce identification. (That is when making deposits, not when withdrawing money.[81]) Therefore, it is peculiar that Scott LJ would excuse a central bank from investigating a transaction involving £45 million.

In another decision involving bankers, Millett J held in *Macmillan v Bishopsgate* that 'account officers are not detectives' and therefore that they should not be expected to investigate every payment. In that case, millions of pounds had been diverted from the Mirror Group pension funds by media mogul Robert Maxwell through the defendant bank. The bank had been sued for knowing receipt of the money when it was paid into bank accounts which the defendant operated. It was held that the bankers were 'entitled to believe that they were dealing with honest men' unless they had some suspicion raised in their minds to the contrary. Similarly, in *El Ajou v Dollar Land Holdings*,[82] Millett J had held that liability for knowing receipt would attach 'in a situation in which any honest and reasonable man would have made inquiry'. In short, the issue is whether or not the circumstances are such as to require a person to be suspicious, so that their conscience would encourage them to make inquiries. It was held that the bank should not be deemed to have had constructive knowledge of the breach of trust behind the deposits because there was nothing suspicious about the transaction which should have brought it to the notice of the defendant bankers. Importantly, money laundering and bank regulation *does* require bankers to be assiduous in identifying fraud – they bear positive obligations to be vigilant and not simply to act passively unless something comes to their attention as being suspicious.[83] Nevertheless, the same approach was taken in *Papadimitriou v Credit Agricole*[84] by the Privy Council, as discussed below at section 19.5.2, when Lord Sumption held that there was no basis for liability unless there was something about the transaction which should have put the defendant on notice.

The banking context raises questions about the circumstances in which it will be the corporate entity can be made liable for having had knowledge or for having acted unconscionably. This issue of corporate liability for knowing receipt, and the decision in *El Ajou v Dollar Land Holdings*, are considered below in section 19.5.1.

19.3.6 Dishonesty in unconscionable receipt

There have been cases in recent past which held that the test for dishonesty which was set out in *Royal Brunei Airlines v Tan* should be applied to the receipt claim. Given that the assistance claim and the receipt claim used to be governed by the same concept of 'knowledge', there is no reason why they should not be governed by the same concept of dishonesty. It was in the Court of Appeal in *Twinsectra Ltd v Yardley* that Potter LJ held that the applicable test for both knowing receipt and dishonest assistance was one of 'dishonesty' as set out in *Royal Brunei Airlines v Tan*. This idea was followed in a line of cases

---

81 I was once questioned by a young cashier, presumably fresh from her training, as to the source of my money when I attempted to deposit a large number of copper coins that I had collected in a jar over the years. I reassured her that I was not drug dealer. And that even if I had been, I was unlikely to have been paid in two pence pieces.

82 *El Ajou v Dollar Land Holdings* [1993] 3 All ER 717; appealed [1994] 2 All ER 685.

83 See generally Hudson, *The Law of Finance*, 2013.

84 [2015] UKPC 13.

including the High Court in *Bank of America v Arnell*[85] and the Court of Appeal in *Heinl and Others v Jyske Bank*.[86] Interestingly, in a subsequent case, the Court of Appeal in *Niru Battery Manufacturing Co v Milestone Trading Ltd*[87] doubted that dishonesty is a requirement of liability for knowing receipt, relying on the decision in *Belmont Finance Corp Ltd v Williams Furniture Ltd*.[88] A preference for a test of unconscionability, which expressly disavows a test of dishonesty in this context, was upheld in *Criterion Properties plc v Stratford UK Properties LLC*.[89] Those two more recent Court of Appeal decisions should have followed the judgment of Potter LJ (which was not doubted in the House of Lords because it was not an issue before that court) in line with the doctrine of precedent, but it was not. No subsequent cases seem to have even cited this opinion thereafter and it is generally overlooked in the textbooks.

This perhaps tells us a deeper truth about the way in which the doctrine of precedent really works in the 21st century – it tells us about some ideas becoming entrenched, almost by chance, in lines of cases coming in quick succession to one another by judges who think those ideas more appropriate than others and by barristers who use some ideas rather than others when presenting their cases. It is a feature of our common law system that with the thousands of judgments which are now available on the internet (as opposed to the very few cases that used to make it into the official law reports) it can be a lottery as to which cases entrench themselves as authorities over time. Even at the Court of Appeal level, there are so many cases decided that not all of them can be treated as authoritative when they are in disagreement with one another. For each edition of this book, for example, there are between 200 and 300 cases mentioning trusts law and equitable concepts in each two-year period. In that flood of case law, some ideas simply get washed away while others establish themselves in later cases.

19.3.7 The current model of unconscionable receipt

The explanation of unconscionable receipt as arising on the basis of dishonesty or of unconscionability had one principal advantage: it recognised that the claim is really based on fault as well as being based on receipt. The fault came from the defendant's unconscionability or dishonesty in receiving property. It is suggested that knowing receipt was also based on the wrong of receiving property in circumstances in which the defendant knew of some factor which should have put her on inquiry or which involved her wilfully shutting her eyes to the obvious.

The judgment of Arden LJ in *Charter plc v City Index Ltd* made unfortunate reference to knowing receipt as being concerned with damages and constructive trusts as being concerned with breach of trust. Arden LJ also referred to liability for receipt of trust property as being divided between 'claims for unjust enrichment based on the wrongful conduct of the defendant (known as knowing receipt) and claims for unjust enrichment based on innocent receipt (often called claims for money had and received)'.[90] This is simply not the case. Knowing receipt is not predicated on unjust enrichment. By definition, a defendant will be liable to account for knowing

85 [1999] Lloyd's Rep Bank 399.
86 [1999] Lloyd's Rep Bank 511.
87 [2004] 2 WLR 1415, para 188, *per* Sedley LJ.
88 [1980] 1 All ER 393.
89 [2003] 2 BCLC 129.
90 *Charter plc v City Index Ltd* [2008] 2 WLR 950, [62].

receipt if she has received trust property knowing of the breach of trust and has since disposed of the property without earning any profit from the transaction. Thus, the defendant need not be enriched to be liable for knowing receipt. Liability is based on the need to compensate the beneficiaries' loss, which is something very different (as discussed in Chapter 26). This is why we must understand the liability as being based on the equitable wrong of knowing and unconscionable receipt of trust property. A claim for money had and received is generally understood as arising when the defendant has acquired an enrichment at the claimant's expense as the result of some unjust factor. Moreover, Arden LJ suggested that the purpose of the doctrine of knowing receipt 'is imposed to deter trustees'; whereas it is suggested that the liability is in fact imposed to compensate the loss suffered by the beneficiaries as a result of the breach of trust.

19.3.8 The nature of the remedy

The defendant will be personally liable to account as a constructive trustee to the beneficiaries for any loss suffered by the breach of trust. This liability is based on the defendant's unconscionability, dishonesty or knowing actions when receiving property further to the breach of trust. It is based on compensating the beneficiaries' loss. It is not concerned to subtract an unjust enrichment from the defendant, even though the property had passed through the defendant's hands at some time.

19.4 DEFENCES

19.4.1 *Bona fide* purchaser for value without notice of the breach of trust

Among the only available defences against a claim for knowing receipt are, first, that the defendant was a *bona fide* purchaser for value without notice of the claimant's rights. Where the defendant can demonstrate that she purchased the property in good faith (which would in any event cancel out a claim for knowing receipt in that the requirement of *bona fides* would require an absence of knowledge or dishonesty).[91] This defence is considered in greater detail in section 20.6 below.

19.4.2 Change of position

In circumstances in which the defendant can demonstrate a change of position in good faith in reliance on receipt of trust property, the defendant would be entitled to resist the claim for personal liability to account.[92] In *Barros Mattos v MacDaniels Ltd*,[93] it was held that where the defendant had knowingly received money which had been stolen from a bank then the defence of change of position would not be available. This defence is considered in detail in section 20.6.

19.4.3 Release

The defendant will be able to defend a claim to dishonest assistance or knowing receipt on the basis that she has been released from liability by the beneficiaries. This defence is considered in greater detail in section 20.6 below.

---

91 *Westdeutsche Landesbank Girozentrale v Islington LBC* [1996] AC 669.
92 *Lipkin Gorman v Karpnale* [1991] 3 WLR 10.
93 [2004] 3 All ER 299.

19.5 LIABILITY TO ACCOUNT IN CORPORATE CONTEXTS

19.5.1 Personal liability to account in corporate contexts

A difficult issue can arise where the defendant is an employee of a company or where the defendant is itself a company. Because companies are not human beings, they have no brains and no limbs; therefore, a company must think and act through human beings. Therefore, if a claimant wants to impose liability on corporate entity then it must identify an individual who has the necessary dishonesty or knowledge and it must prove that it is appropriate for that individual's state of mind to be attributed to the company so that the company in turn will be liable for dishonest assistance or unconscionable receipt.

A company will be liable for anything which its 'controlling mind' knew or any dishonesty which its controlling mind exhibited. It is a question of fact in each case who will be the controlling mind. Ordinarily under company law, anything which was known by the directors will be attributed to the company, as in *Crown Dilmun v Sutton*.[94] This may not always automatically be the case. Otherwise, other employees may be the controlling mind of the company depending on the context.

The clearest example arose in *El-Ajou v Dollar Land Holdings*.[95] A group of Canadian fraudsters defrauded the plaintiff of his money in Geneva and passed the money around the world until they came to London. The traceable proceeds of that money were invested in a London property company called Dollar Land Holdings Ltd ('DLH'). The investment had come to DLH through its chairman, a man who ordinarily took no part in the day-to-day management of the company. The question was whether the chairman was the controlling mind of DLH such that his knowledge of the circumstances could be attributed to DLH, so that DLH in turn could be liable for unconscionable receipt. It was found that only the non-executive chairman had sufficient knowledge of the manner in which the money had come to be invested in DLH for the company to be held liable. The Court of Appeal held that the test for demonstrating that a company has knowledge of something is that 'the controlling mind' or 'the directing mind and will' of the company must have knowledge of whatever has been alleged. On these facts, even though the non-executive chairman of the company ordinarily played no part in the day-to-day management of the company, he had been the person who had organised the investment by the Canadians in DLH and he had acted without any of the requisite resolutions of the board of directors in so doing. It was held that these factors suggested that the chairman was the directing mind and will of the company in this particular context because he had assumed managerial control of this transaction. Moreover, this transaction was sufficiently significant to be appropriate to be attributed to the company. On the facts it was therefore held that the chairman, and consequently DLH by attribution, had had the requisite knowledge of the circumstances which had led to the Canadians making the investment in DLH. The same principle as that in *El Ajou* was applied by the Privy Council in *Lebon v Aqua Salt Co Ltd*.[96]

In the Privy Council in *Meridian Global Funds Management Asia Ltd v Securities Commission*[97] it was held that when deciding the obligation of a company which traded in securi-

---

94 [2004] 1 BCLC 468.
95 [1994] 2 All ER 685; [1994] 1 BCLC 464; [1994] BCC 143.
96 [2009] UKPC 2, [2009] 1 BCLC 549.
97 [1995] 3 All ER 918.

ties to report that it held a given number of a particular type of share so as to comply with securities regulation, the knowledge which should be attributed to the company would be the knowledge of the people who were authorised to acquire those shares on behalf of the company. This approach is not limited to a single person or to a small group of people who run the entire organisation – which would tend to make it difficult to demonstrate knowledge in relation to a large organisation where a function like acquiring shares might be conducted at a much lower level within the company – but rather identifies knowledge in the hands of the individuals who could bind the company in those transactions. Where information comes to the attention of one director of a company, that may be treated as knowledge held by the company even if that director did not inform other board directors of the facts.[98]

19.5.2 The personal liability to account of financial advisors and financial institutions

In the UK, financial institutions and investment advisors are regulated by the Financial Conduct Authority ('FCA') under the Financial Services and Markets Act 2000, and therefore in practice their case law liabilities are only part of the equation because those institutions are also governed by regulatory requirements. Therefore, when identifying what an honest banker should have done or what a banker should have known it is the standards which are set out in those statutory regulations which should be taken to constitute a statement of those objective standards. Consequently, money laundering regulation obliges banks and others to conduct 'know your client' checks on customers and the source of their funds: a regulated entity is expected to have knowledge of information which would reasonably have come to light if they had made the necessary checks. FCA Conduct of Business regulation obliges financial institutions to act in the best interests of their customers and to acquire the best prices and terms ('best execution') for them. These are all positive obligations. It is worth noting that these regulatory standards are the opposite of the approach taken by Scott LJ in *Polly Peck v Nadir* and Millett J in *Macmillan v Bishopsgate* who held that bankers are not expected to conduct inquiries into their clients but rather are only expected to be suspicious of matters which come actively to their attention in ordinary circumstances. Those case law principles are the opposite of the regulatory world in which bankers, financial institutions and their employees operate today.

In *Papadimitriou v Credit Agricole*[99] the Privy Council heard an appeal from the Court of Appeal of Gibraltar which related to a sale of valuable art deco furniture. The furniture had been fraudulently sold by an art dealer for US$15 million. The sale proceeds were then paid into accounts held in different jurisdictions by different companies. The question related to the liability of a bank which received funds from the art dealer through its branch in Gibraltar. It was held by the Court of Appeal in Gibraltar that the bank could be deemed to have had constructive notice of a person's proprietary rights in money that was deposited with it if the bank should have made enquiries which would have revealed the existence of those rights. The question was what a reasonable banker in the defendant's position should have done in the circumstances. The bank argued that there was nothing untoward with the transaction and therefore nothing which ought to have raised a red flag with it. The claimant contended that the bank had knowledge of the 'web of companies' through which the payments were made

---

98 *Jafari-Fini v Skillglass Ltd* [2007] EWCA Civ 261.
99 [2015] UKPC 13.

and that those circumstances, including payments being made through Panamanian and British Virgin Islands entities, should have put the bank on notice. It was argued that if the bank had been put on notice then it could be deemed to have had knowledge of the fraudulent sale of the furniture so that it could have been liable as a constructive trustee. The Privy Council upheld the finding that there was nothing obviously untoward about this transaction which ought to have brought it to the attention of the bank, and that in consequence the bank did not have knowledge of the fraudulent sale.

Lord Sumption held that in this case 'we are in the realm of property rights, and are not concerned with an actionable duty to investigate'. This is an interesting point which underpins the Privy Council's decision. The court assumes that there is no obligation to investigate the source of a payment. Consequently, it is held that unless there is something very unusual or suspicious about the transaction then there is nothing about it which should fix the bank with either constructive notice or constructive knowledge (because Lord Sumption treats them as being the same thing) of the fraud.[100] Of course, European Union banking law (covering Gibraltar) and UK banking law (in general terms) does require that banks conduct so-called 'know your client' and money laundering checks on payments. Therefore, it is incorrect to say that the bank was operating in circumstances in which there was no obligation on it to conduct investigations. The bank was obliged to conduct investigations in general terms by banking regulation. That does not mean that the bank's ordinary checks would have brought this fraud to light but importantly English law on knowing receipt in this area is operating on an unsatisfactory basis if it continues to assume that banks are not supposed to conduct exactly these sorts of checks.

19.6 THE PERSONAL REMEDY IN *RE DIPLOCK*

Where a beneficiary under a will has been underpaid or unpaid, that beneficiary may bring a personal action against any beneficiary who has been overpaid from the assets of the will trust. The remedy is a personal remedy against that overpaid person for the amount of the overpayment. This remedy emerges from the decision of the Court of Appeal in *Re Diplock*.[101]

---

100 *Ibid*, para [33].
101 *Re Diplock* [1948] Ch 465.

Chapter 20

Tracing

CAPSULE SUMMARY

Where a claimant seeks to recover a specific item of property which belonged to her originally in the hands of the defendant, then the claimant will pursue a 'following' action to require the return of that specific item of property. If the claimant seeks to trace from that original item of property into its 'clean substitute' (i.e. where the property is not mixed with other property) then a 'common law tracing' action will be used. In the event that the original property or the substitute property has been mixed with other property then the claimant will only be able to bring an 'equitable tracing' action. An equitable tracing action requires that the claimant had some pre-existing equitable proprietary right in that property. Tracing is the process of identifying property against which a claim will be brought; it is then a separate question which remedy will be claimed. There can be no tracing claim in respect of property which has ceased to exist. In relation to mixtures of trust and other money held in bank accounts, a variety of approaches has been taken in the courts from the application of the old 'first-in, first-out principle', to a rolling charge approach, through to the establishment of proportionate shares in any substitute property. The possible remedies in relation to tracing claims include: the establishment of a constructive trust, an equitable charge, a lien, and subrogation. The defences available in relation to tracing claims include change of position, bona fide purchase of the property for value, estoppel by representation, and passing on.

20.1 INTRODUCTION

20.1.1 The nature of tracing

The law in this chapter is concerned with getting your property back; or, if you cannot get your original property back, then the law on tracing enables you to acquire rights in property which was substituted for your original property. If I take your car and sell it, and use that money to buy a motorbike, then you can trace your property rights into my motorbike. That is the subject of tracing in a nutshell. The law on tracing enables you to 'trace' your original property rights into substitute property which some other person has acquired by using your original property without a lawful excuse. There are then a range of potential remedies which may be claimed over that substitute property and defences which the apparent owner of that property may use to resist your claim. In many commercial contexts, the law on tracing is part of one of the most extensive armouries of weapons in the litigator's arsenal and it is a part of what makes England and Wales such an attractive place to bring commercial law litigation.

20.1.2 Treating tracing as part of the law on breach of trust

It might be useful to think of this chapter as being the third chapter in our examination of all of the ways in which beneficiaries may seek to recover losses caused by a breach of trust. In Chapter 18 we considered the primary liability of the trustees of an express trust. In Chapter 19 we considered the secondary liability of 'strangers' who dishonestly assist a breach of trust or who unconscionably receive property with knowledge of a breach of trust. In this chapter we consider the possibility of recovering the original property which was taken from the trust, and the possibility of tracing through substitutes for that original property in the hands of third parties. It is possible that an action may be brought to claim substitute property without there having been a breach of trust (as we shall see) but when trying to understand how tracing fits into the principles discussed in this book generally then it is alongside the law on breach of trust that it sits most comfortably.

It should be recalled that in practice the beneficiaries will sue all of the potential defendants discussed in Chapters 18 through 20 at once and then they will seek to recoup their losses in the aggregate from those various defendants. All of the various possible defendants will then have responsibility allocated between them at the end of the trial for their contribution to the total loss suffered by the beneficiaries in accordance with the Civil Liability (Contribution) Act 1970. When it is a large trust fund which has been affected then it might mean establishing liability against several defendants to recover the value of the entire trust fund. Therefore, it is in the defendants' interests to join as many parties to the litigation as possible as co-defendants so as to spread the responsibility around.

The law of tracing is concerned with identifying property against which a claim may be brought and then establishing proprietary remedies against that property. This might be preferable to a claim against the trustees for breach of trust (in Chapter 18) or against dishonest assistants or knowing recipients (in Chapter 19) if those people have insufficient funds to compensate the loss to the trust. If the property in question has increased in value then it might also be preferable to bring proprietary rights against it through a tracing action because ownership of property that is increasing in value may be preferable to merely financial compensation. Contrariwise, if the property falls in value then it might be preferable to prioritise the personal claims discussed in Chapters 18 and 19. The advantage of a proprietary right acquired in a tracing action is that it will survive insolvency. Similarly, if the asset remains in England and Wales (or another appropriate jurisdiction) then the action against that property can continue even if the defendant personally has absconded from the jurisdiction. It is also an attraction for some litigants to sue in England and Wales precisely because this sort of remedy is available here even if all of the parties are otherwise resident in other jurisdictions. If there is a valuable asset in England (such as valuable real estate in London or financial instruments) then bringing a tracing action here will be attractive. We shall see that many of the cases discussed in this chapter involved parties who conducted their activities in other jurisdictions but who relied on English law and the presence of assets in this jurisdiction to begin their tracing action. Equally, tracing has the flexibility to cope with complex forms of property (such as money in electronic bank accounts and complex financial instruments) which mean that many of the cases have involved banks or have involved money laundering through bank accounts.

20.1.3 Interesting issues with tracing in property law

Interestingly, a successful tracing action means that the successful claimant is able to impose rights in property which she had not previously owned because that property is a substitute for their original property. If you recall the hypothetical given at the start of this chapter: I stole your car, sold it and used the sale proceeds to buy a motorbike. You will seek to trace your property rights from the car into the motorbike. This is an unusual area of property law precisely because it enables claimants to acquire rights in property which they had never previously owned. The justice of the case is clear: I took your property without a lawful excuse, and therefore you should be able to take whatever property I acquired with it. This sort of action is rare in other jurisdictions. In most jurisdictions the criminal law of theft and the law of tort would be all that would be available. This means that sophisticated criminals can sometimes abscond without recourse in those jurisdictions. If a clever rogue took property through a company under their control and immediately afterwards wound the company up and disappeared, then it would be difficult to bring a claim in tort against that company because it would have no assets left. The claimant would appear to have no recourse. However, the law on tracing enables the claimant to trace their property rights through that company into whichever company or individual's hands the original property or any substitute property then passed. The law on tracing is a very powerful means of providing a remedy to a claimant who has lost property.

Our focus in this chapter will be on *the property rights* which were owned by the claimant and not just on the specific items of property. You may have seen that magician's trick when they lie three playing cards face-down on a table and ask you to pick which one is the Queen after they have moved the cards around quickly. If you allow yourself to become distracted by the magician's moving hands then you will lose sight of the Queen. With tracing, we must not become fixated on the original property. Instead we must think about the property rights. If the claimant lost money from a bank account then that 'money' will be paid into other bank accounts and mixed with other money already in that account. Consequently, it will become very difficult to identify the original money which was taken from the first account. However, if we focus on the property rights in the original money and on the value which was lost, then we can think of those property rights as being transferred to a share in the pool of money in the second account. Therefore, when the money from the second account is used to buy a boat, then we can say that our share of the money in that second account must have acquired a share of that boat. Therefore, we would seek a claim against that boat.

When things become more difficult is when there are other people with shares in the mixed fund in the second bank account. Again, we must not focus on the specific property involved (once we have identified that it is the traceable proceed of other property). Rather, we should consider that each contributor to the mixture has a proportionate share to that mixture and anything bought with it. Clearly, in practice, it can be a very difficult question to prove which money has moved from which account. Many of the recent cases have involved money being moved through bank accounts, and therefore the property involved has been intangible property which is easy to move between accounts and to hide by mixing it with other money. A 'forensic accountant' is often required to prove which moneys can be treated as being the traceable proceeds of the claimant's original property.

20.1.4 Tracing, following and claiming

Distinguishing between tracing, following and claiming

There are some clear divisions in this topic which we should identify at the start. First, if the claimant is seeking to recover a specific item of property which she had previously owned (such as a car identifiable by its registration number) then she would bring a 'following' action to recover that specific car. However, if the original property could not be recovered for some reason (for example, because it had been sold to a *bona fide* purchaser or because it had been transported out of the jurisdiction) then the claimant would need to bring a 'tracing' action to trace those original property rights into any substitute property, such as cash received for the sale of that original item of property (just like the action being brought in relation to the motorbike which was bought when my car was stolen and sold by the defendant).

Second, it is important to distinguish between the 'tracing process' and the remedy which is brought as a result of that tracing process. The tracing process is simply the detective work of identifying property against which a claim may be brought. There is then a separate question of identifying the most appropriate remedy which will be claimed when that property is traced. The remedies are considered below in section 20.4.

Finally, there are two forms of tracing: common law tracing and equitable tracing. Common law tracing is only available where the original property has been subject to a 'clean substitution' – that is, where there has been no mixture of any other property with the substitute for the claimant's original property. If any of these items of property is mixed with other property, then only 'equitable tracing' will be available. For example, if the claimant's original property was sold and the sale proceeds paid into a bank account in which there was other money, then there would be a mixture of moneys and therefore only equitable tracing could be used against that bank account. A clean substitution would take place if the sale proceeds were paid into an empty bank account and never mixed with other money.

Money laundering, tracing and breaking unconscionable

The clearest example of tracing claims in the modern world involve money laundering. 'Money laundering' is the process by which criminals and their agents seek to cleanse 'dirty money' of its stigma of being the proceeds of criminal or similar activity by putting it through so many changes of form that its source is not easily detectable. The best example from modern culture was in the American TV series *Breaking Bad* in which high school chemistry teacher Walter White and one of his former pupils began 'cooking' the highly addictive drug 'crystal meth' in New Mexico, USA.[1] This illegal activity generated a huge profit. However, no career criminal should ever simply spend their ill-gotten gains or else they risk detection and their new-found wealth will be used as evidence against them. Therefore, the criminal needs to 'launder' their money: that means passing it through a number of forms so that its criminal source become difficult or impossible to detect. So, Walter White acquired a large car wash business whose customers often paid in cash. His wife paid the cash acquired from drug deals into the car wash's bank accounts by creating a huge number of false transactions with non-existent customers: in several scenes, after taking money from real customers, she rang fake transactions through the till and printed out receipts for the cash which had actually come from selling crystal meth as though it had come from car wash customers. She was attempting to 'launder' the money by making it appear as though she and her husband had earned it from their car wash business and not from criminal activity. The way in which the law confronts this activity (aside from the criminalisation of money laundering in the UK under the Proceeds of Crime Act 2002 and the creation of an asset recovery agency) is to entitle the victims of this activity to trace their property rights into the eventual form which the laundering process has generated.

In these situations, the State will seek to trace from the criminal proceeds into the accounts of the car wash business. In other circumstances, people who have stolen property will be subject to private law claims seeking to trace from that stolen property into the various forms of property into which the thief may have transformed it. A practical example from the cases of this sort of money laundering activity arose in *Agip (Africa) v Jackson*.[2] Here an accoun-

---

1 The expression 'breaking bad' means 'going beyond bad' in doing something that is so awful or heinous that it is more than merely 'bad'.

2 [1991] Ch 547.

tant acting for the claimant company (and therefore acting in a fiduciary capacity) arranged that money would be passed from the claimant's accounts through a bank account in Egypt which was owned by a 'shell' company which he had created. Shell (or, dummy) companies are used by shysters in these situations to complicate the movement of property. They conduct no business activities and instead are used simply as vessels for holding property. Here, the shell companies' sole purpose was to own bank accounts through which dirty money was passed. The shell companies would then be wound up once the money had passed away in an effort to complicate further the process of tracing the flow of money. The accountant in this case passed the dirty money through several bank accounts owned by a string of shell companies in different jurisdictions, and mixed the money with other money and changed it into different currencies on several occasions. The complex tracing process eventually enabled the claimant to identify which property ultimately represented the money originally taken from it so that a claim could be brought against it.

20.2 TRACING AND FOLLOWING AT COMMON LAW

20.2.1 Introduction

Common law tracing enables the claimant to recover property in two ways. If the claimant can demonstrate that the property claimed is the very property which was owned by them, then that is a 'following' action.[3] Following actions will only be available in very narrow circumstances where the claimant wants to recover their original property: such as, 'that's my phone – give it back'. Alternatively, if the property against which a claim is to be brought is a substitute for the original property, then that will require a 'tracing' action: such as, 'you sold my phone to buy that watch, so I am claiming that watch.' That tracing action can only be brought at common law if the substitute property has not been mixed with any other property.

In *Lipkin Gorman v Karpnale*[4] a solicitors' firm sought to recover money from a casino after one of its solicitors had taken money from a client account and gambled it at the casino. The money was taken by the casino (when it was lost by the hapless solicitor) and paid into its general bank account where it was mixed with other money. Because it was mixed with other money, that money could not be traced at common law. When a mixture takes place, the claimant is required to use equitable tracing (considered in the next section). It has also been held that common law tracing cannot take effect over telegraphic transfers between electronic bank accounts because such intangible property will not be clearly identifiable.[5] Similarly, in *Agip (Africa) v Jackson*,[6] discussed immediately above, the defendant accountants had arranged for money to be taken from the claimant company by means of forged payment orders and passed through a series of dummy companies. These moneys were mixed with other money in other bank accounts owned by the companies under the control of the defendants, and as a result there could be no tracing at common law.

---

3 *Foskett v McKeown* [2000] 3 All ER 97.
4 *Lipkin Gorman v Karpnale* [1991] 2 AC 548.
5 *El Ajou v Dollar Land Holdings* [1993] 3 All ER 717.
6 [1991] Ch 547, 566, *per* Fox LJ.

20.2.2 Understanding the limitations

As is obvious from the two cases considered immediately above, the common law tracing process is very limited. If the property becomes unidentifiable, or if it becomes mixed with any other property, then the common law tracing process will fail. The usual tactic for the money-launderer is therefore to take the original money, to divide it up into randomly-sized portions, pay it into accounts which already contain other money, convert the money into different currencies and move it into accounts in another jurisdiction. This type of subterfuge puts that property beyond the reach of common law tracing because the original money is hopelessly mixed with other money. Instead, the claimant would be required to rely on equitable tracing, as considered at section 20.3 below. It is this limitation in the extent of common law tracing which has led some commentators, such as Sir Peter Millett, to suggest that it should be merged with equitable tracing to form a single doctrine.[7] Ironically, as Millett LJ, his lordship delivered judgment in a case which seemed to expand common law tracing, as discussed next.

20.2.3 A new direction

There scope of common law tracing appeared to widen slightly with the decision of the Court of Appeal in *FC Jones & Sons v Jones*.[8] Mrs Jones received a loan, entirely lawfully, of £11,700 from a partnership of which her husband was a member. Mrs Jones invested the money in commodity futures – that is, a type of financial instrument which speculates on the future price of commodities like potatoes – and she made a large profit. At the end of the period, Mrs Jones had profits of £49,860. Importantly, the original £11,700 and all of the profits earned from the commodity futures were kept in a separate bank account so that there was no mixture with any other money. This separateness of this money is essential to being able to use common law tracing. Subsequently, it transpired that the partnership had been technically bankrupt under the Bankruptcy Act 1914 *before* it had made the loan to Mrs Jones. Consequently, all of the partnership property – including the loan money – was deemed to have passed retrospectively to the Official Receiver. This meant that the Official Receiver was entitled to recover the £11,700 from Mrs Jones. However, that loan money had been spent on commodity futures and then had been transformed into the £49,860 held in that account. It was held that the Official Receiver was able to trace into that £49,860 at common law because there had been no mixture with any other property that was not a clean substitute for the loan moneys and the potato futures. (It was important on those facts to be able to trace at common law because equitable tracing would not have been possible because no money had been held on trust, as we shall discuss next.)

The important advance that was made in this case was that the Official Receiver was not limited to recovering the original £11,700 but rather was entitled to trace into all of the profits (the £49,860) which had flowed from that loan. The nature of the common law tracing right was explained by Millett LJ as being a proprietary right to claim whatever was held in the bank account. What is interesting is that the Court of Appeal in *FC Jones (A Firm) v Jones* appears to have generated an entirely novel proprietary remedy at common law.

---

7 Millett, 1991, 85.
8 [1996] 3 WLR 703; [1996] 4 All ER 721.

20.3 EQUITABLE TRACING

20.3.1 Introduction

Tracing in equity (or, 'equitable tracing') is a considerably more extensive means of tracing property rights than is available at common law. Equitable tracing permits property rights to be traced into mixtures of property so that one of a number of different equitable remedies may be used to reconstitute the claimant's property rights. The pre-requisite for bringing an equitable tracing claim is that the claimant must have had some equitable interest in the original property from which tracing is sought.[9]

This is a two-stage process. The first stage is for the detective work of the tracing process to be carried out so that the claimant is able to identify the property which stands as a substitute for her original property and against which she therefore wishes to bring a claim. The second stage, having traced the property, is to identify which equitable remedy should be imposed over that property. Then we consider whether or not any defences are applicable as a third stage.

20.3.2 Need for a prior equitable interest

The pre-requisite for equitable tracing

It is a pre-requisite for an equitable tracing action that the claimant had some equitable interest in the original property, or that the person who transferred that property away had some fiduciary relationship to the claimant (such as being a trustee).[10] Therefore, it is only possible to begin an equitable tracing action if the claimant has a pre-existing equitable interest.[11] The clearest example of such a pre-existing equitable right entitling a person to begin a tracing action would be for that person to have been a beneficiary under a trust from which property was taken without lawful excuse. That can be any form of trust: express, resulting, constructive or *Quistclose*. It would also cover equitable proprietary rights further to charges, mortgages, leases and so forth.

Liability to equitable tracing even of innocent volunteers

Significantly the defendant need not have acted unconscionably before the claimant may bring an equitable tracing action. In *Re Diplock*[12] the defendant charity had been the recipient of property transferred to them in accordance with the terms of a will. The gift was afterwards held to have been void in other litigation by the House of Lords because its charitable purpose was ineffective.[13] The residuary beneficiary under the trust therefore sought to trace into the property which had been paid to the charity. The Court of Appeal held that the residuary legatee was entitled to sue. The charity had done no wrong but the money had been paid to it mistakenly. The beneficiary's property rights were held to bind

---

9 *Re Diplock's Estate* [1948] Ch 465
10 *Westdeutsche Landesbank v Islington* [1996] AC 669.
11 *Boscawen v Bajwa* [1995] 4 All ER 769.
12 [1948] Ch 465.
13 *Chichester Diocesan Board v Simpson* [1944] AC 341.

'volunteers [such as the charity] provided that as a result of what has gone before some equitable proprietary interest has been created and attaches to the property in the hands of the volunteer'.[14] Therefore, it would not matter that the ultimate recipients were innocent of any breach of trust provided that there had been some preceding breach of an equitable duty by someone else.

This approach was applied by the House of Lords in *Foskett v McKeown*,[15] in circumstances in which a trustee took money from the trust and used it to pay the premiums on an insurance policy which was made out in favour of his own children. It was held that the beneficiaries under the trust were entitled to trace in equity into the proceeds of the insurance policy after the trustee's death, thus illustrating that the limitation on the children's rights in the lump sum paid on the maturity of the insurance policy was subject to the beneficiaries' right to trace even though the children had played no part in the breach of trust.

20.3.3 The benefits of equitable tracing

The benefits

Equitable tracing permits tracing to take effect into mixtures of property, which common law tracing cannot do, as discussed in section 20.4. Equitable tracing also permits a range of different equitable remedies to be used so that a remedy which is appropriate to the circumstances can be used, as discussed in section 20.5.

The clear benefits of equitable tracing over common law tracing appear in money-laundering cases like *Agip (Africa) v Jackson*,[16] which upheld the core principle that there must be a fiduciary relationship which calls the equitable jurisdiction into being at the outset. In *Agip*, on instructions from the plaintiff oil exploration company, the Banque du Sud in Tunis transmitted a payment to Lloyds Bank in London, to be passed on to a specified person. The plaintiff's chief accountant fraudulently altered the payment instruction so that the money was in fact passed on to a company called Baker Oil Ltd. Before the fraud was uncovered, Lloyds Bank had paid out under the chief accountant's instruction to Baker Oil before receiving payment from Banque du Sud via the New York payment system. The account was then closed and the money was transferred via the Isle of Man to a number of recipients controlled by the defendants. The defendants were independent accountants who ran a number of shell companies through which the moneys were paid, their intention being to pass the moneys through these companies so that the funds would become, in effect, untraceable in practice, with the ultimate intention that they would keep those moneys. The defendants were clearly rogues of the lowest sort. The issue arose whether or not the value received by Baker Oil constituted the traceable proceeds of the property transferred from Tunis.

It was held that either principal or agent can sue on the equitable tracing claim, and that the role of plaintiff was not restricted to the Banque du Sud in this case. The bank had not paid Baker Oil with 'its own money' but rather on instruction from the plaintiff oil company which was its customer (albeit that they were fraudulent instructions). Furthermore, it was

14 *Ibid*, 530.
15 [2000] 3 All ER 97.
16 [1991] Ch 547, 566, *per* Fox LJ; [1991] 3 WLR 116; [1992] 4 All ER 451.

impossible to trace the money at common law where the value had been transferred by 'telegraphic transfer' thus making it impossible to identify the specific money which had been misapplied. On these facts, because the plaintiff's fiduciary (that is, its chief accountant) had acted fraudulently, it was held that it was open to the plaintiff to trace the money in equity through the shell companies and into the defendant's hands. There was also a personal liability to account imposed on those persons who had knowingly received misapplied funds, or who had dishonestly assisted in the misapplication of the funds as discussed in Chapter 19. We come to the detail of the tracing process next.

20.4 EQUITABLE TRACING INTO MIXED FUNDS

The most difficult tracing actions involve property which can be mixed inextricably. If you imagine one ton of Fairtrade Demerara sugar being held on trust and then mixed with a ton of Fairtrade Demerara sugar held on the terms of a different trust so that they are held in a single silo, then it would be impossible to separate out the sugar belonging to one trust and the sugar belonging to the other trust. Instead, a common sense solution would be to decide that both sets of beneficiaries would be entitled to half of the sugar held in the silo. This sort of fungible property requires a specific treatment that is different from, for example, claims relating to tangible chattels. Therefore, a different remedy is required for a case in which two cars are parked in a car park in the dark. A quick check of their registration numbers would identify which car belonged to which person and no problem of tracing would arise. When the property is fungible like sugar then the remedies will involve proportionate divisions. Many of the recent cases have involved money paid through electronic bank accounts where the property is both intangible (because it is electronic) and fungible (in that it can be mixed inextricably with other money denominated in the same currency at the slightest touch of a keyboard or a pulse in a computer's memory). In part those cases have involved banks and bank accounts because this litigation can be complex and therefore expensive. In such a situation, equitable tracing and an equitable remedy will be required to identify where my property is deemed to have gone and what recourse I have against the person who is controlling that mixture. It is this sort of intangible, financial situation which will interest us for the remainder of this chapter.

20.4.1 Mixture of trust money with trustee's own money

The first factual situation to be considered in the context of equitable tracing into mixed funds is that where the trustee mixes money taken from the trust with property that is beneficially her own. There are three principal approaches which the courts have taken in this area. As a governing principle, because the trustee has mixed their own property with trust property, everything is assumed against the trustee and in favour of the beneficiaries.

The honest trustee approach

The problem with commingling the trustee's own money with trust property is deciding whether property acquired with money from that mixture is to be treated as having been taken from the trust or as having been taken from the trustee's personal money. On the basis that the trustee is required to invest trust property to achieve the best possible return for the trust,[17] and on the basis that the trustee is required to behave honestly in respect of the trust property, the court may choose to assume that the trustee intended to use trust property to make successful investments for the trust and her own money for any inferior investments. The court would be assuming or pretending that that is the case to reach a suitable outcome.

This clearest example of this approach appeared in *Re Hallett's Estate*.[18] Hallett was a solicitor who held bonds for his client, Cotterill. Hallett also held some of those same bonds on the terms of his own marriage settlement (so that he was among the beneficiaries of that marriage settlement). Hallett sold all of the bonds – those held for Cotterill and those held for his own marriage settlement – and then paid all the sale proceeds into his own bank account. Thus the sale proceeds from the two bond holdings were mixed. Hallett spent some money wisely and just dissipated the other money. He died subsequently. Lord Jessel MR clearly assumed everything in favour of Cotterill and against Hallett because Hallett had been acting as a fiduciary when he mixed the moneys together. His lordship even described Hallett as a solicitor who had 'betrayed his trust'. The way in which Lord Jessel achieved this fair outcome was very interesting. His lordship held that we should assume, where a trustee has money in his own personal bank account to which trust money is added, that the trustee is acting honestly when spending money from that bank account. Therefore, it is assumed that the trustee, Hallett, was spending his own money on his day-to-day living and not the trust money. The court assumed (or pretended to assume) he had been acting honestly. Any money left in the account would be deemed to belong to Cotterill. It was held that:

> where a man does an act which may be rightfully performed . . . he is not allowed to say against the person entitled to the property or the right that he has done it wrongfully.

Lord Jessel meant that there was no problem with Hallett spending his own money out of the mixture on his day-to-day living but it would be wrong for Hallett to spend the trust's money in this way. So, it was not open to Hallett or his personal representatives to claim that it was Cotterill's money which had been spent. Therefore, Lord Jessel chose to pretend that the trustee has rightfully dissipated his own money such that the trust's money remained intact in the bank account.

If the trustee had spent the money on wise investments then the court would have assumed that, as a diligent trustee, Hallett would have spent Cotterill's money for that purpose. What this means for the tracing process is that the beneficiaries of a trust will be able to trace into money remaining in the account and into any wise investments made by the trustee from that mixed account. The question arises: what if the entire mixture had been spent on wise investments? What would each claimant get? The Court of Appeal in *Re Diplock*, as discussed below (under the heading 'Rateable division'), held that the contributors to the mixture would be entitled to trace into substitute property in the same proportions as they contributed to the mixture. (The rules in relation to money held in bank accounts are different, as explained in section 20.4.2 next.) The remedies are discussed in detail below. In essence, the

17 *Cowan v Scargill* [1985] Ch 270.
18 (1880) 13 Ch D 696.

beneficiaries in *Hallett* were entitled to claim either equitable ownership of assets acquired by the trustee, or a lien over those assets.[19]

This is an 'honest trustee' approach in the sense that the court was assuming that Hallett was honest and thus wasting his own money and investing the trust's money wisely as an honest trustee should. That is not the only approach that a court might take.

Beneficiary election approach

A second approach is the 'beneficiary election' approach which appears most clearly in *Re Oatway*.[20] In that case, the trustee held £4,077 in a personal bank account. The trustee then added £3,000 of trust money to this account. Out of the £7,077 held in the account, £2,137 was spent on purchasing shares. The remainder of the money in the bank account was then dissipated. The beneficiaries sought to trace from the £3,000 taken out of the bank into the shares and then to impose a charge over those shares. The shares themselves had risen in value to £2,474. The beneficiaries also sought a further accounting in cash to make up the balance of the £3,000 taken from the trust fund. It was held that where a trustee has wrongfully mixed her own money and trust money, the trustee is not entitled to say that the investment was made with her own money and that the trust money has been dissipated. Importantly, though, the beneficiaries are entitled to elect either that the property be subject to a charge as security for amounts owed to them by the trustee, or that the unauthorised investment be adopted as part of the trust fund: hence us using the term 'beneficiary election approach'.

It is therefore clear that the courts are prepared to protect the beneficiaries at all costs from the misfeasance of the trustee – re-emphasising the strictness of the trustee's obligations to the beneficiaries.[21] So, on the facts of *Oatway* the beneficiaries were able to elect to have the valuable shares subsumed into the trust as opposed simply to taking rights over money (which was to their advantage because it was considered likely that those shares would increase in value in the future), and also to be able to require the trustee to account in cash for the remaining shortfall in the balance taken from the trust fund.

Rateable division

The beneficiary election approach has been expressed as being an exception to the main approach of rateable division of the property in *Foskett v McKeown*[22] in the House of Lords by Lord Millett.[23] In this context, 'rateable division' means a distribution of the mixed property between the claimants in proportion to the size of their contribution to the mixture.

---

19   A lien is a right to take possession of property until one is paid what one is owed. It is clear though that the beneficiary will not now be confined to claiming a lien: *Re Tilley's Will Trusts; Burgin v Croad* [1967] Ch 1179, 1186; [1967] 2 All ER 303, 308; *Scott v Scott* (1963) 109 CLR 649; *Foskett v McKeown* [2000] 3 All ER 97, 123, *per* Lord Millett.

20   [1903] 2 Ch 356.

21   See now *Foskett v McKeown* [2000] 3 All ER 97, 123, *per* Lord Millett.

22   [2000] 3 All ER 97. *Foskett* was followed in *Serious Fraud Office v Lexi Holdings plc* [2008] EWCA Crim 1443, [2009] 1 All ER 586.

23   *Ibid*, 124.

So, you contribute one-third of the mixed fund then you acquire one-third of any property acquired with that fund. Lord Millett held that:

> The primary rule in regard to a mixed fund, therefore, is that gains and losses are borne by the contributors rateably.[24] The beneficiary's right to elect instead to enforce a lien to obtain repayment is an exception to the primary rule, exercisable where the fund is deficient and the claim is made against the wrongdoer and those claiming through him.

Lord Millett relied on similar principles which apply in relation to physical mixtures, where it is said that if the mixture is the fault of the defendant then it is open to the claimant to 'claim the goods'.[25] Importantly, even where the defendant is not at fault in the commingling of property, such an innocent volunteer is not entitled to occupy a better position than the person who was responsible simply by reason of her innocence.[26] This issue of innocents caught up in the affairs of others is considered immediately below.

There is one anomalous case, given the general trend in the cases to assume everything against the trustee who acts wrongfully. In *Re Tilley's Will Trusts*,[27] a trustee took money which she held on trust and paid it into her own personal bank account. The trustee made investments on her own behalf from that bank account. The moneys she took from the trust settled her overdraft on that account in part so that she was able to continue her investment activities because it meant that she was able to keep borrowing against her overdraft. The court held that the beneficiaries had no rights to trace into the investments which the trustee had made with the money taken from that account; rather the court was convinced on the facts that the trust money had simply served to reduce her overdraft but not to pay for her investments. It is suggested that this decision is wrong: the defendant could not have made investments unless trust money had been paid into her account, and therefore the trust money facilitated her investments. An alternative analysis, more in line with *Foskett v McKeown*, would have been to find that if the trust money made the investment possible, then the trust should be taken to have contributed traceable funds to the acquisition of those investments.

20.4.2 Mixture of two trust funds or mixture with innocent volunteer's property

The lay-out of the law relating to tracing into mixtures

The law in this area divides into two. There is a general principle for all cases which do not involve money in current bank accounts and a different set of principles for the cases which involve money in current bank accounts. Most of the litigation in this area relates to money in bank accounts (especially current bank accounts). The cases relating to money in bank accounts divide between the 'first in, first out' principle from the early 19th century, an

---

24 I.e. in proportionate shares.
25 *Lupton v White, White v Lupton* (1808) 15 Ves 432; [1803–13] All ER Rep 336; *Sandeman & Sons v Tyzack and Branfoot Steamship Co Ltd* [1913] AC 680, 695; [1911–13] All ER Rep 1013, 1020, *per* Lord Molton.
26 *Jones v De Marchant* (1916) 28 DLR 561; *Foskett v McKeown* [2000] 3 All ER 97.
27 *Re Tilley's Will Trusts, Burgin v Croad* [1967] Ch 1179.

approach based on a rolling charge, and a general approach of rateable division. These different approaches will be explained below. We begin with the general principle for all cases that do not involve current bank accounts.

The general principle

This section considers the situation in which trust property is misapplied in such a way that it is mixed with property belonging to an innocent third party. The exception from this principle is money mixed in current bank accounts. Therefore, rather than consider the issues which arose in the previous section concerning the obligations of the wrongdoing trustee, it is now necessary to decide how property belonging to innocent parties should be allocated between them. It was held in *Re Diplock*[28] that the entitlement of the beneficiary to the mixed fund should rank *pari passu* (or, 'in equal step'; or, proportionately) with the rights of the innocent volunteer:

> Where an innocent volunteer (as distinct from a purchaser for value without notice) mixes 'money' of his own with 'money' which in equity belongs to another person, or is found in possession of such a mixture, although that other person cannot claim a charge on the mass superior to the claim of the volunteer, he is entitled, nevertheless, to a charge ranking *pari passu* with the claim of the volunteer . . . Such a person is not in conscience bound to give precedence to the equitable owner of the other of the two funds.

Therefore, none of the innocent contributors to the fund is considered as taking any greater right than any other contributor to the fund. Rather, each person has an equal charge over that property. This approach has been adopted in *Foskett v McKeown*[29] by Lord Millett:[30]

> The primary rule in regard to a mixed fund, therefore, is that gains and losses are borne by the contributors rateably.[31] The beneficiary's right to elect instead to enforce a lien to obtain repayment is an exception to the primary rule, exercisable where the fund is deficient and the claim is made against the wrongdoer and those claiming through him.

As considered above, Lord Millett relied on similar principles which apply in relation to physical mixtures, where it is said that if the mixture is the fault of the defendant then it is open to the claimant to 'claim the goods'.[32] It was said at that stage that even where the defendant was not at fault in the commingling of property, such an innocent volunteer would not be entitled to occupy a better position than the person who was responsible simply by reason of her innocence.[33]

---

28   [1948] Ch 465, 524.
29   [2000] 3 All ER 97.
30   *Ibid*, 124.
31   That is, in proportionate shares.
32   *Lupton v White, White v Lupton* (1808) 15 Ves 432; [1803–13] All ER Rep 336; *Sandeman & Sons v Tyzack and Branfoot Steamship Co Ltd* [1913] AC 680, 695; [1911–13] All ER Rep 1013, 1020, *per* Lord Molton.
33   *Jones v De Marchant* (1916) 28 DLR 561; *Foskett v McKeown* [2000] 3 All ER 97.

In the case of *Foskett v McKeown* itself, a trustee had been misusing the trust's funds to pay two of the five premiums on a life assurance policy, of about £20,000, which he had taken out in favour of his wife and children. The trust had therefore contributed 40% of the insurance premiums. The trustee committed suicide and the breach of trust was discovered. The children argued that the claimant was entitled to recover the £20,000 which had been taken from the trust fund. The beneficiaries of the trust argued that because they had contributed 40% of the insurance premiums then they should be entitled to 40% of the insurance pay-out (which was £400,000). It was held by the House of Lords that the beneficiaries of the trust were entitled to trace into 40% of the moneys paid out under the life assurance policy on the basis that their money had been mixed with the trustee's own money to pay for two of the life assurance policy premiums.

Opinion differs greatly over the rights and wrongs of this decision.[34] The House of Lords chose to vindicate the property rights of the beneficiaries by means of recognising that the contributions which the trust fund made to the insurance policy premiums enhanced the final lump sum. Thus, a contribution of only £20,000 landed a 40% share of the £1 million policy pay-out because that £20,000 constituted 40% of all the premiums. This approach reflected the fact that the trustee was supposed to have made investments on behalf of the trust and that this was a successful investment of £20,000 of trust money. An alternative approach, and one which would have recognised the innocence of the children who were expecting to take absolute title in the whole of the lump sum paid out from the insurance policy, would have been to order compensation for the beneficiaries equal to the amount of cash taken from the trust fund to pay the policy's premiums: i.e. £20,000. This approach would have meant that the beneficiaries would not have recovered a proportionate share in the pay-out from the insurance policy.

What the majority decision in the House of Lords achieves is recognition of the fact that the trustee ought to have been investing the trust fund properly, and therefore that for the beneficiaries simply to have the £20,000 in looted cash returned to them would not give them the return they would otherwise have expected on their capital if the trustee had managed and invested it properly. In effect, what is being suggested is that the children would otherwise have received a windfall (in the form of the size of the insurance policy pay-out) without recognising the beneficiaries' unwitting contribution to their wealth. The House of Lords held that tracing constitutes a part of property law, not a part of unjust enrichment (as discussed in Chapter 25). Because this doctrine is part of property law then the purpose of tracing is to 'vindicate' the property rights of the beneficiaries under the trust.

What makes this case difficult is that it involves two sets of innocent parties fighting over the money that is left after the wrongdoing trustee's death. There is no completely satisfactory answer in that one or other of the parties seems likely to receive less money than that to which they would otherwise feel they were entitled. The position of the children who have lost their father to suicide is tragic. The position of the beneficiaries who have lost both money from their trust and the opportunity to earn a profit from that trust is also regrettable. There are no real winners here. Except possibly for the lawyers who were paid to argue this case to the House of Lords.

---

34 E.g., Virgo, 2004 and Rotherham, 2004.

The more difficult situation is that in which the property cannot be divided between the parties rateably because, for example, it is a valuable oil painting which cannot reasonably be cut into pieces and divided. Page Wood VC has held quite simply that:

> if a man mixes trust funds with his own, the whole will be treated as the trust property, except so far as he may be able to distinguish what is his own.[35]

The answer to questions relating to this sort of property (such as a valuable painting which cannot be physically divided) are to be found in the variety of remedies which are available: rather than taking ownership of parts of the property, a charge or a lien may be imposed to permit the property to be sold and the sale proceeds distributed rateably between the parties. The remedies are considered below in section 20.5.

Payments made through current bank accounts

This section considers the principles which apply in relation to tracing payments through current bank accounts. (This is often a key part of exam problems.) The particular problem in cases relating to current bank accounts arises where moneys from different sources are mixed in a bank account and then that money is used to buy other property: the real question is in identifying which contributor to that mixture can trace into which item of property that has been bought from the mixed bank account. We have to imagine a current bank account containing money taken from different people from which payments are made to acquire totally unrelated items of the property. The facts in the following table may illustrate the problem, concerning payments in and out of a current bank account the balance of which stood at zero at the opening of business on 1 June.

On these facts £3,000 was in the account at the end of 2 June, being a mixture of money from two separate trusts (A and B). By 6 June, the traceable proceeds of that property had been used to buy ICI shares, SAFC shares, and BP shares. The problem is then to ascertain the title to those shares. There are two possible approaches: either

Table 20.1

Date	Payments in	Payments out
1 June	£1,000 from trust A	
2 June	£2,000 from trust B	
3 June		£500 to buy ICI Plc shares
4 June		£1,500 to buy SAFC Plc shares
5 June		£1,000 to buy BP Plc shares

---

35 *Frith v Cartland* (1865) 2 Hem & M 417, 420; (1865) 71 ER 525, 526; *Foskett v McKeown* [2000] 3 All ER 97, 125.

particular shares are allocated between the two trust funds, or both funds take proportionate interests in all of the shares.[36] The two scenarios appear in different cases, as considered immediately below.

The first-in, first-out approach

The long-standing rule relating to title in property paid out of current bank accounts is that in *Clayton's Case*.[37] In relation to current bank accounts, the decision in *Clayton's Case* held that the appropriate principle is 'first-in, first-out': that means that the first money to have been paid into the account is deemed to have been the first money to have been paid out of that account. On the facts set out above, the deposit made from Trust A on 1 June is deemed to be the first money to be paid out because it was the first money to have been paid into the account. Consequently, the ICI shares acquired on 3 June for £500 (i.e. the first money to have been paid out) would be deemed to have been acquired solely with money derived from trust A (i.e. the first money to have been paid into the account). So, £500 of the money taken from A would be deemed to be the money which acquired the ICI shares. The tracing process consequently would assign rights in the ICI shares to A.

By the same token, the SAFC shares would be deemed to have been acquired on 4 June with the remaining £500 from trust A and £1,000 from trust B. That is, the last of the money from Trust A is used up and then we start to take money from Trust B (i.e. second in, second out). The BP shares are therefore acquired with the remaining £1,000 from trust B (i.e. last in, last out).

The drawback with the *Clayton's Case* approach is that it would be unfair to trust A if ICI shares were to halve in value while shares in BP were to double in value. That would mean that trust A's £500 investment in ICI would be worth only £250 as a result of the halving in value, whereas trust B's £1,000 investment in BP would then be worth £2,000. That might seem a little arbitrary. After all, the beneficiaries of trust A had no control over how their money was used or when it was added to this bank account.

Proportionate share

The alternative approach would be to decide that each contributor should take proportionate shares in all of the property acquired with the proceeds of the mixed fund. This is the approach taken in most Commonwealth jurisdictions.[38] On the facts in Table 20.1, each party contributed to the bank account in the ratio 1:2 (in that trust A provided £1,000 and trust B provided £2,000). Therefore, all of the ICI shares, the SAFC shares, and the BP shares would be held on trust one-third for Trust A and two-thirds for Trust B. The result is the elimination of any differential movements in value across this property in circumstances in which it is pure chance which beneficiaries would take rights in which property.

A slightly different twist on this approach was adopted in *Barlow Clowes International v Vaughan*.[39] In that case, investors in the collapsed Barlow Clowes organisation had their

---

36 The proportionate approach is probably to be preferred now, although, as will emerge, the authorities are not yet clear on this point: *Foskett v McKeown* [2000] 3 All ER 97.

37 (1816) 1 Mer 572.

38 *Re Ontario Securities Commission* (1985) 30 DLR (4d) 30; *Re Registered Securities* [1991] 1 NZLR 545.

39 [1992] 4 All ER 22, [1992] BCLC 910; noted Birks, 1993, 218.

losses met in part by the Department of Trade and Industry. The Secretary of State for Trade and Industry then sought to recover, in effect, the amounts which had been paid away to those former investors by tracing the compensation paid to the investors into the assets of Barlow Clowes.

At first instance, Peter Gibson J held that the rule in *Clayton's Case*[40] should be applied. The majority of the Court of Appeal favoured a distribution between the rights of the various investors on a sort of proportionate basis, considering *Clayton's Case* too formalistic and arbitrary. Leggatt and Woolf LJJ preferred to use a 'rolling charge' approach culled from the Canadian cases. This rolling charge meant that the investors acquired rights in proportion both to the size of their contribution and also in proportion to the length of time for which it comprised a part of the fund. (An investment of £1 for one year is worth more than an investment of £1 for only one month, after all.) Unfortunately, on the very complicated facts of *Barlow Clowes*, the court found that the sheer mathematical task of calculating the precise proportions owing to the many, many contributors to the investment funds held by the Barlow Clowes organisation made it simply too complex to apply. Therefore, a different approach to *Clayton's Case* was not taken on those facts.

The retreat from Clayton's Case

The general drift of the cases since *Barlow Clowes v Vaughan* has suggested that the English courts would prefer to resile from the *Clayton's Case* principle;[41] but, at the time of writing, *Clayton's Case* has not been formally overruled. What the High Court has done instead is to fix on the following idea mentioned by Woolf LJ in *Barlow Clowes v Vaughan*:[42]

> To throw all the loss upon one [party], through the mere chance of his being earlier in time, is irrational and arbitrary, and is equally a fiction as the rule in *Clayton's Case*. When the law adopts a fiction, it is, or at least it should be, for some purpose of justice. To adopt it here is to apportion a common misfortune through a test which has no relation whatever to the justice of the case.

The effect of these dicta is that when the *Clayton's Case* principle produces results which are 'irrational and arbitrary' then a proportionate share approach should be used.

Using these dicta, Lindsay J refused to follow *Clayton's Case* in *Russell-Cooke Trust Co v Prentis*[43] in a case involving a solicitor who had conducted an investment scheme and who had taken investments from his clients in return for a guaranteed return of 15% on all investments. All of the investments were paid into the solicitor's client account, which meant that those funds were held on trust for the clients in proportionate shares. The Law

---

40 (1816) 1 Mer 572.

41 *Barlow Clowes v Vaughan* [1992] 4 All ER 22; *El Ajou v Dollar Land Holdings (No 2)* [1995] 2 All ER 213, 222, Robert Walker J; *Re Lewis's of Leicester* [1995] 1 BCLC 428; *Sheppard v Thompson* (2001) unreported, 3 December; *Russell-Cooke Trust Co v Prentis* [2003] 2 All ER 478; *Commerzbank AG v IMB Morgan plc* [2004] EWHC 2771 (Ch). Commonwealth jurisdictions have long turned their back on *Clayton's Case* (see *Re Ontario Securities Commission* (1988) 52 DLR (4th) 767 (Sup Ct) in Canada and *Re French Caledonia Travel Service Pty Ltd* (2003) 204 ALR 353, *per* Campbell J, in Australia), as have the courts in the USA (see *Re Walter J Schmidt & Co*, 298 F 314, 316 (1923), *per* Learned Hand J).

42 [1992] 4 All ER 22, 44.

43 [2003] 2 All ER 478.

Society intervened when irregularities in the operation of this fund came to light. Lindsay J held that the *Clayton's Case* approach was still binding but that it was also capable of being distinguished on the facts of any given case. On these facts he considered that it would have been irrational and arbitrary to use the 'first-in, first-out' approach. Similarly, in *Commerzbank AG v IMB Morgan plc*,[44] the same approach to the authority of *Clayton's Case* was taken by Lawrence Collins J. A fraudulent investment scheme was operated through a bank account operated by Commerzbank in which money from several investors was combined. It was held that it would have been unjust and impracticable to have applied *Clayton's Case* on these facts given the complexity and randomness of the investors' contributions to that account.

In the decision of Sir Terence Atherton C in *National Crime Agency v Robb*,[45] his lordship pointed out the practical difficulties associated with applying the 'first-in, first-out' approach. In this case the Serious Organised Crime Agency was proceeding against a criminal who had raised a large amount of money from investors through a bank account in London. The investment scheme was being operated fraudulently. The defendant transferred money from the bank account in London to an account in his own name in Thailand. The question arose as to the basis on which the investors could trace into the account held in Thailand. A large number of investors had paid different amounts of money at different times into the London bank account. It was held that while equitable tracing was possible, it was held that it would be almost impossible to match inputs with outputs from these bank accounts so as to be able to give effect to the *Clayton's Case* analysis. Simply put, it would be very difficult indeed to have identified which money came into the account first and which left the account first, let alone to identify where that money went. Consequently, it was held that it would be better to apply a proportionate share approach on these facts.

A similar issue arose in the case of *Charity Commission v Framjee*.[46] In that case a charitable trust operated a website which purported to raise money for different charities. The Charity Commission investigated this charitable trust and its activities because there was a large shortfall between the amount of money that had been raised through the website and the amount of money which had actually been distributed to charitable purposes. The question arose whether or not tracing would be possible through the amounts given by donors to the website and into the amount that was still held by the charitable trust. Once again, it was held that the sheer volume of payments which had been made through the website made it impracticable to operate the *Clayton's Case* 'first-in, first-out' approach. The 'first-in, first-out' approach requires that it is possible to identify which money came into the account first and which money left the account first, which money came into the account second, and so forth. When a very large number of payments are being made into and out of the account it becomes a very difficult matter indeed to identify precisely the order in which they reach the account and left it: the 'first-in, first-out' approach requires that such an identification of the order of payments can be made. Henderson J held that while it might be possible to perform this calculation (he considered that it would be possible to program

44 [2004] EWHC 2771 (Ch).
45 [2015] 3 WLR 23.
46 [2015] 1 WLR 16.

a computer to do this work), nevertheless it would be too time-consuming and too expensive to be appropriate.

Therefore, on these facts, it was held to be preferable to use a proportionate share analysis. Henderson J was mindful of the remarks made by the Court of Appeal in the *Barlow Clowes v Vaughan* decision on the basis that a rolling charge approach would be very difficult to effect in circumstances in which there had been a large number of payments. He considered that the facts in front of him presented the same problem. Consequently, he preferred the proportionate share approach which had been used in *Ontario Securities*. This meant that the monies held by the charitable trust would be divided into two pools (because there were two categories of claimant) and that the two categories of claimant would be entitled to trace into those pools in proportion to the size of their contribution to their totals. Again, the court was following the approach taken in cases like *Russell Cooke v Prentis* (which was quoted by Henderson J) which refused to apply *Clayton's Case* where it would be irrational, arbitrary or impracticable to apply it.

20.5 LOSS OF THE RIGHT TO TRACE

20.5.1 That there must be identifiable property for tracing

A claimant in a tracing action will lose her right to trace if the property into which she is seeking to trace her rights either ceases to exist or cannot be found. In *Ultraframe (UK) Ltd v Fielding*[47] the claimant sought to claim that the defendant had earned profits by misusing the claimant's intellectual property in breach of trust to manufacture high quality double glazing components.[48] Therefore, the claimant argued, *inter alia*, that the defendant's profits had been derived from the claimant's property. However, the claimant could not prove an unbroken chain of property rights leading from itself to the defendant. Therefore, it was held that where the claimant could not identify any particular item of property as constituting the traceable proceeds of the original trust property, then it would not be possible to trace into any profits which the defendant had made because no link between it and any property taken in breach of trust had been proven. The Court of Appeal in *Serious Fraud Office v Lexi Holdings plc*[49] held similarly that a charge could not be imposed over all of the assets of a bank because the claimant contended that the traceable proceeds of their property must be among the bank's assets somewhere. Rather, the claimant must be able to identify specific property which is to be the subject matter of the tracing action.

20.5.2 The loss of the right to trace, and tracing elsewhere

The more complicated cases arise when money is laundered through several bank accounts. The launderer moves stolen trust money into a bank account owned by dummy company, A Ltd, and mixes it with other money. Then that money is changed into another currency and transferred into an account owned by a different dummy company, B Ltd. Because there is no

---

47 [2005] EWHC 1638 (Ch); [2005] All ER (D) 397.
48 This is a filleted account of a very, very long case indeed which involved a very large number of parties.
49 [2008] EWCA Crim 1443, [2009] 1 All ER 586, [2009] QB 376.

traceable proceed of the trust money left in A Ltd's bank account, the claimant loses a right to trace into A Ltd's account. This is true even if more money is added to that account later because that later money would not be the traceable proceed of the original theft. Significantly, however, the claimant would still be able to trace into the B Ltd account.

This principle was demonstrated most clearly in *Bishopsgate Investment Management v Homan*.[50] Here, in the aftermath of newspaper mogul Robert Maxwell's death, it transpired that amounts belonging to pension trust funds under his control had been misapplied. The amounts had been paid into accounts held by MCC (a company controlled by Maxwell) and other companies. Those accounts had gone overdrawn since the initial deposit of the money. It was held that it was impossible to trace money into an overdrawn account on the basis that the property from which the traceable substitute derives is said to have disappeared.[51] The same approach was taken in *Westdeutsche Landesbank v Islington* where money was paid by a bank to a local authority under a void contract, but the general bank account into which that money was paid went overdrawn. It was held that there could be no tracing into the local authority's general account because no traceable proceeds remained in that account since the account had been run overdrawn. If the destination of that money could have been traced then the tracing process could have continued, but on those facts the money was dissipated on the authority's general expenses and therefore was not traceable.

In *Federal Republic of Brazil v Durant International Corporation*,[52] the Privy Council considered a complex money-laundering scheme in which officers of a Brazilian municipality were alleged to have been involved in the payment of bribes in relation to a public works contract in Brazil. The monies were then laundered through various accounts. It was accepted that the defendants should be constructive trustees of these amounts. The defendants had organised their money-laundering operation so that it would appear as though amounts had been debited from bank accounts before the traced monies had even been paid into them: this would suggest that the two transfers were unconnected. It was accepted by the court that these debits and credits were part of reciprocal transactions. This particular problem was one that is known as 'backwards tracing'. On the facts of this case however Lord Toulson was clear that backwards tracing could be permitted because these particular payment flows had been coordinated and choreographed by the defendants to make it appear as though tracing should be impossible. It is suggested that this is a sensible judgment because it would be too easy for the court to become befuddled by a spurious debit being taken from an account before the traced property is added to that account so that the two appear to cancel one another out such that there is no property to trace. One of the strengths of equitable tracing is that it is able to penetrate the shields which money-launderers seek to erect to protect their ill-gotten gains. The practical difficulties of tracing payments through bank accounts was illustrated again in *Relfo Ltd (in liquidation) v Varsani* where the Court of Appeal identified the difficulty of proving in that case that one payment was indeed the traceable substitute of another when a large

50 [1995] Ch 211; [1995] 1 All ER 347; [1994] 3 WLR 1270; *Law Society of Upper Canada v Toronto Dominion Bank* (1998) 169 DLR (4th) 353 (Ont Ca).
51 The loss of the right to trace was also upheld in *Re BA Peters plc, Atkinson v Moriarty* [2008] EWCA Civ 1604, [2010] 1 BCLC 142, [15], *per* Lord Neuberger where it was held that if the property over which proprietary rights were sought had ceased to exist in the hands of the defendant then there could be no proprietary right in the form of a trust against that defendant.
52 [2015] 3 WLR 599.

number of payments had been made into a bank account.[53] The strength of equity is in being able to look at the substance of a matter rather than being misled by its form.

20.6 CLAIMING: TRUSTS AND REMEDIES

20.6.1 The available forms of remedy

Tracing actions have two parts: first, conduct the tracing process to identify the property against which a claim will be brought; second, identify the appropriate remedy in relation to the particular property in that particular situation. In this section we consider the possible remedies in relation to equitable tracing. Equitable tracing does not carry a single remedy: instead there are four possible remedies on the current state of the authorities. Those remedies are: a constructive trust;[54] a charge;[55] a lien;[56] and subrogation.[57] In this section we shall consider each of those remedies in turn and the circumstances in which each of them would be appropriate in practice. The onus is on the claimant to claim the remedy which is most appropriate in the circumstances. Different types of remedy will be more suitable or more appropriate in different circumstances depending on the nature of the property and whether or not there are innocent third parties involved.

Briefly put, the claimant must consider their objectives in relation to the traced property. In many circumstances the claimant will wish to recover the financial value of property which has been lost to them. If that is the objective then a charge or a lien will grant the claimant a right to be paid an amount of money which is secured over the traced property. A lien entitles the claimant to take possession of property and therefore makes particular sense in relation to identifiable property like a valuable chattel. A charge secures a right to money over property which may be fixed or floating. By contrast, if the claimant wants to take ownership of the traced property, for example because it is particularly valuable, then a constructive trust would be appropriate. Subrogation applies in limited circumstances in which property has been used to discharge a debt. The decision as to which remedy will be the most appropriate will therefore depend on the circumstances.

20.6.2 Constructive trusts in equitable tracing actions

Constructive trusts enable the claimant to acquire equitable ownership of property. In a tracing action, a constructive trust would be desirable in circumstances in which the claimant wanted to take ownership of property which is increasingly valuable or which is intrinsically valuable.

By contrast with ordinary constructive trusts, equitable tracing claims entitle the claimant to a remedy even if the defendant is an innocent volunteer.[58] That means that the defendant need not have acted unconscionably for a constructive trust to be imposed as a response to an equitable tracing claim; rather, such constructive trusts are imposed so as to vindicate the claimant's rights in the traced property. As discussed above in *Re Diplock* there was a

---

53 [2014] EWCA Civ 360.
54 *Westdeutsche Landesbank Girozentrale v Islington LBC* [1996] AC 669.
55 *Re Tilley's Will Trusts* [1967] Ch 1179.
56 *Foskett v McKeown* [2001] 1 AC 102.
57 *Boscawen v Bajwa* [1996] 1 WLR 328.
58 *Re Diplock's Estate* [1948] Ch 465; *Foskett v McKeown* [2001] 1 AC 102; [2000] 3 All ER 97.

successful equitable tracing claim brought against a charity which had received money from a trust by mistake but where it had not acted unconscionably. Thus, equitable tracing does not operate on the basis of unconscionable activity (unless one accepts the argument that it would be unconscionable not to respect the claimant's original property rights). The same point emerges from *Foskett v McKeown* where the defendants had not personally committed any unconscionable act.

In *Westdeutsche Landesbank v Islington LBC*,[59] a bank paid money to a local authority under an interest rate swap contract which was found to have been void *ab initio*. The principal question was whether or not the bank could demonstrate that the local authority should be required to be treated as a constructive trustee of the moneys paid to it such that the bank would be able to trace its money into the local authority's general funds. It was held that the local authority would not be treated as having been a constructive trustee of the moneys paid to it by the bank because, from the time it received the money until the time at which it dissipated those moneys, it had no knowledge that the contract was void *ab initio* and therefore could not have dealt unconscionably with the money.[60] There was no constructive trust, nor any trust of any other kind,[61] and therefore no equitable interest sufficient to found an equitable tracing claim. Furthermore, there could not have been a constructive trust because there was no property over which such a trust could have been imposed, or in relation to which an equitable tracing claim could have been commenced, once the local authority had dissipated the money paid to it by the bank.[62]

20.6.3 Charges and liens in tracing

Equitable charges

Charges take effect in equity.[63] A charge will give the claimant a proportionate right in a fund of property equal to a given value, but without the need for the claimant to segregate property within that fund in the way that would be required for the creation of a trust.[64] Charges can be fixed over specific property, or they can float over a pool of property such that the legal owner of that fund can continue to deal with it. In a tracing action, the benefit of a charge to the claimant would be to grant her a right to be paid whatever amount of money has been awarded by the court further to the tracing action so as to compensate the beneficiaries for their loss, but with the added benefit of a security interest over the charged property which can be seized by order of the court if the defendant fails to make payment. A chargee has a right to apply to the court to seek a right to seize the charged property and to sell it so as to realise the amount owed to it.[65] There is no specific formality for the creation of a charge over

---

59 [1996] AC 669.
60 See generally the discussion of this principle at section 12.1.
61 Particularly no resulting trust, as considered at section 11.1.
62 The moneys had been paid into the local authority's general bank accounts and those accounts had subsequently gone overdrawn, this terminating any possible right of tracing, as considered at section 20.3.
63 *Re Coslett Contractors Ltd* [1998] Ch 495. Explained in Gleeson, *Personal Property Law* (FT Law & Tax, 1997) 235, to be the case because title may not be divided at common law.
64 *Re Goldcorp* [1995] 1 AC 74.
65 *Johnson v Shippen* (1703) 2 Ld Raym 982; *Stainbank v Fenning* (1851) 11 CB 51; *Stainbank v Shepard* (1853) 13 CB 418.

personality.[66] Once a court orders the existence of a charge then the chargee – the claimant in a tracing claim – will have a right to receive money in satisfaction of her rights or to enforce the charge as just described.

Liens

A lien is a right to take possession of another person's property until such time as that other person makes payment in satisfaction of a debt or some other obligation. In equity, it is not necessary for the claimant to have possession of the property before seeking permission to seize that property. A lien is a right only to detain property and not a right to sell it.[67] If the claimant wishes to sell the property to recover amounts owed to her by the defendant, then she must apply to the court for permission.[68] Liens can arise both at common law and in equity. An equitable lien is a right to detain property which then gives rise to an equitable charge.[69] So, an equitable lien is really a manifestation of a jurisdiction accepted by courts of equity to detain property by imposing an equitable charge over it.[70]

In a tracing claim the usefulness of a lien is that it enables the claimant to assume physical control of property until the defendant satisfies her obligations to the claimant. Suppose that the defendant had possession of a stock of uranium which was the traceable proceed of property which had been held on trust for the claimant, and suppose that the claimant was a market trader who worked in cash. The claimant would not want to take property rights in the uranium because it would be difficult to sell without knowing buyers able to buy it and because selling it would require permits. However, the claimant would want to prevent the defendant from moving the uranium before paying over the money that was owed to them under the tracing action. Therefore, a lien would be ideal: the client could keep possession of the uranium until payment is made, and only if payment was not made would the claimant seek to seize the uranium and then to sell it herself.

20.6.4 Subrogation

If Brian used Arthur's money to pay off a debt he owed to Catherine, then Arthur is bound to feel aggrieved. There is an equitable doctrine – 'subrogation' – which allows that debt to be owed by Brian to Arthur instead so that Arthur will receive restitution of what he is owed. The debt which was paid off using Arthur's money can be brought back to life and enforced against Brian by Arthur instead of Catherine. In tracing actions when property is taken from a trust fund and used to pay off the defendant's debts, then the beneficiaries may be subrogated to the defendant's debt – this means that the defendant owes the debt to the beneficiaries instead. This happened in *Boscawen v Bajwa*.[71] A solicitor held money for a client in a trust

---

66 *Cradock v Scottish Provident Institution* (1893) 69 LT 380, affirmed at (1894) 70 LT 718, CA.
67 *Hammonds v Barclay* (1802) 2 East 227.
68 *Larner v Fawcett* [1950] 2 All ER 727.
69 *Ibid; In Re Kent & Sussex Sawmills Ltd* [1947] Ch 177.
70 *Ibid; In Re Kent & Sussex Sawmills Ltd* [1947] Ch 177.
71 [1996] 1 WLR 328. See also section 30.7.3 below. *Ibrahim v Barclays Bank* [2011] EWHC 1897 (Ch) followed *Boscawen v Bajwa*.

account which was intended to be used to purchase a house. Due to an error in the completion process, the purchase moneys were paid over and used to discharge the vendor's mortgage, but the house was not transferred to the purchaser. Therefore, trust money had been used to discharge the defendant vendor's debt. It was held by the Court of Appeal that the defendant vendor should owe his mortgage to the purchaser. The mortgage debt was effectively resuscitated and thus the purchaser acquired a debt on the same terms as it had been originally created by the defendant's mortgagee.

20.6.5 Choice of remedies

Clearly there are a number of remedies potentially available in relation to a tracing claim. No court will permit double recovery in respect of the same loss. Therefore, the equitable doctrine of election arises in such situations to provide that it is open to the claimant to elect between alternative remedies.[72] In *Tang v Capacious Investments*, the possibility of two parallel remedies arose in relation to a breach of trust. It was held that these two remedies existed in the alternative and therefore that the plaintiff could claim both, not being required to elect between them until judgment was awarded in its favour. However, it was held in *Crittenden v The Estate of Charles Albert Bayliss*[73] that it would be an abuse of the process of the court for a claimant to elect not to bring a tracing action and then at a later stage in litigation to seek to bring that tracing action in any event.

20.7 DEFENCES

This section considers the defences to a tracing action. It is suggested, when approaching a problem on the law on tracing, that you analyse the tracing process, then the remedies, and then come to the defences last (just as this chapter has been laid out). In the real world, it must be conceded, one might be tempted to hurry to the defences more quickly because they may neuter a tracing action. Even then, one might choose to decide whether or not tracing is possible first before turning to the defences. Defences arise most naturally only once the principal action has been made out. The following are the principal defences available to a tracing action: change of position, estoppel by representation, and *bona fide* purchaser for value without notice.

20.7.1 Change of position

The basis of the defence of change of position

The defence of change of position allows the court to decide, in essence, whether it would be more just to pass the traced property to the claimant or more just to allow the defendant to keep it. It is an important part of this defence that the defendant must not have acted in bad faith. We should remember that the defendant might have acquired property unwittingly – as in *Re Diplock* – and therefore the change of position defence will tend to

---

72 *Tang v Capacious Investments Ltd* [1996] 1 All ER 193. See Birks, 2000:1, 8.
73 [2005] EWCA Civ 1425.

protect people acting in good faith in that position.[74] As Lord Goff put it in *Westdeutsche Landesbank v Islington LBC*, the defence will apply:[75]

> where an innocent defendant's position is so changed that he will suffer an injustice if called upon to repay or to repay in full, the injustice of requiring him so to repay outweighs the injustice of denying the plaintiff restitution.

Consequently, the court is required to balance the relative justices and injustices of allowing tracing in any given situation.[76] The central statement of this defence was set out by Lord Goff in *Lipkin Gorman v Karpnale*.[77] In that case, the defendant casino had received money from a solicitor who had appropriated that money from a law firm's client accounts and gambled it away at the defendant's premises. The law firm sought to recover the lost moneys from the casino by means of equitable and common law tracing claims, as well as seeking to impose personal liability to account for participation in a breach of trust and a variety of tort claims. With these facts in mind, Lord Goff described the future development of the defence of change of position in the following way:[78]

> It is, of course, plain that the defence is not open to one who has changed his position in bad faith, as where the defendant has paid away the money with knowledge of the facts entitling the plaintiff to restitution; and it is commonly accepted that the defence should not be open to a wrongdoer . . . At present I do not wish to state the principle any less broadly than this: that the defence is available to a person whose position has so changed that it would be inequitable in all the circumstances to require him to make restitution, or alternatively to make restitution in full. I wish to stress however that the mere fact that the defendant has spent the money, in whole or in part, does not of itself render it inequitable that he should be called upon to repay, because the expenditure might in any event have been incurred by him in the ordinary course of things.[79]

Consequently, three points emerge. First, a wrongdoer may not rely on the defence. So, in *Barros Mattos v MacDaniels Ltd*[80] Laddie J held that the defence would not be available to someone who had acted illegally. Second, the defence is intended to avoid the defendant being treated 'inequitably'. This suggests that this remedy is part of equity and not simply part of unjust enrichment. Third, merely spending money does not constitute a change of position unless that expenditure was caused by the receipt of the property. It is worth noting that Lord Goff was careful not to pin down the full extent of the defence. Instead, in time-honoured tradition, he wanted it to develop naturally in the cases to follow. We shall consider some of those developments next.

---

74   *Lipkin Gorman v Karpnale* [1991] 2 AC 548.
75   [1996] AC 669.
76   *Scottish Equitable v Derby* [2000] 3 All ER 793, HC; [2001] 3 All ER 818, CA.
77   [1991] 2 AC 548.
78   *Ibid* at 580.
79   *Ibid.*
80   [2004] 3 All ER 299; [2004] EWHC 1188 (Ch).

The extent of the defence of change of position

The first question is: what will constitute a change of position? We know, from Lord Goff's dicta quoted above, that spending money in reliance on the receipt of property may constitute a change of position. As part of the process the defendant will have to deduct things like earning interest as a result of having the traceable property in their possession.

A salient lesson about life and about change of position arose in *Scottish Equitable v Derby*.[81] A pensioner received a mistaken payment of about £172,400 from his pension provider. The issue arose as to whether or not the pension fund could recover the mistaken payment from the pensioner. The pensioner claimed that he had changed his position in reliance upon receipt of the money. His supposed changes of position were the following. First, he spent £9,600 on repairs to his home. Second, he argued that he had been separating from his wife at the time he received the money and he said that he and his wife would suffer great disappointment if they were required to repay the money. The Court of Appeal held that the pensioner could not claim that he had changed his position by reference to the great disappointment that he would suffer if he was not allowed to keep the money. However, it was held that the pensioner had changed his position in relation to the £9,600 spent on home repairs because, it was found on the facts, that he had only incurred the expense because this windfall had become available to him.[82] Therefore, the pensioner was not entitled to retain the full £172,400, but he could retain (by relying on change of position) the £9,600 which he had spent in good faith. (The salient lesson, it is suggested, is that when you receive a cash windfall then you should start spending it and not save it for a rainy day like your grandmother would probably advise you to do.)

A disquieting decision was reached in *Philip Collins Ltd v Davis*.[83] The company was created to organise the business affairs of 'musician' Phil Collins. The company entered into contracts with his backing musicians to secure their services in the usual way: these contracts typically specify how much everyone is paid for performing live, for performing on recordings, and so forth. By mistake, two of these backing artists – the defendants – were overpaid.[84] The defendants were the horn section for Phil Collins's band and had only played on some of the tracks for which royalties were paid to them. The defendants argued that they had changed their position in reliance on receiving these overpayments. They claimed that they had started to incur more expenses (living a little larger, if you like) as a result of being richer, and that they had given money to friends now that they had money. The company sought to recover the overpayments. It was held that the defendants were entitled to resist recovery of half of the overpayments, on the grounds that they had changed their lifestyles in reliance on having received them. Their change of position was said to be a change in lifestyle as a result of having more money than before. This outcome was the court's assessment of the justice of the situation rather than because the defendants had necessarily spent half of the overpayments.[85] The change of position here is quite opaque.

---

81 [2000] 3 All ER 793.
82 [2001] 3 All ER 818.
83 [2000] 3 All ER 808.
84 It is a moot question how much any backing artist for Phil Collins should be paid.
85 Indeed, this final element – as to the conscionability or reasonableness (where those two terms are taken to be broadly similar in this sense) of the defendant failing to notice that she has received an overpayment – might be considered an important element of this defence in the future. Such an approach would recognise the importance of proof of a link between the conscionability of the change of position, or the hardship that the claimant would suffer, and the receipt of the money. See, for example, *Lloyds Bank v Independent Insurance* [1999] 2 WLR 986; *Home Office v Ayres* [1992] ICR 175.

The equitable element in change of position

The defence of change of position has been treated in several cases as being based on a combination of restitutionary and general equitable principles. (It should be remembered that tracing is part of the law of property, not the law on unjust enrichment.) Lord Goff held that the defence was concerned to prevent the defendant from being treated in an 'inequitable' way in *Lipkin Gorman v Karpnale*.[86] Similarly in *Niru Battery Manufacturing Co v Milestone Trading Ltd* it was held that the essential question is whether on the facts of a particular case it would in all the circumstances be inequitable or unconscionable, and thus unjust, to allow the recipient of money paid under a mistake of fact to deny restitution to the payer'.[87] Sedley LJ considered that the court is required 'to decide whether it is equitable to uphold the defence' and that questions of 'the doctrine of restitution' are concerned with 'looking for the least unjust solution to a residual problem'.[88] Similarly, in *Dextra Bank and Trust Co v Bank of Jamaica* it was held that this defence is 'founded on a principle of justice designed to protect the defendant from a claim to restitution in respect of a benefit received by him in circumstances in which it would be inequitable to pursue that claim'.[89]

Whether incurring future liabilities can amount to a change of position

It is possible to change your position in relation to future amounts of money. For example, it was held by the Privy Council in *Dextra Bank and Trust Co v Bank of Jamaica*[90] that the defendant could invoke the defence where they had made a payment in the expectation that they were to receive the money which the claimant was seeking to trace. In that case, a bank had employed a fraudster who concocted a criminal scheme. He organised for D Bank to lend money to J Bank, and convinced J Bank that this money would be used as part of a foreign exchange transaction whereby a different currency would be paid by J Bank back to D Bank. The claimant bank made its payment first in reliance on the expectation that the other bank would make a payment to it in another currency shortly afterwards. Therefore, the claimant argued that it had changed its position in reliance on the second payment, even though when it changed its position the second payment had not yet been made. It was held that these two payments were clearly contractually linked and therefore it was possible to change one's position in reliance on the expectation of that second payment being made.

Similarly, it was held in *Commerzbank AG v Price*[91] that it is possible for a change of position to have taken place before the property which is being traced has been received by the defendant. There have been other decisions in which it has been held that a change of position can only take place after the traceable property has been received, as in *Pearce v Lloyds Bank* where the defendant tried to take into account obligations to pay VAT which

86 [1991] 2 AC 548 at 580.
87 *Niru Battery Manufacturing Co and Another v Milestone Trading Ltd and Others* [2003] EWCA Civ 1446, para 162, *per* Clarke LJ.
88 *Ibid*, para 192, *per* Sedley LJ.
89 *Dextra Bank and Trust Co v Bank of Jamaica* [2002] 1 All ER (Comm) 193, para 38.
90 *Dextra Bank and Trust Co v Bank of Jamaica* [2002] 1 All ER (Comm) 193.
91 [2003] EWCA Civ 1633.

had not yet arisen.[92] As is usual in any case law field, everything will depend on the circumstances.

20.7.2 Estoppel by representation

In the case of *National Westminster Bank plc v Somer International* a defence of estoppel by representation was used in a situation in which change of position might otherwise be thought to apply.[93] Somer held a US dollar account with the bank into which it paid moneys received from foreign clients. Somer was expecting to receive a sum of between US$70,000 and US$78,000 from one of its clients and informed the bank of this. Subsequently, the bank received a payment of US$76,708 which was intended for another of its account holders but which it mistakenly credited to Somer's US dollar account. The bank informed Somer that the money had been paid into its dollar account and Somer assumed that it was the payment which it was expecting to receive from its own client. Importantly, in reliance on the receipt of the money, Somer shipped US$13,180 worth of goods to the client from which it was expecting the payment. The misunderstanding came to light and the bank sought to deduct the money from Somer's account so as to credit the client who should have received the money. Somer argued that it should be entitled to withhold the sum of US$13,180. It was held by the Court of Appeal that Somer was entitled to withhold the amount of US$13,180 because that represented the value of the goods which it only dispatched to its customer because of the statement which the bank had made to it that payment of US$76,708 had been made to it. It was held that this was an equitable estoppel because Somer had acted in reliance on the statement made by the bank to its detriment.

20.7.3 Passing on

The defence of passing on bears some similarity to the defence of change of position. Passing on requires that the defendant has passed the property on, or that some expense has been incurred such that the value of the property has effectively been passed on, to some third person. The defendant will therefore claim that she does not have possession of the property, nor of its traceable proceeds, because that property has been transferred to another person without receipt of any traceable proceeds. This will depend upon the facts of the case.

20.7.4 *Bona fide* purchaser for value without notice

It is a defence to a tracing action that the defendant was a *bona fide* purchaser of the property without notice of the claimant's rights. This defence was confirmed by Lord Browne-Wilkinson in the House of Lords in *Westdeutsche Landesbank v Islington* to the effect that

> from the date of the establishment of the trust (i.e. receipt or mixing of the moneys by the 'trustee') the original payer will have an equitable proprietary interest in the moneys

---

92 [2001] EWCA Civ 1097.
93 [2002] QB 1286, CA.

so long as they are traceable into whomsoever's hands they come other than a purchaser for value of the legal interest without notice.

Equity protects free markets by ensuring that the *bona fide* purchaser for value without notice of the rights of a beneficial owner is entitled to assert good title in property.

The *bona fide* purchaser defence was considered by the Court of Appeal in *Independent Trustee Services Ltd v GP Noble and Morris*.[94] In matrimonial proceedings, Mr Morris was ordered to pay £1.4 million to his former wife after their divorce. He took a total of £52 million from the claimants' pension funds, taking nearly £5 million for himself personally and using some of it to pay his former wife.[95] The claimants sought to trace after those moneys, *inter alia*, into the funds which had been paid to Mrs Morris. In the meantime, Mrs Morris had learned that her former husband was living in a way that suggested he had more money than had been revealed to her during the divorce proceedings, and therefore she sought to overturn the order made during their divorce. Mrs Morris sought to defend the tracing action on the basis that she was a *bona fide* purchaser of the money from which the payments were made to her. The Court of Appeal held that Mrs Morris was not entitled to this defence because setting aside the order made during the divorce extinguished any argument she had that she had effectively 'bought' the money in exchange for her rights on divorce.

---

94 [2012] EWCA Civ 195; [2012] WLR (D) 55. This case is now the subject of an appeal to the Supreme Court.
95 It took some time for those payments to be made, and there were other matrimonial proceedings necessary to secure payment, but that does not affect the analysis here.

Part 7

Commercial uses of trusts

Chapter 21

Commercial and international trusts law

21.1 INTRODUCTION

Like an onion or garlic in cooking, the trust is a wonderful ingredient in any commercial structure. Almost everything involves trusts: from the most complex tax-avoidance structures to complex financial instruments like the collateralised debt obligations (which were pivotal to the global financial crisis in 2008). Trusts are very significant in international commercial activity and they are wonderful in tax-avoidance structures. An express trust can hide the beneficial ownership of a taxpayer, or it can permit beneficial ownership to be allocated between people, or it can move assets to another jurisdiction. As was discussed in Chapter 2, trusts offer protection against the insolvency of the trustee: so, a buyer of corn can protect themselves against the seller's insolvency by settling their payment on trust until the corn is delivered to them. If the seller went into insolvency before the corn is delivered, the payment would be treated by the terms of the trust as being held on trust for the buyer and therefore would be protected against the seller's insolvency. If the seller made delivery, then the terms of the trust would treat the seller as being the beneficial owner of that money. The flexibility of trusts is the reason why they are used in wills and family trusts at one end of the spectrum, right the way through to billion dollar financial instruments at the other end of the spectrum.

21.2 EQUITY AND COMMERCE

21.2.1 Keeping equity out of commercial transactions

Commercial people like certainty. Or so they say. In truth, financial markets are most profitable for bankers when they are volatile and difficult to predict. That means bank traders make money when prices go up and down quickly. The skill is in spotting when to buy and when to sell. When it comes to their legal arrangements, however, financial people like everything to predictable. Professor Roy Goode identified 'certainty' as being the underlying 'philosophy' of commercial law in his standard textbook *Commercial Law*.[1] That is an interesting concept to identify as a *philosophy*. In this book we have identified equity's philosophy as being based on Aristotle's *Ethics* and on theological theories of conscience (in Chapter 26). Consequently, equity appears to offer a great challenge to commercial law because it is said to be (according to the stereotype that appeared in the thinking of Lord Coke in the 17th century and of Lord Eldon in the early 19th century) unpredictable, discretionary and uncertain. Nevertheless, commercial lawyers have used equitable doctrines more than anyone. Most of the recent litigation in Parts 4 and 6 of this book has been concerned with commercial parties, bankers and so forth. It is the commercial lawyers who use trusts for security, who use *Quistclose* trusts, who use equitable tracing to recover their money, and who sue strangers for intermeddling in breaches of fiduciary duty. Historically, equitable mortgages, floating charges and injunctions have been key parts of commercial practice. Consequently, equity has contributed greatly to commercial practice due to its flexibility, even though its very flexibility causes it to be derided carelessly.

One of the principal interactions between commercial law and equity has been a desire on the part of commercial lawyers to keep equity out of commercial cases.[2] The thinking is this: the law dealing with commercial contracts requires certainty so that commercial people can transact with confidence as to the legal treatment of their activities. Consequently, it is said, discretionary remedies and equitable doctrines are likely to disturb commercial certainties and therefore should be avoided. This issue of certainty is typically linked by the judiciary to a need to protect the integrity of commercial contracts and not to allow other considerations to intrude unless absolutely necessary. The problem is said to be the intervention of some legal principle outwith the expectation of the parties. As Robert Goff LJ has said, recognising the need for certainty in commercial transactions:[3]

> It is of the utmost importance in commercial transactions that, if any particular event occurs which may affect the parties' respective rights under a commercial contract, they should know where they stand. The court should so far as possible desist from placing obstacles in the way of either party ascertaining his legal position, if necessary with the aid of advice from a qualified lawyer, because it may be commercially desirable for action to be taken without delay, action which may be irrecoverable and which may have far-reaching consequences. It is for this reason, of course, that the English courts have time and again asserted the need for certainty in commercial transactions – the simple reason that the parties to such transactions are entitled to know where they stand, and to act accordingly.

The essence of commercial certainty is therefore said to be the minimal use of discretionary remedies, and yet when one commercial party brings a matter to court it is incumbent on a court to consider whether or not justice demands a different outcome from the

---

1 Goode, 1998.
2 Millett, 1998; Goode, 1998.
3 *Ibid*, 257.

straightforward enforcement of a contract or whatever. This manifests itself in loose talk about equity as though it is a threat to commercial activity. As Mason put it:[4]

> there is strong resistance, especially in the United Kingdom, to the infiltration of equity into commercial transactions . . . [arising] from apprehensions about the disruptive impact of equitable proprietary remedies, assisted by the doctrine of notice, on the certainty and security of commercial transactions.

There have been several equity specialists among the judiciary who have identified the need for commercial equity to develop a different culture or different principles from traditional, familial equity. As Lord Browne-Wilkinson has held:

> wise judges have often warned against the wholesale importation into commercial law of equitable principles inconsistent with the certainty and speed which are essential requirements for the orderly conduct of business affairs.[5]

However, what this thinking fails to admit is the need for some ethical norms to govern commercial life. There are few major commercial markets which do not have some sort of government oversight, regulation or licensing. The reason for those sorts of regulation is to prevent unconscionable behaviour in those markets which will affect society more generally.

21.2.2 Developing the commercial trust

There is some talk about whether or not trusts law should adapt itself so as to function specifically in commercial contexts. This is an odd notion given the number of cases since, say, 1990 which have involved commercial parties. Even the cases on certainty of intention and of subject matter in recent years have all involved banks and financial instruments. So, the idea that there needs to be a specifically commercial dimension to trusts law ignores the fact that there is already a large body of authority which deals specifically with commercial situations. Nevertheless, as Lord Browne-Wilkinson held in *Target Holdings v Redferns*:[6]

> In the modern world the trust has become a valuable device in commercial and financial dealings. The fundamental principles of equity apply as much to such trusts as they do to the traditional trusts in relation to which those principles were originally formulated. But in my judgment it is important, if the trust is not to be rendered commercially useless, to distinguish between the basic principles of trust law and those specialist rules developed in relation to traditional trusts which are applicable only to such trusts and the rationale of which has no application to trusts of quite a different kind.[7]

With respect, this does appear to be sculpting the law so as to pander to commercial people, and one wonders what exactly it is that they could want. The principles on, for example,

---

4 Mason, 1997/98, 5.
5 *Westdeutsche Landesbank v Islington LBC* [1996] AC 669, 695.
6 [1996] AC 421.
7 See Nolan, [1996] LMCLQ 161.

certainty of subject matter are well known and commercial lawyers can manipulate their clients' arrangements so as to create valid trusts as easily as anyone else. It is perhaps ironic that Lord Browne-Wilkinson both set out this call for the possible need for equity to adopt a new approach in the commercial context and then delivered the leading speech in the House of Lords in *Westdeutsche Landesbank Girozentrale v Islington LBC*,[8] in which the traditional rules were consolidated.

As Professor Atiyah saw it, there was a clash of moralities between the 'paternal, protective Equity' of the old school and 'the newer individualism [in the late 1970s], stressing risk-taking, free choice, rewards to the enterprising and sharp, and devil take the hindmost'.[9] What better summary of the developing role of equity in the context of commercial markets? The parallel with contract law, however, is one which has been developed further by some commentators, as considered next.

21.2.3 The interaction between trusts law and contract law

The contractarian argument

Following on from the idea that commercial people can be suspicious of equity – especially when a discretionary doctrine means that they do not get the outcome that they wanted – there is an interesting line in the academic discussion of trusts law which has suggested that commercial trusts could develop better if they were understood as being part of the law of contract. The chief advocate of this view has been Professor Langbein who takes the view that all trusts involve a contract between the settlor and the trustees, and therefore that contract law should be used to interpret trusts law.[10] The trustees will often be professionals who, as professionals, will agree to act as trustees only if their duties and liabilities are controlled by contract.[11] Consequently, Langbein considers this contract to be the heart of the trust because it sets out the precise ambit of the trustees' obligations. This would not mean, *inter alia*, that it would be necessary for there to be any beneficiary able to satisfy the beneficiary principle,[12] but rather it would be sufficient to establish a trust if there were a contract demonstrating an intention to create a trust. Such a view means that all questions as to the enforceability of the trust fall to be considered by reference to the law of contract rather than the law of trusts. The advantage for commercial people is said to be that contract law is more familiar to them and therefore that if contract law was used to interpret trusts disputes then that would achieve outcomes which would reassure commercial people.

It is difficult to know what to do with these ideas. First, not all trusts involve any sort of contract. In *Paul v Constance*[13] and *Re Kayford*,[14] for example, there was an express trust found but the parties did not know they were creating a trust. Second, commercial people may well know very little law: it is more important that their legal advisors understand what

---

8   [1996] AC 669.
9   Atiyah, 1979.
10   Langbein, 1995, 625.
11   Section 8.5.1.
12   Section 4.1.
13   [1977] 1 WLR 527.
14   [1975] 1 WLR 279.

the law is. If their advisors are recommending the use of trusts then it is incumbent on them to understand how trusts work. Consequently, I would suggest that we should treat with caution any argument that the principles of express trusts law be overthrown in favour of contractarian or other obligations-based theories.[15]

21.2.4 Exclusion of liability through the trust instrument or through contract

As was discussed in great detail in Chapter 8,[16] one aspect in which the law of trusts has begun to resemble contract law is in its preparedness to permit trustees to limit their liabilities by having a clause included in the trust instrument to that effect.[17] Consequently, a trustee can escape liability for gross negligence on the basis that she has agreed, through the trust instrument, with the settlor to have her liability so excluded. The alternative view would have been to say that, as a fiduciary, the trustee owes certain duties of competence and good faith to the beneficiaries which cannot be excluded by contract. What is new, perhaps, is the idea that the trustee need only act honestly, but not necessarily competently, in the performance of her office as trustee. The courts have apparently accepted the notion that there is nothing wrong in principle with restricting one's liabilities as a trustee.

There is nothing wrong in principle, of course, with the suggestion that my conscience is not affected if I undertake to manage your investments as a trustee on the condition that I will not be liable if I act negligently. Suppose I make this stipulation because I am not a financial expert and therefore do not want to be held to account as though I was one. In such a situation, if the settlor agrees to my stipulation from the outset, I cannot be said to have acted in bad conscience if I do make negligent investments and seek not to be liable for the losses which those investments cause to you. Rather, the concern must be with professional trustees who take large fees based on their assumed professional competence but who then seek to hide behind exclusion of liability clauses in the event that they turn out to be less adept than they had at first suggested. At first blush, the same argument applies to them: they have only agreed to act based on stipulations as to the limits of their liability, and consequently they are entitled to rely on them because otherwise they would not have entered into the contract. However, a professional trustee regulated under the Financial Services and Markets Act 2000 would not be permitted to exclude their regulatory obligations, for example under the Conduct of Business Sourcebook which governs their obligation to act in the best interests of their client and to treat them fairly throughout. Therefore, it does appear that equity's unwillingness to impose objective standards of competence on professional trustees may be out of step with the other commercial standards which are imposed on those professionals.

21.2.5 Themes in international trusts law

There are two principal themes in international trusts law which are dealt with in outline here. The first is the Hague Convention on the Recognition of Trusts, which concerns the recognition of the trusts law of some jurisdictions in other jurisdictions. The second is the use of trusts for tax-avoidance purposes in international trusts law practice.

---

15 Matthews, 2002, 144.
16 Section 8.5.1.
17 *Armitage v Nurse* [1998] Ch 241.

Recognition of trusts

There is an important question within a field of law known as 'private international law' as to whether or not a trust created in one jurisdiction under that jurisdiction's system of law would be enforced in another jurisdiction which had no trusts law or which had different trusts law. Therefore, private international law (sometimes known as 'conflict of laws') develops principles which govern these sorts of issues. Private international law is part of English law. However, English law in this field has signed up to the Hague Convention on the recognition of trusts (that is, 'the Hague Convention on the Law Applicable to Trusts on their Recognition 1985') which was incorporated into English law by the Recognition of Trusts Act 1987. There is insufficient space here to consider this legislation in great detail.[18] Briefly put, the purposes of the Convention are threefold. First, to permit the settlor to provide for the governing law of a trust. That means that the system of rules which governs any disputes as to the trust can be selected by the settlor. The 'governing law' means the system of rules (e.g. English trusts law as discussed in this book) which are used to interpret the trust, the rights of the beneficiaries and the duties of the trustees. The settlor may choose any governing law she wishes. Therefore, the settlor can choose a different governing law from the law in the country in which they are resident. So, a settlor resident in France may choose English law to govern a trust she wishes to create. Secondly, a trust created in that manner is to be recognised in other signatory jurisdictions. Therefore, all states which have signed up to the Convention must recognise trusts created in other states which have signed up to the Convention. Thirdly, the Convention seeks to preclude any signatory state through its trusts law seeking to disapply the more favourable rules of another state.

The Convention applies to trusts which are created voluntarily, and therefore does not apply to trusts implied by law.[19] Also outwith the scope of the Convention are testamentary trusts and lifetime settlements of foreign immovables and movables, in which cases ordinary rules of conflict of laws will apply. The choice of law in relation to a trust which does fall within the Convention is effective only if the system of rules chosen recognises the trust concept.[20] However, significantly, it is not necessary for the system of law chosen to have any connection with the trust, so that, for example, a trust declared in England by an English settlor with English trustees can theoretically have a different system of law from English law. So, if the trusts laws of the Cayman Islands are thought to be advantageous, then that system of law can be chosen to govern that trust. It is also possible to select different systems of law to govern different parts of a trust, so that one system of law could govern clauses dealing with land in France and another system of law could govern clauses dealing with land in England.

Where no express choice of law is made, the 'law with which it is most closely connected' will be the governing law of the settlement.[21] Therefore, the court will look at all the circumstances, including the jurisdiction where the settlor, trustees and beneficiaries are resident, the location of the trust property and so forth. Weighing those factors, it will identify the jurisdiction with which the settlement has the closest connection. Significantly, however, where there are overriding rules of the forum seised of the question, the Convention provides

---

18 The reader is referred to Harris, 2002, generally.
19 Hague Convention, Art 6.
20 *Ibid.*
21 *Ibid*, Art 7.

that that forum so seised is entitled to decide, if the trust has such a weak connection with the jurisdiction of its governing law, that the mandatory rules of the jurisdiction hearing the question should be applied instead.[22]

International trusts law and offshore trusts services

There is a significant area of trusts law practice which deals with the establishment of trusts which permit the residents of one jurisdiction to organise the holding of their assets through trustees resident in a different jurisdiction, with a beneficial tax effect. This is a service which is offered by international trusts service providers. The clearest explanation of these offshore trusts structures is provided by Lord Walker in *Schmidt v Rosewood*[23] in the opening paragraph of his opinion in the following terms:

> It has become common for wealthy individuals in many parts of the world (including countries which have no indigenous law of trusts) to place funds at their disposition into trusts (often with a network of underlying companies) regulated by the law of, and managed by trustees resident in, territories with which the settlor (who may be also a beneficiary) has no substantial connection. These territories (sometimes called tax havens) are chosen not for their geographical convenience (indeed face-to-face meetings between the settlor and his trustees are often very inconvenient) but because they are supposed to offer special advantages in terms of confidentiality and protection from fiscal demands (and sometimes from problems under the insolvency laws, or laws restricting freedom of testamentary disposition, in the country of the settlor's domicile). The trusts and powers contained in a settlement established in such circumstances may give no reliable indication of who will in the event benefit from the settlement. Typically it will contain very wide discretions exercisable by the trustees (sometimes only with the consent of a so-called protector) in favour of a widely-defined class of beneficiaries. The exercise of those discretions may depend upon the settlor's wishes as confidentially imparted to the trustees and the protector. As a further cloak against transparency, the identity of the true settlor or settlors may be concealed behind some corporate figurehead.

Such trusts can be used simply to shelter assets from regulatory oversight. That means, assets are being hidden from the view of taxing authorities or law enforcement authorities. Trusts are not ordinarily required to disclose their beneficiaries to the authorities nor to publish accounts and so forth. Moreover, by having the trustees (and therefore the trust) resident in a different jurisdiction, it becomes difficult as a practical matter as well as a legal matter for the authorities of a jurisdiction like the UK to find out anything about those trusts. There are efforts, as outlined below, to force these 'offshore' jurisdictions to disclose information about such trusts and the professionals who operate them. Some jurisdictions are beginning to introduce registration formalities for trusts which are owned beneficially by people from other jurisdictions. Such offshore trusts are used by international criminal and terrorist organisations to manage their assets as well as by otherwise law-abiding people who simply want to reduce their tax

---

22 *Ibid*, Art 16.
23 [2003] UKPC 26; [2003] 2 AC 709.

bills. Sometimes they are used to achieve objectives which are impossible in the settlor's home jurisdiction, or simply to hide assets from family members and others.

While these structures are executed as trusts, they often also support investment arrangements between the service provider and the settlor-investor. If a UK investor wants to minimise the tax bill on their investments then they might enter into an agreement with an investment bank to move their money to a 'tax haven' from which a trust will invest on behalf of that investor and will benefit from the low taxes payable in that jurisdiction. The trust in such circumstances is merely a vehicle to make the investment possible. The parties' principal intention will be the investment contract between them.

The example of Cayman Islands trusts law

In some jurisdictions there is no need to have a beneficiary to create a valid trust, unlike English trusts law (as discussed in Chapter 4). So in the Cayman Islands there is a statute which creates the 'STAR' trust, named after that jurisdiction's 'Special Trusts (Alternative Regime)' statute of 1997. That statute provides that the beneficiary principle does not apply to STAR trusts from the perspective of the law of the Cayman Islands. Yet, the statute does have a mechanism for protecting the investor in this arrangement from malfeasance by the trustees. This is achieved by an 'enforcer' being appointed to the trust with the power to oversee the activities of the trustees. This device is thought to displace the mischief of the beneficiary principle. Consequently, there is no person who has an equitable interest under this form of trust in the Cayman Islands. Therefore, if the trust earns income then there is no beneficiary who shall bear the tax in the Cayman Islands, but rather tax is only payable by the trustees at the tiny Cayman Islands rates or as a small fixed sum. Importantly, the client who has invested their money into this structure does not bear any tax liabilities in the Cayman Islands. The question, as considered below, is whether the client will bear any tax liabilities in their home jurisdiction.

Clearly, this structure in which the client does not have any equitable interests is very attractive to foreign investors (from the UK and the USA, for example) who want to settle assets (such as shares or other financial instruments) on trust in a way that means they will not personally be liable for tax on any income earned from those assets. By having an enforcer installed it means that there is someone who can oversee the behaviour of the trustees but without there being any beneficial interest which will give rise to tax. The UK taxpayer is hopeful that they will only have to pay a fee to the professional who will act as trustee in the Cayman Islands and that the trustees will only have to pay a small, fixed fee by way of tax to the government of those islands. The risk is whether the UK revenue authorities will finally develop the gumption to track down these sorts of arrangements and whether the English courts will recognise these trusts as being valid. If you are an English trusts lawyer then the problem with the STAR trust is that it has no beneficiary and therefore that it would not be a valid trust under English law (under *Leahy v AG for New South Wales* for example, as discussed in section 4.2). If the trust was not valid under English law then English trusts law would say that the equitable interest passes back to the UK client on resulting trust. If so, the UK client would be liable for the tax just like Mr Vandervell in *Vandervell v IRC*, as discussed in section 5.5. Let us develop that last point in more detail.

The concern of practitioners in offshore jurisdictions is that if English courts will not accept trust structures like STAR trusts as being valid trusts in England, because the trust has no beneficiary, then for the purposes of English trusts law and UK tax law the investor may still be considered to be the beneficial owner of that trust and therefore to be responsible for its profits for tax purposes. The investor would still be considered to be the absolute owner of the property because any property purportedly settled on an ineffective trust would pass back to them on resulting trust principles.[24] If that were the approach taken by the English court then a so-called 'limping trust' would be created[25] on the basis that the parties would have created a trust that was valid under the law of the Cayman Islands but invalid under English law. The argument is advanced by commentators like David Hayton[26] that there is no need to enforce the beneficiary principle strictly if there is some other person (typically dubbed a 'protector' or 'enforcer') who can sue as though a beneficiary under the trust, because that satisfies the mischief of the beneficiary principle (as explained by Goff J in *Re Denley* to be the need for someone in whose favour the court can decree performance) by other means.

Some also make the suggestion that English law should therefore ditch the beneficiary principle so that these tax havens can expand their trusts services businesses. That daft, immoral suggestion will only increase the amount of tax avoidance that is conducted by British people through those islands. The only outcome from that unwelcome change in the law would be that there would be a huge fall in the tax take in the UK with the result that fewer hospitals, schools and railways could be built in this country. The tax burden would fall on lower income people in the UK. It is a proposal which should be dismissed out of hand.

Sinister uses of international trusts

There is another, even more sinister use of international trusts in the modern age. This has come to the attention of the OECD (the respected international Organisation for Economic Cooperation and Development), the FATF and other bodies. The principal use of trusts in many jurisdictions (like England and Wales) is that there is no registration of the existence of trusts nor any registration of the ownership of trust assets. In relation to companies created in the UK under the Companies Act 2006, for example, there are a wide number of requirements for the registration of the company itself, of its shareholders, of anyone controlling shares in the company, of the company's accounts annually, of a variety of directors' reports, and so forth. There is literally no requirement of this sort in relation to trusts. So, if you want to keep your ownership of assets a secret then holding those assets on a trust is the best way of doing that.

There are many criminal organisations which want to keep their ownership of assets a secret. The most sinister, of course, are international terrorist organisations which need to move money around the world and which want to be able to invest their money so as to increase their wealth. In Chapter 17 *A Politics of Trusts Law*, we considered the steps which a person might take to use trusts to fund and organise a criminal or terrorist organisation. The principal goal of any organisation of this sort is to 'launder' their money by passing it through numbers of front organisations (trusts, companies and other organisations) which appear to 'wash' their money free of the stigma of having been owned by criminal organisations.

If you have seen TV programmes like *Breaking Bad* or *The Sopranos*, then you will be aware of the need criminals have so as to be able to spend their money without the police being able to prove that it is 'criminal property' (as under the UK Proceeds of Crime Act

---

24 *Vandervell v IRC* [1967] 2 AC 291, HL.
25 Waters, 2002.
26 Hayton, 2001.

2002). In *Breaking Bad* a drug dealer purchased a large car wash business and falsified the amount of money which it received (by means of his wife running fictional purchases of car washing facilities through the till) so as to pretend that his huge amounts of cash had come from somewhere legitimate; and Tony Soprano, a mafia boss in New Jersey, operated a bar, a pork butcher and a rubbish collection business so that he could pretend that his criminal earnings came from legitimate sources in *The Sopranos*. This is known as 'money-laundering' and the use of tax havens for this purpose has been legendary over the years. Since the attack on the World Trade Center in September 2001, the world changed and the impetus to combat the activities which are conducted in these offshore jurisdictions increased markedly. It is a change which has put trusts law at the centre of geopolitics.

Quistclose trusts

CAPSULE SUMMARY

A *Quistclose* trust comes into existence in relation to a loan contract when the intention of the parties is that the borrower is required to use the loan moneys for a specified purpose. In the event that the borrower goes into insolvency, the loan moneys are deemed to have been held on trust for the lender. The issue is as to the basis on which this trust comes into existence. In *Barclays Bank v Quistclose* Lord Wilberforce held that a primary trust took effect over the loan moneys until they were used for their assigned purpose, and a secondary trust came into existence so as to carry the equitable interest back to the lender if that primary purpose was not performed. This was interpreted by many commentators as being a resulting trust. Lord Wilberforce himself expressed this as a combination of common law and equitable principles such that an equitable remedy granted property rights to the lender in the event that the terms of the contract were not performed. In *Twinsectra v Yardley* Lord Millett considered that this was a resulting trust which operated so that sufficient title was transferred to the borrower to carry out the terms of the loan contract but that the lender otherwise retained the equitable interest in the loan moneys.

22.1 INTRODUCTION

The philosopher Ludwig Wittgenstein thought that we know what things are because we know what they are called. So, we know what a table is because it has the word 'table' attached to it.[1] With *Quistclose* trusts, which are the subject of this chapter, we know what they are called but we have no agreement as to what they are. Thus, *Quistclose* trusts cause an interesting philosophical problem and quite a few interesting legal problems.

In essence, the purpose of a *Quistclose* trust is to provide protection for people who lend money against the insolvency of the borrower of that money. So, if a lender includes a term in their loan contract with a borrower which specifies the purpose for which the borrower can use that money, then a *Quistclose* is imposed over that money if the borrower attempts to use it for any other purpose. If the borrower goes into insolvency, for example, then the lender has the benefit of a *Quistclose* trust over the loan moneys so that those moneys cannot be used, for example, to pay off the borrower's debts to its unsecured creditors. It is simple and effective: if the correct sort of term is put into the loan contract then the lender has a trust automatically imposed over the loan moneys which protects the lender against the money being misused. If the loan moneys were paid away by the borrower to a third party in breach of the term of the contract restricting the use of those moneys, then the lender would have an equitable interest in that money which would enable it to begin an equitable tracing claim in relation to the funds received by that third party.

What is problematic about a *Quistclose* trust is that it is unclear whether it works as a resulting trust, as an express trust, or as some other sort of trust entirely. The judges and the commentators have argued about this for decades. It is likely that a question in your trusts law module about *Quistclose* trusts would ask you to compare the various arguments about the nature of *Quistclose* trusts. This chapter is organised so as to explain the leading cases in this area and then to lead you through the most important models of *Quistclose* trusts in the literature. That should provide you with a structure for discussing these trusts in an essay.

Before we begin, however, I would proffer just one idea about *Quistclose* trusts which is never considered by trusts lawyers. One of my other fields is finance law. In my book *The Law of Finance*,[2] I discuss the law governing lending transactions in great detail. For any practising banking lawyer, this area looks entirely different from the way it looks to a trusts lawyer. If you are a banking lawyer advising a bank about the terms of its loan contract in relation to a particularly risky borrower, then you would draft that loan contract so that you make the terms and nature of your *Quistclose* trust very clear indeed. Therefore, no banking lawyer worth their salt would ever leave the effect of their banking contract to be analysed by the court by reference to a series of unknown, vague academic categories because they would expect to be sued for negligence if they did. Consequently, this entire discussion should be considering the terms of loan contracts first, before acknowledging that the debate about *Quistclose* trusts in the academic journals is just a debate about the exceptional categories of trust in circumstances in which lawyers have failed to draft the banks' loan contracts properly.

---

1   Wittgenstein, *Tractatus Logico-Philosophicus*. Before his untimely death, Wittgenstein changed his mind about all this.
2   Hudson, 2013.

22.2 THE FUNDAMENTALS OF LOAN CONTRACTS

This section explains the legal basis of loan contracts as a background to *Quistclose* trusts. Loan contracts are very simple. When the contract is created, the lender agrees to pay an amount of money to the borrower; and the borrower agrees to repay the equivalent amount of money at a given date in the future and in the meantime to pay an identified rate of interest (whether a fixed or a floating[3] rate) periodically to the lender. All of this takes place at common law and there is no need for the involvement of trusts law at all. In property law terms, when the loan contract is created what happens is that the lender transfers ownership of the loan money outright at the moment when it is paid into the borrower's bank account. The borrower is therefore the outright owner of that money from the moment that she receives it. Again, trusts law plays no part in this. Ordinarily, the borrower is then entitled to spend that money in any way they please. Their only contractual obligations are to pay amounts of interest periodically and to repay the amount of the loan at the time identified in the loan contract. Importantly, in property law terms, the money that is repaid at the end of the loan term is different money from the original money which was paid by the lender to the borrower at the beginning of the loan. This is obvious because the borrower must be able to spend the money or else the loan would be pointless.

The big question arises: how does the lender protect itself against the risk that the borrower will not repay the loan? There are many well-known means of taking protection. The best known is to take a guarantee from some reputable third party or else to take security, for example by way of a mortgage or other charge, over some identified property. There is another way of taking security, however, and that is the *Quistclose* trust. A *Quistclose* trust is created by inserting a term into the loan contract which says that the borrower can only use the money for a specific purpose: for example, the loan contract might say that 'the borrower may only use this money to buy a new computer for her business and for no other purpose'. The *Quistclose* trust would then bite if the borrower wanted to use the money to buy a new car instead of a computer. *Quistclose* trusts are usually intended to be used if the borrower goes into insolvency but there is no reason why these trust rights cannot operate more generally than that, as we shall see.

Another technique which commercial lawyers use to take security is to 'retain title' in property.[4] So, if you are providing a machine for your business partner to use in manufacturing shoes, you might specify that 'the shoe machine remains my property throughout the life of our partnership' so that there is no question about whose machine that is when the partnership dissolves in the future. Some lawyers think of *Quistclose* trusts as being a similar sort of device to retain property rights for the lender, as we shall see below in relation to Lord Millett's explanation of these *Quistclose* trusts in *Twinsectra v Yardley*.

22.3 THE FUNDAMENTALS OF *QUISTCLOSE* TRUSTS

22.3.1 *Quistclose* trusts in outline

A general definition of the Quistclose *trust*

A *Quistclose* trust is a means by which a lender of money can protect themselves against the insolvency or misfeasance of the borrower by inserting a clause into the loan contract which specifies that the loan money may only be used by the borrower for a specified purpose.

---

3 A 'floating' rate is a rate of interest which changes, usually when Bank of England base rates change.
4 *Aluminium Industrie Vaassen BV v Romalpa Aluminium Ltd* [1976] 1 WLR 676.

This clause in the loan contract creates a trust in the event that the borrower does go into insolvency or that the money is purportedly used for another purpose.

Let us summarise some of the questions that this simple structure raises before we consider the detail of the case law. The usual explanation for this arrangement is that a *Quistclose* trust creates a resulting trust which carries the equitable interest in the loan moneys back to the lender.[5] The question is knowing whether or not that resulting trust comes into existence only after the borrower would go into insolvency, or whether it existed before the insolvency, or whether it is created at the same moment as the insolvency. (It is worth noting that any well-drafted loan contract should make this clear from the outset, but the discussion in the cases and the journals does not consider that contingency because this point is always discussed on the basis of pure trusts law.) If the resulting trust only came into existence after the insolvency, then that would be useless because the right would come into existence too late. It is important that the trust must pre-date the insolvency or the property will be locked up in the insolvency proceedings. Lord Millett held in *Twinsectra v Yardley* that the lender should be interpreted as retaining an equitable interest throughout the transaction, and that it would be a resulting trust which came into existence on the borrower's insolvency. (This raises a problem which we shall consider below.) The strength of this model is that the lender's equitable interest comes into existence before the insolvency.

The approach that is taken in Australia is that a *Quistclose* trust should be interpreted as creating an express trust over the loan moneys from the moment that the contract is created. This has the virtue that the equitable interest comes into existence from the very moment that the loan contract is created. The borrower is then deemed to have a power to use the money for the purpose that is specified in the loan contract.

Interestingly, the leading case in this area – *Barclays Bank v Quistclose* – does not identify which type of trust is in existence. The reason for this is simple: the judge who delivered the leading speech, Lord Wilberforce, thought about this area of law completed differently from the trusts law commentators. While the trusts law commentators are obsessed with the type of trust that is in existence here, and while they generally interpret Lord Wilberforce as having intended a resulting trust, Lord Wilberforce knew a lot more about taking security in loan contracts. As explained above in relation to the legal analysis of loan contracts, it is common law which dominates loan contracts. Any legal problem relating to a loan concerns a debt being owed by the borrower to the lender at common law which is governed by contract law. It is only when something goes wrong and the money is about to be misused, says Lord Wilberforce, that the 'remedies of equity' are used to protect the lender. It is at this moment that a trust of some sort (a 'secondary trust') is created, in the opinion of Lord Wilberforce. As we shall see in the next section when we analyse this case in detail, Lord Wilberforce saw this as common law and equity working together to protect the lender. So, his lordship was not particularly concerned about what type of trust was at issue because he saw it as being a question about equity and common law cooperating with one another.

22.3.2 The decision in *Barclays Bank v Quistclose*

The *Quistclose* trust takes its name from the decision of the House of Lords in *Barclays Bank v Quistclose*.[6] In that case, a loan contract was created. Quistclose lent money to

---

5 *Twinsectra v Yardley* [2002] 2 AC 164.
6 [1970] AC 567.

Rolls Razor Ltd. There was a condition in the contract that the loan moneys were only to be used to pay a dividend to a particular class of shareholders. That money was held in a bank account with Barclays Bank which was separate from all other moneys. Subsequently Rolls Razor went into insolvency before the dividend was paid. The loan money stayed in the bank account. When Rolls Razor went into insolvency, Barclays Bank purported to take the loan money from that bank account and to use it to pay off an overdraft which Rolls Razor had run up. Quistclose sued Barclays Bank on the basis that the money in the dividend bank account should be deemed to be held on trust for Quistclose because it had inserted a clause in the loan contract which specified that that money was only to be used to pay a dividend to specific shareholders. It was held that the money in that account was indeed held on trust for Quistclose and therefore Barclays could not use the money to discharge the overdraft.

The question in the appeal was whether or not there was a resulting trust over that money and the House of Lords granted the appeal: therefore, it is generally assumed that this case created a resulting trust. However, Lord Wilberforce did not use the term 'resulting trust' in his judgment. It is important to focus in detail on what his lordship actually said so as to understand this area of law. What his lordship did hold was the following:[7]

> There is surely no difficulty in recognising the co-existence in one transaction of legal and equitable rights and remedies: when the money is advanced, the lender acquires an equitable right to see that it is applied for the primary designated purpose:[8] when the purpose has been carried out (that is, the debt paid) the lender has his remedy against the borrower in debt: if the primary purpose cannot be carried out, the question arises if a secondary purpose (that is, repayment to the lender) has been agreed, expressly or by implication: if it has, the remedies of equity may be invoked to give effect to it, if it has not (and the money is intended to fall within the general fund of the debtor's assets) then there is the appropriate remedy for recovery of a loan.

This passage means that there is no problem with having obligations at common law (that is, to repay the loan) and also obligations in equity (that is, to hold the money on trust until it is used for the specified purpose). Thus, if the purpose is performed then the lender has rights against the borrower at common law under the terms of the contract (that is, he 'has his remedy in debt'). The 'secondary obligation' arises in equity either on the express terms of the contract or impliedly from the circumstances. The 'remedies of equity' in this context are the 'secondary trust' which requires that the loan money is held on trust if it is not used for the specified purpose. Interestingly, though, Lord Wilberforce expressed this in terms of being a general 'equitable right' rather than explicitly a resulting trust in the following passage:

> I can appreciate no reason why the flexible interplay of law and equity cannot let in these practical arrangements, and other variations if desired: it would be to the discredit of both systems if they could not. In the present case the intention to create a secondary trust for the benefit of the lender, to arise if the primary trust, to pay the dividend, could not be carried out, is clear and I can find no reason why the law should not give effect to it.

---

7 *Ibid* at 581–582.
8 *In re Rogers*, 8 Morr 243, *per* Lindley LJ and Kay LJ.

Therefore, the *Quistclose* trust arises from the interplay of the ordinary principles of the contract of loan at common law and the equitable principles which prevent ownership of the loan money being passed to a third party if it is misused.

A similar formulation has been used by Lord Millett in *Twinsectra v Yardley,*[9] and approved by Evans-Lombe J in *Cooper v PRG Power Ltd,*[10] to the effect that 'when the money is advanced, the lender acquires a right, enforceable in equity, to see that it is applied for the stated purpose, or more accurately to prevent its application for any other purpose': again, it is an equitable ability to prevent misuse of the money. What this account misses, however, is the understanding of the *Quistclose* arrangement as depending on the common law rules on contract and debt in the first place.

Importantly, the manner in which Lord Wilberforce decides that the *Quistclose* trust arises is then by means of a 'secondary trust' coming into existence for the benefit of the lender if the 'primary trust . . . cannot be carried out'. Two points emerge. First, this trust was based on that interaction of primary and secondary trusts being the intention of the parties, an idea which has been approved in subsequent cases.[11] Secondly, this does not require that the borrower must have misused the money; instead, it only requires that the purpose 'cannot be carried out' for whatever reason, whether because of the borrower's insolvency or some other event.

22.3.3 The decision in *Twinsectra v Yardley*

Lord Millett set out another explanation of the *Quistclose* trust in his judgment in *Twinsectra v Yardley*.[12] Lord Millett was the only one of the judges in the House of Lords who took the *Quistclose* point; whereas the others focused on the dishonest assistance issue discussed in Chapter 19. The approach advanced there was that the *Quistclose* trust should be considered to be akin to a retention of title by the lender whereby the lender effectively retains an equitable interest in the property throughout the transaction. In that case a solicitor permitted loan moneys to be used by his client in breach of the express terms of a loan contract. On this analysis, a *Quistclose* trust enables a party to a commercial contract to retain their equitable interest in property provided as part of a commercial agreement by way of a resulting trust.

While Lord Millett upheld the theory of the *Quistclose* trust being a resulting trust, he explained it a different way from Lord Wilberforce in the *Quistclose* case. We shall focus on two passages in particular from his lordship's speech. First, paragraph 81 of Lord Millett's judgment compared the *Quistclose trust* to the retention of title structure considered above in section 22.2:

> On this analysis, the *Quistclose* trust is a simple commercial arrangement akin . . . to a retention of title clause (though with a different object) which enables the borrower to have recourse to the lender's money for a particular purpose without entrenching on the lender's property rights more than necessary to enable the purpose to be achieved. The

---

9   [2002] 2 AC 164, para [69].
10 [2008] BCC 588, para [13].
11 *Re Niagara Mechanical Services International Ltd (in admin.)* [2001] BCC 393; *Shalson v Russo* [2003] EWHC 1637 (Ch); [2005] Ch 281; *Cooper v PRG Power* [2008] BCC 588.
12 [2002] UKHL 12; [2002] 2 AC 164.

money remains the property of the lender unless and until it is applied in accordance with his directions, and insofar as it is not so applied it must be returned to him. I am disposed, perhaps pre-disposed, to think that this is the only analysis which is consistent both with orthodox trust law and with commercial reality.

The second sentence is very problematic: 'The money remains the property of the lender unless and until it is applied in accordance with his directions, and insofar as it is not so applied it must be returned to him.' There is a clear contradiction in terms here: if the money *remains* the property of the lender then how can it possibly be *returned* to him? If I retain property then I cannot possibly ask you to return it to me later because I have kept it. Imagine that you ask to borrow my lawnmower and I refuse to lend it to you.[13] If I were to come to your front door the next day and demand that you return my lawnmower to me, you would say 'well, you kept your lawnmower so how can I possibly return it to you?' It is the same problem with Lord Millett's formulation here: if the lender retains the money, it cannot logically be returned to him. What we might take Lord Millett to mean is that *ownership* of the money in equity remains with the lender even if *possession* of the money is passed to the borrower, such that the borrower has to return *possession* of the money to the lender. Similarly, Lord Millett's reference to 'the property' is unclear because we cannot know if it means retention of absolute title (which would negate the possibility of there being a trust) or whether it is supposed to mean only retention of an equitable interest under a trust.

The following paragraph 100 from Lord Millett's speech also presents problems when trying to understand the nature of a *Quistclose* trust:

> As Sherlock Holmes reminded Dr Watson, when you have eliminated the impossible, whatever remains, however improbable, must be the truth. I would reject all the alternative analyses, which I find unconvincing for the reasons I have endeavoured to explain, and hold the *Quistclose* trust to be an entirely orthodox example of the kind of default trust known as a resulting trust. The lender pays the money to the borrower by way of loan, but he does not part with the entire beneficial interest in the money, and in so far as he does not it is held on a resulting trust for the lender from the outset. Contrary to the opinion of the Court of Appeal, it is the borrower who has a very limited use of the money, being obliged to apply it for the stated purpose or return it. He has no beneficial interest in the money, which remains throughout in the lender subject only to the borrower's power or duty to apply the money in accordance with the lender's instructions. When the purpose fails, the money is returnable to the lender, not under some new trust in his favour which only comes into being on the failure of the purpose, but because the resulting trust in his favour is no longer subject to any power on the part of the borrower to make use of the money. Whether the borrower is obliged to apply the money for the stated purpose or merely at liberty to do so, and whether the lender can countermand the borrower's mandate while it is still capable of being carried out, must depend on the circumstances of the particular case.

---

13 I can be capricious like that, especially with umbrellas because you never get them back.

Again, as with paragraph 81, there is a problem in that we are told that the money 'remains throughout in the lender' and yet that 'the money is returnable to the lender'. Furthermore, the *Quistclose* trust is held explicitly to be a resulting trust, even though ownership of the money is said to *remain* with the lender. Therefore, this is not a resulting trust as Professor Birks has explained it because a resulting trust ordinarily requires that equitable ownership of the property has passed away and that it then 'jumps back'[14] to the lender. That cannot happen if the lender *retains* equitable ownership of the loan money throughout the loan contract. Alternatively, we must reject Professor Birks's analysis of a resulting trust and instead accept that Lord Millett has established that resulting trusts are merely a 'default trust' in which a court of equity simply recognises that when there is a question as to the ownership of property then we should recognise that the last owner of that property is still its owner.

22.4 CATEGORISING THE *QUISTCLOSE* TRUST

22.4.1 The issues

There are two principal problems which arise in relation to a *Quistclose* trust. First, does the equitable interest under that trust arise before or after the borrower has purported to misuse the money? Does that model of the trust provide protection against insolvency? If the rights only come into existence after the borrower has gone into insolvency then it does not provide security. Second, does the *Quistclose* trust arise by operation of law (for example as a resulting trust) or does it arise by agreement of the parties (for example as an express trust contained in the parties' loan contract)? It will be important to know whether the lender 'retains' a right in the original loan moneys throughout the life of the loan contract, or whether that right only comes into existence for the first time when the borrower disobeys the terms of the loan contract, or whether the right comes into existence in some other way. It is important to consider how the precise terms of any loan contract may alter the appropriate analysis on the facts of any given case. This section will consider the different explanations of the *Quistclose* trust.

22.4.2 Resulting trust

The argument for resulting trust: Are there two different types of resulting trust here?

The first explanation of the nature of a *Quistclose* trust, which has been attributed to Lord Wilberforce in *Barclays Bank v Quistclose*[15] and which was explicitly approved by Lord Millett in the House of Lords in *Twinsectra v Yardley,*[16] is that the *Quistclose* trust operates on resulting trust principles. The most common understanding of a resulting trust (as discussed in Chapter 11) is that it comes into existence so as to carry property back to its original owner, as in *Vandervell v IRC*. This analysis suggests that title in the loan moneys passes away from the lender to the borrower, under Lord Wilbeforce's 'primary trust', before then bouncing

---

14 See section 11.1 of this book.
15 [1970] AC 567.
16 [2002] 2 AC 164.

back to the lender on resulting trust when the 'secondary trust' comes into existence at the moment when the borrower has breached the terms of the loan contract. This analysis might mean that the property rights have to move away before they can be brought back: what if the property rights (i.e. the loan moneys) have been moved into another jurisdiction which does not recognise the *Quistclose* trust? In those circumstances, the trust would arise too late and the lender would have no effective property rights.

However, if we follow the model of the resulting trust advanced by Harman J in *Re Gillingham Bus Disaster Fund* then we would understand each resulting trust as arising on its own terms (i.e. *sub modo*) and therefore we could consider the resulting trust to be the same as a constructive trust in this context as arising automatically when the money is about to be in breach of the loan contract so that the equitable interest is caught before it can pass away. This model of resulting trust would give greater flexibility in the operation of *Quistclose* trusts.

The *Twinsectra* model of the resulting trust advanced by Lord Millett, as discussed above, suggested that possession of the loan moneys passes to the borrower and that the lender in some unclear way also retains property rights in that money on resulting trust principles. This resulting trust appears to exist throughout the life of the loan contract and does not operate like the *Vandervell* resulting trust to make property rights bounce back to the lender at a later date.

22.4.3 Express trust

The analysis of the *Quistclose* trust as a form of express trust would proceed as follows. The lender enters into a contract of loan with the borrower. That contract does not conform to the ordinary presumption of a loan contract that the lender intends to transfer outright all of the interest in the loan moneys but rather contains an express contractual provision which precludes the borrower from using the money for any purpose other than that provided for in the contract. That contract, if it were well-drafted, should provide explicitly that there is an express trust over the loan moneys such that the borrower holds the money on trust for the lender unless the borrower uses the money for the purpose identified in the loan contract. The borrower, as trustee, would have a power to use the money for this purpose; or alternatively the borrower could be identified as a second beneficiary under the trust with a right to have the money applied for their benefit provided that that application of the money is for the purpose identified in the loan contract.[17]

Everything depends upon the precise phrasing of the loan contract and the provisions within that agreement which create the express trust. In banking law practice, a competent lawyer would be required to structure and word these provisions appropriately so that the lender's rights are made crystal clear from the outset. It should not be a question of identifying the best analysis to be imposed by an unclear, hotly-contested area of the law on implied trusts. The contract should make all of this sufficiently clear.

---

17 Those terms would continue: if the borrower purports to use the loan moneys for any other purpose then the borrower will be acting in excess of her power, such that the exercise of the power will be void, and those loan moneys would continue to be held on trust for the benefit of the lender. The lender would be able to trace the loan moneys into the hands of any third party and so recover them, as considered in Chapter 20. The borrower would be liable to account to the lender for any breach of trust, as considered in Chapter 18.

This express trust analysis has been upheld in Australia[18] but not yet in England. This form of express *Quistclose* trust has been explained on the basis of having two limbs:[19] one granting a power to the borrower to use the loan moneys for the contractually specified purpose and the second which provides that any misuse of the loan moneys causes the entire equitable interest to be held for the lender.[20] This analysis could have been applied in the English case of *Templeton Insurance Ltd v Penningtons Solicitors LLP*.[21] There, money had been lent by Templeton to clients of Penningtons, a firm of solicitors, to purchase a 'brownfield' development site. Those moneys were lent on the condition that the loan moneys would be held by Penningtons subject to a solicitor's undertaking that the money was to be used to complete the purchase of that land; or, in the event that the sale could not be completed, on the condition that the loan money would be held in Pennington's client bank account on trust for the lender. It was held that this constituted a *Quistclose* trust in favour of Templeton. While Lewison J analysed this transaction as being a resulting trust following the judgment of Lord Millett in *Twinsectra v Yardley*, it would have been possible to say that Penningtons held the money as trustee under an express trust which could be inferred from the circumstances of paying the money into a client account (as in *Re Kayford*)[22] and that Penningtons had a limited power as trustee to advance the loan moneys to complete the purchase of the development land. The principal argument against the express trust model is that in *Barclays Bank v Quistclose* and in *Twinsectra v Yardley*, two differently constituted Houses of Lords have not found that there was an intention to create an express trust.

22.4.4 Constructive trust

A *Quistclose* trust could conceivably be considered to be a constructive trust on the general basis that it would be unconscionable for the lender to assert title to that money if it was not used for the purpose for which it was lent. The *Quistclose* trust principle was stated in *Carreras Rothmans Ltd v Freeman Mathews Treasure Ltd*[23] to be that:

> equity fastens of the conscience of the person who receives from another property transferred for a specific purpose only and not therefore for the recipient's own purposes, so that such person will not be permitted to treat the property as his own or to use it for other than the stated purpose.

This statement could be taken to be authority for one of three competing understandings of the *Quistclose* arrangement. At first blush, the reference to the 'conscience' of the recipient equates most obviously to a constructive trust. The principal argument against the imposition of a constructive trust is that the equitable interest of the lender appears to exist *before* the borrower seeks to perform any unconscionable act in relation to the property. As the speech of Lord Browne-Wilkinson in *Westdeutsche Landesbank v Islington*[24] reminds us, a

---

18 *Re Australian Elizabethan Theatre Trust* (1991) 102 ALR 681, 691, *per* Gummow J.
19 See Thomas and Hudson, 2010, para 9.84.
20 *General Communications Ltd v Development Finance Corporation of New Zealand Ltd* [1990] 3 NZLR 406, 432.
21 [2006] EWHC 685 (Ch).
22 As was the case in *Target Holdings v Referns* [1996] AC 421 and in *Boscawen v Bajwa* [1996] 1 WLR 328.
23 [1985] Ch 207, 222.
24 [1996] AC 669.

constructive trust only comes into existence when the trustee has knowledge of some factor which affects her conscience. In the context of a *Quistclose* arrangement the rights of the lender arise under the contract and therefore pre-date the transfer of the loan moneys. A constructive trust would seem to require that the borrower misapply the loan moneys before her conscience could be affected so as to create a constructive trust. This may not bring the trust into existence in good time.

Part 8

Charities

Chapter 23

Charities

CAPSULE SUMMARY

The case law on charitable trusts divided between trusts for the relief of poverty; trusts for the advancement of education; trusts for the advancement of religion; and trusts for other purposes beneficial to the community. However, the enactment of the Charities Act 2011 has had the effect of expanding the categories of 'charitable purpose' beyond those categories set out by the case law. The first three categories – the prevention and relief of poverty, the advancement of religion and the advancement of education – remain, but the fourth category has been replaced by a statutory list of purposes. There are now 13 categories of charitable purpose. That statutory list includes: the advancement of health or the saving of lives; the advancement of citizenship or community development; the advancement of the arts, culture, heritage or science; the advancement of amateur sport; the advancement of human rights, conflict resolution or reconciliation or the promotion of religious or racial harmony or equality and diversity; the advancement of environmental protection or improvement; the relief of those in need by reason of youth, age, ill-health, disability, financial hardship or other disadvantage; the advancement of animal welfare.

Trusts for the relief of poverty must relieve the poverty of some person. 'Poverty' means 'something more than going short' but does not require absolute destitution. It is apparently the case that it need not be a broad section of the community which stands to benefit from the trust. Rather, trusts for the relief of poverty are presumed to have a generally altruistic motivation and are therefore enforceable as being charitable. There have been subtle but significant alterations to poverty charities in the Charities Act 2011: a public benefit may now be required. This calls into question trusts for the relief of the poverty which will benefit only a small number of people: they were valid under the old case law.

Trusts for the advancement of education require that there is some institution of education benefited, or that the purpose of the trust is to generate research which will be published for the public benefit. In many cases, educational charitable trusts have been used as fronts for the provision of benefits to a private class of individuals. Consequently, the courts have developed a requirement that there be a sufficient public benefit, which requires that there is no 'personal nexus' between the people who stand to benefit and the settlor of the trust.

Trusts for the advancement of religion are required to have a sufficient public benefit, such that, for example, the works done and the prayers said by a cloistered order of nuns, though religious, would not be charitable in legal terms. Religion is concerned with 'man's relations with God' and therefore excludes many modern new-age religions and cults.

23.1 INTRODUCTION

23.1.1 Context

The place of charity in British society

In ordinary parlance, charities are organisations which work for 'good causes'. The British are a charitable people and you will frequently see charity workers and volunteers rattling collecting boxes on station forecourts and in shopping centres to raise money for those good causes in the UK and around the world. There are approximately 164,000 registered charities in the UK for a population of approximately 60 million people. That is approximately one charity for every 365 people. The televised London Marathon is an annual procession of people in outrageous costumes raising money for their favourite charities through sponsorship; the bi-annual Comic Relief and Children in Need telethons similarly provoke ordinary people into extraordinary acts of benevolence. At this level, charity seems to be a very simple exercise in doing good works for the benefit of other people.

In its legal sense, however, 'charity' is considerably more complicated than that. Charities law stretches from the complex legal question as to when a purpose will be a 'charitable purpose' for 'the public benefit' which attracts all the legal, social and fiscal benefits of charitable status, right through to the regulatory machinery administered by the Charity Commission which is necessary to combat the fraud and tax avoidance which are perpetrated through charities so often in practice. As we shall see, many of the leading cases relating to the definition of what is 'charitable' in law are combating the misuse of charities to avoid tax. This chapter focuses on the various categories of charitable purpose under statute and in the case law, and it examines the statutory rules and structures contained in the Charities Act 2011 which govern this field.

The law relating to charities is a subject which in itself is separate from the ordinary law of trusts. That the law of charities is treated as forming part of trusts law is an accident of history. In English history, charity was administered in local parishes by the Church. This meant that the principal forms of charity related to the relief of poverty, the advancement of religion, and the advancement of education (because the Church oversaw the provision of relief for the poor and education for ordinary people who could not afford private tutors).[1] Consequently, due to their roots in the activities of the Church, charities were originally overseen by the ecclesiastical courts. This part of the ecclesiastical jurisdiction was subsumed by the Courts of Chancery, in particular by those Lords Chancellor who were themselves bishops, and charities were consequently administered in a manner that was superficially similar to express trusts.

The purpose of charities in the modern world

It is important to understand the role of charities in Western societies. As the welfare state is shrinking in countries like the UK, many of the activities which were once undertaken and funded out of central taxation are now the subject of governmental initiatives to involve the private sector or 'the third sector' in the provision of public services. This concept of the 'third sector' includes the charitable sector. It stands somewhere between the public sector and the private sector. The Conservative-led Coalition government promoted a policy between 2010 and 2015 of encouraging 'the Big Society' in which it was hoped that philanthropic, volunteer organisations (including charities) would undertake many of the works that were previously performed by the State in their local communities. This was expected to devolve power in effect to local communities and to take it away from central government. It was also hoped to reduce the amount of money which the State would need to spend in providing those services. The policy had little effect on the surface. However, under the surface there has been a large-scale reallocation of resources in areas such as the health service, for example, to private enterprise and a greater involvement of charities in work of all kinds. Therefore, charities have become an important part of public policy, in particular a push from the centre and the right-wing in British politics to reorder the nature of the state.

Charities are significant in many other senses too. Charities are exempt from most taxes. (The complexities of charity taxation are beyond the scope of this book. That charities are exempt from most taxes and business rates is all that we need to know. It is important in many of the cases we shall discuss.) Therefore, whereas other organisations would pay tax on certain forms of income, charities do not pay those taxes. Consequently, the State is funding charitable activities by exempting them from taxation. This raises political questions about the sorts of activities which do, and which do not, receive this indirect State support. The are many problems in charities law which makes it appear to be straightforwardly political. That private schools receive charitable tax exemptions, when organisations seeking to ban vivisection (i.e. laboratory experiments on animals) do not, makes it appear to be a political decision to support one type of activity but not another: the children of the rich are more important than rabbits, in this example. As we shall see from the case law, an organisation which teaches warfare can be charitable, whereas an organisation which seeks to promote peace will not be. Charities law has many quirks. For example, the activities of Catholic nuns will not necessarily be accepted as being a charitable purpose for the advancement of religion, even though Catholic

---

1 Ironically, those early schools were known as 'public schools' and have metamorphosed into the elite, private schools which we know today.

doctrine considers nuns to be 'brides of Christ'. So, you can be married to the son of God but that is not enough to impress English charities law. Clearly, charities law has very complicated priorities.

As will emerge in the discussion of the decided cases to follow, a very large number of important charities cases have related to tax-avoidance scams which have sought to abuse charities' tax exempt status. The Charity Commission expressed great concern in a report in 2013 that the amount of fraud and money laundering being effected through charities (often through small, inconspicuous charities) is increasing rapidly.[2] In 2015, at the time of writing this book, the well-known charity Kids Company collapsed under the weight of allegations about mismanagement and misuse of funds. Kids Company was a good example of a charity which was replacing activities which would otherwise have had to be performed by the State. Even charities which do exemplary work may be mismanaged or used by third parties to further their own unlawful goals. These concerns of charities law are all a far cry from well-meaning people stumbling across London's Tower Bridge dressed in a Bugs Bunny costume to raise money for children suffering from cystic fibrosis.

23.1.2 The structure of this chapter: The changes effected by the Charities Act 2011

The Charities Act 2006 effected important changes in charities law which have now been consolidated into the Charities Act 2011. The Charities Act 2011 is therefore the principal statute in relation to charities law. Whereas the case law had created only four categories of charitable purpose before 2006 – the relief of poverty, the advancement of religion, the advancement of education, and 'other purposes beneficial to the community' – the Charities Act 2011 has 13 categories of charitable purpose. It was a matter of public policy to expand the range of charitable purposes so as to encourage more philanthropic activity by the public in their local communities. As will emerge below, the courts had tended to be very narrow-minded about the sorts of activity which would be considered to be charitable before the statutory changes were first introduced by the Charities Act 2006 (which was consolidated into the 2011 Act). The law from before 2006 remains important today. Therefore, this chapter sets out the new statutory heads of charity and analyses the case law (much of it from before 2006) which deals with those various heads of charity. Importantly, the statute explicitly retains the case law analyses, as is considered next. The remainder of the chapter then considers two issues: first, the new regulatory structure for the administration of charities by the Charity Commission and, secondly, the *cy-près* doctrine.

23.1.3 Answering problem questions on charities law

The law of charities can be a comparatively straightforward option in problem questions at exam time. The structure to answering a problem question is simple. First, identify which category (or categories) of charity from s 3 of the CA 2011 might apply to your problem question, and then discuss whether or not your problem fits in with the applicable case law. Second, consider whether or not your problem shows sufficient 'public benefit' (as required

---

2 Charity Commission, 'The Charity Commission strategy for dealing with fraud, financial crime and financial abuse of the charity sector', 2013.

by statute and as conceptualised in the case law). Third, consider whether any possible vitiating factor (e.g. the presence of an unlawful political purpose or a lack of exclusively charitable purpose) could prevent your case from being a charitable purpose. Fourth, if appropriate, consider whether the *cy-près* doctrine might apply to rescue an ineffective charitable purpose.

23.1.4 The definition of 'charitable purposes' under the Charities Act 2011

The role of the Charities Act 2011

The Charities Act 2011 is primarily a consolidating statute which transposes the previous statutory scheme for charities contained in the Charities Act 2006. The 2006 Act had marked a sea-change in the categories of charity because it created nine new categories of charity which had not been settled in the earlier case law. The intention of the Labour government in 2006 had been to broaden the type and number of charities in existence, not least so that the shrinking welfare state could be supplemented by charitable activity in areas of perceived social need. Some of the new charitable purposes (such as the emphasis on the environment) mark very new political priorities for charities law; whereas other new purposes (such as the acceptance of sport as a potentially charitable activity) resolve long-standing difficulties in the case law. There was a lot of similarity between the commitment of the Blair government in 2006 to the third sector and the commitment of the Coalition government before 2015 to the same goals.

The meaning of 'charity' as disclosing a 'charitable purpose'

A 'charity' is defined in s 1 of the Charities Act 2011 as being 'an institution', which can be a trust or a company under English law, 'which is established for charitable purposes only' and which 'falls to be subject to the control of the High Court in the exercise of its jurisdiction with respect to charities'.[3] Thus, to know whether or not a trust purpose will constitute a charity we must establish whether or not that purpose can be defined as being a 'charitable purpose', as considered in the next section.

The definition of 'charitable purposes' in the Charities Act 2011

A 'charitable purpose' is one which fulfils two requirements, as set out in s 2(1) of the Act. First, it must fall within the list of purposes set out in s 3(1) of the 2011 Act, as considered in the remainder of this section; and, second, it must satisfy the 'public benefit' test, as is considered in the next section of this chapter. So, the definition of 'charitable purposes' in the Charities Act 2011 is found in s 3(1) in the following form. There are 13 categories, of which the first three and the last one refer back to the pre-existing case law on the definition of a charitable purpose:

(a) the prevention or relief of poverty;
(b) the advancement of education;
(c) the advancement of religion.

---

3 Charities Act 2011, s 1(1).

These first three categories are therefore very similar to the initial three case law categories of charitable purpose, as considered in detail below. By contrast, the following nine categories were new to charities law in 2006:

(d) the advancement of health or the saving of lives;
(e) the advancement of citizenship or community development;
(f) the advancement of the arts, culture, heritage or science;
(g) the advancement of amateur sport;
(h) the advancement of human rights, conflict resolution or reconciliation or the promotion of religious or racial harmony or equality and diversity;
(i) the advancement of environmental protection or improvement;
(j) the relief of those in need by reason of youth, age, ill-health, disability, financial hardship or other disadvantage;
(k) the advancement of animal welfare;
(l) the promotion of the efficiency of the armed forces of the Crown, or of the efficiency of the police, fire and rescue services or ambulance services;
(m) any other purposes within subs (4) [that is, categories of charitable purpose which already existed under the case law on charities].

Each of these new categories of charitable purpose is considered in turn later in this chapter in section 23.6, after a discussion of the existing heads of charity set out in categories (a) to (c) above. The importance of the new categories is that they either give validity to some purposes which the case law refused to recognise as being charitable, or that they bring novel purposes under the umbrella of charitable purposes as part of government policy. Among the purposes which are now included in the list of charitable activities, but which might otherwise have been excluded from being charitable by the old case law, are purposes such as animal welfare, campaigning for human rights and environmental protection. These sorts of new category in the statute gives us a flavour of the new political priorities in this area. The detail of these changes is considered later in the chapter. Before that we need to introduce some more of the essential features of charities law.

The continued validity of charitable purposes accepted in the old case law

What is particularly important is that categories of charity which have been accepted in the old case law continue to be valid under the 2011 Act. It is provided in s 4(3) of the Charities Act 2011 ('CA 2011') that any purposes which are 'recognised as charitable purposes under existing charity law', for example under the old case law, will continue to be recognised as charitable purposes. Moreover, it is provided in s 3(1)(m)(i) of the 2011 Act that any purposes which are 'recognised as charitable purposes by virtue of s 5 (recreational and similar trusts, etc.) or under the old law' are recognised as being charitable purposes under the 2011 Act. Thus, categories of charity under 'the old law' will still be valid charities even if they are not explicitly contained in the s 3(1) list. Similarly, any purposes which 'may reasonably be regarded as analogous to, or within the spirit of' any of the categories in paragraphs (a) to (l) will be charitable purposes, as will any types of trust which are 'analogous to, or within the spirit of' the old charities law. Therefore, in effect, other types of charitable purpose under the old case law will continue to be recognised as charitable purposes regardless of whether or not they appear explicitly in the list of charitable purposes in s 3(1) of the 2011 Act. Consequently, it is still important to consider those categories of charitable purpose which have been upheld by the pre-2011 case law precisely because the 2011 Act maintains their validity.

The statutory test of 'public benefit'

As considered above, it is a pre-requisite of a trust purpose being held to be a charitable purpose that it is 'for the public benefit' under s 2(1)(b) of the 2011 Act. This statutory requirement of public benefit is expressly stated to be a public benefit as currently understood under the case law in the law of charities.[4] So, it is important to consider what the case law has defined a 'public benefit' to be. There are detailed discussions later in this chapter about the concept of 'public benefit' in relation to the case law on educational purposes and on religious purposes in particular. In the following section we will acquire a rough rule of thumb as to what will constitute a 'public benefit' and in the section after that it is suggested that the case law, however, did not require that charities for the relief of poverty needed be for the public benefit. Therefore, it will remain a complex matter for us to know what constitutes a public benefit in charities law until future case law clarifies matters.

23.2 THE SPECIAL FEATURES OF CHARITIES

23.2.1 The trusts law advantages of charitable status

Charities are not required to comply with the perpetuities rules nor with the beneficiary principle as discussed in Chapter 4. Charities do not have beneficiaries. Consequently, so-called 'charitable trusts' are very different from express trusts. We shall refer to charities as being 'public trusts' because they must have a 'public benefit' but no beneficiaries; and we shall refer to the different kind of express trusts already considered in Part 2 of this book as being 'private trusts' (because they were created for the benefit of their private beneficiaries).

23.2.2 The tax advantages of charitable status

Charities are exempt from most taxes, with the principal exception of VAT. That is the central message in relation to tax. Significantly, through schemes like 'Gift Aid', if I make a donation to a charity then the charity can recover from the government the tax that I paid when earning that money. So, not only do charities receive an indirect public subsidy in the form of exemption from most taxes, but charities can also recover the tax already paid by many of their donors. The detail of this area of tax law is too complex for us here: the only point to absorb is that charities occupy a particularly privileged position in relation to taxation. This means that charities can be used as a way to syphon money off without paying tax on it – if I could 'sell' my post-tax salary to an unscrupulous charity, then that charity could recover the tax I had paid and pass all that money back to me in some clandestine way (offshore or under a pseudonym), while pocketing a fee for doing the deal. I would get my salary almost tax-free and the charity would pocket a small fee from me. This would be a fraud but it is not entirely unknown in this area.

---

4 *Ibid*, s 3(3).

The question which arises is always the following one: if the charity is being used for tax-avoidance purposes, does that mean that the charity is not acting in the public benefit? If the charity is not acting in the public benefit, then it is not a charity at all and therefore it will lose both its purported charitable status and its tax-exempt status. For example, in *IRC v Educational Grants Association*[5] the executives of a large company created a charity through that company which purported to pay the school fees of supposedly any child in the country who would attend expensive private schools. In practice, the charity only paid for the school fees of the children of the company's executives. Thus, the executives were having their children's school fees paid by a charity which paid no tax on the money it received from the company. They were pretending that any child in the country could benefit, while actually operating the charity as a private trust. Therefore, those executives were getting a part of their salary paid to them indirectly and tax-free because it was used to fund their children's expensive educations. The tax authorities spotted this tax-avoidance scam and it was found that this activity was not a 'charitable purpose' because it was not being done for the 'public benefit'. Rather, it was being done for the benefit of a small group of private individuals.

However, charities are still used to avoid tax. So, when the British bank Northern Rock crashed into insolvency in 2007, it emerged that the complex corporate reorganisation of that entity had included assets being held offshore in a discretionary trust which included among its beneficiaries a small charity registered perfectly lawfully in a domestic residence in South Shields. It seems that this ridiculously complex arrangement was put together for tax purposes (with charities and discretionary trusts having many tax advantages in different contexts). The people who operated that perfectly legitimate charity were reported to have told journalists that they had no idea about the existence of this discretionary trust arrangement. This sort of arrangement is more common than you might like to think.

Do not worry if this seems confusing. From the tax avoider's perspective, it is supposed to be confusing. It is supposed to confuse Her Majesty's Revenue and Customs in particular. You are not expected to know the tax law. Rather, the lesson to learn here is that the tax-exempt status of charities is very attractive to third parties who want to avoid tax, just as a person holding a large umbrella is very attractive to people trying to avoid heavy rain. Therefore, in many of the cases which are discussed in this chapter (especially in relation to educational charitable purposes), charities are being used (or abused) so as to avoid tax. This is a long way from the good-hearted activity of rattling a bucket to raise money for disadvantaged children outside a train station dressed as Harry Potter. It is not what most people think about when they hear the word 'charity'.

23.3 FACTORS NEGATING CHARITABLE STATUS: CHARITABLE INTENTION, BUT NO POLITICAL PURPOSES

23.3.1 Sufficient intention to create a charitable trust

The settlor must have had an exclusively charitable intention in creating her trust for it to be a valid charitable purpose. So, for example, where a trust was left for a 'charitable or benevolent' purpose then that would fail to be a valid charitable purpose because it could

5 [1967] Ch 123.

also be a benevolent purpose, as was held in the leading case of *Chichester Diocesan Board of Finance v Simpson*.[6] The problem is that (read very literally by the courts) a 'benevolent' purpose might not be a 'charitable' purpose. Those two words might mean different things. The purpose must be exclusively charitable. It is a little like saying that you want a red car but you are presented with a contract which say you can be provided with a car that could be 'red or pink': that would not be an exclusively red car. This case illustrates the strict approach which was generally taken in the older cases to the requirement of the exclusivity of the charitable purpose. If a settlor has two purposes behind his trust, one charitable and the other not, then the trust may be held to be an invalid charity on this approach. In cases in which the settlor has provided that money is to be held for 'charitable *or* other purposes' then the use of the word 'or' has been taken to suggest that those other purposes could be something different from charitable purposes, and therefore the trust has been held invalid.[7] By contrast, if the settlor provides that money is to be held for 'charitable *and* other purposes' then the use of the word 'and' has been taken to connote that the use will definitely be charitable even if it will also be something else simultaneously, and therefore the trust has been held to be a valid charity.[8]

This literal reading of a trust instrument still takes place in modern cases. In *St Andrews (Cheam) Lawn Tennis Club Trust*[9] the members of the trust had played tennis happily for many years until the point was raised as to whether or not the trust was valid as a charity at all. Arnold J held that the terms in the trust instrument which provided that the trustees could use its funds for 'any other purposes in connection with St Andrew's Church' meant that the trust did not have an exclusively charitable purpose because it could be used for 'any other purposes'. Consequently, the trust was found to have been an invalid private purpose trust and not a charity.

In more recent cases some courts have proved themselves willing to validate a genuinely charitable purpose wherever they find one.[10] Thus, in *Re Koeppler*,[11] Slade LJ looked to the general charitable intention of a testator (who had sought to leave money for the furtherance of a charitable project on which he worked) and overlooked looseness in the drafting which suggested that there were two possible purposes. By looking to the settlor's general intention it was possible to interpret the wording so as to validate the trust as a charity. It is suggested, in the wake of more benign constructions like that in *Guild v IRC*[12] and *Re Hetherington*[13] in recent years, that the courts are less likely to invalidate trusts on the basis of lack of exclusivity of purpose than was the case in many of the older cases. However, that does not mean that the courts will accept as charitable those trusts which are not exclusively charitable. Rather, they will be prepared to accept both that the underlying intention can be *construed* as being charitable and that the trustees will *in practice apply* the trust property so as to make it operate as a charitable trust, even if the wording suggests something different. For example, the trust in *Re Hetherington* was prima facie invalid because it

---

6 [1944] AC 341.
7 *Re Macduff* [1896] 2 Ch 451.
8 *Blair v Duncan* [1902] AC 37.
9 [2012] 1 WLR 3487.
10 *Re Hetherington* [1990] Ch 1.
11 [1984] 2 WLR 973.
12 [1992] 2 AC 310.
13 [1990] Ch 1.

provided for the saying of Catholic mass in private and therefore was not 'for the public benefit'. It was held that if this trust was operated in practice so that mass was made available to the public then it could be a valid trust. Thus, the drafting error was overlooked provided that the trustees acted in an appropriately charitable way. The message to take from these cases is that the courts in recent charities law cases have demonstrated a preparedness to re-interpret poor drafting so as to make charitable trusts valid. These cases are discussed below.

In *Re Harding*[14] Lewison J applied this notion of validating charitable, testamentary gifts wherever possible in relation to a purpose which in itself was so broadly drafted that it could not have disclosed an exclusively charitable purpose. The bequest provided that property was to be held 'in trust for the black community of Hackney, Haringey, Islington and Tower Hamlets'. As drafted, that did not require that purpose was exclusively charitable. Lewison J held that this purpose should be interpreted so as to make it valid. As Lewison J put it in the final substantive sentence of his judgment '[t]he precise nature of the trusts can be dealt with by a scheme'[15] (which means that a method of operating the trust can be identified which would be acceptable to the court). This approach does seem to require the trustees to resettle the property by deciding what they think an appropriate charitable use for this property would be. To that extent, charitable trusts operate very differently from private express trusts.

23.3.2 Political purposes

In general terms, no purpose can be charitable if it is political. The rationale for this rule is that the courts should not be required to judge whether one political objective is better than another. So, in *McGovern v Attorney-General*[16] the human rights campaigning organisation Amnesty International was held not to be charitable because it campaigned for changes in the laws of numerous countries. The leading case of *National Anti-Vivisection Society v IRC*[17] before the House of Lords considered the question whether or not the society's political campaigning for the banning of vivisection[18] would prevent its purposes from being defined as being charitable. The type of political campaigning undertaken was to procure a change in the law so that vivisection would be banned outright. Lord Simonds considered the society's aims to be too political to qualify as a charity on the basis that an aim to change legislation is necessarily political. Consequently, the society was found not to be charitable and therefore not exempt from income tax. Somewhat differently in *Bowman v Secular Society*[19] Lord Normand held that a society could be charitable where its *predominant* aim was charitable, even though it had a subsidiary aim which was to change the law. It is a question of degree whether a society seeks to change the law as its main focus, or whether it espouses ends which incidentally require a change in the law.

---

14 [2008] 2 WLR 361.
15 *Ibid*, para [27].
16 [1982] 2 WLR 222.
17 *Ibid*.
18 'Vivisection' means animal experimentation.
19 [1917] AC 406.

23.4 PREVENTION AND RELIEF OF POVERTY

23.4.1 Introduction

The statutory principle

The first category of charitable purpose relates to poverty. Section 3(1)(a) of the CA 2011 provides for 'the *prevention* or relief of poverty' which is a change from the old case law in that 'prevention' has now been added to the old concept of the 'relief' of poverty. In the discussion to follow, we shall consider the leading case on trusts for the relief of poverty which was decided before the Act came into force, on the basis that it is provided in s 4(3) of the CA 2011 that any purposes which are 'recognised as charitable purposes under existing charity law', for example under the old case law, will continue to be recognised as charitable purposes. We will, however, need to consider some old cases known as the 'poor relatives' cases more carefully in the light of the 2011 Act.

The leading case: Dingle v Turner

The leading case in relation to the relief of poverty is the decision of the House of Lords in *Dingle v Turner.*[20] The trust in *Dingle v Turner* concerned a bequest of £10,000 to be applied 'to pay pensions to poor employees of E Dingle & Company'. Those arguing that the bequest should be held invalid relied on two cases relating to the 'education' category (*Oppenheim v Tobacco Securities Trust*[21] and *Re Compton*[22]) in which it had been held that a trust could not be charitable if 'the benefits under it are confined to the descendants of a named individual or company'.[23] Lord Cross found that the trust was valid. He explained that the rule in *Re Compton* was not one of universal application across the whole of the law of charities. Therefore, it did not apply to trusts for the relief of poverty. His speech had two main points: first, that the *Compton* principle was intellectually unsound in itself and, second, that trusts for the relief of poverty required a different test from other forms of charitable trust which did not require a public benefit.

The *Compton* principle held that for a trust to be for the public benefit, it must be for more than 'a mere fluctuating body of private individuals'. Lord Cross held that there were plenty of examples of classes which would be for the public benefit which were still bodies of private individuals. The example he gave was of the inhabitants of the Royal London Borough of Kensington and Chelsea: that was undoubtedly a section of the public and yet membership of that class comprised a fluctuating body of private individuals (in that the inhabitants were all private individuals and they would fluctuate in the sense that people would move into and out of the borough, and people would be born and die in the borough too). Equally, a link through employment would not necessarily disprove that the people were insufficiently numerous to be a section of the public. For example, the Post Office employs 125,000 postmen and postwomen at the time of writing, whereas there are approximately 158,000 people living in the Royal Borough of Kensington and Chelsea

---

20 [1972] AC 601.
21 [1951] AC 297.
22 [1945] Ch 123.
23 *Oppenheim* is a case relating to educational purpose trusts, considered below at section 27.3.3.

today. Therefore, a trust in favour of postal delivery workers would have almost as many people benefited as the accepted public class of inhabitants of Kensington. However, a trust for postal workers would fail under a literal application of the *Compton* test because those workers would all be connected by a common employment. Lord Cross held that these sorts of problems with the *Compton* test meant that it could not be considered to be sound. Moreover, Lord Cross held that it was not a test which should cover all of charities law. The cases of *Compton* and *Oppenheim* involved tax avoidance (that is, people seeking an 'undeserved fiscal immunity' in the words of Lord Cross) and therefore had their own rationale. By contrast, held Lord Cross, 'much must depend on the purpose of the trust'. Trusts for the relief of poverty could usually show a genuine charitable purpose if there was some poverty which was being relieved. Thus, a genuine charitable purpose became the standard which Lord Cross considered appropriate, as opposed to the rigidity of the *Compton* formula, in poverty cases.

Having considered the leading case, it is worth exploring the requirements for a charitable trust for the relief of poverty. There are two core questions concerned with the relief of poverty: first, what is 'poverty', and second, what is 'relief'? These two questions will be considered in turn. Later we shall consider the new statutory idea of the 'prevention' of poverty.

23.4.2 What is 'poverty'?

There are few clear statements in the cases as to the meaning of 'poverty'. It is a term which social scientists debate constantly: does it relate to a single level of income, or there always poverty below a given proportion of the average wage, or does poverty involve the lack of identified criteria (such as the lack of a broadband connection, or the lack of sufficient food)? In *Mary Clark Homes Trustees v Anderson*,[24] Channell J held that poverty was a relative term and that someone would be considered to be poor if he was in 'genuinely straitened circumstances and unable to maintain a very modest standard of living for himself and the persons (if any) dependent upon him'.[25] Interestingly, this conceptualisation of poverty does not require outright destitution; merely reduced living and straitened circumstances. (It is worth noting that that is probably how most undergraduate students live in their second year at university.) At one end of the spectrum, poverty must involve something which is more than simply 'going short'.[26] Nevertheless, there are a number of examples of situations in which the courts have held cases of financial hardship, rather than grinding poverty, to be within the technical definition of 'poverty'. For example, a trust for 'ladies of limited means' has been held to be charitable[27] together with the (gloriously expressed) trust for the benefit of 'decayed actors'.[28] (In the 17th century this term 'decayed' had as one of its meanings 'to have declined in prosperity'.) Another example of a valid charitable trust for the relief of poverty was the establishment of an organisation for people who have 'fallen on evil days', an expression which would have been too vague an expression for ordinary private trusts purposes.[29]

---

24 [1904] 2 KB 745.
25 Quotation taken from Tudor, 1995, 29.
26 *Re Coulthurst's Will Trusts* [1951] Ch 661, at 666 (more than 'going short').
27 *Re Gardom* [1914] 1 Ch 662.
28 *Spiller v Maude* (1881) 32 Ch D 158.
29 *Re Young* [1951] Ch 344.

It was held in *Re Sanders' WT*[30] that the 'working class' do not constitute a section of the poor. However, in the specific circumstances of *Re Niyazi's WT*[31] it was held that a gift for the construction of a working men's hostel in an area of extreme poverty in Cyprus created a valid charitable trust for the relief of poverty. In this second case there was demonstrable poverty in that part of Cyprus which would be alleviated by the construction of this hostel. It was not the same as assuming that the working class as a whole were poor.

23.4.3 What is meant by 'relief' and by 'prevention'?

The relief of poverty

The term 'relief' of poverty is not intended to cure the impoverished people of their poverty; rather, it is enough that there is some relief from that poverty. So, it is enough that a charity provides food but the charity does not need to provide sufficient money to make the poor into rich people as well.[32] A soup kitchen for the benefit of the genuinely impoverished will be a valid charity for the relief of poverty.[33] It does not also need to pay a salary to the poor people who use it. Importantly, however, there must be some poverty which will be relieved. So, in *Re Gwyon*[34] a trust for the provision of clothing for boys was held to be invalid on the basis that there was no necessary requirement that the boys in question had to be in poverty.

The prevention of poverty

The Charities Act 2011, s 3(1)(a) added the notion of the 'prevention' of poverty to this category. The principal effect of this change would be to remove the requirement that the people who are to be helped must already be in poverty. Thus it would be a valid charitable purpose if someone anticipated that a person was going to fall into poverty and so took some action by constituting a trust to prevent that state of affairs arising.

23.4.4 Limits on the class of people taking a benefit

The case law on the relief of poverty did not require that there must be a public benefit. However, the CA 2011 requires both that all charitable purposes must be for the public benefit and also that the statute must be interpreted in the light of existing charities law. Therefore, the following question arises: henceforth, will all charities for the relief of poverty which are not for the public benefit be void; or will the statute be interpreted so that the public benefit requirement does not apply to poverty trusts in the same way as the rest of charities law? It was held in *Dingle v Turner*[35] that a trust for the relief of poverty does not have to be shown to be for the general public benefit, as long as it does go beyond the relief of the poverty of a single, individual beneficiary. It could be argued, as a result, that a poverty trust would be valid as being for the public benefit if the term public benefit is interpreted as meaning 'for the benefit of more than a single individual' in this context.

---

30 [1954] Ch 265.
31 [1978] 1 WLR 910.
32 *Joseph Rowntree Memorial Trust Housing Association Ltd v Attorney-General* [1983] 1 All ER 288.
33 *Biscoe v Jackson* (1887) 35 Ch D 460.
34 [1930] 1 Ch 255.
35 [1972] AC 601.

The most problematic cases in this regard are the 'poor relations' cases in which valid charitable trusts were created for the benefit of relatives of the settlor. These cases, which were approved in *Dingle v Turner*, were clearly not for the public benefit because there was a relationship of blood, and therefore clearly a 'nexus', between the settlor and the people who would benefit from the trust. However, it was required in those cases that there was some poverty which was being relieved. So in *Re Scarisbrick*[36] a testatrix provided that property be held on trust 'for such relations of my said son and daughters as in the opinion of the survivor of my said son and daughters shall be in needy circumstances'. It was held by the Court of Appeal that this was a valid charitable trust for the relief of the poverty of such persons.[37] It is from this line of decisions that trusts for the benefit of poor relations have been upheld as being valid charitable trusts. This line of cases would be overruled if the public benefit test in s 4 (as required by s 2(1)(b)) of the CA 2011 were interpreted as applying to trusts for the relief of poverty because there is clearly a nexus between the settlor and the people who are intended to benefit from the trust. Such trusts would clearly be private express trusts except for the fact that the relatives are impoverished. Section 4(3) of the CA 2011 provides that the 'reference to the public benefit is a reference to the public benefit as that term is understood for purposes of the law relating to charities'. This provision could be understood to mean that the requirement for a public benefit under the statute is to be interpreted in accordance with the understanding of the term 'public benefit' as applied in the case law on charities before 2006 (when the statutory concept was first introduced). Before 2006, the concept of public benefit did not apply, in effect, to poverty cases.

It was held in *Joseph Rowntree Memorial Trust Housing Association Ltd v Attorney-General* that a trust to establish a home for elderly Presbyterians would constitute a sufficiently broad public benefit, even though the category of people who could have benefited was limited to members of that religion of an appropriate age.[38] In that case there was sheltered accommodation provided by a company which both charged occupants for their accommodation and which made that accommodation available only to a limited number of people. There was an argument as to whether or not an organisation could be a charity if it charged for its services. It was held by Peter Gibson J that neither of these factors disqualified the purpose from qualifying as a charitable purpose. By contrast, in *IRC v Society for the Relief of Widows and Orphans of Medical Men*,[39] Rowlatt J had held (60 years earlier) that charity is to be provided by way of 'bounty and not bargain', which had always been read as a prohibition on charities charging for their services. There, an organisation which had assumed responsibility for the maintenance and management of many properties from a local authority was held not to have exclusively charitable purposes because it conferred private benefits on individual tenants as part of its activities.[40] Also, it was not clear that all of the occupants in that case would have been in poverty. The more benign approach in *Joseph Rowntree* accepted that charities can only deal with the poverty of limited numbers of people at a time and yet that that constitutes a public benefit; and moreover that it is reasonable for a housing charity to charge some rent (albeit low rent) for occupation of their properties. If we want to encourage housing charities, then perhaps we need to accept the more benign

36 *Ibid.*
37 *Attorney-General v Price* (1810) 17 Ves 371.
38 [1983] 1 All ER 288.
39 (1926) 11 TC 1.
40 *Helena Housing Ltd v Revenue and Customs Commissioners* [2011] STC 1307, TCC.

approach that such charities will have to have some criteria for selecting their tenants and that the provision of low rent accommodation for the poor is charitable in itself.

23.5 TRUSTS FOR THE ADVANCEMENT OF EDUCATION

23.5.1 Introduction

The discussion in this section considering the nature of charitable educational trusts falls into two halves. The first half will discuss what is meant by the term 'education' in this context. The second half will consider the meaning of 'public benefit', and in particular the tax-avoidance cases in which corporations sought to benefit their employees by using sham charities. The concept of 'public benefit' was particularly significant in those cases.

23.5.2 What is 'education'?

The first issue is to decide what exactly is meant by the term 'education' in the context of the law of charities. Clearly trusts purposes involving schools and universities have always been considered to be charitable under the case law. There are more difficult questions relating to education beyond those sorts of institutions and in relation to research. The term 'education' in the charitable sense is not limited to teaching activities in schools and universities. Education can involve activities not in the classroom such as sport[41] or the establishment of a choir.[42] The issue is as to the extent of education beyond those sorts of easy cases. For example, in *Re Holburne*[43] the foundation of an art museum was held to be of public utility for the purposes of education because it would educate the public about art. However, that does not mean that all art galleries will be treated as being educational. In *Re Pinion*[44] a collection of eclectic *objets d'art* was argued to be educational when it was made available to the National Trust. However, the court could not see any public utility in this particular gift because the objects were described in evidence as being 'atrociously bad'.[45] Therefore, everything will depend upon the circumstances. Ordinarily, gifts to established museums will be charitable as being educational purposes.[46] The courts will be slow to make value judgments as to the quality of works of art or different approaches to education, except in extreme cases like *Re Pinion*.

Whether research is 'educational' in the legal sense can be a difficult question. Ironically perhaps, research has shown that most academic articles are read, on average, by only a few people – which means that there must be some articles which are read by almost no-one. It is difficult to see how 'the public' benefits if only five people read an article. The argument is made that the research is available to the public and that researchers who work in the public interest in that field will have access to that research. In practice, of course, huge multinational corporations now control access to most academic research journals, which means that only people with access to specialist libraries which have subscribed to those corporations'

---

41 *IRC v McMullen* [1981] AC 1; *London Hospital Medical College v IRC* [1976] 1 WLR 613 (sport in universities).
42 *Royal Choral Society v IRC* [1943] 2 All ER 101.
43 (1885) 53 LT 212; (1885) 1 TLR 517.
44 [1965] Ch 85.
45 See also *Re Hummeltenberg* [1923] 1 Ch 237.
46 *British Museum Trustees v White* (1826) 2 Sm & St 594.

products can access that research in reality. Those commercial issues are unlikely to affect the law in this area, however. Slade J set out the principles on which a court would typically find that research work would be held charitable in *McGovern v Attorney-General*.[47] In essence, the proposed research must be in 'a useful subject of study', it must be intended that 'the knowledge acquired . . . will be disseminated to others', and the knowledge must be for the benefit of the public. It is not necessary that this research is linked to a school or university. The research need only be disseminated to some 'others' and therefore it would appear to be sufficient that a small group of specialist researchers are the only people who can or will access it.

While the courts usually refrain from making value judgments, it is difficult not to identify patterns in their judgments. Take the revisionist work of the Francis Bacon Society which aims to show, *inter alia*, that Shakespeare's works were actually written by Francis Bacon. One of their beliefs, to simplify somewhat, is that Shakespeare was just a glove-maker's son from the Midlands whereas Bacon was a brilliant, Oxford-educated man who is far more likely to have been the author of *Hamlet* and *King Lear* as a result. (An answer to this question is suggested by Shapiro's excellent book *Contested Will* which disposes of the arguments that Shakespeare did not write Shakespeare's works.) In *Re Hopkins*[48] it was held that a bequest to the Francis Bacon Society was an educational purpose because the Society would publish its research. By contrast, in *Re Shaw*[49] a bequest was made by the great socialist playwright George Bernard Shaw to fund research into a new alphabet with the intention of developing a new language which would be common to all nations so that there could be greater peace and understanding between those nations. It was held by Harman J that this purpose was not a charitable purpose because it involved propaganda. The 'propaganda' appeared to be in the idea that it would be a good idea to prevent future wars. So, to summarise these two cases: conducting research in an effort to stop war is not a charitable purpose, whereas proving that only social elites can create great art is.

Before the Charities Act 2006, it was difficult to know whether or not sporting activities would constitute a charitable, educational purpose. In *IRC v McMullen*[50] the House of Lords held that playing football (as well as playing and coaching of other sports) would be charitable if it was done within schools or other educational establishments. Lord Hailsham took the view that a healthy mind and a healthy body went together, and therefore that playing sport was educational in that context. More generally, sport was not considered to be charitable in itself. Indeed, playing games more generally presented difficulties to the courts. In *Re Dupree's Deed Trusts*[51] Vaisey J was uneasy when validating a trust which would fund an annual chess tournament because

> one is on rather a slippery slope. If chess, why not draughts? If draughts, why not bezique, and so on, through to bridge and whist, and by another route, to stamp collecting and the acquisition of birds' eggs?

---

47 [1982] Ch 321: see also that judge in *Re Besterman's Will Trusts* (1980) *The Times*, 21 January.
48 [1965] Ch 699.
49 [1958] 1 All ER 245. See also *Re Shaw's WT* [1952] Ch 163.
50 [1981] AC 1.
51 [1945] Ch 16, 20.

The approach which underpins the CA 2011 is that sport is a good thing in general terms, not least for the nation's health.

23.5.3 The 'public benefit' requirement

The leading case on the 'public benefit' test in relation to education is *Oppenheim v Tobacco Securities Trust*.[52] The House of Lords considered a trust which was intended to generate income to pay for the education of the children of employees of British-American Tobacco Co Ltd ('BAT'). That company was a very large multinational company employing a large number of people. The trust would have been void as a private trust on the basis that it lacked a perpetuities provision. It was argued, however, that the purpose was charitable and therefore that no perpetuities provision was necessary. This was a tax dodge. What BAT was doing was providing a perk for its senior employees by paying for their children's school fees. If the trust paid for those fees then that was a tax-free way of supplying that benefit to those employees, instead of the employees having to pay for the fees themselves out of their taxed income. Lord Simonds followed *Re Compton*[53] in holding that there was a requirement of public benefit to qualify as an educational charity and that on these facts there was a connection (or, 'nexus') between the individuals who would take a benefit and the company, BAT. As Lord Simonds expressed the test: a group of persons may be numerous, but, if the nexus between them is their personal relationship to a single *propositus* or to several *propositi*, they are neither the community not a section of the community for charitable purposes.

So, a nexus between the people who benefit will prevent them from being a section of the public for the purposes of the 'public benefit' test. The critique of this test by Lord Cross in *Dingle v Turner* was set out above in relation to trusts for the relief of poverty.

Two other cases have taken interesting perspectives on this test. There was an epidemic of tax avoidance through charities in the 1960s and 1970s at a time of high taxes. If these trusts could be shown to be charities then they would not have to pay tax. In *IRC v Educational Grants Association*[54] a trust had been created with the objective of holding property on trust 'for the education of the children of the UK'. Read at face value, that appears to be a charitable purpose for the public benefit. However, in reality the trust was operated as to 80% of its income by the trustees to provide funds for the education of children of employees of the company Metal Box Plc. The remaining 20% was applied for the education of people unconnected with the company. It appeared that the trustees were using that 20% in that way in an attempt to pacify the tax authorities. It was held that this was a *de facto* private trust and therefore that it could not qualify for a charity's tax exemptions. In the older case of *Re Koettgen*[55] Upjohn J upheld a trust as being charitable in circumstances in which the assets were applied 75% as a private trust and only 25% for the public benefit. It was held that the charity tax exemption could only be permitted to the extent that the charity was being operated for the public benefit. So, in that case, there was only 25% of the tax relief available because only 25% of the assets were being used for the public benefit.

The most contentious aspect of the law of charities is the status of independent, fee-charging schools as being charities. The so-called 'public schools' of England and Wales

52 [1951] AC 297.
53 [1945] Ch 123.
54 [1967] Ch 123.
55 [1954] Ch 252.

are charities at present and therefore they do not pay tax on their profits, which means that the state is effectively supporting them. If those schools were not charities then their fees would have to be much higher to meet the tax bills they would then suffer. Those tax bills, it is said, would bankrupt many of those schools. In *Independent Schools Council v Charity Commission*[56] the Upper Tribunal considered whether or not such independent schools were charities concerned with the advancement of education in the public benefit. It was held that a public benefit was required to be something which was both of benefit to the community and directed at a sufficiently large section of the community.[57] That a purpose was educational did not necessarily mean that it was of benefit to the community nor that it was directed at a sufficiently large section of it. So, in deciding whether or not a sufficient section of the community was benefited, the Charity Commission would have to consider the number of people who would be able to pay the fees charged by that school and then to consider whether or not that suggested a charitable purpose. The core issue which the Upper Tribunal was asked to consider was whether or not independent schools provided a benefit which was directed at a sufficiently wide section of the community so as to constitute a 'public benefit'. It was held that schools which charged fees for pupils to attend them could not be charities because they excluded poor people and their children from their educational services. By contrast, a school which admitted students no matter what their ability to pay the fees (whether by making bursaries available to the families of pupils who required them or otherwise) could be a charity because it was available to the community in general. Therefore, the Charity Commission would have to consider each school by reference to its own circumstances.

23.6 TRUSTS FOR RELIGIOUS PURPOSES

23.6.1 Introduction

This section considers trusts for the advancement of religion. English charities law has an odd relationship with the supernatural. On the one hand, 'man's relations with God' as opposed to 'man's relations with man' is said to be the distinction between religion and mere humanism. On the other hand, religions which have no single god (such as Buddhism) are accepted as being charitable religious purposes because it would be difficult not to do so. It is important to note as we begin that the Charities Act 2011 makes reference to 'gods' as well as to 'god', thus moving beyond the Judeo-Christian belief in a single god. Oddly, to be a nun, and thus to have devoted oneself to a life of religious devotion, does not constitute a religious, charitable purpose unless that is done for the 'public benefit' in contact with the rest of the world. So, the requirement of public benefit has prevented the validity of bequests to contemplative orders of nuns in *Gilmour v Coats*[58] because they do not come into contact with the public in their religious observance. What is interesting about this area is that any attempt to define 'religion' usually generates as many difficult questions as it answers. In this section we shall consider the meaning of 'religion' in this area of charities law before considering the public benefit test as it applies in this context.

---

56   [2012] 2 WLR 100.
57   *Jones v Williams* (1767) Amb 651; *Oppenheim v Tobacco Securities Trust Co Ltd* [1951] All ER 31.
58   [1949] AC 426.

23.6.2 What is a 'religion' in charities law?

We shall begin by considering the key definitions of 'religion' which have emerged in the case law. In *Re South Place Ethical Society*,[59] Dillon J gave the following, pithy definition 'religious purpose' in the law of charity: 'religion, as I see it, is concerned with man's relations with God.' Therefore, on the facts of *South Place*, the study and dissemination of ethical principles was held not to constitute religion because 'ethics are concerned with man's relations with man', as opposed to any relationship with a god. He continued: 'It seems to me that two of the essential attributes of religion are faith and worship: faith in a god and worship of that god.' The focus is therefore on a system of belief in a god or the promotion of spiritual teaching connected to such religious activity.[60]

The effect of s 3 of the Charities Act 2011 will be profound in two ways: by changing the concept of 'god' and by making god optional in religion. First, s 3(2)(a)(i) of the CA 2011 provides that belief in 'gods', in the plural, as well as 'god', in the singular, counts as a religion for the purposes of charities law. Thus, major faiths like Hinduism with more than one god are explicitly accepted as constituting religions in this legal sense as opposed merely to being accepted in practice by the Charity Commission. Second, s 3(2)(a)(ii) of the CA 2011 introduces the theologically delicious idea of 'a religion which does not involve belief in a god'.[61] Clearly, leading world faiths which do not worship a god, such as Buddhism, are therefore embraced by the statute. The further question is what other activities could be accepted as being religions on this basis.

The Scientology cult, for example, does not have a god and could therefore seek charitable status now. Historically, the courts were aggressively hostile to the idea that Scientology should be accepted as being a religion.[62] In *Hubbard v Vosper*[63] Lord Denning described Scientology as 'dangerous material' and Goff J described it as 'pernicious nonsense' in *Church of Scientology v Kaufman*.[64] In the Supreme Court decision in *R (on the application of Hodkin) v Registrar General of Births, Marriages and Deaths*,[65] which did not relate directly to charities law, it was held that Scientology does constitute a religion for the purposes of licensing its premises to be used as places of marriage under the Places of Worship Registration Act 1855. The definition of a 'religion' which Lord Toulson advanced[66] was that it is:

> a spiritual or non-secular belief system, held by a group of adherents, which claims to explain mankind's place in the universe and relationship with the infinite, and to teach its adherents how they are to live their lives in conformity with the spiritual understanding associated with the belief system.

---

59 [1980] 3 All ER 918.
60 *Keren Kayemeth Le Jisroel Ltd v IRC* [1931] 2 KB 465.
61 *Ibid*, s 2(3)(a)(ii).
62 In essence, the Scientologists believe in the writings of L Ron Hubbard, a science fiction novelist, seemingly to the effect that human beings were placed on Earth by aliens millions of years ago (flying craft that looked just like B-52 bombers) and that, through a process of auditing themselves, they make themselves ready for the return of said aliens.
63 [1972] 2 QB 84, 96.
64 [1973] RPC 635, 658.
65 [2013] UKSC 77.
66 [2013] UKSC 77, [57].

This definition involves a number of problematic concepts. Why must the religion be shared by a group? Why must it explain mankind's place in the universe? Would that explanation of our place in the universe involve a belief in the correctness of astrophysics which is held by a group of adherents in the physics departments of our universities? Some yoga classes try to teach their participants how to live in accordance with a quasi-spiritual understanding of the world: is that a religion? After all, a 'backwards dog' is just 'god'.[67]

The *Shorter Oxford English Dictionary* defines 'religion' as involving a:

> belief in or sensing of some superhuman controlling power or powers, entitled to obedience, reverence, and worship, or in a system defining a code of living, esp. as a means to achieve spiritual or material improvement.[68]

The requirement for some 'superhuman being' is interesting given the ubiquity of superheroes in our popular culture. Does a belief in Spider Man as a force for good in the universe count as a religion? There have also been two fairly pedestrian films about the Marvel character Thor. Outside the cinema, Thor has been a Norse god for centuries. The entirety of the earliest runs of Thor comics published by Marvel were based strictly on the Norse legends about Odin and his sons, Thor and Loki. This is an ancient religious tradition with several gods. So, when does genuine religious belief in Thor the Norse god merge into a belief in a fictitious comic book character who rescues Natalie Portman from a variety of dangerous situations? Does belief in the cinematic version of Thor count as a religion? Does belief in the divinity of Natalie Portman count as a religion? You may think it laughable that a film character could be a religion but L Ron Hubbard was simply a novelist before Scientology took off, the Norse religion had existed for centuries before Hollywood appropriated one of their key gods, and most religions rely on sharing stories (some of which may have been embellished in the re-telling).

And what of new religions? For example, Rastafarianism is a belief practised most widely in Jamaica in which the Rastafarians developed a belief in the divinity of Haile Selassie I (who was Emperor of Ethiopia from 1930 until 1974). He was a human being living at the same time as belief in his divinity began. One of the most famous adherents of this religion was Bob Marley. If you were to listen to his magnificent live album *Babylon by Bus* then it is clear from the introduction to the opening track that this is religious music. At what point does such a belief system become a religion? When it has enough adherents? How could we create a new religion today? There were 300,000 people in the UK who identified their religion as being 'Jedi' in the last census. If it is just about numbers then 'Jedi Knight' is a *bona fide* religion because there are as many people attending Star Wars events as some churches. If it is not just about the number of adherents, then a qualitative measurement of other people's belief and seriousness is necessary. That returns us to the difficult task with which we began: what is the sort of belief which constitutes a *bona fide* religion? Why should L Ron Hubbard's science fiction tropes constitute a religion but George Lucas's ideas should not? This is the sort of question you can answer for yourself, and then read the cases and consider whether or not you agree with the judges. This is clearly an ideal topic for a seminar discussion and for essays.

---

67 Think about it. The downward dog is a yoga position; and the spelling of 'dog' backwards is something quite different, as Neil pointed out during *The Inbetweeners Movie*.

68 Does the requirement for 'obedience' include the sort of acts depicted in the quasi-pornographic novel *Fifty Shades of Grey*? There is a lot of stylised 'worship' in there and it is very popular nowadays.

23.6.3 The requirement of public benefit

All charities must be for the public benefit.[69] This can be a difficult concept in relation to religious purposes. In the leading case of *Gilmour v Coats*[70] the House of Lords held that mere religious observance was not enough to make a contemplative order of nuns a charitable purpose unless there was also some demonstrable public benefit. The argument that the prayers of a cloistered order of nuns would be for the benefit of mankind was not considered to be a valid charitable purpose for the advancement of religion. Nevertheless, in *Thornton v Howe*[71] it was accepted that the writings of Joanna Southcott, who had ecstatic visions through which she claimed to have been impregnated by the Holy Ghost and to have become pregnant with the new Messiah, would be for the public benefit if they were published. In contrast to publication of such spiritual works, the trust at issue in *Gilmour v Coats*[72] was a trust created for the benefit of an order of contemplative Carmelite nuns. The trust was held not to have been charitable on the basis that the order contemplated in private, thus failing to communicate any benefit to the public. Lord Simonds required tangible proof that the works of the trust would convey a benefit to the public, as opposed simply to the adherents' belief that the power of prayer would necessarily be of benefit to the public. This point has been accepted in a number of cases.[73] In *Dunne v Byrne*[74] the point is made that such activities of nuns in a convent would be accepted as being 'religious' in a general sense but not 'charitable' in the legal sense. It does not seem that the tangible benefit of the publication of the thoughts of Ms Southcott was subjected to the same test: it might have made more sense if that was accepted as being an educational purpose for the publication of theological research.

The courts have begun to adopt increasingly relaxed approaches to the interpretation of such charitable purposes. In *Neville Estates v Madden*[75] the issue arose whether a trust to benefit members of the Catford Synagogue could be a charitable purpose. The central issue was whether the members of that synagogue could be considered to be a sufficient section of the population to constitute a 'public benefit'. It was held that, because the religious observance practised in the synagogue was (in theory) open to the public, then the requirement of public benefit would be satisfied.[76] In the imaginative decision in *Re Hetherington*[77] there was a trust to provide income for the saying of Catholic masses in private. By definition, saying mass in private would not have any connection with the public. Nevertheless, Browne-Wilkinson VC construed the gift as being a gift to say masses in public (so that it would be a charitable purpose) on the basis that that would render it valid. On those facts, his lordship found it possible that the masses could be heard in public in practice and found a further public benefit in that the funds provided by the trust would relieve church funds in paying for the stipends of more priests. This was a straightforwardly purposive interpretation of the circumstances. While his lordship relied on authorities like *Gilmour v Coats*,[78] *Yeap Cheah*

---

69   Charities Act 2011, s 2(1)(b).
70   [1949] AC 426.
71   (1862) 31 Beav 14.
72   [1949] AC 426.
73   *Cocks v Manners* (1871) LR 12 Eq 574; *Leahy v Attorney-General for NSW* [1959] AC 457.
74   [1912] AC 407.
75   [1962] Ch 832.
76   See also *Bunting v Sargent* (1879) 13 Ch D 330.
77   [1990] Ch 1.
78   [1949] AC 426.

Neo v Ong[79] and *Hoare v Hoare*,[80] the outcome was clearly much more expansive than the approach taken in those earlier decisions.

23.7 OTHER PURPOSES BENEFICIAL TO THE COMMUNITY

23.7.1 Introduction

This fourth category of charitable purpose under the case law was clearly broader in scope than the other three heads. It acted as a reservoir for a number of the miscellaneous trusts which had struggled to qualify as being charitable despite their seemingly benevolent aim. This category no longer exists intact as a result of the passage of the CA 2011. However, that Act does provide in s 3(1)(m)(iii) that any charities found valid under the case law will still be considered to be valid after 2011.

23.7.2 The nature of the fourth head: other purposes beneficial to the community

It was held by Lord Macnaghten in *Pemsel's Case*[81] that to fall under this head the trust must either be analogous with the categories cited in the Preamble to a Statute of 1601 or with the principles deriving from decided cases.

23.7.3 The requirement of a public benefit

This head of charity included a requirement that the purpose be 'beneficial to the community'. The roots of the case law are established in the dicta of Sir Samuel Romilly in *Morice v Bishop of Durham*[82] making reference to a requirement of 'general public utility' to satisfy this fourth head. Trusts for the maintenance of a town's bridges, towers and walls have been upheld as valid charitable purposes[83] as has a trust for the support of a crematorium.[84] As a general rule of thumb it was suggested in *ICLR v Attorney-General*[85] by Russell LJ that where a trust purpose removes the need for statutory or governmental action by providing a service voluntarily, then the organisation providing that service should be deemed to be charitable.

There is a necessary requirement that there be sufficient benefit to the community. In *Verge v Somerville*[86] Lord Wrenbury held that:

> The inhabitants of a parish or town or any particular class of such inhabitants, may, for instance, be the objects of such a gift, but private individuals, or a fluctuating body of private individuals cannot.

---

79 (1875) LR 6 PC 381.
80 (1886) 56 LT 147.
81 [1891] AC 531.
82 (1805) 10 Ves 522.
83 *Attorney-General v Shrewsbury Corp* (1843) 6 Beav 220.
84 *Scottish Burial Reform and Cremation Society v Glasgow Corp* [1968] AC 138.
85 [1972] Ch 73.
86 [1924] AC 496.

Therefore, the community must be something more than 'a fluctuating body of private individuals'. You might recall that this was precisely the concept which was criticised in *Dingle v Turner*[87] as being a reasonable definition of a section of the community (as discussed in section 23.4.1).

As outlined at the beginning of this chapter, there are two competing views in the cases as to the meaning of 'public benefit'. This is an opportunity for you, when answering problem questions, to demonstrate that you understand how these different tests would apply to the question in front of you (and that one test applies to poverty, while the other applies to education and religion). Demonstrating the ability to apply those two different tests to a set of facts and to recognise that they would often produce different outcomes, is a key way of acquiring a good mark.

23.7.4 The remaining purposes beneficial to the community under the Charities Act 2011

The principal effect of the Charities Act 2011 in relation to the definition of 'charitable purpose' has been to break out a number of the key, contested categories of 'other purposes beneficial to the community' in an attempt to make clear that they should now be considered to be valid heads of charity in their own right. Consequently, the law of charities appeared to have broadened and modernised. Unfortunately, there is a problem. The decision of Lewison J in *Hanchett-Stamford v Attorney-General*[88] threatens to limit the effect of the Act quite remarkably by taking the position (in relation specifically to animal welfare, as considered below at section 23.8.9) that if the charitable purpose was invalid under the old case law then the Act should not be taken as necessarily having any effect in broadening that category of charitable purpose. If this approach were repeated then this would mean that the Parliamentary intention of modernising and expanding the categories of charitable purpose would be frustrated by the courts.

23.8 THE NEW CATEGORIES OF CHARITABLE PURPOSE UNDER THE CHARITIES ACT 2006

23.8.1 An introduction to the Act

This section considers the other categories of charitable purpose which are set out in the CA 2011 beyond the three main categories considered above. In relation to many of these categories there are no decided cases at present.

23.8.2 The advancement of health or the saving of lives

This head includes the 'prevention or relief of sickness, disease or human suffering' along with the advancement of health.[89] Research into medical procedures would ordinarily have fallen under educational purposes under the research category in any event. The '*advancement*

---

87   [1972] AC 601.
88   [2008] EWHC 330 (Ch).
89   Charities Act 2006, s 2(3)(b).

of health' could encompass activities which promote healthy eating – such as celebrity chef Jamie Oliver's campaigning for the improvement of dinners in schools – or public information campaigns promoting sexual health. The 'saving of lives' could encompass anything from medical care to lifeboat services which save lives at sea.[90]

23.8.3 The advancement of citizenship or community development

Section 2(2)(e) deals with 'the advancement of citizenship or community development'. This means very little, of course, as it is drafted but it is entirely in line with government policy since 1997. The Act contains a gloss to the effect that this concept includes 'rural or urban regeneration' and 'the promotion of civic responsibility, volunteering, the voluntary sector or the effectiveness or efficiency of charities'.[91] What is difficult to see is how these intangible – but potentially important – improvements in social life will tally with the judges' historical aversion to services or activities which do not lead to any tangible benefit to identifiable groups of people. Moreover, community development may often seem to be a political purpose in practice.

23.8.4 The advancement of the arts, culture, heritage or science

This category refers to 'the advancement of the arts, culture, heritage or science'. None of these terms is defined in the Act and therefore we must develop our own understandings of these provisions and guess as to the future. First, the reference to 'the arts' in the plural is not a reference simply to 'art', which presumably encompasses street theatre. What about those people who paint themselves silver and pretend to be statues for tourists? What about graffiti artists painting their tags on railway arches? Are they art, or part of 'the arts'? The meaning of the term 'culture' is one which is hotly contested among social theorists and could encompass almost any aspect of human interaction. It remains to be seen which forms of culture will be accepted as being charitable.[92] High culture, like opera? Or 'low' culture, like non-league football matches or rap battles in disused warehouses? Scientists describe mould in a Petri dish as being 'a culture' after all.

23.8.5 The advancement of amateur sport

This category refers to 'the advancement of amateur sport'. Under the old case law the mere advancement of sport did not in itself constitute a charitable purpose (unless it was played at a school or university): thus paying for a cup for a yachting competition and to promote yachting was held not to be a charitable purpose,[93] nor was the promotion of cricket.[94] Recreational charities have been held valid under the old case law as charitable purposes; but only if they improved the conditions of life of the people using them and either if they were available to all members of the population without discrimination or if they were made

---

90 *Re David* (1889) 43 Ch D 27.
91 Charities Act 2011, s 3(2)(c).
92 Taken literally, of course, 'culture' could refer to mould or fungus.
93 *Re Nottage* (1885) 2 Ch D 649.
94 *Re Patten* [1929] 2 Ch 276.

available by reason of their users' 'youth, age, infirmity, disability, poverty or social and economic circumstances'. All of these terms were contained in the Recreational Charities Act 1958, which is considered in detail below in section 25.8.12. The Charity Commission has, however, changed its view and decided that it will accord charitable status to 'the promotion of community participation in healthy recreation by providing facilities for playing particular sports'.[95] Consequently, in practice there are unlikely to be any further cases on this topic because the Charity Commission will not challenge genuine trusts created to achieve these goals.

23.8.6 The advancement of human rights, conflict resolution or reconciliation or the promotion of religious or racial harmony or equality and diversity

This category deals with 'the advancement of human rights, conflict resolution or reconciliation or the promotion of religious or racial harmony or equality and diversity'. Purposes of this kind would previously have run the risk of being held to be void purposes on the basis that they sought a change in the law or that they were more generally political purposes.[96] The old case law had not recognised the pursuit of better relations between groups or nations – such as the British and the Boers after the Boer War – as being charitable.[97] The Charity Commission, however, doubtless emboldened now by the new Act, has expressed its view that promoting good race relations ought to be considered to be a charitable purpose in the future and as being self-evidently for the public benefit.

23.8.7 The advancement of environmental protection or improvement

This category is concerned with 'the advancement of environmental protection or improvement'. The environment can be taken to refer to particular items of flora and fauna, at one end of the spectrum, right the way through to combating climate change or global warming at the other end. Again, the problem here is that many environmental activities shade into campaigning for a change in the law, and thus would be invalid political purposes.

23.8.8 The relief of those in need by reason of youth, age, ill-health, disability, financial hardship or other disadvantage

The contents of this category are 'the relief of those in need by reason of youth, age, ill-health, disability, financial hardship or other disadvantage'. Activities involving the National Society for the Prevention of Cruelty to Children have been upheld as being charitable purposes,[98] as has the provision of a children's home.[99] This category seems to enact a part of the old fourth head under the case law.

---

95 Charity Commission, *RR 11: Charitable Status and Sport* (2003).
96 See *National Anti-vivisection Society v IRC* [1940] AC 31.
97 See *Re Strakosch* [1949] Ch 529.
98 See *D v NSPCC* [1978] AC 171.
99 *Re Sohal's WT* [1958] 1 WLR 1243.

23.8.9 The advancement of animal welfare

This category relates to 'the advancement of animal welfare'. This would encompass the good works of the Royal Society for the Prevention of Cruelty to Animals or the Royal Society for the Protection of Birds, being organisations committed to the care of animals. Equally, the provision of hospices for animals or even the provision of veterinary services may be charitable purposes. Under the old case law there was a public benefit in animal welfare only if there could be shown to be some moral improvement to the *human* community by dint of treating animals better.[100]

The Court of Appeal has held that a trust intended for the prevention of cruelty to animals would contribute to public morality and therefore that it would be a valid charitable trust.[101] In *Re Moss*[102] a trust for a specified person 'for her work for the welfare of cats and kittens needing care and attention' was held to be a valid charitable purpose by Romer J.[103] Similarly, a trust *inter alia* to 'stimulate humane and generous sentiments in man towards lower animals' has been upheld as a charitable purpose where it was attached to the establishment of an animal refuge.[104] However, the Court of Appeal in *Re Grove-Grady*[105] held that a will providing for a residuary estate to be used to provide 'refuges for the preservation of all animals or birds' was not a charitable purpose because there was no discernible benefit to the community. In that case, Russell LJ held that there was no general rule that trusts for the preservation and care of animals would necessarily be of benefit to the community: rather, each case should be considered on its own merits.

In spite of the express inclusion of a category of animal welfare for the first time in the Charities Act 2006 (which has now been consolidated into the CA 2011), Lewison J chose to limit the future possible development of charitable animal welfare purposes in *Hanchett-Stamford v Attorney-General*.[106] In that case a couple had long maintained an unincorporated association ('The Performing and Captive Animals Defence League') which sought to achieve a change in the law so as to ban the use of performing animals. The association had been denied charitable status on the basis that it sought to effect a change in the law. Lewison J held, correctly it is suggested, that the Charities Act 2006 had not effected any change in the law on preventing charities from seeking a change in the law. A political purpose of that sort will still prevent a purpose from being charitable. In relation specifically to animal welfare, however, the claimants argued that the inclusion of the category of animal welfare into the Charities Act 2006 when taken together with the provisions of the Animal Welfare Act 2006 (which created offences of causing distress to animals) had effected a significant change in the law. Lewison J held that animal welfare purposes had generally been invalid under the case law prior to the 2006 Act and therefore that the Act should not be interpreted as having changed the scope of that position under charities law. The purpose was held to be invalid as a charitable purpose. This is a surprisingly narrow interpretation of the legislation and, it is suggested, is clearly contrary to the will of Parliament when it included this category in the legislation for the first time. There is nothing in the Act to suggest that it should be interpreted

---

100 *Re Wedgwood* [1915] 1 Ch 113.
101 *Ibid.*
102 [1949] 1 All ER 495.
103 *Re Douglas* (1887) 35 Ch D 472; *Re Murawski's WT* [1971] 2 All ER 328.
104 *Re Wedgwood* [1915] 1 Ch 113.
105 [1929] 1 Ch 557.
106 [2008] EWHC 330 (Ch), [2008] 4 All ER 323.

as being limited to the position under the old case law. To apply Lewison J's position across the whole of charities law after 2011 would be to limit all of the new statutory purposes to old attitudes in the case law which the Act was intended to reverse.

23.8.10 The promotion of the efficiency of the armed forces of the Crown

'The promotion of the efficiency of the armed forces of the Crown' was a late addition to the legislation. It had previously been the case that trusts to promote national defence through the armed forces would have been considered to be a purpose for the public benefit.[107] It would, however, be a quirky notion of charity which extended to the acquisition of weapons.

23.8.11 The promotion of the efficiency of the police, fire rescue and ambulance services

'The promotion of the efficiency of the police, fire rescue and ambulance services' perhaps simply codifies the previous position whereby trusts to promote the three emergency services were considered to be charitable as a purpose beneficial to the community.[108] The old case law would require that these purposes were directed at the services' professional functions and not at the general condition of their officers. So, in *IRC v Glasgow City Police*[109] it was held that the provision of facilities for the recreation of police officers would not be a charitable purpose.

23.8.12 Recreational charities

In general terms, the courts did not uphold recreational purposes as being charities. Section 5 of the CA 2011 provides that it is charitable to provide 'recreational' or 'other leisure-time occupation' activities, provided that those activities are 'in the interests of social welfare'. This, it is suggested, is in line with the general approach of the Recreational Charities Act 1958.

Under the case law, charitable status was not given to social clubs or sports clubs which did not alleviate any material lack in the lives of a section of the public. For example, in *IRC v Baddeley*[110] it was held that recreation for a restricted class of people in a specific geographic area would not be charitable. As a result, the Recreational Charities Act 1958 was introduced to bring such purposes within the heads of charity. The 1958 Act is effectively re-enacted in s 5 of the CA 2011. The 1958 Act established a 'public benefit test' to legitimise recreational charities as charitable trusts. The facilities were to be provided with the intention of improving the conditions of life of the people benefiting. There are two further, alternative requirements that either those persons must have a need of those facilities on grounds of their social and economic circumstances or that the facilities will be available to both men and women in the

---

107 The 'setting out of soldiers' was included in the 1601 Preamble.
108 *Re Wokingham Fire Brigade Trusts* [1951] Ch 373.
109 [1953] AC 380.
110 [1955] AC 572.

public at large. In explaining the ambit of the 1958 Act, the majority of the House of Lords in *IRC v McMullen*[111] held that it was only if the persons standing to benefit from the trust were in some way deprived at the outset that their conditions of life could be said to have been improved.

A more liberal interpretation was taken by a differently constituted House of Lords in *Guild v IRC*[112] in relation to a bequest 'to the town council of North Berwick for the use in connection with the sports centre in North Berwick or some similar purpose in connection with sport'. It was accepted that this sports centre would be available to the general public as required by the Act. The principal question was whether or not this sports centre could be said to be connected with 'social welfare' as required by s 1(1) of the Act. Lord Keith made it plain that he was prepared to adopt a 'benignant construction' of the bequest in this case. It was a bequest which demonstrated that the testator's intention was to benefit a sports centre the facilities of which were available to the public at large. Consequently, it was held that this constituted a valid charitable purpose.

23.9 *CY-PRÈS* DOCTRINE

23.9.1 The case law position

The *cy-près* doctrine permits the court to redirect the purpose of a failed charitable trust to a similar purpose, as opposed to finding the trust void. Where the charitable objects do not exist or are uncertain, the court has the power to order an application of the trust fund for alternative charitable purposes which are in accordance with the settlor's underlying intentions.[113]

If the trust is impossible to perform from the outset then the *cy-près* doctrine will not apply. As a result, the property settled on trust passes on resulting trust back to the settlor's estate.[114] For example, in *Re Rymer*[115] a legacy to the rector of an identified seminary could not be applied *cy-près* when that seminary ceased to exist. It was held that the bequest was so specific to that seminary that it did not disclose a general charitable intention.

The *cy-près* doctrine can be applied where the terms of the trust disclose a general charitable intention beyond an intention merely to benefit the identified charity. So, if the legacy in *Re Rymer* had not been directed at a particular seminary but rather for a more general religious purpose, then a *cy-près* application would have been possible. In *Biscoe v Jackson*[116] the settlor sought to create a soup kitchen and a cottage hospital 'in the parish of Shoreditch'. When the intended land could not be acquired, the Court of Appeal held that the settlor had disclosed a general charitable intention to provide those sorts of facilities somewhere in the general area such that the fund could be applied *cy-près*. In such cases where no specific

111 [1981] AC 1.
112 [1992] 2 AC 310.
113 Mulheron, 2005.
114 *Re Rymer* [1895] 1 Ch 19; *Re Wilson* [1913] 1 Ch 314; *Re Packe* [1918] 1 Ch 437. Cf. *Bath and Wells Diocesan Board of Finance v Jenkinson* (2000) *The Times*, 6 September.
115 [1895] 1 Ch 19.
116 (1887) 35 Ch D 460.

charity is identified or where there is a long list of potential charities, then the courts are more likely to find that there was a general charitable intention beyond the benefit of any one charity.[117] Alternatively, the charity may have continued in another form and so the courts may apply the *cy-près* doctrine to benefit the successor entity.[118]

23.9.2 Exclusivity of purpose

The operation of the *cy-près* doctrine is dependent on the underlying purpose of the settlor being exclusively charitable.[119] Alternatively, it is open to the court to apportion a trust fund between valid charitable purposes and other objects. It is possible that non-charitable objects will fail but that the charitable objects will be severed from those other provisions and validated separately, as was held in *Re Clarke*.[120]

23.9.3 The mechanics of the *cy-près* doctrine under statute

The Charities Act 1960 sought, *inter alia*, to expand the operation of the *cy-près* doctrine: the provisions of the 1960 Act have been re-enacted in the Charities Act 2011, Part 6. The principal change was to extend the operation of the doctrine beyond requirements of mere impossibility or impracticability into other situations in which the trustees may prefer to apply the funds for other (charitable) purposes than those identified by the settlor. The key provision in this context is s 62 of the Charities Act 2011 which sets out the following situations in which a *cy-près* application can be made. They are as follows:

It must be demonstrated that there is a general charitable intention; and either –

(1) where the purposes have been 'as far as may be fulfilled';
(2) where the purposes cannot be carried out as directed or within the spirit of the gift;
(3) where the purpose provides a use for only part of the gift;
(4) where the property can be more usefully applied along with other property applied for similar purposes;
(5) where the area of the original purpose is no more; or
(6) where the original purposes are adequately provided-for purposes such as statutory services, or are harmful to the community, or useless to the community, or are no longer an effective use of the property.

Attention must also be paid to the spirit of the gift and to the social and economic circumstances at the time of altering the purposes of the trust when making the decision about a *cy-près* application.

---

117 *Re Davis* [1902] 1 Ch 876.
118 *Re Faraker* [1912] 2 Ch 488; *Re Finger's WT* [1972] 1 Ch 286.
119 *Chichester Diocesan Fund v Simpson* [1944] AC 341.
120 [1923] 2 Ch 407.

23.10 THE REGULATION OF CHARITIES

Charities are regulated by the Charity Commission[121] which maintains the register of charities.[122] Mindful of the intermittent concerns expressed about the abuse of charities, the Charity Commission has five key objectives:[123]

(1) The public confidence objective is to increase public trust and confidence in charities.

(2) The public benefit objective is to promote awareness and understanding of the operation of the public benefit requirement.

(3) The compliance objective is to increase compliance by charity trustee with their legal obligations in exercising control and management of the administration of their charities.

(4) The charitable resources objective is to promote the effective use of charitable resources.

(5) The accountability objective is to enhance the accountability of charities to donors, beneficiaries and the general public.

These regulatory objectives do not create legal rights in the hands of the people who are mentioned in the text of the objectives, but rather they anticipate that the Charity Commission will consider the interests of those people when exercising their regulatory function. The general functions of the Commission are then to decide whether or not purposes are charitable, to encourage better administration of charities, to investigate mismanagement in the administration of charities, to determine the suitability of public collections certificates, and to disseminate information about its activities and to advise government ministers.[124] A Charity Appeal Tribunal has been created in relation to the activities and decisions of the Commission, with appeal to the High Court.[125]

---

121 Charities Act 2006, s 6.
122 *Ibid*, s 9.
123 *Ibid*, s 7, inserting s 1B to the Charities Act 1993.
124 Charities Bill 2006, s 7, inserting s 1C to the Charities Act 1993.
125 *Ibid*, s 8.

Part 9

Equitable remedies

Injunctions

CAPSULE SUMMARY

Injunctions are an equitable remedy and their use is widespread in practice in every area of law from family law to commercial law. The courts have a broad inherent jurisdiction to award injunctions in any circumstances where it is 'just and convenient' to do so, under s 37 of the Senior Courts Act 1981. The House of Lords in *Mercedes Benz v Leiduck* underlined the inherent nature of the jurisdiction of the courts to award injunctions to avoid injustice. The ability of the courts to create new forms of injunction is shown by freezing orders, search orders and super-injunctions. This chapter focuses on describing the principal forms of injunction and on the recent, newsworthy disputes about super-injunctions and privacy.

24.1 NATURE OF INJUNCTIONS

24.1.1 Introduction: The power of the courts to grant injunctions

The law on injunctions is central to English equity. Injunctions are an equitable remedy which are available in a very wide range of circumstances spanning across English civil law from family law to commercial law. Such is their ubiquity in our legal system that their roots in equity are often overlooked. The central proposition which it is important to absorb is that judges have an inherent jurisdiction to award injunctions in circumstances in which they consider it necessary to avoid injustice. As Lord Nicholls made plain in the House of Lords in *Mercedes Benz AG v Leiduck*:[1]

> The court may grant an injunction against a party properly before it where this is required to avoid injustice . . . The court habitually grants injunctions in respect of certain types of conduct. But that does not mean that the situations in which injunctions may be granted are now set in stone for all time . . . The exercise of the jurisdiction must be principled, but the criterion is injustice.

Therefore, injunctions arise on the basis of principles of justice at their most primitive level. The courts have an inherent jurisdiction to grant injunctions where it is necessary to prevent injustice, and they are able to create new forms of injunction where necessary. In this chapter, for example, we shall consider several types of commercial injunction which were created in the 20th century by the courts to meet the justice of the case. While the power to grant injunctions is unfettered by statute (i.e. the judges have an unfettered ability to grant injunctions where they consider it to be appropriate), there is a broad statutory root for the power to grant injunctions. The most significant statutory source for injunctions (in all of the many forms of injunction that exist in the world) is s 37(1) of the Senior Courts Act 1981 which provides that:

> The High Court may by order (whether interlocutory or final) grant an injunction . . . in all cases in which it appears to the court to be just and convenient to do so.

> (1) Any such order may be made either unconditionally or on such terms and conditions as the court thinks just.

Again, the general language of equity is visible in this provision: injunctions may be awarded where it is 'just and convenient to do so'. This runs in parallel with the principle in *Leiduck* that was advanced by Lord Nicholls that injunctions are aimed at avoiding injustice. As Spry has pointed out in *Equitable Remedies*[2] the court's jurisdiction towards injunctions operates 'without limits, and can be exercised either in support of any legal right, or in the creation of a new equitable right, as the court thinks fit in the application of equitable principles'.

Clearly, this is a potentially enormous topic. This chapter will focus principally on two things (whereas my other book *Equity & Trusts* considers this area of law in much greater detail). First, we shall consider the various, principal categories of injunction in outline.

---

1   [1996] AC 284, 308.
2   Spry, 2010, 331.

Second, we shall focus on super-injunctions and on injunctions in relation to privacy and 'confidences' because they have been so newsworthy in recent years and because they are a focus of many university equity and trusts courses as a result.

24.1.2 The different types of injunction

Injunctions fall into several different categories. At root, we must bear in mind that the injunction is an equitable remedy and that courts have, first, the inherent jurisdiction acknowledged in *Leiduck* to award injunctions and, second, the statutory power to award injunctions where it is 'just and convenient to do so' under the Senior Courts Act. Injunctions have many uses: they can be used either as a part of litigation (sometimes as part of a strategy to dictate the behaviour of the other party to litigation) or as a final remedy at the end of a trial. Injunctions divide between those that require some action from the respondent (mandatory injunctions), those that require the respondent to refrain from some action (prohibitory injunctions) and those that seek to prevent some action that it is feared may be performed in the future (injunctions *quia timet*).

Injunctions may be awarded during litigation or before litigation begins to preserve the status quo until the court can hear the case in full. These injunctions are known as 'interim injunctions'. This may be done to prevent property being taken out of the jurisdiction (so-called 'freezing injunctions') or to permit searches to be conducted to identify and preserve evidence (so-called 'search orders'). These different types of injunctions are outlined below. Alternatively, injunctions may be awarded at the end of litigation as the final remedy. These injunctions are known as 'final injunctions'.

24.1.3 How equity really functions: Creating principle out of discretionary powers

What we have learned so far is that the law on injunctions covers almost the whole of civil litigation potentially, and that there are particular statutory contexts in which injunctions may be ordered (for example in family law and child law cases). This section considers how injunctions operate in practice because the principles on which they are based are very broad indeed. So broad, in fact, that this might awaken all of those concerns which were discussed in Chapter 1 about equity being too broad and too discretionary for the stomach of some judges even in the 17th century. The simple point to make at the outset is that *in practice* English judges are generally uncomfortable with making awards of injunctions entirely arbitrarily and therefore they prefer to award injunctions where they accord with precedent. (There are situations in which novel injunctions will be awarded, however, as considered below.) These concepts were created by judges and developed over time in accordance with the doctrine of precedent. There is a tendency for English judges to take a statutory power like s 37 of the Senior Courts Act 1981 and to move immediately to restrict their own powers by setting out the considerations which should be taken into account when deciding whether or not to make such an order.

The decision of the Court of Appeal in *Jaggard v Sawyer*[3] is a very good example of this tendency. In that case, the applicant sought an injunction to prevent his neighbour from

---

3 [1995] 1 WLR 269.

developing a road between their land in breach of covenant incumbent on their respective plots of land. The issue arose whether an injunction would be appropriate or whether the court should simply award damages instead. Sir Thomas Bingham MR analysed the four elements required for the award of an injunction which had been set out in the 19th century case of *Shelfer v City of London Electric Lighting Co.*[4] His lordship accepted these four requirements which must be satisfied before a court will award damages instead of an injunction in circumstances where an injunction might otherwise be awarded:

(a) the harm suffered by the applicant must have been comparatively slight;
(b) the harm suffered must be capable of being quantified in financial terms;
(c) the harm suffered must be such that it can be compensated adequately by payment of damages; and
(d) it must have been oppressive to the respondent to have granted the injunction sought.[5]

This is significant because it indicates how modern judges tend to deal with discretionary, equitable powers and doctrines: they begin by identifying the sorts of factors which will inhibit the use of their power. Thus a potentially enormous discretion is limited by the judges themselves developing limitations on the ways in which they will use that discretion. The answer to most of the objections about equity being too discretionary are found in this observation: while equitable doctrines often operate on the basis of high-level principles, the courts tend to implement them by reference to clear precedent or by establishing principles of the sort set out in *Jaggard v Sawyer*.

24.2 GENERAL EQUITABLE PRINCIPLES GOVERNING INJUNCTIONS

There are several, general equitable principles which govern the court's decision whether or not to award an injunction. First, an injunction will not be awarded if cash damages or some other common law remedy would provide a suitable remedy.[6] However, where the court feels that, while damages are available, they would not be an adequate remedy, an equitable remedy (such as an injunction) will be awarded.[7] The equitable remedy of injunction will only be applied where the common law will not achieve justice between the parties. Second, an applicant for an injunction must come to equity with clean hands. It is a key part of any equitable remedy that the applicant is not seeking that remedy to advance some inequitable purpose.[8] Third, there must not be any delay in bringing proceedings because the purpose of an injunction, in general terms, is that it is necessary to protect or preserve some right that the applicant has.[9] Avoiding delay is one of the core equitable principles.[10] Delay will typically be taken as a sign of acquiescence in the actions of the defendant and thus disqualify

---

4 [1895] 1 Ch 287.
5 *Ibid, per* AL Smith LJ.
6 *London and Blackwall Railway Co v Cross* (1886) 31 Ch D 354.
7 *Beswick v Beswick* [1968] AC 58.
8 *Tinsley v Milligan* [1994] 1 AC 340, *per* Lord Goff.
9 *Jaggard v Sawyer* [1995] 1 WLR 269.
10 *Gafford v Graham* [1999] 41 EG 157.

the claimant from obtaining an injunction[11] and from damages in connection with any such injunction.[12] Fourth, equity will not act in vain – which means that the court will not award an injunction if it would achieve nothing. Fifth, there must be some right of the applicant which is being affected, and therefore injunctions will not be awarded in thin air. As Sir George Baker P held in *Paton v British Pregnancy Advisory Service Trustees*:[13] 'the first and basic principle is that there must be a legal right enforceable in law or in equity before the applicant can obtain an injunction from the court to restrain an infringement of that right'. Sixth, and importantly, the award of the injunction must not cause disproportionate hardship or harm to the respondent. In this sense, the respondent will only be able to resist the award of an injunction if it would be oppressive of them.

Many courts, however, can tend to lapse into the habit of simply measuring which party would suffer more harm out of the two of them. In *Jaggard v Sawyer*,[14] Sir Thomas Bingham MR pointed out that 'the test is one of oppression, and the court should not slide into the application of a general balance of convenience test'. In practice, applications for interim injunctions, for example, usually end up being a bun-fight over which person would suffer more harm if the court awarded or did not award the injunction. For example, if the applicant for the injunction is seeking to stop the respondent from using their vans to deliver bread to their chain of sandwich shops in Kent so that the applicant can bring an action for repossession of the vans, and if the respondent would suffer great loss of business if she could not use the vans, then counsel for both sides will simply spend their time trying to convince the judge that it is their client who would suffer greater hardship. Each party's counsel will then try to prove the hardship that would be suffered by their client, while rubbishing the other party's arguments. The respondent's counsel would estimate the cost of the loss of business (possibly with a surprising lack of transparency as to where those figures came from); the applicant's counsel would argue that replacement vans could be rented in the meantime, or that deliveries could be made from the respondent's own Toyota Renegade, and that the respondent's cash flow estimates are a fiction. And so forth. Most lawyering at this level is entirely about common sense.

Courts will often err on the side of keeping everything in position until trial, but they have a weakness for not preventing people from carrying on their businesses for the many months that can pass until a trial is held. Sometimes seeking an injunction at a sufficiently early stage in litigation can panic the other party into settling (for example if they might lose a lot of business) or frighten them about how costly and time-consuming the litigation will become if there are too many applications for injunctions and so forth.

24.3 INTERIM INJUNCTIONS

24.3.1 Introduction

The interim injunction is an injunction made during litigation which is binding on the parties only up to the date of final judgment. This is opposed to permanent injunctions, which are binding on the parties from the date of judgment in perpetuity (or until the

---

11 *Ibid.*
12 *Ibid.*
13 [1979] QB 276.
14 [1995] 1 WLR 269.

judge expresses them to expire, or until a successful appeal against the injunction). In relation to a final injunction, the court will have heard full evidence from all relevant parties and will have conducted a full trial of all relevant issues. In that context, the court is able to reach an informed decision on the most suitable means for disposing of the differences between the parties. In the case of an interim injunction, there will not have been a trial of the issues between the parties. Therefore, the court will not have had the opportunity to form an opinion on the merits of the case. To award an injunction in favour of one party (the applicant) will prevent the other party (the respondent) from acting as they otherwise would. It is possible that the respondent would win the trial and therefore would have suffered detriment for the period of the injunction. However, if the respondent were permitted to continue to act freely, and then lost at trial, this might cause even greater loss to the applicant.

24.3.2 The core test – 'balance of convenience'

The classic test for the availability of an interim injunction was contained in *American Cyanamid v Ethicon Ltd*.[15] In the words of Lord Diplock, 'The court must weigh one need against another and determine where "the balance of convenience" lies.' His lordship held that there were four factors which were necessary for the award of an interim injunction: that the balance of convenience between the parties (i.e. who would suffer less, the applicant or the respondent); whether or not the applicant can demonstrate a 'strong prima facie case' (i.e. that they have a good chance of winning at the final trial); that there is a serious issue to be resolved at trial; and that the applicant can give an undertaking to pay damages for the harm caused to the respondent by the injunction if the applicant is unsuccessful at the eventual trial. His lordship also pointed out that it is impossible for the court at an interim stage to reach a firm conclusion as to the merits of the case.[16] In practice, therefore, the parties have to give as strong an indication as possible of their chances of success at a future trial when making the application for an interim injunction possibly many months beforehand.

These principles can be difficult to apply in practice because the judge hearing an application for an interim injunction long before the trial is held is having to indulge in a little guesswork about many of these factors. An explanation of these principles which was presented by Laddie J[17] was that Lord Diplock must have required the court to consider the comparative strengths of the parties' cases but without needing to resolve any difficult issues of fact or law (because that is something which can only be done at trial with all the witnesses being heard and so forth). Some subsequent cases have cast doubt on the breadth of the applicability of *American Cyanamid*.[18] In *Cambridge Nutrition Ltd v British Broadcasting Association*,[19] in a dissenting judgment, Kerr LJ held that the *American Cyanamid* principle is not a principle of universal application.

---

15 [1975] AC 396.
16 Cf. *Hoffmann La Roche & Co v Secretary of State for Trade and Industry* [1973] AC 295.
17 *Ibid*.
18 [1975] AC 396.
19 [1990] 3 All ER 523.

24.4 FREEZING INJUNCTIONS

The freezing injunction was formerly known as the 'Mareva injunction' on account of the case in which it first appeared: *Mareva Compania Naviera SA v International Bulk Carriers SA*.[20] A freezing injunction stops a respondent from taking assets or property out of the jurisdiction before trial. Clearly, if a party had no assets left in England and Wales, then it would make it very difficult for the applicant to enforce any judgment which they might win at trial. So, the freezing injunction is a form of interim injunction which is acquired before trial so as to ensure that there are assets left in the jurisdiction.

If we can liken commercial litigation to being like a war (and I think that most commercial litigators would rather like that), then a freezing injunction (and the search order, considered next) are like Special Forces being sent behind enemy lines to cut the opposition's supply lines before the real artillery bombardments begin. In the quiet, office-bound life of a commercial litigator, there are only three forms of excitement. First, opening pay cheques and buying sports cars. Second, telling other people about your international travel schedule. Third, roaring onto a dockside, into a warehouse or into an office building at a ridiculously early time in the morning holding a copy of the court order aloft, surrounded by security and other personnel hired for the occasion, and shouting loudly at confused cleaners that you have come to enforce a court order. Men of my generation, I am sure, think they are in *The Sweeney* or *The Professionals* when they do this sort of thing.[21] Men and women of your generation will probably imagine themselves to look like Jason Statham, Vin Diesel or Angelina Jolie (with Brad Pitt in *Mr and Mrs Jones*).

For a freezing injunction, the applicant is required to demonstrate three things: a good arguable case; that there are assets within the jurisdiction; and that there is a real risk of the dissipation of those assets which would otherwise make final judgment nugatory. This is an interim injunction, so the judge is having to make an educated guess as to the future. If the respondent had a history of taking assets out of the jurisdiction, or if the respondent had no other links with England and stood to lose a lot of money, then these might be circumstances which would point towards the award of a freezing injunction. The applicant would usually be required to make a cogent case as to the risk of assets being moved out of the jurisdiction.[22] Another formulation has provided that freezing injunctions will be awarded when the court is convinced that the applicant will recover judgment against the defendant, that there is good reason to believe that the defendant has assets within the jurisdiction to meet that liability, and that the respondent may well take steps to put those assets beyond the applicant's reach.[23]

It was held in *Fourie v Le Roux*[24] that the courts will not impose such an injunction if the burden placed on the defendant would be more than is just and convenient. The applicant before the House of Lords in *Fourie v Le Roux* was involved in litigation with the respondents in South Africa. Through various forms of deception, assets against which the

---

20 [1975] 2 Lloyd's Rep 509.
21 Watch the re-runs on ITV4. They are always storming into warehouses or disused docks. That was what the 1970s were like. Today, every inch of warehouse or disused dock is a restaurant, coffee shop or internet start-up.
22 I was once involved in a case in which the application before the court was abandoned as we arrived because we were told that the valuable artwork we were seeking to restrain had just been loaded onto a plane bound for Colombia.
23 *Z Ltd v A-Z* [1982] QB 558, 585.
24 *Ibid.*

applicant might have brought a claim had been moved to England. The applicant therefore sought a freezing order over those assets in England. That order was made by the High Court. The respondents appealed on the basis that the applicant had not yet brought any substantive proceedings against the respondents and therefore that the court had no jurisdiction to make a freezing order. Lord Scott held that the trial judge had had jurisdiction to make an order in the strict sense that the assets and the parties were properly parties before an English court.

Extraordinarily, the English courts have decided that they have the jurisdiction to grant freezing injunctions over assets held outside England and Wales: the so-called 'worldwide freezing injunction'. The power is said to arise further to s 37(1) of the Senior Courts Act 1981 and to obtain in the event that the defendant is properly before the court.[25] In *Derby v Weldon*,[26] the Court of Appeal was of the view that the defendants were a corporation with sufficient know-how to put assets beyond the reach of the applicant even if the applicant was successful at trial. Therefore, the Court of Appeal held, exceptionally, that the freeze on the defendants' assets would be required to be global in scope for the applicant to be certain of receiving adequate compensation in the event of success at trial. In a comparative relaxation of the principle, the Court of Appeal in *Credit Suisse Fides Trust v Cuoghi*[27] held that the worldwide freezing injunction can be granted in circumstances in which 'it would be expedient', rather than being limited to a situation in which exceptional circumstances justify the order. In *JSC BTA Bank v Ablyazov (No 11)*[28] a bank resident in Kazakhstan had commenced litigation against its former chairman and majority shareholder alleging misappropriation of funds from the bank. The claimant bank sought a worldwide freezing order against the defendant. It was held by the Court of Appeal that the claimant had established a good arguable case at first instance and that on the balance of probabilities, on the information available at time, it was reasonable for the freezing order to have been made.

24.5 SEARCH ORDERS

The search order is a form of injunction which entitles the applicant to seize the defendant's property to protect evidence. The order will be made on the satisfaction of three criteria: there must be an 'extremely strong prima facie case'; the potential or actual damage must be 'very serious for the applicant'; and there must be clear evidence that the defendants have in their possession 'incriminating documents or things with a real possibility that they may destroy such material before an application could be made to the court'.[29] In *Anton Piller KG v Manufacturing Processes Ltd*,[30] Lord Denning MR held that such an order should be made 'only in an extreme case where there is grave danger of property being smuggled away or of vital evidence being destroyed'.

25 *Derby & Co Ltd v Weldon (Nos 3 and 4)* [1990] Ch 65, 93, *per* Neill LJ.
26 *Ibid.*
27 [1997] 3 All ER 724.
28 [2015] 1 WLR 1287.
29 *Anton Piller KG v Manufacturing Processes Ltd* [1976] Ch 55, 62.
30 [1976] Ch 55, 61.

24.6 CONFIDENCES IN EQUITY

24.6.1 Confidential information in equity and in tort

Since at least the 16th century, equity has sought to protect confidences – such as commercial secrets, intellectual property, secrets contained in private correspondence, and so on – by awarding injunctions to prevent the dissemination of confidential information. One of the leading cases in this area, *Prince Albert v Strange*,[31] involved Queen Victoria's husband suing Mr Strange when Strange had gained access to some etchings of paintings which Queen Victoria and her family had made of their private life, their pets and so on. Strange had intended to exhibit those etchings to a paying public and to publish a catalogue of the contents of that exhibition. It was held by the House of Lords that the contents of this catalogue (let alone the etchings themselves) were private information and that the publication of this private information would be prevented by a permanent injunction. The principle which was set down by Lord Cottenham was that the court will enjoin the publication of confidential information where that would constitute a 'breach of trust, confidence, or contract'. Some of the most significant cases have involved the publication of information passed between husband and wife, which is necessarily considered to be private. So, in *Duke of Argyll v Duchess of Argyll*[32] the Duke of Argyll was enjoined from publishing information about his wife's attitudes to sexual morals and the sanctity of marriage in a story in *The People* newspaper.[33]

In *Coco v AN Clark (Engineering) Ltd*[34] Megarry J held that there are three prerequisites in this area: the information must be confidential or have arisen in a confidential context; the information must have been passed in a context which suggested it was confidential; and the use of the information must be unauthorised and to the detriment of its owner. These principles were upheld in the Court of Appeal in *Imerman v Tchenguiz*,[35] when Lord Neuberger emphasised the difference between common law and equitable principles in this area. There a husband was entitled to have his personal data, which had been stored on a server which he used in common with his brother-in-law, kept in confidence and not used in divorce proceedings. The same approach to the protection of confidential information, such as wedding photographs at a private ceremony, was taken in *Douglas v Hello! Ltd*.[36]

24.6.2 The movement towards tort law in this context

Latterly, Lord Nicholls explained in *Campbell v MGN*[37] how the traditional equitable doctrine was now giving way in the context of privacy specifically to a 'tort of the misuse of private information' which would provide a remedy in damages but which would continue to provide a right to injunctions to prevent publication. Otherwise, the equitable doctrine continues in existence as before, as evidenced by *Imerman v Tchenguiz*.[38] It is in relation to this

---

31 (1849) 41 ER 1171.
32 [1967] Ch 302.
33 The verb which runs with the expression 'the grant of an injunction' is 'to enjoin': thus a court enjoins a person from continuing with an action.
34 [1969] RPC 41.
35 [2011] 2 WLR 592.
36 [2001] QB 967.
37 [2004] 2 AC 457.
38 [2011] 2 WLR 592.

tort and injunctions sought in relation to it that the issues relating to super-injunctions have arisen. The law on super-injunctions and injunctions to protect privacy are considered next.

24.7 SUPER-INJUNCTIONS AND PRIVACY

24.7.1 The law on super-injunctions

The public debate about super-injunctions

There was a media storm through 2010 and 2011 about the freedom of the Press to report whatever it chose to report. In particular there was great concern about the use of so-called 'super-injunctions' by the courts so as to prevent the Press from reporting not only the detail of legal proceedings but also from reporting the fact that an injunction had been awarded. After all, if the newspapers could not report a first story under the headline 'Alastair Hudson commits atrocity' then it would be nearly as good if the newspapers could report a second story under the headline 'Alastair Hudson obtains atrocious injunction to prevent reporting of what he gets up to'. So, the super-injunction prevented the newspapers from reporting the second story as well as the first: that is, the Press could not report the existence of the injunction as well as being prohibited from reporting the underlying story. Furthermore, the 'super-injunction' made the parties anonymous so that it was impossible to report the identities of the parties in any event. At the outset these cases were principally concerned with footballers, pop stars, television presenters and senior bankers trying to keep their extra-marital, sexual affairs secret. Frankly, if you had any interest in the finer things in life, it was impossible to care about many of the individual stories (except for the appalling one affecting the Dowler family whose daughter Milly had disappeared and some others affecting people's children); but the general issue about whether a free Press should be allowed to wallow about in the gutter like this, or whether this is a necessary price to pay for a free Press in a democratic country, is very important.

All of this issue became bound up, in the public debate at least, with a different scandal concerning the habit of journalists at News International and other corporations, and the private detectives whom they hired, to 'hack' into the voicemail accounts of celebrities and non-celebrities alike; something which was a criminal offence. (They often did this by assuming that these people would not change their PIN codes for their voicemail services from the factory setting of '1234' and thus were able to listen to their voicemails.) The Press argued that they had a right to freedom of expression which militated against super-injunctions; whereas the celebrities argued that they had a right to privacy, that the tabloid press was out of control and that super-injunctions were consequently necessary to protect their privacy. The allegation that the voicemail of a teenage murder victim, Milly Dowler, had been hacked into by journalists, and her messages deleted (with the tragic result that her parents thought she was still alive and had deleted her own messages) led to a step-change in the seriousness with which the general public began to take these issues. Suddenly it was clear that these issues affected ordinary people and not just those who made their fortunes from their exposure in the same Press which they now demonised.

On the one hand there were grave concerns about the way in which the Press operated (including examples of widespread illegal activity which have now led to several criminal convictions), and on the other hand there were concerns about the ability of the Press to report court proceedings freely (part of the long-established principle of 'open justice' in Britain) in the shadow of the courts creating super-injunctions. In turn, this led to the establishment of the 'Leveson Inquiry into the Culture, Practice and Ethics of the Press' in 2011 and, significantly for present purposes, the publication of a report by a committee empanelled by the Master of the Rolls titled the *Report of the Committee on Super-Injunctions* in 2011. As emerged from the latter report, all of the 18 cases involving applications for super-injunctions decided at that time had had reasoned judgments published by the relevant judges and all of those injunctions (where they had been granted) had been only temporary in nature. Therefore, the public debate about super-injunctions had appeared to be slightly overblown when it was alleged that the judges were silencing the Press.

24.7.2 The nature of super-injunctions

The term 'super-injunction' has been bandied around in the Press so as to cover a number of different legal devices. From a lawyer's perspective, it is important to distinguish between a 'super-injunction' and an 'anonymised injunction', and other forms of injunction. All super-injunctions are at root just interim injunctions (as discussed above) with the following added features described by the Master of the Rolls in the *Report of the Committee on Super-Injunctions* as being:

> an interim injunction which restrains a person from:
>
> (i)   publishing information which concerns the applicant and is said to be confidential or private; and
>
> (ii) publicising or informing others of the existence of the order and the proceedings (the 'super' element of the order).

So, a super-injunction is an injunction which prevents publication of information and which prevents the publication of the existence of such an injunction. It is important to remember that these are merely temporary injunctions pending a trial of the underlying issues. It is often argued by journalists that even a temporary delay in publication can, in effect, destroy a story by making it old news. Although, if such a story does quickly become old news then it is unclear to what extent it was an important story in the first place. The revelations about the behaviour of the vile Jimmy Savile and other public figures from the 1970s were decades old when they were published: a genuinely important story will not lose its significance with the passage of time.

Much of the public debate in the newspapers and in the media conflated super-injunctions with 'anonymised injunctions' where the parties' identities are kept anonymous. Journalists were concerned that if the parties to super-injunction litigation were kept anonymous then that would prevent them from publishing compelling stories. An 'anonymised injunction' was defined in the report as being:

> an interim injunction which restrains a person from publishing information which concerns the applicant and is said to be confidential or private where the names of either or both of the parties to the proceedings are not stated.

It is common to have anonymised proceedings in criminal and in family law matters. Most child law cases turn the parties' names into initials so that the identities of the parties remain secret. Consequently, the ability of the courts to anonymise the parties' names was not considered to be an issue in itself. The principles governing interim injunctions generally apply to super-injunctions and therefore the same balancing acts will be conducted in those cases as in any other. However, it is in relation to the area of privacy in particular that super-injunctions have acquired their own peculiar lustre; after all, the media is never more excited than when talking about the media or about celebrities, as will emerge in the following section.

24.7.3 The balancing act in relation to awards of injunctions for privacy

The debates about the law on super-injunctions and the law on other injunctions seeking to protect the applicant's privacy have therefore run together. The principles of equity in relation to confidences have given way in this particular context to the law of tort and, significantly, to the principles of human rights law which were incorporated into UK law by the Human Rights Act 1998. In *Murray v Express Newspapers plc*[39] Sir Anthony Clarke MR held that, in deciding whether or not to award an injunction to protect private information, the courts must balance the claimant's human right to respect for her private and family life under Art 8 of the European Convention on Human Rights with the competing right to free expression of newspapers and others under Art 10 of that Convention. As Lord Steyn made clear in the House of Lords in *In re S (A Child) (Identification: Restrictions on Publication)*,[40] neither the right to privacy nor the right to freedom of expression necessarily has supremacy over the other; instead the court must apply the concept of proportionality when deciding in any given context which of the two is to take priority in any given circumstances.

The procedure works as follows. It is only if there is a situation which calls the Art 8 right into existence will the court consider whether or not that should be outweighed on the facts by the Art 10 right to freedom of expression. What is clear is that the courts are prepared to allow a very broad range of material to be published as being in the public interest which might otherwise be thought of as mere tittle-tattle: for example, the 'news' that a supermodel had lied in interviews about having taken drugs when she was in fact receiving treatment for drug addiction in *Campbell v MGN*,[41] and the 'news' that the chief executive of a bank had had an extra-marital sexual relationship with a fellow employee of that bank in *Goodwin v NGN Ltd*.[42]

Therefore, the court must first consider whether or not the information is such that there will be a right under Art 8 at all on the facts of the case. If Art 8 does not apply, then no injunction nor any other remedy will be granted. In general terms, sexual activity (e.g. *Donald v Ntuli*[43]) and information relating to the existence of children outside a marriage would be the sorts of matters which would ordinarily fall within Art 8. The decided cases have tended to involve this sort of circumstance. However, where the applicant in *Hutcheson v News Group Newspapers Ltd*[44] sought to keep the existence of his second family secret, it was held that the fact that their existence was already publicly known would prevent Art 8

---

39 [2009] Ch 481.
40 [2005] 1 AC 593.
41 [2004] 2 AC 457.
42 [2011] EWHC 1437 (QB).
43 [2010] EWCA Civ 1276.
44 [2011] EWCA Civ 808.

from applying. In the leading case of *Campbell v MGN*[45] it was held that the fact that a supermodel was receiving treatment for drug addiction was something which would fall within Art 8 and require protection of her privacy. The court is likely to seek to protect children in general terms: as in *CTB v News Group Newspapers Ltd*[46] where a famous footballer sought to keep an adulterous relationship a secret in part to protect his children, or more importantly in *Re S* where the identity of a young boy was kept confidential when his mother was on trial for the murder of that young boy's brother.[47] This was also the approach where the Press took unauthorised photographs of a famous novelist's children in *Murray v Express Newspapers*.[48]

What is particularly important, of course, is that significant matters which impact on our political system (such as the MPs' expenses scandal disclosed first in the *Daily Telegraph*), or on our national security (as with the Wikileaks and Snowden disclosures), or on public safety (such as the allegations of dumping of toxic waste in the *Trafigua* case) are able to be made public. As part of the concern about super-injunctions, Paul Farrelly MP raised a question in Parliament about the dumping of toxic waste in the *Trafigua* case which, unbeknown to him or the Parliamentary authorities, had been made subject to a confidentiality order and an anonymised injunction. This raised the concern about politicians potentially misusing Parliamentary privilege (which allows MPs to raise any issue in Parliament without fear of litigation) in the future so as to publicise things which the courts had ordered should remain confidential. There is a clear principle that Parliament can and should debate anything which it considers to be appropriate. Nevertheless, to do so when a court has issued a temporary injunction requiring confidentiality is to interfere with the independence and freedom of the judiciary. These constitutional issues are considered in detail in the *Report of the Committee on Super-injunctions*. Ultimately, it is difficult to create an objectively correct answer to issues of this sort which are essentially political and which essentially depend on one's of point of view – assuming, that is, you can get through the miasma of nonsense in our free Press about celebrities' nocturnal activities so as to learn the facts on which you can make an informed opinion. And do note that this section has been completed without mentioning a single footballer: something which the newspapers have been unable to do when discussing this issue.

45 [2004] UKHL 22.
46 [2011] EWCA Civ 42.
47 [2005] 1 AC 593.
48 [2009] Ch 481.

Part 10

Academic themes in equity and trusts

Chapter 25

Essay: Restitution of unjust enrichment

CAPSULE SUMMARY

A claimant may bring an action for unjust enrichment where the defendant has been 'enriched' as a result of some 'unjust factor' at the claimant's expense. The academic work done on 'unjust enrichment' is a mooted replacement for equity. The judiciary have been less enthusiastic about the scholarly models. That unjust enrichment is a part of English law emerged from the decisions of the House of Lords in *Lipkin Gorman v Karpnale* and in *Woolwich v IRC*. The intention of its proponents is that this model should replace equity. However, its presence has been on the wane for some time. The role of unjust enrichment as the explanation for a variety of equitable doctrines has been rejected in relation to resulting trusts (in *Westdeutsche Landesbank v Islington*), tracing (in *Foskett v McKeown*), and knowing receipt (in *BCCI v Akindele*). The sole outpost of unjust enrichment thinking in a major field of equity has been as an explanation for subrogation – an old equitable doctrine – as held in *Guinness Mahon v Kensington*.

25.1 INTRODUCTION

25.1.1 The roots of restitution in England and Wales

The law of unjust enrichment presents a different way of thinking about private law from the traditional concepts of equity, contract, tort and so forth. As such it is attractive to many young scholars as an iconoclastic exercise in re-imagining the entire structure of private law. Unjust enrichment, in truth, only addresses a narrow range of doctrines which have existed in equity for centuries, and provides no explanation for the remainder. The philosophical underpinnings of equity – in Aristotle's *Ethics* and in the questions about conscience considered in Chapter 26 of this book – tie a much larger range of doctrines together than unjust enrichment ever could.

A claim in unjust enrichment operates on the following, very simple basis. A claimant may bring an action for unjust enrichment where the defendant has been 'enriched' as a result of some 'unjust factor' at the claimant's expense. The unjust factors are presented in a list compiled by Birks and Chambers in the *Restitution Research Resource*;[1] and other lists are presented in other publications by other academics: the contents of each list are hotly debated among the academics who belong to this 'restitutionist' school. They include well-known actions such as mistake, undue influence, duress and so forth, which are said to trigger a claim for unjust enrichment. The responses which the law should give are also listed. By way of illustration, it is said that a resulting trust could be understood as identifying an enrichment in the defendant's hands in the form of an item of property which, for example, the defendant had acquired by mistake, and then pulling that property (i.e. the enrichment) back into the claimant's hands. However, this model of the resulting trust was rejected by the House of Lords in *Westdeutsche Landesbank v Islington*.[2] The law on tracing, resulting trust, subrogation and so forth has been analysed through this lens, as discussed in earlier chapters. The question is whether unjust enrichment thinking offers any better answers to these questions than does equity at present.

25.1.2 The roots of unjust enrichment thinking

Methodology

The methodology which Birks and the restitutionists used is known as 'taxonomy'. In the natural sciences, a taxonomy is an ordering of the scientists' observations into scientific categories. In biology, for example, the various types of moths are organised within the insects, are differentiated from butterflies, are organised into sub-categories depending on size, number of wings, and so forth. However, when legal academics use a 'taxonomy' they are not observing things as they exist in the natural world. Instead, they are creating an ideology of the way in which they believe the law should be re-ordered so as to fit in with their fundamentalist beliefs in order. For 'order' is the principal belief of the restitutionist. In that sense, they are the inheritors of the mantle of Lord Eldon and Lord Hardwicke in their suspicion of equity from earlier centuries (as discussed in Chapter 1).

---

1 Birks and Chambers, 1995.
2 [1996] AC 669.

For all that the restitutionists urge pragmatism and order on us all, it is worth remembering the philosopher Friedrich Nietzsche's remark that:[3]

> It is the powerful who made the names of things into law, and among the powerful it is the greatest artists in abstraction who created the categories.

The restitutionists would like to think that creating this list of categories is an entirely technical activity. However, creating the categories is itself an ideological act. By excluding from the list of unjust factors claims in family law, claims for injunctions in equity, and claims involving company law, the restitutionists are making an ideological decision (or omission). In truth, equity does this work much better with its centuries of principle which react to the factual situations which face judges in practice. Consequently, in equity a web of principle is bound to ideas of unconscionability and so forth by those authorities, and thus the law on injunctions, trusts and so forth are all brought together. The restitutionists are artists in abstraction, not certainty, when they create their categories. The greater problem which they face is that the members of their school are involved in a seemingly perpetual argument about the content of the categories (on a technical, not a theoretical, level). It is unlikely that the judiciary will jettison centuries of precedent when the advocates of the new theory cannot agree what their new theory means.

The core of unjust enrichment and the scope of this essay

The basis of unjust enrichment is straightforward.[4] The claimant may bring an action for 'unjust enrichment' in circumstances in which the defendant has been enriched as a result of some unjust factor (such as a mistake, undue influence or the failure of a contract) at the claimant's expense. Some of the problems are caused by the restitutionists' own debates among themselves about what the unjust factors should be, what an enrichment is, and so forth. Like a group of terriers worrying at a piece of fabric, after a while the original cloth looks nothing like it did at the start. Other problems arise when the theory meets existing legal rules and principles, or when external questions are brought to bear: such as the key objection to the first generation unjust enrichment model that was raised in *Westdeutsche Landesbank v Islington* – what happens if one of the parties is insolvent? The pattern which our discussion is the following: first, we shall examine the differences between Goff and Birks in thinking about restitutionary questions; second, we shall consider the supposed roots of unjust enrichment thinking in Roman law and in older English authorities; and, third, we shall examine the three generations of Birksian unjust enrichment thinking.

25.2 COMPETING MODELS OF UNJUST ENRICHMENT

25.2.1 The differences in outline

There are two competing models of unjust enrichment thinking which are significant in England and Wales (there is simply not space to consider the thinking in other jurisdictions, especially the USA). The principal academic model is that advanced by Birks and the Oxford

---

3 Nietzsche, *The Will to Power*, para 513.
4 Virgo, 1999.

restitution school. The principal judicial model (which was also published in book form[5]) was that propounded by Lord Robert Goff in his brilliant judicial career. This section considers the differences between those two.

25.2.2 Lord Robert Goff

Birks' model of unjust enrichment was more dogmatic than that suggested by Goff and Jones in their book *The Law of Restitution*. Birks had no time for philosophical debates about justice in the courtroom. Instead, the unjust factors are simply listed. If your claim is not on the list, then you are not getting in.[6] Conceptual neatness and order are his watchwords.

By contrast, in his judgments, Lord Goff demonstrated an affection for 'justice' in the broadest sense: not a generalised justice but rather a reasoned sense of right and wrong. Examples of his approach which we have met in this book are the judgments in *Tinsley v Milligan*[7] and in *Westdeutsche Landesbank v Islington* (both discussed in Chapter 11). Lord Goff was in the grand Aristotelian tradition of equity in the sense that he was always in search of a just, principled result and not simply an arbitrary one which followed the law obediently. In *Tinsley v Milligan*, Lord Goff would not agree with the majority in finding a resulting trust interest in a house for someone who had been a party to a criminal conspiracy to commit housing benefit fraud. He preferred the high-minded principle that one cannot have the benefit of an equitable doctrine if one has acted unconscionably. In *Westdeutsche Landesbank v Islington*, where unjust enrichment thinking had its most fateful hour when the majority chose to continue with traditional equitable concepts of conscience in the law of trusts, Lord Goff said that it was not the role of judges to debate the theoretical nature of the law. Instead, he said, 'the function of your Lordships' House is simply to decide the questions at issue before it in the present case'.

It was in the leading case of *Lipkin Gorman v Karpnale Ltd*[8] in the House of Lords that Lord Goff was able to stake out territory for restitution on grounds of unjust enrichment. That judgment recognised the existence of unjust enrichment in English law but it did not presume to set out a textbook for the way in which those principles would work. Lord Goff preferred to allow the law to develop, rather than stipulating in advance how the details should work. For example, when confirming that a defence of change of position (as discussed in Chapter 19) should exist in English law, Lord Goff said the following:

> . . . if a thief steals my money and pays it to a third party who gives it away to charity, that third party should have a good defence to an action for money had and received. In other words, bona fide change of position should of itself be a good defence in such cases as these . . . I am most anxious that, in recognising this defence to actions of restitution, nothing should be said at this stage to inhibit the development of the defence on

---

5 Goff and Jones, 1966.

6 That sentence was meant to be a play on the famous nightclub bouncer's line: 'If your name's not on the list, you're not getting in'. Maybe the joke doesn't work if I have to explain it.

7 [1994] 1 AC 340.

8 [1991] 2 AC 548.

a case by case basis, in the usual way . . . At present I do not wish to state the principle any less broadly than this: that the defence is available to a person whose position has so changed that it would be inequitable in all the circumstances to require him to make restitution, or alternatively to make restitution in full.

Two things are clear from this important passage which creates the defence of change of position in English law. First, while Lord Goff was imaginative enough to create new doctrines as a judge, he was nevertheless sufficiently pragmatic to leave those doctrines broadly stated so that they could react to circumstances in future cases. This is the opposite of the Birksian model of unjust enrichment which wants to rigidify everything from the start. Second, Lord Goff was prepared to use terms such as 'inequitable' when setting out these 'restitutionary' principles. For him, this was a matter of evolution in the debates about common law and equity, as opposed to the Birksian revolution.

25.2.3 Birks's works

By contrast, Birks had no truck with ideas of 'justice' in the general sense of that word. The concept of '*unjust* enrichment' in his scheme meant a list of unjust factors which were set out in advance in a rigid taxonomy,[9] such that the law would not respond to injustice in general terms but rather only where there were 'unjust factors' of the sort which appeared on that list. That list, as set out below, involved traditional doctrines of English law like mistake, duress and so forth. There was certainly not to be any general principle in Birks's scheme of the sort that is found in equity. The idea of 'conscience' as an organising principle was an anathema to Birks because he considered it to be too vague. The Birksian model, and its roots in Roman law, are considered next.

25.3 A CHRONOLOGY OF UNJUST ENRICHMENT THINKING

25.3.1 Introduction

The principal objective of English model of unjust enrichment is to create order: in particular a conceptual clarity so that it is possible to know exactly which event gives rise to which claim and calls for which remedy. This conceptual clarity was modelled on Roman law.

25.3.2 The Roman roots of unjust enrichment

The Roman Emperor Justinian reigned during the introduction of a code of law which divided between 'actions, people, and things'. In this spirit of orderliness, and to emulate *Justinian's Institutes* in Roman law, Birks suggested the following reorganisation of English private law into the three categories of consent, wrongs and unjust enrichment.[10] However, there are problems with the use of Justinian as a role model. First, Justinian's *Pandects* were an important source of equity on which 19th century equity scholars like

---

9   Where a 'taxonomy', as was explained in Chapter 1, is the sort of ordering commonly undertaking by biologists
      to organise living things into different categories and sub-categories for a better understanding of their natures.
10   Birks and McLeod, 1987; Birks, 1997.

Professor Story relied.[11] Indeed, Roman law used the concept of *aequitas* ('equity') to achieve equity in many cases. It should be remembered, the Romans borrowed largely from Greeks like Aristotle.

Second, and far more salaciously, Justinian was a swine of the first water. The celebrated Roman historian Procopius is the principal source for what we know about Justinian, from his book *The Secret History*. In *The Secret History*, Justinian and his wife Theodora are revealed to be corrupt, lascivious and deeply wicked. Far from being an upholder of the law, Justinian received bribes from wealthy murderers not to prosecute them, he created new criminal offences to persecute his enemies, he took bribes in relation to land disputes, and so on. There was no rule of law in Justinian's empire. As Procopius tells us:[12]

> The maintenance of established institutions meant nothing to [Justinian]: endless innovations were his constant preoccupation. In a word, he was a great destroyer of well-established institutions.[13] . . . No law or contract retained any force on the secure basis of the established order, but everything turned to growing violence and confusion, and the government was indistinguishable from a tyranny – not, however, a stable tyranny but one that changed every day and was forever starting afresh.

So, the *Institutes* which are so prized for their order concealed endless innovations in the law (exactly in the way that restitutionists criticise equity) and that same law was implemented in a tyrannical way. The French essayist Michel de Montaigne understood the limits of Justinian's *Institutes*:[14]

> I hardly agree, therefore, with the opinion of that man [Justinian] who tried to curb the authority of his judges by a multitude of laws, thus cutting their meat up for them. He did not understand that there is as much liberty and latitude in the interpretation as in the making of them.

It is not enough to create a rigid scheme of rules like a child assembles Lego buildings. The real work comes in the application of those rules and principles in practice. That is something for which equity's principles are better suited.

25.3.3 The organisation of unjust enrichment based on *Moses v Macferlan*

Any new theory needs to capture the *zeitgeist* or it needs to show that it has historical roots. The use of Roman law, albeit one of the most unlikely emperors, was a part of that project. Another key part of unjust enrichment thinking was the list of actions set out by Lord Mansfield in *Moses v Macferlan*[15] because Birks used it to supply him with a large part of his list of unjust factors and actions. That case related to a claim for money had and received (as

---

11 Story, 1839.
12 Procopius, 2007, 31.
13 Procopius, 2007.
14 Montaigne, 1958.
15 (1760) 2 Burr 1005.

did *Westdeutsche Landesbank v Islington*). Lord Mansfield CJ listed some of the key heads of claim as follows:

> The action for money had and received, an equitable action to recover money which the defendant ought not in justice to keep . . . lies for money paid by mistake; or upon a consideration which happens to fail; or for money got through imposition (express or implied;) or extortion; or oppression; or an undue advantage taken of the plaintiff's situation, contrary to laws made for the protection of persons under those circumstances. In one word, the gist of this kind of action is, that the defendant, upon the circumstances of the case, is obliged by the ties of natural justice and equity to refund the money.

Unjust enrichment scholars use the list of actions in that passage (mistake, failure of consideration, and so forth) as constituting the basis for their taxonomy. Significantly, however, this action is described as being 'equitable' and as arising on the basis of 'natural justice and equity' as opposed to a taxonomic list of actions. Therefore, even this root case is actually adhering closely to equity and its traditional methodology, as opposed to the Birksian scheme. It is the bedrock of restitution's taxonomy, and yet it is a decision predicated clearly on equity. It is only if you fail to read what the judge actually said in *Moses v Macferlan* that you can kid yourself that it has something to do with unjust enrichment.

25.4 THE COMPONENT PARTS OF 'RESTITUTION OF UNJUST ENRICHMENT'

25.4.1 Models of unjust enrichment at work

The component parts of 'restitution of unjust enrichment'

The classic three-step test in the traditional restitution model operated as follows: there must have been an enrichment taken by the defendant; that enrichment must have been made at the claimant's expense; and that enrichment must have arisen as a result of some unjust factor. It is said that restitution is concerned to reverse an enrichment of the defendant where that enrichment has been made as a result of some unjust factor. Reversal is achieved by the 'subtraction' of the enrichment from the defendant. In short the claimant is entitled to say: 'You have made an enrichment at my expense, so give me that enrichment.' The form of the enrichment may therefore either be the acquisition of a specific piece of property, or it may be the acquisition of some cash value. The problem for restitution lawyers is therefore whether the remedy ought to be personal or proprietary.

The unjust factors are to be identified from a list of unjust factors and are *not* to be identified by the courts when they consider it to be appropriate by reference to some general moral principle. So, you might ask: do we have a complete list of the unjust factors? The answer is: no. Birks and Chambers took the view that there were 43 of them.[16] However, each unjust

---

16 Birks and Chambers, 1997.

enrichment scholar has their own view as to the number of unjust factors there are. One account suggests that there is only one unjust factor which is to be identified by reference to a general principle.[17]

On this model, the law of restitution creates a new right, rather than giving effect ex post facto to a pre-existing right. That right is generated by the receipt of the unjust enrichment with the effect of depriving the defendant of the value received at the plaintiff's expense. In Birks' terms: 'Restitution is that active or creative response at the moment of enrichment.'[18] That means that the rights would only come into existence at the date of the court order prospectively, which was an idea that was rejected by the House of Lords in *Westdeutsche Landesbank v Islington* in relation to constructive and resulting trusts.

In the House of Lords in *Lipkin Gorman v Karpnale*[19] it was held by Lord Goff, when considering the liability of a casino for receiving money from on a solicitor which he had taken from accounts which were held on trust for the firm's clients, that:

> I accept that the solicitors' claim [for money had and received] in the present case is founded upon the unjust enrichment of the club, and can only succeed if, in accordance with the principles of the law of restitution, the club was indeed unjustly enriched at the expense of the solicitors.

At this moment, it became clear that unjust enrichment in some form was a part of English law.

Specific remodelling of equitable doctrines by unjust enrichment

The goal of unjust enrichment scholarship has been to re-explain existing doctrines so that they fit into the restitutionary framework. A large part of that work has attempted to re-model equitable doctrines so as to fit into the new theory. The restitutionary understanding of resulting trusts was set out by Chambers in *Resulting Trusts*.[20] The suggestion was that resulting trusts would come into existence when an enrichment had been taken as a result of some unjust factor, at the claimant's expense. The resulting trust would then carry the equitable interest in that property back to the claimant. However, the House of Lords in *Westdeutsche Landesbank v Islington*[21] rejected this theory.

The restitutionary understanding of the law of tracing was set out by Smith in *The Law of Tracing*. In essence, tracing would become one doctrine (instead of dividing between common law and equity) and it would operate to carry property rights back to a claimant when a defendant had received an enrichment, in the form of property rights, at the claimant's expense as a result of some unjust factor. Again, resulting trusts would be the principal remedy. However, the House of Lords in *Foskett v McKeown*[22] held that tracing is part of the law of property and not part of the law of unjust enrichment.

---

17 Meier and Zimmerman, 1999.
18 *Ibid*, 14.
19 [1991] 2 AC 548.
20 Chambers, 1997.
21 [1996] AC 669.
22 [2001] 1 AC 102.

The restitutionary understanding of subrogation was set out by Mitchell in *The Law of Subrogation*.[23] In essence, the purpose of subrogation was to act as a remedy where the defendant was unjustly enriched at the claimant's expense by using property to discharge a debt. The House of Lords in *Guinness Mahon v Kensington*[24] did hold that subrogation was a restitutionary device, contrary to centuries of authority which saw subrogation as an equitable device which came into existence when justice required it.

Birks claimed that knowing receipt was a doctrine which effected unjust enrichment in some circumstances so as to effect restitution of property which had been transferred away from a trust in breach of that trust.[25] However, unconscionable receipt actually comes into existence not to effect restitution but rather to compensate the beneficiaries for the loss that they suffer as a result of the recipient's participation in the breach of trust by knowingly receiving that property. It does not come into existence to disgorge an enrichment from the defendant; but rather it comes into existence to compensate the beneficiaries. It has nothing to do with unjust enrichment.

25.4.2 The purely technical meaning of the word 'unjust'

A claim for unjust enrichment begins with an enrichment, and then requires that there was one of the 'unjust factors' on the list of unjust factors in play at the time. While one might expect that a theory of '*unjust* enrichment' has at its heart a moral project, in truth its goals are entirely positivist, and so not concerned with morals. Birks was clear on this point:[26]

> 'Unjust' here is technical. An enrichment is unjust if the circumstances are such that the law requires its recipient to make restitution.

This is a particularly circular sentence. How do we know if something is unjust? Well, if the recipient must make restitution. And when must they make restitution? When their enrichment is unjust. So, how do we know if something is unjust? Oh. Look. We are back where we started.

Beyond that logical feedback loop, one of the more difficult aspects of the restitution project is its determined amorality and its equally determined refusal to explain what its philosophical underpinnings are. Instead, what restitutionists present is an insistence on order for its own sake. As Birks put it:[27]

> We are not all as brave as Cranmer but like him we know it is better to burn than to live in a world which has abandoned rationality.

Of course, we are not sure that this is true. Particularly when it is not rationality which has been abandoned, but rather an obsession with having everything in straight lines. As Ralph

---

23 Mitchell, 1994.
24 [1998] 2 All ER 272.
25 Birks and Pretto, 2002.
26 Birks, 2000, 6.
27 *Ibid*, 8.

Waldo Emerson put it, 'a foolish consistency is the hobgoblin of little minds'. To use open-textured moral principles to decide cases on a case-by-case basis in accordance with precedent and in a way that reflects constantly on the meaning and application of those moral principles, is not a failure to think. Instead, it is a different way of thinking.

25.4.3 The final phase: 'Analogous to a mistake'

Birks had embarked on the third version of his theory before his untimely death. The third version of Birks's scheme provides that the law on unjust enrichment operates in relation to any set of facts which is 'analogous to mistake'.[28] This version has moved from taxonomic certainty into metaphysics. It was unclear what was meant by the idea that something must be 'analogous to a mistake': how analogous? In what way? What sort of mistake? Behind Birks lay a veritable bar fight made up of unjust enrichment scholars arguing over the number of unjust factors which could give rise to a right to unjust enrichment, the viability of the so-called 'quadration thesis', what exactly might be meant 'by analogy with mistake'; whether a remedy can achieve restitution or whether restitution is itself the remedy; and other intellectual niceties. Restitution is not neat: rather it is bedevilled by the uncertainties which are all part and parcel of any properly functioning system of private law – namely, the need to reach the best result on the facts of any given case.

25.4.4 The retreat from restitution

The courts have begun to mix restitutionary concepts with equitable concepts in a way that suggests they are considered to be the same thing, especially in recent cases on tracing. The general principle on which the Court of Appeal in *Niru Battery Manufacturing Co v Milestone Trading Ltd* has recognised the operation of the defence of change of position is by reference to 'whether on the facts of a particular case it would in all the circumstances be inequitable or unconscionable, and thus unjust, to allow the recipient of money paid under a mistake of fact to deny restitution to the payer'.[29] Sedley LJ has expressed the same process in terms that the courts 'are to decide whether it is equitable to uphold the defence' of change of position.[30]

What is clear from these dicta is that the defence of change of position is being applied on the basis of equitable doctrines.[31] References to 'the doctrine of restitution' notwithstanding, there is no explanation of these principles by reference to unjust enrichment on this model. Similarly, in *Dextra Bank and Trust Co v Bank of Jamaica*, the keynote of the defence of change of position has become its transformation into a general, equitable form of defence which is:

> founded on a principle of justice designed to protect the defendant from a claim to restitution in respect of a benefit received by him in circumstances in which it would be inequitable to pursue that claim, or to pursue it in full.[32]

---

28 Birks, 2005.
29 *Niru Battery Manufacturing Co and Another v Milestone Trading Ltd and Others* [2003] EWCA Civ 1446, para 162, *per* Clarke LJ.
30 *Ibid*, para 192, *per* Sedley LJ.
31 See *Credit Suisse (Monaco) SA v Attar* [2004] EWHC 374 (Comm), para [98], *per* Gross J.
32 *Dextra Bank and Trust Co v Bank of Jamaica* [2002] 1 All ER (Comm) 193, para 38.

Thus, restitution – in a general conception of recovery or return of property – has become equated with general notions of equity and as such need not be based on restitution of unjust enrichment.[33] Having understood the limits which the courts are now placing on the theory of unjust enrichment, we shall turn to consider how conscience works in equity.

33 Smith, 1997.

Chapter 26

Essay: The concept of conscience in equity

CAPSULE SUMMARY

Most of the problems with the discussion of conscience in the case law arise from a perception that a conscience is subjective. A conscience is an objectively constituted part of the psyche through which society's values are imported into the individual's mind. The model of conscience that is advanced by Freud and Jung in psychoanalysis, by Kant in philosophy, and even in the form of etymology of the word 'conscience', all perceive it as being outside the conscious mind and as being comprised of objective elements. If the conscience is objective in that sense then it is an appropriate measuring device for assessing the behaviour of defendants.

26.1 INTRODUCTION

26.1.1 The development of conscience from theology

The conscience-based equity that is used in England and Wales grew through the centuries from a theological idea about the monarch's conscience and the need for individual defendants to cleanse their consciences through the courts, into a very important part of our system of law (governing pension funds, ownership of the home and so forth) which is based on a moral concept of good conscience in the treatment of other people and their property. This chapter tells the story of equity. It is a story about archbishops and their relation to their Queen, it is a story about lesbian architects, and it is a story about a little wooden puppet who just wanted to be a real boy.

26.1.2 The golden metwand versus the Lesbian rule

In Chapter 1 we considered the development of equity in outline.[1] We learned that judges like Chief Justice Fortescue were clear that in the early courts of equity 'we argue conscience not the law', meaning that only equitable principles and discretion were to be used, not common law rules.[2] By contrast, Lord Coke, the leading common lawyer at the beginning of the 17th century, took the opposite view because he thought that:

> all causes should be measured by the golden and straight metwand of the law, and not the incertain and crooked cord of discretion.[3]

A metwand is a metal measuring rod which is entirely straight and which gives entirely predictable measurements. Its opposite is the 'crooked cord of discretion'. Like a coil of damp rope left lying on a filthy floor, this crooked cord is said to be useless in giving predictable measurements because it is not straight and regular like the metwand of the common law. Coke wanted to rid English law of equity entirely and to replace it with the golden metwand of the common law.

Meanwhile, the adherents to equity are from a different party. The early judges in the courts of equity[4] were ecclesiastics. They took their inspiration from different places: from the Bible and from Aristotle. Let us think about God first. Principally, the ecclesiastics' motivations were religious and the conscience which they espoused was a sublime conscience derived from God (with a capital 'G'). As Cardinal Newman described this process in the Christian tradition centuries later, 'the conscience is the aboriginal vicar of Christ'.[5] That peculiar expression means that, once an individual receives their religious teaching in infancy, that teaching builds up the attitudes in their conscience which controls or judges their behaviour throughout life. Ultimately, we are all judged by God, in the Christian tradition, and the conscience was considered to be the voice of God inside the individual's mind. Those courts would use torture to wring confessions from defendants in the Tudor period. Literally, the clerics who oversaw this system of so-called justice considered that the individual's conscience was in danger if they did not confess, and therefore to cleanse their conscience (and so prepare them for the afterlife) they must be brought to contrition. If

---

1 Section 1.1.3.
2 Mitch 31 Hen VI, Fitz Abr, *Subpena*, pl 23, cited by Baker, 2002, 108.
3 Coke, 4 Inst. 41. In *Keighley's Case* (1609) 10 Co. Rep. 139a he suggested that discretion should be 'limited and bound with the rule of reason and law'.
4 There were several such courts in England aside from the Court of Chancery but it is on that court which we shall concentrate.
5 It is 'aboriginal' in the sense of wandering wherever the individual goes, and it is a 'vicar' in the sense of ministering between god and the individual.

that necessitated torture, then so be it. It is this sense that the early courts talked of acting *in personam* against the conscience of the individual.

As the clouds of these dark ages began to lift, the idea of conscience began to change. Lord Chancellors like Sir Christopher Hatton were known as 'the Keeper of the Queen's Conscience'. Bishops who were Lord Chancellors during the reign of Henry VIII administered the monarch's conscience through the bureaucracy of the Chancery and also in an ecclesiastical role. As judgments in Chancery cases began to be reported more reliably (although the note-taking in cases before the advent of formal law reports in the 19th century remained patchy) the focus of the idea of conscience began to shift to the unethical conduct of the defendant according to categories of behaviour which the courts considered to be unacceptable in earlier cases – such as theft, fraud and undue influence – and away from purely religious ideas of conscience.

There is a line of judges from Lord Nottingham (especially in cases like *Cook v Fountain* in 1676[6]) through to Lord Eldon (especially in cases like *Morice v Bishop of Durham*[7] and *Gee v Pritchard* in 1818[8]) who sought to make equity more certain. Instead of allowing the idea of conscience to be entirely at the whim of the individual judge in a court of equity, a system of precedents and of principles and rules on which the courts acted was introduced. Lord Eldon considered that he would be embarrassed if he left his post as Lord Chancellor with a perception behind him that he had allowed equity to continue to be comprised of discretionary doctrines. All was not perfect, however. By the time we reach Lord Chancellor Cottenham in the late Victorian period, we encounter a Court of Chancery which has become legendary for its delays and its ponderous approach to thought as well as litigation. Lords Eldon and Cottenham would sometimes take an unconscionably long time to deliver judgment (meaning that some litigants had to wait years after their trial had finished to find out who had won, and whether or not they could get their hands on any property), and even had to order cases to be retried because they had simply forgotten the facts by the time they finally sat down to write their judgments. It was Lord Cottenham who was satirised as being that 'most floundering and pestilential of sinners' who sits at the centre of the fog at the opening of Charles Dickens' *Bleak House*. It was this Lord Chancellor (many of whose judgments are indeed very poorly reasoned) who is the *animus grise* at the centre of one of the greatest novels in the English language.

So, the reformist Lord Chancellors in the 19th century were also some of the most inefficient judges of all time. They left us with some clearer rules at the heart of express trusts law, for example, but they were hellishly ineffective from the perspective of solving the disputes that came before them. At this point, we should reflect on the debates which were being conducted about equity between the 16th century and the 19th century because they are exactly the same debates that we are having in equity and trusts law in the 21st century, except that they were conducted in much more colourful language.

Let us wind the tape back to Lord Coke at the turn of the 17th century, espousing the virtues of a common law that was a golden metwand (not just a metwand, but a golden one!) as compared to the crooked cord of equity. The equity which was espoused by Lord Chancellor Ellesmere in his judgment in the *Earl of Oxford's Case* in 1615 was one which

---

6   (1676) 3 Swan 585.
7   (1805) 10 Ves 522.
8   (1818) 2 Swan 402.

was based on Aristotle's model of equity in his *Ethics*[9] when he held that 'men's actions are so diverse and infinite that it is impossible to make a general law which may aptly meet with every particular and not fail in some circumstances'.[10] This was the reason Aristotle gave for equity being 'superior' to formal systems of justice like the common law, because common law and statutory rules are drafted for the 'universal' case and will therefore generate injustices (or, 'errors') in individual cases in which their application seems unfair.

Importantly, Aristotle had also thought through the sort of complaint that Lord Coke would raise centuries later about the common law being a golden metwand which would be an ideal sort of ruler for measuring out justice. The problem with having a hard, metal rule is that it is useless for measuring anything that is not dead straight. As Aristotle said, when explaining the benefits of equity over formal justice:

> An irregular object has a rule of irregular shape, like the leaden rule of Lesbian architecture: just as this rule is not rigid but is adapted to the shape of the stone . . .

The architects on the island of Lesbos were famous for their intricate stonework. The type of rule they used to measure stone which would be carved into intricate shapes was made of a malleable form of lead which was of a definite length and which could be manipulated so as to follow the irregular shape of the stone so as to measure exacts lengths and dimensions. In England, builders still used to refer to a 'Lesbian rule' of this sort in the 20th century.[11] A rigid metwand would have been useless. So, Aristotle considered that equity was like this malleable ruler: it could be fashioned so that it would fit the circumstances perfectly, as opposed to a dead straight ruler which would only be appropriate in limited types of situation. Aristotle used this metaphor as an explanation of why equity would sometimes be 'superior' to formal codes of justice:[12]

> . . . equity, although just, is better than a kind of justice . . . it is a rectification of law in so far as law is defective on account of its generality. This in fact is also the reason why everything is not regulated by law [as opposed to equity]: it is because there are some cases that no law can be framed to cover, so that they require a special ordinance [or judgment]. An irregular object has a rule of irregular shape, like the leaden rule of Lesbian architecture: just as this rule is not rigid but is adapted to the shape of the stone, so the ordinance [or judgment] is framed to fit the circumstances.

To create a balanced system of civil law in England and Wales, we need to balance out a system of formal, predictable rules on the one hand (at common law, in statute and in most of express trusts law) with a system of equitable principles which will permit the courts to reach just outcomes on the other hand (in equity). It was also Aristotle's view that the two systems should work together to ensure that justice is achieved for the individual because if the legal

---

9 The same concepts of equity appear in both the *Nicomachean Ethics* and in the *Eudemian Ethics*.

10 (1615) 1 Ch Rep 1, at 6.

11 The sexual meaning of 'lesbian', which is the one you had running round your internet-addled mind, is a much later sense of the word.

12 *Ibid.*

system as a whole is predicated on the need for justice, then there does not need to be conflict between the common law and equity because they should both be directed ultimately at that same goal.[13] To belabour the Aristotelian metaphor one last time: in architecture, rigid rules will not always work because the thing that is being measured will not always be straight and simple; just as in law, rigid rules will not always work because the thing that is being judged will not always conform to rigid patterns.

26.1.3 The crooked timber of humanity

As the philosopher Immanuel Kant put it: 'from the crooked timber of humanity no straight thing was ever made'.[14] This is true of litigation and the problems that real life throws up against the legal system: because nothing straight will emerge from people, we cannot assume that our laws can always operate in entirely straight lines. Importantly, I am not advocating that we abandon rationality and that we abandon having rules. Far from it. Even within equity, the predictability of the certainties in the creation of express trusts is necessary to enable people to know whether they have created a valid trust. Laws give structure to society and their enforcement gives us a sense of the mores of the society in which we live. However, in such a rapidly changing world, there is necessarily a need to build some flexibility into our justice system so that we can know that it is generating justice for each of our citizens. In the modern world, we are not prepared to accept that some individuals may suffer harm or loss because the greater goal of protecting the sanctity of our legal system requires it. Instead, individuals require that they are treated as being individually valuable (just as Kant required us to think of individual human beings as being ends in themselves and not just a means to achieve other ends). If we are to treat individuals as being ends in themselves then we need an area of our law which can award injunctions or award proprietary estoppel remedies or recognise the existence of constructive trusts where there has been unconscionable behaviour. There is a need for equity.

26.1.4 The development of an English equity

The development of the specifically English equity, building on Aristotle's theory, was signalled with the use of the idea of conscience. As Lord Ellesmere put it in the *Earl of Oxford's Case*:[15]

> The office of the Chancellor is to correct men's consciences for frauds, breach of trusts, wrongs and oppressions, of what nature soever they be, and to soften and mollify the extremity of the law . . .

The significance of the court 'correcting' someone's conscience is to be found in the idea, mentioned above, that the early courts would extract confessions from defendants in some cases through force so as to cleanse, and thus correct, their consciences. Things are a little less visceral for defendants today, although the impact of their lives of winning or losing

---

13   *Cowper v Cowper* 2 PW 752, *per* Sir Joseph Jekyll: 'The discretion which is exercised here, is to be governed by the rules of law and equity, which are not to oppose, but each in its turn to be subservient to the other.'
14   Kant, 1784, proposition 6.
15   *Ibid.*

cases in equity can be equally significant: they can lose their homes or their pensions. At least there is no question of the court being able to remove their souls.

26.2 THE MEANING OF 'CONSCIENCE'

26.2.1 Defining 'conscience'

Moral theory and conscience

The debate between the commentators and judges on equity fell into two halves, which is still the case today. On one side were the enthusiasts for equity. Here we find Ashburner's *Equity*, a very influential practitioner's textbook on equity from the early 20th century, which identifies Aristotle's *Ethics* as being the source of English equity. Lord Chief Justice Mansfield was a great proponent of equitable ways of thinking being incorporated into the common law so as to achieve justice – a presaging of the modern debates about fusing the concepts of law and equity. There are judges like Lord Denning who prized discretionary and creative law-making; albeit that this sometimes exposed some undesirable attitudes (for example his thoughts on the differences between men and women, discussed in Chapter 17) which in turn bring into relief the potential dangers of allowing judges too much discretion on some occasions.

Examples of the modern beneficiaries of this sort of open-textured equity, using discretionary doctrines, were the claimant in *Baker v Baker* whose pressing *need* for nursing care was prioritised by the Court of Appeal over potentially useless property rights, and the litigants in *Jennings v Rice* who saw a testatrix's unpaid helpers being rewarded with £200,000 but who also saw the intended owners of her large house receive that property by means of her will. This flexibility in proprietary estoppel cases and in cases relating to the home (discussed in Chapters 13 and 15) is mirrored in the creativity in identifying appropriate remedies in tracing cases (discussed in Chapter 20) ranging from liens, charges and subrogation through to constructive trusts. The law on dishonest assistance and unconscionable receipt has demonstrated a creativity in providing compensation for breaches of trust. The endless creativity of this open-textured, imaginative equity has proved to be a boon in commercial as well as family cases.

On the other side of the debate were ranged a large number of commentators. So great was the antipathy to equity as a concept that Richard Francis was forced to begin his *Maxims of Equity*, published in 1739,[16] by confronting the assertion that decisions of courts of equity were 'uncertain and precarious' because they were 'not . . . bound by any established Rules or Orders'. His answer to this charge was that conscience would not cause judges to act arbitrarily but rather that each of those judges would 'be guided by that infallible Monitor within his own Breast': that is, his conscience. However, that defence almost makes the point for the other side: if we think of the judge as simply looking to his own conscience then doesn't that make equity a very subjective field? Remarkably, Chief Justice Hale said when giving judgment in *Rosecarrick v Barton* in 1672 that 'By the growth of equity on equity the heart of the common law is eaten out.'[17] So, the Chief Justice considered that equity's creativity

16 Francis, 1739.
17 (1672) 1 Ch Cas 217, 219.

was destroying the common law: eating out its heart. That is a very aggressive metaphor for a judge to use about other judges.

The meaning of 'conscience'

The etymology of the English word 'conscience' is a combination of the word 'con', meaning 'with', and the word 'science', meaning 'knowledge'. This idea of 'knowledge with' comes from the ancient Greek 'suneidenai' and refers to a person having 'knowledge of oneself with oneself'. In particular, the root of the Greek word suggested specifically 'sharing knowledge *of a defect* held with oneself'.[18] This particular meaning of that Greek word was something that was developed in Greek drama of that period. Significantly, the individual has two separate components in their conscious mind – their conscious self and their conscience – which share knowledge of a defect together. Consequently, a conscience is not simply subjective knowledge of oneself, but rather it recognises the existence of a conscious self and an entirely different self within one's mind.

26.2.2 The psychological understanding of an objective conscience

This model of a conscience is found in the psychological literature too. In Chapter 1, we mentioned Freud and Jung in this regard. Sigmund Freud explained the creation of the conscience as a psychological phenomenon in *Civilisation and Its Discontents* in the following way:[19]

> . . . a portion of the ego [sets] itself up as the super-ego in opposition to the rest [of the psyche], and is now prepared, as 'conscience', to exercise the same severe aggression against the ego that the latter would have liked to direct towards other individuals. The tension between the stern super-ego and the ego that is subject to it is what we call a 'sense of guilt'; this manifests itself as a need for punishment. In this way civilisation overcomes the dangerous aggressivity of the individual, by weakening him, disarming him and setting up an internal authority to watch over him, like a garrison in a conquered town.

Thus, the conscience is assembled inside the mind with inputs from outside that individual mind. During infancy those messages come from parents and other family members; during childhood they also come from schoolteachers and others; and then during adulthood there is the legal system, the media and so forth all directing different inputs to the individual's mind.[20] The result is a conscience which contains an aggregation of individual responses to those social messages.

26.2.3 Understanding the objective conscience

This idea of an objective conscience can be explained by an analogy with aesthetics: the philosophical study of why human beings find some things beautiful, especially works of art. Theodor Adorno, in an essay titled 'Subject and Object',[21] rejected the idea that there is

18 Sorabji, 2014, 12.
19 Freud, 1930, 77.
20 Elias, 2001.
21 Adorno, 1978.

anything which is objectively great art. Instead, he argued that all we have is a sufficiently large accumulation of individual opinions that a particular work of art is great that everyone accepts that it is great. So, that would seem to suggest that all appreciation of art is entirely subjective, and there need to be enough 'votes' in favour of one work of art for it to be accepted as being great. However, Adorno also argued that there is no such thing as a subjective opinion of an artwork because we are all conditioned and educated to believe that certain types of art are great and that other things are possibly not even art at all. Therefore, there is no subjectivity at all, in Adorno's view, because everything we believe is subjective to us is actually an accumulation of objective messages which we have absorbed through our lives or when we have visited art galleries and been presented with something on the wall as being 'great'.

The same, I believe, is true of conscience. All of the beliefs which you have inside your own mind, including the dictates of your conscience, come from outside you. Over time you have assimilated them into your mind. They are accumulations of experiences which almost everyone in your society will have had (murder is wrong, theft is wrong, adultery is wrong) and also experiences which are unique to you (lemon boiled sweets make you feel sick, the over-use of plastic bags is wrong, cruelty to dogs is shocking). However, even those experiences which are unique to you (because they arose in your life and not as part as any formal instruction as to the attitudes you should have) only became your attitudes to life because the outside world confronted you with them. Your aversion to lemon boiled sweets was only formed because your mother gave you a lemon boiled sweet on a long car journey when you were young, you said you felt sick and your father was smoking cigarettes with the windows rolled up. (That one is clearly specific to me.) It was only when you first saw a dog being mistreated that you formed the view that such cruelty was shocking. (That one is a commonly held view in the UK but not in parts of South East Asia, which shows that those attitudes are societal.) So, your attitudes are objective in the sense that they are formed in reaction to the world outside you. At the same time, many of the attitudes which the courts will absorb into law are subjective opinions of this sort which are accepted across society as being wrong. So, murder is outlawed but lemon boiled sweets are still sold openly on our streets. The former is outlawed because almost everyone agrees that murder is wrong; whereas that issue with lemon boiled sweets is only held by a few weirdoes like you, and therefore it cannot become law.

The point is that the conscience is subjectively-situated but it is objectively-constituted. It is subjectively-situated in that we experience our own conscience inside our own minds and therefore it feels very immediate and very personal to us. Nevertheless, it is objectively-constituted in that the attitudes it contains were either put there by other people intentionally (parents, teachers, etc.) or they were grown there in reaction to confrontation with the outside world. An objectively-constituted conscience is, at the very least, an appropriate metaphor or standard for a system of principles within our law which seeks to judges defendants against the way that they should have behaved. So, the conscience can be the underpinning for equity because it is objective and therefore defendants are being measured against an objective model of conscience and not simply their own subjective beliefs.

26.2.4 The objective conscience in popular culture: *Pinocchio* and *Deadpool*

In Chapter 1, we considered in outline the concept of a conscience. The example that was used there to illustrate the objective conscience was Walt Disney's *Pinocchio* where the entire plot was organised around the idea that for a wooden puppet to become 'a real boy' he needed to have a conscience. The conscience that was appointed for him was a creature that lived outside Pinocchio's wooden head: Jiminy Cricket. As Pinocchio tells one of the naughty boys he meets later in the story: 'He's my conscience. He tells me what's right and wrong.'[22] The conscience is a 'he' that is literally outside Pinocchio's head. This understanding of the conscience as being something which is distinct from the conscious mind, and which nags at the conscious mind when it does wrong, is in line with all of the psychological and cultural understandings of conscience in our culture. The conscience is objective in that sense. It is only the legal commentators who seem to have been stuck with the idea that the conscience is entirely subjective.

This understanding of the conscience as being two different phenomena inside the same mind – one subjective and the other objective – appears even in the most popular of popular culture: the comic book anti-hero Deadpool. In *Deadpool: Drinking Game*,[23] the 'mercenary with a mouth' Wade Wilson (aka Deadpool) is about to take advantage of the troubled alcoholic Tony Stark (aka Iron Man) by plying him with booze when he realises that he is about to do something wrong. Deadpool says:

> I can almost hear another voice starting to yell in my head. Ugh. Is this what having a conscience is like?

Yes, that is exactly what having a conscience is like. The conscience comes unbidden to your conscious mind to tell it that you have done something unethical. The conscience comes even if your conscious mind wants to do the unethical thing (eat the last cake, take the plaudits you have not earned, have sex). You have no control over what your conscience thinks. You cannot switch your conscience off. Either it nags at you or it does not. Even a character as immoral as Deadpool is assailed by conscience when he does something self-evidently immoral. Deadpool makes his living from killing people for money, and yet he is surprised that he has a conscience which reproaches him for pouring booze into recovering alcoholic Stark. This is something that we know ought to bother any right-thinking person because we all have a shared understanding of how people ought to behave in most circumstances. Previously, Deadpool had never been bothered by his conscience but suddenly it renders him incapable of acting.

The ancient Anglo-Saxon expression for a pang of conscience is an 'agenbite of inwit': literally, the agonising bite of inside wit. The conscience bites when it strikes. It is not gentle. It is outside the control of the conscious mind. This is why it is an appropriate standard for equity: the conscience stands for the messages which should have gone into the individual's mind. Therefore, it is appropriate for courts to judge whether or not that defendant has complied with those moral standards which should have been in their head because they come from outside.

---

22 This causes Lampwick to ask: 'What? You mean you take orders from a grasshopper?'
23 Duggan and Posehn, 2014.

26.2.5 The usefulness of an objective conscience in English equity

Recognising that a conscience is actually an objective phenomenon is the answer to many of the troublesome debates within equity because it refutes the suggestion that any judgment based on conscience is merely a subjective judgment. Instead, recognising that a conscience is an objective phenomenon allows us to realise that the courts are holding the defendant to an objective standard of what a person ought to have done in those circumstances and judging them accordingly. The business of law in its practice is exactly that: judging people. At some point, a line has to be drawn.

The restitutionists, discussed in the previous chapter, would like to draw their lines on their word processors and then apply their rules like automatons. They do this as though their creation of those rules were not ideological value judgments in themselves. By contrast, equity reserves its judgment until it has evaluated the justice of the case between the parties where the rigid rules will not answer the case. This is a different way of thinking and it also involves value judgments, but in cases involving injunctions or ownership of the home, and so forth, that is the only appropriate way to proceed. As Chadwick LJ held in *Jones v Morgan*:[24]

> The enquiry is not whether the conscience of the party who has obtained the benefit . . . is affected in fact; the enquiry is whether, in the view of the court, it ought to be.

This is the point: the courts are measuring what a person *ought to have* thought, or done or not done. The court is assessing what that defendant's conscience ought to have prompted them to do. The court is able to do that because the court stands for an objective statement of the values which should have been input to a person's conscience. So, in our discussion of the law on dishonest assistance in the next chapter, we shall see that when Lord Nicholls established his objective test for dishonesty in *Royal Brunei Airlines v Tan*,[25] what he was doing was requiring the judge to ask what an honest person would have done in the circumstances (i.e. what should their ethics have required any member of this society to do in that situation) and to judge them against that standard, when the standard of unconscionability is used it is to establish an objective idea of proper behaviour, when fiduciaries are prevented from taking secret profits that is part of the establishment of an objective morality, and so on.

So, we have established a model of the idea of conscience which justifies its use deontologically within equity. In the next chapter, on a consequentialist, case-by-case approach, we consider how the courts have developed this idea of conscience and its technical cousin 'unconscionability' through some of the key cases discussed in this book.

24 [2001] EWCA Civ. 995, [35].
25 [1995] 2 AC 378.

Chapter 27

Essay: Modern equity

27.1 INTRODUCTION

27.1.1 The purpose of this chapter

The purpose of this chapter, building on the preceding discussion of conscience in Chapter 26, is to explain how the ideas of conscience and unconscionability work in equity and trusts law by reflecting back on the case law and the discussions which we have already had in this book. The underlying objective of this chapter is to revise the key cases which we have studied together. You should therefore experience a comforting sensation of revisiting ground which you know very well. (If you do not, then you are advised to go back and re-read what you do not remember.)

27.1.2 The essence of equity

Equity deals in essential truths; and it also deals in technical detail. The quintessential truth is that in the modern world each of us demands that we are treated as being valuable individuals. Equity is one of the ways in which we do that. As James LJ put it in *Fowkes v Pascoe*,[1] in relation to rebutting the arbitrary presumptions of advancement,[2] the court should listen to our story (about how we came to have property in that instance) and craft

---

1 (1875) 10 Ch App Cas 343
2 See section 11.4.2.

its judgment accordingly. That is all we want as human beings: to be heard, to be valued and to be treated fairly. As Aristotle recognised, strict legal rules will not deal fairly with every situation and therefore equity is necessary to generate that fairness.[3] While equity was considered in the 16th century to be arbitrary (because it had granted its judges complete discretion to reach whatever judgments they deemed to be appropriate), modern equity cannot be accused of the same failing. As *Jaggard v Sawyer*[4] illustrates, the first instinct of any English judge applying equitable principles (such as the award of an injunction) is to identify and schematise the factors which must be considered by a court before making such an award. Even in the use of discretionary doctrines like injunctions, equity operates on the basis of precedent and, in line with fields as disparate as family law and financial regulation, it uses high-level principles to guide the use of those precedents in individual cases.

27.1.3 Complex but free; improvisational but firmly patterned

It seems to me that a review of the improvisational 1950s jazz band, The Dave Brubeck Five, from *Time* magazine in 1954, could define equity perfectly:

> It is tremendously complex, but free. It flows along, improvising constantly but yet it is held together by a firm pattern . . . The essence is the tension between improvisation and order; between freedom and discipline.

Dave Brubeck's five musicians were extremely talented. Their improvisation was not arbitrary; just as modern Chancery court judges do not use equitable principles in an arbitrary way. They were skilled musicians conducting improvisations that were based on their shared experience and skill. This movement – along with Miles Davis, Dizzie Gillespie, Charlie Parker, and the sublime Charles Mingus – was very progressive. It was simply another way of playing music, just as equity is simply another way of thinking about law. Equity is 'complex' because it is comprised of centuries of case law establishing many different doctrines. It is 'free' in the sense that it develops new doctrines and it uses existing doctrines to identify the right approach for litigants in any given case. This freedom is now balanced out by the predictability which adherence to the doctrine of precedent and textbooks on equity have brought. As the *Time* review continues: 'It flows along, improvising constantly but yet it is held together by a firm pattern.' Improvisational jazz musicians worked in bands. They did not have four or five musicians playing discordantly in entirely separate keys on separate melodies. Instead, one musician at a time would improvise on identified phrases – for example, in Miles Davis' *Sketches of Spain* the band improvised with phrases from traditional Spanish music – and thus to develop new melodies and ideas that were based on the established musical principles worked out among those musicians.

This is how equity works. When deciding whether or not to award an injunction or a constructive trust, the judge is using principles which have been established by earlier judges but applying them to novel factual situations. That judge is not acting arbitrarily but rather is

---

3 Aristotle, 1955.
4 [1995] 1 WLR 269.

improvising with existing patterns to meet the needs of an individual case. Just like the jazz trumpeter who takes their turn to improvise, they apply the melodies and patterns used by their bandmates to their own work. Then the baton is passed to another band member, and so on. Equity has a firm pattern: like a river, it follows the course set by its banks just like courts of equity follow precedent and doctrine. When a judge applies a remedial doctrine like proprietary estoppel, they are not acting entirely randomly, but rather they are improvising on the pattern of what was established before.

'The essence is the tension between improvisation and order, between freedom and discipline.' Equity is not simply a doctrine which improvises and acts on discretionary whim. Instead equity has its own sense of order and discipline in its doctrines. In express trusts law this is clearly true: the rules on certainties, the detailed rules on the duties of trustees, the beneficiary principle, the formalities in the creation of some trusts and in the constitution of others, are all examples of equity developing strict rules in a context in which those rules are required. Where the court needs to be free to identify when an interim injunction is required, then there is flexibility. In some contexts – such as constructive trusts over unauthorised profits taken by fiduciaries from their offices – the courts of equity have developed 'inflexible rules' (as in *Bray v Ford*[5]) to impose a constructive trust. By contrast, the constructive trust is at its most flexible when identifying rights in the home.

Equity is neither entirely one thing, nor entirely the other. (That is why it is important to study the whole of equity and not simply to focus on small parts of it.) All of life is a synthesis of day and night, rain and sun, warmth and cold. A successful legal system is a synthesis of freedom and order; a successful system of private law is a synthesis of common law and equity.

What we shall do now is to take some examples of equitable doctrines from the second half of the book and consider how they fit into this equity based on conscience.

27.2 CONSCIENCE-BASED EQUITY AT WORK

27.2.1 *Quistclose* trusts as 'remedies of equity'

Let us begin with a good example of a doctrine (discussed in Chapter 22) which exemplifies the freedom in equity but which is often mistaken by the commentators as needing to be limited to a particular type of trust. The *Quistclose* trust is a device which continues to vex the commentariat on trusts law: is it a resulting trust? If so, how does it work? How does it protect against insolvency? Is it an express trust? Is it a unique type of trust which arises *sui generis*?

A large part of this discussion misses two very important facts. First, only a negligently drafted loan contract would fail to specify what type of trust and beneficial interest is created for the lender. Therefore, nearly all competently drafted loan contracts (i.e. those specifying a purpose for the use of the loan money) will create *Quistclose* arrangements which are express trusts. Nothing will be left to chance.

5 [1896] AC 44.

Second, and more importantly perhaps, the commentators tend not to read Lord Wilberforce's excellent judgment in *Barclays Bank v Quistclose*[6] at face value. The commentators are so keen to identify the type of trust that Lord Wilberforce must have meant, that they do not read what his lordship actually said. Lord Wilberforce was not a trusts law obsessive and so he did not see the entire universe in terms of equitable interests held by trustees. Instead, he identified that a loan contract involves common law concepts of debt. If the contract contains provisions about the repayment of the money then a contract law analysis of those provisions will govern the arrangement in ordinary circumstances. It is only if the money cannot be used (or has not been used) for the purpose specified in the loan contract that 'the remedies of equity' are introduced for the first time. Equity comes to assist the common law by creating a primary trust (to enable the proper use of the loan moneys) and a secondary trust (to protect the interests of the lender).

The 'equity' which is at use here is a flexible equity which, like the Lesbian architects' rule discussed by Aristotle, moulds itself to the circumstances so as to fit the needs of the case. It is not the rigid equity of the trusts lawyers who need to know in which pigeon hole (resulting, express, constructive) the *Quistclose* trust sits. It does not matter. Let it be a unique kind of trust then, if that is thought necessary; but its real role is to achieve just outcomes whereby the lender is protected under the terms of the loan contract. It is a truly equitable doctrine, and not just a part of trusts law.

Interestingly, in *Carreras Rothmans v Freeman Mathews*[7] we have an explanation of the *Quistclose* as operating such that 'equity fastens on the conscience of the person who receives from another property transferred for a specific purpose only'.[8] This approach is very similar to Lord Wilberforce's model in the *Quistclose* case itself: equity is simply protecting the right of someone who would otherwise be unconscionably treated. That makes it a simply equitable doctrine.

The most satisfying explanation of this sort of trust is the one which Lord Wilberforce actually gave: equity is moulding an appropriate remedy in this circumstance to support the common law concepts governing debts and loan contracts. Equity is really very simple. When detailed answers are unsatisfactory, we should not be afraid of the intuitive explanations which work on the basis of high-level principles.

27.2.2 Constructive trusts

The decision in *Boardman v Phipps*[9] often strikes students as being harsh because the solicitor in that case used his brain and risked his own money to make a profit for himself and the trust. Long before Lord Herschell gave judgment in *Bray v Ford*[10] in 1895 it had been an 'inflexible rule of equity' that a fiduciary may not take an unauthorised profit from their office. Boardman was a solicitor, so he should have known that. That he did not protect himself against a suit to recover his profits was entirely down to his own professional incompetence. More to the point, as a solicitor Boardman should have known that

---

6 [1970] AC 567.
7 [1985] 1 Ch 207.
8 [1985] Ch 207, 222.
9 [1967] 2 AC 46.
10 [1896] AC 44.

fiduciaries occupy a different legal category from other offices and duties: that is the entire point of their existence. Therefore, Boardman should have known that it was unconscionable of him to use his office to gain the information which he exploited for his own gain. The reason for having a category of fiduciary offices is precisely so that there is a category of duties which recognises that consciable behaviour involves a higher standard than in other circumstances.

A clearer example of unconscionable behaviour is the receipt of a bribe. If you think about it, anyone who is worth bribing must be defined as occupying a fiduciary office in that particular context, or else why would anyone bother to bribe them? The point was made clearly in *AG for Hong Kong v Reid*[11] that a constructive trust is imposed over a bribe because bribery is 'an evil practice' and because it is therefore 'unconscionable'. Consequently, any profit taken from that bribe is also held on constructive trust; and moreover the recipient is required to account for any diminution in the value of the property acquired with the bribe (or the bribe itself). The error made in *Sinclair v Versailles Trading*,[12] whereby no bribes would have been held on constructive trust unless trust property was used to earn them, was reversed by the Supreme Court in *FHR European Ventures v Cedar Capital*.[13] If cases involving insolvency do require different treatment (as was suggested in *Sinclair v Versailles*), then the insolvency statutes should be altered to cater for the problem. Otherwise, the only way of preventing a wrongdoer from taking the benefit of their unconscionable (or in the case of bribery, illegal) act is to require them to hold the bribe on constructive trust from the moment of its receipt. To do anything else is not only unconscionable but it also creates a different rule for bribery from every other type of unconscionable activity.

Similarly, taking a benefit from unlawful killing leads to the imposition of a constructive trust over any property acquired in that way. This rule prevented the convicted murderer Dr Crippen from taking a benefit from his wife's estate after he was convicted of murdering her.[14] Equity is very simple in this context, contrary to Birks' concerns that it is not clear on what basis a constructive trust arises.

Trusts law has developed a series of categories of unconscionable action, including bribery, killing, taking unauthorised profits as a fiduciary, and so forth. The common thread between them is the idea – restated in *Westdeutsche Landesbank v Islington* – that any knowing, unconscionable act in relation to property leads to that property being held on constructive trust by its legal owner. Consequently, any new case which falls into one of the established categories will lead to the imposition of a constructive trust. The thing that triggers the existence of that constructive trust is knowing that an unconscionable act is being (or has been) committed. If the new case falls outside the established categories, then the judge must consider whether or not the defendant has acted unconscionably and knowingly. The trigger for this constructive trust would be, once more, the combination of knowledge and an unconscionable act. After all, it would be a reproach to our system of jurisprudence if unjust and inequitable acts could not be treated in this way by the courts.

---

11   [1994] 1 AC 324.
12   [2011] EWCA Civ 347.
13   [2014] 3 WLR 535.
14   *In re Crippen* [1911] P 108.

27.2.3 Where could equity go next?

One thing about equity which often goes unremarked is how it has been a predominantly bourgeois area of law. The trusts law of the 18th and 19th centuries was clearly only interested in the landed classes. The vote was not made available to all adults in the UK until 1928. It was not until the beginning of the 21st century that we began to see people from outside the upper middle classes bringing litigation contesting ownership of their homes, and that was the result of the skewed British economy which has presided over an unprecedented boom in house prices while no other economic indicator (including wages) has kept pace with that rate of growth. A house costing £4,000 in a London suburb in 1970 may now sell for £600,000. Significantly, however, equity remains primarily the preserve of commercial people and the wealthy in other contexts. The case law on certainties in Chapter 3 involves the estates of very wealthy, multinational industrialists (like Gestetner and Gulbenkian) or peers (as in *Bowring-Hanbury* and *Ogden*), or the affairs of investment banks. The working classes rarely get a look-in (as in the unusual case of *Paul v Constance*).

There is a serious point here. If Aristotle was concerned that *no one* should be overlooked by the legal system when they were subject to an unjust rule, then that should apply to tenants of local authority and social housing more than anyone. The rights of such tenants are dominated by statute. Appeals against decisions made in relation to their homes are dominated by a bureaucratic structure which each local authority is required to create. There is apparently no space for equity here because these people are dealt with entirely by statutory rules, guidance notes issued by central government for the instruction of local authority officers, and appeals procedures which are heard by the same people who made the original decision against which the appeal is being brought. If a tenant, for example, wants to appeal against the local authority's appeals decision, then they have to bring very expensive judicial review proceedings. They are not allowed to bring, for example, a claim that they suffered detriment as a result of relying on a representation which a local authority officer made to them, nor a general claim that they have been treated unconscionably. In a democratic country (even though we have had full adult suffrage for less than a hundred years) it is difficult to understand why an area of law which is avowedly intended to bring justice to individual litigants has only ever been available to a narrow band of the population.[15] Why is equity only available to the rich?

There are opportunities to broaden the utility of equity. In planning law, for example, there are cases in which individuals have simply cheated the system. My suggestion is that these areas of law could easily and usefully adopt principles of equity which are similar to the economists' notion of equity which focuses on fair and equal access to public goods like the law. An example of what I have in mind emerges from *Arun DC v First Secretary of State*[16] in which a woman received planning permission for an extension to her home on the condition that the extension remained part of one single dwelling. Instead, the woman began to use the extension as a separate, second dwelling in breach of the permission. However, the manner in which the legislation had been drafted meant that, even though this woman deliberately flouted the terms on which planning permission had been granted to her originally, because she had committed this particular breach by changing the use of the extension four years after the permission was granted, then the ordinary rules as to breach of planning

---

15 See generally Alastair Hudson, *The Law on Homelessness*, 1997.
16 [2007] 1 WLR 523.

permission conditions did not apply on a literal reading of the legislation. In a short judgment, Sedley LJ held that:

> the discovery that Mrs Brown has – not to put too fine a point on it – cheated on a conditional grant of permission, to the detriment of her neighbours and of planning control, may well be a matter of time and chance.[17]

My suggestion would be that the courts could develop a notion of equity even in relation to quasi-public law contexts like this in which a statute has, effectively, been used as an engine of fraud. In a private law context it would be possible to say that the defendant was taking unconscionable advantage of the statute and therefore that equity should be entitled to disapply the advantage which the defendant would otherwise receive, as was the case in *Rochefoucauld v Boustead*[18] and in relation to proprietary estoppel in *Yaxley v Gotts*.[19] After all, as Sedley LJ pointed out in this instance, the defendant had 'cheated' on the conditions on which she had been granted planning permission and clearly the Court of Appeal was reluctant to find that she could benefit from a mismatch in the drafting of the legislation relating to the limitation period applicable to this sort of planning grant. It would, it is suggested, be only a short step to introduce general notions of equity and of unconscionability in this sort of context. For the future, then, it would be a larger question whether or not the discussion of 'equity' in the other social sciences, relating to fairness and equality of treatment, can be developed by English public law.

27.2.4 Dishonest assistance

The test of 'dishonesty' in *Royal Brunei Airlines v Tan*[20] as framed by Lord Nicholls explicitly refused to allow it to be collapsed into a general concept of unconscionability. Nevertheless, the concept of measuring the defendant's behaviour against the standards which could be expected from an objectively honest person has great similarity to that model of equity which is concerned to measure the defendant's actions against the objective idea of good conscience (as discussed in Chapter 26). As a result of *Tan*, the judge must establish what an objectively honest person would have done in that situation: the defendant is considered to be 'dishonest' if they did not live up to that standard. A conscience is objectively-constituted, as discussed in Chapter 26, and therefore any finding of *un*conscionability, should be taken to be an assessment that the defendant's conscience should have told them that their behaviour was contrary to the ethical standards which their objectively-constituted conscience ought to have contained. In essence, this methodology is the same. It is suggested that Lord Nicholls was rejecting a subjective conception of unconscionability, which was rejected in Chapter 26.

The rejection of Lord Hutton's analysis in *Twinsectra v Yardley*[21] is telling. Lord Hutton wanted to transform the test of dishonesty into a subjective-heavy, hybrid test of the defendant failing to do what an honest person would have done in the circumstances and also

---

17 *Ibid*, 532, para [36].
18 [1897] 1 Ch 196. See section 5.2.2 above.
19 [2000] Ch 162. See section 13.3.4.
20 [1995] 2 AC 378.
21 [2002] 2 All ER 377.

being aware that an honest person would think that. This would be a transformation into the subjective concept of conscience which commentators like Peter Birks have criticised for so long. Yet, that did not happen. The Privy Council reversed this change in the law in *Barlow Clowes v Eurotrust*,[22] and the subsequent cases have all held that the test must be objective: it cannot matter what the defendant thought was honest (or claims to think was honest).[23] Therefore, the equitable methodology remains the assessment of the behaviour of an individual against objective standards of proper behaviour. There is no arbitrary discretion here; rather, the courts have developed a clear and reasoned test which still matches the morality of the situation.

27.2.5 Fairness and ownership of the home

Two of the more troublesome concepts in the equitable firmament at present are the concept of 'common intention' and the concept of 'fairness' as set out in *Jones v Kernott*.[24] At one level, it may be unclear how they correlate with the rest of the law discussed in this book. The concept of 'unconscionability' is used in Australia as the root of the law on ownership of the home. The focus on that model is on ensuring that neither party is treated unconscionably, a little like the model of proprietary estoppel which was established in *Jennings v Rice*[25] and *Gillett v Holt*,[26] but very different from the common intention concept introduced in *Gissing v Gissing*.[27]

The English concept of common intention anticipates the existence of an intention that is common to the parties. There is a lot about that which is unclear: on some models, it is required that the intention was common to the parties at the date of the acquisition of the home,[28] on other models it is demonstrated simply by contribution to the mortgage repayments, on other models that intention emerges over time from the way in which the parties cohabit, and on yet other models that common intention may change over time. By focusing on the purchase price of the property in *Lloyds Bank v Rosset*,[29] there is potential unfairness on those who were not able to contribute to the purchase price (due to lack of earning power, due to being misled by their partner, or otherwise). Other models have required that we undertake a survey of the entire course of dealing between the parties, and therefore that we do not limit our analysis to the purchase price. It is less clear what we are supposed to be looking for when we undertake this survey, however. In *Midland Bank v Cooke*[30] itself, Waite LJ found a sufficiently large interest (half of the equity) with the result that the Cookes were able to resist the mortgagee's claim for repossession of their home because Mrs Cooke was found to have half of the equitable interest in the home.

It is in *Jones v Kernott* that we have a clearer route map as to what happens when the search for the 'phantom' common intention is fruitless. Lady Hale and Lord Walker, and Lord Kerr, have held that the court should look for what is 'fair' when there is no common

---

22 [2005] UKPC 37; [2006] 1 WLR 1476.
23 See section 20.2.
24 [2011] UKSC 53.
25 [2002] EWCA Civ 159.
26 [2001] Ch 210.
27 [1971] AC 886.
28 [1991] 1 AC 1.
29 [1995] 4 All ER 562.
30 *Ibid.*

intention. There is no clarity as to what this fairness might involve. A little like a principle of family law, the court is left to develop its own response to the facts in front of it by reference only to that general principle. The default setting for the division of property in divorce cases (which can be adjusted by any suggestive factor to the contrary) is equality. Therefore, one approach which the courts could take in trusts of homes cases is to begin with an assumption that co-owners are presumptively to acquire equal rights, and then to work away from that assumption if the facts require a different outcome.

That 'equality is equity' is a long-standing principle of equity. Vaisey J considered the doctrine of 'equality is equity' in the following way:

> I think that the principle which applies here is Plato's definition of equality as a 'sort of justice': if you cannot find any other, equality is the proper basis.[31]

Fairness is taken by the philosopher John Rawls in his book *A Theory of Justice* to constitute equality.[32] In that theory, Rawls took the view that society as a whole would be reorganised on the basis of equality if we were all required to redesign our society and to vote (in complete ignorance of what our own roles would be in the new society) on how that society should be organised. Rawls considered that everyone would vote for each of us to be treated in the same way in all aspects of our lives. From this premise, he made an argument that the level of inequality in our societies is something which we should not accept and that equality would be more just.

The Australian concept of 'unconscionability' would offer greater compatibility with the rest of English trusts law (especially the general law on constructive trusts) if the rights in the home were re-arranged in accordance with the idea that all of the beneficial owners of the property should not be treated unconscionably by being denied rights in the property as a result of contributing to the purchase price, or contributing to the cohabiting unit by caring for children, undertaking costly repairs, meeting other domestic outgoings, and so forth. The parties' common intention from the outset would be a clear part of that concept of unconscionability (a little like the New Zealand concept of recognising the parties' legitimate expectations from their cohabiting) in that it would be unconscionable to deny someone rights which they had been led to believe they would receive if the parties' had organised (and continued to organise) their cohabitation around that understanding. Cases like *Oates v Stimson*[33] have seen the Court of Appeal take exactly this approach. During argument in the Supreme Court in *Jones v Kernott*, Lady Hale did remark that it was a pity that trusts law did not permit a means of achieving fair outcomes. It is suggested that the constructive trust or proprietary estoppel (as considered in the previous chapter) can do exactly that.

27.3 CONCLUSION

There is something remarkably humane in the development of equity. It creates a means by which private law can achieve fair outcomes in individual cases. It can recognise human beings as valuable individuals, and not simply as chess pieces against which abstract rules

---

31 *Jones v Maynard* [1951] Ch 572, 575.
32 Rawls, 1971.
33 [2006] EWCA Civ 548.

are enforced. In delineating the respective spaces of common law and equity, it is important to ensure that a balance is maintained between the two – that the willowy suppleness of equity is not displaced by a brittle demand for common law certainty. It is only through equity that we can extricate the human being from the impersonal machinery of the legal system. The flexibility of equity brings equilibrium to our private law in a way that provides balance with the certainties of common law. Through this synergy we can achieve harmony. We must resist the temptation to try to impose too much order on what will remain a fundamentally chaotic universe.

Bibliography

Adams, J, (1975) 39 Conv 94

Adorno, T, 'Subject and object', in Arato, A and Gerbhardt, E (eds), *The Essential Frankfurt School Reader*, 1978, New York: Continuum

Allen, 'Bribes and constructive trusts: *A-G Hong Kong v Reid*' (1995) 58 MLR 87

American Law Institute, *Restatement of the Law of Restitution*, 1937, St Paul, Minn: ALI

Annetta, V, 'Priority rights in insolvency – the doctrinal basis for equity's intervention' (1992) 20 ABLR 311

Aristotle, *The Nicomachean Ethics*, 1955, Thomson (trans), Harmondsworth: Penguin

Arora, A, 'The bank's liability as a constructive trustee' [1990] JBL 217

Arrowsmith, S, 'Ineffective transactions and unjust enrichment: a framework for analysis' (1989) 9 LS 121

Atiyah, P, *The Rise and Fall of Freedom of Contract*, 1979, Oxford: Clarendon

Atiyah, P, *Essays on Contract*, 1986, Oxford: Clarendon

Auchmuty, R, 'The fiction of equity', in Scott-Hunt, S and Lim, H (eds), *Feminist Perspectives on Equity and Trusts*, ed., 2001, London: Cavendish, 1

Austin, R, 'Constructive trusts', in Finn, P (ed), *Essays in Equity*, 1985, Sydney: LBC, 196

Bamforth, N, 'Unconscionability as a vitiating factor' [1995] LMCLQ 538

Barker, K, 'Rescuing remedialism in unjust enrichment law: why remedies are right' [1998] CLJ 301

Barlow, A, 'Rights in the family home: time for a conceptual revolution?', in Hudson, AS (ed), *New Perspectives on Property Law, Human Rights and the Home*, 2003, London: Cavendish Publishing, 53

Barnsley, DG, 'Co-owners' rights to occupy trust land' [1998] CLJ 123

Bartlett, R, 'When is a "trust" not a trust? The National Health Service Trust' [1996] Conv 186

Battersby [1995] CFLQ 59

Beatson, J, 'Restitutionary remedies for void and ineffective contracts' (1989) 105 LQR 179

Beatson, J, *Use and Abuse of Unjust Enrichment*, 1991, Oxford: Clarendon

Beatson, J, 'The relationship between regulations governing the financial services industry and fiduciary duties under the general law', in McKendrick, E, *Commercial Aspects of Trusts and Fiduciary Obligations*, 1992, Oxford: Clarendon, 55

Bevan, A, *In Place of Fear* (1952), 1978, London: Quartet

Birks, P, *Introduction to the Law of Restitution*, 1989, Oxford: Clarendon (1989:1)

Birks, P, 'Restitution and resulting trusts', in Goldstein (ed), *Equity: Contemporary Legal Developments*, 1992, Jerusalem, 335

Birks, P, 'Persistent problems in misdirected money' [1993] LMCLQ 218 (1993:1)

Birks, P, 'No consideration: restitution after void contracts' (1993) 23 UWALR 195 (1993:2)

Birks, P, 'Establishing a proprietary base' [1995] RLR 83 (1995:1)

Birks, P, 'Overview: tracing, claiming and defences', in Birks, P (ed), *Laundering and Tracing*, 1995, Oxford: Clarendon, 289 (1995:2)

Birks, P, 'Equity in the modern law: an exercise in taxonomy' (1996) 26 UWALR 1

Birks, P, 'Trusts raised to avoid unjust enrichment: the *Westdeutsche* case' [1996] RLR 3 (1996)

Birks, P, 'On taking seriously the difference between tracing and claiming' (1997) 11 Trusts Law International 2

Birks, P, 'Definition and division: a meditation on *Institutes* 313', in Birks, P (ed), *The Classification of Obligations*, 1997, Oxford: Clarendon, 1 (1997:2)

Birks, P, 'Misnomer', in Cornish, W, Nolan, R, O'Sullivan, J and Virgo, G (eds), *Restitution, Present and Future: Essays in Honour of Gareth Jones*, 1998, Oxford: Hart, 1 (1998:2)

Birks, P, 'Rights, wrongs and remedies' (2000) OJLS 1 (2000:1)

Birks, P, (ed), *Private Law*, 2000, Oxford: Oxford University Press (2000:3)

Birks, P, 'The content of fiduciary obligations' (2002) 16 Trusts Law International 34

Birks, P, 'Receipt', in Birks, P and Pretto, A (eds), *Breach of Trust*, 2002, Oxford: Hart (2002:2)

Birks, P, *Unjust Enrichment*, 2003, Oxford: Oxford University Press

Birks, P and Chambers, R, *Restitution Research Resource*, 1997, Oxford: Mansfield, 1–6 (1997:1)

Bostock, C, *Aristotle's Ethics*, 2000, Oxford: Oxford University Press

Bottomley, A, 'Our property in trust: things to make and do', in Scott-Hunt, S and Lim, H (eds), *Feminist Perspectives on Equity and Trusts*, 2001, London: Cavendish Publishing

Browne, D, *Ashburner's Principles of Equity*, London: Butterworths, 1933.

Bryan, M, 'The conscience of equity in Australia' (1990) 106 LQR 25

Burrows, A (ed), *Essays in the Law of Restitution*, 1991, Oxford: Clarendon (1991:1)

Burrows, A, 'Public authorities, *ultra vires* and restitution', in Burrows, A (ed), *Essays in the Law of Restitution*, 1991, Oxford: Clarendon (1991:2)

Burrows, A, *The Law of Restitution*, 1993; 2nd edn, 2002, London: Butterworths

Burrows, A, 'Swaps and friction between common law and equity' [1995] RLR 15

Burrows, A, 'Understanding the law of restitution: a map through the thicket', in *Understanding the Law of Obligations*, 1998, Oxford: Hart, 45

Burrows, A, 'Proprietary restitution: unmasking unjust enrichment' (2001) 117 LQR 412

Burrows, A, 'We do this at common law but that in equity' (2002) 22 OJLS 1

Buxton, R, 'The Human Rights Act and private law' (2000) 116 LQR 48

Campbell, D, 'Facism and legality' (1946) 62 LQR 141

Carr, A and McNulty, M, *The Handbook of Clinical Adult Psychology*, 2006, London: Routledge

Chambers, R, 'Restitution, trusts and compound interest' (1996) 20 Mel UL Rev 848

Chambers, R, *Resulting Trusts*, 1997, Oxford: Clarendon

Chambers, R, 'Constructive trusts in Canada', Pt 1 (2001) 15 Trusts Law International 214; and Pt 2 (2002) 16 Trusts Law International 2

Clarke, A, 'Property law' (1995) 48 CLP 117

Conaglen, M, 'Equitable compensation for breach of fiduciary dealing rules' (2003) 119 LQR 246

Cooke, A and Hayton, D, 'Land law and trusts', in Hayton, D (ed), *Law's Futures*, 2000, Oxford: Hart, 433

Cooke, E, 'Equitable accounting' [1995] Conv 391

Cooke, E, *The Modern Law of Estoppel*, 2000, Oxford: Clarendon

Cooke, E, 'In the wake of *Stack v Dowden*: the tale of TR1' [2011] Fam Law 1142

Cotterrell, R, *Sociology of Law*, 1993, London: Butterworths (1993:1)

Cotterrell, R, 'Trusting in law: legal and moral concepts of trust' (1993) 46(2) CLP 75 (1993:2)

Crane, R, 'After the deserted wife's licence' (1965) 29 *The Conveyancer*, 254

Cretney, S, *Family Law in the Twentieth Century: A History*, 2005, London: Sweet & Maxwell

Croft, C, 'Lord Hardwicke's use of precedent in equity' (1989) Aust Bar Rev 29

Cross (1956) 72 LQR 182

Davey, N, (1988) 8 LS 92

Denning, *The Due Process of Law*, 1980, London: Butterworths

Dewar, J, 'The development of the remedial constructive trust' (1982) 60 Can BR 265

Dewar, J, *Law and the Family*, 2nd edn, 1992, London: Butterworths

Dewar, J, 'The normal chaos of family life' (1998) 61 MLR 467

Dixon, M, 'The never-ending story: co-ownership after *Stack v Dowden*' (2007) 71 Conv 456

Douzinas, C, *The End of Human Rights*, 2000, Oxford: Hart

Duxbury, N, *The Nature and Authority of Precedent*, 2008, Cambridge: Cambridge University Press

Dworkin, R, *Law's Empire*, 1986, Cambridge, Mass: Harvard University Press

Eleftheriadis, P, 'The analysis of property rights' (1996) OJLS 31

Elias, G, *Explaining Constructive Trusts*, 1990, Oxford: Clarendon

Elias, N, *The Society of Individuals*, 2001, New York: Continuum

Elliott, S and Mitchell, C, 'Remedies for dishonest assistance' (2004) 67 MLR 16

Emery, C, 'The most hallowed principle – certainty of beneficiaries of trusts and powers of appointment' (1982) 98 LQR 551

Encarta World Dictionary, Hudson (ed), 'Law', 1999, London: Bloomsbury

Enzensberger, HM, *Mediocrity and Delusion, Collected Diversions*, 1992, London: Verso

Evans, J, 'Economic globalisation: the need for a social dimension', in Foden, D and Morris, P (eds), *The Search for Equity*, 1998, London: Lawrence and Wishart

Evans, S, 'Rethinking tracing and the law of restitution' (1999) 115 LQR 469

Ferguson, P, 'Constructive trusts: a note of caution' (1993) 109 LQR 114

Finn, P (ed), *Fiduciary Obligations*, 1977, Sydney: LBC

Finn, P (ed), *Essays in Equity*, 1985, Sydney: LBC

Finn, P (ed), *Equity and Commercial Relationships*, 1985, Sydney: LBC (1985:1)

Finn, P (ed), *Essays on Restitution*, 1990, Sydney: LBC

Finn, P, 'Fiduciary law in the modern commercial world', in McKendrick, E (ed), *Commercial Aspects of Trusts and Fiduciary Obligations*, 1992, Oxford: Clarendon

Ford, H, 'Public unit trusts', in Austin, RP and Vann, R (eds), *The Law of Public Company Finance*, 1986, Sydney: LBC, 400

Ford, H and Lee, W, *The Law of Trusts*, 3rd edn, 1996, Sydney: LBC

Foucault, M, *The Archaeology of Knowledge* (1969), 1972, London: Tavistock

Foucault, M, *The History of Sexuality* (1976), 1979, London: Allen Lane

Foucault, M, *Power/Knowledge: Selected Interviews and Other Writings 1972–1977*, Gordon (ed), 1981, London: Routledge

Fox, D, 'Constructive notice and knowing receipt: an economic analysis' [1998] CLJ 391

Freedland, 'Public and private finance' [1998] PL 288

Freud, S, *Beyond The Pleasure Principle*, 1923, Harmondsworth: Penguin

Freud, S, *Civilisation and its Discontents*, 1930, Harmondsworth: Penguin

Fried, C, *Contract as Promise*, 1981, Oxford: Clarendon

Friedmann, D, (1991) 11 LS 304

Friedmann, D and Cohen, N, *The International Encyclopaedia of Comparative Law*, 1991, Lancaster, 24n 177

Fukuyama, F, *The End of History and the Last Man*, 1992, New York: Free Press

Fukuyama, F, *Trust*, 1995, London: Hamish Hamilton

Fuller, L, *The Morality of Law*, 1964, New Haven: Yale University Press

Gardner, S, *Introduction to the Law of Trusts*, 1990, Oxford: Clarendon

Gardner, S, 'Rethinking family property' (1993) 109 LQR 263

Gardner, S, 'Rethinking family property' (1996) 112 LQR 56

Gardner, S and Davidson, K, 'The future of *Stack v Dowden*' (2011) 127 LQR 13

Garton, J, 'The role of the trust mechanism in the rule in *Re Rose*' [2003] Conv 364

Getzler, J, *Rationalizing Property, Equity and Trusts*, 2003, London: LexisNexis

Giddens, A, *Modernity and Self-Identity*, 1991, Cambridge: Polity

Giddens, A, *Beyond Left and Right*, 1994, Cambridge: Polity

Gleick, J, *Chaos: Making a New Science*, 1988, London: Heinemann

Glover, J, 'Bankruptcy and constructive trusts' (1991) 19 ABLR 98

Goff, R and Jones, G, *The Law of Restitution*, 6th edn, 2002, London: Sweet & Maxwell

Goode, R, (1983) 3 LS 283

Goode, R, 'Ownership and obligation in commercial transactions' (1987) 103 LQR 433

Goode, R, 'Property and unjust enrichment', in Burrows, A (ed), *Essays on Restitution*, 1991, Oxford: Clarendon, Chapter 9

Goode, R, 'Charges over book debts: a missed opportunity' (1994) 110 LQR 592

Goode, R, *Commercial Law*, 2nd edn, 1997, Harmondsworth: Penguin (1997:2)

Goulding, S, 'Equity and the money-launderers' [1992] Conv 367

Grantham, R, 'Doctrinal bases for the recognition of proprietary rights' (1996) OJLS 561 (1996:1)

Grantham, R, 'Restitution, property and ignorance – a reply to Mr Swadling' [1996] LMCLQ 463 (1996:2)

Grantham, R and Rickett, C, 'Trust money as an unjust enrichment: a misconception' [1988] LMCLQ 514

Grantham, R and Rickett, C, 'On the subsidiarity of unjust enrichment' (2001) 117 LQR 273

Gravells, N, 'Public purpose trusts' (1977) 40 MLR 397

Gray, K, 'Equitable property' [1994] CLP 157

Gray, K and Gray, F, *Elements of Land Law*, 6th edn, 2009, London: Butterworths

Grbich, Y, 'Baden: awakening the conceptually moribund trust' (1974) 37 MLR 643

Green, B, 'The dissolution of unincorporated non-profit associations' (1980) 43 MLR 626

Green, B, '*Grey, Oughtred* and *Vandervell* – a contextual reappraisal' (1984) 47 MLR 385

Griffiths, G, 'Missed or misguided? Formality, land contracts and the statute of frauds', in Hudson, AS (ed), *New Perspectives on Property Law, Obligations and Restitution*, 2003, London: Cavendish Publishing

Grubb, A, 'Powers, trusts and classes of objects' [1982] Conv 432

Gummow J, 'Unjust enrichment, restitution and proprietary remedies', in Finn, PD (ed), *Essays on Restitution*, 1990, Sydney: LBC, Chapter 3

Habermas, J, *Legitimation Crisis* (1973), 1988, Cambridge: Polity

Hackney, J, *Understanding Equity and Trusts*, 1987, London: Fontana

Hackney, J, 'A trace of the old philosophy', in Birks, P (ed), *The Classification of Obligations*, 1997, Oxford: Clarendon

Ham, R, 'Trustees' liability' (1995) 9 Trusts Law International 21

Hammond (1990) 106 LQR 207

Hanbury, HG, *Essays in Equity*, 1934, Oxford: Clarendon

Hanbury, HG, *Modern Equity*, 1st edn, 1935, London: Stevens

Hanbury, HG and Martin, J, *Modern Equity*, 13th edn, 1993, London: Sweet & Maxwell

Harpum, C, 'The stranger as constructive trustee' (1986) 102 LQR 114

Harpum, C, 'Overreaching, trustee's powers, and the reform of the 1925 legislation' (1990) 49 CLJ 277

Harpum, C, [1991] CLJ 409

Harpum, C, 'The basis of equitable liability' in Birks, P (ed), *The Frontiers of Liability, Vol 1*, 1994, Oxford: Oxford University Press, 9

Harpum, C, 'Knowing assistance and knowing receipt: the basis for equitable liability', in Birks, P (ed), *The Frontiers of Liability*, 1994, Oxford: Clarendon (1994:1)

Harpum, C, 'Accessory liability for procuring or assisting a breach of trust' (1995) 111 LQR 545

Harpum, C, *Megarry and Wade's Law of Real Property*, 6th edn, 2000, London: Sweet & Maxwell

Harris, J, 'Trust, power, or duty' (1971) 87 LQR 31

Harris, J, (1975) 38 MLR 557

Harris, J, *Variation of Trusts*, 1975, London: Sweet & Maxwell (1975:1)

Harris, J, *Property and Justice*, 1996, Oxford: Oxford University Press

Harris, T, *The Hague Trusts Convention*, 2002, Oxford: Hart

Hayton, D, 'Constructive trusts' (1985) 27 Malaya L Rev 313

Hayton, D, 'Remedial constructive trusts of homes; an overseas view' [1988] Conv 259

Hayton, D, 'Constructive trusts: is the remedying of unjust enrichment a satisfactory approach?', in Youdan (ed), *Equity, Fiduciaries and Trusts*, 1989, Zurich: Carswell

Hayton, D, 'Equitable rights of cohabitees' [1990] Conv 370 (1990:1)

Hayton, D, 'Investment management problems' (1990) 106 LQR 89 (1990:2)

Hayton, D, 'Equitable rights of cohabitees', in Goldstein (ed), *Equity and Contemporary Legal Developments*, 1992, Jerusalem

Hayton, D, 'Constructive trusts: a bold approach' [1993] LQR 485

Hayton, D, 'Equity's identification rules', in Birks, P (ed), *Laundering and Tracing*, 1995, Oxford: Clarendon, 6–19 (1995:2)

Hayton, D, 'The irreducible core content of trusteeship', in Oakley, A (ed), *Trends in Contemporary Trust Law*, 1996, Oxford: Oxford University Press, 47

Hayton, D, 'Fiduciaries in context', in Birks, P (ed), *Privacy and Loyalty*, 1997, Oxford: Clarendon

Hayton, D (ed), *Modern International Developments in Trust Law*, 1999, The Hague: Kluwer

Hayton, D, 'Developing the obligation characteristic of the trust' (2001) 117 LQR 96

Hayton, D (ed), *Extending the Boundaries of Trusts and Similar Ring-fenced Funds*, 2002, Hague: Kluwer Law International

Hayton, D, Matthews, P and Mitchell, C, *Underhill and Hayton's Law of Trusts and Trustees*, 18th edn, 2010, London: Butterworths

Hayton, D and Cooke, E, 'Land law and trusts', in Hayton, D (ed), *Law's Futures*, 2000, Oxford: Hart, 433

Hayton, D and Marshall, *Cases and Commentary on the Law of Trusts and Equitable Obligations*, 11th edn, 2001, London: Sweet & Maxwell

Hayton, D, Kortmann, S and Verhagen, H (eds), *Principles of European Trusts Law*, 1999, The Hague: Kluwer

Hedley, S, 'Unjust enrichment as the basis of restitution – an overworked concept' (1985) 5 LS 56

Hedley, S, 'The taxonomy of restitution', in Hudson, AS (ed), *New Perspectives on Property Law, Obligations and Restitution*, 2003, London: Cavendish Publishing

Hegel, GWF, *Philosophy of Right* (1821), trans Knox, 1952, Oxford: Oxford University Press

Hicks, A, 'The Trustee Act 2000 and the modern meaning of "investment"' (2001) 15 *Trusts Law International* 203

Hobsbawm, E, *The Age of Capital: 1848–1875*, 1975, London: Weidenfeld & Nicolson

Hodge, D, 'Secret trusts: the fraud theory revisited' [1980] Conv 341

Hoggett, B, Pearl, D, Cooke, E and Bates, P, *The Family, Law and Society*, 4th edn, 1996, London: Butterworths

Hohfeld, WN, *Fundamental Legal Conceptions as Applied in Judicial Reasoning*, Cook (ed), 1919, London: Yale University Press

Holdsworth, Sir W, *A History of English Law*, vol iv, 1945, London: Sweet & Maxwell

Holland (1945) 9 CLJ 17

Honoré, A, 'Trusts: the inessentials', in Getzler, J (ed), *Rationalizing Property, Equity and Trusts*, 2003, London: LexisNexis

Hopkins, J, 'Certain uncertainties of trusts and powers' [1971] CLJ 68

Howe, HR (ed), *Concepts of Property In Intellectual Property Law*, 2013, Cambridge: Cambridge University Press

Howell, J, 'Land and human rights' [1999] Conv 287

Hudson, AH, 'Abandonment', in Palmer, N and McKendrick, E (eds), *Interest in Goods*, 1993, London: Lloyd's

Hudson, AS, *The Law on Homelessness*, 1997, London: Sweet & Maxwell (1997:1)

Hudson, AS, 'Proprietary rights in financial transactions' (1997) *Amicus Curiae*, 2 November, 27 (1997:2)

Hudson, AS, 'Justice in a reasonable period' (1997–98) KCLJ 8, 133–36

Hudson, AS, 'Void interest swaps: restitution not reinforcement' (1998) 19(6) Company Lawyer 181–82 (1998:2)

Hudson, AS, *Swaps, Restitution and Trusts*, 1999, London: Sweet & Maxwell (1999:1)

Hudson, AS, *Towards a Just Society: Law, Labour and Legal Aid*, 1999, London: Pinter (1999:2)

Hudson, AS, 'Money as property in financial transactions' (1999) 14:06 JIBL, 170–77 (1999:3)

Hudson, AS, 'The regulatory aspect of private law in financial transactions', in Hudson, AS (ed), *Modern Financial Techniques, Derivatives and Law*, 1999, London: Kluwer (1999:4)

Hudson, AS, 'Assessing mistake of law in derivatives transactions' [1999] 14:03 JIBL 1–5 (1999:5)

Hudson, AS, 'Seller liability in credit derivatives', in Hudson, AS (ed), *Credit Derivatives*, 1999, London: Sweet & Maxwell (1999:6)

Hudson, AS, 'Termination and restitution of credit derivatives', in Hudson, AS (ed), *Credit Derivatives*, 1999, London: Sweet & Maxwell (1999:7)

Hudson, AS, *The Law on Investment Entities*, 2000, London: Sweet & Maxwell (2000:1)

Hudson, AS, 'Law of finance', in Birks, P (ed), *Lessons from the Swaps Cases*, 2000, London: Mansfield (2000:2)

Hudson, AS, 'The unbearable lightness of property', in Hudson, AS (ed), *New Perspectives on Property Law, Obligations and Restitution*, 2004, London: Cavendish Publishing, 1 (2004:1)

Hudson, AS, 'Equity, individualisation and social justice', in Hudson, AS (ed), *New Perspectives on Property Law, Human Rights and the Home*, 2004, London: Cavendish Publishing, 1 (2004:2)

Hudson, AS, 'Rapporteur: between morality and formalism in property, obligations and restitution', in Hudson, AS (ed), *New Perspectives on Property Law, Obligations and Restitution*, 2004, London: Cavendish Publishing (2004:3)

Hudson, AS, 'Rapporteur: differentiation in property and obligations', in Hudson, AS (ed), *New Perspectives on Property Law, Human Rights and the Home*, 2004, London: Cavendish Publishing (2004:4)

Hudson, AS (ed), *New Perspectives on Property Law, Obligations and Restitution*, 2004, London: Cavendish Publishing (2004:5)

Hudson, AS (ed), *New Perspectives on Property Law, Human Rights and the Home*, 2004, London: Cavendish Publishing (2004:6)

Hudson, AS, 'The liability of trusts service providers in international finance law', in Glasson J and Thomas GW (eds), *The International Trust*, 2006, Bristol: Jordans (2006:2)

Hudson, AS, 'The regulation of trustees', in Dixon and Griffiths (eds), *Developments in Contemporary Property Law*, 2007, Oxford: Oxford University Press

Hudson, AS, with Thomas, GW, *The Law of Trusts*, 2nd edn, 2010, Oxford: Oxford University Press

Hudson, AS, *Understanding Company Law*, 1st edn, 2011, London: Routledge

Hudson, AS, 'Trusts and Finance Law', in Hayton D (ed), *The International Trust*, 3rd edn, 2012, Bristol: Jordans, Chapter 12

Hudson, AS, 'Asset Protection Trusts', in Hayton D (ed), *The International Trust*, 3rd edn, 2012, Bristol: Jordans, Chapter 6

Hudson, AS, *The Law on Financial Derivatives*, 5th edn, 2012, London: Sweet & Maxwell

Hudson AS, *Securities Law*, 2nd edn, 2013, London: Sweet & Maxwell

Hudson AS, *The Law of Finance*, 2nd edn, 2013, London: Sweet & Maxwell, Classics Series

Hudson AS, *The Law and Regulation of Finance*, 2nd edn, 2013, London: Sweet & Maxwell

Hudson AS, 'Equity, Confidentiality and the Nature of Property', in HR Howe (ed), *Concepts of Property In Intellectual Property Law*, 2013, Cambridge: Cambridge University Press

Hudson AS, 'The synthesis of public and private in finance law', in K Barker and D Jensen (eds), *Private Law: Key Encounters with Public Law*, 2013, Cambridge: Cambridge University Press

Hudson, AS, *Understanding Equity & Trusts*, 6th edn, 2014, Oxford: Routledge

Hudson, AS, 'Conscience as the Ordering Concept in Equity', (2016) *Canadian Journal of Comparative and Contemporary Law*, 1

Hudson, AS, *Equity & Trusts*, 9th edn, 2016, Oxford: Routledge

Hudson, AS, *Text, Cases and Materials in Equity & Trusts*, 2017, Oxford: Routledge

Hunt, A, 'A socialist interest in law' (1992) 192 New Left Rev 105

Hunt, M, 'The "horizontal effect" of the Human Rights Act' [1998] Public Law 423

Ibbetson, D, *A Historical Introduction to the Law of Obligations*, 1999, Oxford: Oxford University Press

Jackson, J and Doran, S, *Judge without Jury: Diplock Trials in the Adversary System*, 1995, Oxford: Clarendon

Jaffey, P, 'Restitutionary damages and disgorgement' [1995] RLR 30

Jaffey, P, [1996] RLR 92

Jaffey, P, *The Nature and Scope of Restitution*, 2000, Oxford: Hart

Jennings, *Jarman on Wills*, 8th edn, 1951, London: Sweet & Maxwell

Jones, G, (1968) 84 LQR 474

Jones, G, 'Unjust enrichment and the fiduciary's duty of loyalty' (1968) 84 LQR 472

Jones, G, 'Remedies for the recovery of money paid by mistake' (1980) 39 CLJ 275

Jones, G, *Restitution in Public and Private Law*, 1991, London: Sweet & Maxwell

Jones, G, [1996] CLJ 432

Jung, C, 'Structure of the psyche' (1927), in Storr (ed), *Essential Jung*, 1998, London: Fontana

Kant, I, *The Metaphysics of Morals*, 1996 (1758), Cambridge: Cambridge University Press

Kennedy, I, 'The fiduciary relationship – doctors and patients', in Birks, P (ed), *Wrongs and Remedies in the 21st Century*, 1996, Oxford: Clarendon

Langbein, J, 'The new American trust-investment Act' (1994) 8 Trusts Law International 123

Langbein, J, 'The contractarian basis of the law of trusts' (1995) 105 Yale LJ 625

Langbein, J and Posner, R, 'Social investing and the law of trusts' (1980) 79 Michigan Law Review 72

Larkin, P, *High Windows*, 1974, London: Faber & Faber

Law Commission, *Fiduciary Duties and Regulatory Rules*, 1992, 124

Law Commission, *Restitution: Mistakes of Law and Ultra Vires Public Authority Receipts and Payments*, Law Com No 227, 1994

Law Commission, *Fiduciary Duties and Regulatory Rules*, Law Com No 236, 1995

Law Commission, *Sharing Homes*, Law Com No 278, 2002

Law Commission, *Cohabitation: The Financial Consequences of Relationship Breakdown*, Law Com No 307, 2007

Law Commission, *Illegality Defence*, Law Com Consultation Paper No 189, 2009

Lewin, R, *Complexity*, 1993, London: Phoenix

Lewin, T, *A Practical Treatise on the Law of Trusts and Trustees*, 1837, London: Maxwell

Leyden, W von, *Aristotle on Equality and Justice: His Political Argument*, 1985, London: Macmillan

Lim, H, 'The waqf in trust', in Scott-Hunt, S and Lim, H (eds), *Feminist Perspectives on Equity and Trusts*, 2001, London: Cavendish Publishing

Litman, MM, 'The emergence of unjust enrichment as a cause of action and the remedy of constructive trust' (1988) 26 Alberta LR 407

Loughlan, P, 'The historical role of equitable jurisdiction', in Parkinson, P (ed), *The Principles of Equity*, 2nd edn, 2003, Sydney: LBC

Lowry, J and Edmunds, R, 'Excuses', in Birks, P and Pretto, A (eds), *Breach of Trust*, 2002, Oxford: Hart, 269

Lupoi, M, *Trusts: A Comparative Study*, 2000, Cambridge: Cambridge University Press

McCormack, G, [1989] LMCLQ 198

McCormack, G, 'Assisting in a breach of trust: principles of accessory liability' (1995) TLI 102 (1995:1)

McCormack, G, *Reservation of Title*, 2nd edn, 1995, London: Sweet & Maxwell (1995:2)

McCormack, G, 'Mistaken payment and proprietary claims' [1996] Conv 86 (1996:1)

McCormack, G, 'The eye of equity: identification principles and equitable tracing' [1996] JBL 225 (1996:2)

McCormack, G, 'Fiduciary obligations in a changing commercial climate', in Rider, B and Andenas, M (eds), *Developments in European Community Law*, 1996, London: Kluwer, Vol 1, 33 (1996:3)

McCormack, G, (1998) 19(2) The Company Lawyer 39

McGhee, J, *Snell's Equity*, 31st edn, 2005, London: Sweet & Maxwell

McGregor, H, 'Restitutionary damages', in Birks, P (ed), *Wrongs and Remedies in the 21st Century*, 1996, Oxford: Clarendon, 203

McKendrick, E, 'Tracing misdirected funds' [1991] LMCLQ 378

McKendrick, E, *Commercial Aspects of Trusts and Fiduciary Obligations*, 1992, Oxford: Clarendon

McKendrick, E, 'Local authorities and swaps: undermining the market?', in Cranston, R (ed), *Making Commercial Law: Essays in Honour of Roy Goode*, 1997, Oxford: Clarendon

Maitland, FW, *Equity – A Course of Lectures*, 2nd edn, 1936, Cambridge: Cambridge University Press

Maloney, W, Smith, G and Stoker, G, 'Social capital and human capital revisited', in Baron, S, Field, J and Schuller, T (eds), *Social Capital*, 2000, Oxford: Oxford University Press, 212

Mann, F, 'On interest, compound interest and damages' (1985) 101 LQR 30

Mann, F, *The Legal Aspect of Money*, 5th edn, 1992, Oxford: Oxford University Press

Martin, J, 'Tracing, fraud and *ultra vires*' [1993] Conv 370

Martin, J, 'Certainty of subject matter: a defence of *Hunter v Moss*' [1996] Conv 223

Martin, J, *Hanbury and Martin, Modern Equity*, 15th edn, 1997, London: Sweet & Maxwell

Marx, K and Engels, F, *Critique of the Gotha Programme*, 1959, Harmondsworth: Penguin

Mason, A, 'Equity's role in the twentieth century' (1997/98) 8 KCLJ 1

Matthews, P, 'The true basis of the half-secret trust?' [1979] Conv 360

Matthews, P, 'The efficacy of trustee exemption clauses in English law' [1989] Conv 42

Matthews, P, 'A problem in the construction of gifts to unincorporated associations' [1995] Conv 302 (1995:1)

Matthews, P, 'The legal and moral limits of common law tracing' in Birks, P (ed) *Laundering and Tracing*, 1995, Oxford: Clarendon (1995:2)

Matthews, P, 'The new trust: obligations without rights?' in Oakley, A (ed), *Trends in Contemporary Trusts Law*, 1996, Oxford: Oxford University Press, 1

Matthews, P, 'From obligation to property, and back again? The future of the noncharitable purpose trust', in Hayton, D (ed), *Extending the Boundaries of Trusts and Similar Ring-fenced Funds*, 2002, Hague: Kluwer Law International

Maudsley, R, 'Proprietary remedies for the recovery of money' (1959) 75 LQR 234

Maurice, 'The office of custodian trustee' (1960) 24 Conv 196

Meagher, R and Gummow, WMC, *Equity: Doctrines and Remedies*, 3rd edn, 1992, Sydney: Butterworths

Meagher, R, Heydon, D and Leeming, M, *Meagher, Gummow and Lehane's Equity: Doctrines and Remedies*, 4th edn, 2002, Sydney: Butterworths

Mee, J, [1992] Conv 202

Mee, J, *The Property Rights of Cohabitees*, 1999, Oxford: Hart

Miller, D, *Social Justice*, 1976, Oxford: Oxford University Press

Millett, P, 'The *Quistclose* trust: who can enforce it?' (1985) 101 LQR 269

Millett, P, 'Tracing the proceeds of fraud' (1991) 107 LQR 71, 85

Millett, P, 'Bribes and secret commissions' [1993] RLR 7

Millett, P, (1995) 7 Trusts Law International 35

Millett, P, 'Equity's place in the law of commerce; restitution and constructive trusts' (1998) 114 LQR 214

Millett, P, 'Restitution: taking stock', delivering the Society of Advanced Legal Studies Lecture, Institute of Advanced Legal Studies, London, 23 July 1998 (1998:1)

Millett, P, 'Restitution and constructive trusts' (1998) 114 LQR 399 (1998:2)

Mitchell, C, *The Law of Subrogation*, 1994, Oxford: Oxford University Press

Mitchell, C, 'Apportioning liability for trust losses', in Birks, P and Rose (eds), *Restitution and Equity, Vol 1*, 2000, Oxford: Mansfield, 211

Mitchell, C, 'Assistance', in Birks, P and Pretto, A (eds), *Breach of Trust*, 2002, Oxford: Hart

Moffat, *Trusts Law*, 3rd edn, 1999, London: Butterworths

Moriarty, 'Tracing, mixing and laundering', in Birks, P (ed), *Laundering and Tracing*, 1995, Oxford: Clarendon, 73

Mowbray, J *et al*, *Lewin on Trusts*, 32nd edn, 2010, London: Sweet & Maxwell

Mulheron, R, *The Modern Cy-Près Doctrine*, 2006, London: UCL Press

Murphy, T and Roberts, S, *Understanding Property Law*, 3rd edn, 1998, London: Sweet & Maxwell

Lord Nicholls, 'Trustees and their broader community: where duty, morality and ethics converge' (1995) 9 Trusts Law International 71

Lord Nicholls, 'Knowing receipt: the need for a new landmark', in Cornish, W (ed), *Restitution: Past, Present and Future*, 1998, Oxford: Hart

Nolan, R, 'How knowing is knowing receipt?' [2000] CLJ 421

Nolan, R, '*Vandervell v IRC*: a case of overreaching' [2002] CLJ 169

Nolan, R, 'Property in a fund' (2004) 120 LQR 108

Oakley, A, 'The pre-requisites of an equitable tracing claim' (1975) 28 CLP 64

Oakley, A, [1995] CLJ 377

Oakley, A, *Constructive Trusts*, 3rd edn, 1997, London: Sweet & Maxwell

Oakley, A, Parker and Mellow, *The Modern Law of Trusts*, 7th edn, 1998, London: Sweet & Maxwell

Oliver, P, 'New model trusts' (1997/98) 8 KCLJ 147

O'Sullivan, J, 'Undue influence and misrepresentation after *O'Brien*', in Rose, F (ed), *Restitution and Banking Law*, 1998, London: Mansfield

Paciocco, DM, 'The remedial constructive trust: a principled basis for priorities over creditors' (1989) 68 Can BR 315

Panesar, S, *General Principles of Property Law*, 2001, London: Longman

Parkinson, P, 'Reconceptualising the express trust' [2002] CLJ 657

Pawlowski, M, *The Doctrine of Proprietary Estoppel*, 1996, London: Sweet & Maxwell

Pawlowski, M, 'Equitable wrongs: common law damages or equitable compensation?' (2000) 6(9) T & T 20

Payne, J, '*Quistclose* and resulting trusts', in Birks, P and Rose, F (eds), *Resulting Trusts and Equitable Compensation*, 2000, Oxford, Mansfield

Pearce, 'A tracing paper' (1976) 40 Conv 277

Penner, J, *The Idea of Property in Law*, 1997, Oxford: Oxford University Press

Penner, J, 'Exemptions', in Birks, P and Pretto, A (eds), *Breach of Trust*, 2002, Oxford: Hart, 241

Penner, J, 'Lord Millett's analysis', in Swadling, W (ed), *Quistclose Trusts*, 2004, Oxford: Hart, 41

Phillipson, G, 'The Human Rights Act, "horizontal effect" and the common law: a bang or a whimper?' (1999) 62 MLR 824

Picarda, H, *The Law and Practice Relating to Charities*, 4th edn, 2007, London: Butterworths

Piska, N, 'Intention, fairness and the presumption of resulting trust after *Stack v Dowden*' (2008) 71 MLR 120

Pollard, D, '*Schmidt v Rosewood*' (2003) 17 Trusts Law International 90

Pollock, Sir F and Maitland, FW, *History of English Law*, 1895, vol ii

Pound, R, 'The progress of law' (1920) 33 Harv L Rev 420

Probert, R, 'Family law and property law: competing spheres in the regulation of the family home', in Hudson, AS (ed), *New Perspectives on Property Law, Human Rights and the Home*, 2003, London: Cavendish Publishing, 37

Probert, R, 'Equality in the family home?' (2007) *Feminist Legal Studies*, 341

Rajani, S, 'Equitable assistance in the search for security', in Rajak, H (ed), *Insolvency Law: Theory and Practice*, 1993, London: Butterworths, Chapter 2

Rawls, J, *Theory of Justice*, 1971, Oxford: Oxford University Press

Rawls, J, 'Justice as fairness: political not metaphysical' (1985) 14 Philosophy & Public Affairs 223

Raz, J, *The Morality of Freedom*, 1986, Oxford: Clarendon

Riches (1997) PCB 5

Rickett, C, (1979) 38 CLJ 260

Rickett, C, (1991) 107 LQR 608

Rickett, C, 'The remedial constructive trust in Canadian restitution law' [1991] Conv 125

Rickett, C, 'Compensating for loss in equity', in Birks, P and Rose, F (eds), *Restitution and Equity, Vol 1*, 2000, Oxford: Mansfield, 172

Rickett, C, 'Completely constituting an *inter vivos* trust: property rules?' [2001] Conv 515

Rickett, C and Grantham, R, 'Resulting trusts – a rather limited doctrine', in Birks, P and Rose, F (eds), *Restitution and Equity, Vol 1*, 2000, Oxford: Mansfield, 39

Rider, B, 'The fiduciary and the frying pan' [1978] Conv 114

Robertson, 'Land and post-apartheid South Africa', in Bright, S and Dewar, J (eds), *Land Law: Themes and Perspectives*, 1998, Oxford: Oxford University Press, 311

Rose, F, 'Gratuitous transfers and illegal purposes' (1996) 112 LQR 386

Rose, F (ed), *Restitution and Banking Law*, 1998, Oxford: Mansfield

Rotherham, C, *Proprietary Remedies in Context*, 2002, Oxford: Hart

Rotherham, C, 'Property and unjust enrichment: a misunderstood relationship', in Hudson, AS (ed), *New Perspectives on Property Law, Obligations and Restitution*, 2003, London: Cavendish Publishing

Rutherford [1996] Conv 260

Scott, AW and Fratcher, WF, *The Law of Trusts*, 3rd edn, 1967, Boston: Little, Brown

Scott-Hunt, S and Lim, H (eds), *Feminist Perspectives on Equity and Trusts*, 2001, London: Cavendish

Sealy, L, 'Fiduciary relationships' [1962] CLJ 69

Shapiro, J, *Contested Will: Who Wrote Shakespeare*, 2010, Faber

Sherrin, CH, Barlow, RFD and Wallington, RA, *Williams's Law Relating to Wills*, 6th edn, 1987, London: Butterworths, Vol 1, 326

Sherwin, E, 'Constructive trusts in bankruptcy' [1989] University of Illinois L Rev 297

Smith, L, 'Presents, principles and trusts principles' [1982] Conv 352

Smith, L, 'Tracing into the payment of a debt' [1995] CLJ 290 (1995:1)

Smith, L, 'Tracing in *Taylor v Plumer*: equity in the Court of King's Bench' [1995] LMCLQ 240 (1995:2)

Smith, L, *The Law of Tracing*, 1997, Oxford: Clarendon

Smith, L, 'Tracing and electronic funds transfer', in Rose, F (ed), *Restitution and Banking Law*, 1998, Oxford: Mansfield, 120

Smith, L, 'Constructive trusts and constructive trustees' [1999] CLJ 294

Smith, L, 'Unjust enrichment, property, and the structure of trusts' (2000) 116 LQR 412

Smith, R, 'Oral contracts for the sale of land' [2000] 116 LQR 11

Snell, *Equity*, 1868, 1st edn

Sparkes, P, *A New Land Law*, 1999, Oxford: Hart

Spry, I, *Equitable Remedies*, 8th edn, 2010, Sydney: LBC

Spry, I, *The Principles of Equitable Remedies*, 8th edn, 2010, London: Sweet & Maxwell

Stephenson, 'Co-trustees or several trustees?' (1942) 16 Temple ULQ 249

Stevens, 'Election between alternative remedies' [1996] RLR 117

Story, J, *Commentaries on Equity Jurisprudence*, 1839, Boston: Little and Brown

Story, J, *Commentaries on Equity Jurisprudence*, 13th edn, ed. Bigelow, 1886, Little and Brown

Swadling, W, [1994] All ER Rev 259 (1994:1)

Swadling, W, [1994] RLR 195 (1994:2)

Swadling, W, 'A new role for resulting trusts?' (1996) 16 LS 110

Swadling, W, 'Property and conscience' (1998) 12 Trusts Law International 228

Swadling, W, 'A hard look at *Hodgson v Marks*', in Birks, P and Rose, F (eds), *Resulting Trusts and Equitable Compensation*, 2000, Oxford: Mansfield, 61

Swadling, W, *Quistclose Trusts*, 2004, Oxford: Hart

Swadling, W, 'The common intention constructive trust in the House of Lords: an opportunity missed' (2007) 123 LQR 511

Tee, L, 'A merry-go-round for the millennium' [2000] CLJ 23

Tettenborn, A, [1980] CLJ 272

Tettenborn, A, *The Law of Restitution in England and Ireland*, 2nd edn, 1997, London: Cavendish Publishing

Tettenborn, A, 'Misnomer: a response', in Cornish, W, Nolan, R, O'Sullivan, J and Virgo, G (eds), *Restitution, Present and Future: Essays in Honour of Gareth Jones*, 1998, Oxford: Hart, 31

Teubner, G, *Law as an Autopoietic System*, 1994, Oxford: Blackwell

Thomas, G, 'James I, equity and Lord Keeper John Williams' (1976) English Historical Rev 506

Thomas, G, *Powers*, 2nd edn, 2012, Oxford University Press

Thomas, GW and Hudson, AS, *The Law of Trusts*, 2nd edn, 2010, Oxford: Oxford University Press

Thompson, EP, *The Making of the English Working Class*, 1963, London: Victor Gollancz; references are to the Penguin 1968 edition

Thompson, M, 'Constructive trusts, estoppel and the family home' [2004] Conv 1

Townsend, P, *Poverty in the United Kingdom*, 1979, Harmondsworth: Penguin

Tudor, OD, *Tudor on Charities*, 9th edn, 2003, London: Sweet & Maxwell

Underhill, A, *A Practical and Concise Manual of the Law Relating to Private Trusts and Trustees*, 3rd edn, 1889, London: Butterworths

Underhill, A and Hayton, D, *The Law of Trusts and Trustees*, 16th edn, 2002, London: Butterworths

Virgo, G, 'Undue influence and misrepresentation after *O'Brien*', in Rose, F (ed), *Restitution and Banking Law*, 1998, London: Mansfield, 70

Virgo, G, *Principles of the Law of Restitution*, 1999, Oxford: Oxford University Press

Virgo, G, 'Vindicating vindication: *Foskett v McKeown* reviewed', in Hudson, AS (ed), *New Perspectives on Property Law, Obligations and Restitution*, 2003, London: Cavendish Publishing

Warburton, J, [1987] Conv 217

Waters, D, *The Constructive Trust*, 1964, London: Athlone

Waters, D, 'Reaching for the sky – taking trusts laws to the limit, in Hayton, D (ed), *Extending the Boundaries of Trusts and Similar Ring-fenced Funds*, 2002, Hague: Kluwer Law International, 59

Watson, J, *Psychology from the Standpoint of the Behaviourist*, (1919), 1994, London: Routledge

Watts, P, (1996) 112 LQR 219

Weil, S, 'Human Personality', reproduced in Miles, S (ed), *Simone Weil – An Anthology*, 2005, London: Penguin, 69 (originally published by Virago Press, 1985)

Wilken, S and Villiers, T, *Waiver, Variation and Estoppel*, 1999, London: John Wiley

Wittgenstein, L, *Tractatus Logico-Philosophicus*, 1922, London: Kegan Paul.

Wong, S, 'Constructive trusts over the family home: lessons to be learned from other Commonwealth jurisdictions' (1998) 18 LS 369

Wong, S, 'When trust(s) is not enough: an argument for the use of unjust enrichment for home-sharers' (1999) 7(1) FLS 47

Wong, S, 'Rethinking *Rosset* from a human rights perspective', in Hudson, AS (ed), *New Perspectives on Property Law, Human Rights and the Home*, 2003, London: Cavendish Publishing, 79

Wooldridge [1987] JBL 329

Worthington, S, *Proprietary Interests in Commercial Transactions*, 1996, Oxford: Clarendon

Worthington, S, 'Reconsidering disgorgement for wrongs' (1999) 62 MLR 218 (1999:1)

Worthington, S, 'Fiduciaries: when is self-denial obligatory?' [1999] 58 CLJ 500 (1999:2)

Youdan, T, 'Formalities for trusts of land, and the doctrine in *Rochefoucauld v Boustead*' [1984] 43 CLJ 306

Youdan, TG (ed), *Equity, Fiduciaries and Trusts*, 1989, Toronto

Zimmerman, *The Law of Obligations: Roman Foundations of the Civilian Tradition*, 1996, Oxford: Oxford University Press

Index